STREET ATLAS

UNRIVALLED DETAIL FROM THE BEST-SELLING ATLAS RANGE*

NAVIGATOR®
BUCKINGHAMSHIRE
AND MILTON KEYNES

www.philips-maps.co.uk
Published by Philip's, a division of
Octopus Publishing Group Ltd
www.octopusbooks.co.uk
Carmelite House
50 Victoria Embankment
London EC4Y 0DZ
An Hachette UK Company
www.hachette.co.uk

First edition 2023
First impression 2023
BUCFA

ISBN 978-1-84907-633-3 (spiral)

© Philip's 2023

This product includes mapping data licensed from Ordnance Survey® with the permission of the Controller of His Majesty's Stationery Office. © Crown copyright 2023. All rights reserved. Licence number 100011710.

CONTENTS

III Key to map symbols

IV Key to map pages

VI Route planning

VIII Major administrative and Postcode boundaries

1 Street maps at 3½ inches to 1 mile

214 Index of towns, villages, streets, hospitals, industrial estates, railway stations, schools, shopping centres, universities and places of interest

T0329517

STREET ATLAS

PHILIP'S

UNRIVALLED
DETAIL FROM THE
BEST-SELLING
ATLAS RANGE

NAVIGATOR
BUCKINGHAMSHIRE
AND MILTON KEYNES

Key to map symbols

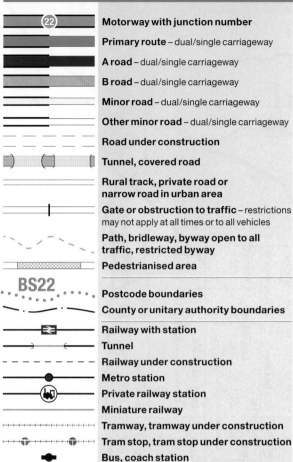

	Motorway with junction number (22)
	Primary route – dual/single carriageway
	A road – dual/single carriageway
	B road – dual/single carriageway
	Minor road – dual/single carriageway
	Other minor road – dual/single carriageway
	Road under construction
	Tunnel, covered road
	Rural track, private road or narrow road in urban area
	Gate or obstruction to traffic – restrictions may not apply at all times or to all vehicles
	Path, bridleway, byway open to all traffic, restricted byway
	Pedestrianised area
BS22	Postcode boundaries
	County or unitary authority boundaries
	Railway with station
	Tunnel
	Railway under construction
	Metro station
	Private railway station
	Miniature railway
	Tramway, tramway under construction
	Tram stop, tram stop under construction
	Bus, coach station

♦	Ambulance station
♦	Coastguard station
♦	Fire station
♦	Police station
✚	Accident and Emergency entrance to hospital
H	Hospital
+	Place of worship
i	Information centre – open all year
⊞ P	Shopping centre, parking
P&R PO	Park and Ride, Post Office
Ⓧ ⊟	Camping site, caravan site
▶ ✕	Golf course, picnic site
ROMAN FORT	Non-Roman antiquity, Roman antiquity
Univ	Important buildings, schools, colleges, universities and hospitals
	Woods, built-up area
River Medway	Water name
	River, weir
	Stream
	Canal, lock, tunnel
	Water
	Tidal water
58 ◀ 87 / 246	Adjoining page indicators and overlap bands – the colour of the arrow and band indicates the scale of the adjoining or overlapping page (see scale below)

The dark grey border on the inside edge of some pages indicates that the mapping does not continue onto the adjacent page

The small numbers around the edges of the maps identify the 1-kilometre National Grid lines

Abbreviations

Acad	Academy	Meml	Memorial
Allot Gdns	Allotments	Mon	Monument
Cemy	Cemetery	Mus	Museum
C Ctr	Civic centre	Obsy	Observatory
CH	Club house	Pal	Royal palace
Coll	College	PH	Public house
Crem	Crematorium	Recn Gd	Recreation ground
Ent	Enterprise		
Ex H	Exhibition hall	Resr	Reservoir
Ind Est	Industrial Estate	Ret Pk	Retail park
IRB Sta	Inshore rescue boat station	Sch	School
		Sh Ctr	Shopping centre
Inst	Institute	TH	Town hall / house
Ct	Law court	Trad Est	Trading estate
L Ctr	Leisure centre	Univ	University
LC	Level crossing	W Twr	Water tower
Liby	Library	Wks	Works
Mkt	Market	YH	Youth hostel

The map scale on the pages numbered in blue is 3½ inches to 1 mile
5.52 cm to 1 km • 1:18 103

0	¼ mile	½ mile	¾ mile	1 mile

0	250m	500m	750m	1km

Key to map pages

113 Map pages at 3½ inches to 1 mile

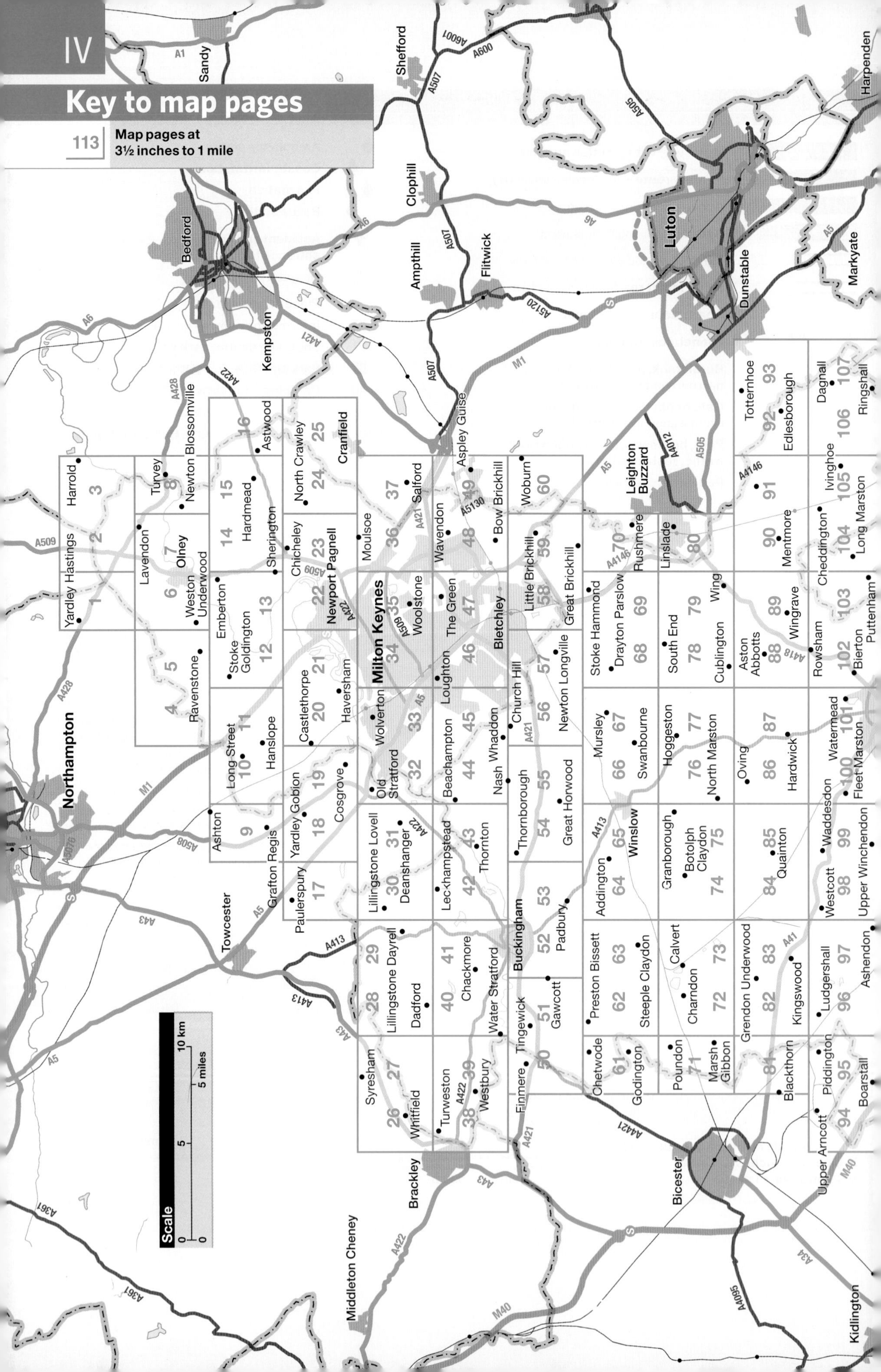
Sandy
Shefford
Harpenden
Clophill
Bedford
Luton
Ampthill
Flitwick
Kempston
Dunstable
Markyate
Newton Blossomville
Astwood
Aspley Guise
Cranfield
North Crawley
Harrold
Turvey
Hardmead
Salford
Leighton Buzzard
Totternhoe
Dagnall
Eddlesborough
Ringshall
Lavendon
Olney
Sherington
Chicheley
Moulsoe
Wavendon
Bow Brickhill
Woburn
Ivinghoe
Yardley Hastings
Emberton
Weston Underwood
Newport Pagnell
Milton Keynes
Woolstone
The Green
Bletchley
Little Brickhill
Great Brickhill
Rushmere
Linslade
Mentmore
Cheddington
Long Marston
Stoke Goldington
Ravenstone
Haversham
Castlethorpe
Wolverton
Loughton
Stoke Hammond
Drayton Parslow
South End
Wing
Cublington
Aston Abbotts
Wingrave
Rowsham
Bierton
Puttenham
Northampton
Long Street
Hanslope
Cosgrove
Old Stratford
Beachampton
Nash
Whaddon
Church Hill
Newton Longville
Mursley
Swanbourne
Hoggeston
North Marston
Oving
Hardwick
Watermead
Fleet Marston
Ashton
Grafton Regis
Yardley Gobion
Lillingstone Lovell
Deanshanger
Leckhampstead
Thornton
Thornborough
Great Horwood
Winslow
Granborough
Botolph Claydon
Quainton
Waddesdon
Upper Winchendon
Towcester
Paulerspury
Addington
Westcott
Buckingham
Padbury
Lillingstone Dayrell
Dadford
Chackmore
Water Stratford
Tingewick
Gawcott
Preston Bissett
Steeple Claydon
Calvert
Charndon
Grendon Underwood
Kingswood
Ludgershall
Ashendon
Syresham
Whitfield
Turweston
Westbury
Finmere
Chetwode
Godington
Poundon
Marsh Gibbon
Blackthorn
Piddington
Boarstall
Upper Arncott
Brackley
Bicester
Middleton Cheney
Kidlington
Scale
5 miles
10 km

A1081 · A5183 · Redbourn · St Albans · A414 · A4147 · M1 · Hemel Hempstead · A4251 · A41 · M10 · M25 · Kings Langley · Radlett · M1 · A41 · Bushey · Watford · A412 · A411 · Rickmansworth · A404 · A409 · A4008 · Harrow · A4090 · A404 · Ruislip · A40 · A4180 · Southall · Ealing · Brentford · A4127 · Hounslow · A312 · A4020 · Hayes · A437 · Harmondsworth · Feltham · Ashford · A316 · A30 · A308 · Staines · Egham · A3044 · Stanwell · West Drayton · Cowley · Yiewsley · Uxbridge · South Harefield

146 Felden Bovingdon	156 Flaunden Chenies	167 Chorleywood	178 Maple Cross	190 South Harefield	201 Uxbridge	208 West Drayton	213 Colnbrook
120 Aldbury Little Gaddesden	135 Northchurch	145 Ashley Green	155 Latimer	166	177 Chalfont St Peter	189 Higher Denham	200 Iver Heath	207	212 Datchet
121	134 Berkhamsted	144 Botley	154 Amersham	165 Winchmore Hill	176 Seer Green	188 Gerrards Cross	199 Wexham Street	206 Upton	211 Windsor Old Windsor
119 Wilstone Green	133 Hastoe	143 Chartridge	153 Little Missenden	164 Amersham Old Town	175 Beaconsfield	187 Hedgerley	198 Farnham Common	205 Slough	210 Boveney Clewer Green
118 Tring Wigginton	132 Cholesbury St Leonards	142 Lee Common	152 Great Missenden	163 Hazlemere	174 Loudwater	186 Wooburn Common	197 Burnham	204 Eton Wick	209
117 Aston Clinton	131 Wendover	141 Wendover Dean	151 Prestwood	162 Cryers Hill	173 High Wycombe	185 Flackwell Heath	196 Cookham	203 Maidenhead Bray	
116 Weston Turville	130 Ellesborough	140 Little Hampden	150 Speen	161 Naphill	172 Booker	184 Little Marlow	195 Cookham Rise Taplow	202	
115 Bishopstone	129 Little Kimble	139 Longwick	149 Lacey Green	160 West Wycombe	171 Lane End	183 Marlow Bottom	194 Bisham	193 Mill End	
114 Stone	128 Ford	138 Princes Risborough	148 Rout's Green	159 Stokenchurch	170 Frieth	182 Lower Woodend Marlow	192 Hurley	191 Henley-on-Thames	
113 Cuddington	127 Haddenham	137 Henton	147 Crowell	158 Bledlow Ridge	169 Turville	181 Hambleden	180 Fawley		
112 Westlington	126 Kingsey		136 Chinnor	157 Lewknor	168 Christmas Common	179 Maidensgrove			
111 Chilton Upper Pollicott	125 Long Crendon								
110 Brill	124	Thame	Milton Common						
123 Ickford	122 Horton-cum-Studley Oakley	Worminghall	Shabbington Tiddington						

Aylesbury · A413 · A4010 · A4128 · A404 · A4094 · A4155 · A4130 · A404 · M40 · A413 · A355 · A412 · M25 · A40

Oxford · A40 · A4142 · A4074 · A34 · A4183 · A4165 · A415 · Abingdon-on-Thames · Didcot · A4130 · A417 · Wallingford · A4074 · A329 · Goring · Sonning Common · Reading · A4 · A33 · M4 · A329 · A340 · A4155 · Twyford · A321 · Wokingham · Binfield · Bracknell · A322 · A329 · A3095 · A330 · A332

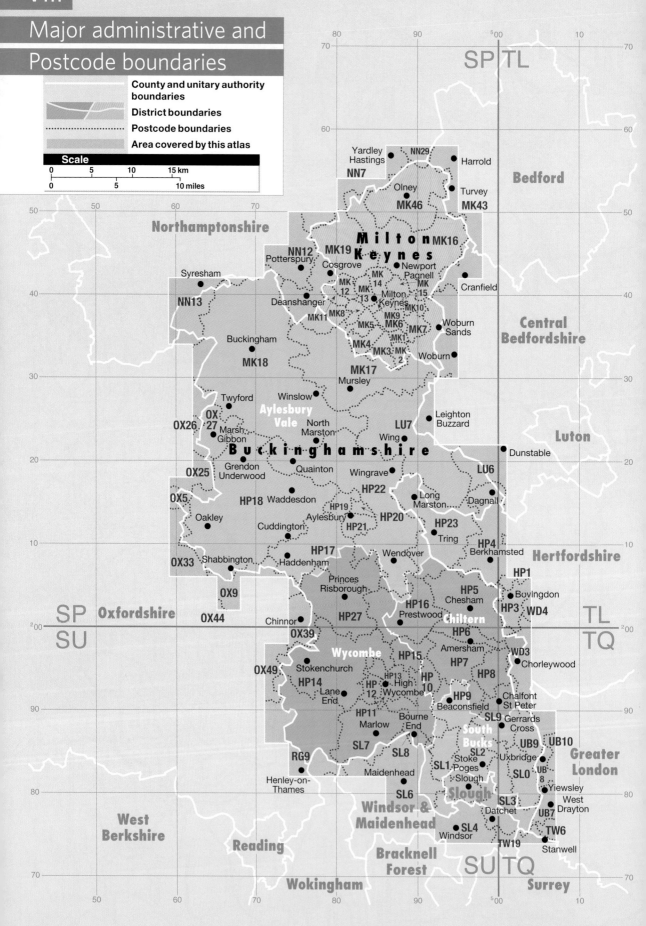

County and unitary authority
boundaries
District boundaries
Postcode boundaries
Area covered by this atlas

Scale

0   5   10   15 km
0   5   10 miles

SP TL

Bedford

Northamptonshire

Central
Bedfordshire

Luton

Hertfordshire

Greater
London

Oxfordshire

SP
SU

TL
TQ

West
Berkshire

Reading

Wokingham

Bracknell
Forest

Surrey

SU TQ

Milton Keynes

Aylesbury Vale

Buckinghamshire

Chiltern

Wycombe

South Bucks

Slough

Windsor &
Maidenhead

Yardley Hastings
NN29
Harrold
NN7
Olney
Turvey
MK46
MK43
Cranfield
NN12
Potterspury
MK19
Cosgrove
MK16
Newport Pagnell
MK14
MK
12
MK
13
MK
15
Milton Keynes
MK10
MK9
Woburn Sands
MK8
MK5
MK6
MK7
MK11
MK1
Deanshanger
MK4
MK3
MK
2
Woburn
Syresham
NN13
Buckingham
MK18
MK17
Mursley
Twyford
Winslow
OX
27
OX26
Marsh Gibbon
North Marston
LU7
Leighton Buzzard
Wing
OX25
Grendon Underwood
Quainton
Wingrave
LU6
OX5
HP18
Waddesdon
HP22
Long Marston
Dagnall
Oakley
HP19
Aylesbury
HP20
HP23
Cuddington
HP21
Tring
Dunstable
OX33
Shabbington
HP17
Haddenham
Wendover
HP4
Berkhamsted
OX9
Princes Risborough
HP1
HP5
Chesham
Bovingdon
OX44
Chinnor
HP16
Prestwood
HP3
WD4
SP
SU
TL
TQ
HP27
Chiltern
HP6
OX39
Amersham
WD3
Chorleywood
Wycombe
HP15
OX49
Stokenchurch
HP7
HP8
HP14
HP13
High Wycombe
HP
10
HP9
Chalfont St Peter
Lane End
HP
12
Beaconsfield
SL9
Gerrards Cross
HP11
Bourne End
UB9
UB10
Marlow
Stoke Poges
SL2
Uxbridge
RG9
SL7
SL8
SL1
Slough
SL0
UB
8
Yiewsley
Henley-on-Thames
Maidenhead
SL3
Datchet
UB7
West Drayton
SL6
TW6
SL4
Windsor
TW19
Stanwell

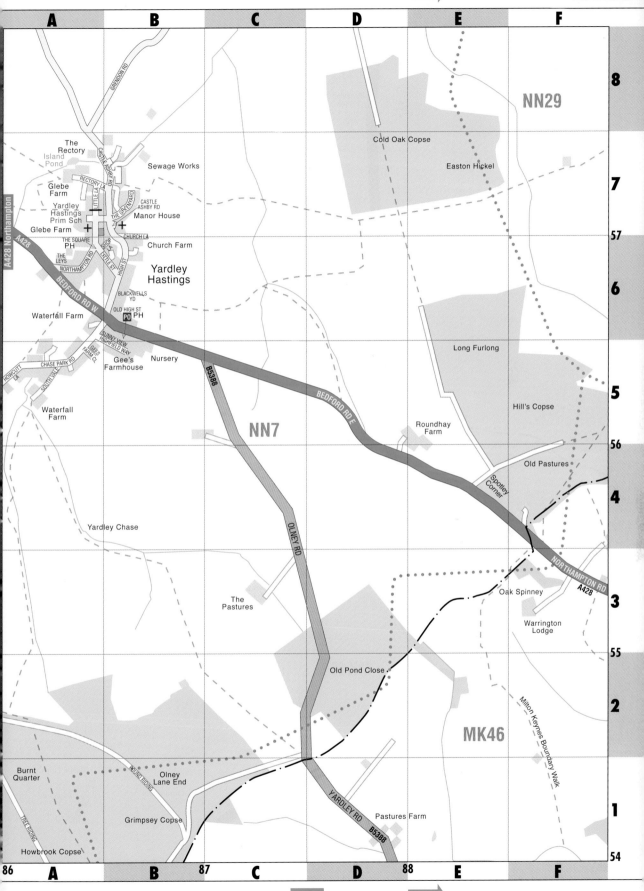

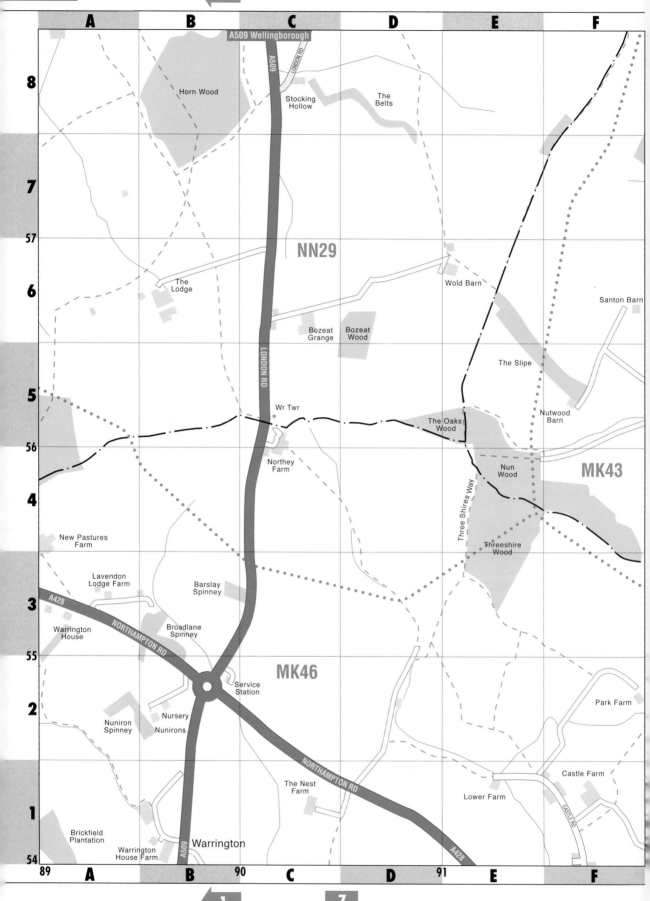

A509 Wellingborough

A B C D E F

8

Horn Wood

Stocking Hollow

The Belts

7

57

NN29

The Lodge

6

Wold Barn

Santon Barn

Bozeat Grange

Bozeat Wood

The Slipe

LONDON RD

5

Wr Twr

The Oaks Wood

Nutwood Barn

56

Northey Farm

Nun Wood

MK43

Three Shires Way

4

New Pastures Farm

Threeshire Wood

Lavendon Lodge Farm

Barslay Spinney

3

A428

Warrington House

NORTHAMPTON RD

Broadlane Spinney

MK46

55

Service Station

2

Park Farm

Nuniron Spinney

Nursery

Nunirons

NORTHAMPTON RD

Castle Farm

The Nest Farm

Lower Farm

CASTLE RD

1

Brickfield Plantation

A509

Warrington

A428

54

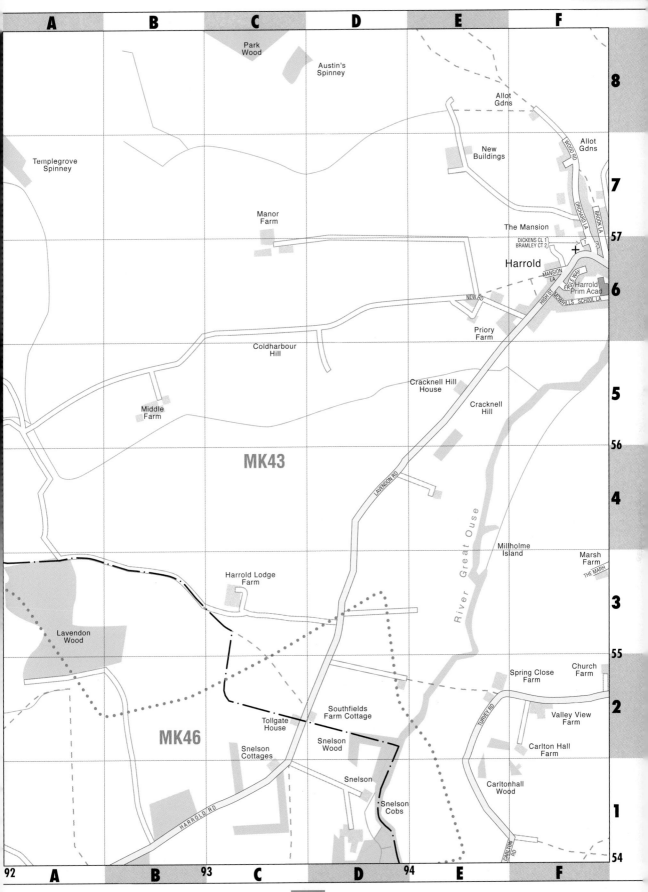

8

7

57

6

5

56

4

55

3

2

1

54

Park
Wood

Austin's
Spinney

Allot
Gdns

Templegrove
Spinney

New
Buildings

WOOD RD

Allot
Gdns

BROOK LA

The Mansion

ORCHARD LA

Manor
Farm

DICKENS CL 1
BRAMLEY CT 2

Harrold

MANSION
LA

HIGH ST

EAGLE WAY

Harrold
Prim Acad

MOWBALLS

SCHOOL LA

NEW RD

Priory
Farm

Coldharbour
Hill

Cracknell Hill
House

Cracknell
Hill

Middle
Farm

MK43

LAVENDON RD

Millholme
Island

Marsh
Farm

THE MARSH

River Great Ouse

Lavendon
Wood

Harrold Lodge
Farm

Spring Close
Farm

Church
Farm

TURVEY RD

Valley View
Farm

MK46

Tollgate
House

Southfields
Farm Cottage

Snelson
Cottages

Snelson
Wood

Carlton Hall
Farm

Snelson

Carltonhall
Wood

Snelson
Cobs

HARROLD RD

CARLTON RD

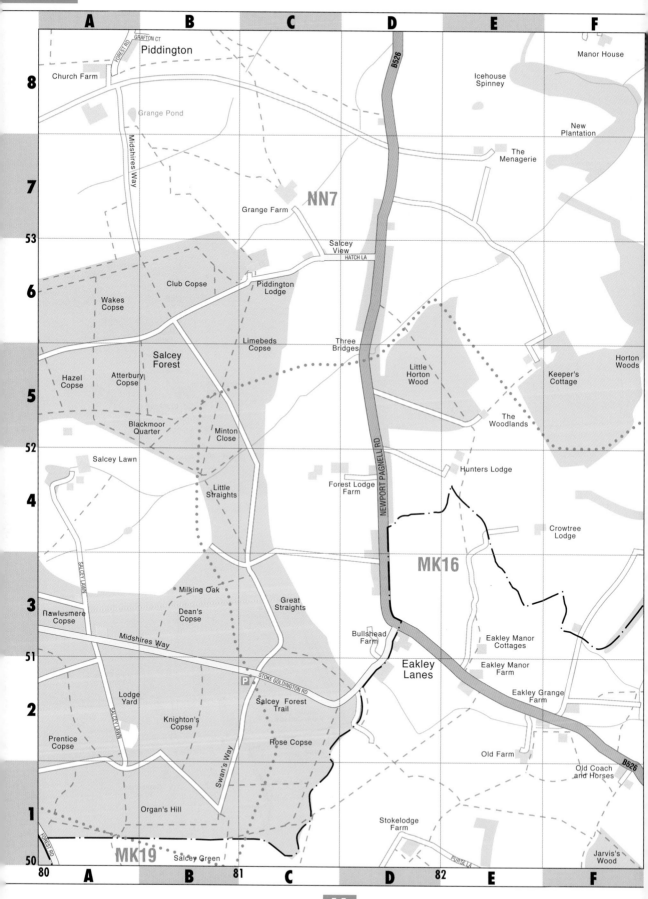

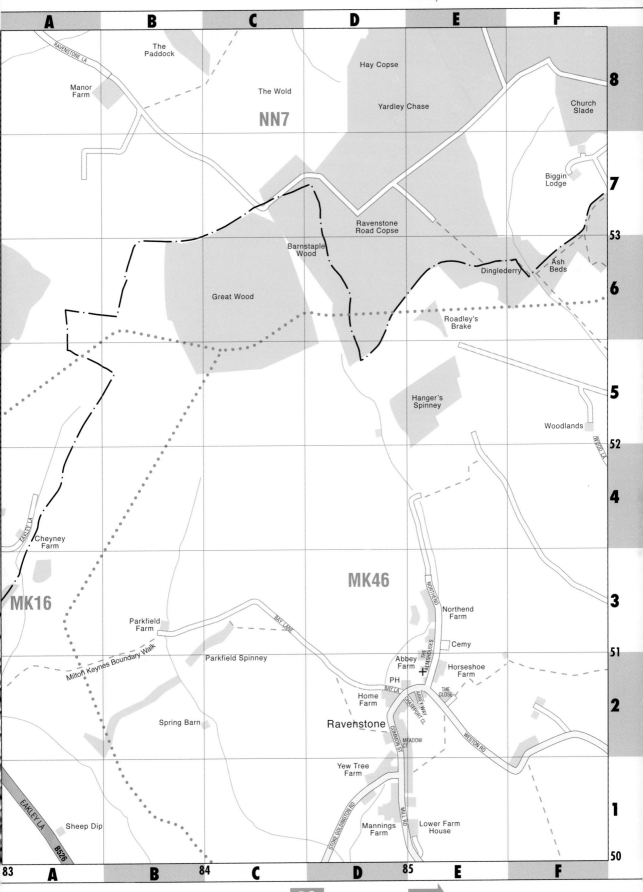

A B C D E F

8

The Paddock

Manor Farm

The Wold

Hay Copse

Yardley Chase

Church Slade

NN7

Biggin Lodge

7

53

Ravenstone Road Copse

Barnstaple Wood

Ash Beds

Great Wood

Dinglederry

6

Roadley's Brake

Hanger's Spinney

5

Woodlands

WESTON LA

52

4

Cheyney Farm

EAKLEY LA

MK46

Northend Farm

3

MK16

NORTHEND

Parkfield Farm

BAY LANE

Cemy

THE FARMHOUSES

51

Milton Keynes Boundary Walk

Parkfield Spinney

Abbey Farm

Horseshoe Farm

PH

THE CLOSE

BAY LA

ABBEY WAY

CHASEPORT CL.

2

Home Farm

Spring Barn

Ravenstone

COMMON ST

MEADOW CT

WESTON RD

Yew Tree Farm

1

EAKLEY LA

B526

Sheep Dip

STOKE GOLDINGTON RD

Mannings Farm

MILL RD

Lower Farm House

50

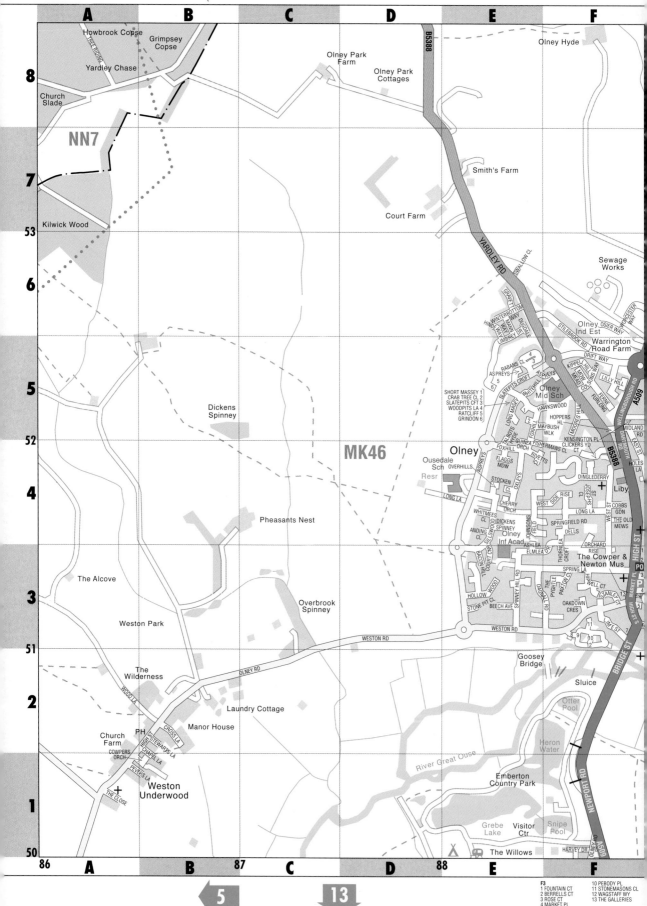

A 8 Howbrook Copse
Grimpsey Copse
Yardley Chase
Church Slade
NN7
Kilwick Wood
53
6

B5388
Olney Hyde
Olney Park Farm
Olney Park Cottages

Smith's Farm

Court Farm

Sewage Works

YARDLEY RD

Warrington Road Farm
Olney Osier Way
Olney Ind Est
DRIFT WAY
LILLY HILL
WORCESTER WAY
A509

5

Dickens Spinney

MK46

SHORT MASSEY 1
CRAB TREE CL 2
SLATEPITS CFT 3
WOODPITS LA 4
RATCLIFF 5
GRINDON 6

Olney Mid Sch
HAWKSWOOD
HOPPERS HL
MAYBUSH WLK

52

Ousedale Sch
OVERHILLS

Olney

KENSINGTON PL
CLICKERS YD
RIVETTS CL
FLAGGS MDW
STOCKEN

Liby
MIDLAND RD
B5388
COBBS GDN
THE OLD MEWS

4

LONG LA

CHERRY ORCH

WEST SIDE
RISE
LONG LA
WEST ST

SPRINGFIELD RD
ORCHARD

Pheasants Nest

WHITMEES CL
ANDING CL
DICKENS Spinney
Olney Inf Acad

JOHNSONS FIELD
DELLS
ASHLEA
ELMLEA

THORNLEA CROFT
SPRING LA

The Cowper & Newton Mus
HIGH ST

The Alcove

Overbrook Spinney

HOLLOW
STONE PIT CL
BACON HILL
COURT CL

BEECH AVE
SPINNEY HILL RD
DARVAL RD
PAXTON CL

WELL CT
OAKDOWN CRES
STANLEY CT

PO

3

Weston Park

WESTON RD

WESTON RD

Goosey Bridge
Sluice
BRIDGE ST

51

The Wilderness

OLNEY RD

Otter Pool

NEWPORT RD

2

WOOD LA

Laundry Cottage
Manor House

Heron Water

Church Farm
PH
STEWARTS LA
HIGH ST
CROSS LA
CHAPEL LA
COWPERS ORCH
FEVERS LA

River Great Ouse

Emberton Country Park

1

THE CLOSE
Weston Underwood

Grebe Lake
Visitor Ctr
Snipe Pool
The Willows
HARVEY DR
GOSE RD

50

86   A   B   87   C   D   88   E   F

F3
1 FOUNTAIN CT
2 BERRELLS CT
3 ROSE CT
4 MARKET PL
5 OSBORNS CT
6 CHURCH ST
7 PEMBROKE HO
8 CHANTRY RI
9 CLAY PIT LA
10 PEBODY PL
11 STONEMASONS CL
12 WAGSTAFF WY
13 THE GALLERIES

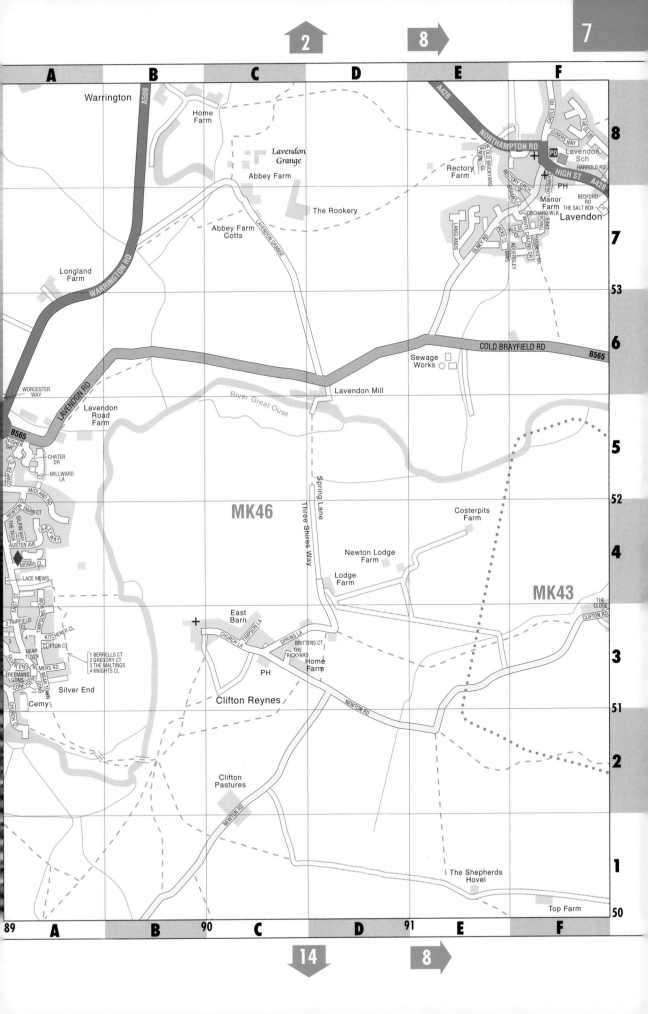

A **B** **C** **D** **E** **F**

8

Snip Wood

New Barn

Copymoor

THE GLEBE

HARROLD RD

Uphoe Manor Farm

7

A428

Cemy

OLD STONEYARD CL

New Park

Cricket Ground

CARLTON RD

53

MK46

Cemy

6

B565

Turvey House

Turvey Prim Sch

HAWTHORN CL

GROVE RD

MAY RD

NORFOLK RD

New Gains Farm

Turvey

Chantry Farm

VINE ROW

THE PROSPECT

LAWS CL

BARN

BAMFORDS LA

THE ROW

CHURCH TERR

PO

DET END

BEDFORD RD

Turvey Bridge

CRANES CL

ELMWK

ABBEY SQ

Cold Brayfield

Waterfield Farm

THE ROW

BRIDGE ST

HIGH ST

BEDFORD RD

A428

A428 Bedford

5

Brayfield Farm

Turvey Mill

MILL GN

THE GREEN

Turvey Loop

LADYBRIDGE TERR

BAMFORDS YD

Ford

Turvey Abbey

BRAYFIELD HO

TANDYS CL

NEWTON RD

BAKERS CL

52

Lodge

Long Belt

Abbey Farm

4

Newton Blossomville

THE RICKYARD

NEWTON LA

Top Lodge

Mossy Bank Wood

PH

CLIFTON RD

Newton Blossomville CE Sch

THE ROW

BROOK LA

Turvey Cottage

River Great Ouse

Woodside Cottage

New Wood

3

HARDMEAD RD

Home Farm

Westfields Barn

MK43

Keepers Cottage

51

Turvey Hall

2

Newton Park

Gullet Wood

Clifton Spinney

Two Chimneys

1

Sheepwalks Spinney

Mast

Newton Wood

Turvey Lodge Farm

50

92 **A** **B** **93** **C** **D** **94** **E** **F**

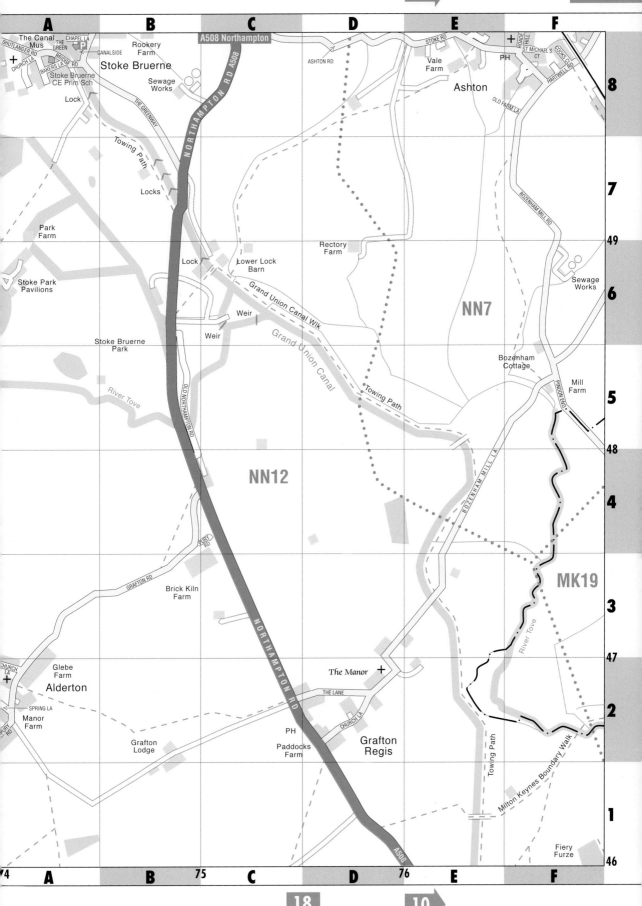

A   B   C   D   E   F

The Canal Mus
CHAPEL LA
THE GREEN
CANALSIDE
Rookery Farm
A508 Northampton
Ashton RD
STOKE RD
Vale Farm
PH
St MICHAEL'S CT
ROADE HILL
COCKS CT
HARTWELL RD

SHUTLANGER RD
CHURCH LA
BRIDGE RD
BAKERS LA
Stoke Bruerne CE Prim Sch
Stoke Bruerne
Sewage Works
Lock
Ashton
OLD FARM LA

THE GREENWAY
Towing Path
Locks
NORTHAMPTON RD A508
BOZENHAM MILL RD

Park Farm
Rectory Farm
NN7
Sewage Works

Stoke Park Pavilions
Lock
Lower Lock Barn
Grand Union Canal Wlk
Bozenham Cottage
Mill Farm
PINDON END

Weir
Weir
Grand Union Canal
Stoke Bruerne Park
OLD NORTHAMPTON RD

River Tove
Towing Path
48

NN12
BOZENHAM MILL LA
MK19

BURY RD
Brick Kiln Farm
River Tove

GRAFTON RD
NORTHAMPTON RD

CHURCH LA
Glebe Farm
The Manor
Alderton
THE LANE
47

SPRING LA
CHURCH LA
Manor Farm
BURY RD
Grafton Lodge
PH
Paddocks Farm
Grafton Regis
Towing Path
Milton Keynes Boundary Walk

A508
Fiery Furze

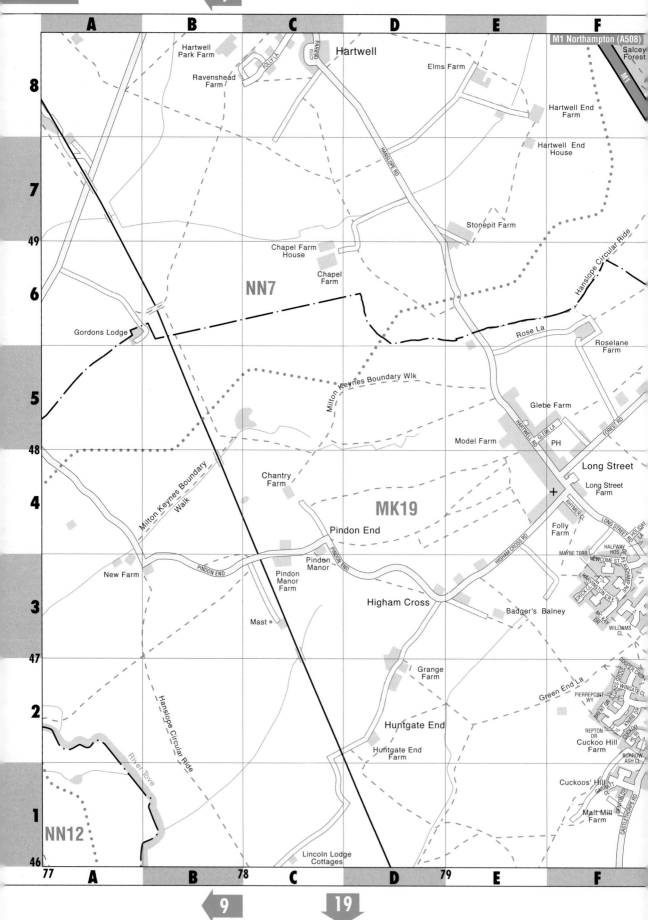

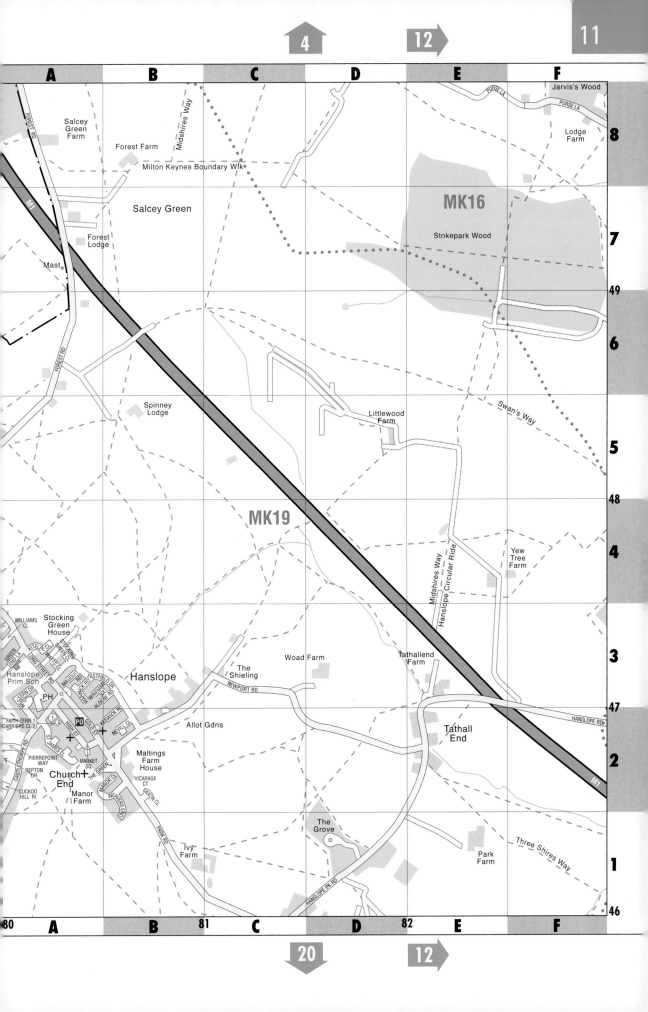

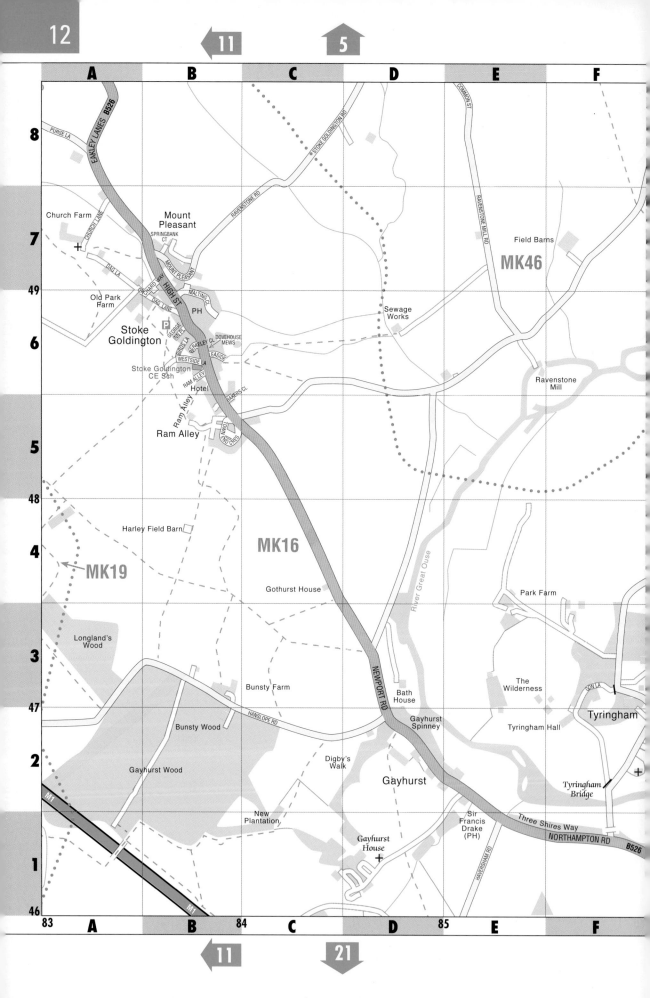

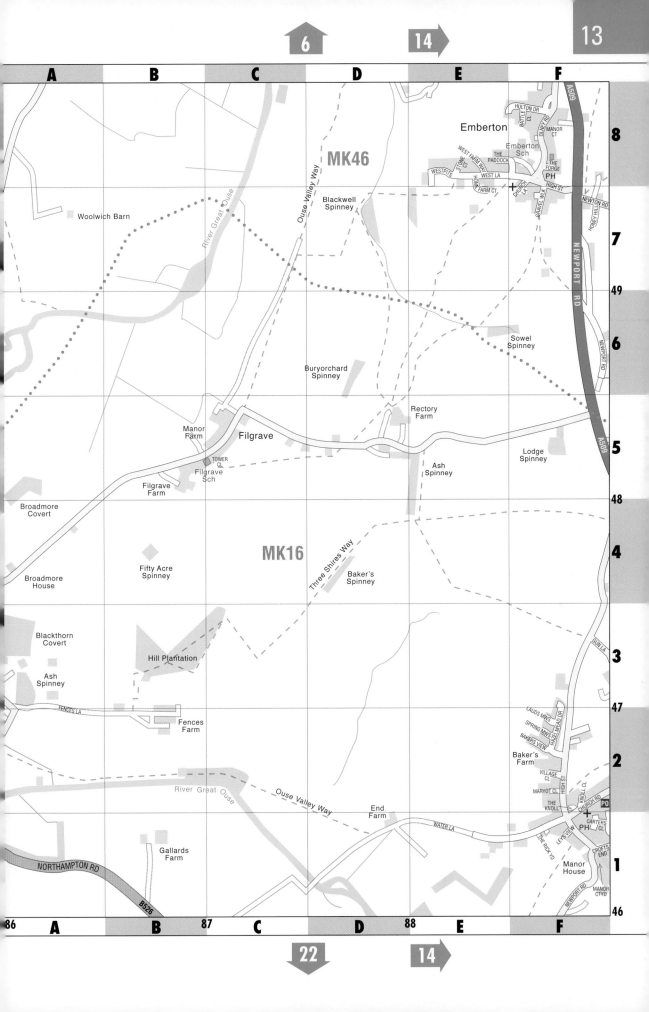

A   **B**   **C**   **D**   **E**   **F**

Emberton

HULTON DR
OLNEY RD
BATTLE CL
MANOR CT

MK46

Emberton Sch

WEST FARM WAY
STONE CT
WESTPITS
THE PADDOCK
WEST LA
HOME FARM CT
GRAVEL WLK
CHURCH LA
THE FORGE
PH
HIGH ST

8

NEWTON RD
HONEY HILL

A509

Woolwich Barn

River Great Ouse

Blackwell Spinney

Ouse Valley Way

NEWPORT RD

7

49

Sowel Spinney

NEWPORT RD

6

Buryorchard Spinney

Rectory Farm

A509

Manor Farm

Filgrave

Ash Spinney

Lodge Spinney

5

TOWER CL
Filgrave Sch

Filgrave Farm

48

Broadmore Covert

MK16

Three Shires Way

Baker's Spinney

4

Broadmore House

Fifty Acre Spinney

Blackthorn Covert

Hill Plantation

SUN LA

3

Ash Spinney

FENCES LA

Fences Farm

LAUDS MWS
SPRING MWS
HAZEL MEAD DR
BAKERS VIEW

47

Baker's Farm

VILLAGE CL
MARYOT CL
HIGH ST
KNOLL CL
CHURCH RD
PO

2

River Great Ouse

Ouse Valley Way

End Farm

WATER LA

THE KNOLL
LEYS VIEW
THE RICK YD
PH
CARTERS CL
CROFTS END

Gallards Farm

NORTHAMPTON RD

Manor House

MANOR CTYD

1

B526

NEWPORT RD

46

A B C D E F

8

Three Shires Way
NEWPORT RD

Rectory Farm

Petsoe Manor Farm

7

PETSOE END

Petsoe End

Petsoe Manor

Hill Farm

Clay Farm

Grange Farm

49

MK46

6

Hollington Wood

Wood Farm

Mulducks

Parrages Wood

5

Seven Acre Covert

Short Wood

48

A509 NEWPORT RD

4

3

MK16

Gowle's Farm

Thickthorn Wood

47

GUN LA
FIELD CL
PH
PARK RD
CHURCH RD
CHURCH END

2

Sherington
Sherington CE Prim Sch

SCHOOL LA
GRIGGS ORCH
PERRY LA

Grange Farm

Brickyard Cottage

CARTERS CL
CROFTS END
PERRY LANE
HILLVIEW
BEDFORD RD

BEDFORD RD

A422

Chicheley Brook

Crofts End

Bedlam

BEDLAM WLK
BEDLAM LA

1

A509

Brandon's Wood

46

89 A B 90 C D 91 E F

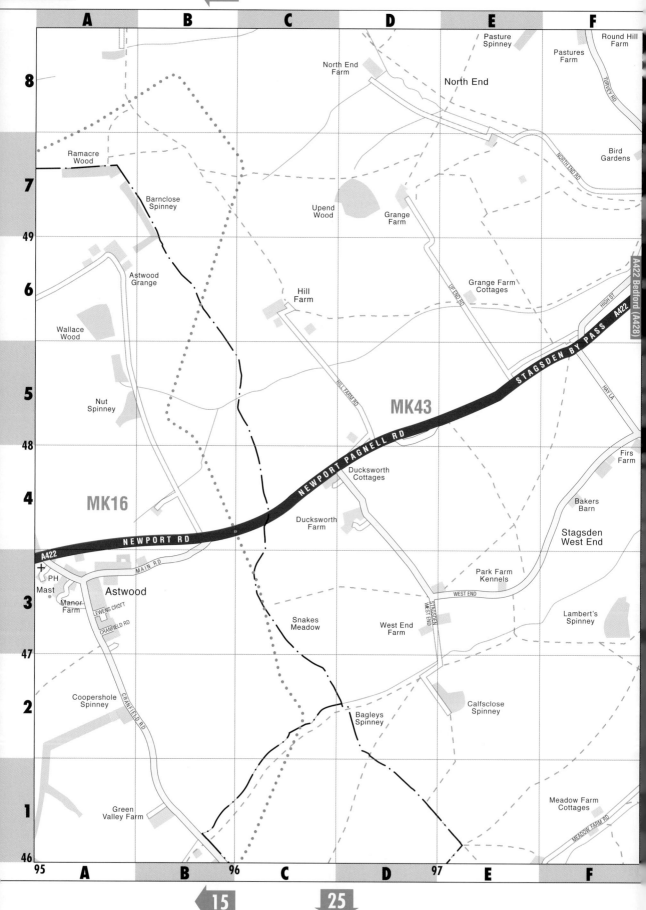

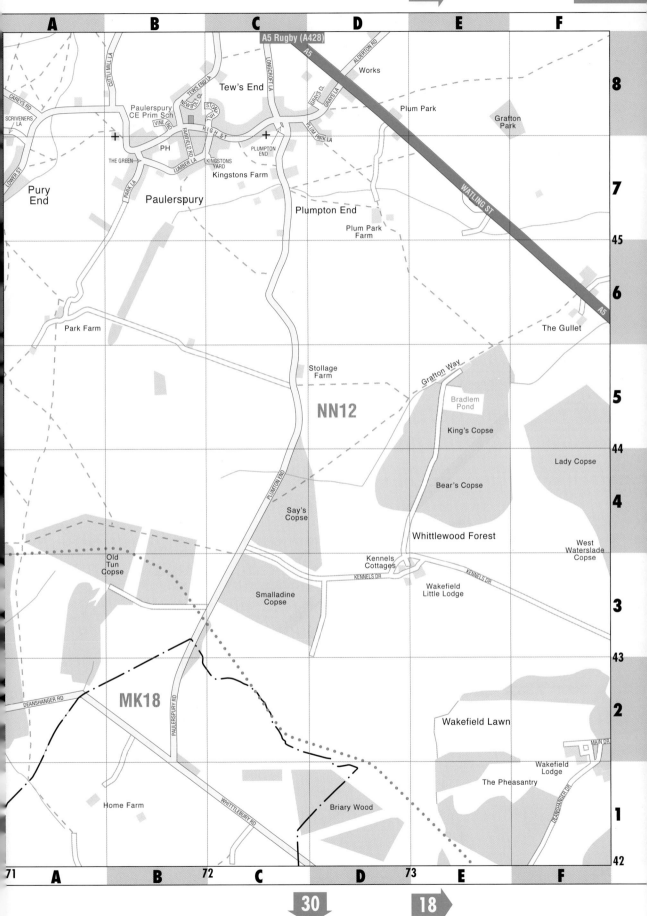

A5 Rugby (A428)

Works

Tew's End

Plum Park

Grafton Park

Paulerspury
CE Prim Sch

SCRIVENERS
LA

CAREYS RD

LOWER ST

THE GREEN

PH

Kingstons
Yard

Plumpton
End

Kingstons Farm

Paulerspury

Plumpton End

Pury
End

Plum Park
Farm

Watling St

The Gullet

Park Farm

Stollage
Farm

Grafton Way

Bradlem
Pond

NN12

King's Copse

Lady Copse

Bear's Copse

Say's
Copse

Whittlewood Forest

West
Waterslade
Copse

Old Tun
Copse

Kennels
Cottages

Kennels Dr

Kennels Dr

Wakefield
Little Lodge

Smalladine
Copse

MK18

Deanshanger Rd

Paulerspury Rd

Wakefield Lawn

Wakefield
Lodge

Main Dr

Deanshanger Dr

The Pheasantry

Home Farm

Whittlebury Rd

Briary Wood

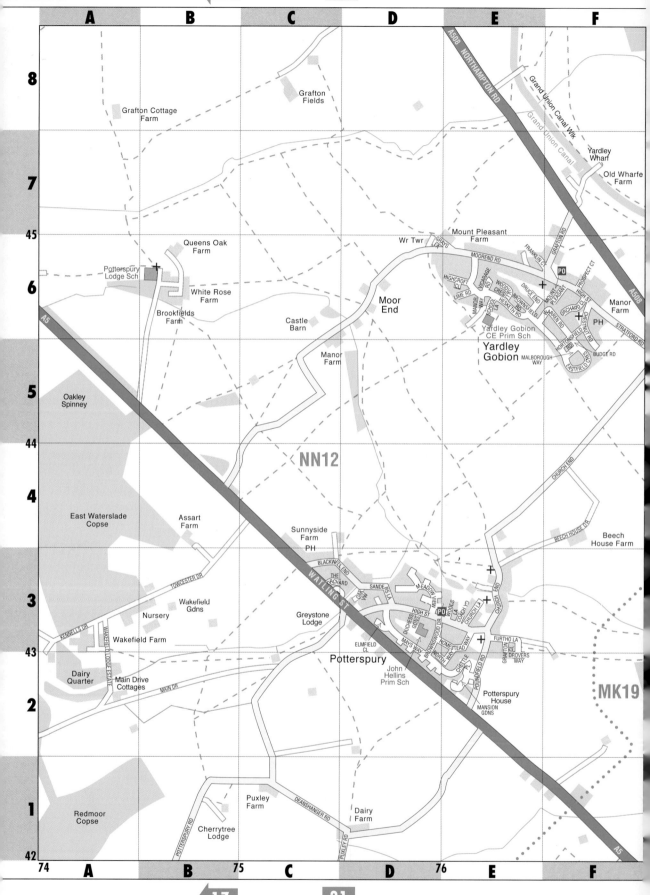

A B C D E F

8

7

45

6

5

44

4

3

43

2

1

42

74 A B 75 C D 76 E F

Grafton Fields

Grafton Cottage Farm

A508 NORTHAMPTON RD

Grand Union Canal Wlk

Grand Union Canal

Yardley Wharf

Old Wharfe Farm

Queens Oak Farm

Potterspury Lodge Sch

White Rose Farm

Brookfields Farm

Castle Barn

Manor Farm

Moor End

Mount Pleasant Farm

Wr Twr

GRAY'S LA

MOOREND RD

FRANKLIN CL

GRAFTON RD

PO

PROSPECT CT

A508

HIGHCROFT CL

VICARAGE RD

WOODL CREST

DRUCE END

MANOR WAY

SCHOOL RD

LIME RD

HESKETH RD

BROWNSWD

MOUNT PLEASANT

WARREN RD

HIGH ST

Manor Farm

STRATFORD RD

Yardley Gobion CE Prim Sch

ORCHARD LA

PH

CHESTNUT RD

BUDGE RD

HORTONSFIELD RD

Yardley Gobion

EASTFIELD

MALBOROUGH WAY

A5

Oakley Spinney

NN12

East Waterslade Copse

Assart Farm

CHURCH END

BEECH HOUSE DR

Beech House Farm

Sunnyside Farm PH

TOWCESTER DR

Wakefield Gdns

Nursery

BLACKWELL END

THE ORCHARD

WATLING ST

OAK WY

SANDE RS LA

MEADOW VIEW

SCHOOL LA

COACH YD

WOODS LA

CHURCH LA

PO

CHAPEL END

Greystone Lodge

HIGH ST

DUCHESS GDNS

BROWNSWOOD DR

HOMESTEAD

MK19

KENNELLS DR

WAKEFIELD LODGE ESTATE

Wakefield Farm

Dairy Quarter

Main Drive Cottages

MAIN DR

ELMFIELD CL

MAYS WAY

Potterspury

John Hellins Prim Sch

NORTH CRES

CHET LE

CASTLE WAY

GRAFTON RD

POUNDFIELD RD

FURTHO LA

DROVERS WAY

Potterspury House

MANSION GDNS

Redmoor Copse

POTTERSPURY RD

Cherrytree Lodge

Puxley Farm

DEANSHANGER RD

PUXLEY RD

Dairy Farm

A5

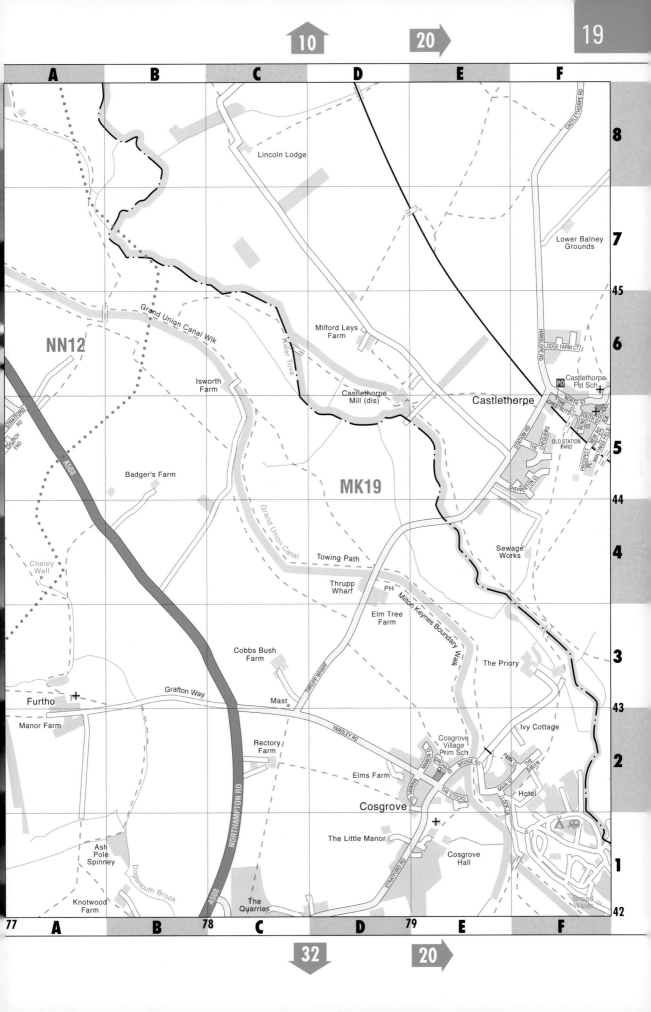

A   B   C   D   E   F

8

Manor Farm

Long Plantation

Mast
Park House

Narrow Leys

Swan's Way
Midshires Way

Hanslope Park

MK16

Hanger Quarter

7

Bullington End

45

Hanslope Lodge

Glenmore Farm

New Buildings

6

THRUPP CL
TYRELL CL

NORTH ST
COVERT LA

Castlethorpe

Leamington Farm

Swan's Way
Midshires Way

SOUTH ST

5

Maltings Farm

PADDOCK CL
MALTINGS CT

WOLVERTON RD

Pineham Farm

44

Hanslope Circular Ride

MK19

Pikes Farm

Field House Farm

4

Water Tower

Fox Covert

Otley Farm

GRANARY CL

3

Lodge Farm Bsns Ctr

Haythorn Spinney

Crossroads Farm

THE STABLES

43

Haversham

HIGH ST

PH

2

CHALMERS AVE
ROWAN DR
KEEPEL AVE

Haversham Village Sch

BROOKFIELD RD

MANOR DR

Haversham Manor

BEECH TREE CL

THE CRESCENT

HAVERSHAM RD

1

River Great Ouse

MK12

P

42

MK13

80   A   81   B   C   82   D   E   F

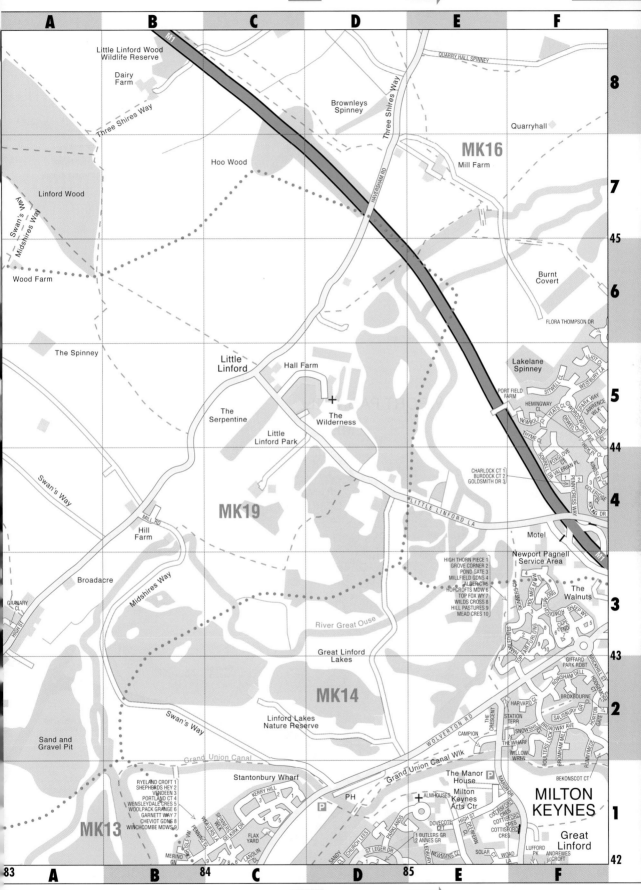

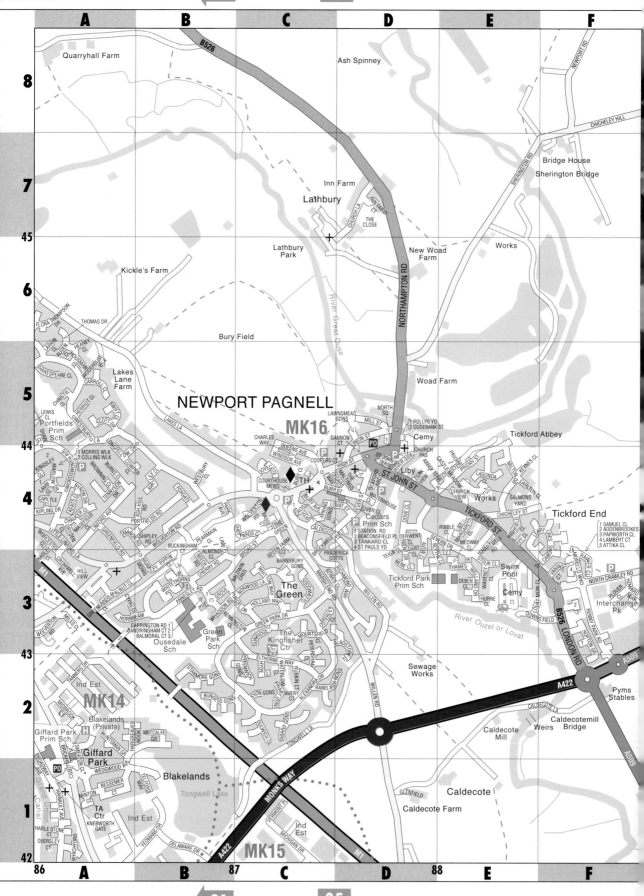

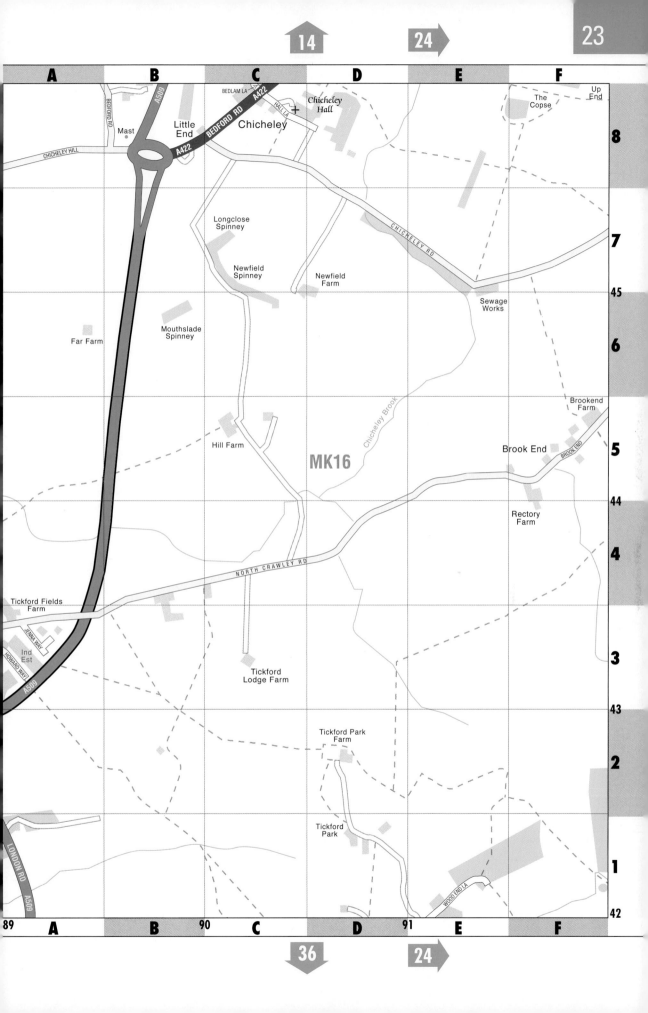

23
15

	A	B	C	D	E	F

Up End

8

606 LA

Little
Crawley
Farm

Horncastle
Farm

Dollars Grove
Farm

7

Gumbrills
Farm

CHICHELEY RD

POUND LA

Dollars
Grove

Chicheley Brook

Old
Moat
Farm

East
End
Farm

45

ORCHARD WAY

HACKETT PL.

HALPIN LA

Quaker's
Farm

BRYANT CRES

STOW CL

Crawley
Grange

6

North
Crawley

HIGH ST

PH

Rookery
Farm

EAST END

Manor
Farm

East End

BROOK END

North
Crawley
CE Sch

CHURCH
WLK

CHEQUERS LA

Church
Farm

Broadmead

Ford

MK16

5

FOLLY LA

Lodge Farm

CRANFIELD RD

Ringtail Farm

44

Ring Croft
Farm

CRAWLEY RD

SHIRE LANE

4

Murtland's
Farm

Rings Wharley
Farm

Hurstend Farm

3

Hurst End

Sewage
Works

Wharley Farm

FEDDEN HQ

43

ROYCE RD

WEST RD

EAST RD

HENSON CL

REYNOLDS CL

HANDLEY
PAGE CL

Conference
Ctr

MITCHELL
RD

DUNCAN RD

MERCHANT LA

THE DRIVE

PRINCE PHILIP AVE

THE
GREEN

2

THE
CRESCENT

COLLEGE RD

LANCHESTER RD

PO

CENTRAL AVE

The Cottage

Cranfield
Univ

Wharley
End

Liby

MK43

Moulsoe Old Wood

Chapelclose
Spinney

UNIVERSITY WAY

Wharley End
Farm

Cranfield
Airport

1

42

| 92 | A | | 93 | B | | C | | D | 94 | E | | F |

23
37

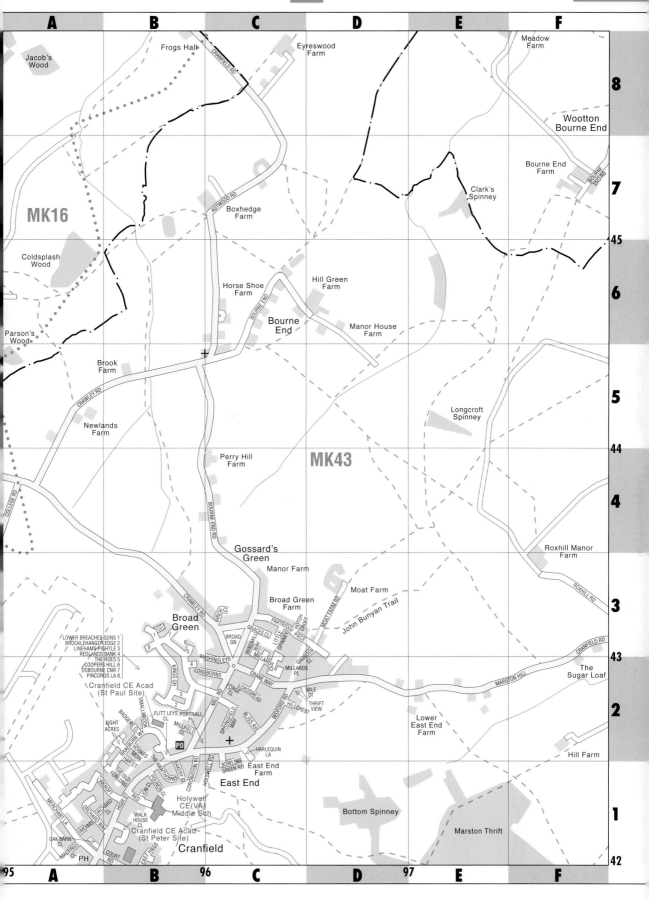

A B C D E F

8

Jacob's Wood

Frogs Hall

Eyreswood Farm

Meadow Farm

Wootton Bourne End

7

MK16

Astwood Rd

Boxhedge Farm

Clark's Spinney

Bourne End Farm

Bourne End Rd

45

Coldsplash Wood

Horse Shoe Farm

Hill Green Farm

6

Bourne End

Manor House Farm

Parson's Wood

Brook Farm

Crawley Rd

5

Newlands Farm

Longcroft Spinney

Perry Hill Farm

MK43

44

College Rd

Bourne End Rd

4

Gossard's Green

Roxhill Manor Farm

Roxhill Rd

Manor Farm

Broad Green Farm

Moat Farm

John Bunyan Trail

3

Crawley Rd

Broad Green

Birch Cl

Graces Cl

Partridge Piece

Little Spinney

Hotch Croft

Moat Farm Rd

Cranfield Rd

The Sugar Loaf

43

LOWER BREACHES GDNS 1
BROCKLEHANGER EDGE 2
LINEHAMS PIGHTLE 3
REDLANDS BANK 4
THE ROES 5
COOPERS HILL 6
OSBOURNE CNR 7
PINCORDS LA 8

Broad Gn

Windmill Way

Millards

Gadsden Cl

Millards Pl

Marston Hill

Washingleys

Kings Gr

Longborns

Mill Rd

Crane Way

Lordsmead

Vale Ct

Thrift View

Cranfield CE Acad (St Paul Site)

Forge Cl

Springfield Way

Bliss Ave

Bedford Rd

Hillcrest

Lower East End Farm

2

Badgers Cl

Smallbrook

Flitt Leys

Portnall Pl

Millfield Cl

Eight Acres

Braybrooke Wy

Harcourt

The Hawthorns

Bakers Ct

Coronation Rd

Holywell Rd

Bowling Green Rd

Harlequin La

East End Farm

Hill Farm

PO

East End

Merchant La

Lagcroft

Orchard Cl

Orchard Way

High St

Simpsons

Pounds Cl

Red Lion Cl

Walk House Cl

Holywell CE(VA) Middle Sch

Bottom Spinney

Marston Thrift

1

Oak Barn Cl

Maltings Cl

PH

The Old Furlong

Court Rd

East Hills

Cranfield CE Acad (St Peter Site)

Cranfield

42

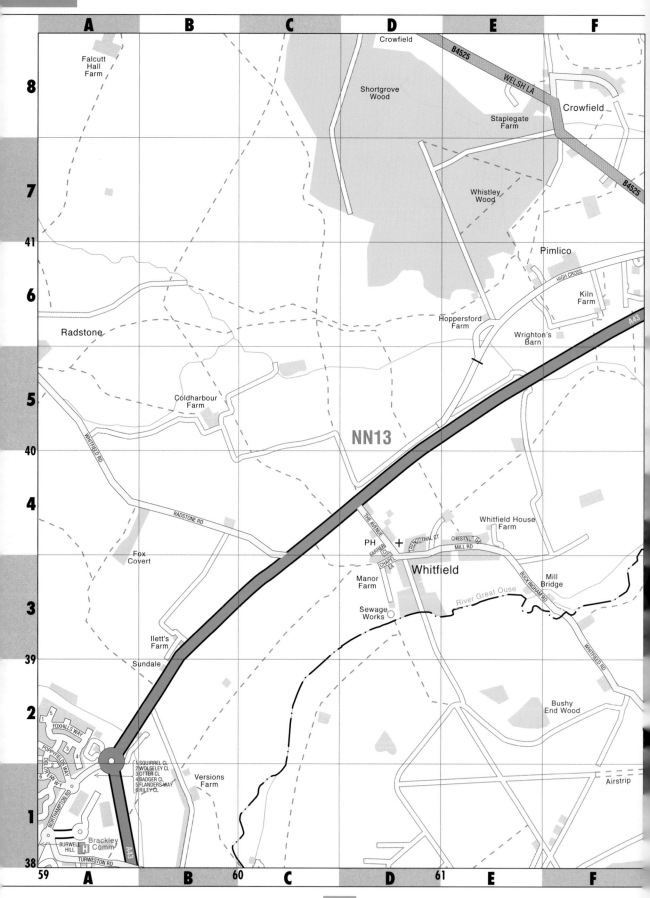

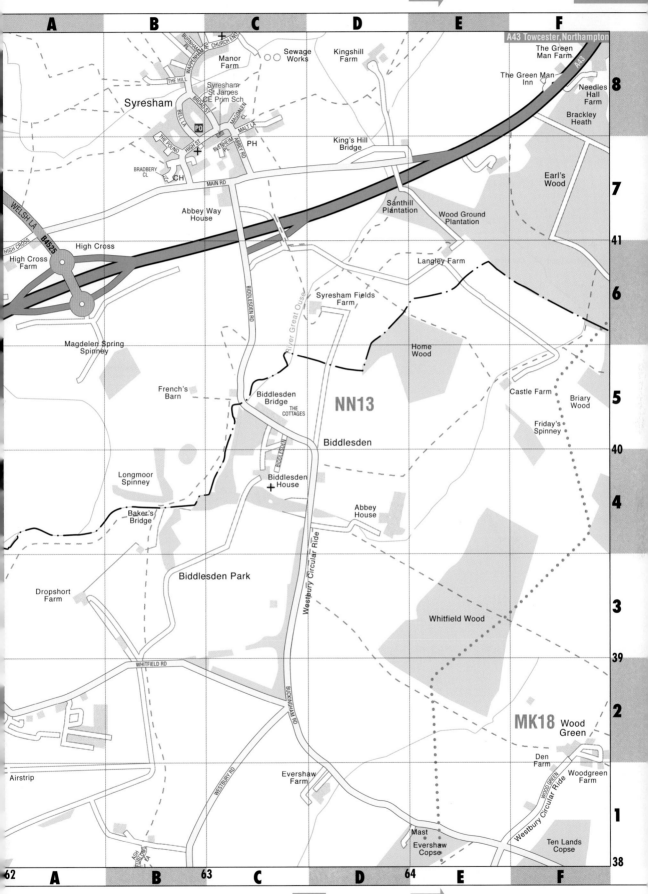

A43 Towcester, Northampton

The Green
Man Farm

The Green Man
Inn

Needles
Hall
Farm

Brackley
Heath

Earl's
Wood

Manor
Farm

Sewage
Works

Kingshill
Farm

Syresham
St James
CE Prim Sch

Syresham

THE HILL

BURNHAM PL
WAPPENHAM PL

CHURCH END

BROAD ST

BELL LA

MAGDELEN CL

MALT LA

THE POUND

HIGH ST

BLENHEIM PL

ABBEY RD

PO

PH

CH

BRADBERY CL

MAIN RD

King's Hill
Bridge

Santhill
Plantation

Wood Ground
Plantation

WELSH LA

B4525

HIGH CROSS

High Cross

High Cross
Farm

Abbey Way
House

Langley Farm

Magdelen Spring
Spinney

BIDDLESDEN RD

River Great Ouse

Syresham Fields
Farm

Home
Wood

Castle Farm

Briary
Wood

French's
Barn

Biddlesden
Bridge

THE
COTTAGES

NN13

Biddlesden

Friday's
Spinney

Longmoor
Spinney

BIDDLESDEN

Biddlesden
House

Abbey
House

Baker's
Bridge

Westbury Circular Ride

Biddlesden Park

Dropshort
Farm

Whitfield Wood

WHITFIELD RD

BUCKINGHAM RD

MK18 Wood
Green

Den
Farm

Woodgreen
Farm

WESTBURY RD

Airstrip

Evershaw
Farm

WOOD GREEN

Westbury Circular Ride

Ten Lands
Copse

Mast

Evershaw
Copse

ASH FURLONG LA

8

7

41

6

5

40

4

3

39

2

1

38

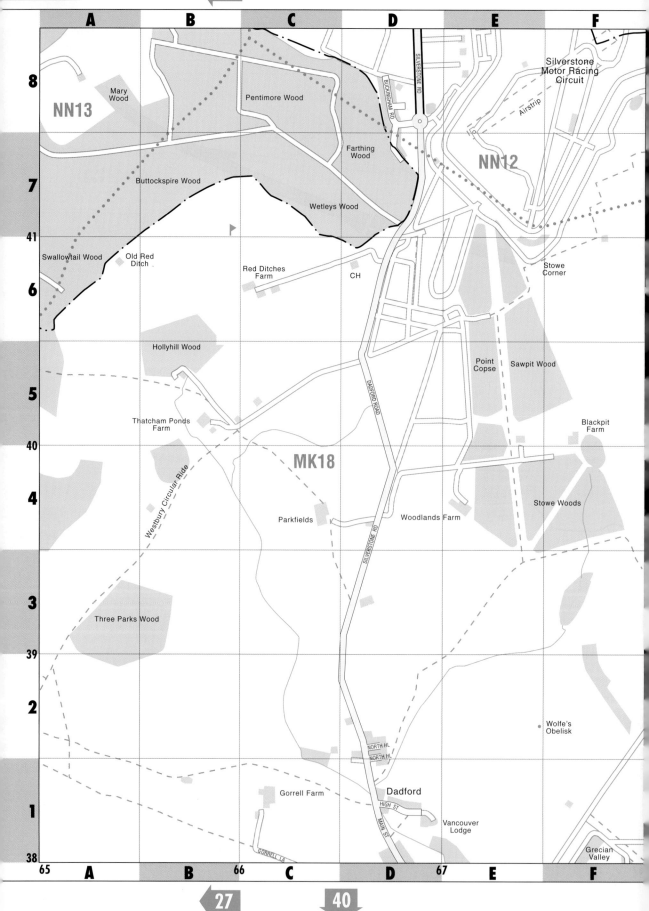

A B C D E F

8

NN13

Mary
Wood

Pentimore Wood

Buckingham Rd

Silverstone Rd

Silverstone
Motor Racing
Circuit

Airstrip

NN12

7

Buttockspire Wood

Farthing
Wood

Wetleys Wood

Stowe
Corner

41

Swallowtail Wood

Old Red
Ditch

Red Ditches
Farm

CH

6

Hollyhill Wood

Point
Copse

Sawpit Wood

5

Thatcham Ponds
Farm

Dadford Road

Blackpit
Farm

40

MK18

Westbury Circular Ride

4

Parkfields

Woodlands Farm

Silverstone Rd

Stowe Woods

3

Three Parks Wood

39

2

Wolfe's
Obelisk

North Hl

North Hl

Gorrell Farm

Dadford

High St

1

Main St

Vancouver
Lodge

Grecian
Valley

38

Gorrell La

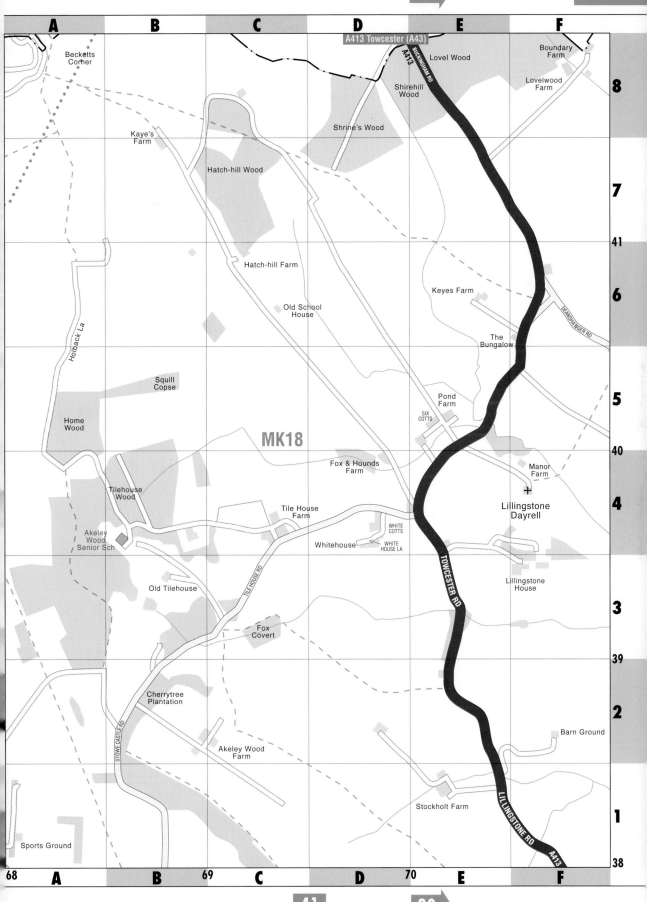

A B C D E F

Beckett's Corner

A413 Towcester (A43)

A413

BUCKINGHAM RD

Lovel Wood

Boundary Farm

Lovelwood Farm

Shirehill Wood

Shrine's Wood

Kaye's Farm

Hatch-hill Wood

Hatch-hill Farm

Keyes Farm

DEANSHANGER RD

Old School House

The Bungalow

Holback La

Squill Copse

Pond Farm

Home Wood

SIX COTTS

MK18

Manor Farm

Fox & Hounds Farm

Lillingstone Dayrell

Tilehouse Wood

Tile House Farm

WHITE COTTS

Whitehouse

WHITE HOUSE LA

Lillingstone House

Akeley Wood Senior Sch

TILE HOUSE RD

TOWCESTER RD

Old Tilehouse

Fox Covert

Barn Ground

Cherrytree Plantation

STOWE CASTLE RD

Akeley Wood Farm

Stockholt Farm

LILLINGSTONE RD

A413

Sports Ground

68 A B 69 C D 70 E F

8 7 41 6 5 40 4 3 39 2 1 38

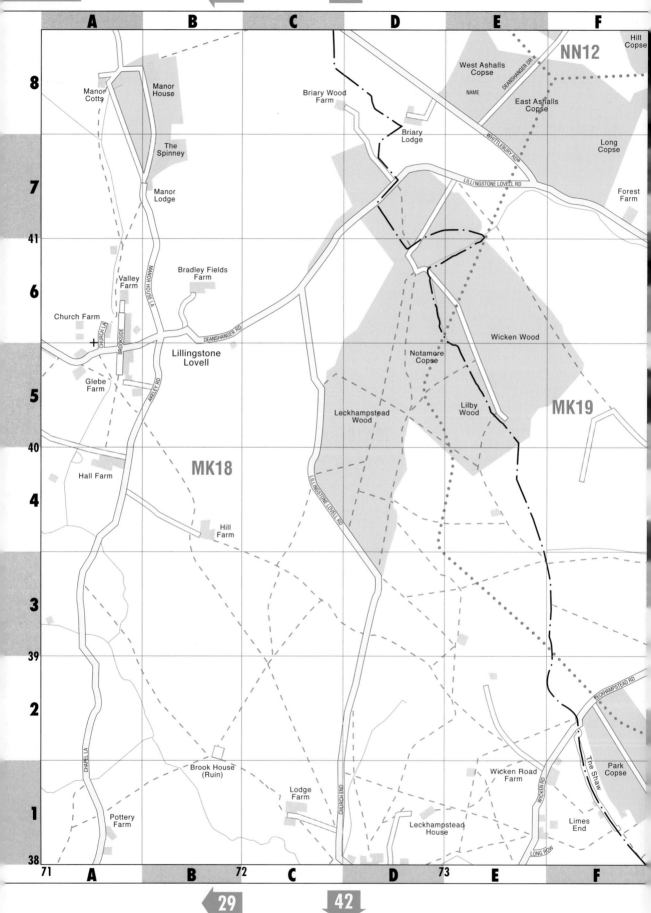

| | A | B | C | D | E | F |

8

Manor Cotts

Manor House

The Spinney

Briary Wood Farm

West Ashalls Copse

NAME

East Ashalls Copse

Hill Copse

NN12

DEANSHANGER DR

Briary Lodge

Long Copse

WHITTLEBURY RD

7

Manor Lodge

LILLINGSTONE LOVELL RD

Forest Farm

41

MANOR HOUSE LA

Valley Farm

Bradley Fields Farm

Church Farm

BROOKSIDE

CHURCH LA

DEANSHANGER RD

Wicken Wood

6

Glebe Farm

AKLEY RD

Lillingstone Lovell

Notamare Copse

MK19

5

Leckhampstead Wood

Lilby Wood

40

Hall Farm

MK18

4

Hill Farm

LILLINGSTONE LOVELL RD

3

39

LECKHAMPSTEAD RD

2

Brook House (Ruin)

Wicken Road Farm

WICKEN RD

The Shaw

Park Copse

1

CHAPEL LA

Pottery Farm

Lodge Farm

CHURCH END

Leckhampstead House

LONG ROW

Limes End

38

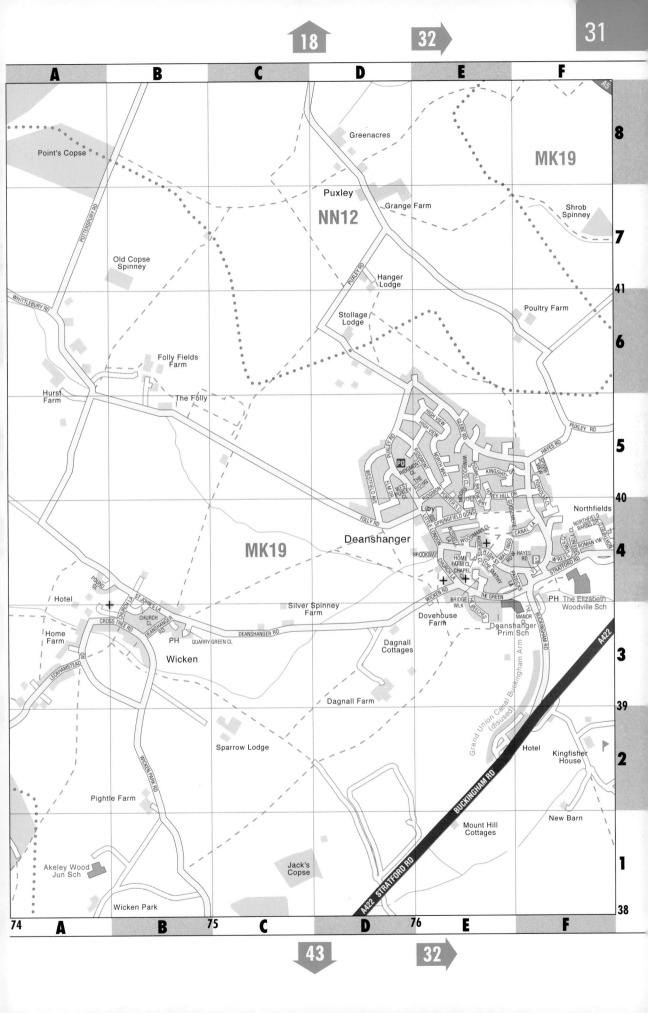

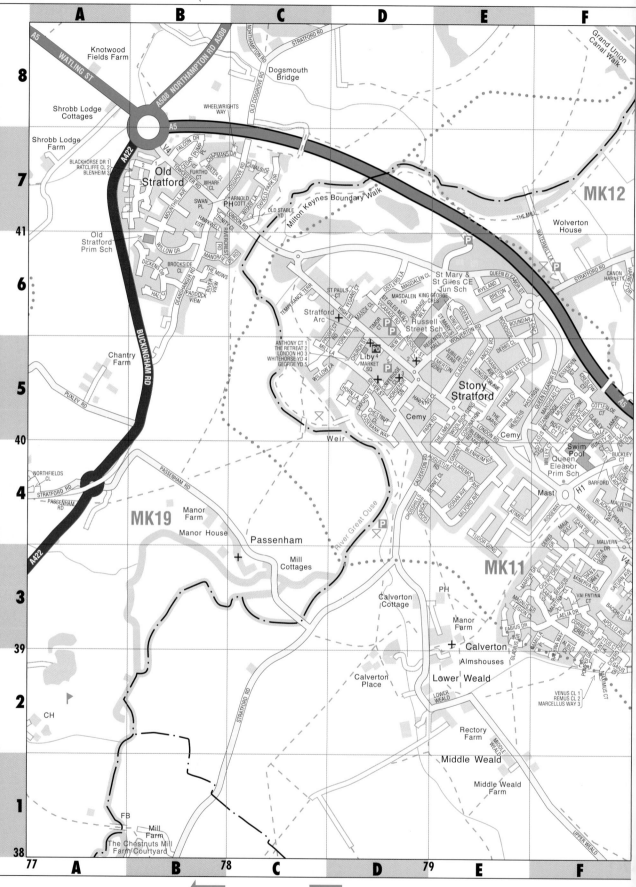

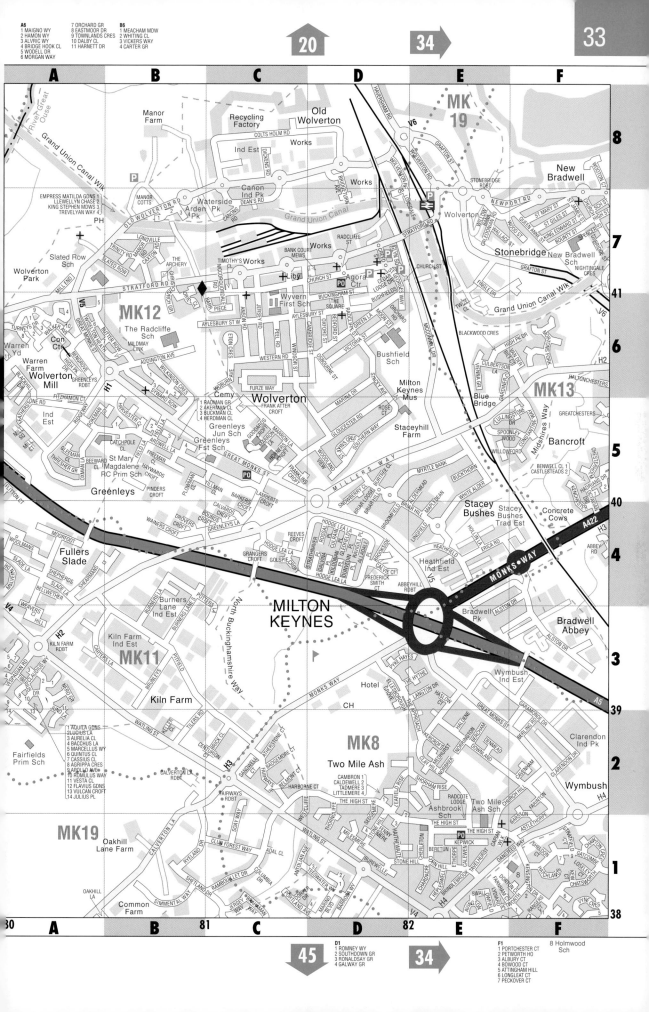

33 21

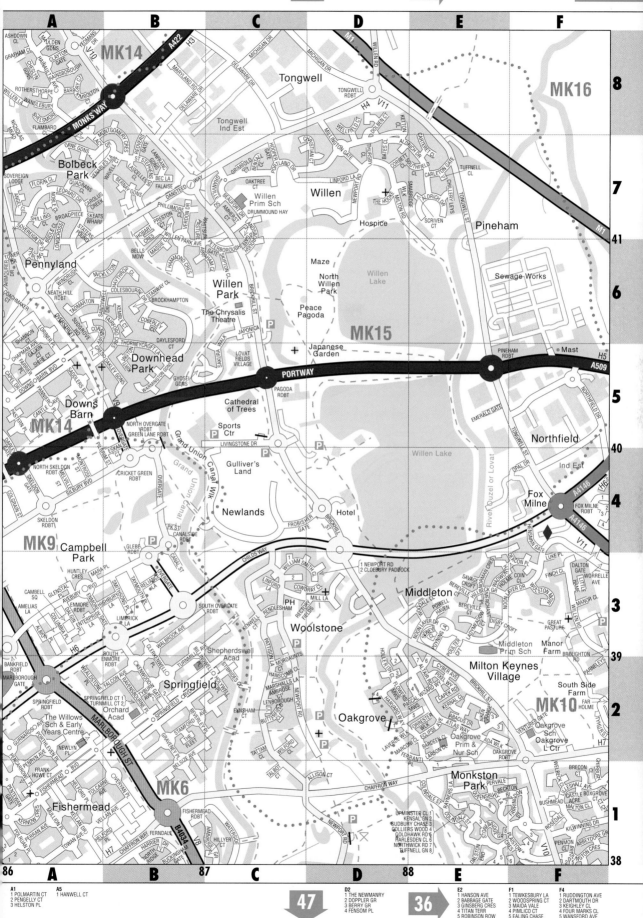

A1
1 POLMARTIN CT
2 PENGELLY CT
3 HELSTON PL

A5
1 HANWELL CT

47

D2
1 THE NEWMANRY
2 DOPPLER GR
3 BERRY GR
4 FENSOM PL

36

E2
1 HANSON AVE
2 BABBAGE GATE
3 GINSBERG CRES
4 TITAN TERR
5 ROBINSON ROW
6 GAMBIT AVE
7 ALTAIR RD

F1
1 TEWKESBURY LA
2 WOODSPRING CT
3 MAIDA VALE
4 PIMLICO CT
5 EALING CHASE
6 ISLINGTON GR

F4
1 RUDDINGTON AVE
2 DARTMOUTH DR
3 KEIGHLEY CL
4 FOUR MARKS CL
5 WANSFORD AVE

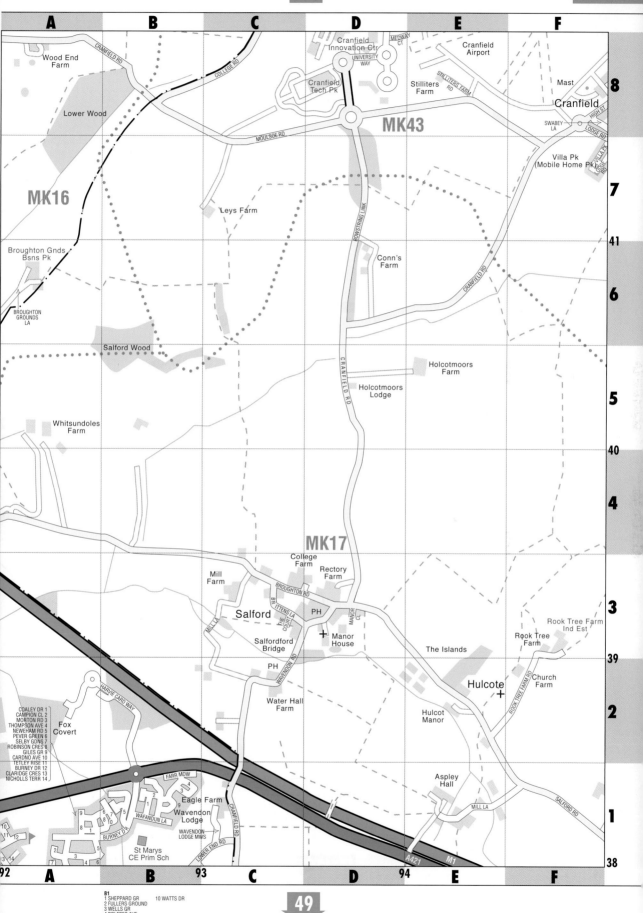

A B C D E F

8

Wood End Farm

Lower Wood

CRANFIELD RD

COLLEGE RD

MOULSOE RD

Cranfield Innovation Ctr

MEDWAY CT

UNIVERSITY WAY

Cranfield Tech Pk

Cranfield Airport

Stilliters Farm

STILLITERS FARM RD

Mast

Cranfield

HIGH ST

SWABEY LA

LODGE RD

MK43

Villa Pk (Mobile Home Pk)

VILLA PK

LODGE RD

MK16

7

Leys Farm

BOWSTRING LINK

Conn's Farm

CRANFIELD RD

41

Broughton Gnds Bsns Pk

BROUGHTON GROUNDS LA

6

Salford Wood

CRANFIELD RD

Holcotmoors Farm

Holcotmoors Lodge

5

Whitsundoles Farm

40

4

MK17

College Farm

Rectory Farm

Mill Farm

BROUGHTON RD

BRITTENS LA

THE COURT

MILL LA

Salford

PH

MANOR CL

3

Rook Tree Farm Ind Est

Rook Tree Farm

Salfordford Bridge

Manor House

The Islands

39

PH

WAVENDON RD

ROOK TREE FARM RD

Church Farm

Hulcote

COALEY DR 1
CAMPION CL 2
MORTON RD 3
THOMPSON AVE 4
NEWEHAM RD 5
PEVER GREEN 6
SELBY GDNS 7
ROBINSON CRES 8
GILES GR 9
CARDNO AVE 10
TETLEY RISE 11
BURNEY DR 12
CLARIDGE CRES 13
NICHOLLS TERR 14

HARVIE CARD WAY

Fox Covert

Water Hall Farm

Hulcot Manor

2

FARR MDW

Eagle Farm

WAFANDUN LA

BURNEY DR

Wavendon Lodge

WAVENDON LODGE MWS

CRANFIELD RD

LOWER END RD

St Marys CE Prim Sch

Aspley Hall

MILL LA

SALFORD RD

1

A421

M1

38

92 A B 93 C D 94 E F

B1
1 SHEPPARD GR
2 FULLERS GROUND
3 WELLS GR
4 BOLEBEC AVE
5 COURTENAY CROFT
6 WATSON DR
7 STURGESS AVE
8 BELL GR
9 ABBATS WOOD

10 WATTS DR

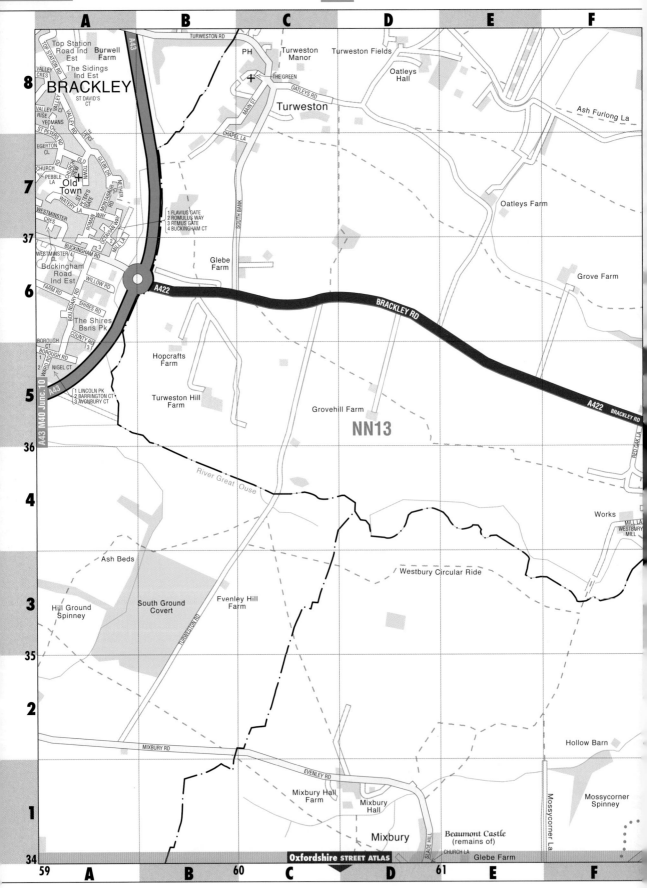

BRACKLEY

Top Station Road Ind Est
Burwell Farm
The Sidings Ind Est
VALLEY CRES
ST DAVID'S CT
VALLEY RISE
ST PETERS RD
YEOMANS CL
EGERTON CL
CHURCH
PEBBLE LA
CHURCH RD
Old Town
NETHER PETER'S GATE
WATERY LA
OLD TOWN
GLEBE DR
ROMAN WAY
MONTGOMERY
WESTMINSTER CRES
BUCKINGHAM RD
WESTMINSTER CL
Buckingham Road Ind Est
FARM RD
WILLOW RD
BOUNDARY RD
SHIRES RD
The Shires Bsns Pk
COUNTY RD
BOROUGH CT
BOROUGH RD
WHD CT
Nigel CT

1 FLAVIUS GATE
2 ROMULUS WAY
3 REMUS GATE
4 BUCKINGHAM CT

1 LINCOLN PK
2 BARRINGTON CT
3 AVONBURY CT

A43 M40 Junc. 10
A43

TURWESTON RD
Turweston Manor
Turweston Fields
PH
THE GREEN
MAIN ST
CHAPEL LA
Turweston
Oatleys Hall
Ash Furlong La

SOUTH BANK
Oatleys Farm
Grove Farm

Glebe Farm
A422
BRACKLEY RD
A422 BRACKLEY RD

Hopcrafts Farm
Turweston Hill Farm
Grovehill Farm

NN13

RED OAK LA

River Great Ouse

Works
MILL LA
WESTBURY MILL

Ash Beds
Westbury Circular Ride

Hill Ground Spinney
South Ground Covert
Evenley Hill Farm

TURWESTON RD

Hollow Barn

MIXBURY RD
EVENLEY RD
Mixbury Hall Farm
Mixbury Hall
Mossycorner Spinney

Mossycorner La

Mixbury
SLADE HILL
Beaumont Castle (remains of)
CHURCH LA
Glebe Farm

59   A   B   60   C   D   61   E   F

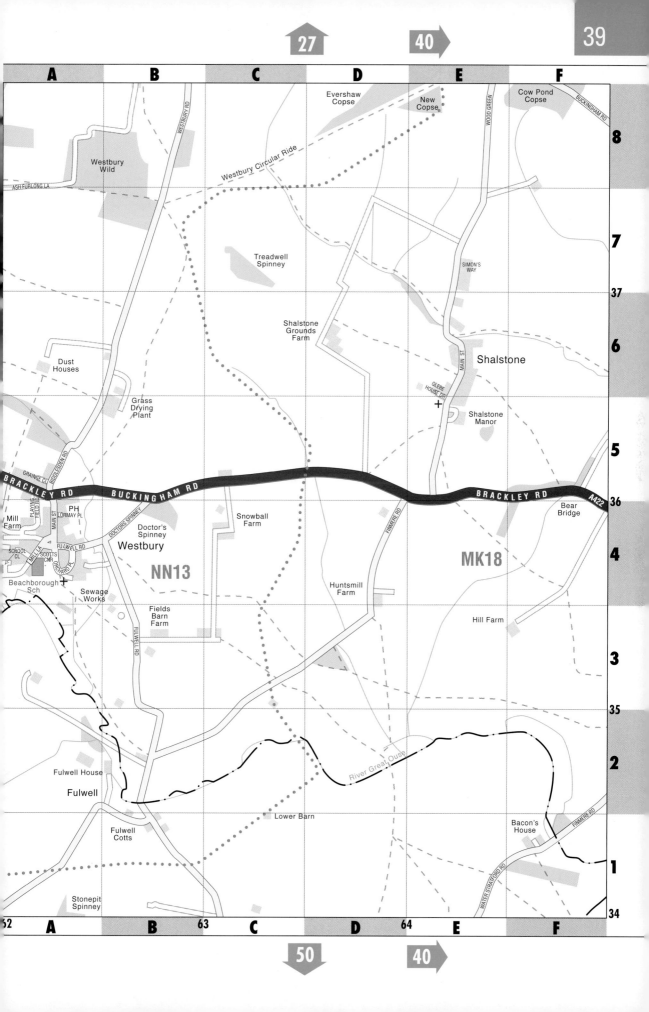

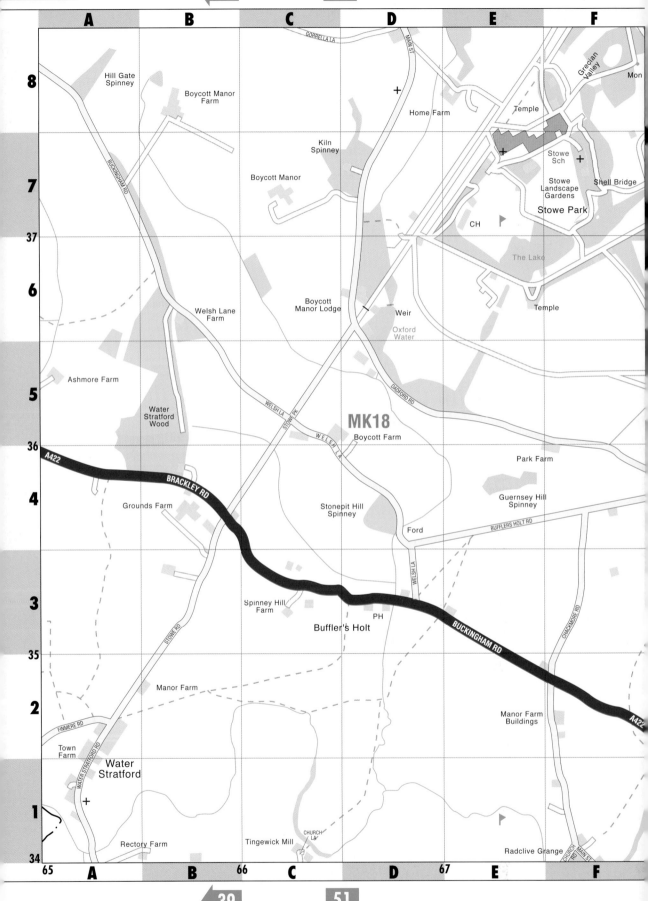

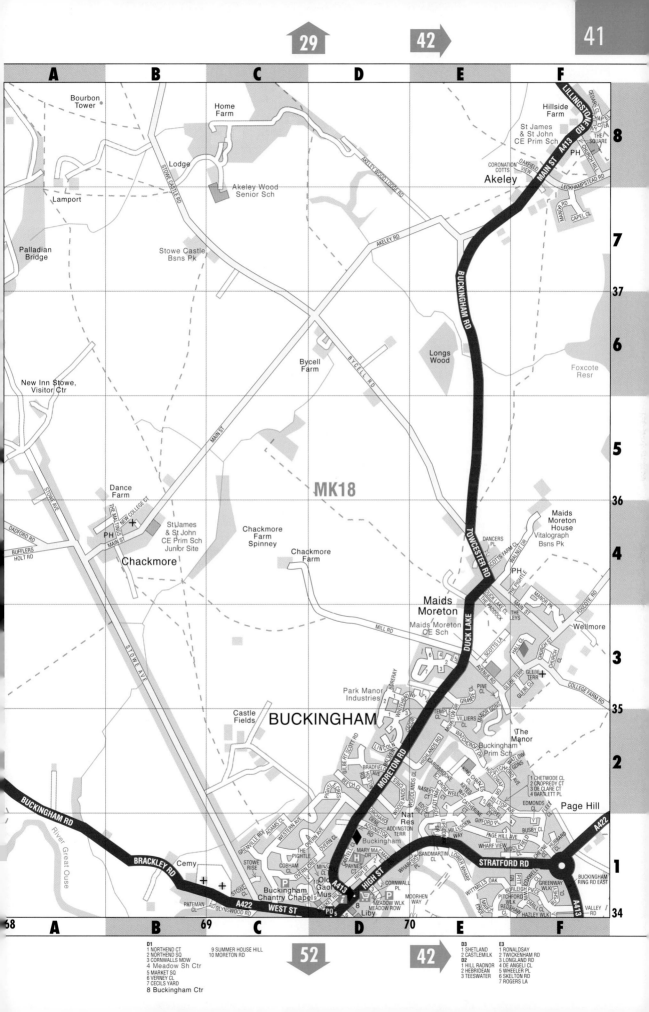

A B C D E F

8 7 37 6 5 36 4 3 35 2 1 34

Bourbon Tower
Home Farm
Hillside Farm
St James & St John CE Prim Sch
LILLINGSTONE RD
CEDARS CL
CHAPEL
THE SQUARE
Lodge
PH
CHURCH HILL
MAIN ST
A413
OAKFIELD
Lamport
STOWE CASTLE RD
Akeley Wood Senior Sch
CORONATION COTTS
VIEW
LECKHAMPSTEAD RD
Akeley
MANOR RD
CAPEL CL
Palladian Bridge
Stowe Castle Bsns Pk
AKELEY WOOD LODGE RD
AKELEY RD
BUCKINGHAM RD
New Inn Stowe, Visitor Ctr
Bycell Farm
BYCELL RD
Longs Wood
Foxcote Resr
STOWE AVE
MAIN ST
MK18
Dance Farm
Chackmore Farm Spinney
Chackmore Farm
TOWCESTER RD
Maids Moreton House Vitalograph Bsns Pk
DADFORD RD
THE MALTINGS
NEW COLLEGE CT
St James & St John CE Prim Sch Junior Site
DANCERS PL
SCOTTS FARM CL
WALNUT DR
MAIN ST
MANOR PK
BUFFLERS HOLT RD
PH
MAIN ST
Chackmore
DUCK LAKE CL
THE PIGHTLE
THE LEYS
PH
FOSSOTE RD
Maids Moreton
DUCK LAKE
Wellmore
MILL RD
Maids Moreton OE Sch
SCOTTS LA
AVENUE RD
HALL CL
GLEBE TERR
CHURCH
COLLEGE FARM RD
PINE CL
GLEBE TERR
Park Manor Industries
BORERAY
WHITEMEADOW
GRANS
GLEBE RD
The Manor
STOWE AVE
Castle Fields
BUCKINGHAM
TEMPLE
VILLIERS CL
MANOR GDNS
Buckingham Prim Sch
MORETON RD
LINCOLN
WATCHCROFT
WATLOW GDNS
1 CHETWODE CL
2 CROPREDY CT
3 DE CLARE CT
4 BARTLETT PL
GILBERT SCOTT RD
CAWKWELL WAY
BRADFIELD AVE
BEECH CL
HOLTON
HORNTON
NASEBY CT
CROMWELL
KING CHARLES
EDGE HILL
KEYES
HILLTOP AVE
EDMONDS CL
Page Hill
A422
River Great Ouse
BUCKINGHAM RD
GRENVILLE RD
ADAMS CL
WESTERN AVE
PIGHTLE CT
BRUCE CL
WOODLANDS RD
CATHERINE
EDGCOTT WAY
LIPSCOMB
GIFFORD PL
BUSBY CL
PAGE HILL AVE
CHEYNE CL
GREENWAY WLK
Buckingham Ring Rd East
Cemy
BRACKLEY RD
STOWE RISE
COBHAM AVE
OVERN AVE
OVERN CRES
OVERN CL
MINSHULL CT
ORCHARD DENE
ADDINGTON TERR
Nat Res Buckingham
SANDMARTIN CL
LOWER WHARF
STRATFORD RD
WHARF VIEW
MIDDLEFIELD
HUBBARD
BURLEIGH PIECE
A413
VALLEY RD
STOWE CL
PATEMAN CL
GLYNSWOOD RD
Buckingham Chantry Chapel
PAYNES CT
THE PIGHTLE
MARY MACKIE CT
CANTELL
CORNWALL PL
WHARFSIDE
MOORHEN WAY
WITTMILLS OAK
PITCHFORD WLK
REDSHAW WLK
HAZLEY WLK
A422
WEST ST
Old Gaol Mus
HIGH ST
A413
PO
Liby
MEADOW WLK
MEADOW ROW
MARSH

D1
1 NORTHEND CT
2 NORTHEND SQ
3 CORNWALLS MDW
4 Meadow Sh Ctr
5 MARKET SQ
6 VERNEY CL
7 CECILS YARD
8 Buckingham Ctr

9 SUMMER HOUSE HILL
10 MORETON RD

D3
1 SHETLAND
2 CASTLEMILK
D2
1 HILL RADNOR
2 HEBRIDEAN
3 TEESWATER

E3
1 RONALDSAY
2 TWICKENHAM RD
3 LONGLAND RD
4 DE ANGELI CL
5 WHEELER RD
6 SKELTON RD
7 ROGERS LA

68   69   70

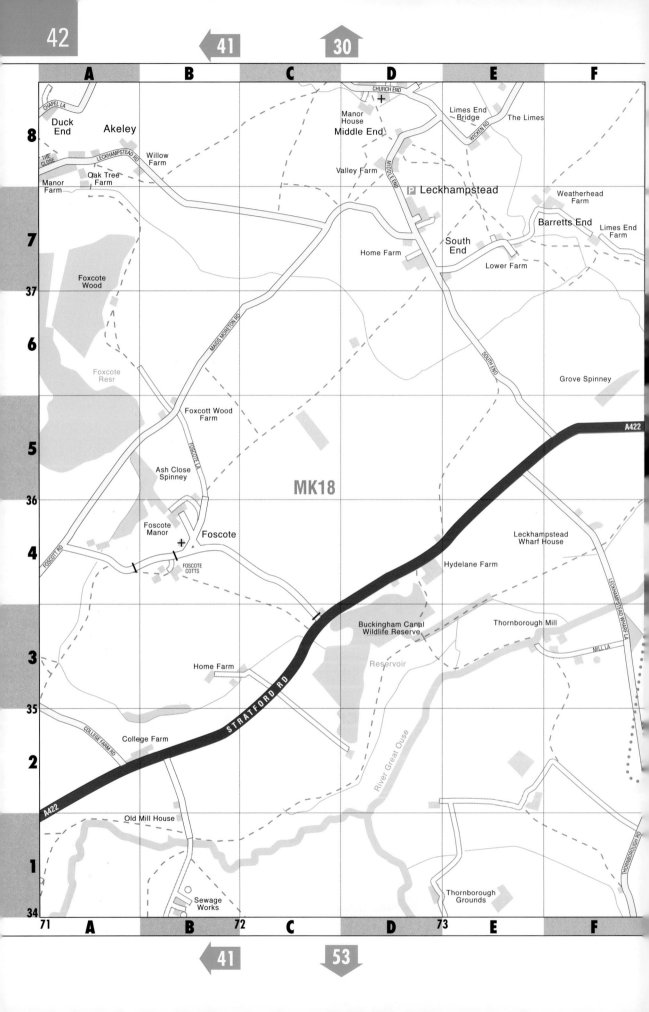

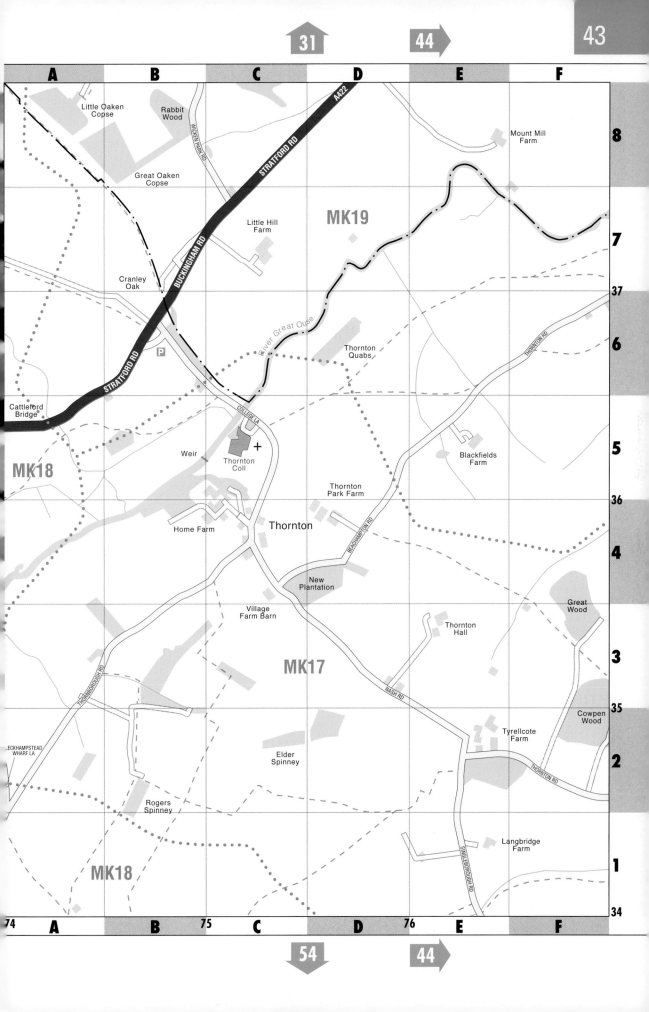

A   B   C   D   E   F

8

Little Oaken
Copse

Rabbit
Wood

Great Oaken
Copse

MK19

Little Hill
Farm

7

37

Cranley
Oak

STRATFORD RD

A422

BUCKINGHAM RD

WICKEN PARK RD

P

River Great Ouse

Thornton
Quabs

Thornton RD

6

STRATFORD RD

Cattleford
Bridge

COLLEGE LA

Weir

Thornton
Coll

+

Blackfields
Farm

5

MK18

Thornton
Park Farm

36

Home Farm

Thornton

4

BEACHAMPTON RD

New
Plantation

Great
Wood

Village
Farm Barn

Thornton
Hall

MK17

3

THORNBOROUGH RD

NASH RD

Cowpen
Wood

35

Tyrellcote
Farm

ECKHAMPSTEAD
WHARF LA

Elder
Spinney

THORNTON RD

2

Rogers
Spinney

Langbridge
Farm

SINGLEBOROUGH RD

1

MK18

34

A   B   C   D   E   F

8

River Great Ouse

Blacon
Spinney

Upper
Weald

UPPER WEALD

Beachampton
Hall

STRATFORD RD

Milton Keynes Boundary Walk

7

Manor
Farm

Hill Farm

37

THORNTON RD

Beachampton

MK19

PH

MAIN ST

Home Farm

WATERY LA

6

ELMERS CT

Red
House
Farm

Beachampton
Grove

Grange
Farm

NASH RD

Grove Farm

5

36

School
Furze

The Oaks

4

Beachampton
Bsns Pk

Potash
Farm

3

Furzenfield
Farm

35

Elm
Farm

2

MK17

NASH RD

Yew Tree
Farm

Basshill
Farm

WHADDON RD

STRATFORD RD

THORNTON RD

Holywell
Cottages

PANTERS CL

Town
End

North Buckinghamshire Way

Holywell Farm

The
Hill

HIGH ST

Nash

1

STRATFORD RD

ALL SAINTS
CL

WINSLOW RD

Barnhill
Farm

THORNBOROUGH
RD

OLD ENGLISH

34

77   A   B   78   C   D   79   E   F

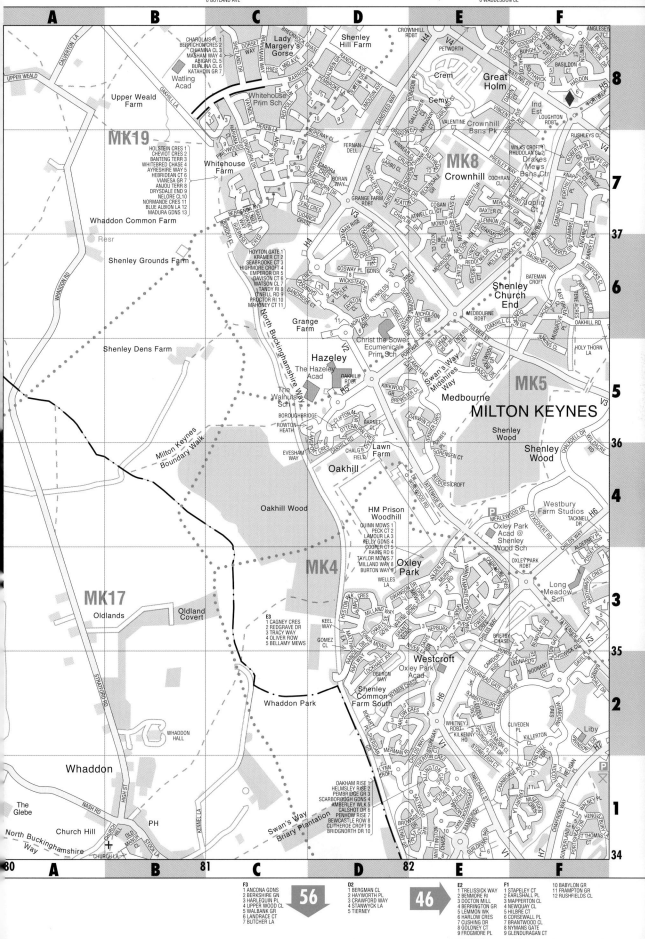

D8
1 DALESBREDGR
2 SIMFORD WAY
3 PORTLAND AVE
4 HEREFORD WY
5 JACOB GR
6 GOTLAND AVE
7 ZUBRON GR
8 BEULAH GR
9 CANARIA CL
10 SALORN WAY

33

46

F8
1 ALBURY CT
2 MENTMORE CT
3 HOUGHTON CT
4 HUNTINGBROOKE
5 HAMPTON
6 WADDESDON CL
7 VYNE CRES

45

Map Labels

MK19

MK17

MK8 — Crownhill

MK5

MK4

MILTON KEYNES

Upper Weald Farm

Whitehouse Farm

Whaddon Common Farm

Shenley Grounds Farm

Shenley Dens Farm

Oldlands

Oldland Covert

Whaddon Hall

Whaddon

Whaddon Park

The Glebe

Church Hill

North Buckinghamshire Way

Oakhill Wood

Grange Farm

Hazeley

The Hazeley Acad

The Walnuts Sch

Boroughbridge

Rowton Heath

Oakhill

HM Prison Woodhill

Shenley Church End

Christ the Sower Ecumenical Prim Sch

Medbourne

Shenley Wood

Westbury Farm Studios

Oxley Park Acad @ Shenley Wood Sch

Long Meadow Sch

Oxley Park

Westcroft

Oxley Park Acad

Shenley Common Farm South

Lady Margery's Gorse

Shenley Hill Farm

Great Holm

Crem

Crownhill Bsns Pk

Drakes Mews Bsns Ctr

Ind Est

Watling Acad

Whitehouse Prim Sch

Upper Weald

F3
1 ANCONA GDNS
2 BERKSHIRE GN
3 HARLEQUIN CL
4 UPPER WOOD CL
5 WALBANK GR
6 LANDRACE CT
7 BUTCHER LA

56

D2
1 BERGMAN CL
2 HAYWORTH PL
3 CRAWFORD WAY
4 STANWYCK LA
5 TIERNEY

46

E2
1 TRELISSICK WAY
2 BENMORE RI
3 DOCTON MILL
4 BERRINGTON GR
5 LEMMON WK
6 HARLOW CRES
7 CUSHING DR
8 GOLDNEY CT
9 FROGMORE PL

F1
1 STAPELEY CT
2 EARLSHALL PL
3 MAPPERTON CL
4 NEWQUAY CL
5 HILBRE CT
6 CORSEWALL PL
7 BRANTWOOD CL
8 NYMANS GATE
9 GLENDURAGAN CL

10 BABYLON GR
11 FRAMPTON GR
12 RUSHFIELDS CL

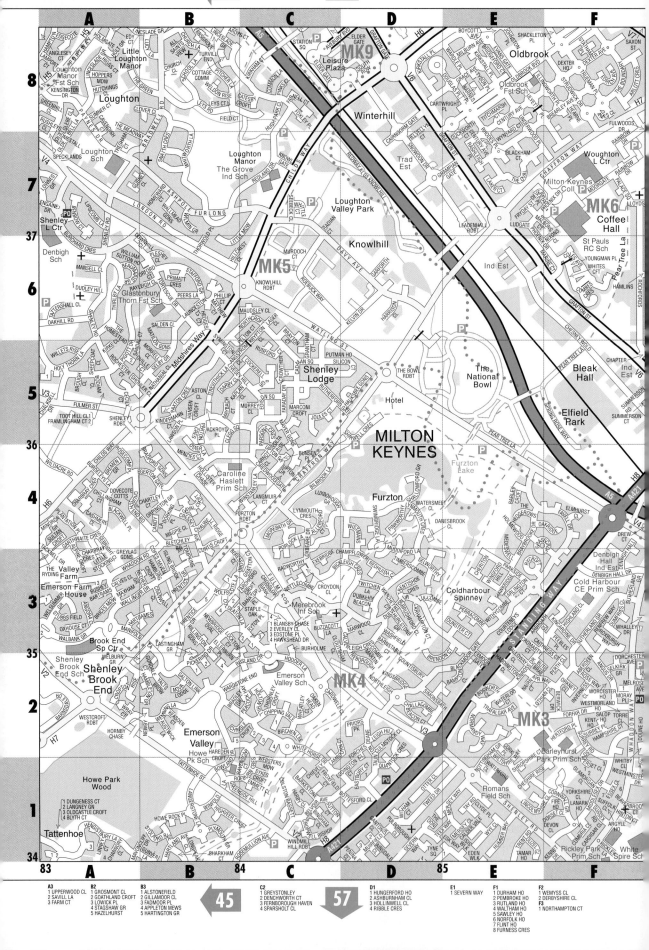

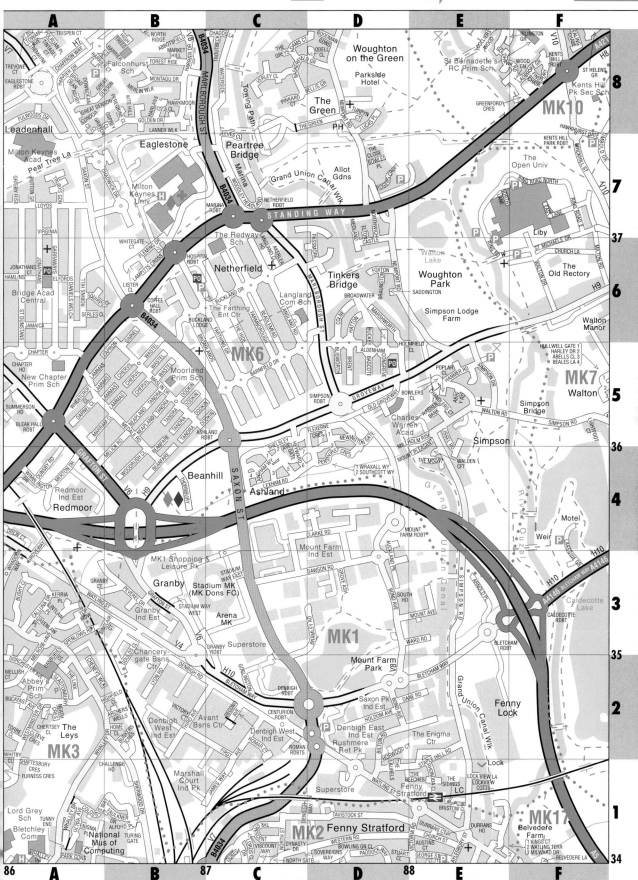

C4
1 THE MARTLET
2 FELSTAR WK
3 WETHERINGSETT
4 GENESIS GN
5 KELSALE CHASE
6 FENLANDIA
7 YEARL STONE SQ

48

47

36

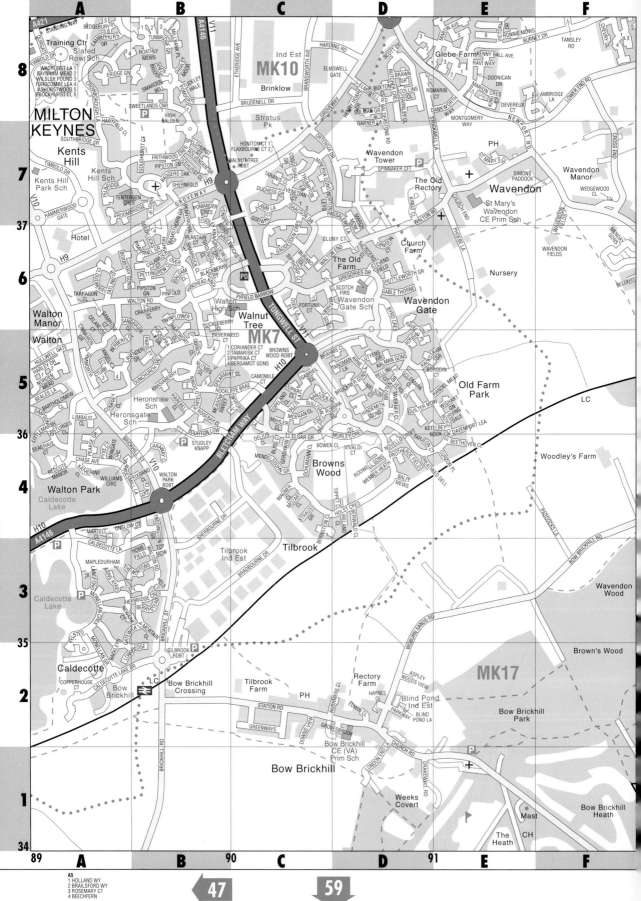

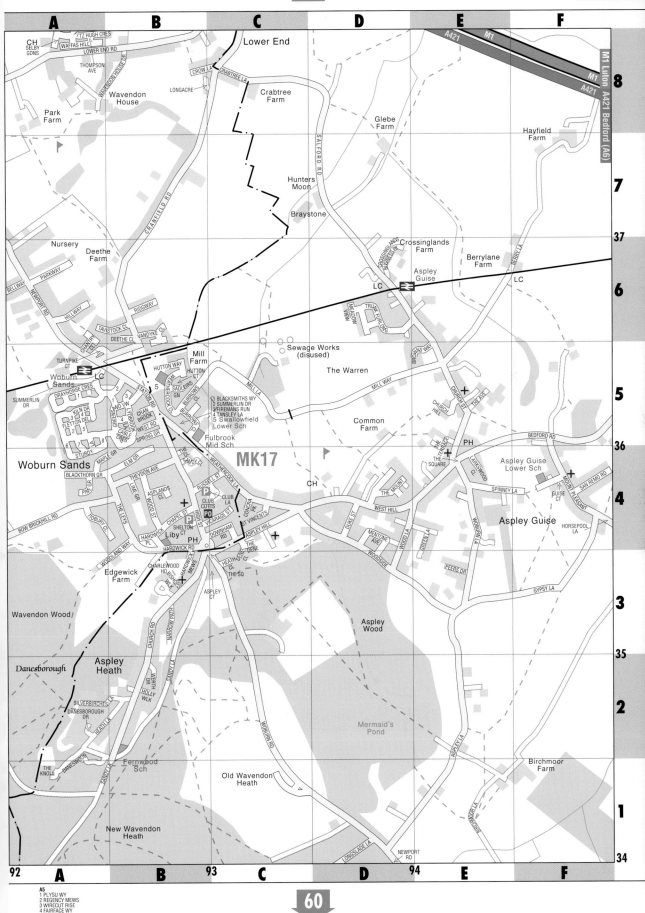

A5
1 PLYSU WY
2 REGENCY MEWS
3 WIRECUT RISE
4 FAIRFACE WY
5 CLAY GDNS
6 EASTAFF CROFT
7 BADGERS HOLT
8 WILKIE CT

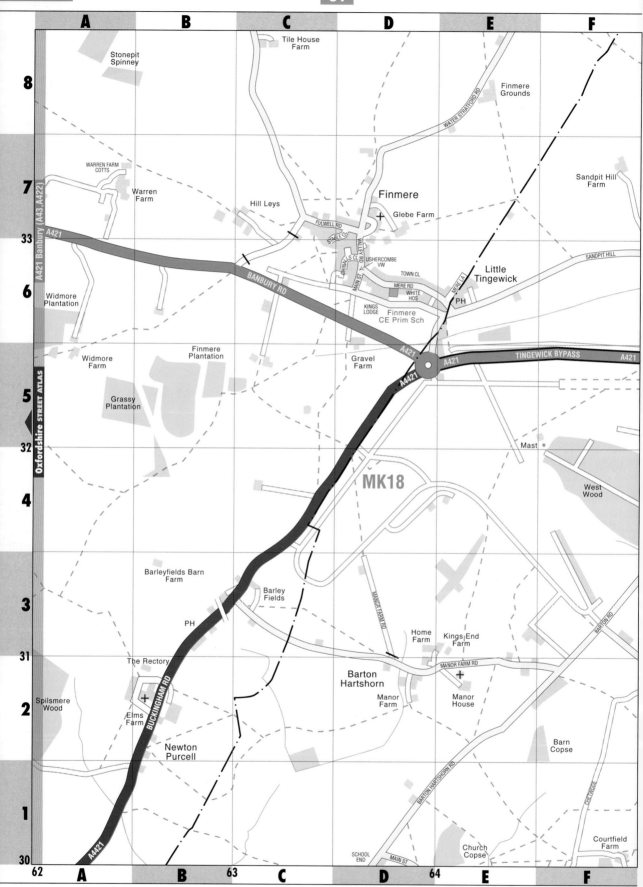

Stonepit
Spinney

Tile House
Farm

Finmere
Grounds

Sandpit Hill
Farm

WARREN FARM
COTTS

Warren
Farm

Hill Leys

Finmere

Glebe Farm

Little
Tingewick

Sandpit Hill

A421

FULWELL RD

STABLE CL

VALLEY RD

MAIN ST

S CL

LS CL

USHERCOMBE
VW

TOWN CL

MERE RD

WHITE
HOS

MERE LA

PH

BANBURY RD

Widmore
Plantation

Widmore
Farm

Finmere
Plantation

KINGS
LODGE

Finmere
CE Prim Sch

Gravel
Farm

A421

TINGEWICK BYPASS   A421

A4421

Grassy
Plantation

Mast

West
Wood

MK18

Barleyfields Barn
Farm

Barley
Fields

MANOR FARM RD

Home
Farm

Kings End
Farm

BARTON RD

PH

The Rectory

BUCKINGHAM RD

Barton
Hartshorn

MANOR FARM RD

Spilsmere
Wood

Elms
Farm

Manor
Farm

Manor
House

Barn
Copse

Newton
Purcell

BARTON HARTSHORN RD

CHETWODE

Courtfield
Farm

A4421

SCHOOL
END

MAIN ST

Church
Copse

Oxfordshire STREET ATLAS

A421 Banbury (A43, A422)

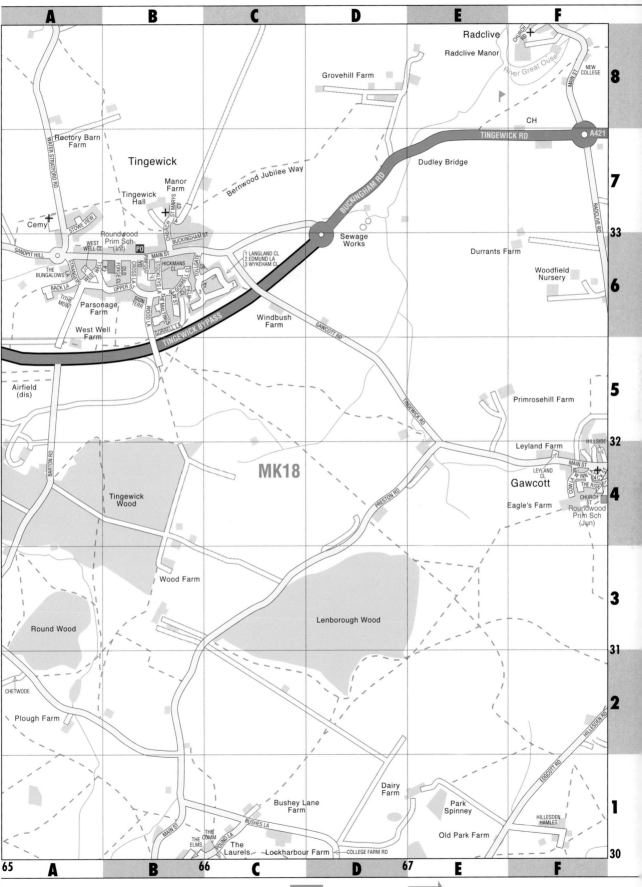

A B C D E F

8
7
33
6
5
32
4
3
31
2
1
30

Radclive
Radclive Manor
CHURCH RD
River Great Ouse
NEW COLLEGE
CH
MAIN ST
TINGEWICK RD
A421
RADCLIVE RD
Grovehill Farm
Dudley Bridge
BUCKINGHAM RD
Tingewick
Bernwood Jubilee Way
Durrants Farm
Woodfield Nursery
Manor Farm
Tingewick Hall
Tingewick Hall
CHURCH LA
ST MARYS CT
BUCKINGHAM ST
Cemy
STOWE VIEW
Roundwood Prim Sch (Inf)
WEST WELL CL
PO
MAIN ST
HICKMANS CL
1 LANGLAND CL
2 EDMUND LA
3 WYKEHAM CL
SANDPIT HILL
THE BUNGALOWS
STRANGERS
WEST WELL
OLD FORGE CL
PINFOLD YD
CROSS ST
STOCKLEYS LA
S M GORREL CL
THE MALTINGS
GORREL FIELD
LYTTLE
Sewage Works
WEST WELL CL
BACK LA
TITHE MDW
UPPER ST
SION TERR
WOOD LA
GORRELL LA
Parsonage Farm
West Well Farm
Windbush Farm
GAWCOTT RD
TINGEWICK BYPASS
Airfield (dis)
Primrosehill Farm
Leyland Farm
HILLSIDE
MK18
LEYLAND CL
MAIN ST
NEW INN
COCK RD
THE RISE
Gawcott
CHURCH ST
Roundwood Prim Sch (Jun)
Eagle's Farm
TINGEWICK RD
BARTON RD
Tingewick Wood
PRESTON RD
Wood Farm
Round Wood
Lenborough Wood
CHETWODE
Plough Farm
HILLSDEN RD
EDGCOTT RD
Dairy Farm
Park Spinney
Bushey Lane Farm
Old Park Farm
HILLESDEN HAMLET
BUSHES LA
MAIN ST
THE COMM
THE ELMS
POUND LA
The Laurels
Lockharbour Farm
COLLEGE FARM RD

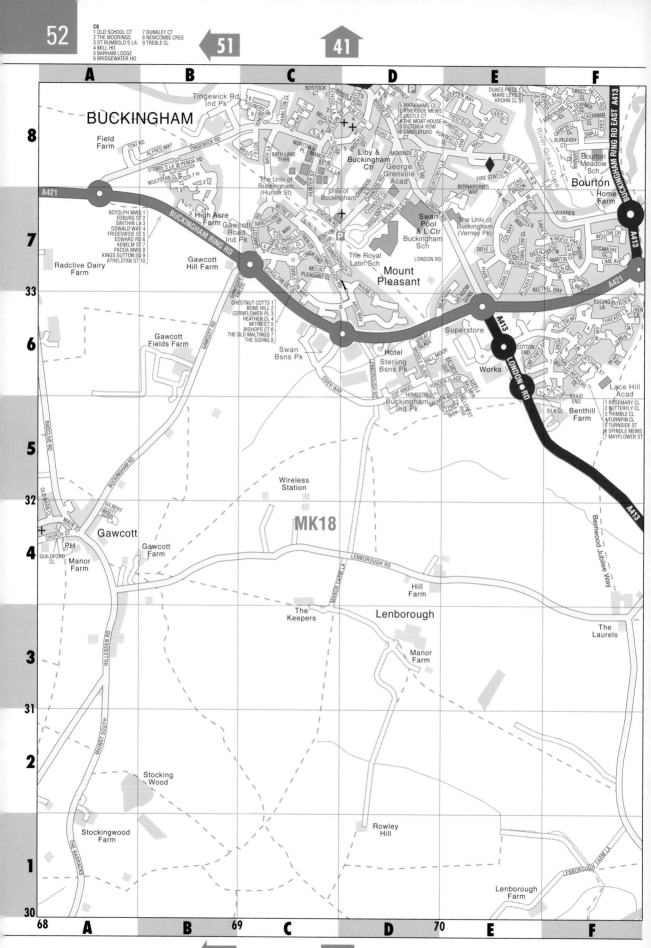

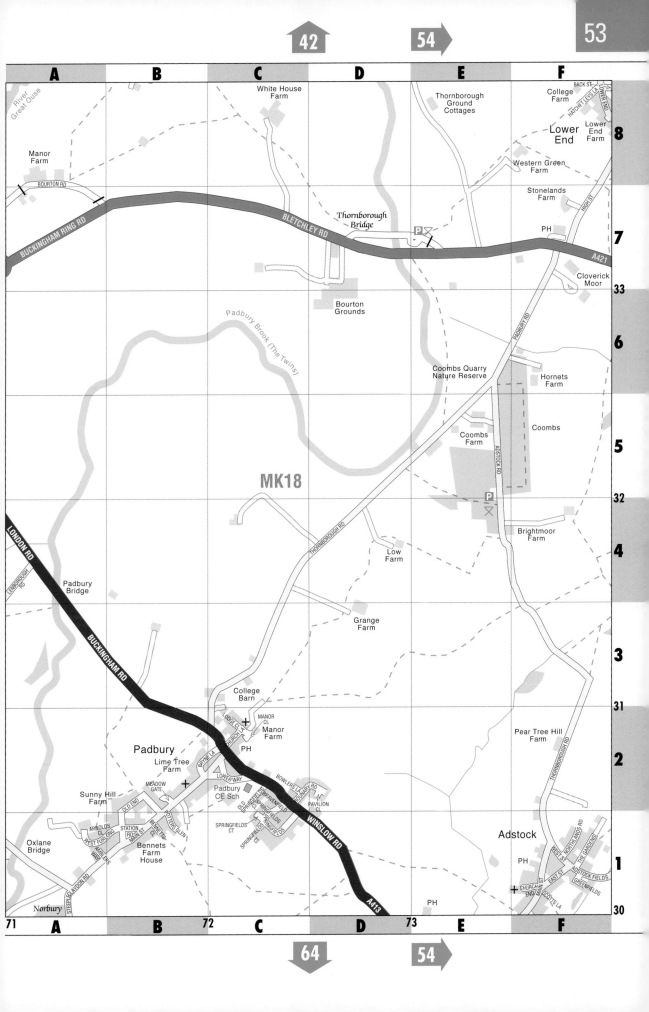

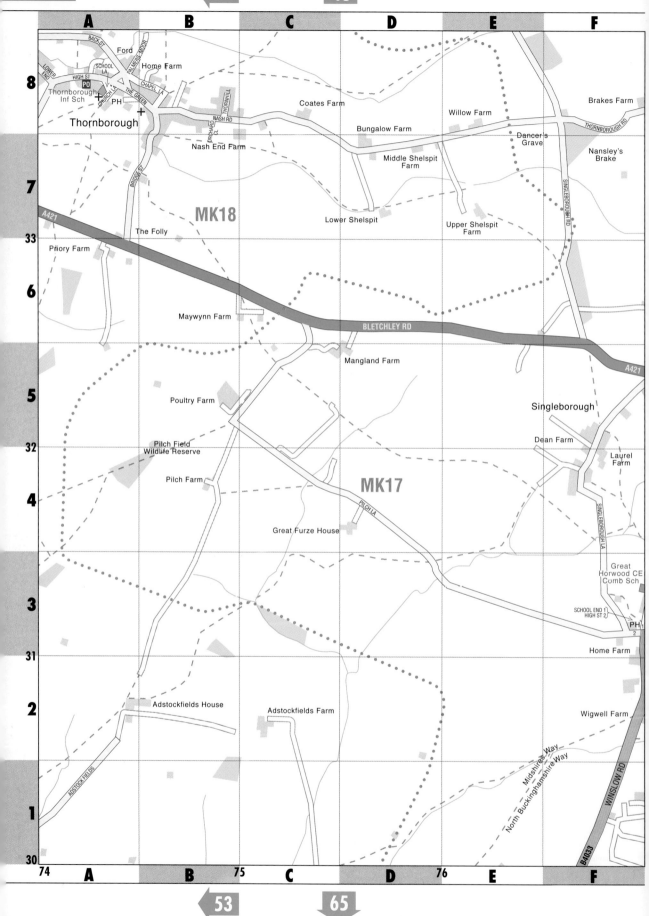

A   B   C   D   E   F

8

Back St

Ford

Home Farm

Lower End

School La

High St

PO

Thornborough Inf Sch

Palmers Moor

Chapel La

The Green

Thornborough

PH

Nash Rd

Thornhill

Orchard Cl

Coates Farm

Willow Farm

Brakes Farm

Thornborough Rd

Nash End Farm

Bungalow Farm

Dancer's Grave

Nansley's Brake

Middle Shelspit Farm

MK18

7

A421

The Folly

33

Lower Shelspit

Upper Shelspit Farm

Singleborough Rd

Priory Farm

6

Maywynn Farm

BLETCHLEY RD

A421

Mangland Farm

5

Poultry Farm

Singleborough

Dean Farm

Laurel Farm

Pilch Field Wildlife Reserve

32

Pilch Farm

MK17

4

Singleborough La

Pilch La

Great Furze House

Great Horwood CE Comb Sch

3

School End 1

High St 2

PH

Home Farm

31

Adstockfields House

Adstockfields Farm

Wigwell Farm

2

Adstock Fields

Midshires Way

North Buckinghamshire Way

Winslow Rd

1

B4033

30

74   A   B   75   C   D   76   E   F

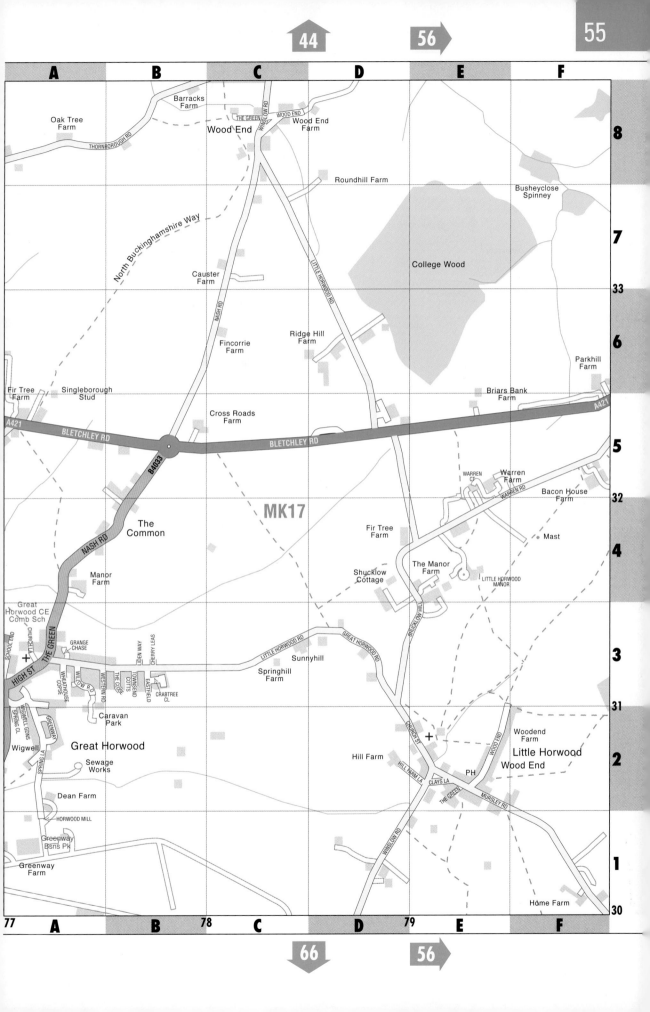

F8
1 BALCARY GR
2 THORPENESS CROFT
3 JEROME WY
4 CHAFFRON WAY
5 SNELSHALL ST

A B C D E F

8

Church-hill Farm

Church Hill

CHURCH LA
Whaddon CE First Sch
KENNEL LA
VICARAGE RD
STOCK LA
LADY MEAD
BRIARY VIEW

SHENLEY RD

17 SNELSHALL ST
18 CHAFFRON WAY

Bottlehouse Farm

KINGSMEAD RDBT
SHENLEY RD
BUDFORD AVE
INCE WY
WALMER WY
HATTON WAY
ST ABBS CT
PORTISHEAD GR
GREAT ORMES

Tattenhoe Bare Farm

Priory Rise Sch
CANTERBURY MEWS
PRIESTLEY DR
MITCHELL WY
FORRESTER GDNS
BRONTE AVE

MK4

Tattenhoe Park

THWAIN WY

7

Coddimoor Farm

Thickbare Wood

CODDIMOOR LA

STEINBECK CRES

33

Coddimoor Farm

Coddimoorhill Wood

Whaddon Chase

6

Hogpound Wood

Woodpond Farm

BOTTLE DUMP RDBT

STANDING WAY   A421

BUCKINGHAM RD

A421   BLETCHLEY RD

BLETCHLEY RD

Thrift Farm

Thrift Wood

Bottledump

WHADDON RD

Bletchley Leys Farm

WARREN RD
FERNFIELD

Broadway Wood

E8
1 TENBY GR
2 CAISTER CT
3 SALTWOOD AVE
4 WHITTINGTON CHASE
5 GOODRICH GN
6 BYWELL CT
7 ASKERTON CRES
8 CARTINGTON GDNS
9 WHADDON RD
10 SUDELEY PL
11 PONTEFRACT AVE
12 HEVER CL
13 DUNSTANBURGH CL
14 TUTBURY LA
15 WHITECASTLE WAY
16 CAREW CT
17 MAXSTOKE GR
18 PENARD CRES
19 CALSHOT DR

5

Fernfield Farm

32

4

Stearthill Farm

WHADDON RD

MK17

Chase Farm

CHASE FARM BARNS

NURSEL RD

Midshires Way

Swan's Way

Weasels'

Lower Salden Farm

Salden Wood

3

Norbury Coppice

Salden Crabtree Farm

31

Crabtree Farm

(dis)

SALDEN LA

2

Springfield Farm

Middle Salden Wood

1

Aqueduct

30

80   A   81   B   C   82   D   E   F

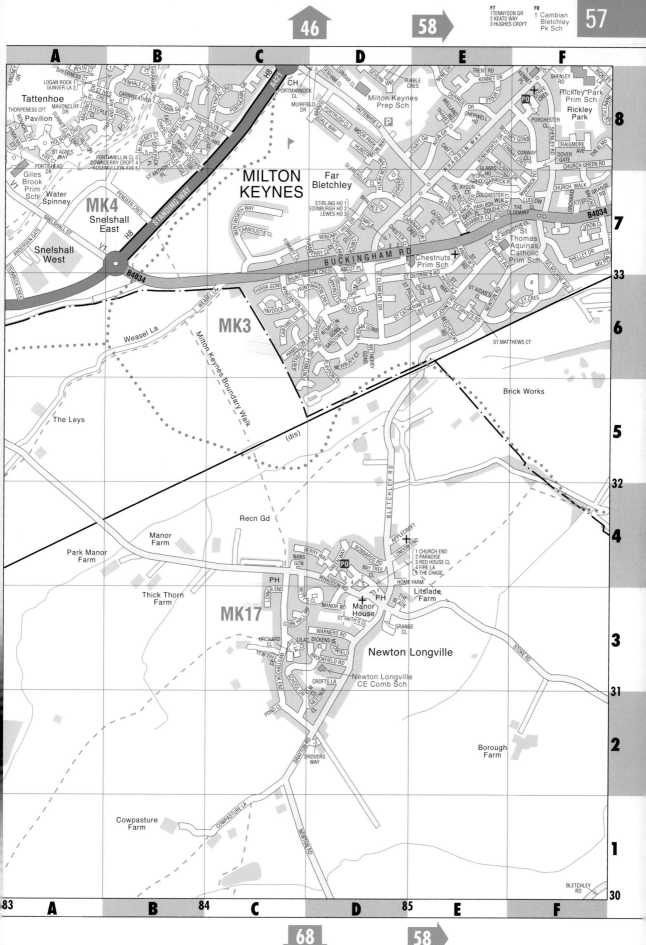

B8
1 HOMERTON ST
2 ROBINSON ST

C8
1 ALEXANDER HO
2 LEE HO
3 CHRISTINE HO
4 WOODWARD WY
5 CAWKWELL WY
6 THE CONCOURSE

7 Agora Ctr

57

47

D8
1 BOWLING GREEN CL
2 KNIGHTS CRES
3 MARQUESS DR
4 BOWLING GN CL

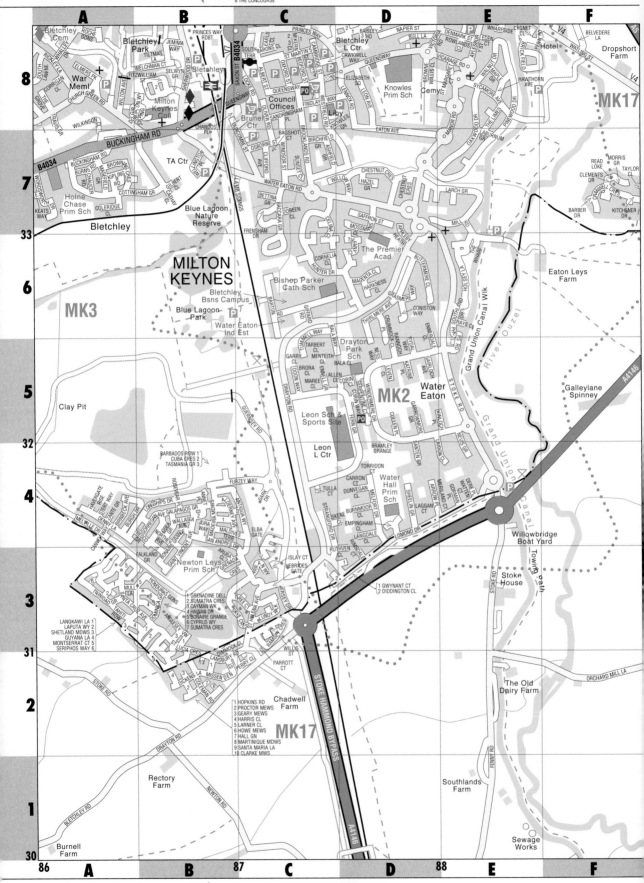

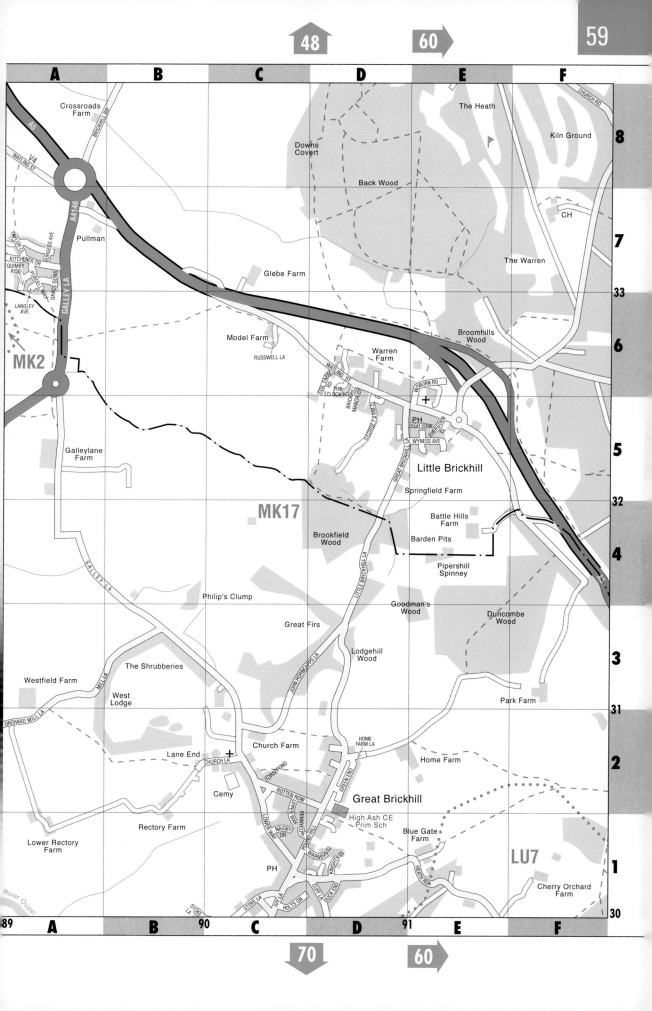

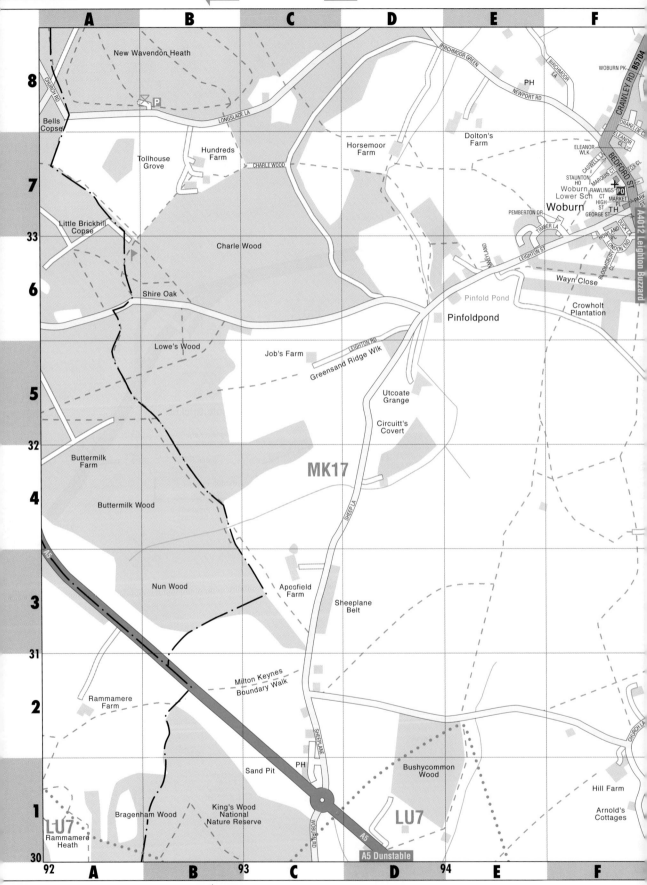

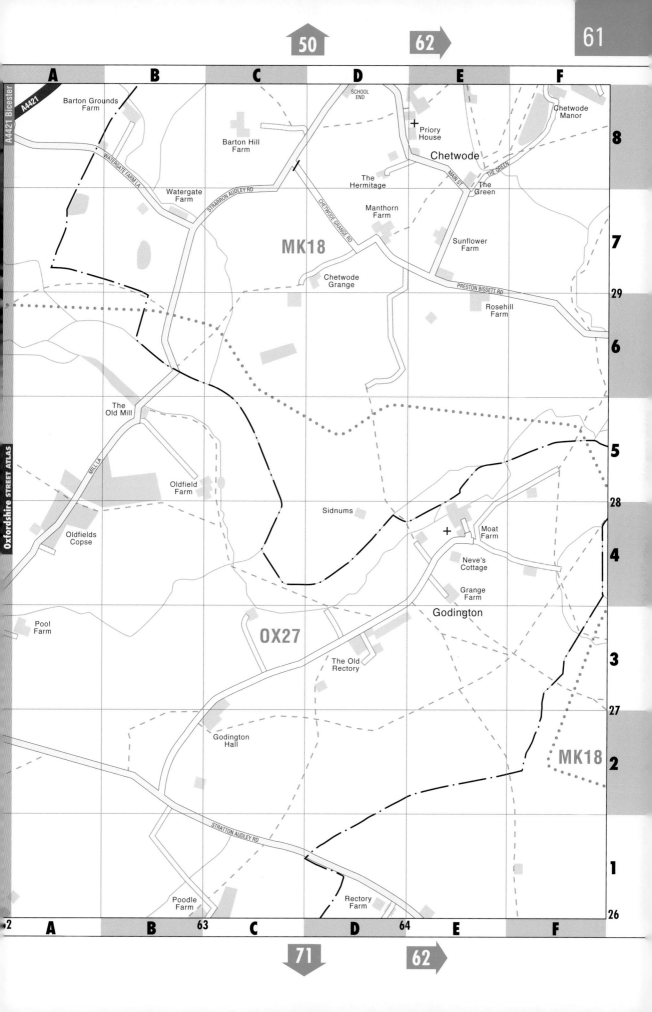

A4421 Bicester

Oxfordshire STREET ATLAS

A4421

Barton Grounds Farm

WATERGATE FARM LA

Watergate Farm

Barton Hill Farm

STRARRON AUDLEY RD

SCHOOL END

Priory House

Chetwode

The Hermitage

MAIN ST

THE GREEN

The Green

CHETWODE GRANGE RD

Manthorn Farm

MK18

Sunflower Farm

Chetwode Grange

PRESTON BISSETT RD

29

Rosehill Farm

6

The Old Mill

MILL LA

Oldfield Farm

Sidnums

5

28

Moat Farm

Oldfields Copse

Neve's Cottage

4

Grange Farm

Pool Farm

Godington

OX27

The Old Rectory

3

27

Godington Hall

MK18

2

STRATTON AUDLEY RD

1

Poodle Farm

Rectory Farm

26

Chetwode Manor

8

7

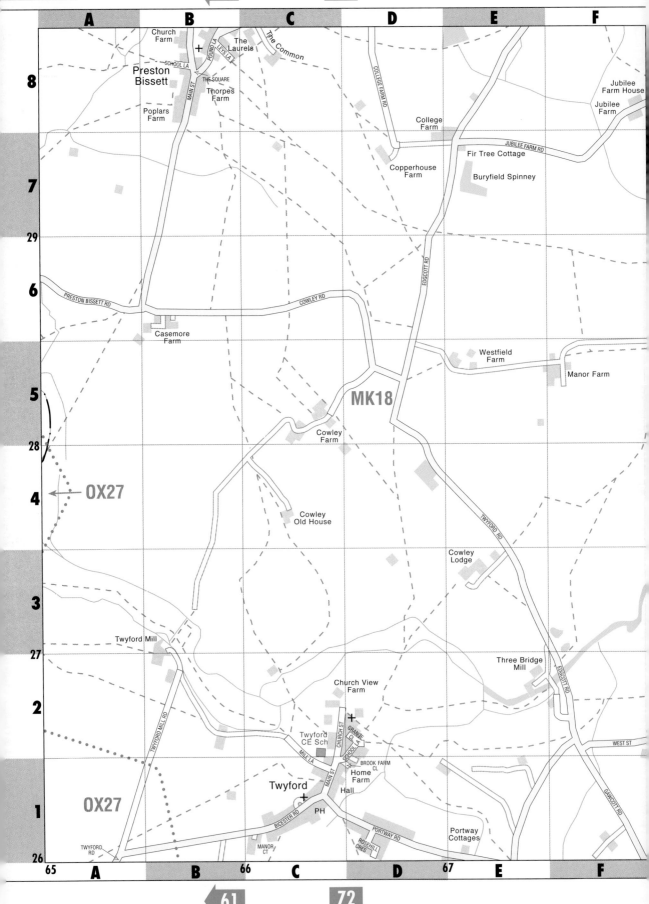

Map labels

Preston Bissett

Church Farm
The Laurels
The Common
SCHOOL LA
POUND LA
LEYS LA
MAIN ST
THE SQUARE
Thorpes Farm
Poplars Farm

College Farm
COLLEGE FARM RD
Copperhouse Farm
Fir Tree Cottage
JUBILEE FARM RD
Buryfield Spinney
Jubilee Farm House
Jubilee Farm

PRESTON BISSETT RD
COWLEY RD
EDGCOTT RD
Casemore Farm

Westfield Farm
Manor Farm

MK18

Cowley Farm

OX27

Cowley Old House

Cowley Lodge
TWYFORD RD

Twyford Mill
TWYFORD MILL RD

Three Bridge Mill
EDGCOTT RD

Church View Farm

Twyford CE Sch
CHURCH ST
GRANGE CL
SCHOOL LA
BROOK FARM CL
Home Farm
MILL LA
Hall
MAIN ST
Twyford
PH
BICESTER RD
PORTWAY RD
Portway Cottages
ROSEHILL CRES
WEST ST
GARCOTT RD

OX27
TWYFORD RD
MANOR CT

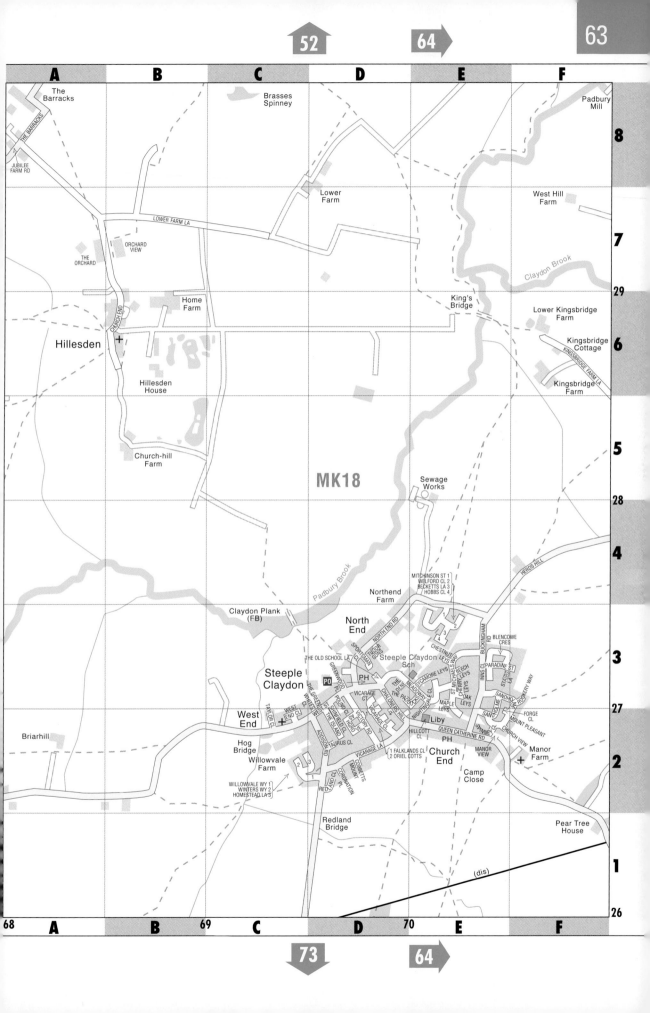

A **B** **C** **D** **E** **F**

The Barracks

THE BARRACKS

Brasses Spinney

Padbury Mill

8

JUBILEE FARM RD

Lower Farm

West Hill Farm

LOWER FARM LA

7

ORCHARD VIEW

Claydon Brook

THE ORCHARD

29

King's Bridge

Lower Kingsbridge Farm

CHURCH END

Home Farm

Hillesden

Kingsbridge Cottage

6

KINGSBRIDGE FARM LA

Hillesden House

Kingsbridge Farm

Church-hill Farm

5

Sewage Works

MK18

28

4

HERDS HILL

Padbury Brook

MITCHINSON ST 1
WELFORD CL 2
BECKETTS LA 3
HOBBS CL 4

Claydon Plank (FB)

Northend Farm

North End

NORTH END RD

CHESTNUT

BUCKINGHAM RD

BLENCOWE CRES

3

SPORTS LAND

Steeple Claydon Sch

BEECH

PARADINE ST

THE OLD SCHOOL LA

GREENWOOD RD

SYCAMORE LEYS

ST MICHAELS WAY

INNS CL

ST BIRINUS LA

Steeple Claydon

PO

PH

VICARAGE CT

MAPLE LEYS

CHERRY LEYS

OAK LEYS

ROOKERY WAY

THE GREEN

WHITES CL

POUND CL

THE MEADOW

CHALONERS HILL

SANDY

HOLME

FORGE CL

Mount Pleasant

27

West End

TAYLOR CL

WEST END CL

THE ISLAND

SHIFIELD CL

VICTORY RD

SAMS

SPINNEY

CHURCH VIEW

Liby

Briarhill

Hog Bridge

ADDISON RD

TAURUS CL

QUEEN CATHERINE RD

PH

Manor Farm

Willowvale Farm

VICARAGE LA

HILLCOTT CL

MANOR VIEW

2

WILLOWVALE WY 1
WINTERS WY 2
HOMESTEAD LA 3

CORBETTS

MOUNT PL

CORONATION

RED

1 FALKLANDS CL
2 ORIEL COTTS

Church End

Camp Close

Redland Bridge

Pear Tree House

(dis)

1

26

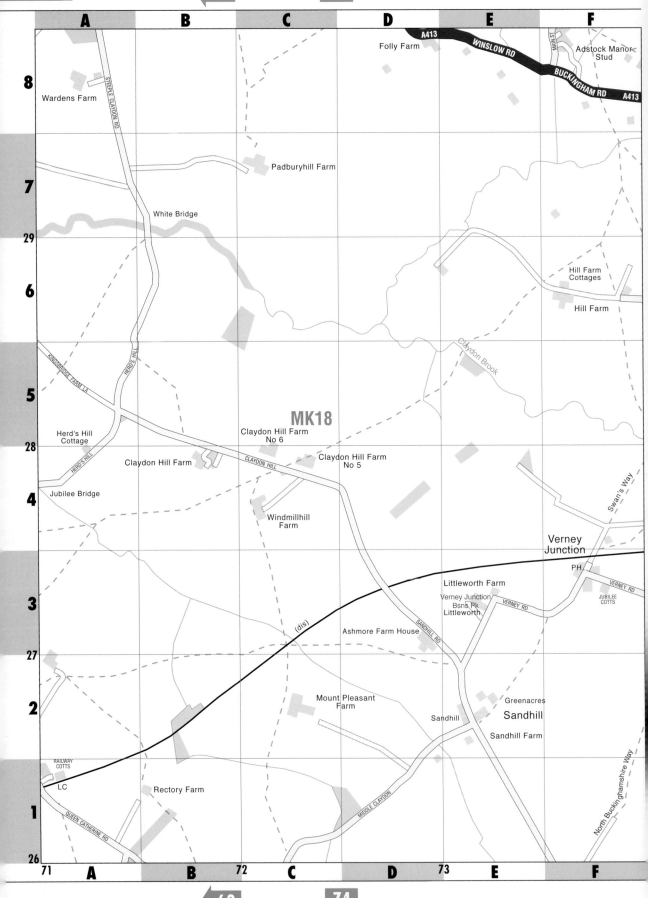

A B C D E F

8

Wardens Farm

Folly Farm

A413 WINSLOW RD

BUCKINGHAM RD A413

MAIN ST

Adstock Manor Stud

STEEPLE CLAYDON RD

Padburyhill Farm

7

White Bridge

29

Hill Farm Cottages

6

Hill Farm

Claydon Brook

KINGSBRIDGE FARM LA

HERD'S HILL

5

MK18

Claydon Hill Farm No 6

Herd's Hill Cottage

28

Claydon Hill Farm

CLAYDON HILL

Claydon Hill Farm No 5

Swan's Way

Jubilee Bridge

4

Windmillhill Farm

Verney Junction

PH

HERD'S HILL

Littleworth Farm

VERNEY RD

3

Verney Junction Bsns Pk Littleworth

VERNEY RD

JUBILEE COTTS

(dis)

Ashmore Farm House

SANDHILL RD

27

Mount Pleasant Farm

Greenacres

2

Sandhill

Sandhill

Sandhill Farm

North Buckinghamshire Way

RAILWAY COTTS

LC

Rectory Farm

MIDDLE CLAYDON

1

QUEEN CATHERINE RD

26

71 A B 72 C D 73 E F

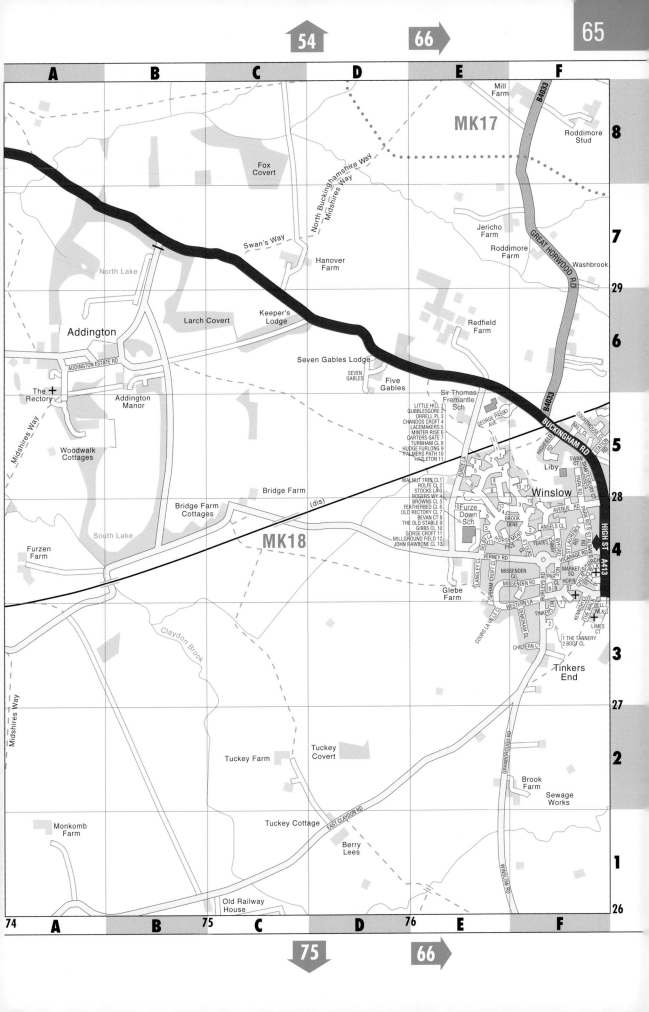

A B C D E F

MK17

Mill Farm

B4033

Roddimore Stud

8

Fox Covert

North Buckinghamshire Way
Midshires Way

Jericho Farm

7

Swan's Way

Roddimore Farm

Washbrook

GREAT HORWOOD RD

29

North Lake

Hanover Farm

Larch Covert

Keeper's Lodge

Redfield Farm

6

Addington

ADDINGTON ESTATE RD

Seven Gables Lodge

SEVEN GABLES

Five Gables

B4033

The Rectory

Addington Manor

Sir Thomas Fremantle Sch

GEORGE PASSO AVE

BUCKINGHAM RD

COURTHOUSE CL
MILL CL
STATION RD

Midshires Way

Woodwalk Cottages

LITTLE HILL 1
GUBBLESGORE 2
ORRELL PL 3
CHANDOS CROFT 4
LACEMAKERS 5
MINTER RISE 6
CARTERS GATE 7
TURNHAM CL 8
HUDGE FURLONG 9
PALMERS PATH 10
HAZLETON 11

HIGHFIELD RD

SWAN CT
Liby

SHAFTESBURY CT
PARK RD

5

FURZE LA

Winslow

28

Bridge Farm

WALNUT TREE CL 1
ROLFE CL 2
STOCKS LA 3
ROGERS WY 4
BROWNS CL 5
FEATHERBED CL 6
OLD RECTORY CL 7
BEVAN CT 8
THE OLD STABLE 9
GIBBS CL 10
GORSE CROFT 11
MILLGROUND FIELD 12
JOHN RAWBONE CL 13

Furze Down Sch

BROOK DENE

AVENUE

ANGELS CL

PARK RD
ST LAURENCE RD

HIGH ST A413

4

Bridge Farm Cottages

(dis)

MK18

South Lake

Furzen Farm

HORSEMED PIECE

SELBY LA

ST STOCKS

YEATES CL

VERNEY RD

LANGLEY CL

ISHAM CROFT CL

MISSENDEN CL

MISSENDEN RD

BURLEYS RD

MARKET SQ

PAR CL
NO 1
HORN ST

BYORD

CHURCH ST
CHURCH WLK

VICARAGE RD

KENNISH CL

BELL WLK

1 THE TANNERY
2 BOOT CL

LIMES CT

Glebe Farm

COURS LA VILLE CL

WESTERN LA

DENHAM RD

TINKERS

CHILTERN CT

THE WALK

3

Tinkers End

27

Tuckey Farm

Tuckey Covert

GRANBROUGH RD

Brook Farm

2

Sewage Works

Claydon Brook

Tuckey Cottage

EAST CLAYDON RD

Berry Lees

WINSLOW RD

Midshires Way

Monkomb Farm

Old Railway House

1

26

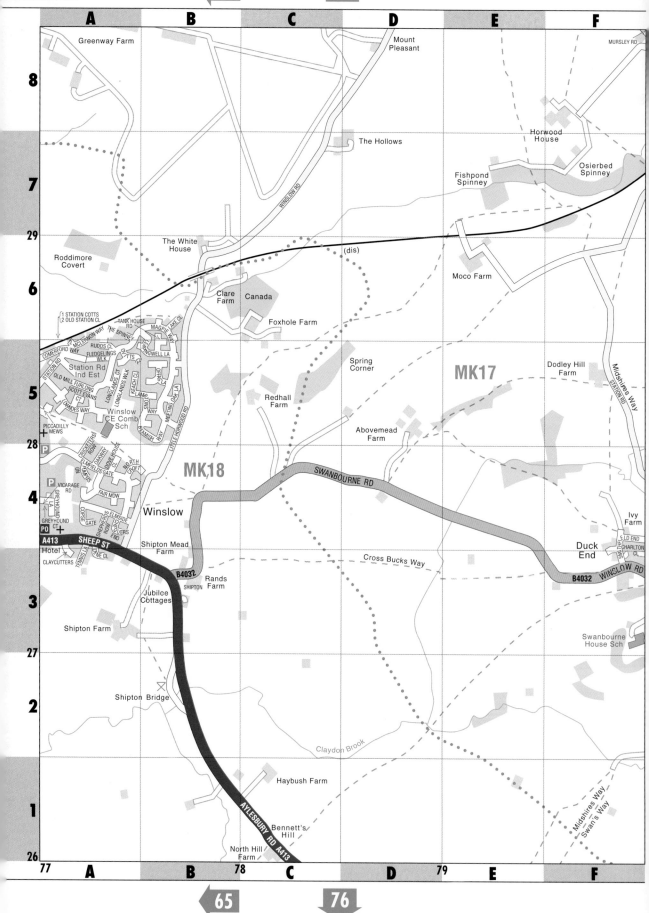

A B C D E F

8

Greenway Farm

Mount Pleasant

MURSLEY RD

The Hollows

Horwood House

7

WINSLOW RD

Fishpond Spinney

Osierbed Spinney

29

The White House

(dis)

Roddimore Covert

Moco Farm

6

Clare Farm

Canada

Foxhole Farm

1 STATION COTTS
2 OLD STATION CL

Spring Corner

MK17

Dodley Hill Farm

TANK HOUSE RD

THE SPINNEY

MAGPIE WAY

LAKE CL

MCLERNON WAY

RUDDS CL

COMERFORD WAY

FLEDGELINGS WLK

SPANGWELL LA

STATION RD IND EST

STATION RD

OLD MILL FURLONG

LONGLANDS CT

LONGLANDS WLK

KEACH CL

MEETING OAK LA

JOHNS CL

TITTS

Redhall Farm

MIDSHIRES WAY

STATION RD

5

SCOTT EVANS CT

LOWNDES WAY

Winslow CE Comb Sch

LITTLE HORWOOD RD

LAMB WAY

BEAMISH WAY

Abovemead Farm

28

PICCADILLY MEWS

P

CRICKETERS ROW

OAKWAY

LIDDLE HOUSE

NORTH CROFT

GT HORWOOD

P

VICARAGE RD

ELMFIELDS GATE

MK18

SWANBOURNE RD

Ivy Farm

4

GREYHOUND RD

LA

ELMFIELDS

FAIR MDW

Winslow

OLD END

CHARLTON CL

PHILLIPS

Duck End

B4032

WINSLOW RD

GREYHOUND CT

SHEPHERDS CL

ELMSIDE

CLAYCUTTERS

COPSE

GATE

Shipton Mead Farm

Cross Bucks Way

Hotel

A413

SHEEP ST

CLAYCUTTERS

TENNIS LA

CLYNE CL

B4032

Rands Farm

SHIPTON

Swanbourne House Sch

Jubilee Cottages

3

Shipton Farm

27

Shipton Bridge

2

Claydon Brook

Haybush Farm

Midshires Way

Swan's Way

1

AYLESBURY RD A413

Bennett's Hill

North Hill Farm

26

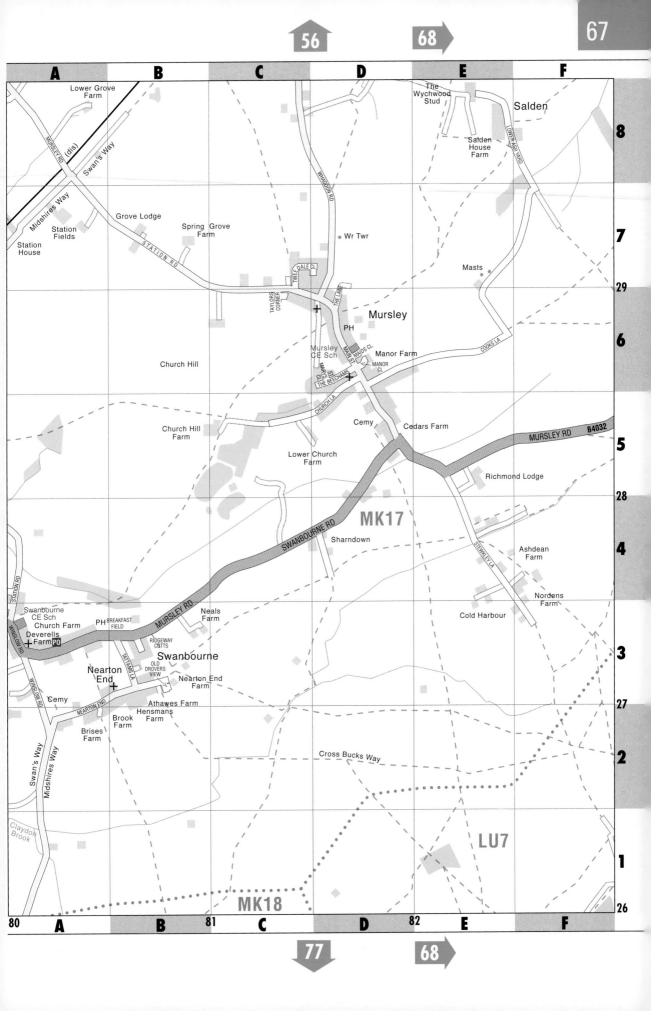

A B C D E F

8
7
29
6
5
28
4
3
27
2
1
26

Lower Grove Farm

Swan's Way

Midshires Way

Station Fields

Station House

Grove Lodge

STATION RD

Spring Grove Farm

MURSLEY RD (dis)

WHADDON RD

Wr Twr

The Wychwood Stud

Salden

Salden House Farm

LOWER ASH YARD

Masts

TWEEDALE CL

TAYLORS CORNER

THE LANE

Mursley

PH

MAIN ST

MAIDS CL

Manor Farm

MANOR CL

COOKS LA

Church Hill

Mursley CE Sch

MARY'S CL

THE BEECHAMS

CHURCH LA

Cemy

Cedars Farm

MURSLEY RD B4032

Church Hill Farm

Lower Church Farm

Richmond Lodge

MK17

SWANBOURNE RD

Sharndown

STEWKLEY LA

Ashdean Farm

Nordens Farm

STATION RD

MURSLEY RD

Neals Farm

Cold Harbour

Swanbourne CE Sch

PH

BREAKFAST FIELD

Church Farm

Deverells Farm PO

WINSLOW RD

TATTAMS LA

RIDGEWAY COTTS

Swanbourne

OLD DROVERS VIEW

Nearton End

Nearton End Farm

Cemy

WINSLOW RD

NEARTON END

Athawes Farm

Hensmans Farm

Brook Farm

Brises Farm

Swan's Way

Midshires Way

Cross Bucks Way

LU7

Claydon Brook

MK18

80 81 82

67
57

A **B** **C** **D** **E** **F**

8

Ash Farm

Highfield

Villiers Farm

BLETCHLEY RD

NEWTON RD

Drayton Crossroad Farm

7

29

Prospect Farm

MK17

CARRINGTON HALL RD

HIGH AWY

Newmans Clyd

PROSPECT CL

FOX LA

STONES WY

6

Drayton Parslow Village Sch

Chestnut Farm

The Lower Farm

LOVE ROW

Sewage Works

STEWKLEY RD

Manor Farm

PH

BATES CL

SALDEN CL

BELL

NORTH CL

CHAPEL LA

NEW RD

NEW RD

Drayton Parslow

Kingsland Farm

Bungler's Hall

MAIN RD

CHURCH END

5

B4032

Church End

Stokeroad Farm

28

Merrymead

MURSLEY RD

4

Old Leighton Farm

HOLLINGDON RD

BLETCHLEY RD

3

Grange Farm

LU7

The Grange

HAYWOOD PK

GRUBBS CL

27

Lansdowne Farm

North End

Heywood House

Lower Dean Farm

White Horse Lodge

Laurel Farm

Stewkley House

2

Upper Dean Farm

HIGH ST N

HIGH ST NORTH

STOCKHALL CRES

SYCAMORE CL

Stewkley

DEAN RD

CRICKETERS CL

Bonham Farm

Stewkley Dean

Dean Farm

Sycamore Farm

PH

CHAPEL SQ

IVY LA

Church Farm

1

FISHWEIR

Dean Tithe Farm

St Michael's CE Comb Sch

SCHOOL

ST MICHAELS CL

26

TYTHE GDNS

SOULBURY RD B4032

83 **A** **B** **84** **C** **D** **85** **E** **F**

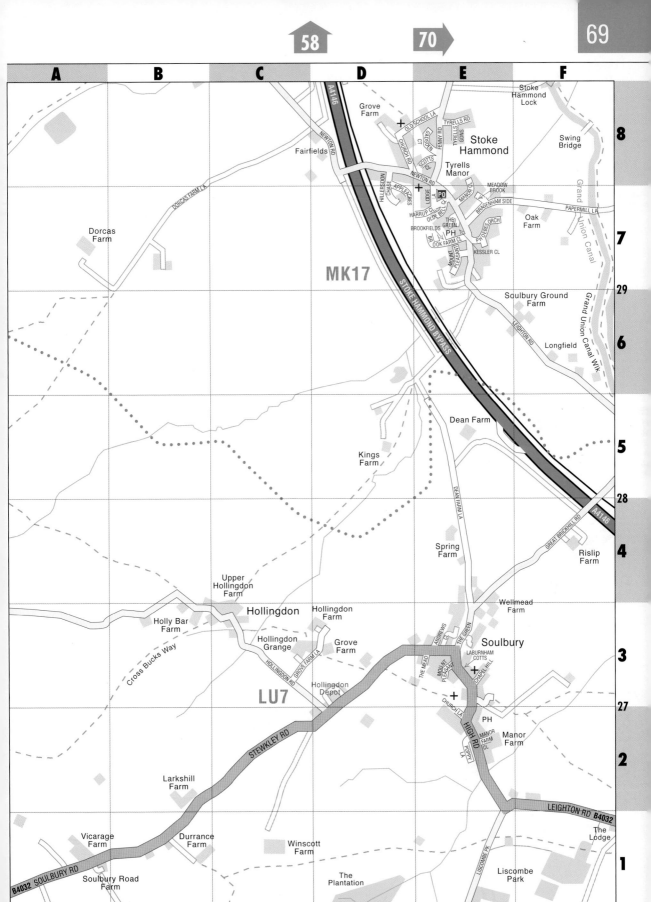

A   B   C   D   E   F

8

Grove Farm

Stoke Hammond Lock

Swing Bridge

Fairfields

OLD SCHOOL LA

TYRELLS RD

Stoke Hammond

Grand Union Canal

NEWTON RD

CHURCH RD

FENNY RD

TYRELLS RD

SNOS

Tyrells Manor

PAPERMILL LA

7

Dorcas Farm

DORCAS FARM LA

HILLERSDON CHASE

APPLEACRES

MOUNT PLEASANT

NEWTON RD

SCOTTS CL

MANOR CL

MEADOW BROOK

BRAGENHAM SIDE

Oak Farm

HARRUP CL

OLDE BELL CL

BROOK FARM CL

THE GREEN

PH

PW DEREK ORCH

KESSLER CL

MK17

Soulbury Ground Farm

29

STOKE HAMMOND BYPASS

LEIGHTON RD

6

Longfield

Grand Union Canal Wlk

Dean Farm

5

Kings Farm

DEAN FARM LA

28

A4146

Spring Farm

GREAT BRICKHILL RD

4

Rislip Farm

Upper Hollingdon Farm

Wellmead Farm

Hollingdon

Hollingdon Farm

ANDREWS

THE GREEN

Soulbury

Holly Bar Farm

Hollingdon Grange

HOLLINGDON RD

GROVE FARM LA

Grove Farm

LABURNHAM COTTS

THE MEAD

MOUNT PLEASANT

CHAPEL HILL

3

Cross Bucks Way

Hollingdon Depot

LU7

CHURCH LA

PH

27

STEWKLEY RD

HIGH RD

MANOR FARM CL

POPPY LA

Manor Farm

2

Larkshill Farm

LEIGHTON RD B4032

The Lodge

Vicarage Farm

Durrance Farm

Winscott Farm

LISCOMBE PK

Liscombe Park

1

B4032 SOULBURY RD

Soulbury Road Farm

The Plantation

26

86   A   B   87   C   D   88   E   F

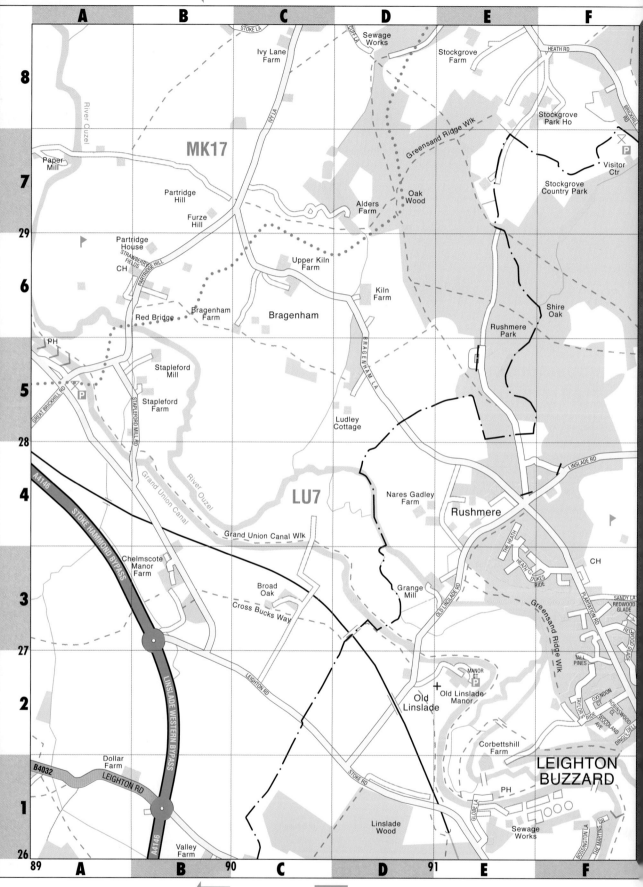

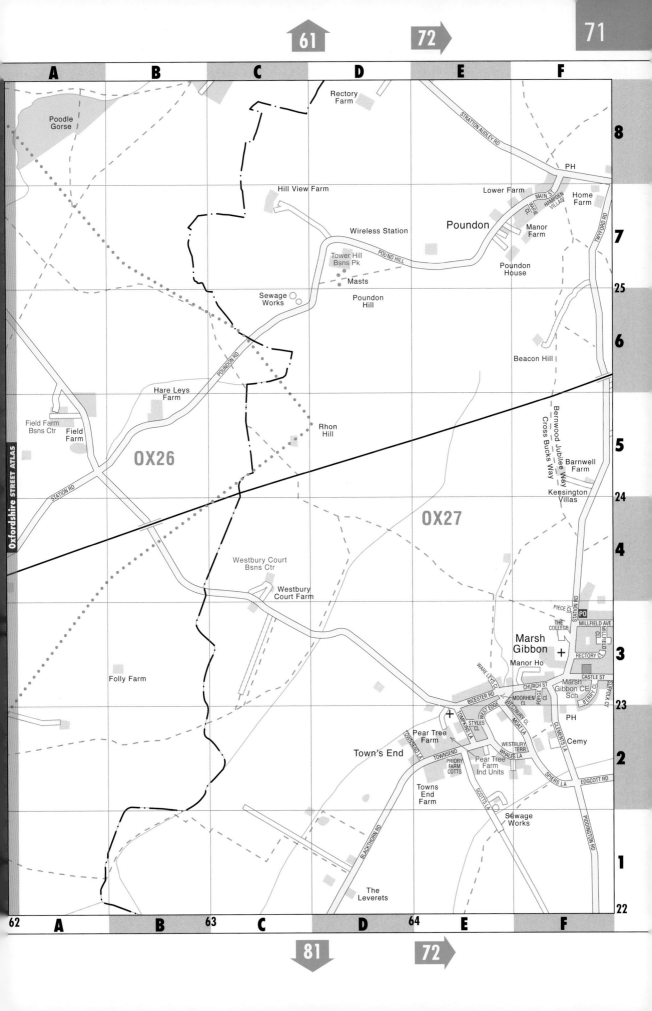

A B C D E F

8
7
25
6
5
24
4
3
23
2
1
22

Poodle
Gorse

Rectory
Farm

Hill View Farm

Wireless Station

Tower Hill
Bsns Pk

Masts

Sewage
Works

Poundon
Hill

STRATTON AUDLEY RD

PH

Lower Farm

Home
Farm

Poundon

Manor
Farm

Poundon
House

Beacon Hill

POUND HILL

MAIN ST
MARIE CL
HAMPDEN VILLAS
TWYFORD RD

POUNDON RD

Hare Leys
Farm

Field Farm
Bsns Ctr

Field
Farm

OX26

Rhon
Hill

STATION RD

Bernwood Jubilee Way
Cross Bucks Way

Barnwell
Farm

Kensington
Villas

OX27

Westbury Court
Bsns Ctr

Westbury
Court Farm

Folly Farm

PIECE CL
PO
MILLFIELD AVE
THE COLLEGE
MILLFIELD CL
STATION RD

Marsh
Gibbon

RECTORY C

Manor Ho

Marsh
Gibbon CE
Sch

CASTLE ST

SUFFOLK CT

WARE LEYS CL

CHURCH ST

BERRY CL

MOORHEN CL

WESTBURY CL

CLEMENTS LA

PH

Cemy

Bicester Rd

WEST EDGE

TOMPKINS LA

STYLES CL

MOAT LA

WHALES LA

WESTBURY
TERR

SPIERS LA

EDGCOTT RD

Pear Tree
Farm

Town's End

TOWNSHOLD LA

TOWNSEND

PRIORY
FARM
COTTS

Pear Tree
Farm Ind Units

Towns
End
Farm

SCOTTS LA

Sewage
Works

PIDDINGTON RD

BLACKTHORN RD

The
Leverets

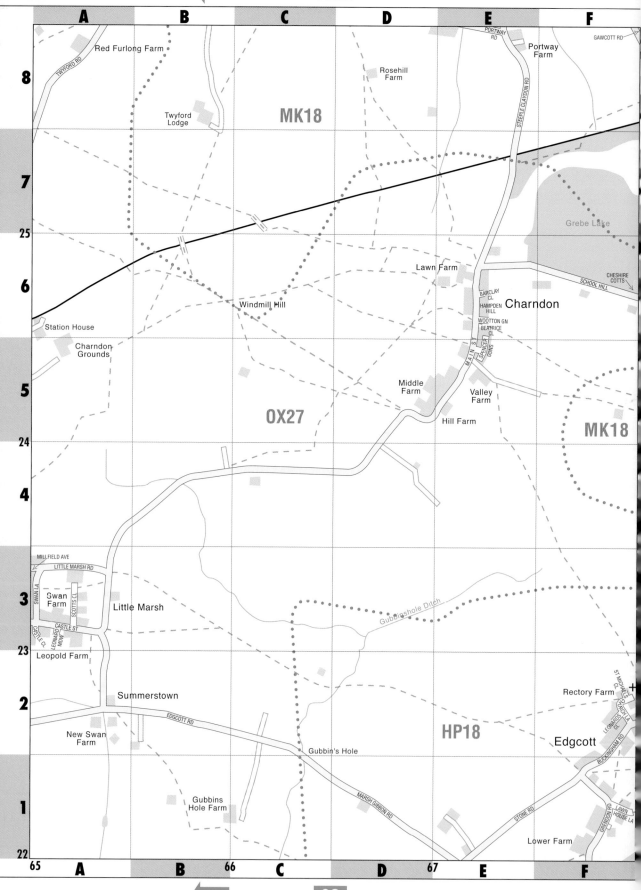

A **B** **C** **D** **E** **F**

GAWCOTT RD

Red Furlong Farm

TWYFORD RD

8

Twyford
Lodge

MK18

Rosehill
Farm

PORTWAY
RD

Portway
Farm

STEPLE CLAYDON RD

7

Grebe Lake

25

Lawn Farm

CHESHIRE
COTTS

SCHOOL HILL

6

Windmill Hill

BARCLAY
CL

HAMPDEN
HILL

Charndon

Station House

WOOTTON GN
BEATRICE
CL

MAIN ST

SPENCER
GDNS

Charndon
Grounds

5

Middle
Farm

Valley
Farm

MK18

OX27

Hill Farm

24

4

MILLFIELD AVE

LITTLE MARSH RD

SWAN LA

Swan
Farm

SCOTTS CL

Little Marsh

Gubbinshole Ditch

3

CASTLE ST

CASTLE CL

LEONARD
MDW

23

Leopold Farm

St MICHAELS
CROFT

Rectory Farm

Summerstown

LEONARDS
CL

2

EDGCOTT RD

HP18

Edgcott

New Swan
Farm

BUCKINGHAM RD

Gubbin's Hole

Gubbins
Hole Farm

MARSH GIBBON RD

STONE RD

1

GRENDON RD

LAWN
HOUSE LA

Lower Farm

22

65 **A** **B** **66** **C** **D** **67** **E** **F**

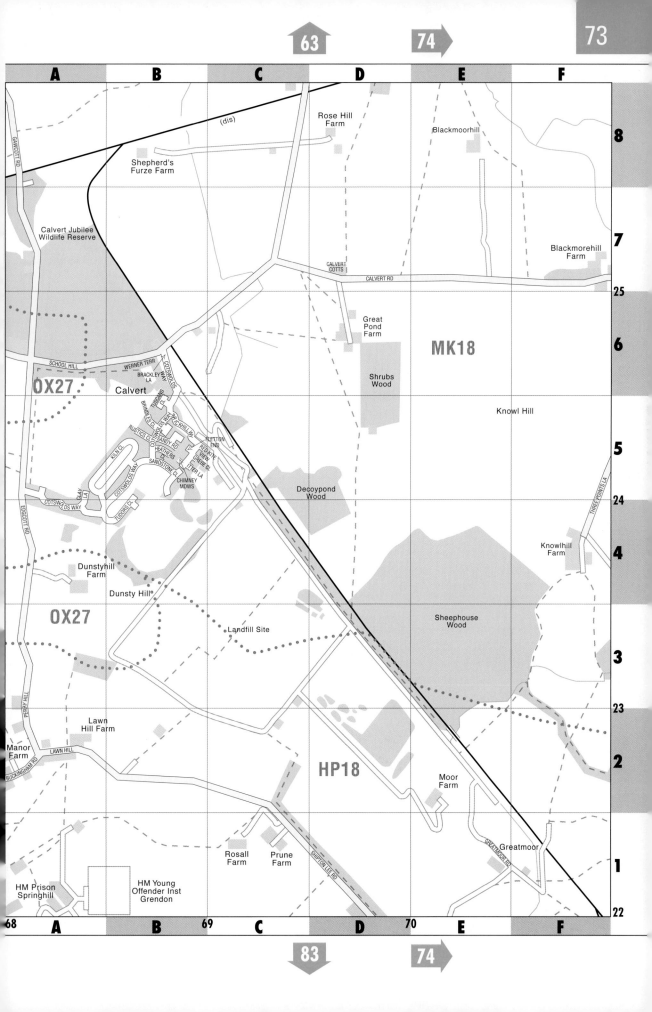

A　B　C　D　E　F

8

Blackmoorhill

Rose Hill
Farm

(dis)

Shepherd's
Furze Farm

7

Calvert Jubilee
Wildlife Reserve

Blackmorehill
Farm

CALVERT
COTTS

CALVERT RD

25

Great
Pond
Farm

6

WERNER TERR

SCHOOL HILL

MK18

BRACKLEY
LA

COTSWOLDS
WAY

Shrubs
Wood

OX27

Calvert

Knowl Hill

TUSCANS
CL

BRINDLES CL

CK HILL WY

RUSTICS CL

COTS 2ND SANDY RD

FLETTON
END

5

KILN CL

HEATHERS
CL

RED KYTE
VIEW

SANDSTONE CL

GREBE CL

OTTER LA

CLAY
LA

COTSWOLDS WAY

CHIMNEY
MDWS

Decoypond
Wood

24

COTSW LDS WAY

TUDORS CL

Knowlhill
Farm

THREE POINTS LA

Dunstyhill
Farm

4

OX27

Dunsty Hill

Sheephouse
Wood

Landfill Site

EDGCOTT RD

3

23

PERRY HILL

Lawn
Hill Farm

Manor
Farm

LAWN HILL

2

HP18

BUCKINGHAM RD

Moor
Farm

Greatmoor

GREATMOOR RD

SHIPTON LEE RD

1

Rosall
Farm

Prune
Farm

HM Prison
Springhill

HM Young
Offender Inst
Grendon

22

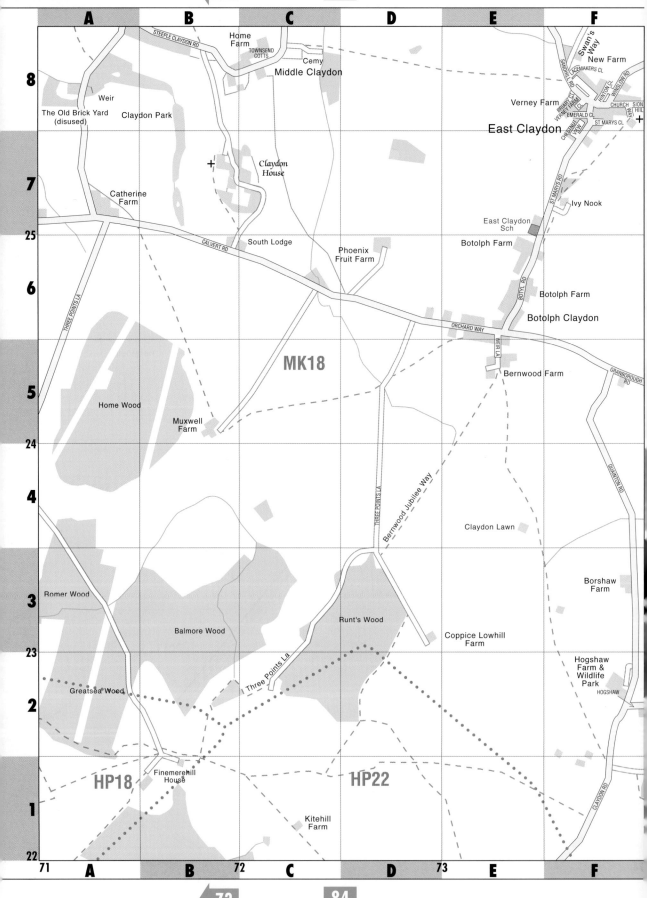

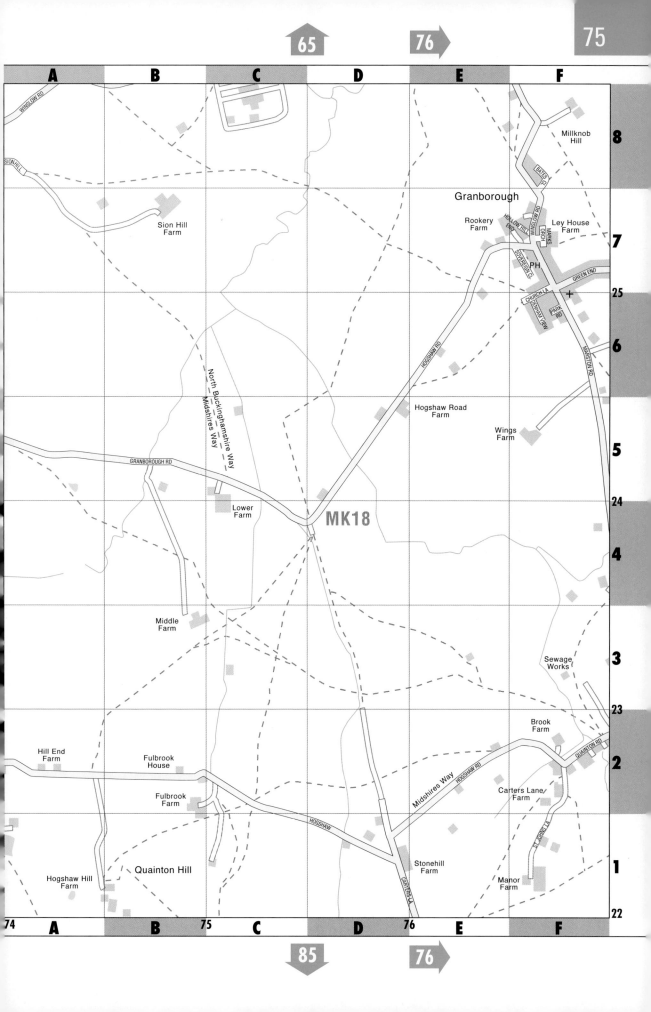

A B C D E F

8

7

25

6

5

24

4

3

23

2

1

22

WINSLOW RD

SION HILL

Sion Hill
Farm

Millknob
Hill

Granborough

Rookery
Farm

BATES CL

MISLOW HILL

HOLLOW HILL END

ORCH

MARKS

Ley House
Farm

PH

SOVEREIGN CL

CHURCH LA

CHELTENHAM VIEW

PARK RD

GREEN END

MARSTON RD

+

Hogshaw Road
Farm

HOGSHAW RD

Wings
Farm

North Buckinghamshire Way
Midshires Way

GRANBOROUGH RD

Lower
Farm

MK18

Middle
Farm

Sewage
Works

Brook
Farm

QUAINTON RD

Hill End
Farm

Fulbrook
House

Fulbrook
Farm

Quainton Hill

Hogshaw Hill
Farm

HOGSHAW

Midshires Way

HOGSHAW RD

Carters Lane
Farm

ST JOHNS LA

Stonehill
Farm

CARTERS LA

Manor
Farm

	A	B	C	D	E	F

8

A413
North Hill Farm
AYLESBURY RD
Oakham Farm
Swan's Way

Holcombe Cottages

7 Green End
GREEN END
Lower Green End Farm
CHRISTMAS GORSE LA
Christmas Gorse
Buxlow Farm

Grange Farm
25
Green End Farm
The Neptune Farm
WINSLOW RD
MAIN ST

6
Lathwells Farm

Midshires Way
MK18

A413
5
Maynes Hill Farm

24
Marstonfields Farm

4
The Bungalow
Crandon Farm

Swan's Way
Buttermilkhall Farm
3
Guy's Thorns

Stevens Farm
GRANBOROUGH RD
GIBBINGS CL
23
ELMERS MDW
HP22
QUAINTON RD
HILL FARM
North Marston CE Sch
MARSTONFIELDS RD
SHEPHERDS CL
CARTERS MDW
DUDLEY CL
PH
2
Manor Farm
HIGH ST
SCHOOL HILL
Townsend
Ramhill Farm
CHURCH ST
Glebe Farm

North Marston
MORTON CL
SCHOOL LA
Burnaby Farm
PULPIT LA
MEADWAY
PORTWAY
1

22

	A	B	C	D	E	F
78 79

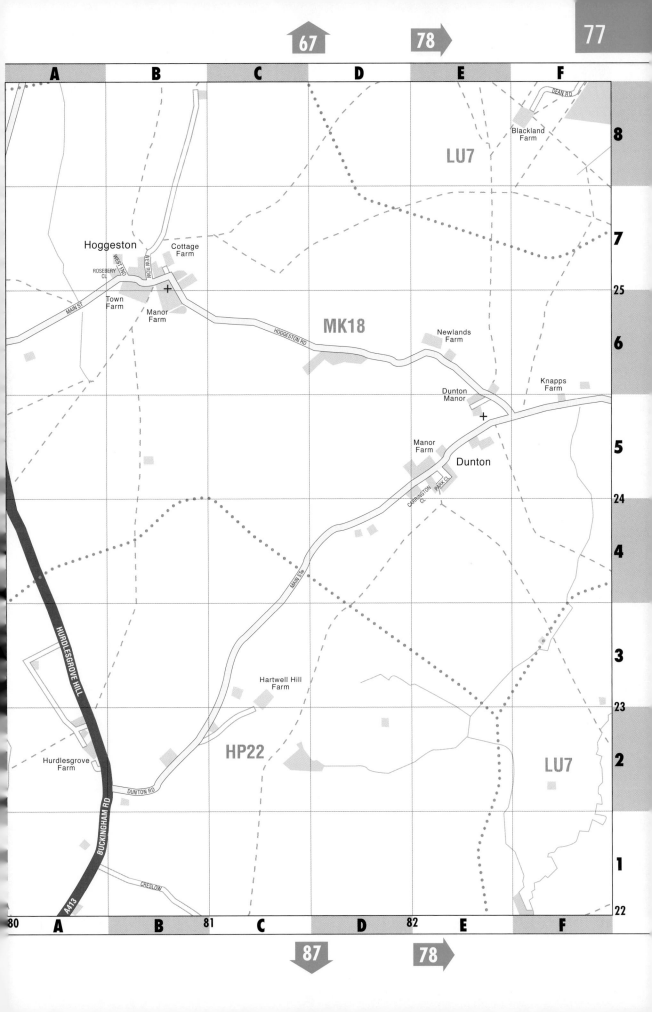

A　　B　　C　　D　　E　　F

8

7

25

6

MK18

Littlecote

5

24

4

LU7

3

23

2

1

22

83　　A　　84　　B　　C　　84　　D　　85　　E　　F

Red Barn
Farm

Manor
House

TYTHE
GDNS

PARSONS
CL

SOULBURY
RD

B4032

FOLDING CL

DOVE ST

OLD
MANOR CL

MANOR DR

ORKNEY CL

WALDUCKS CL

CHAPPELL WAY

FENNELL DR

GRIFFIN FIELD

LOVETTS
END

HIGH ST

MALTINGS CL

COURTNEIDGE
CL

South End

ORCHARD LA

Breach Farm

TAYLORS LA

KINGS ST

PH

OLD COAL
YARD

South LA

Wing Road
Farm

Kiln Farm

DUNTON RD

Sewage
Works

WING RD

Forge
Farm

North Farm

Penton Farm

Warren Farm

MAIN RD

LIDCOTE

Littlecote Dairy
Farm

Mount Pleasant
Farm

LITTLECOTE

P

DUNTON RD

Kingsbridge
Farm

P

Poultry Farm

DUNTON RD

Steart Farm

Acorn
Bsns Ctr

New Dairy
Farm

STEWKLEY RD

Cedars Farm

Lockharts

South Tinkers
Hole Farm

Poultry
Farm

READS LA

Neales Farm

Cublington

ST NICHOLAS CL 1
CHENEY CL 2
MEADOW CL 3

CHURCH PATH

SILVER ST

The Olde
Manor

Old Manor
Farm

CUBLINGTON RD

STEWKLEY RD

Old
House
Farm

HIGH ST

BELL CL

WING RD

Manor
Farm

RIDINGS WAY

WHITCHURCH RD

PH

ROSES
CL

ASTON ABBOTTS RD

Southend Farm

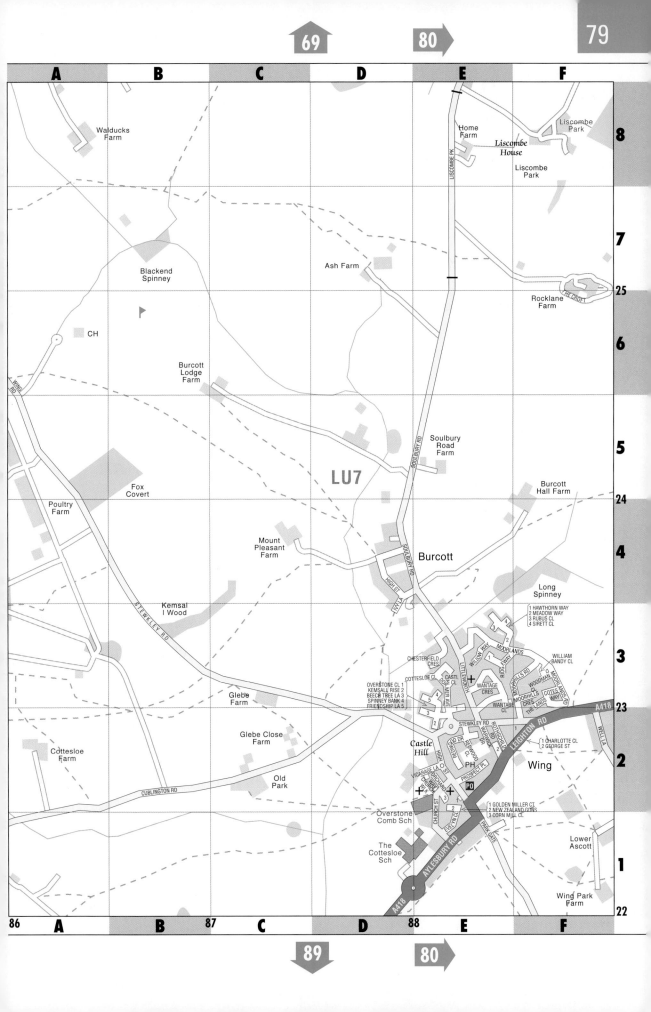

A B C D E F

8

Walducks
Farm

Home
Farm

Liscombe
Park

Liscombe
House

Liscombe
Park

7

Blackend
Spinney

Ash Farm

25

Rocklane
Farm

THE CROFT

CH

6

Burcott
Lodge
Farm

WING RD

Soulbury
Road
Farm

5

SOULBURY RD

Fox
Covert

LU7

Burcott
Hall Farm

24

Poultry
Farm

Mount
Pleasant
Farm

Burcott

Long
Spinney

4

SOULBURY RD

HIGH ST

IVY LA

Kemsal
l Wood

STEWKLEY RD

1 HAWTHORN WAY
2 MEADOW WAY
3 RUBUS CL
4 SIRETT CL

3

CHESTERFIELD
CRES

WILLOW WAY

MOORLANDS

RIDGEWAY

WILLIAM
BANDY CL

WOODMAN
CRES

MOORHILLS RD

COTES
WAY

MOORHILLS RD

Glebe
Farm

COTTESLOE CL

CASTLE
CL

LITTLEWORTH

COSMER AVE

WANTAGE
CRES

MOORHILLS
CRES

THE LANDS

OVERSTONE CL 1
KEMSALL RISE 2
BEECH TREE LA 3
SPINNEY BANK 4
FRIENDSHIP LA 5

WANTAGE
CL

A418

23

Glebe Close
Farm

STEWKLEY RD

LEIGHTON RD

WELL A

Cottesloe
Farm

Old
Park

RICHMOND DR

REDWOOD

RUSHCHILL

WARWICK
DR

1 CHARLOTTE CL
2 GEORGE ST

Wing

2

CUBLINGTON RD

Castle
Hill

HIGH ST

VICARAGE LA

ORCHARD
CL WAY

PROSPECT PL

PH

PO

1 GOLDEN MILLER CT
2 NEW ZEALAND GDNS
3 CORN MILL CL

Overstone
Comb Sch

CHURCH ST

EVZEL'YN CL

AYLESBURY RD

PARK GATE

Lower
Ascott

1

The
Cottesloe
Sch

A418

Wing Park
Farm

22

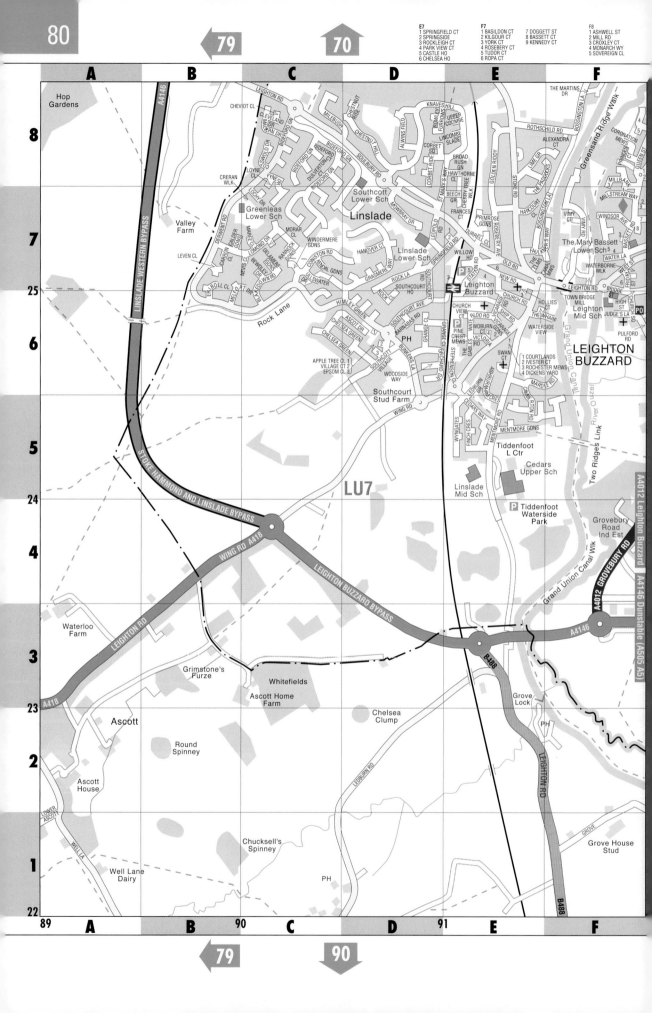

A   B   C   D   E   F

Hop
Gardens

8

Valley
Farm

LEVEN CL

7

Greenleas
Lower Sch

Southcott
Lower Sch

Linslade

Linslade
Lower Sch

The Mary Bassett
Lower Sch

Waterborne
Wlk

25

Rock Lane

Leighton
Buzzard

LEIGHTON RD

Leighton
Mid Sch

LEIGHTON BUZZARD

6

Southcourt
HO

APPLE TREE CL 1
VILLAGE CT 2
EPSOM CL 3

WOODSIDE
WAY

1 COURTLANDS
2 IVESTER CT
3 ROCHESTER MEWS
4 DICKENS YARD

Southcourt
Stud Farm

WING RD

5

Tiddenfoot
L Ctr

Cedars
Upper Sch

Two Ridges Link

24

LU7

Linslade
Mid Sch

Tiddenfoot
Waterside
Park

Grovebury
Road
Ind Est

4

WING RD A418

LEIGHTON BUZZARD BYPASS

GROVEBURY RD

A4146

Waterloo
Farm

Grove
Lock

3

A418

Grimstone's
Furze

Whitefields

Ascott Home
Farm

Chelsea
Clump

PH

B488

23

Ascott

Round
Spinney

2

Ascott
House

Chucksell's
Spinney

LEIGHTON RD

Grove House
Stud

1

Well Lane
Dairy

PH

B488

22

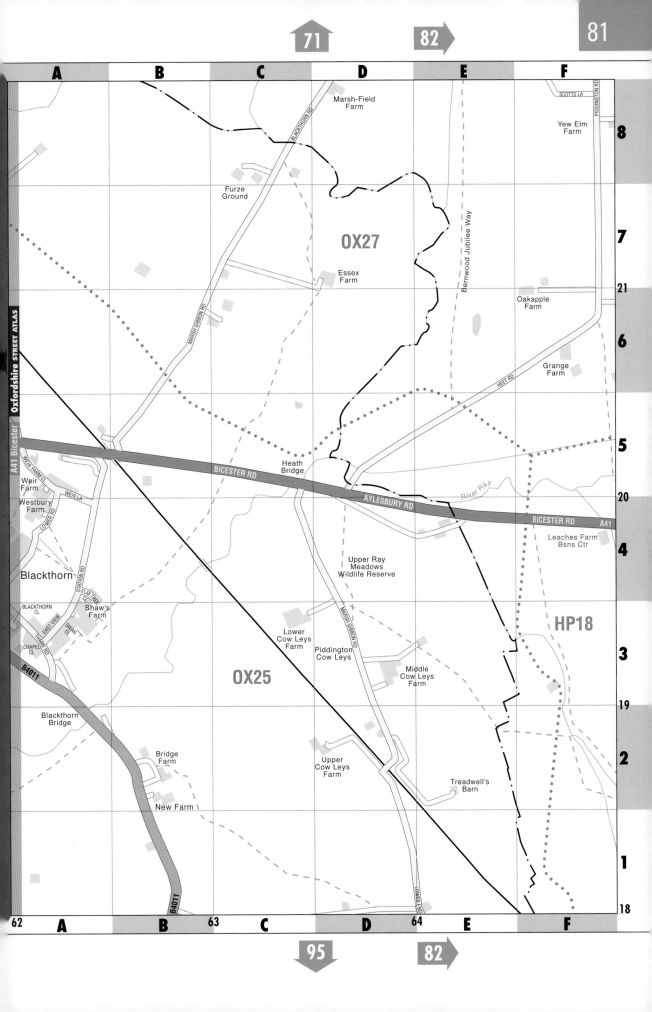

81
72

A **B** **C** **D** **E** **F**

8 Yew Elm Farm

Gubbinshole Ditch

OX27

Tudor Farm

Dunmead Farm

MARSH GIBBON RD

GRENDON RD

SPRINGHILL RD

PARK P.

SPRINGHILL RD

MOAT VIEW

7

HALL COTTS

21

+

EDGCOTT RD

Manor Farm

MIDSUMMER DR

MILLERS

GL ST

MAIN ST

RUMPTONS PADDOCK

SHAKESPEARE ORCH

SAWE & SELE CL

6

River Ray

Shakespeare Farm

LEAR LA

Three Points

5

BROADWAY

20

Winding Brook

HP18

White House Farm

Tetchwick Brook

A41

4 Cub Pond

Gallow's Bridge

BICESTER RD

A41

3

Tetchwick Farm

19

Tetchwick

TETCHWICK FARM RD

2

New Barn Farm

BICESTER RD

Sewage Works

1

Tittershall Wood

18

65 **A** **B** 66 **C** **D** 67 **E** **F**

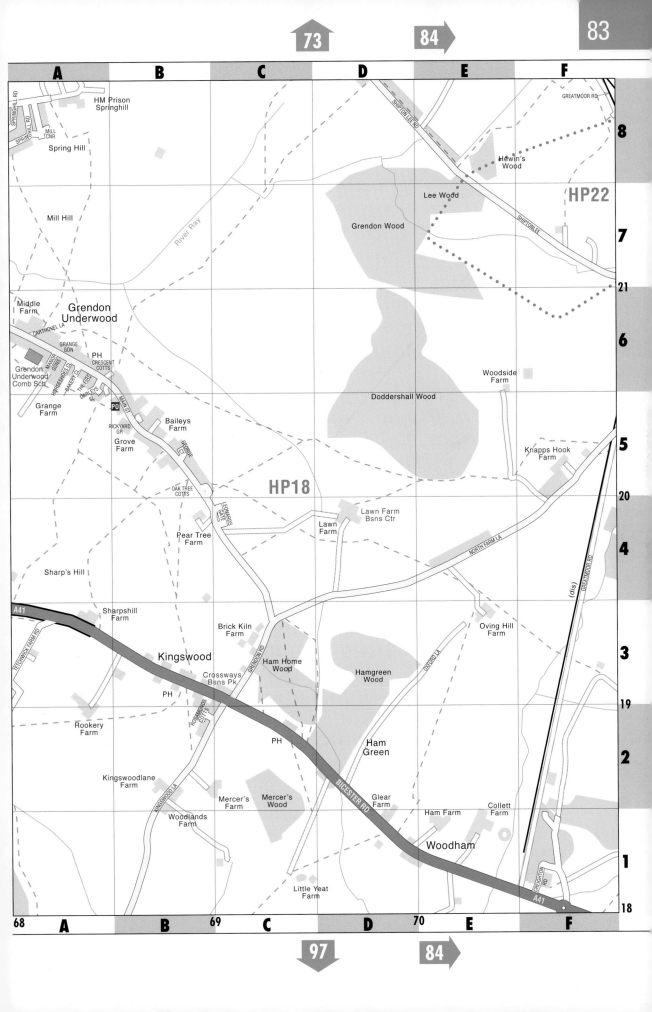

A **B** **C** **D** **E** **F**

SPRINGHILL RD

HM Prison
Springhill

MILL
CNR

Spring Hill

Mill Hill

River Ray

GREATMOOR RD

SHIPTON LEE RD

Hewin's
Wood

Lee Wood

Grendon Wood

SHIPTONLEE

HP22

8

7

21

Middle
Farm

Grendon
Underwood

CARTHONEL LA

GRANGE
GDN

PH
CRESCENT
COTTS

MANOR
GDNS

Grendon
Underwood
Comb Sch

HORSESHOES CL

THE CLOSE

BAKERY CL

DARLEYS CL

PO

MAIN ST

RICKYARD
GR

Grange
Farm

Grove
Farm

Baileys
Farm

GEORGE CL

OAK TREE
COTTS

Woodside
Farm

Doddershall Wood

Knapps Hook
Farm

HP18

6

5

20

LEONARDS
GATE

Pear Tree
Farm

Sharp's Hill

Lawn
Farm

Lawn Farm
Bsns Ctr

NORTH FARM LA

Oving Hill
Farm

OXCORD LA

GREATMOOR RD

(d/s)

4

A41

Sharpshill
Farm

LETCHWICK FARM RD

Kingswood

PH

Brick Kiln
Farm

GRENDON RD

Ham Home
Wood

Hamgreen
Wood

3

19

Rookery
Farm

ROSAMONDS
COTTS

PH

Ham
Green

2

Kingswoodlane
Farm

KINGSWOOD LA

Mercer's
Farm

Mercer's
Wood

BICESTER RD

Glear
Farm

Ham Farm

Collett
Farm

CREIGHTON RD

1

Woodlands
Farm

Woodham

A41

Little Yeat
Farm

18

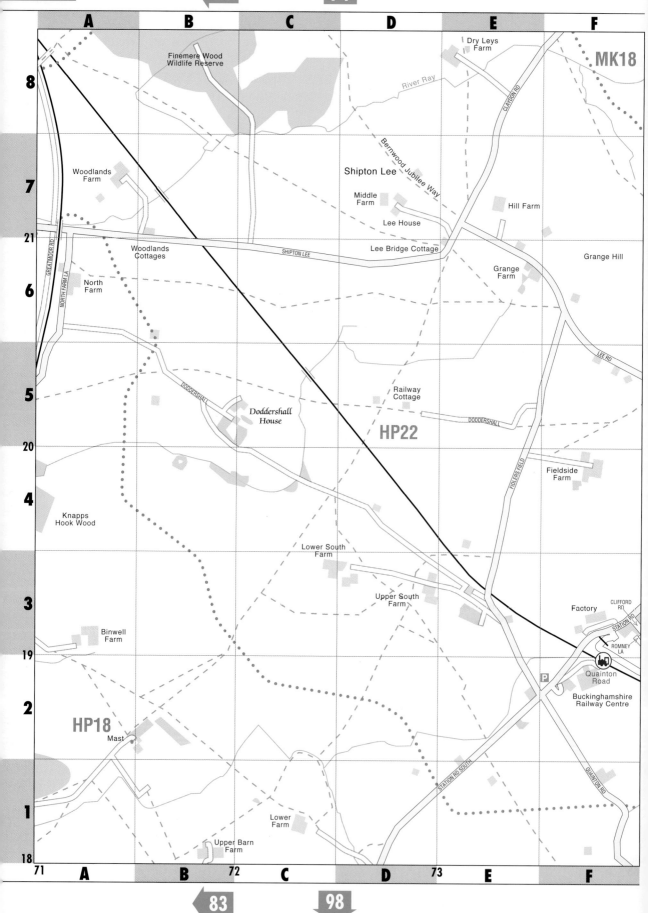

A B C D E F

MK18

8

Dry Leys
Farm

Finemere Wood
Wildlife Reserve

River Ray

Bernwood Jubilee Way

Shipton Lee

CLAYDON RD

7

Woodlands
Farm

Middle
Farm

Hill Farm

Lee House

21

Woodlands
Cottages

SHIPTON LEE

Lee Bridge Cottage

Grange Hill

6

North
Farm

Grange
Farm

GREATMOOR RD

NORTH FARM LA

DODDERSHALL

LEE RD

5

Doddershall
House

Railway
Cottage

DODDERSHALL

HP22

20

FIDLERS FIELD

Fieldside
Farm

4

Knapps
Hook Wood

Lower South
Farm

3

Upper South
Farm

Factory

CLIFFORD
RD

STATION RD

Binwell
Farm

ROMNEY
LA

19

P

Quainton
Road

2

HP18

Buckinghamshire
Railway Centre

Mast

STATION RD SOUTH

QUAINTON RD

1

Lower
Farm

Upper Barn
Farm

18

71 A B 72 C D 73 E F

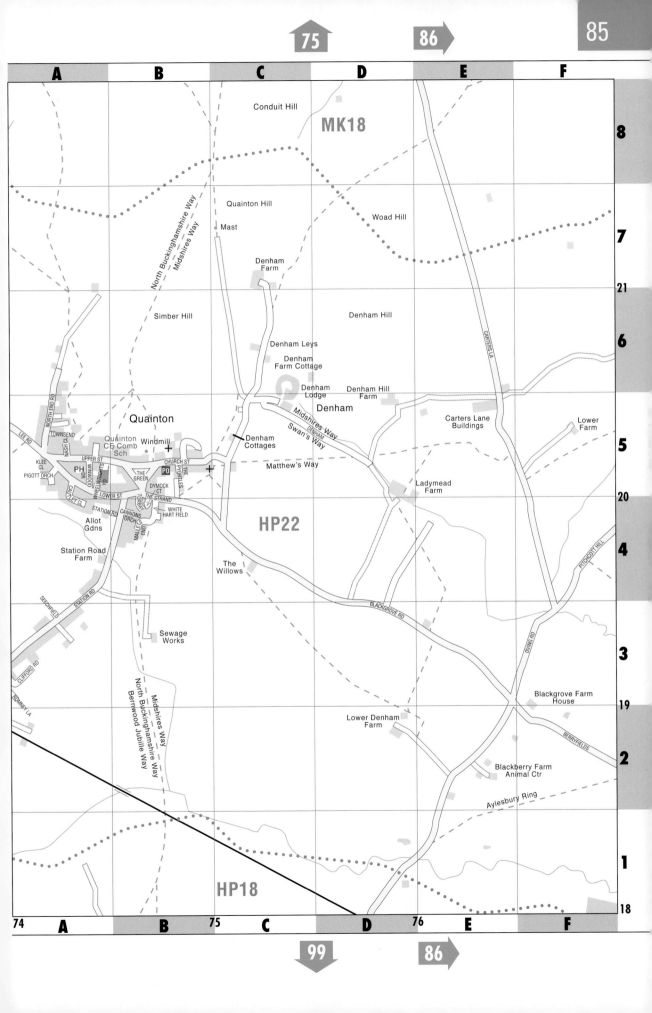

A B C D E F

8
7
21
6
5
20
4
3
19
2
1
18

Conduit Hill

MK18

Quainton Hill

Woad Hill

Mast

Simber Hill

Denham Farm

Denham Hill

Denham Leys

Denham Farm Cottage

Denham Lodge

Denham Hill Farm

Denham

North Buckinghamshire Way
Midshires Way

CARTERS LA

Quainton

Windmill

Midshires Way

Swan's Way

DENHAM

Carters Lane Buildings

Lower Farm

TOWNSEND

LEE RD

NORTH END RD

NASH CL

KLEE CL

PIGOTT ORCH

PH

WINDMILL

WHEELWRIGHTS CL

UPPER ST

Quainton CE Comb Sch

THE GREEN

LOWER ST

CAULEY CL

STATION RD

THE PYGHTLES

CHURCH ST

PO

THE STRAND

DYMOCK CT

CANNONS ORCH

TORRIL

MALLERY END

WHITE HART FIELD

Denham Cottages

Matthew's Way

HP22

Ladymead Farm

PITCHCOTT HILL

Allot Gdns

Station Road Farm

SEECHFIELD

STATION RD

CLIFFORD RD

ROMNEY LA

The Willows

Sewage Works

Midshires Way
North Buckinghamshire Way
Bernwood Jubilee Way

BLACKGROVE RD

OVING RD

Lower Denham Farm

Blackgrove Farm House

BERRYFIELDS

Blackberry Farm Animal Ctr

Aylesbury Ring

HP18

A B C D E F

8

MK18

PORTWAY

MARSTON HILL

Bushy Farm

PULPIT LA

MEADWAY

Home Farm

Crossroads Farm

WHITCHURCH LA

Oving

FOUR ACRES

BOWLING ALLEY

THE PIGHTLE

Matthew's Way

Church Farm

PH

Recn Gd

Whitchurch Comb Sch

NORTH MARSTON LA

NEWMANS CL

ASHGROVE GDNS

ASHGROVE GDNS

THE MEADOWS

BUCKINGHAM RD

A413

7

CHURCH LA

STONE VIEW

21

MANOR RD

DARK LA

Oving House

BALUK RD

WHITCHURCH RD

GREEN ACRES CL

ASHGROVE GDNS

OVING RD

CRABS GR

MT PLEASANT

RICKYARD

MARKET HILL

Pitchcott Hill

PITCHCOTT RD

Bunshill

CASTLE LA

WEIR LA

6

Pitchcott Hill Farm

Holbornhill Farm

Scotshill Farm

Pitchcott

Dunn Mill

5

Manor Farm

PITCHCOTT HILL

20

HP22

4

19

Aylesbury Ring

FOLLY FARM RD

Folly Farm

2

Upper Blackgrove Farm

Cow Ground Buildings

Middle Blackgrove Farm

BERRYFIELDS

Whitesfield Farm

1

18

Whitesfield Farm Cottages

77 A 78 B C 78 D 79 E F

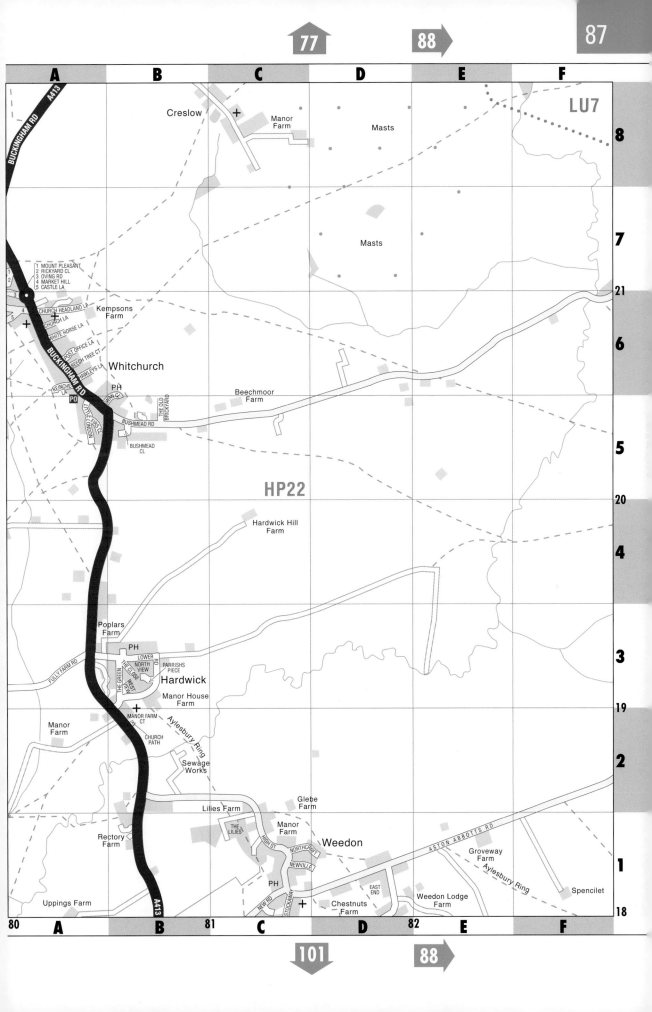

LU7

Creslow

Manor Farm

Masts

Masts

8

7

21

A413
BUCKINGHAM RD

1 MOUNT PLEASANT
2 RICKYARD CL
3 OVING RD
4 MARKET HILL
5 CASTLE LA

CHURCH HEADLAND LA
CHURCH LA

Kempsons Farm

WHITE HORSE LA

POST OFFICE LA
BEECH TREE CT
HAWLEYS LA

Whitchurch

6

BUCKINGHAM RD

KEINCHE LA
PH
PO

SWAN CT

LITTLE LONDON

THE OLD BRICKYARD

BUSHMEAD RD

Beechmoor Farm

BUSHMEAD CL

5

HP22

20

Hardwick Hill Farm

4

Poplars Farm

FULLY FARM RD

PH

LOWER NORTH RD

THE CLOSE
THE GREEN
WEST VIEW

PARRISHS PIECE

Hardwick

Manor House Farm

3

Manor Farm

MANOR FARM CT

CHURCH PATH

Aylesbury Ring

19

Sewage Works

2

Glebe Farm

Lilies Farm

THE LILIES

Manor Farm

HIGH ST

NORTHCROFT

NEWVILLE

Weedon

ASTON ABBOTTS RD

Groveway Farm

Aylesbury Ring

1

Rectory Farm

PH

NEW RD

STOCKAWAY

EAST END

Chestnuts Farm

Weedon Lodge Farm

Spencilet

Uppings Farm

A413

18

← 87
78

A   B   C   D   E   F

8

WHITCHURCH RD

ASTON ABBOTTS RD

Sewage Works

LU7

Red Barn

7

21

Willowbrook Farm

The Hay Barn Bsns Pk

Red Barn Farm

Vicarage Farm

6

CUBLINGTON RD

Longmoor Farm

Sewage Works

Freemasons Wood

Church Farm

5

Aston Abbotts

Norduck Farm

The Abbey

CHAPMANS LEA
RISS RD
THE OLD BAKERY
HUMPHREYS CL
PH

20

MOAT LA

THE GREEN

BRIDGSTOCK

NASHS FARM

HUNTERS WAY

NEW ZEALAND COTTS

WINGRAVE RD

WINGRAVE CROSS RDS

A418

Windmill Hill Farm

THE LINES

WINSLOW RD

HP22

4

Windmill Hill

LINES HILL

Fox Covert

Barns Farm

3

19

WEEDON RD

AYLESBURY RD

Lower Burston Farm

2

Burston Hill Farm

Burston Hill

1

Manor Farm

18

Aylesbury Ring

MANOR RD

A418

BREWHOUSE LA

Hale Farm

83   A   B   84   C   D   85   E   F

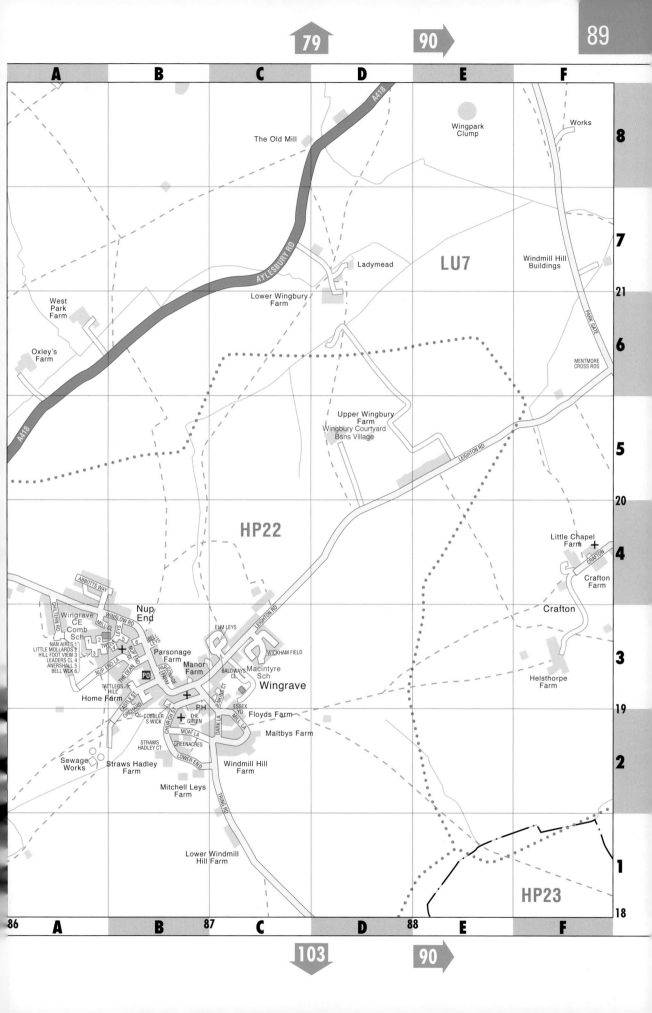

89
80

A **B** **C** **D** **E** **F**

Manor Farm

MANOR FARM LA

LEDBURN

LAKES COTTS

LEYBURNE CL

Ledburn

8

WELL LA

Ledburn Farm

B488

LEIGHTON RD

The Lodge

7

Windmill Hill

LEDBURN

Rowden Farm

21

ROWDEN FARM LA

B488

6

CHEDDINGTON RD

LU7

5

LEDBURN RD

Mentmore Stud Farm

20

CRAFTON LA

The Belt

CHEDDINGTON RD

Mentmore

MENTMORE CT

Wing Lodge

THE GREEN

HOWELL HILL CL

CRAFTON

4

+

PH

Big Wood

Mentmore Towers

Home Farm

Mansom

CRAFTON LODGE RD

Mentmore Park

ROSEBERY MEWS

Crafton Stud Farm

New Spinney

MENTMORE

3

Crafton Lodge

Mentmore Park Farm

19

The Belt

CH

Cheddington Lodge

2

MENTMORE RD

HP23

1

STATION RD

18

89 **A** **B** 90 **C** **D** 91 **E** **F**

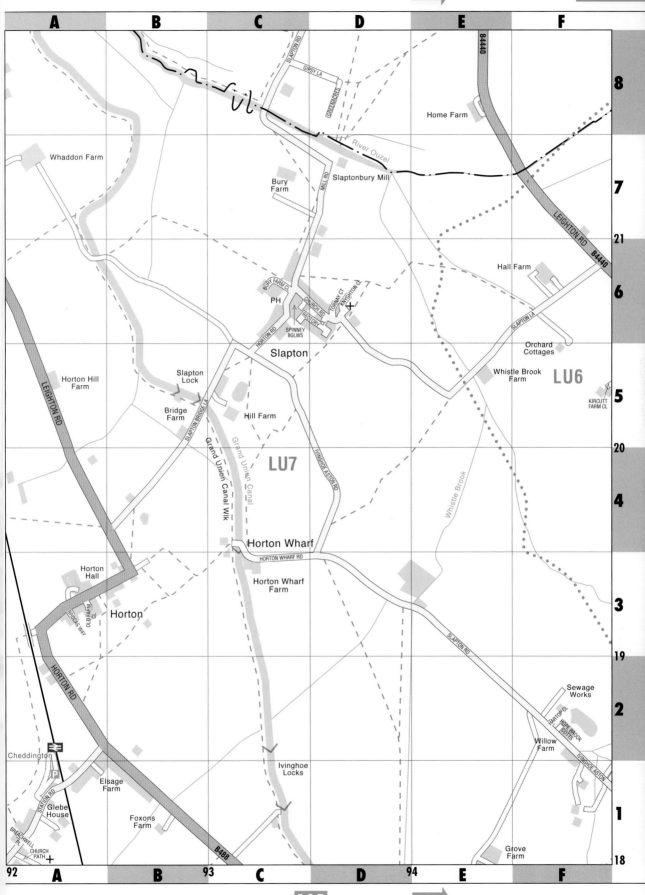

A B C D E F

8
7
21
6
5
20
4
3
19
2
1
18

Home Farm
Whaddon Farm
Bury Farm
River Ouzel
Slaptonbury Mill
LEIGHTON RD
B4440
GIPSY LA
GREENACRES
SLAPTON RD
MILL RD
Hall Farm
Slapton LA
Orchard Cottages
Whistle Brook Farm
LU6
KIRCUTT FARM CL
BURY FARM CL
CHURCH RD
TOPMAY CT
KNIGHTON CL
RECTORY CL
SPINNEY BGLWS
HORTON RD
PH
Slapton
Horton Hill Farm
Slapton Lock
Bridge Farm
Hill Farm
SLAPTON BRIDGE LA
Grand Union Canal Wlk
Grand Union Canal
LU7
IVINGHOE ASTON RD
Whistle Brook
Horton Wharf
HORTON WHARF RD
Horton Wharf Farm
Horton Hall
Horton
BROCAS WAY
OLD FARM CL
SLAPTON RD
Sewage Works
HARTOP CL
HOPE BROOK COTTS
Willow Farm
IVINGHOE ASTON
HORTON RD
Cheddington
STATION RD
BREACHWELL PL
CHURCH PATH
Glebe House
Elsage Farm
Foxons Farm
Ivinghoe Locks
B488
Grove Farm

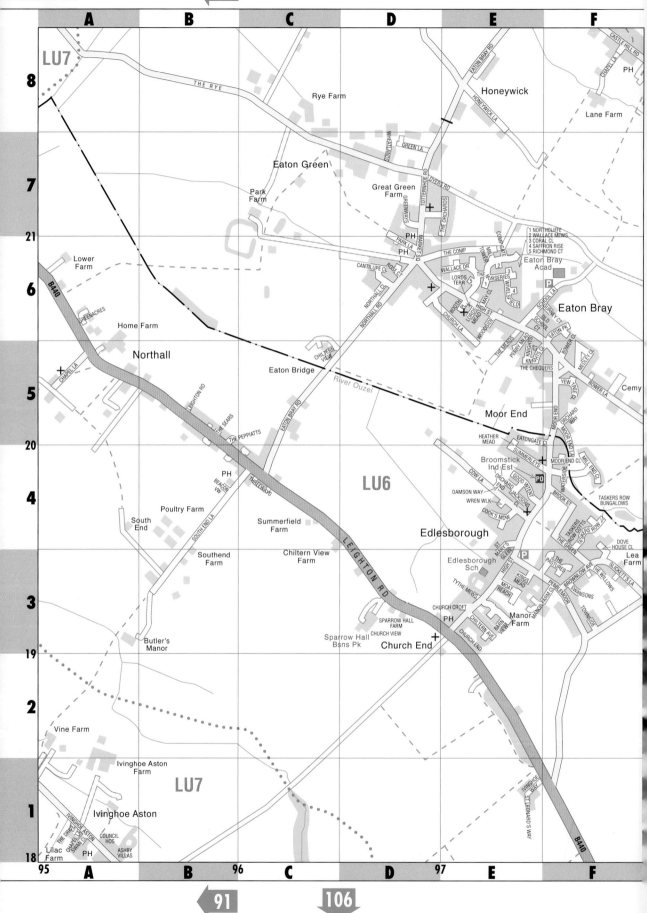

A B C D E F

8

LU7

THE RYE

Rye Farm

EATON BRAY RD

Honeywick

HONEYWICK LA

CASTLE HILL RD

CHAPELLA

PH

Lane Farm

7

Eaton Green

Park Farm

GREEN LA

WHEATLANDS

Great Green Farm

DYERS RD

TOTTERNHOE RD

GREENWAYS

THE ORCHARDS

21

PARK LA

PH

PH

MARKET SQ

CANTILUPE CL

ROSE CT

THE COMP

WALLACE DR

MILL TOWER

COMP GATE

THE COMP

1 NORTHCLIFFE
2 WALLACE MEWS
3 CORAL CL
4 SAFFRON RISE
5 RICHMOND CT

L2

Eaton Bray Acad

P

6

B440

Lower Farm

GREENACRES

Home Farm

NORTHALL RD

LORDS TERR

BOOTH

PL

MAY CL

HIGH ST

NURSERIES

SCHOOL LA

SCHOOL CT

EATON PK

Eaton Bray

BOWER CL

MEGG'S CL

Cemy

CHAPEL LA

Northall

LEIGHTON RD

CHILTERN VIEW

Eaton Bridge

River Ouzel

CHURCH LA

WOODSIDE

THE MEADS

PERRY MEAD

KNS

THE CHEQUERS

YEW TREE CL

BOWER LA

5

20

THE SEARS

THE PEPPIATTS

EATON BRAY RD

Moor End

HEATHER MEAD

EATONGATE CL

SUMMERLEYS

Broomstick Ind Est

MOOR END

ORCHARD WAY

MOOR END CL

MILL END CL

MOOR END

PO

TASKERS ROW BUNGALOWS

4

PH

BEACON VW

THREEWAYS

SOUTH END LA

Poultry Farm

South End

Summerfield Farm

Chiltern View Farm

LU6

COW LA

ORCHARD END

DAMSON WAY

WREN WLK

COOK'S MDN

JACKSONS CL

GOOD WITHN

WATERSIDE

BROOK ST

Edlesborough

TASKERS ROW COTTS

TASKERS ROW

THE GREEN

DOVE HOUSE CL

Lea Farm

SLICKETT'S LA

3

Southend Farm

Butler's Manor

LEIGHTON RD

Edlesborough Sch

P

ST MARY'S GLEBE

TYTHE MEWS

CHURCH CROFT

Sparrow Hall Farm

CHURCH VIEW

Sparrow Hall Bsns Pk

PH

Church End

CHILTERN AVE

CHURCH END

CHURCH END

KINGS MEAD

MOAT REACH

HIGH ST

BARN VIEW

MANOR FARM

Manor Farm

THE PASTURES

BROWNLOW AVE

PEBBLEMOOR

SWANSONS

TOWNSIDE

THE WILLOWS

19

Vine Farm

2

Ivinghoe Aston Farm

LU7

IVINGHOE WAY

ST LEONARD'S WAY

B440

1

Ivinghoe Aston

THE DRIVE

IVINGHOE ASTON

CHAPEL LA

SWAN CL

COUNCIL HOS

PH

ASHBY VILLAS

18

Lilac Farm

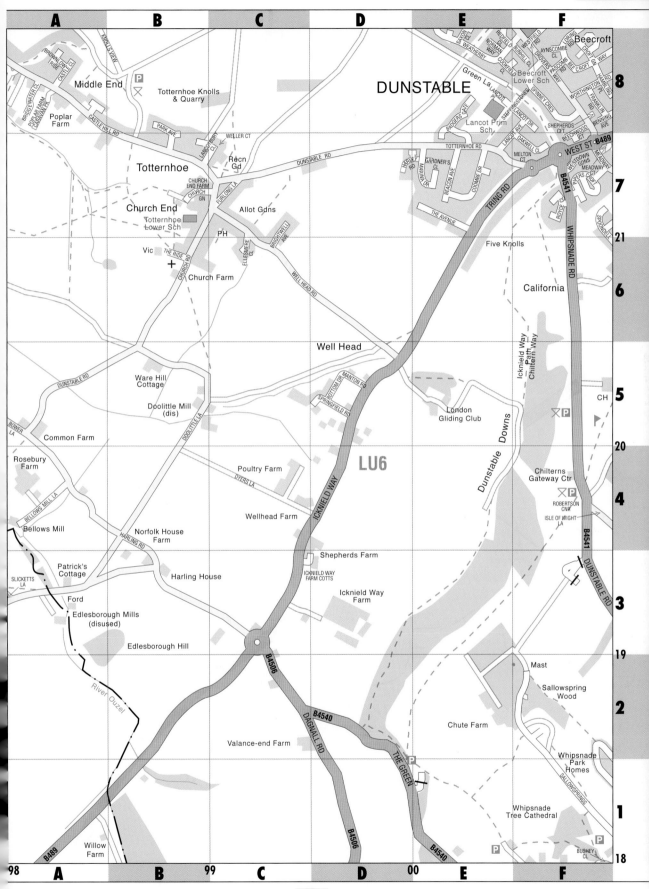

A   B   C   D   E   F

8

DUNSTABLE

Beecroft

Middle End

Poplar
Farm

Totternhoe Knolls
& Quarry

Green La

Beecroft
Lower Sch

Lancot Prim
Sch

Totternhoe

WEST ST

7

Totternhoe Rd

21

Recn
Gd

Church End

Totternhoe
Lower Sch

Allot Gdns

Dunstable Rd

Five Knolls

California

6

Vic

Church Farm

Well Head Rd

Well Head

20

Ware Hill
Cottage

Doolittle Mill
(dis)

Manton Rd

London
Gliding Club

CH

Dunstable Downs

5

Common Farm

Springfield Rd

LU6

Chilterns
Gateway Ctr

Rosebury
Farm

Poultry Farm

DYERS LA

Icknield Way

ROBERTSON
CNR

ISLE OF WIGHT
LA

4

Bellows Mill

Norfolk House
Farm

Wellhead Farm

Shepherds Farm

Icknield Way
Farm Cotts

Icknield Way
Farm

Mast

3

Patrick's
Cottage

Harling House

Sallowspring
Wood

Ford

Edlesborough Mills
(disused)

B4506

B4540

Chute Farm

2

Edlesborough Hill

River Ouzel

Valance-end Farm

DAGNALL RD

THE GREEN

Whipsnade
Park Homes

19

Whipsnade
Tree Cathedral

1

B489

Willow
Farm

B4506

B4540

BUSHEY
CL

18

98   A   B   99   C   D   00   E   F

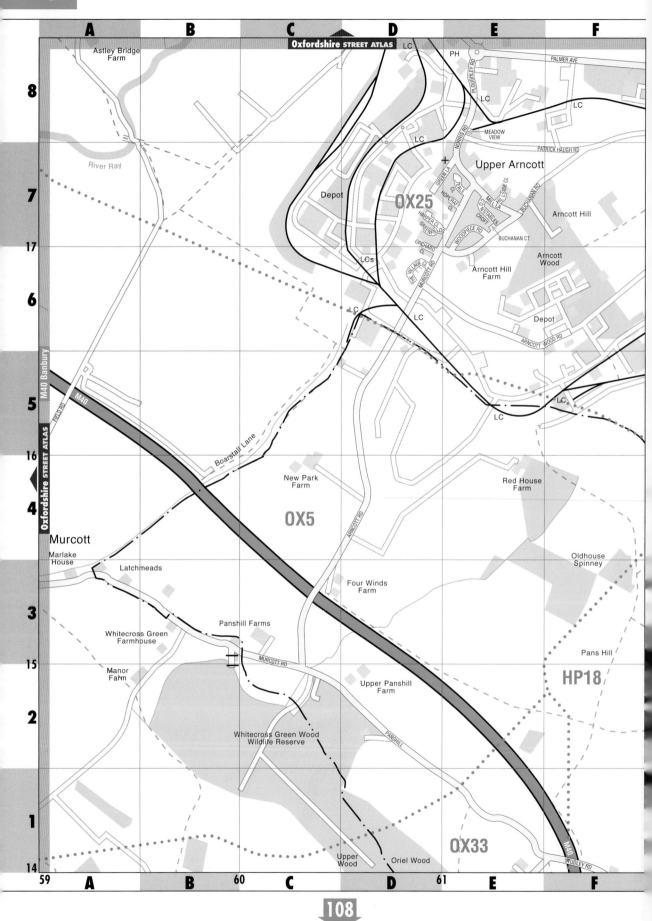

Astley Bridge Farm

8

River Ray

7

17

Depot

OX25

LC
PH
PALMER AVE
LC
LC
MEADOW VIEW
PATRICK HAUGH RD
Upper Arncott
GREEN LA
HORCRAFT CL
NORRIS RD
PLOUGHLEY RD
BUCHANAN RD
MILL LA
CO STABLES
CROFT
Arncott Hill
HARPER CL DS
GREEN
WOODPIECE RD
BUCHANAN CT
Arncott Wood
ORCHARD CL
THE VILLAGE CL
MURCOTT RD
Arncott Hill Farm
Depot

6

LCs
LC
LC
LC
ARNCOTT WOOD RD

M40 Banbury

5

M40
FIELD RD

Boarstall Lane

16

New Park Farm

OX5

Red House Farm
LC
LC
LC

4

Murcott

Marlake House

Latchmeads

Oldhouse Spinney

ARNCOTT RD

Four Winds Farm

3

Whitecross Green Farmhouse

Panshill Farms

MURCOTT RD

Pans Hill

15

Manor Farm

Upper Panshill Farm

HP18

2

Whitecross Green Wood Wildlife Reserve

PANSHILL

1

OX33

Upper Wood

Oriel Wood

STUDLEY RD
M40

14

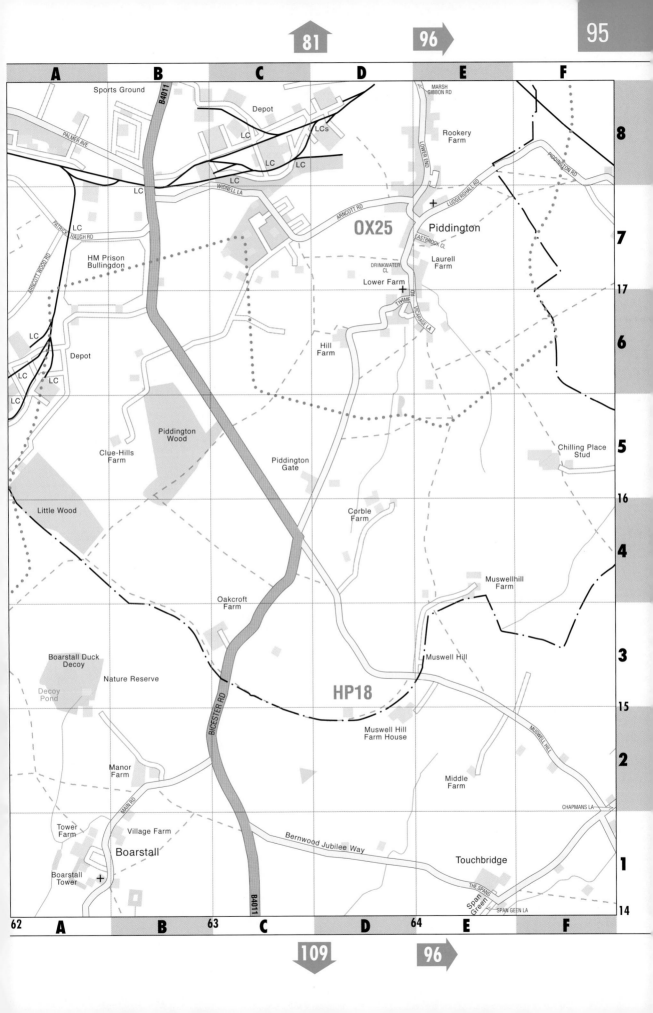

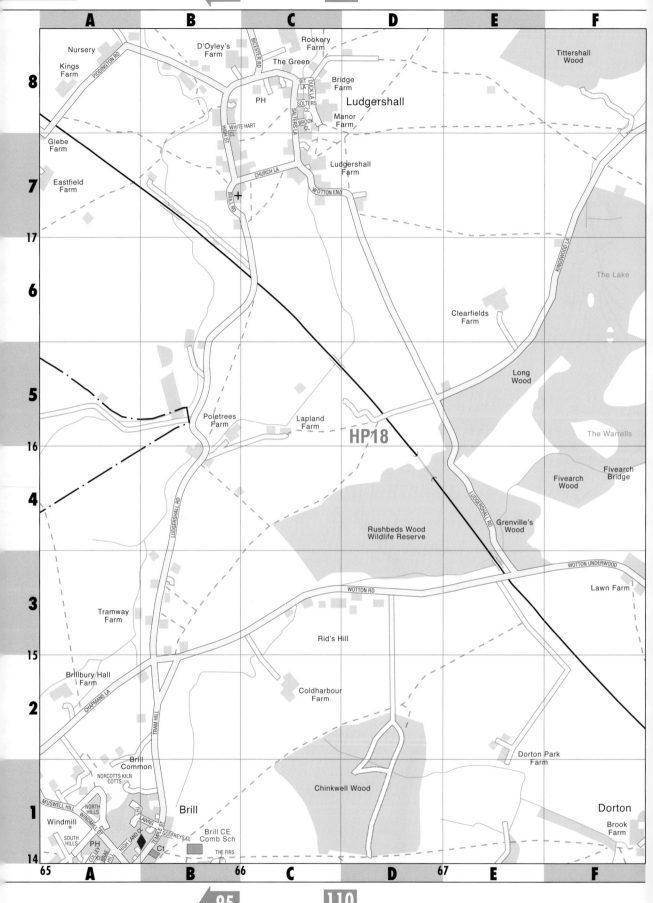

95
82

A   B   C   D   E   F

8

Nursery

Kings
Farm

D'Oyley's
Farm

PIDDINGTON RD

Rookery
Farm

The Green

BICESTER RD

BIT
LA

DUCK LA

Bridge
Farm

Ludgershall

Tittershall
Wood

PH

SOLTERS
CL

Manor
Farm

WHITE HART

HIGH ST

SALTERS LA

BROOK
CL

Glebe
Farm

7

Eastfield
Farm

CHURCH LA

Ludgershall
Farm

WOTTON END

BRILL RD

17

6

Clearfields
Farm

The Lake

KINGSWOOD LA

5

Long
Wood

Poletrees
Farm

Lapland
Farm

HP18

The Warrells

16

Fivearch
Bridge

4

Fivearch
Wood

LUDGERSHALL RD

Rushbeds Wood
Wildlife Reserve

Grenville's
Wood

WOTTON UNDERWOOD

Lawn Farm

WOTTON RD

3

Tramway
Farm

Rid's Hill

CHAPMANS LA

15

Brillbury Hall
Farm

Coldharbour
Farm

2

TRAM HILL

Dorton Park
Farm

Brill
Common

NORCOTTS KILN
COTTS

Chinkwell Wood

Dorton

MUSWELL HILL

NORTH
HILLS

THE LAWNS

Brill

1

Windmill

SOUTH
HILLS

PH

WINDMILL ST

HIGH LAND CT

TEMPLE ST

GODFREYS CL

Brill CE
Comb Sch

Brook
Farm

COLL

BRAE
HILL

Ct

THE FIRS

14

65   A   B   66   C   D   67   E   F

95
110

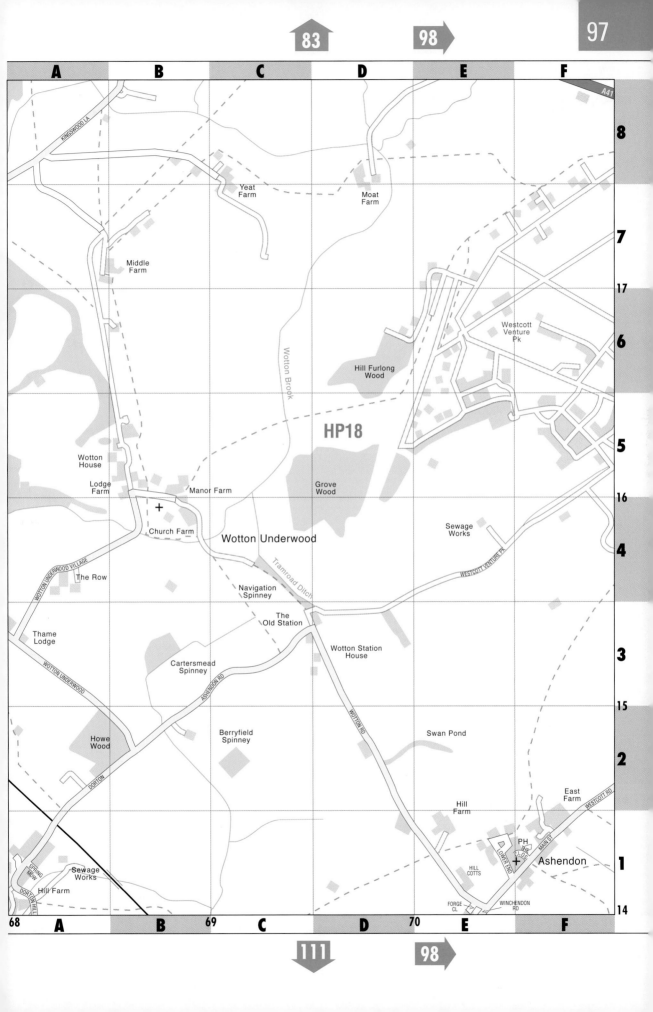

83
98

A41

A   B   C   D   E   F

8

KINGSWOOD LA

Yeat
Farm

Moat
Farm

7

17

Middle
Farm

Westcott
Venture
Pk

6

Wotton Brook

Hill Furlong
Wood

HP18

5

Wotton
House

Grove
Wood

16

Lodge
Farm

Manor Farm

Sewage
Works

Church Farm

Wotton Underwood

WESTCOTT VENTURE PK

4

Tramroad Ditch

The Row

Navigation
Spinney

WOTTON UNDERWOOD VILLAGE

The
Old Station

Thame
Lodge

Cartersmead
Spinney

Wotton Station
House

WOTTON UNDERWOOD

3

ASHENDON RD

15

Berryfield
Spinney

Howe
Wood

WOTTON RD

Swan Pond

2

DORTON

East
Farm

Hill
Farm

WESTCOTT RD

MAIN ST

SPRING MDW

Sewage
Works

LOWER END

THE CLOSE

PH

Ashendon

1

DORTON HILL

Hill Farm

HILL
COTTS

FORGE
CL

WINCHENDON
RD

14

68   A   B   69   C   D   70   E   F

111
98

A **B** **C** **D** **E** **F**

8

A41

Newhouse
Farm

WESTCOTT VENTURE PK

South View
Farm

BICESTER RD

Littleton Middle
Farm

Hall
Farm

STATION RD SOUTH

WELLINGTON DR

7

BURN FARM RD

HIGH ST

Westcott
CE Sch

CHURCH LA

SWAN CT

Westcott

Waddesdon
Gardens

Waddesdon
Farm

A41 HIGH ST

17

WHITCHURCH
CL

AYLESS
CL

LOWER GREEN

KINGS
CL

QUEEN ST

Waddesdon
Dairy

6

Works

Westcott
Farm

ASHENDON RD

RAVEN
CRES

Lodge Hill

WADDESDON
MANOR
FLATS

WADDESDON MANOR EST

Waddesdon
Manor

Westcott
Venture
Pk

LINES DR

Westcott
Field
Farm

WADDESDON MANOR EST

5

Windmill
Plantation

16

SILK ST

HP18

4

Gypsy
Bottom

Windmill Hill
Farm

Watbridge
Farm
Cottages

3

15

WESTCOTT RD

2

Grassy
Dell

Decoy
Farm

1

Watbridge
Farm

Decoy
Wood

14

71

A **B** **72** **C** **D** **73** **E** **F**

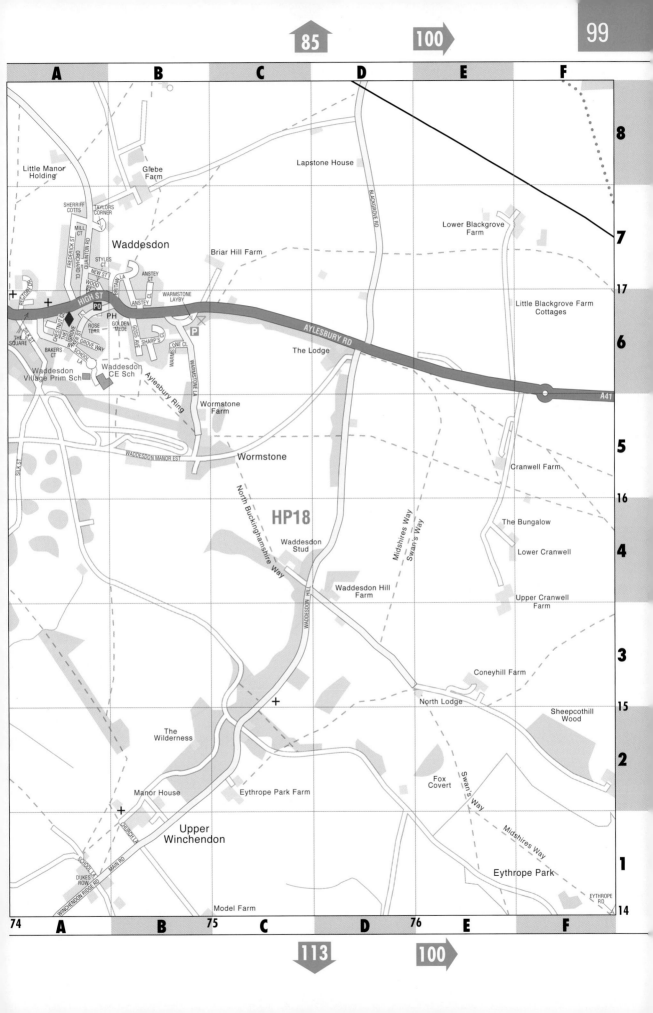

A B C D E F

8

7

17

6

5

16

4

3

15

2

1

14

Little Manor Holding

Glebe Farm

Lapstone House

Lower Blackgrove Farm

SHERRIFF COTTS

TAYLORS CORNER

MILL CT

FREDERICK ST

SCHOOL CT

QUAINTON RD

Waddesdon

STYLES CT

NEW ST

WOOD ST

ANSTEY CT

BRITTAIN LA

ANSTEY CL

ANSTEY

Briar Hill Farm

WARMSTONE LAYBY

Little Blackgrove Farm Cottages

RECTORY DR

HIGH ST

PO

PH

GOLDEN MEDE

ROSE TERR

AYLESBURY RD

SILK ST

THE SQUARE

THE GROVE

CHESTNUT CL

BAKER ST

BAKERS CT

BAKER GROVE WAY

SHARP'S CL

GOSS AVE

SCHOOL LA

WARMSTONE CL

WARMSTONE LA

The Lodge

A41

Waddesdon Village Prim Sch

Waddesdon CE Sch

Aylesbury Ring

Wormstone Farm

Cranwell Farm

SILK ST

WADDESDON MANOR EST

Wormstone

The Bungalow

HP18

North Buckinghamshire Way

Midshires Way

Swan's Way

Lower Cranwell

Waddesdon Stud

Waddesdon Hill Farm

WADDESDON HILL

Upper Cranwell Farm

Coneyhill Farm

North Lodge

Sheepcothill Wood

The Wilderness

Fox Covert

Swan's Way

Manor House

Eythrope Park Farm

CHURCH LA

Upper Winchendon

Midshires Way

SCHOOL LA

DUKES ROW

WINCHENDON RIDGE RD

MAIN RD

Eythrope Park

EYTHROPE RD

Model Farm

A B C D E F

8

HP22

Lower Farm

Lower Fleetmarston Farm

7

17

D5
1 NORTHCLIFFE WY
2 MORGAN DR
3 FREYBERG DR
4 KIRKES WAY
5 MERRYWEATHER ST
6 DAMSON RD
7 FARLEIGH DR
8 MIRABELLE CL
9 MARJORIE CL
10 HERMAN ST
11 HONEYPIN DR
12 MOORE CRES
13 BENNET WAY
14 WOOLBROCK CL
15 LEVELLER WAY

6

Fleet Marston Cottages

Fleet Marston Farm Hunters Farm Ind Est

ASHMEAD ST
BRAEBURN RD
EMPIRE CL
JUPITER CL
LAKELAND DR
TOPAZ LA
MONAR
RUBY CRES

A41 AYLESBURY RD

Green Ridge Prim Acad

NEWTON AVE
GRIEVEN RD
BRAMLEY RD
D'ARCY CL
LIMELIGHT AVE
BRAMLEY RD

10 WINSTON MEWS
11 GILLIFLOWER ST
12 DERBY PL
13 DISCOVERY ST
14 GREENSLEEVES DR
15 BREEDON DR
16 GALA RD
17 FORTONE CL
18 KESWICK ST

WHINHAM GN 1
VALERIE WAY 2
KEEPSAKE WAY 3
DENBIGH CL 4
SENECA CL 5
BLUE ROCK DR 6

Berryfield

5

BICESTER RD

Berryfields Farm

GLENTON GN
MARLET WAY
PRESIDENT RD
PIXIE RD
RUSSEL RD
DOMINO WY
PIPPIN RD
AMBER CL
ARCH GR
SIDDINGTON DR
COTTINGTON DR
CALVILLE GDNS
MELBA ST

1 POMEROY CT
2 AVERDAL DR
3 TYDEMANS CL
4 AMOROSA GDNS
5 ALDERMAN DR
6 PERRINE CL
7 CLEMENS RD
8 CARDINAL DR
9 ELMORE ST

16

INCITA
OLYMPIA WAY
MENDIP ST
MERTON
ELDERBERRY RD
HOWATE

Berryfields CE Prim Sch

MORELLO CL 1
LAMBERT RD 2
COLNEY RD 3
BENTON MEWS 4
APOLLO CL 5
OXYARD 6
THE WARREN 7
PONDECROFT 8
BROKEND 9
BANKS YARD 10
COW GROUND 11
GEORGE HAMMOND LA 12

QUINDELL CL
CONCORDE SQ
CAMEO CT
NIMROD ST
PARADISE ORCHARD

1 CRAWFORD RD
2 OLDFIELD ST
3 BRANDY ST
4 SPARTLET MEWS
5 CARRICK ST
6 THORNLEY CL
7 BARLAND WY
8 RITSON LA
9 IDAHO ST
10 CONFERENCE RD
11 ZOE ST

4

Fleet Marston

HP18

NOBLE CRES
WHATLEY
FERRY RD
OX GROUND
PARADISE ORCHARD
JOHN FITZ JOHN AVE
FORD LA

Aylesbury Vale Acad

NICHOLAS CHARLES CRES
SEABRIGHT WAY 1
VICTOR CL 2
KENTISH ST 3
ELTON CL 4

WESTERN LINK RD
MOORCROFT LA
SIERRA RD

Putlowes Cottages

PUTLOWES DR

SIR HENRY LEE CRES
P&R

Aylesbury Vale Parkway

Billingsfield Cottages

1 READING CL 1
NAPPIN CL 2
ROBINSON CL 3

HAYWOOD WAY
GRIMMER CL
FLETCHER CL
DICKS WAY
BELGRAVE RD
LANDER RD
EELES CL
ATKINS CL

3

Fleet Marston Spinney

Putlowes

SIR HENRY LEE CRES

1 OPAL MEWS
2 EXCALIBUR RD

VALOR DR
AVALON DR
PERSHORE WY

GAINSBOROUGH PL

BICESTER RD

Haydon Hill

A41

15

River Thame

Sewage Works

MULLINS WAY 1
CONSTABLE PL 2
AILWARD RD 3

REMBRANDT END
MONET
GOYA PL
LATTICE WAY
PICASSO PL
RUBENS RD
DICKENS WAY
FRONT CL
THACKERAY
BRONTE
AUSTEN CL
BAGRICK RD

2

Sheepcote Hill Farm

HP19

Rabans Lane Ind Est

MEREDITH DR
CARRIE CL
SCOTT
TENNYSON WAY RD

SMEATON CL
ANGIER CL
BRUNEL RD
TELFORD WY

1

Eythrope

Bear Brook

EDISON RD
BESSEMER CRES
HARTWELL VIEW

Bell Bsns Pk

RABANS CL
RABANS LA
THOMPSON
CHELSEA
LONDON RD
NAPIER RD
ABINGTON WAY
BRIMMERS WAY

EYTHROPE RD

Haydon Mill Farm

HUDSON MS
GROSVENOR WY

FIRS CL

14

77 A B 78 C D 79 E F

F1
1 SPRUCE RD
2 HIGHGATE MEWS
3 KENSINGTON PATH
4 CRAFTON PL
5 PINE ST
6 COLDHARBOUR WAY
7 HAMPSTEAD CL
8 CAVENDISH WY

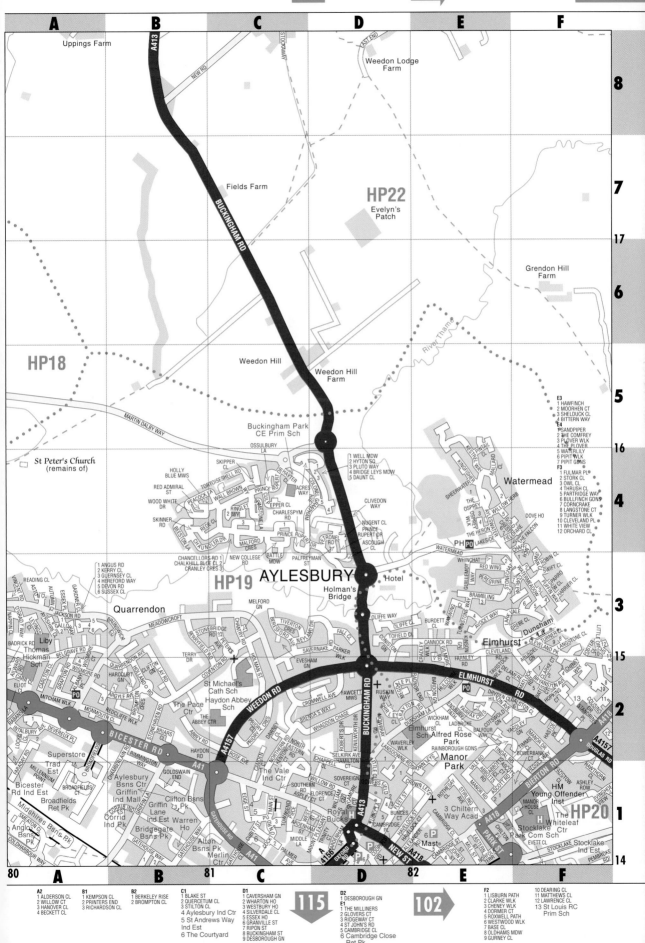

101
88

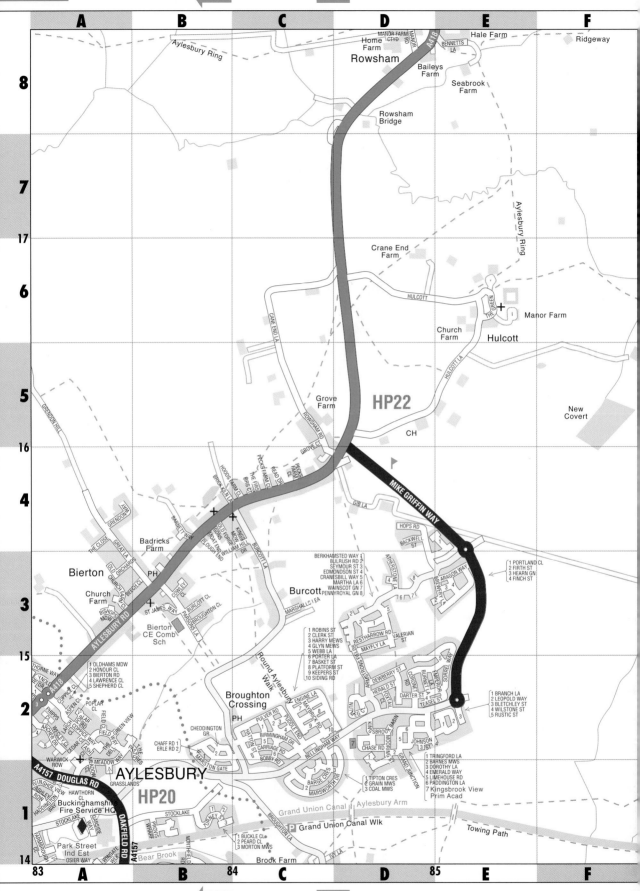

101
116

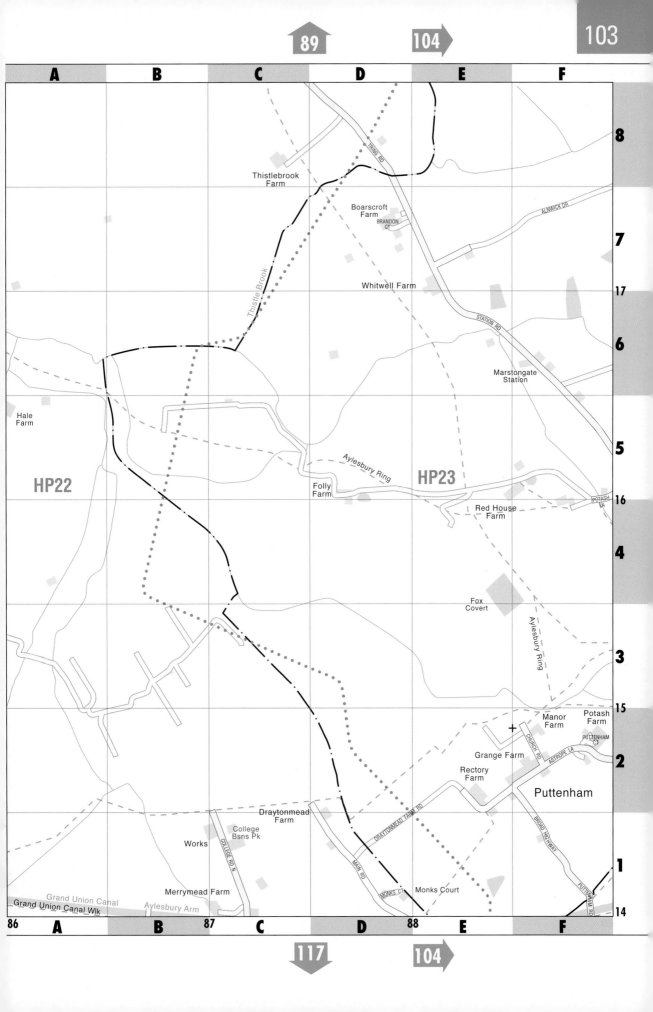

A   B   C   D   E   F

8

Thistlebrook
Farm

Boarscroft
Farm
BRANDON
CT

ALNWICK DR

7

Whitwell Farm

17

STATION RD

6

Marstongate
Station

Hale
Farm

5

Aylesbury Ring

HP23

Folly
Farm

HP22

Red House
Farm

POTASH
LA

16

4

Fox
Covert

Aylesbury Ring

3

15

Manor
Farm

Potash
Farm

PUTTENHAM
CT

CHURCH RD

ASTROPE LA

Grange Farm

2

Rectory
Farm

Puttenham

Draytonmead
Farm

DRAYTONMEAD FARM RD

BROAD HIGHWAY

College
Bsns Pk

Works

COLLEGE RD N

MAIN RD

PUTTENHAM RD

1

Grand Union Canal

Merrymead Farm

Grand Union Canal Wlk

Aylesbury Arm

MONKS CT

Monks Court

14

103
90

A B C D E F

8

Broadmead
Farm

Cheddington

BLENHEIM
CL

STATION RD

REYNOLDS
MEAD

ALNWICK DR

Alnwick
Farm

CHURCH
HILL

WESTMORE RD

MERRY LEYS

HORSESHOE
CL

WESTWARD
DR

PONIES CL

CARTRIDGE

LU7

Manor
House

7

Betlow
Farm

West End
Farm

WEST END RD

THE BAULK

BERRYFIELD

MANOR RD

NEW ST

SUNNY BANK

HILL SIDE

GOOSE
ACRE

BROWNLOW
LA

17

Westend
Hill

6

Mast

Old Airfield
Ind Est

LONG MARSTON RD

Southend
Hill

5

Long Leys
Farm

CHEDDINGTON LA

POTASH LA

16

Old
Toms
Farm

Central
Farm

ALDERPARK
MDW

4

BROMLEY

CHURCH VIEW

STATION RD

CHAPEL LA

PH

HP23

1 RAVENS CT
2 THE OLD FORGE

Old Church
Farm

Long Marston
VA CE
Prim Sch

MARSTON CT

LOXLEY
STABLES

2
1

Long
Marston

Great
Farm

ASTROPE LA

Astrope

Millfield

TRING RD

Gubblecote

LONDON GR

LUKES LA

LONG MARSTON RD

Sewage
Works

Church
Farm

CHURCH FARM LA

Lower
End

15

GREGORYS FIELD

3

Astrope
Farm

WATERY LA

Gubblecote
Farm

LOWER END

SLIP LA

2

ASTROPE LA

Dover
Castle

College
Farm

WINGRAVE RD

Moat
Farm

Gurney's
Farm

PH

VICARAGE RD

CHURCH LA

AYLESBURY RING

DIXON'S
WHARF

Locks

Grand Union Canal

WILSTONE
WHARF

Aylesbury Arm

Dixon's Gap
Bridge

Locks

MARSWORTH
WHARF

LUKES LEA

1

Grand Union Canal Wlk

Wilstone
Bridge

Locks

Wilstone

SANDBROOK LA

THE MILL

GRANGE RD

ROSEBARN LA

PH

Startop's
End

Startop
Farm

WATERY LA

LOWER ICKNIELD WAY

PH

B489

14

89 A 90 B C D 91 E F

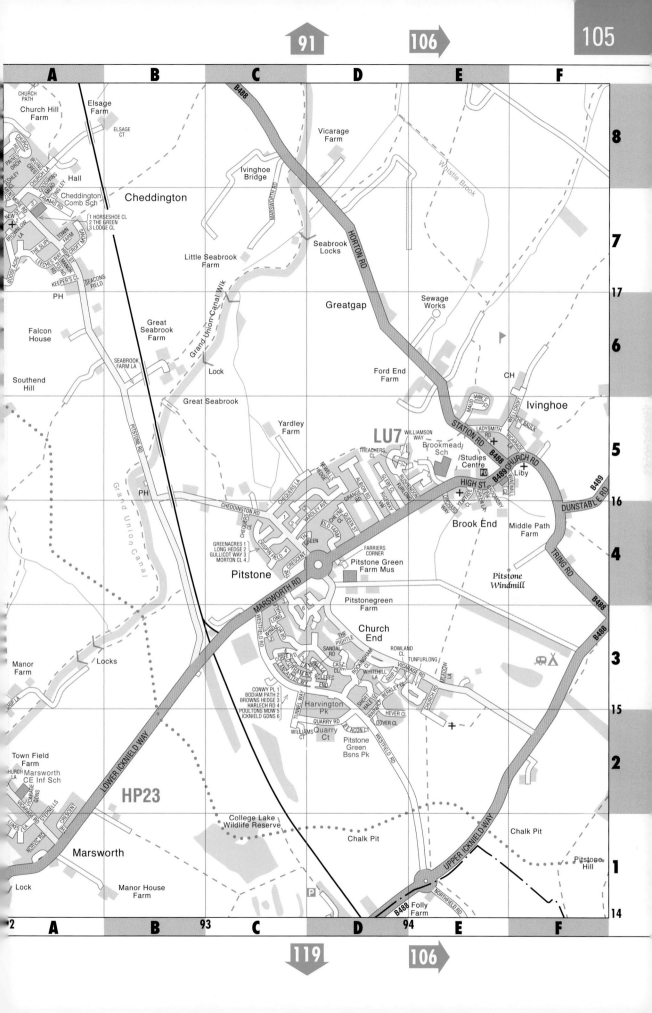

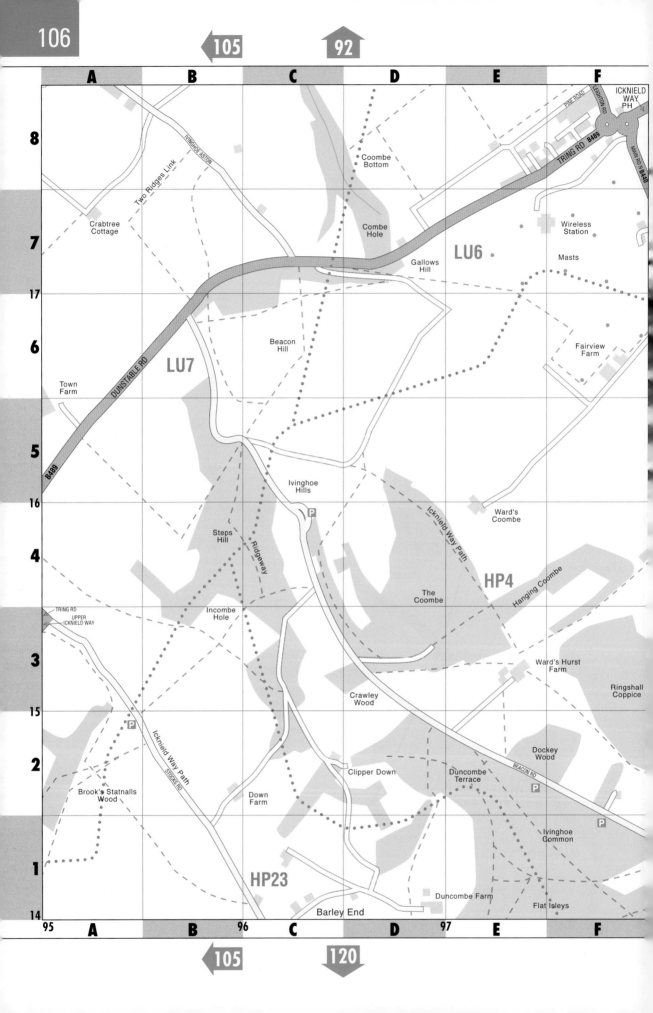

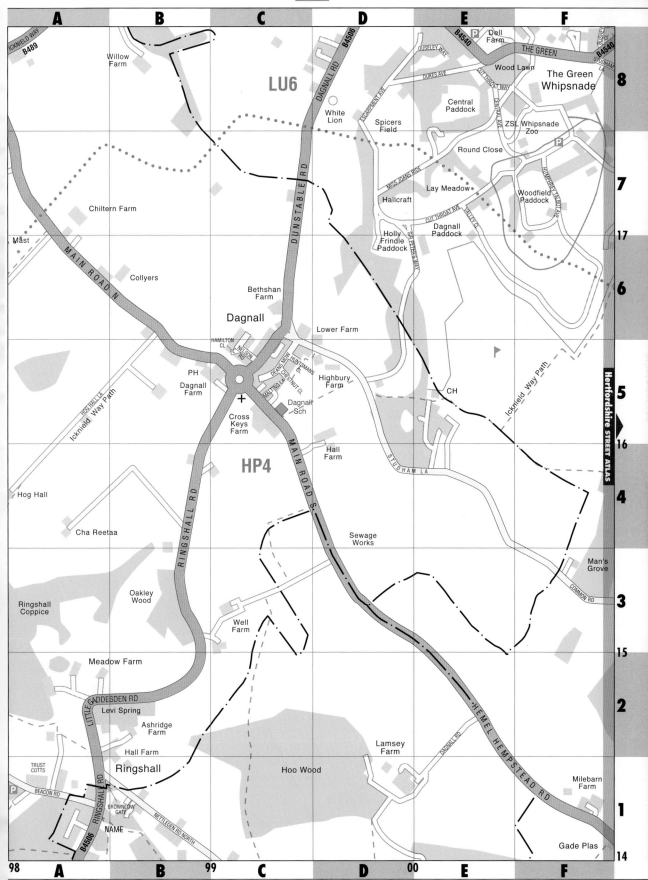

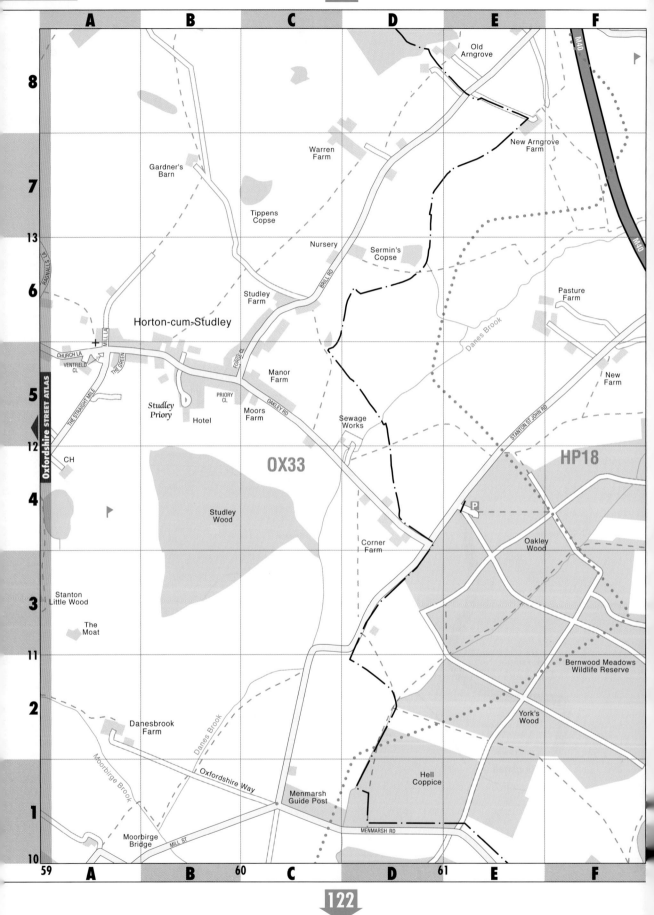

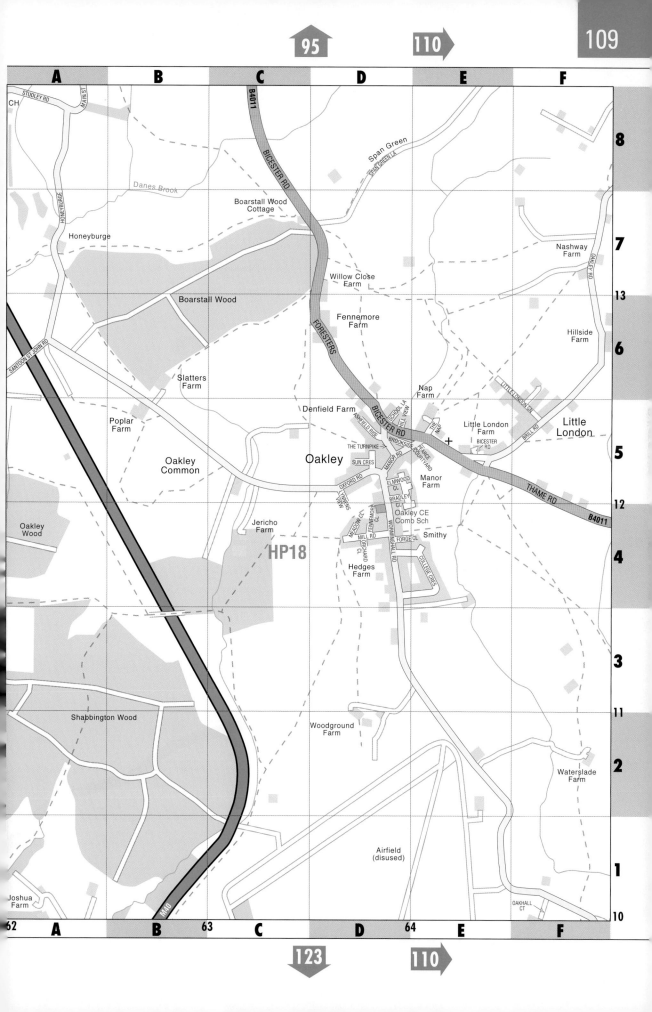

A B C D E F

8
7
13
6
5
12
4
3
11
2
1
10

STUDLEY RD
CH
MAIN ST
HONEYBURGE

Danes Brook

B4011
BICESTER RD

Span Green
Span Green La

Boarstall Wood
Cottage

Honeyburge

Nashway
Farm

OAKLEY RD

Boarstall Wood

Willow Close
Farm

13

Fennemore
Farm

Hillside
Farm

FORESTERS

6

SANTCOM ST JOHN RD

Slatters
Farm

Nap
Farm

LITTLE LONDON GDN

BRILL RD

Poplar
Farm

Denfield Farm

BICESTER RD
SCHOOL LA
HILL VIEW
THE NAP

Little London
Farm

Little
London

Oakley
Common

Oakley

ASHFIELD RISE
BROOKSIDE
THE TURNPIKE
SUN CRES
MANOR RD
PEARCE
COURTYARD

+

BICESTER
RD

5

OXFORD RD
MILL RD
ELMWOOD
CL
BRADLEY
CL

Manor
Farm

THAME RD

Oakley
Wood

Jericho
Farm

MEADOW CL
FENNEMORE
CL
WORMINGHALL RD

Oakley CE
Comb Sch

B4011

12

HP18

ORCHARD CL
MILL RD
FORGE CL
COLLEGE CRES

Smithy

4

Hedges
Farm

3

Shabbington Wood

Woodground
Farm

11

M40

Waterslade
Farm

2

Airfield
(disused)

1

Joshua
Farm

OAKHALL
CT

10

109
96

A **B** **C** **D** **E** **F**

COLLEY CL
SOUTH HILLS
BRAE HILL
PRIMROSE TERR
TEMPLE ST
Brill
HARRIS CL
MANOR HO
HIGH ST
THE SQUARE
OAKLEY RD
CLARKES FIELD
CHURCH ST
THE GREEN
SPA CL
THE FIRS
CHURCH ST

Manor Farm

Brill House

Spa Farm

Ashfold Sch
Dorton House

Dorton Park

Spa Wood

8

THAME RD

7

Parkpale Farm

Chiltonpark Farm

13

6

Ryman's Farm

Leap Hill

Chilton Grove

Leatherslade Farm

NEWTON'S LA

5

Buttermilk Hall

12

B4011

HP18

Grove Spinney

4

BRILL RD

Addingrove Farm

THAME RD

3

11

Meads Farm

Hornage Farm

2

BICESTER RD

Ixhill Farm

Hornage Copse

B4011

1

10

65 **A** **B** 66 **C** **D** 67 **E** **F**

109
124

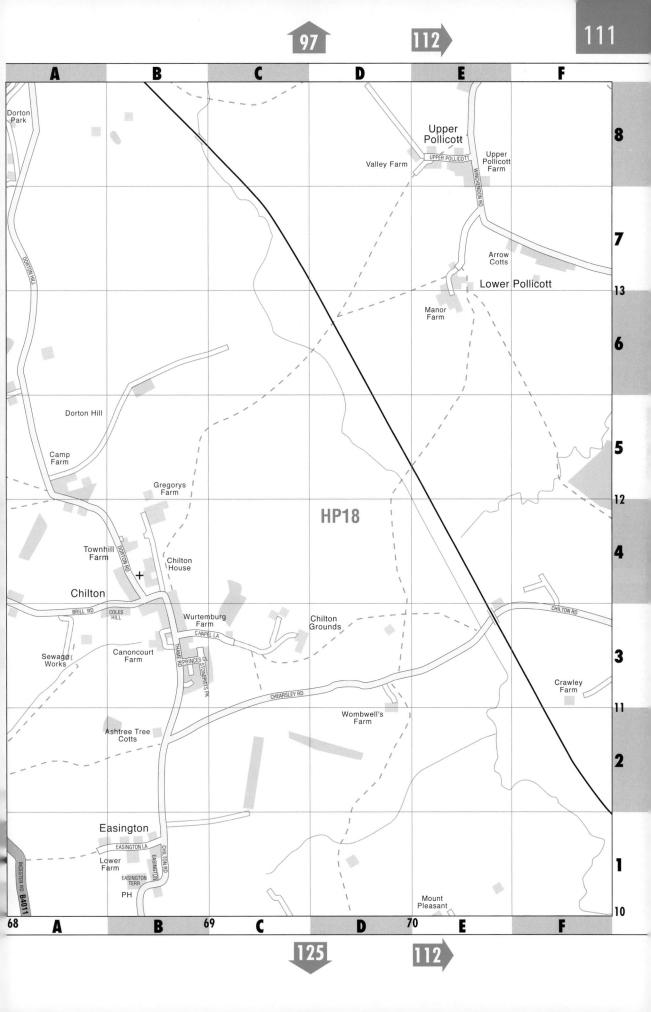

A B C D E F

8

7

13

6

5

12

4

11

3

2

1

10

Dorton
Park

DORTON HILL

Upper
Pollicott

Valley Farm

UPPER POLLICOTT

Upper
Pollicott
Farm

WINCHENDON RD

Arrow
Cotts

Lower Pollicott

Manor
Farm

Dorton Hill

Camp
Farm

Gregorys
Farm

HP18

Townhill
Farm

DORTON RD

Chilton
House

Chilton

BRILL RD

COLES
HILL

Wurtemburg
Farm

Chilton
Grounds

CHILTON RD

Crawley
Farm

Sewage
Works

Canoncourt
Farm

THAME RD

CHAPEL LA

PRINCES CL

ST AGNES PK

CHEARSLEY RD

Wombwell's
Farm

Ashtree Tree
Cotts

Easington

EASINGTON LA

CHILTON RD

EASINGTON

Lower
Farm

EASINGTON
TERR

PH

Mount
Pleasant

BICESTER RD

B4011

111
98

A **B** **C** **D** **E** **F**

8
7
13
6
12
5
4
3
11
2
1
10

71 · 72 · 73

WINCHENDON RD

Musk Hill Farm

Marsh Farm

WINCHENDON RIDGE RD

Cedarwood Bungalow

Obsy

Winchendon Hill Farm

BARRACK HILL

Hall

Nether Winchendon or Lower Winchendon

Brackwell Farm

WINCHENDON RD

CANNONS HILL

Manor Farm

The Old Mill

Chearsley Furze

HP18

Whaddonfield Farm

The Villas

NETHER WINCHENDON

Nether Winchendon House

Sewage Works

River Thame

Holyman's Farm

FROG LA

LOWER GN

SPICKETTS

ABBEY'S LA

LOWER CHURCH LA

GREAT STONE

SWAN ST

Cuddington Bridges

MILL LA

CUDDINGTON HILL

UPPER CHURCH LA

PO

SPURT ST

PH

Cuddington & Dinton CE Sch (Inf)

THE GREEN

AYLESBURY RD

SWAN CL

SWAN COTTS

BERNARD CL

DADBROOK

Cuddington Mill Farm

BRIDGEWAY

Welford Way

WELFORD WAY

HILLSIDE COTTS

CHILTON RD

1 COUSINS PIECE
2 EVANS CL

Furze Farm

WILLOW GATE

AYLESBURY RD

LAMMAS LA

LAMMAS PATH

DADBROOK CL 1
DADFIELD CL 2

Chearsley Hill House

STONEY FURLONG

WINCHENDON RD

OLD PLOUGH CL

SCHOOL LA

Bernwood Jubilee Way
Thame Valley Walk

Dadbrook House

Chearsley

PH

THE GREEN

TURNIP CL

DARK LA

LOWER GREEN LA

Lower Green Farm

WATTS GN

SHUPS LA

ELM BROOK CL

CHURCH LA

Manor Farm

CRENDON RD

BOTTOM ORCH

Dad Brook

HP17

Bettymoor Plantation

A418
AYLESBURY RD

Grove Farm

CHEARSLEY RD

Hawks Bridge

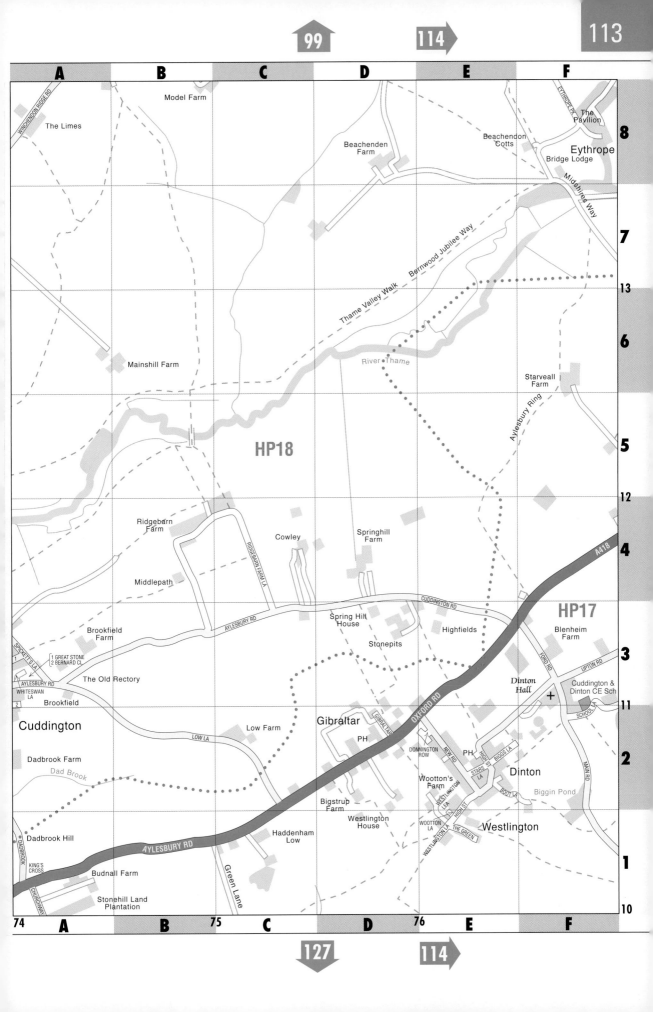

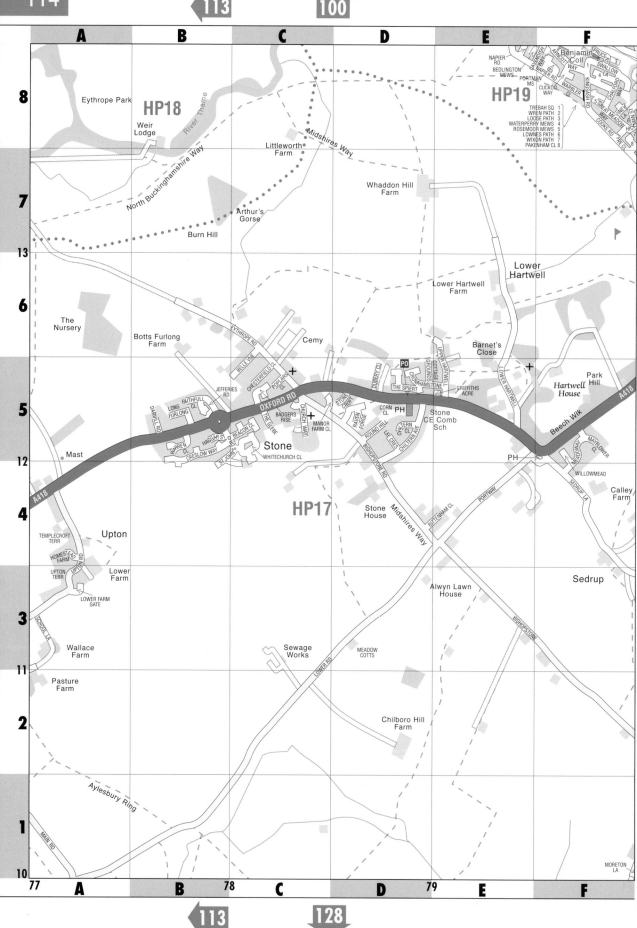

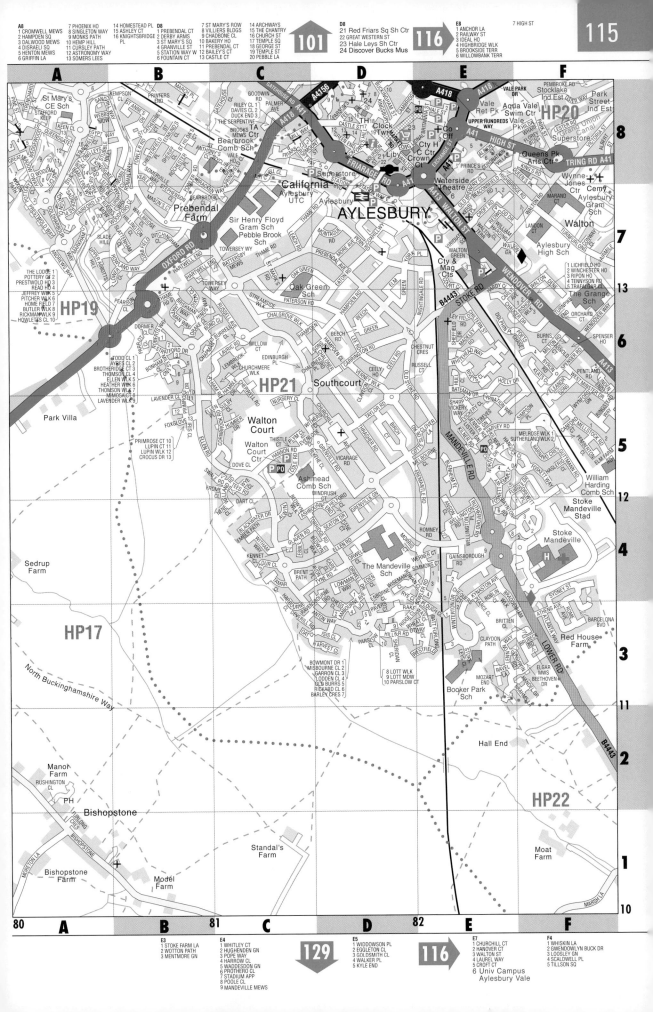

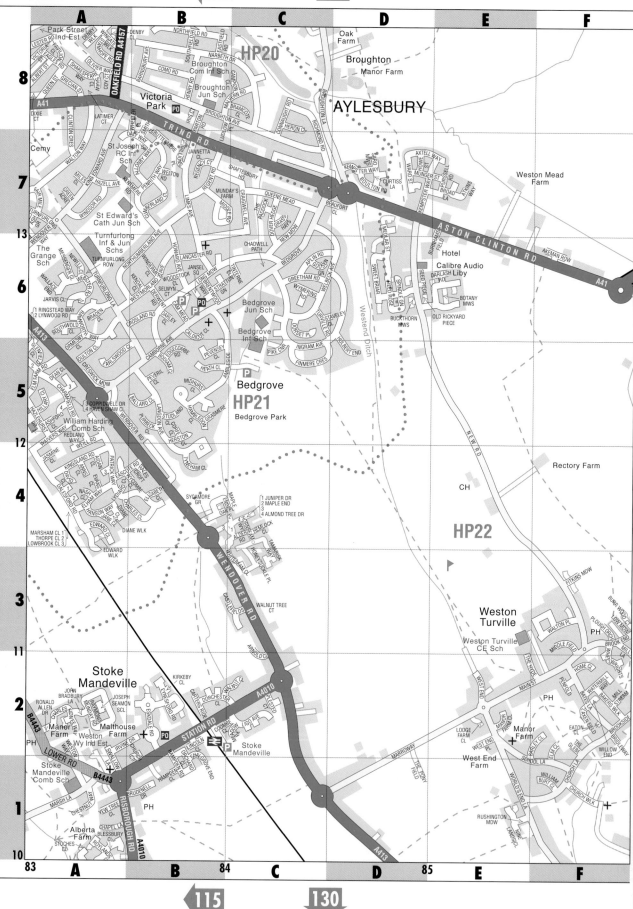

115
102

HP20

Oak Farm

Broughton Manor Farm

Victoria Park

AYLESBURY

Weston Mead Farm

ASTON CLINTON RD

Cemy

The Grange Sch

St Edward's Cath Jun Sch

Turnfurlong Inf & Jun Schs

Chadwell Path

Hotel

Calibre Audio Liby

BOTANY MWS

Old Rickyard Piece

Bedgrove Jun Sch

Bedgrove Inf Sch

Westend Ditch

Bedgrove

HP21

Bedgrove Park

William Harding Comb Sch

HP22

Rectory Farm

CH

Weston Turville

Weston Turville CE Sch

Stoke Mandeville

Kirkeby

Manor Farm

Malthouse Farm

Weston Wy Ind Est

LOWER RD

Stoke Mandeville Comb Sch

Stoke Mandeville

West End

Lodge Farm

Manor Farm

West End Farm

Alberta Farm

Rushington Mdw

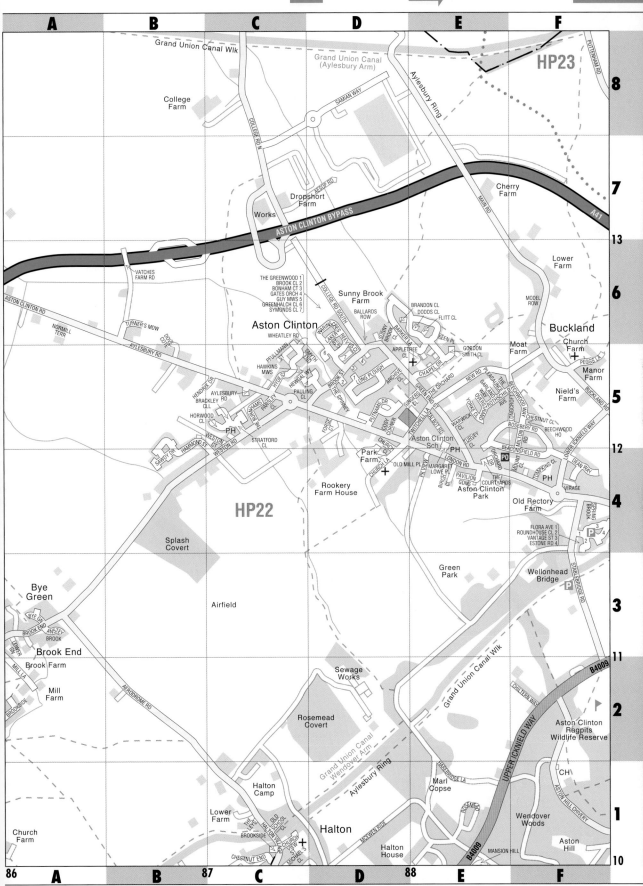

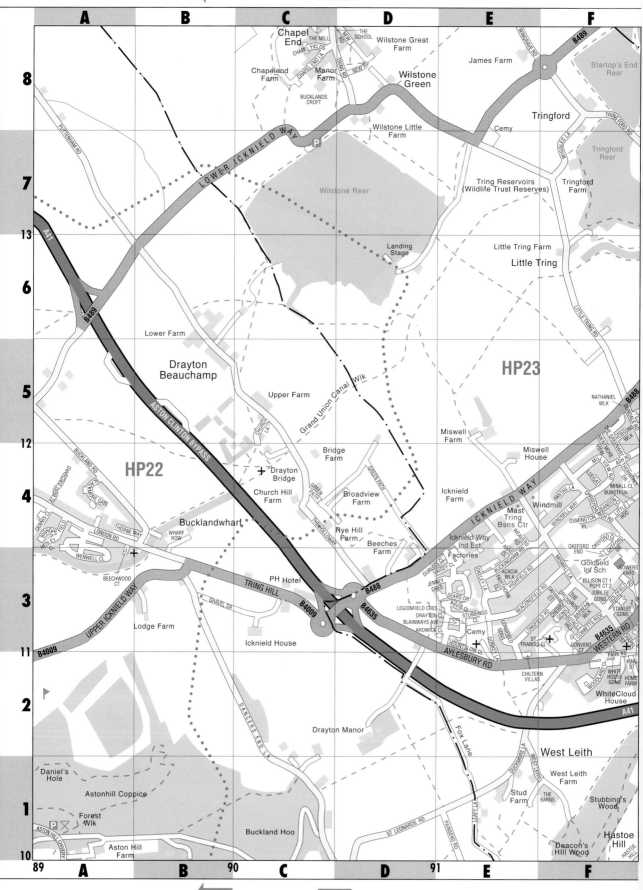

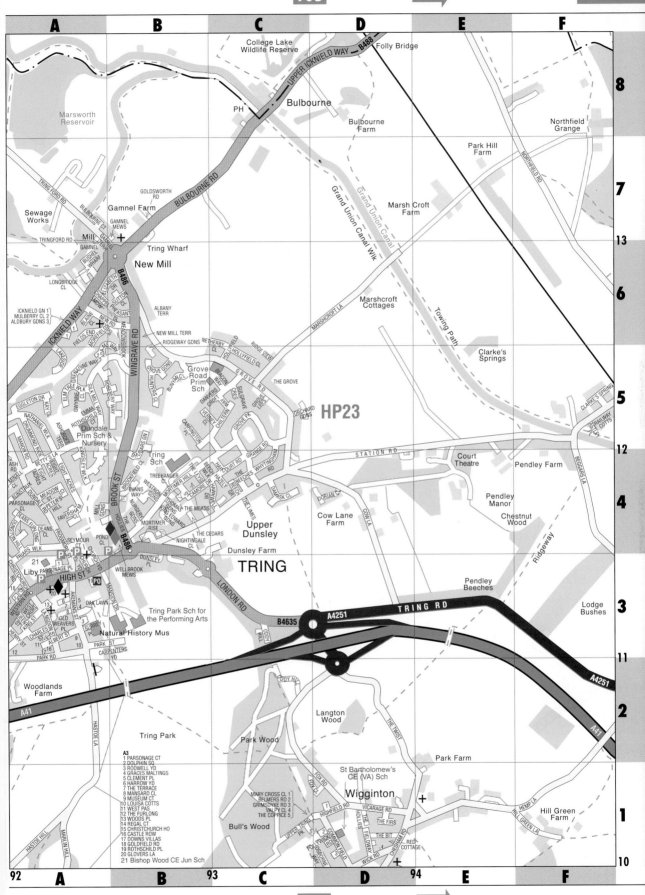

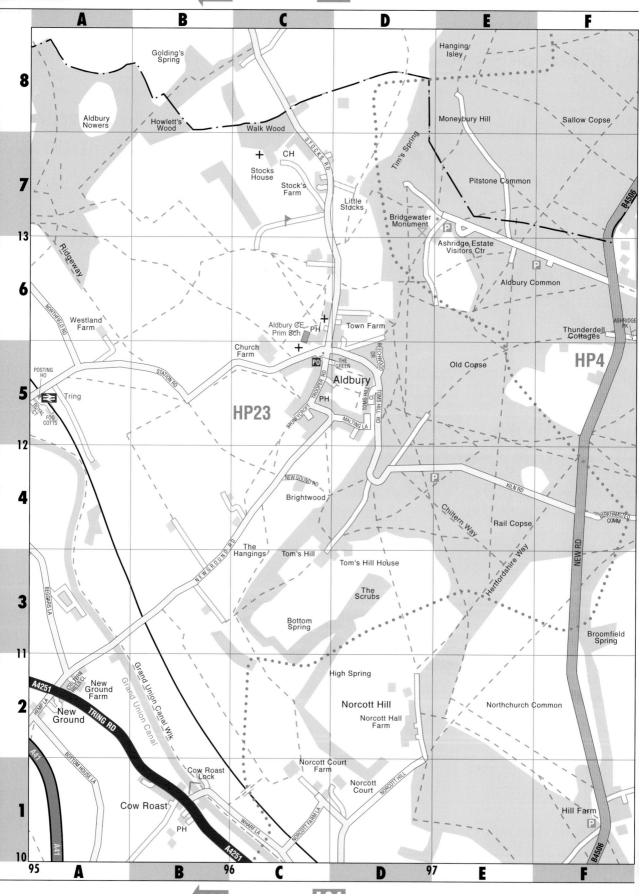

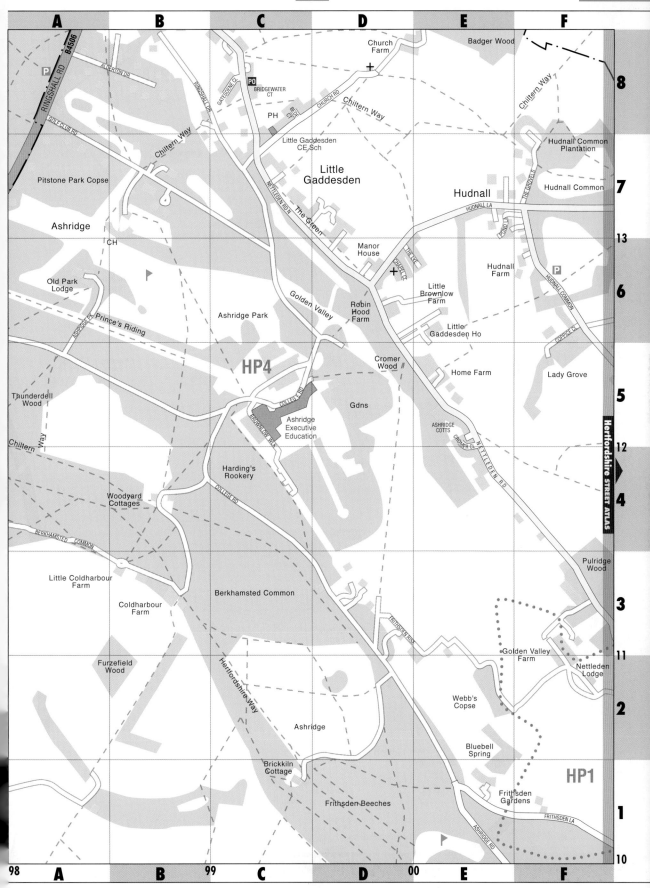

A B C D E F

8

7

09

6

5

08

4

3

07

2

1

06

Oxfordshire STREET ATLAS

Mill St

Moorbirge Brook

Clearsale

Hursthill

HP18

Wood Farm

MENMARSH RD

Waterperry Common

Bernwood Forest

Commonleys Farm

Waterperry Wood

Polecat End

Drunkard's Corner

Park Farm House

Park Farm

Oxfordshire Way

Polecat End Hollows

Marsh Copse

Parson's Farm

Ledall Cottage

POLECAT NOLA

Holton Wood

OX33

Buryhook Barn

Holton Brook

M40

B4027

Keeper's Cottage

Warren Farm

Pond Farm

Warren Wood

WHEATLEY RD

Lyehill Quarries (dis)

Old Park Farm

Cottage Copse

A40 Oxford

B4027

BURYHOOK CNR

Warwick Close Farm

Recn Gd

HOME CL

Wheatley Park Sch

John Watson Sch

BARNS CL

Holton

The Rectory

Holton Place

Liby

Park Sports Ctr

Wheatley

LONDON RD

PARK HILL

A40

Church Farm

Moat

Garden Copse

WESTFIELD RD

LONDON RD

WESTFIELD RD

Oxford Brookes Univ (Wheatley Campus)

COLLEGE CL

Waterperry Rd

M40

A B C D E F

8

7

09

6

HP18

Worminghall

5

08

4

3

07

2

1

06

Hill Coppice

MENMARSH RD

Long Spinney

Field Farm

Airfield (disused)

WORNAL PK

Wornal Park

Works

Catsbrain Farm

Sewage Works

Brownacre

Field Barn

Thomley Hall Farm

Town Farm

OLD FARM CL

KINGS CL

SILVER MEAD

BISHOPS WAY

CLIFTON RD

WATERPERRY RD

MENMARSH RD

OAKLEY RD

ICKFORD RD

ALMSHOUSES

THE AVENUE

Brissenden Farm

Lappingford Bridge

SHABBINGTON RD

PH

Sewage Works

Court Farm

Lower Brook Farm

Baker's Spinney

Baker's Farm

POPLAR WY

Manor Farm

PH

OLD THORNBURY RD

GOLDER'S CL

FARM CL

CHURCH RD

SHELDON RD

Ickford Sch

Church Farm

Ickford

Townsend Farm

Townsend

OX33

WATERPERRY COMMON

Oxfordshire Way

WORMINGHALL RD

GREEN GROUND

River Thame

BRIDGE RD

Manor Farm

MANOR COURT YD

Rectory Farm

WATERPERRY

SPINNEY COTTS

Boathouse Spinney

Ickford Bridge

Waterperry

Waterperry Gardens

STOCKWELL LA

Jubilee Covert

ICKFORD RD

ORLYCOTT

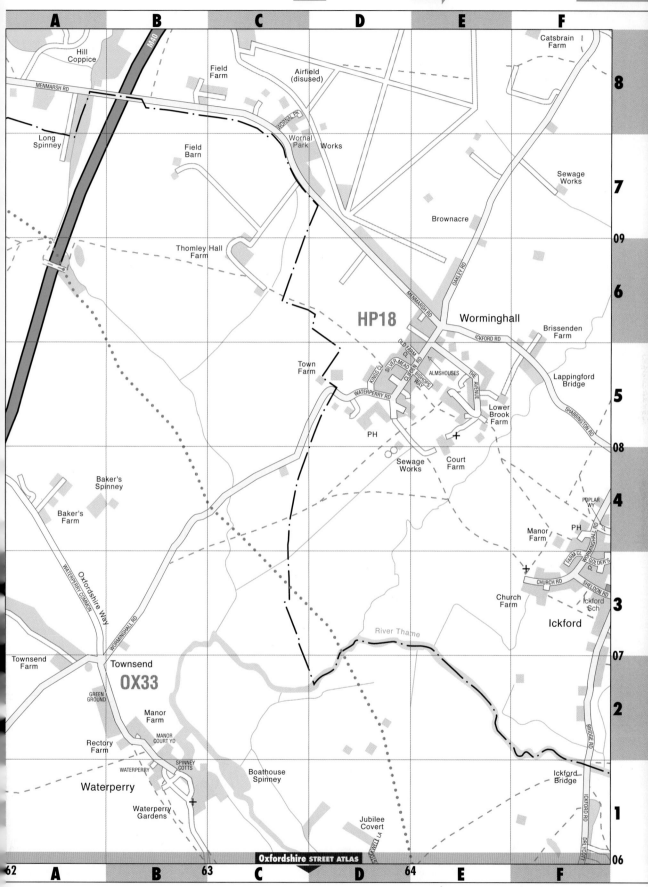

123
110

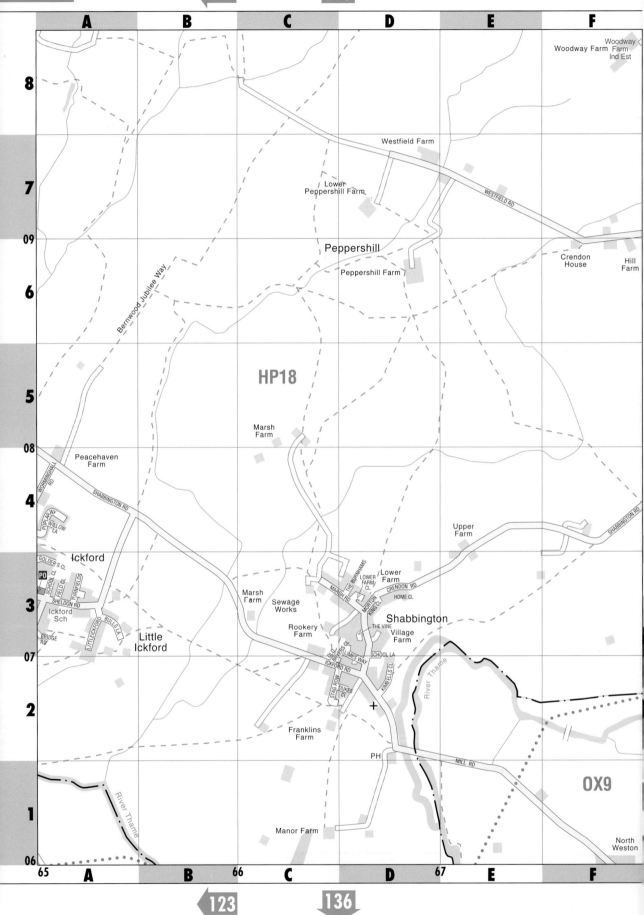

123
136

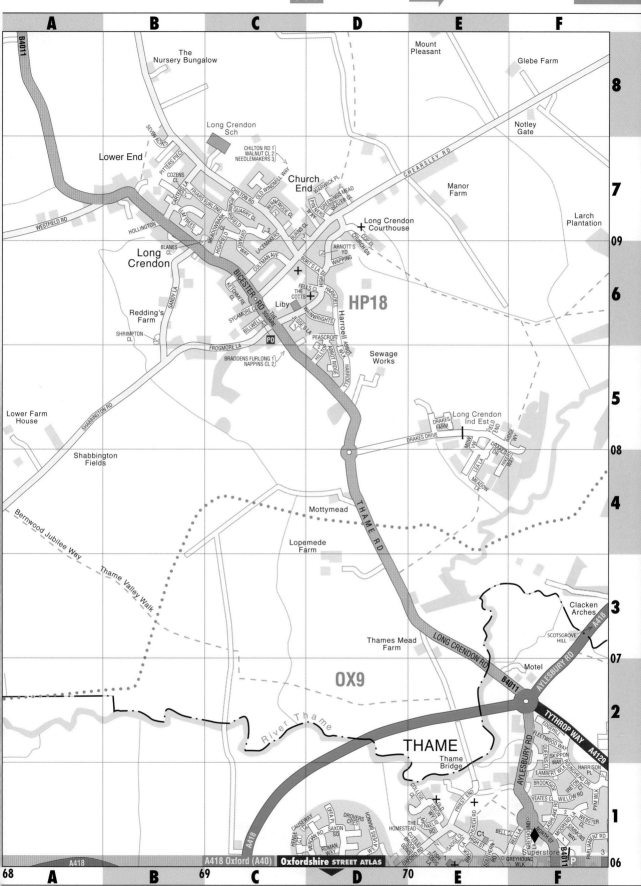

A · B · C · D · E · F

8
7
09
6
5
08
4
3
07
2
1
06

The Nursery Bungalow

Mount Pleasant

Glebe Farm

Lower End

Long Crendon Sch

CHILTON RD 1
WALNUT CL 2
NEEDLEMAKERS 3

Church End

CHEARSLEY RD

Notley Gate

Manor Farm

Larch Plantation

WESTFIELD RD

HOLLINGTON

BLANES CL

Long Crendon

WARWICK PL

Long Crendon Courthouse

Arnott's Yd

WAPPING

HP18

Redding's Farm

SHRIMPTON CL

FROGMORE LA

Liby

THE COTTS

PO

BRADDENS FURLONG 1
NAPPINS CL 2

PEASCROFT

Harroell

Sewage Works

Lower Farm House

SHABBINGTON RD

Shabbington Fields

Long Crendon Ind Est

DRAKES FARM

FIELD END

DRAKES DRIVE

DRAKES DRAGONS RIDGE WY

MEADOW LK

Bernwood Jubilee Way

Mottymead

THAME RD

Thame Valley Walk

Lopemede Farm

Clacken Arches

SCOTSGROVE HILL

A418

Thames Mead Farm

LONG CRENDON RD

Motel

AYLESBURY RD

B4011

OX9

River Thame

THAME

TYTHROP WAY

A4129

Thame Bridge

AYLESBURY RD

FLEETWOOD WAY

SKIPPON WAY

HARRISON PL

LAMBERT WLK

BROOKSIDE

IRETON CT

WILLOW RD

YEATES CL

PYM WLK

WEBSTER CL

MOORES

SIMMONS CL

PARLIAMENT RD

Superstore

The Homestead

PRIEST END

CHURCH RD

HIGH ST

Ct

BELL CT

BELL LA

NORTH ST

GREYHOUND WLK

P

B4011

E1
1 St Joseph's Cath Prim Sch

F1
1 ABINGDON CL
2 GREENWAY
3 Barley Hill Prim Sch

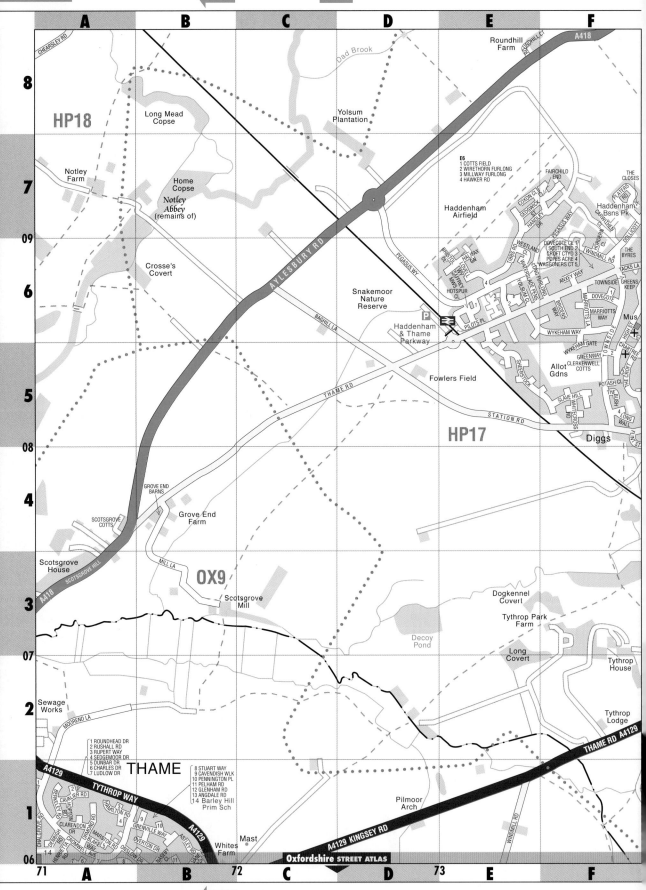

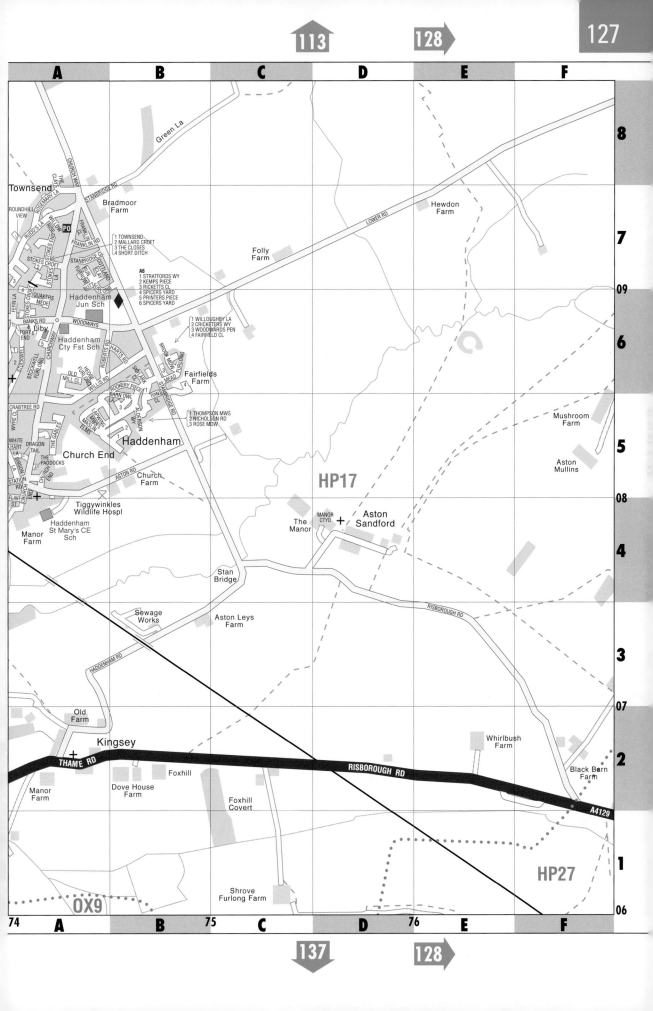

127
114

A B C D E F

8

LOWER RD

BRIDGE FARM BLDGS

Moat Farm

Moreton Village

PH

WATER LA

Ford

Moreton Farm

MAIN RD

Manor Farm

7

FRAUCUP CL

BURGESS LA

LINDEN WAY

Ford Farm

CHAPEL RD

09

North Buckinghamshire Way

Midshires Way

6

Aylesbury Ring

HP17

MORETON RD

5

Lower Waldridge Farm

Fox Covert

08

Pollard Farm

Poplar Farm

4

OWLSWICK RD

Waldridge Manor

3

Waldridge Village

Black Barn

07

Swan's Way

KIMBLEWICK RD

Midshires Way

Pasture Farm

2

Stockwell Lane Farm

Hill Ground Farm

HP27

A4129

RISBOROUGH RD

Midshires Way

OWLSWICK

Owlswick Farm

STOCKWELL LA

Green Lane Farm

GREEN LA

Owlswick

1

THAME RD

Little Acre Farm

Manor Farm

A4129

ILMER LA

Ray Farm

06

77 A B 78 C D 79 E F

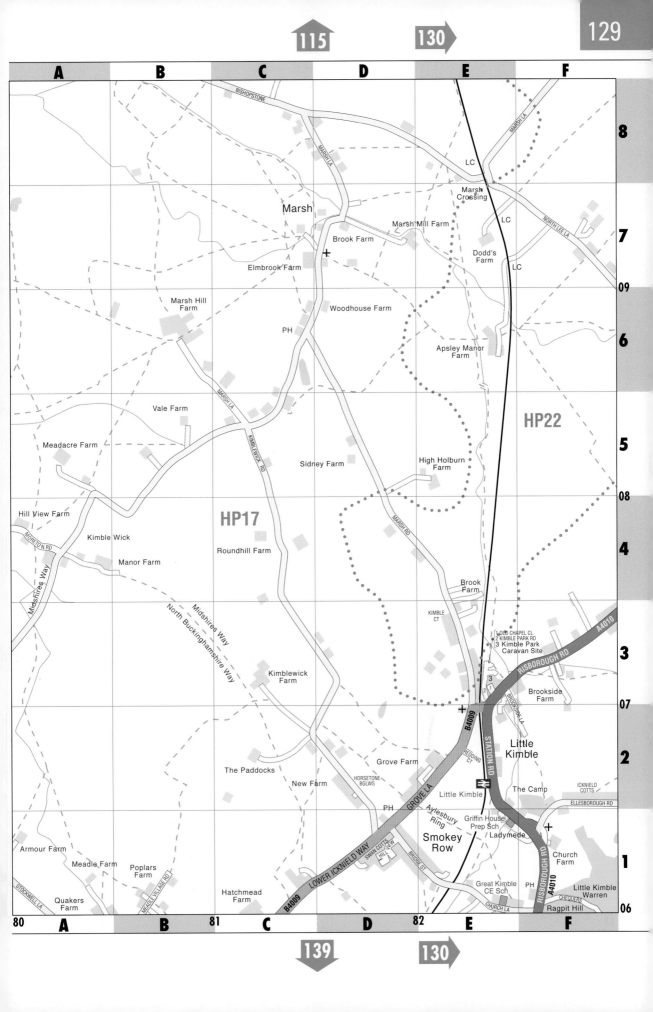

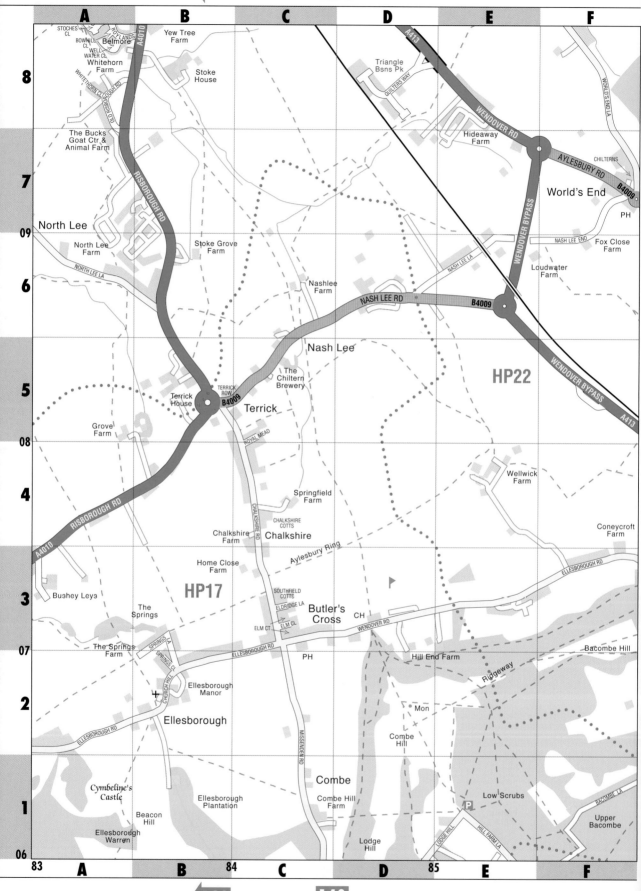

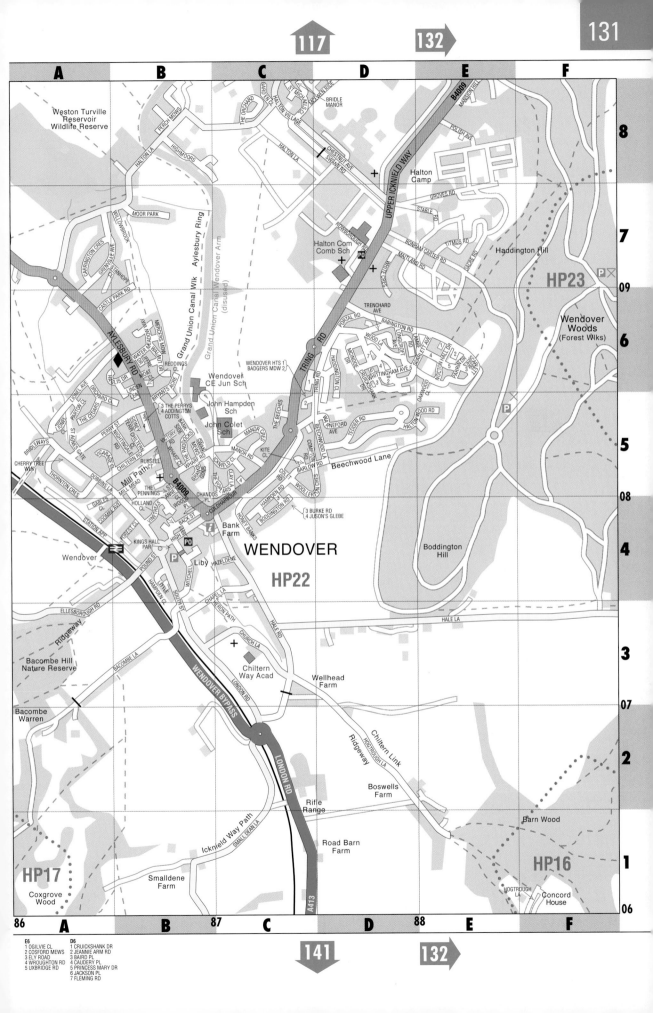

A B C D E F

8 7 09 6 5 08 4 3 07 2 1 06

Weston Turville
Reservoir
Wildlife Reserve

Moor Park

CARRINGTON CRES
WILLOWBROOK
GREVILLE AVE
STANHOPE
CASTLE PARK RD
AYLESBURY RD

Grand Union Canal Wlk
Aylesbury Ring
Grand Union Canal Wendover Arm
(disused)

HALTON LA
HIGHMOORS
PERCH MDWS
THE ORCHARD
GARD EN CL
HALTON VILLAGE
ST. MICHAEL'S CL
HALTON LA
CHESTNUT AVE
SWANN RD
McEWEN RISE
BRIDLE
MANOR

UPPER ICKNIELD WAY
B4009
MANSION HILL
POLISH AVE
Halton Camp
Halton Com
Comb Sch
GROVES RD
STABLE RD
ROWBOROUGH RD
BONHAM CARTER RD
WHITE CRES
MAITLAND RD
TITMUS RD
DEGRE RD

Haddington Hill

HP23
P
Wendover
Woods
(Forest Wlks)

TRING RD
TRENCHARD AVE
PORTAL RD
BABINGTON RD
WOOD LA
McINDOE DR
HADDINGTON DR
LONGCROFT AVE
LAMB CRES
SCARLETT AVE
DANWOOD RD
TARRINGTON
PARTRIDGE
MUGSTON HALTON
HALTON WOOD RD

WENDOVER HTS 1
BADGERS MDW 2
Wendover
CE Jun Sch
3 THE PERRYS
4 ADDINGTON COTTS
John Hampden Sch
John Colet Sch
THE BEECHES
WHITTINGHAM AVE 5
ONEFORD AVE
FEEDER RD
BEECHWOOD LA
Beechwood Lane
HALTON WOOD RD

REDDINGS CL
BRYANTS ACRE
LINDEN
LEA
MERCERS MDW
WATER SIDE
NIGHT IN GALE RD
MOAT
HALLS DR
LIONEL AVE
ORCHARD CL
PASTURE CL
LIONEL AVE
THE CEDARS
ST AGNES GATE
VICARAGE RD
PERRY ST
NIGHTINGALE RD
CHILTERN RD
RUSSELL
DOBBINS LA

MANOR CL
MANOR RD
KITE CL
CLAY LA
HAMPDEN RD
BODDINGTON RD
COLET
WOOLLERTON
COMPTON
BARLOW RD
3 BURKE RD
4 JUSON'S GLEBE

Mill Path
BRIDLEWAYS
CHERRY TREE
WLK
THORNTON CRES
GABLES CL
COMBE AVE
STATION APP
FOREST CL
HOLLAND CL
VINE TREES
THE PENNINGS
Mill Mead
B4009
CHANDOS
PL
COLDHARBOUR
VICTORY
BANK
WHARF
SWAN
GRANGE
ICKNIELD CL
HONEY BANKS
BACK ST
HIGH ST
Bank
Farm
Liby
HAZELDENE
SOUTH ST
WITCHEL
HAMPDEN CL
LITTLE
POUND ST
KINGS HALL
PAR
CHAPEL LA
CAMERON PATH
HALE RD
LONDON RD
CHURCH LA

Wendover
WENDOVER
HP22

Bacombe Hill
Nature Reserve
Ridgeway
Bacombe
Warren
BACOMBE LA

ELLESBOROUGH RD

WENDOVER BYPASS
LONDON RD
A413

Chiltern Way Acad
Wellhead
Farm
HALE LA

Boddington
Hill

Chiltern Link
Ridgeway
HOGTROUGH LA
Boswells
Farm
Rifle
Range
Road Barn
Farm
Barn Wood
HP16
HOGTROUGH LA
Concord
House

HP17
Coxgrove
Wood
Icknield Way Path
SMALL DEAN LA
Smalldene
Farm

E6
1 OGILVIE CL
2 COSFORD MEWS
3 ELY ROAD
4 WROUGHTON RD
5 UXBRIDGE RD

D6
1 CRUICKSHANK DR
2 JEANNIE ARM RD
3 BAIRD PL
4 CAUDERY PL
5 PRINCESS MARY DR
6 JACKSON PL
7 FLEMING RD

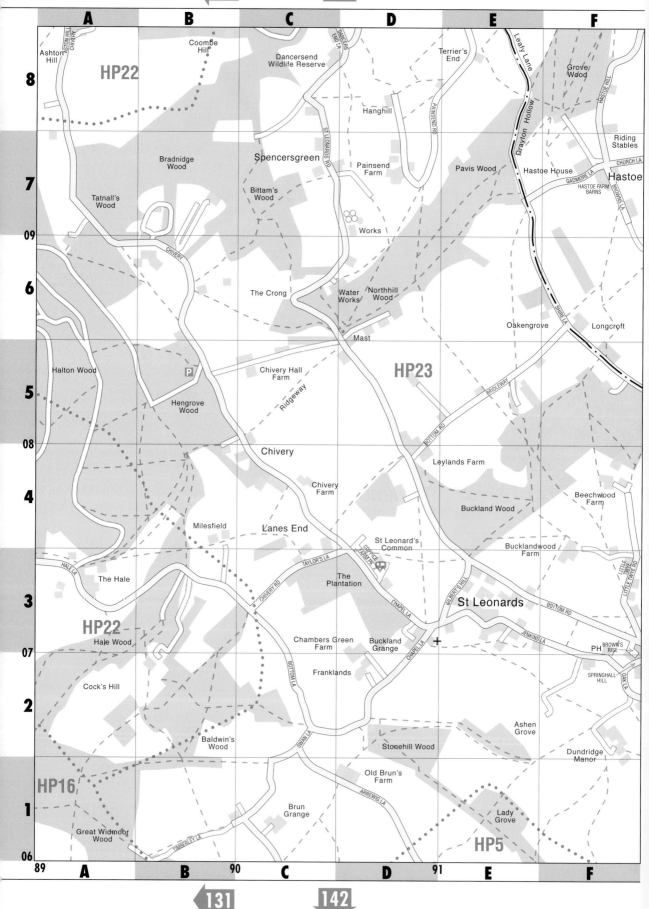

A **B** **C** **D** **E** **F**

Ashton Hill

HP22

Coombe Hill

Dancersend Wildlife Reserve

Terrier's End

Grove Wood

8

Hanghill

Riding Stables

Bradnidge Wood

Spencersgreen

Painsend Farm

Pavis Wood

Hastoe House

Hastoe

Tatnall's Wood

Bittam's Wood

7

Hastoe Farm Barns

Works

09

CHIVERY

The Crong

Water Works

Northhill Wood

6

Halton Wood

Mast

Oakengrove

Longcroft

Chivery Hall Farm

HP23

5

Hengrove Wood

Ridgeway

BRIDLEWAY

08

Chivery

Leylands Farm

Beechwood Farm

4

Chivery Farm

Buckland Wood

Milesfield

Lanes End

St Leonard's Common

Bucklandwood Farm

The Hale

The Plantation

St Leonards

3

HP22

Hale Wood

Chambers Green Farm

Buckland Grange

PH

Brown's Rise

Franklands

Springhall Hill

Cock's Hill

2

Ashen Grove

Dundridge Manor

Baldwin's Wood

Stonehill Wood

07

HP16

Old Brun's Farm

Lady Grove

1

Great Widmoor Wood

Brun Grange

HP5

06

89 **A** **B** **90** **C** **D** **91** **E** **F**

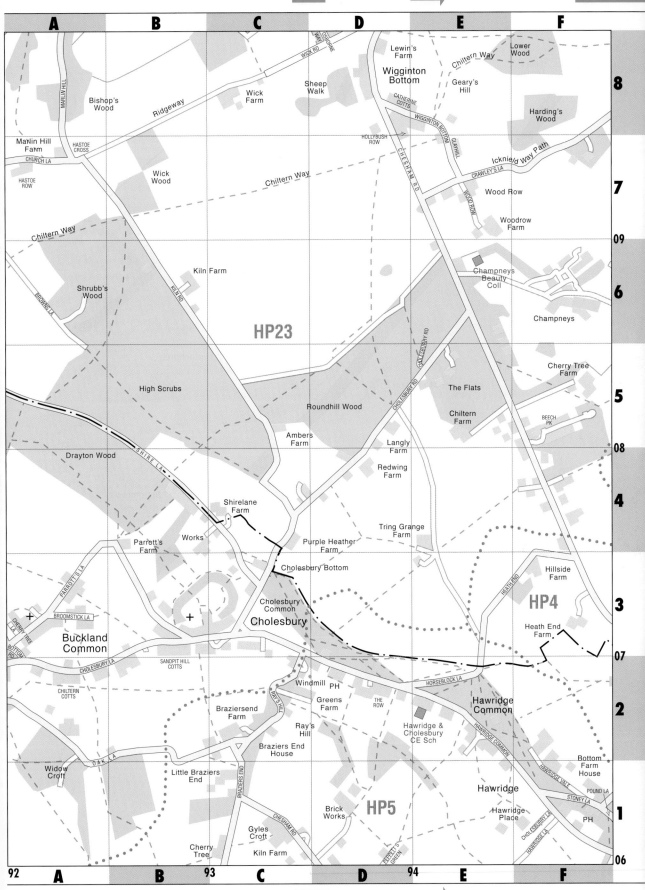

A B C D E F

8 7 6 5 4 3 2 1

09 08 07 06

Marlin Hill

Bishop's
Wood

Ridgeway

Wick Farm

Sheep
Walk

Lewin's
Farm

Wigginton
Bottom

Chiltern Way

Lower
Wood

Geary's
Hill

Harding's
Wood

Marlin Hill
Farm

HASTOE
CROSS

CHURCH LA

HASTOE
ROW

Wick
Wood

Chiltern Way

HOLLYBUSH
ROW

CATHERINE
COTTS

WIGGINTON BOTTOM

CLAYHILL

CRAWLEY'S LA

CHESHAM RD

Icknield Way Path

Wood Row

WOOD ROW

Woodrow
Farm

Chiltern Way

Kiln Farm

KILN RD

BROWNS LA

Shrubb's
Wood

Champneys
Beauty
Coll

Champneys

HP23

High Scrubs

Roundhill Wood

Ambers
Farm

CHOLESBURY RD

CHOLESBURY RD

The Flats

Chiltern
Farm

Cherry Tree
Farm

BEECH
PK

Langly
Farm

Redwing
Farm

Drayton Wood

SHIRE LA

Shirelane
Farm

Works

Tring Grange
Farm

Purple Heather
Farm

Parrott's
Farm

PARROTT'S LA

Cholesbury Bottom

Hillside
Farm

HEATH END

HP4

Heath End
Farm

CHERRY TREE BOTTOM RD

+

BROOMSTICK LA

+

Buckland
Common

CHOLESBURY LA

SANDPIT HILL
COTTS

Cholesbury
Common
Cholesbury

HORSEBLOCK LA

Hawridge
Common

CHILTERN
COTTS

OAK LA

Braziersend
Farm

RAY'S HILL

Windmill PH

Greens
Farm

THE
ROW

Hawridge
& Cholesbury
CE Sch

HAWRIDGE COMMON

Ray's
Hill

Braziers End
House

Widow
Croft

BRAZIERS END

Little Braziers
End

CHESHAM RD

Gyles
Croft

Brick
Works

HP5

PEPPETT'S
GREEN

Bottom
Farm
House

POUND LA

STONEY LA

Hawridge

Hawridge
Place

PH

HAWRIDGE LA

CHOLESBURY LA

HAWRIDGE VALE

Cherry
Tree

Kiln Farm

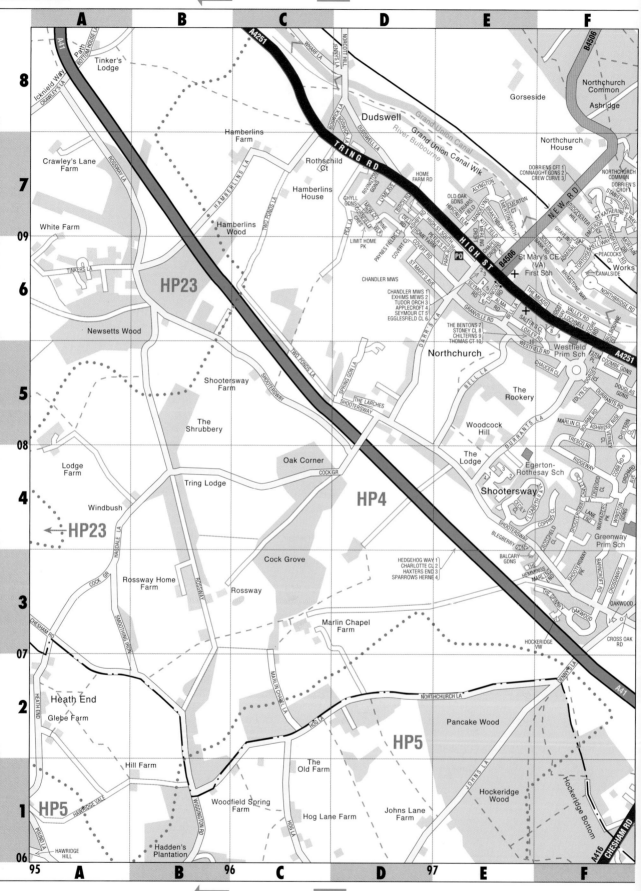

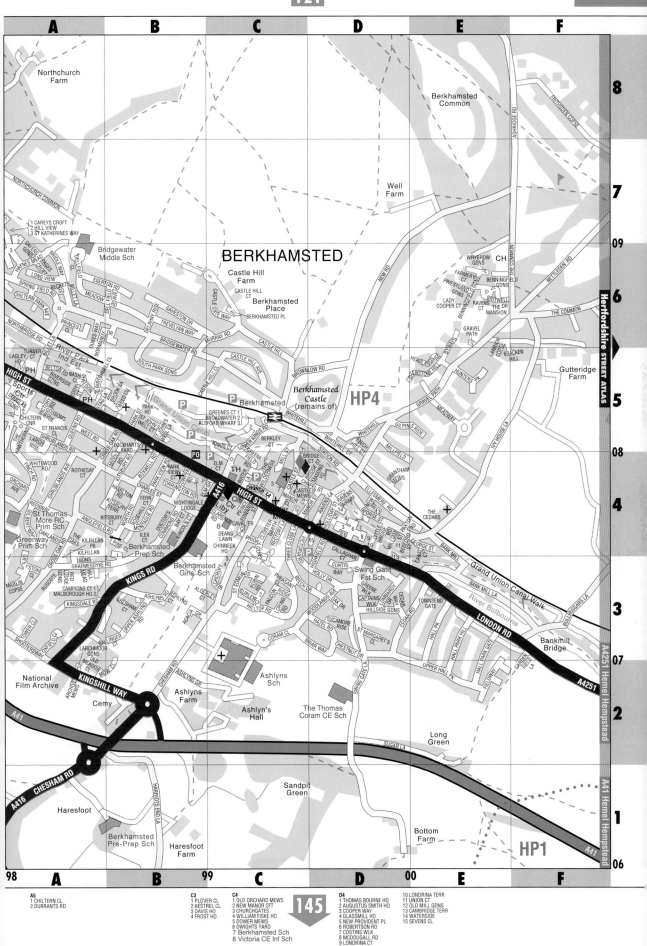

BERKHAMSTED

HP4

HP1

A5
1 CHILTERN CL
2 DURRANTS RD

C3
1 PLOVER CL
2 KESTREL CL
3 DAVIS HO
4 FROST HO

C4
1 OLD ORCHARD MEWS
2 NEW MANOR CFT
3 CHURCHGATES
4 WILLIAM FISKE HO
5 DOWER MEWS
6 DWIGHTS YARD
7 Berkhamsted Sch
8 Victoria CE Inf Sch

D4
1 THOMAS BOURNE HO
2 AUGUSTUS SMITH HO
3 COOPER WAY
4 GLASSMILL HO
5 NEW PROVIDENT PL
6 ROBERTSON RD
7 COSTINS WLK
8 MCDOUGALL RD
9 LONDRINA CT

10 LONDRINA TERR
11 UNION CT
12 OLD MILL GDNS
13 CAMBRIDGE TERR
14 WATERSIDE
15 SEVENS CL

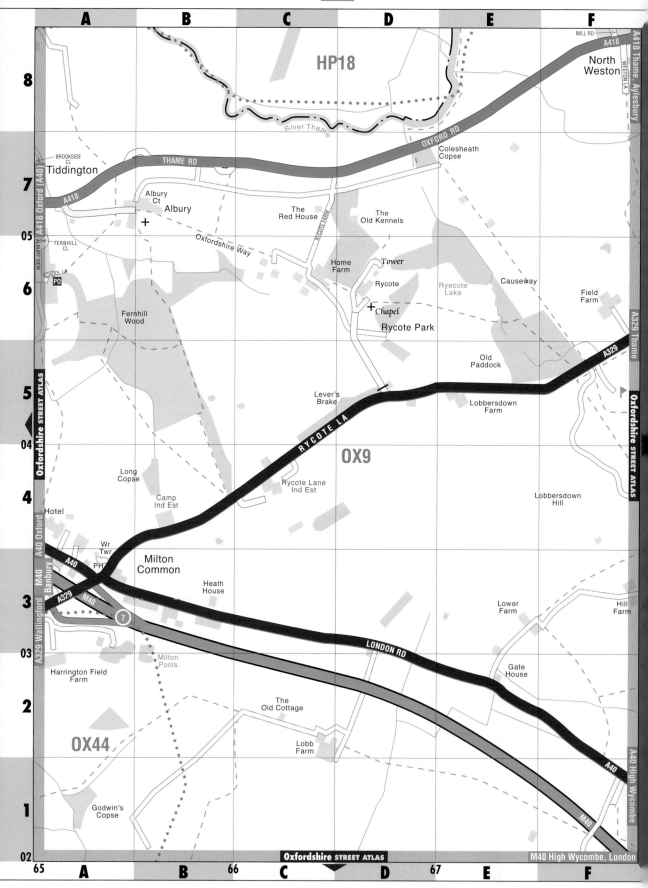

A   B   C   D   E   F

HP18

North Weston

Coleesheath Copse

THAME RD

Tiddington

Albury Ct
Albury

The Red House

The Old Kennels

Oxfordshire Way

Home Farm

Tower

Rycote

Ryecote Lake

Causeway

Field Farm

Fernhill Wood

Chapel

Rycote Park

Old Paddock

Lever's Brake

Lobbersdown Farm

OX9

RYCOTE LA

Long Copse

Rycote Lane Ind Est

Lobbersdown Hill

Camp Ind Est

Hotel

Milton Common

Heath House

Lower Farm

Hill Farm

LONDON RD

Harrington Field Farm

Milton Pools

Gate House

OX44

The Old Cottage

Lobb Farm

Godwin's Copse

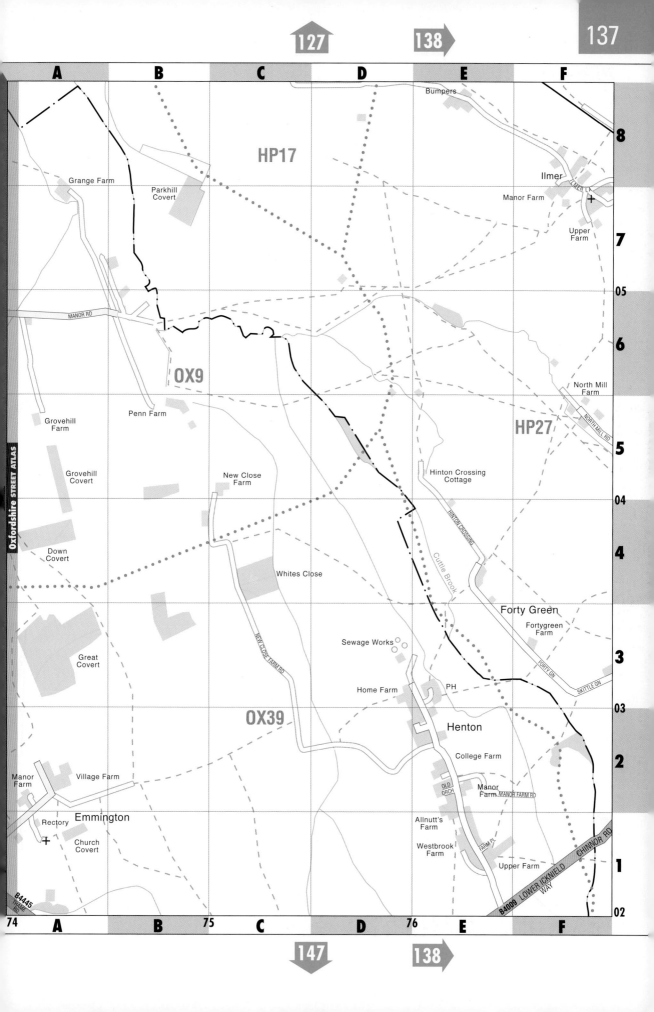

A   B   C   D   E   F

8
7
05
6
5
04
4
3
03
2
1
02

Oxfordshire STREET ATLAS

HP17

Grange Farm

Parkhill Covert

Bumpers

Ilmer

ILMER LA

Manor Farm

Upper Farm

MANOR RD

OX9

Penn Farm

North Mill Farm

NORTH MILL RD

HP27

Grovehill Farm

Grovehill Covert

New Close Farm

Hinton Crossing Cottage

HINTON CROSSING

Down Covert

Cuttle Brook

Whites Close

Forty Green

Fortygreen Farm

FORTY GN

SKITTLE GN

Great Covert

NEW CLOSE FARM RD

Sewage Works

OX39

Home Farm

PH

03

Henton

College Farm

Manor Farm

Village Farm

OLD ORCH

Manor Farm

MANOR FARM RD

Emmington

Rectory

Church Covert

Allnutt's Farm

Westbrook Farm

FARM PL

Upper Farm

CHINNOR RD

LOWER ICKNIELD WAY

B4009

B4445 THAME RD

137
128

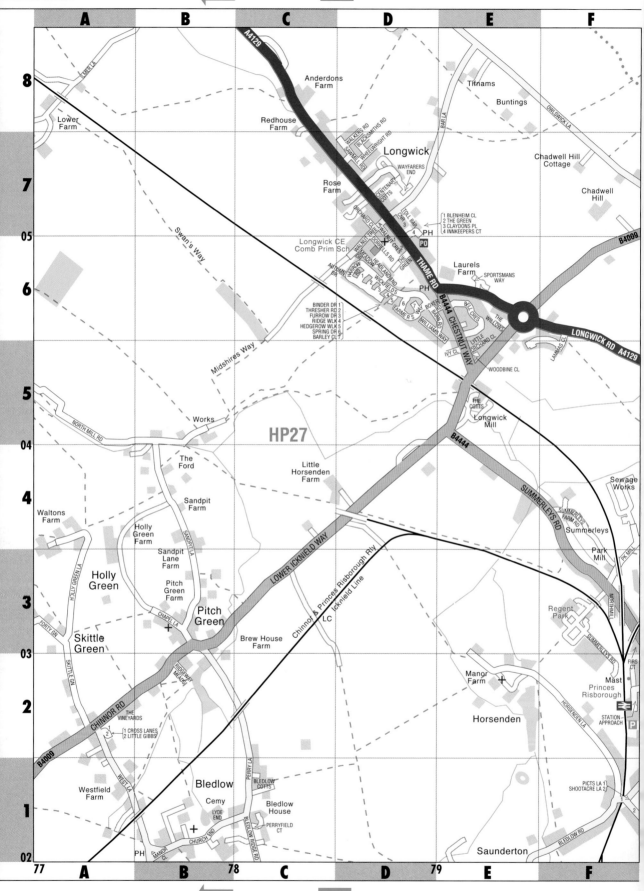

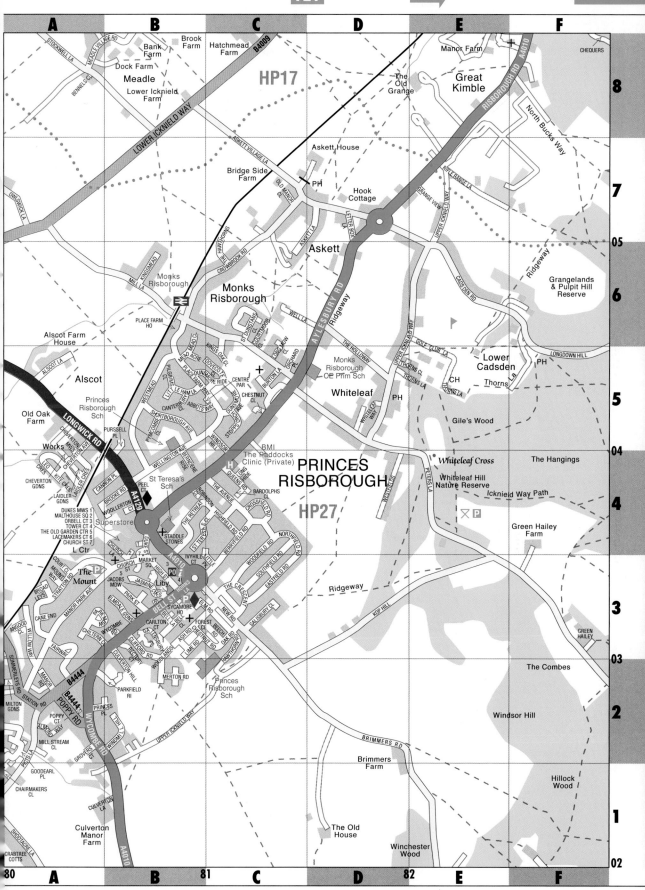

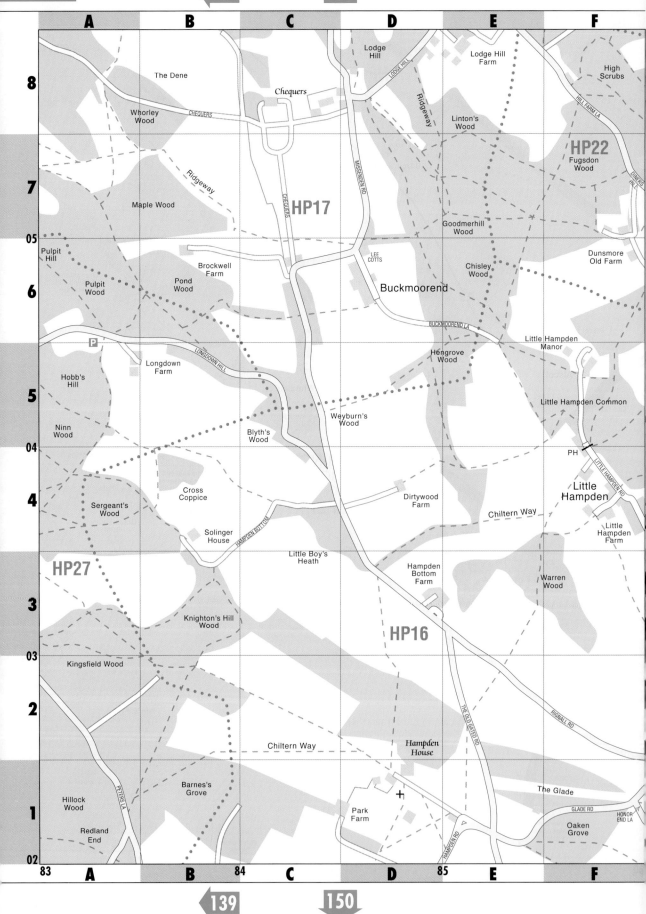

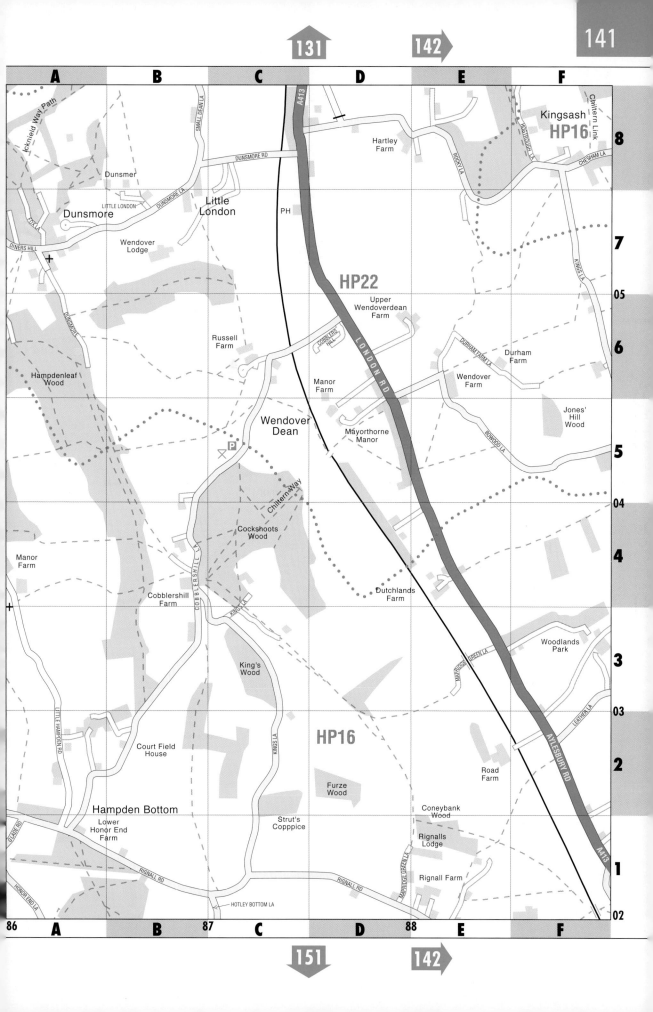

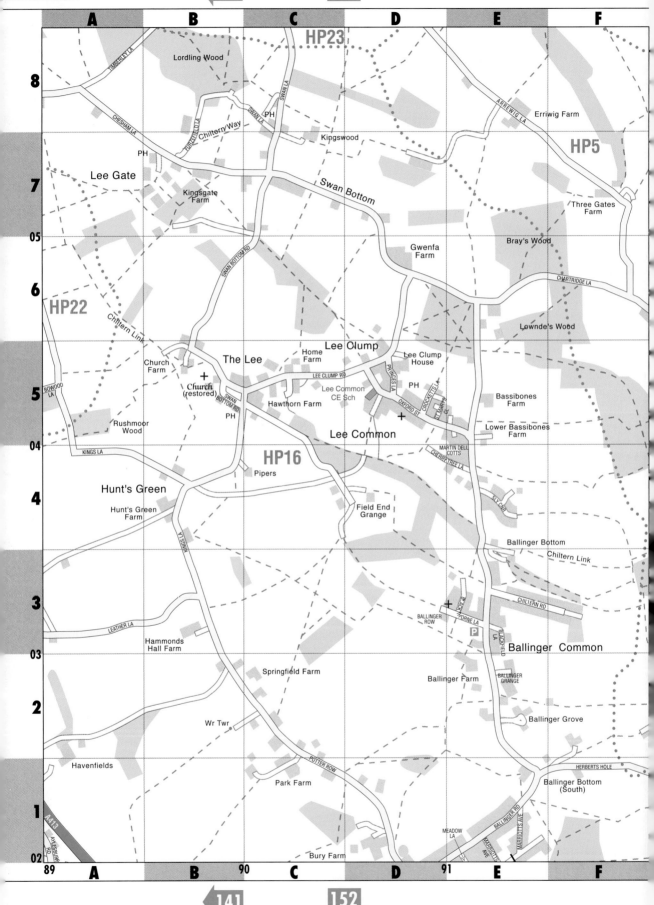

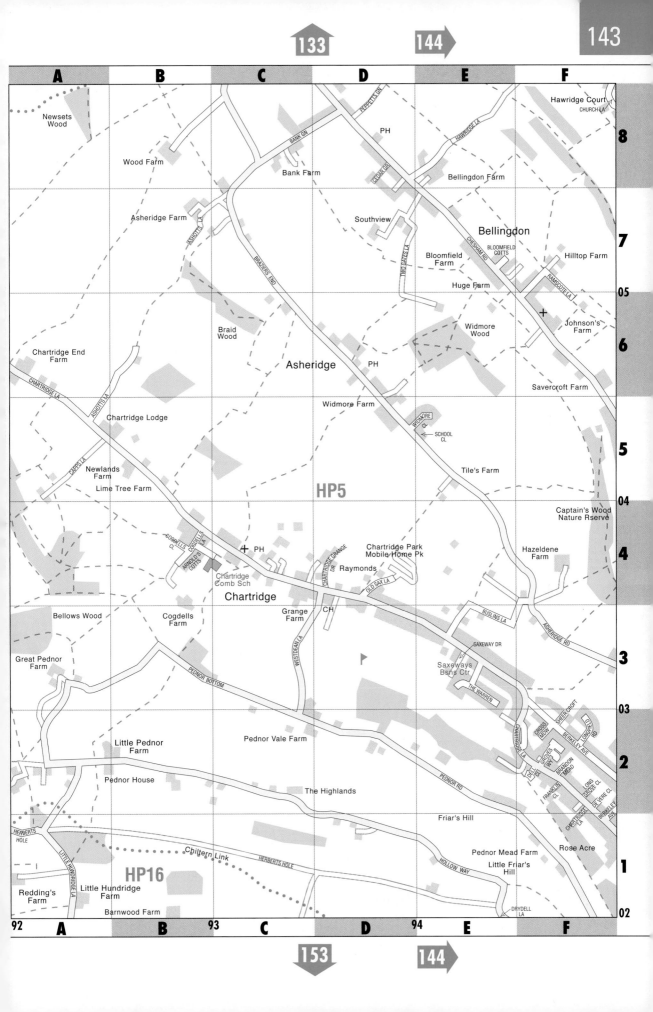

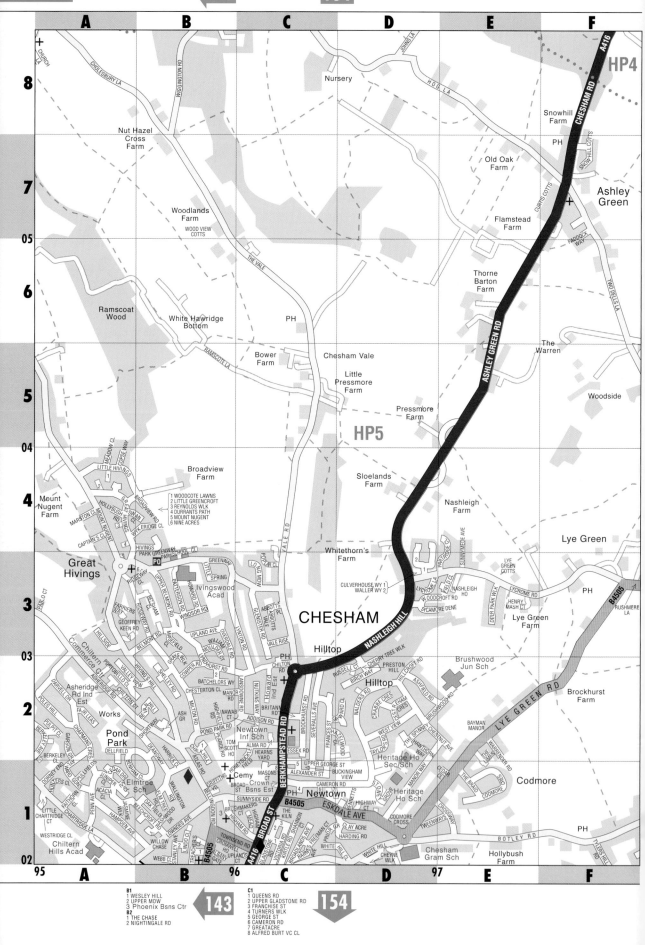

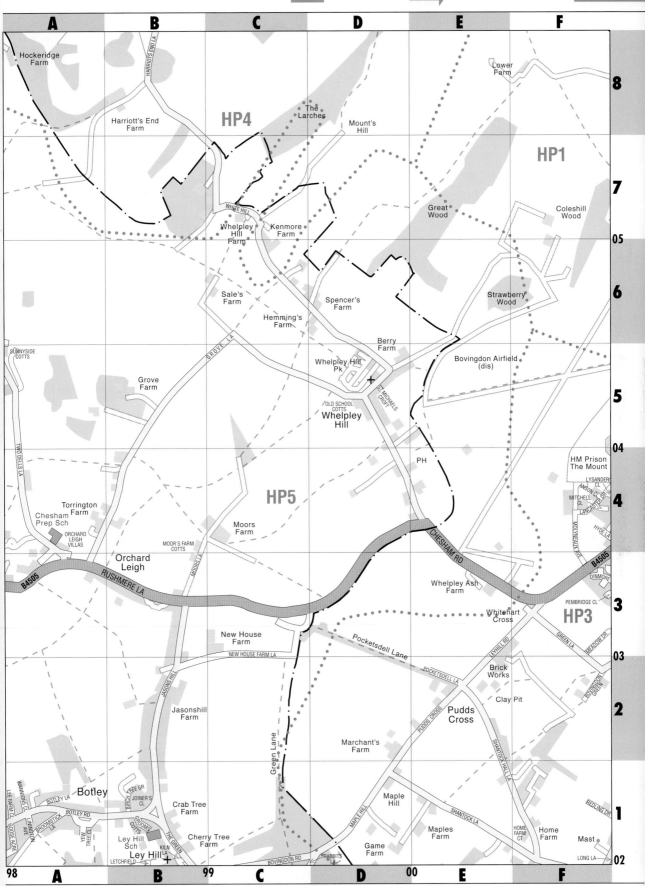

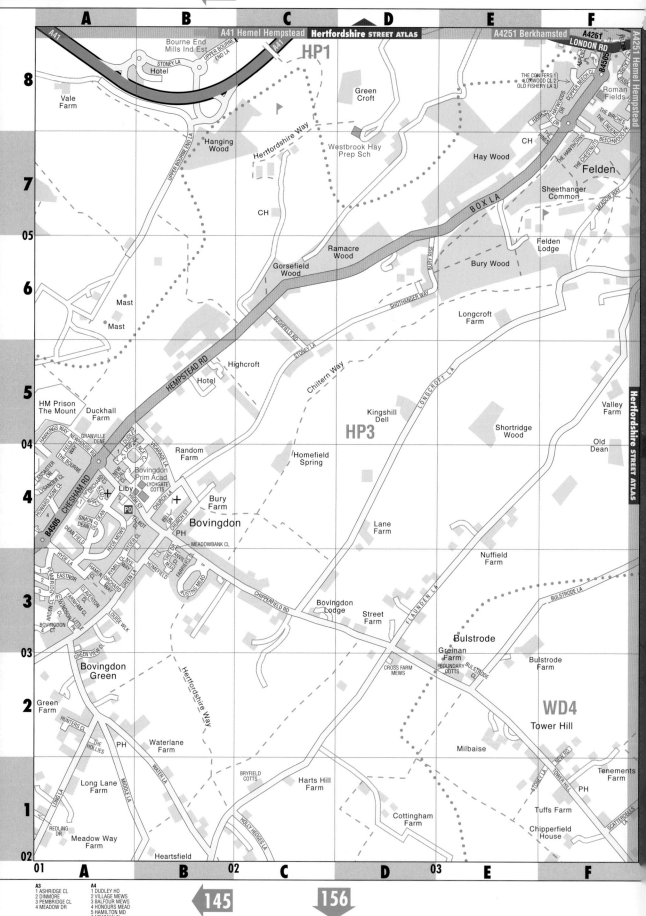
HP1

Vale Farm

Bourne End Mills Ind Est

STONEY LA

Hotel

UPPER BOURNE END LA

Hanging Wood

Hertfordshire Way

CH

Green Croft

Westbrook Hay Prep Sch

THE CONIFERS 1
LOXWOOD CL 2
OLD FISHERY LA 3

Roman Fields

THE BIRCHES

THE LINDENS

CH

Hay Wood

Felden

Sheethanger Common

BOX LA

Felden Lodge

Ramacre Wood

Gorsefield Wood

BURY RISE

Bury Wood

SHOTHANGER WAY

Longcroft Farm

Mast

Mast

BUSHFIELD RD

STONEY LA

Chiltern Way

LONGCROFT LA

HEMPSTEAD RD

Highcroft

Hotel

Kingshill Dell

HP3

Shortridge Wood

Valley Farm

Old Dean

HM Prison The Mount

Duckhall Farm

Random Farm

Homefield Spring

HAWKINGS WAY
THE BOURNE
NEWHOUSE RD
GRANVILLE DENE
VICARAGE LA
LAWRENCE CL

Bovingdon Prim Acad

LYCHGATE COTTS

Liby

Lane Farm

Nuffield Farm

CHESHAM RD

B4505

Bury Farm

Bovingdon

PH

Chipperfield Rd

Bovingdon Lodge

Street Farm

Bulstrode

Greinan Farm

BULSTRODE LA

Bulstrode Farm

CROSS FARM MEWS

BOUNDARY COTTS
BULSTRODE CL

FLAUNDEN LA

WD4

Tower Hill

Bovingdon Green

Hertfordshire Way

Green Farm

HUNTERS CL

THE HOLLIES

PH

Waterlane Farm

WATER LA

MIDDLE LA

Milbaise

TOWER HILL

STONE LA

PH

Tenements Farm

Long Lane Farm

LONG LA

BRYFIELD COTTS

HOLLY HEDGES LA

Harts Hill Farm

Cottingham Farm

Tuffs Farm

Chipperfield House

SCATTERDELLS LA

REDLING DR

Meadow Way Farm

Heartsfield

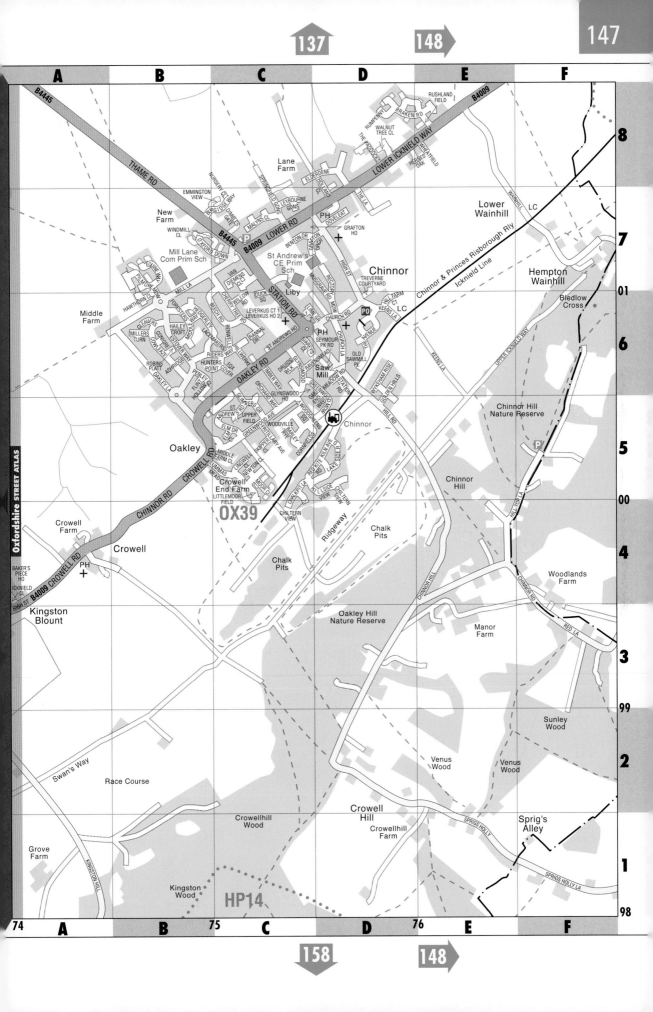

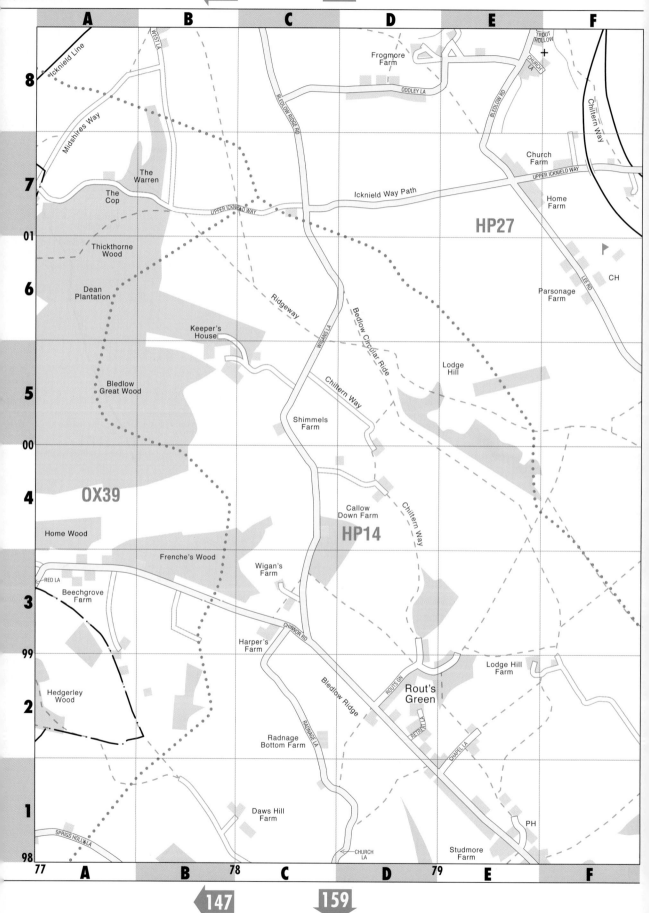

A   B   C   D   E   F

Icknield Line

8

Midshires Way

WEST LA

Frogmore
Farm

ODDLEY LA

TROUT
HOLLOW

CHURCH
LA

BLEDLOW RD

CHILTERN Way

The Warren

7

The
Cop

Upper Icknield Way

Icknield Way Path

Church
Farm

UPPER ICKNIELD WAY

Home
Farm

HP27

01

Thickthorne
Wood

Parsonage
Farm

LEE RD

CH

6

Dean
Plantation

Ridgeway

Bledlow Circular Ride

Keeper's
House

WIGANS LA

Lodge
Hill

5

Bledlow
Great Wood

Chiltern Way

Shimmels
Farm

00

4

OX39

Callow
Down Farm

HP14

Chiltern Way

Home Wood

Frenche's Wood

Wigan's
Farm

3

RED LA

Beechgrove
Farm

CHINNOR RD

Harper's
Farm

Bledlow Ridge

Lodge Hill
Farm

99

ROUTS GN

Rout's
Green

RETREAT

2

Hedgerley
Wood

RADNAGE LA

Radnage
Bottom Farm

CHAPEL LA

1

Daws Hill
Farm

PH

Studmore
Farm

SPRIGS HOLLOW LA

CHURCH
LA

98

77   A   B   78   C   D   79   E   F

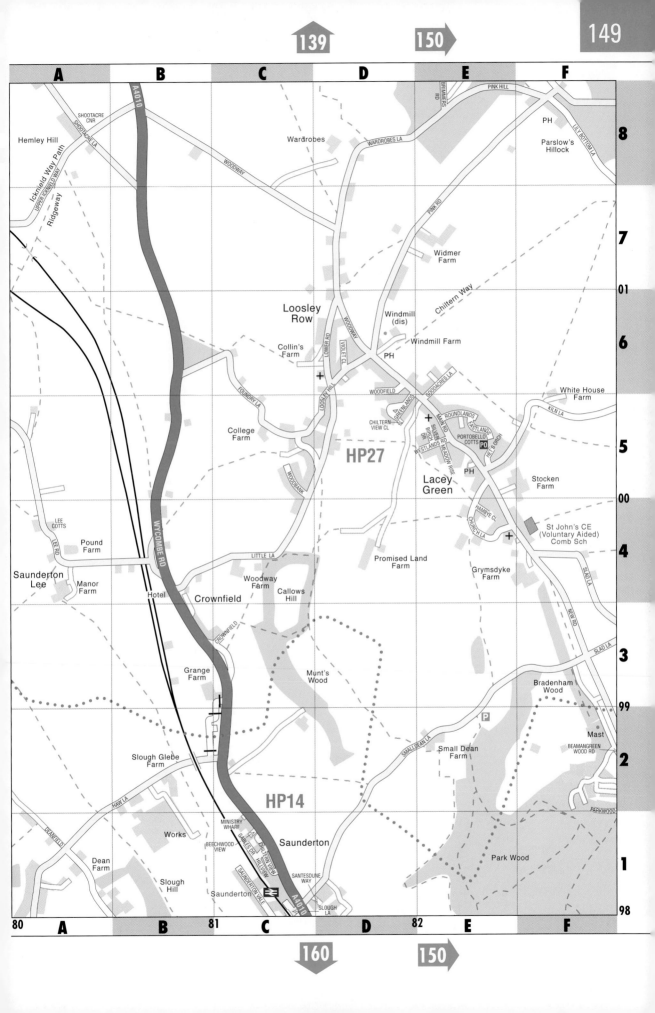

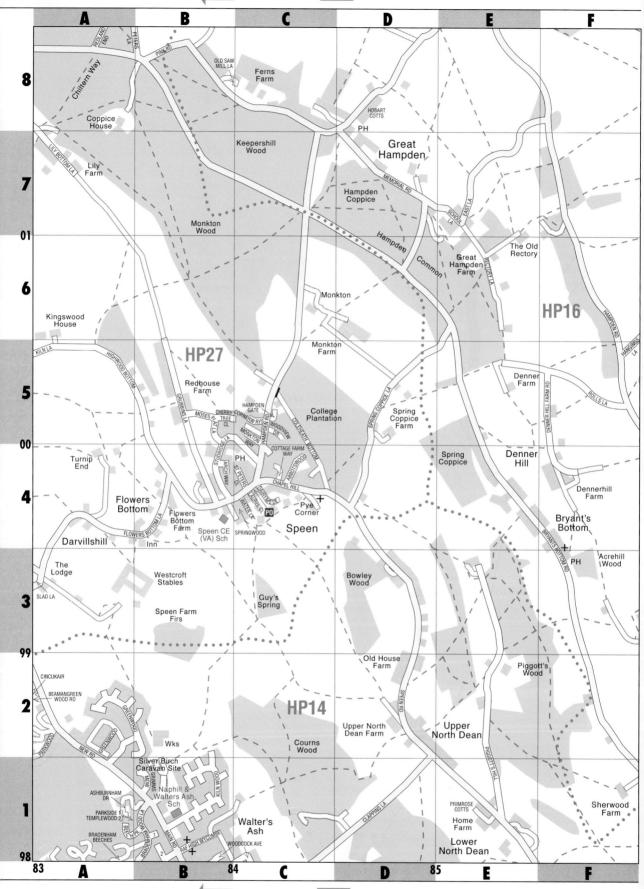

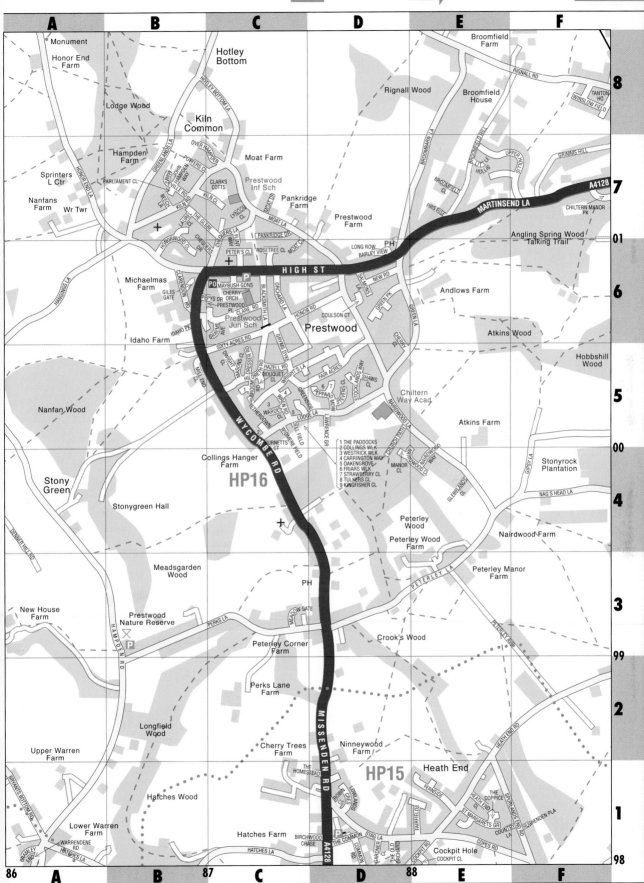

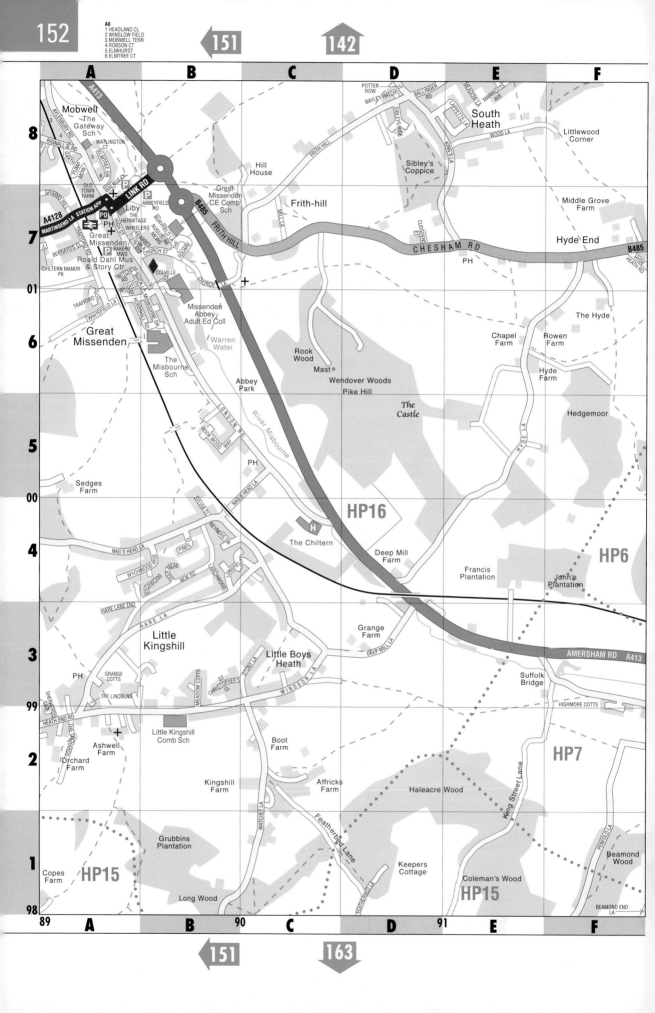

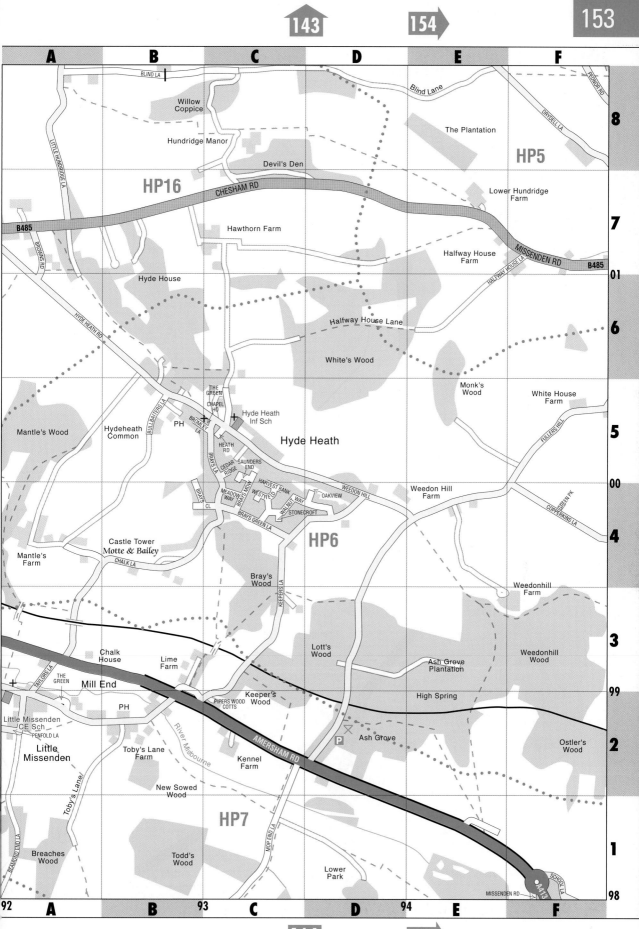

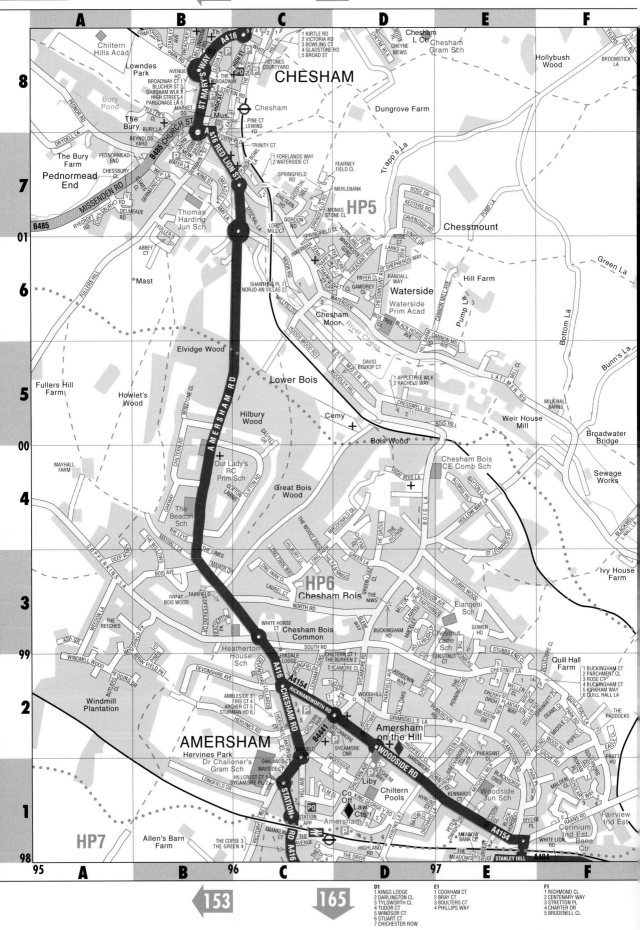

CHESHAM

HP5

Chessmount

Waterside

Lower Bois

Bois Wood

HP6
Chesham Bois

AMERSHAM

Amersham
on the Hill

HP7

D1
1 KINGS LODGE
2 DARLINGTON CL
3 TYLSWORTH CL
4 TUDOR CT
5 WINDSOR CT
6 STUART CT
7 CHICHESTER ROW

E1
1 COOKHAM CT
2 BRAY CT
3 BOULTERS CT
4 PHILLIPS WAY

F1
1 RICHMOND CL
2 CENTENARY WAY
3 STRETTON PL
4 CHARTER DR
5 BRUDENELL CL

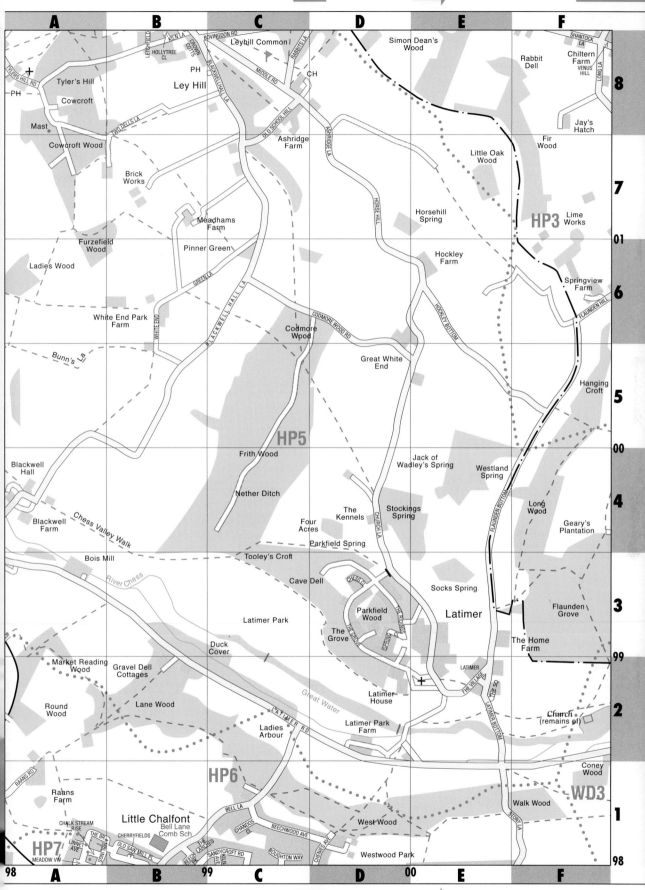

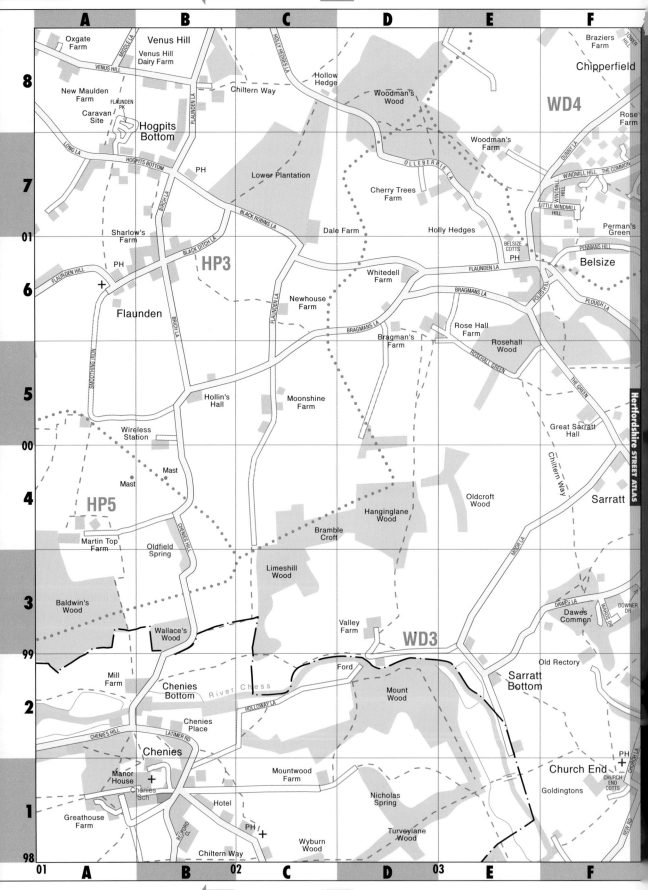

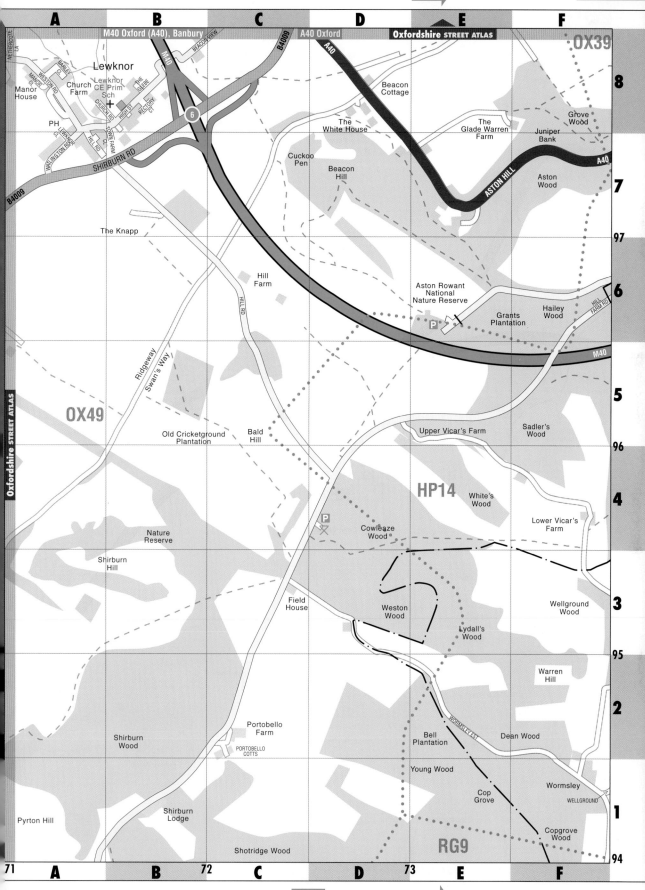

Oxfordshire STREET ATLAS

OX39

A B C D E F

8
7
97
6
5
96
4
3
95
2
1
94

M40 Oxford (A40), Banbury
A40 Oxford

Lewknor

Manor House

Church Farm

Lewknor CE Prim Sch

PH

The Glebe

6

Beacon Cottage

The White House

The Glade Warren Farm

Grove Wood

Juniper Bank

SHIRBURN RD

B4009

The Knapp

Cuckoo Pen

Beacon Hill

Aston Wood

ASTON HILL

A40

HILL RD

Hill Farm

Aston Rowant National Nature Reserve

Grants Plantation

Hailey Wood

HILL FARM RD

P

M40

OX49

Ridgeway

Swan's Way

Old Cricketground Plantation

Bald Hill

Upper Vicar's Farm

Sadler's Wood

Nature Reserve

HP14

White's Wood

Lower Vicar's Farm

Shirburn Hill

P

Cowleaze Wood

Field House

Weston Wood

Lydall's Wood

Wellground Wood

Warren Hill

Shirburn Wood

Portobello Farm

PORTOBELLO COTTS

Bell Plantation

WORMSLEY RD

Dean Wood

Pyrton Hill

Shirburn Lodge

Young Wood

Cop Grove

Wormsley

WELLGROUND

Shotridge Wood

RG9

Copgrove Wood

71 A 72 B C 73 D E F

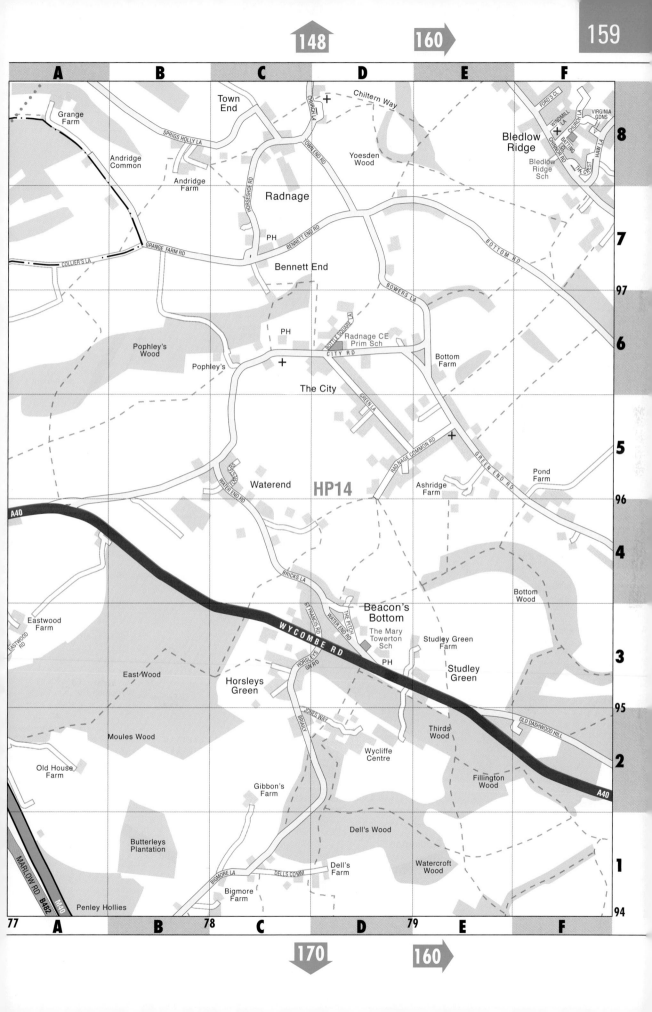

A   B   C   D   E   F

8

Town End
Chiltern Way
Bledlow Ridge
FORD'S CL
WINDMILL LA
VIRGINIA GDNS
CHURCH LA
BAITING
CHINNOR RD
THE CREST
HAW LA
Bledlow Ridge Sch

SPRIGS HOLLY LA
Grange Farm
Andridge Common
Andridge Farm
HORSESHOE RD
TOWN END RD
CHURCH LA
Yoesden Wood
Radnage

7

97

GRANGE FARM RD
COLLIER'S LA
PH
BENNETT END RD
Bennett End
BOTTOM RD
BOWERS LA

6

Pophley's Wood
PH
BOTTLE SQUARE LA
CITY RD
Radnage CE Prim Sch
Bottom Farm
Pophley's
The City
GREEN LA
RADNAGE COMMON RD
GREEN END RD

5

96

A40
WATER END RD
ASS. SPORT
Waterend
HP14
Ashridge Farm
Pond Farm

4

BRICKS LA
Bottom Wood

3

95

Eastwood Farm
EASTWOOD RD
East Wood
ST FRANCIS RD
WATER END RD
THE PITCH
WYCOMBE RD
HORSLEYS GN RD
Horsleys Green
Beacon's Bottom
The Mary Towerton Sch
PH
Studley Green Farm
Studley Green
OLD DASHWOOD HILL

Moules Wood
JONES WAY
BRIARLY
Thirds Wood

2

Old House Farm
Gibbon's Farm
Wycliffe Centre
Fillington Wood
A40

MARLOW RD
B482
M40
Butterleys Plantation
BIGMORE LA
DELL'S COMM
Dell's Farm
Dell's Wood
Watercroft Wood

1

94

Penley Hollies
Bigmore Farm

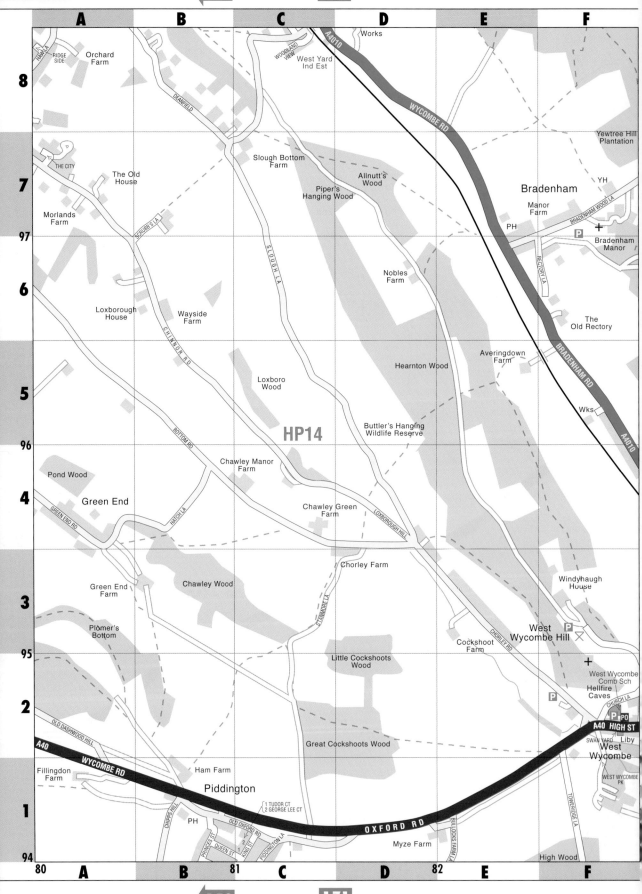

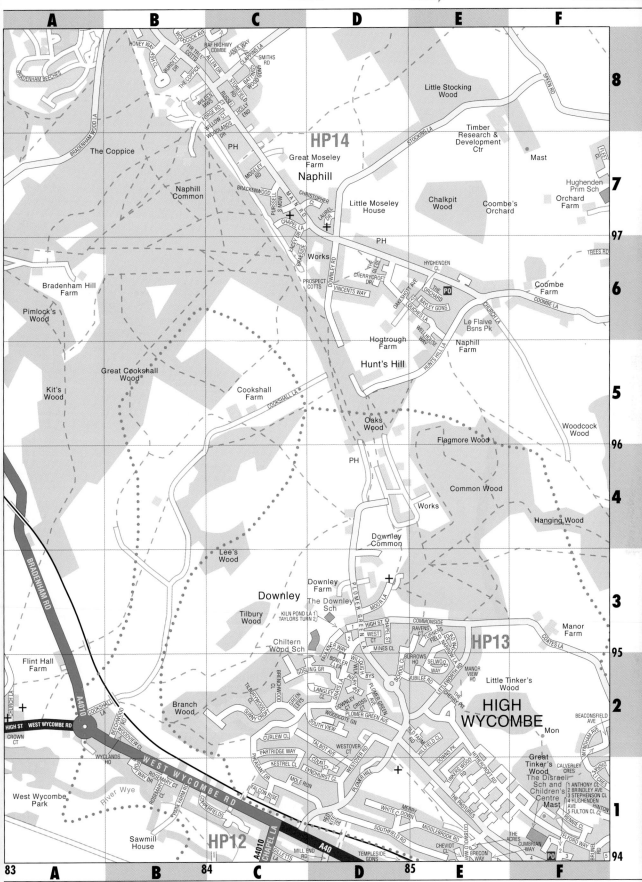

HP14

Naphill

HP13

HP12

HIGH WYCOMBE

Downley

BRADENHAM BEECHES

The Coppice

Naphill Common

Bradenham Hill Farm

Pimlock's Wood

Kit's Wood

Great Cookshall Wood

Cookshall Farm

Flint Hall Farm

West Wycombe Park

Sawmill House

Great Moseley Farm

Little Moseley House

Little Stocking Wood

Timber Research & Development Ctr

Mast

Hughenden Prim Sch

Orchard Farm

Chalkpit Wood

Coombe's Orchard

Coombe Farm

Hogtrough Farm

Hunt's Hill

Naphill Farm

Le Flaive Bsns Pk

Oaks Wood

Flagmore Wood

Common Wood

Hanging Wood

Woodcock Wood

Works

Downley Common

Lee's Wood

Downley Farm

The Downley Sch

Tilbury Wood

Chiltern Wood Sch

Branch Wood

Manor Farm

Little Tinker's Wood

Manor View Ho

Great Tinker's Wood

The Disraeli Sch and Children's Centre

Mast

West Wycombe Rd

River Wye

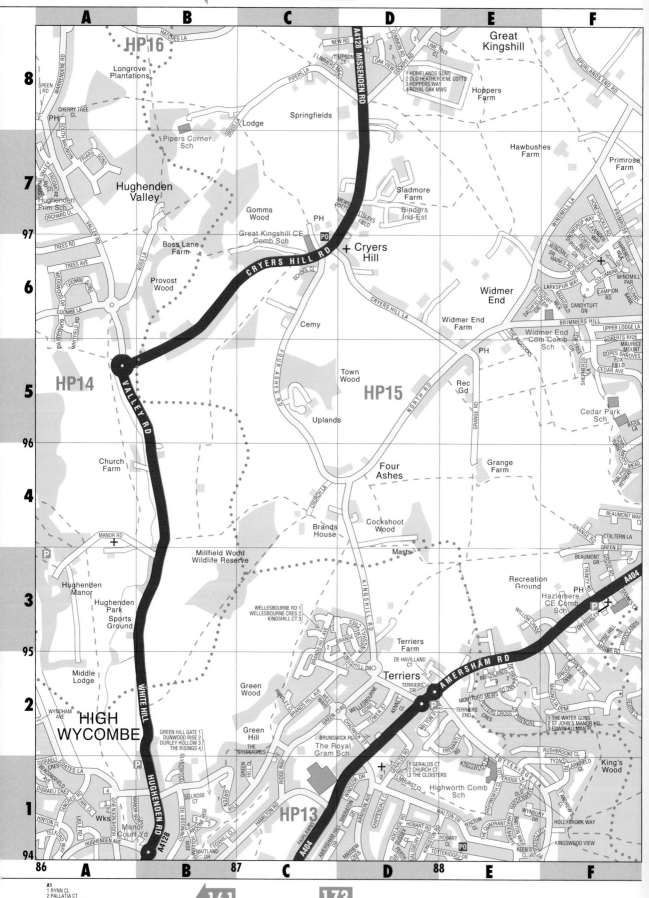

A1
1 RYNN CL
2 PALLATIA CT
3 HARRISONS WAY
4 JUMELLE MEWS

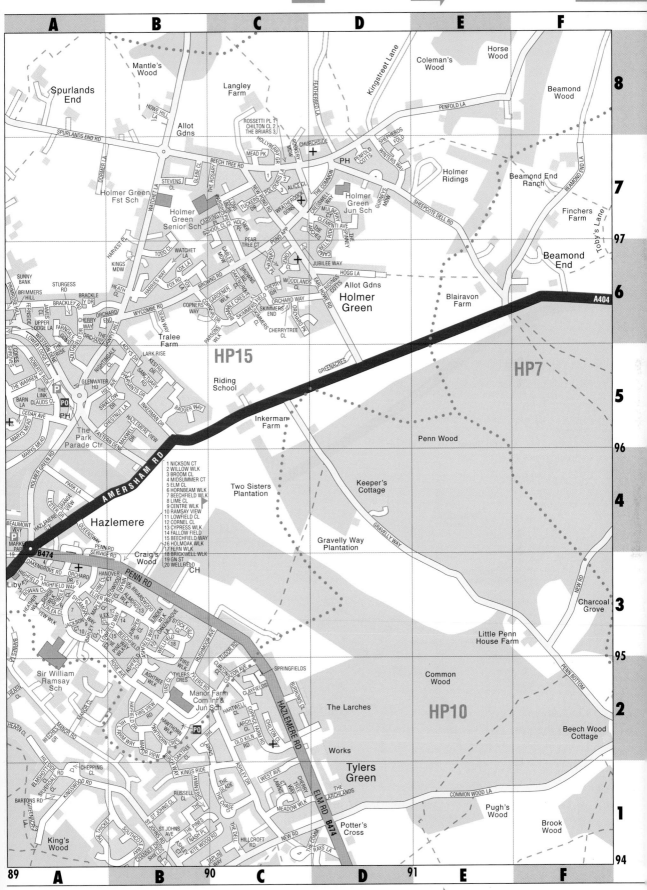

163
153

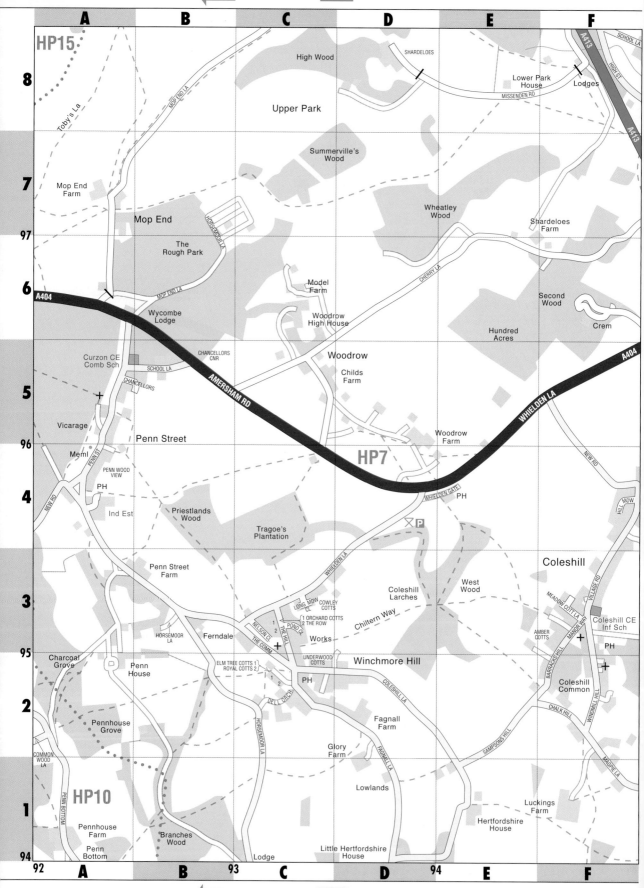

163
175

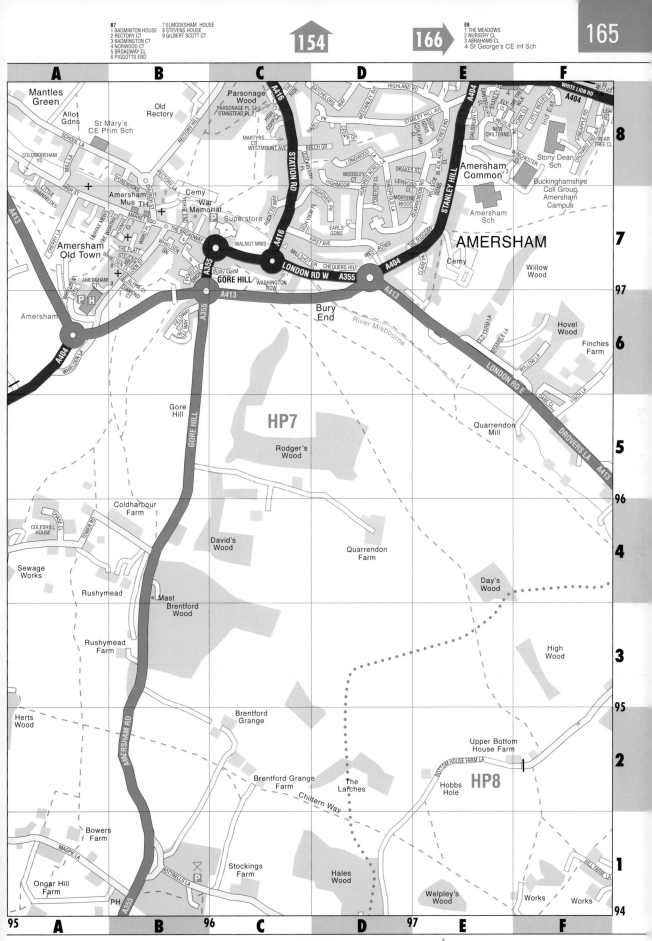

B7
1 BADMINTON HOUSE
2 RECTORY CT
3 BADMINGTON CT
4 NORWOOD CT
5 BROADWAY CL
6 PIGGOTTS END
7 ELMODESHAM HOUSE
8 STEVENS HOUSE
9 GILBERT SCOTT CT

E8
1 THE MEADOWS
2 NURSERY CL
3 ABRAHAMS CL
4 St George's CE Inf Sch

154
166
176
166

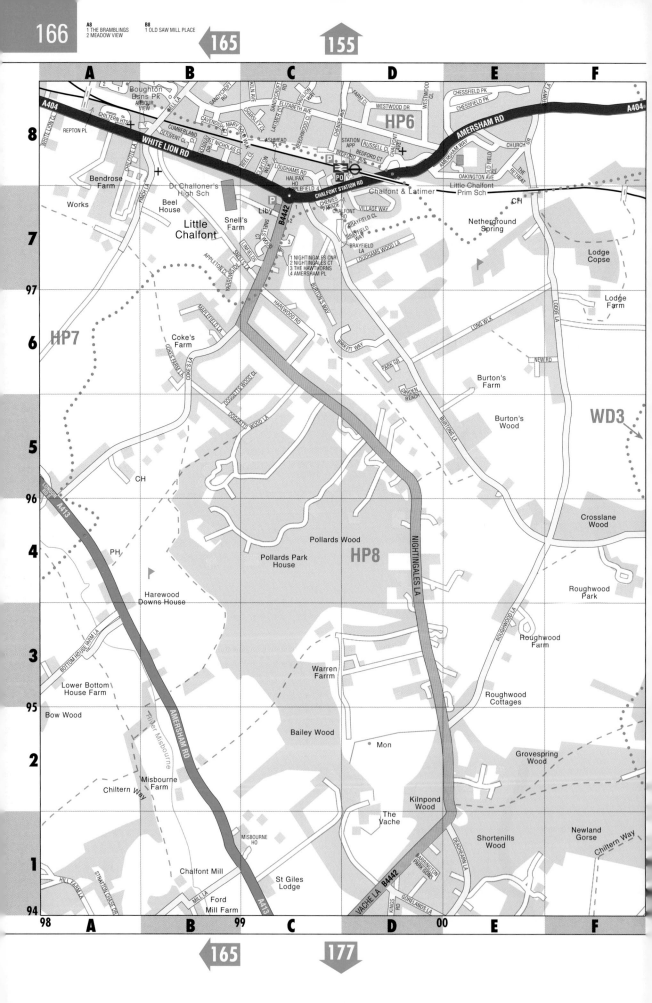

A8
1 THE BRAMBLINGS
2 MEADOW VIEW

B8
1 OLD SAW MILL PLACE

◀ 165
155

A B C D E F

A404

WHITE LION RD

Boughton
Bsns PK
ARBOUR
VIEW
CHILTERN HTS
SANDYCROFT RD
KILN AVE
SANDYCROFT RD
CHARSLEY CL
PAVILION WAY
FARM CL
WESTWOOD DR
WESTWOOD CL
CHESSFIELD PK
CHESSFIELD PK
TONY LA
A404
AMERSHAM RD

HP6

8

REPTON PL
WHITE LION CL
PHILCOTE LA
FINCH LA
CUMBERLAND
DERWENT CL
KENRICK ST NICHOLAS CL
CAVENDISH
MARY NICHOLAS
ASHMEAD
PL
CLAXTON
WLK
LOUDHAMS RD
BEECHWOOD CL
CHENIES AVE
ELIZABETH AVE
LATIMER CL
STATION
APP
RUSSELL CL
BEDFORD CT
BEDFORD AVE
AMERSHAM WAY
CHURCH GR
OLD FIELD
THE RETREAT

Bendrose
Farm
Works
Dr Challoner's
High Sch
Beel
House
BELL CL
Little
Chalfont
Snell's
Farm
SNELLS WOOD
Liby
B4442
LINKFIELS
APPLETON CL
YABBOW GDNS
Halifax
HO
APPLEFIELD
CHENIES
PARADE
CHALFONT
RD
CHALFONT STATION RD
VILLAGE WAY
BRAYFIELD CL
BRAYFIELD
WAY
BRAYFIELD
LA
LOUGHAMS WOOD LA
P
PO
Chalfont & Latimer
Little Chalfont
Prim Sch
Netherground
Spring
OAKINGTON AVE
CH
Lodge
Copse
Lodge
Farm

7

1 NIGHTINGALES CNR
2 NIGHTINGALES CT
3 THE HAWTHORNS
4 AMERSHAM PL

97

HP7

6

Coke's
Farm
COKES FARM LA
COKE'S LA
MAPLEFIELD LA
DOGGETTS WOOD CL
DOGGETTS WOOD LA
HAREWOOD RD
BURTON'S WAY
BIRKETT WAY
PARK GR
GARDEN
REACH
LONG WLK
BURTONS LA
LODGE LA
NEW RD
Burton's
Farm
Burton's
Wood
WD3

5

CH

96

A413
LONDON RD

PH

Harewood
Downs House

Pollards Wood
Pollards Park
House
HP8
NIGHTINGALES LA
ROUGHWOOD LA
Crosslane
Wood
Roughwood
Park
Roughwood
Farm
Roughwood
Cottages

4

3

BOTTOM HOUSE FARM LA
Lower Bottom
House Farm
AMERSHAM RD
River Misbourne
Warren
Farrm
Grovespring
Wood

2

95
Bow Wood
Misbourne
Farm
Chiltern Way
Bailey Wood
Mon
Kilnpond
Wood
The Vache
Shortenills
Wood
Newland
Gorse
Chiltern Way

1

HILL FARM LA
STRATTON CHASE DR
MILL LA
Misbourne
HO
Chalfont Mill
Ford
Mill Farm
St Giles
Lodge
A413
VACHE LA
B4442
KINGS RD
GORELANDS LA
CARRINGTON PARK GDNS
DEADMAN LA

94

98 A 99 B C 00 D E F

◀ 165
177

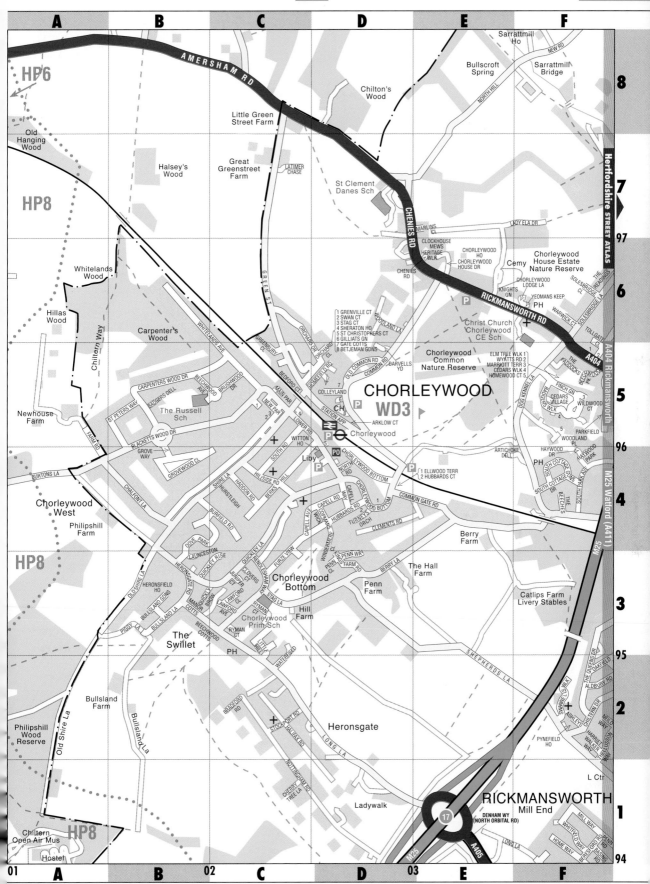

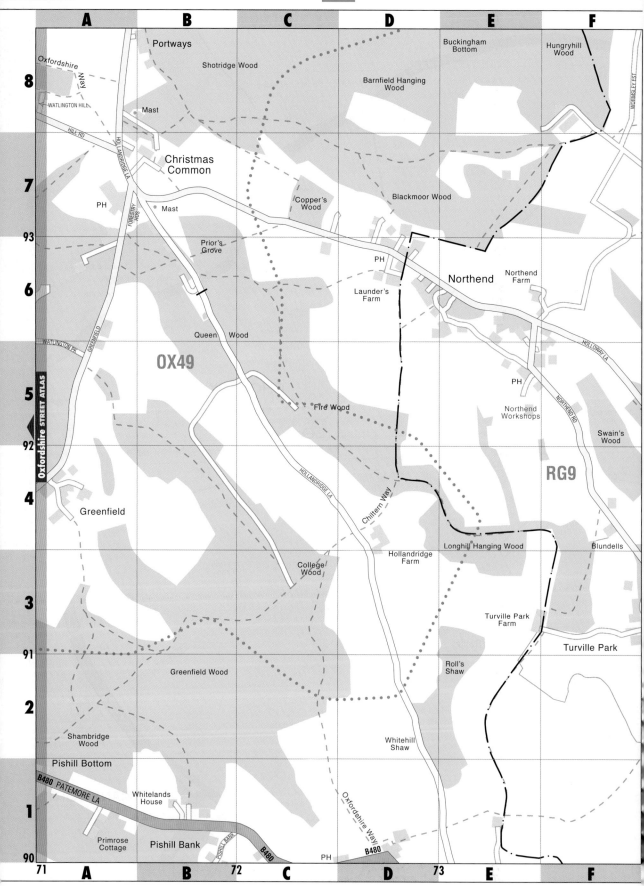

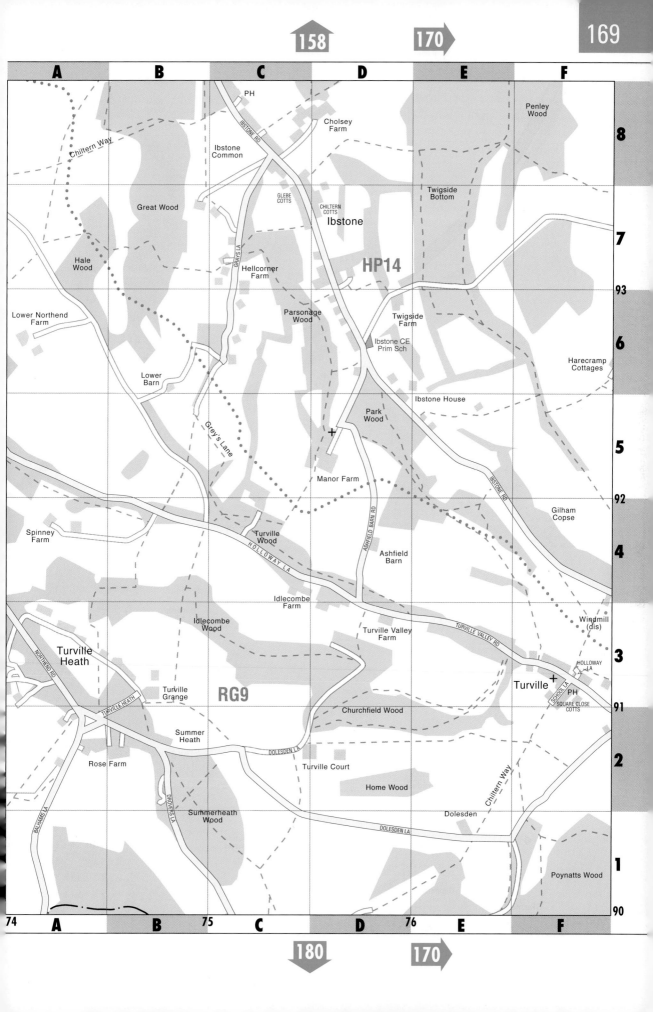

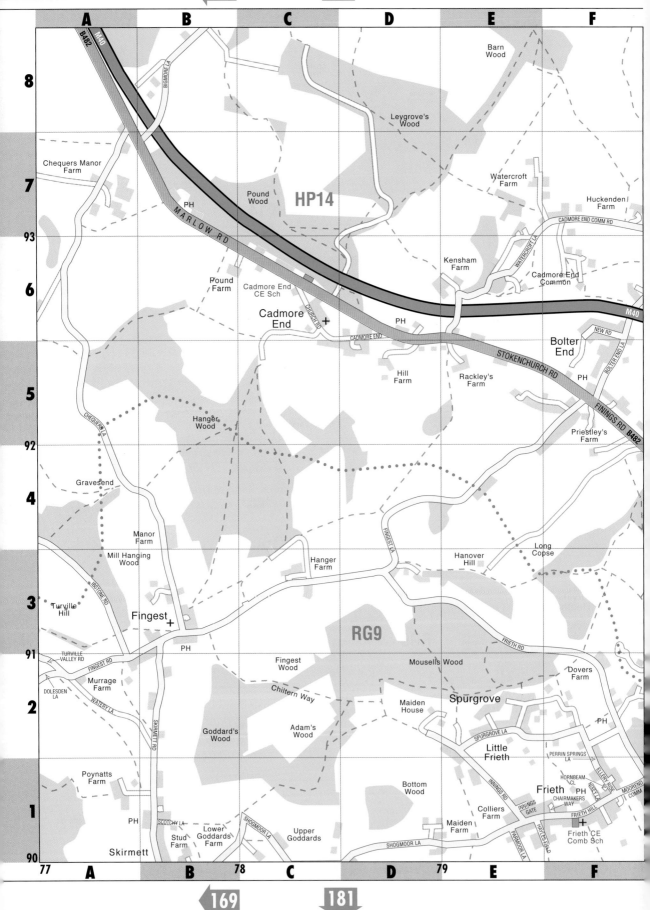

A **B** **C** **D** **E** **F**

8

M40
B482

Chequers Manor Farm

7

PH

MARLOW RD

Pound Wood

HP14

Barn Wood

Leygrove's Wood

Watercroft Farm

Huckenden Farm

CADMORE END COMM RD

93

Pound Farm

Cadmore End CE Sch

Cadmore End

CHURCH RD

CADMORE END

Kensham Farm

WATERCROFT LA

Cadmore End Common

M40

6

PH

STOKENCHURCH RD

NEW RD

Bolter End

BOLTER END LA

Hill Farm

Rackley's Farm

PH

FININGS RD B482

5

Hanger Wood

Priestley's Farm

CHEQUERS LA

92

Gravesend

Hanover Hill

Long Copse

4

Manor Farm

FINGEST LA

Mill Hanging Wood

INSTONE RD

Hanger Farm

3

Turville Hill

Fingest

RG9

FRIETH RD

Dovers Farm

PH

91

TURVILLE VALLEY RD

FINGEST RD

PH

Fingest Wood

Mousells Wood

Spurgrove

DOLESDEN LA

Murrage Farm

WATERY LA

SKIRMETT RD

Chiltern Way

Maiden House

SPURGROVE LA

Little Frieth

PH

PERRIN SPRINGS LA

2

HORNBEAM CL

ELLERY RSE

MOOREND COMM

Goddard's Wood

Adam's Wood

Frieth

PH

CHAIRMAKERS WAY

Poynatts Farm

INNINGS RD

Colliers Farm

INNINGS GATE

HAYES FLD

FRIETH HILL

1

PH

SCOTCHV LA

Stud Farm

Lower Goddards Farm

SHOGMOOR LA

Upper Goddards

Bottom Wood

Maiden Farm

SHOGMOOR LA

PARMOOR LA

Frieth CE Comb Sch

90

Skirmett

A B C D E F

Chipp's Manor
Jane's Wood
Bullocks Farm
Upper Dorrels Wood
Lower Dorrels Wood
West Wycombe Park
TOWERIDGE LA
Towerage
Towerage Farm
8

Laurel Farm
PRINCES ST
WELLFIELD RD
KING ST
CHIPPS HILL
Old Ridge Farm
PIDDINGTON LA
BULLOCKS FARM LA
Great Wood
Hellbottom Wood
HP12
7

Wheeler End Common
PH
CHAPEL ROW
ORCHARD ROW
BOLTER END LA
Denham Farm
Denham Wood
93

Wheeler End
WHEELER END COMM
Rickett's Farm
PH
Pyatts Farm
Fryers Farm
Sunter's Wood
6

DENHAM RD
SIDNEY CL
PARK CL
PUSEY WAY
IVY PL
MOUNT PLEASANT
NURSERY DR
LINES RD
WRIGHTS CL
SMITHS LA
RUSTIC CL
PYATTS FARM LA
Sandage Wood
Grove Farm
FRYERS FARM LA
SPRING COPPICE
5

Finings Farm
HANDLETON COMM
JOHNSON RD
BLACKWELL RD
SANDAGE RD
HARRIS RD
THE PIN
DISC CL
CORONATION RD
WIDDENTON VIEW
PARK FARM WAY
BEECH AVE
OAK TREE DR
HP14
PARK LA
LANE END RD
92

B482
FININGS RD
LAMMAS WAY
MANCHESTER TERR
P
ARCHERS WAY
TAPPING
FORGETTS RD
SHOTFIELD
SLATER RD
SIMMONS WAY
M40
92

Bolter End Farm
DAISY COTTS
OAKWOOD PL
HIGH ST
CHURCH PATH
IND EST
PO
SCATER RD
SAXHORN RD
Lane End
Resr
HP12
4

Fining Wood
Wr Twr
THE OLD BAKERY
PH
FRAMERS CT
ELLIS WAY
POND COTTS
CLAYTON RD
PHILP'S PL
RIDGE CL
BASSET
SOMERLY
Lane End Prim Sch
1 JAMES RD
2 HOBBS RD
3 ELWES RD
4 OLD SUN CL
5 SPRINGBANK RD

Cutler's Farm
Widdenton Park Wood

Wycombe Court Farm
CHALKY FIELD

Ditchfield
DITCHFIELD COTTS
GUINYARD PL
CHURCH RD
Ditchfield Common
PANLEIGH COTTS
3

Muswell Farm
Moor Farm
91

MOOR COMM
MOOR END COMM
Moor Common
Wycombe Air Park
2

MARLOW RD
SL7

Moorend Common
Moor Copse
Moor Wood
Garden Centre

RG9
Strawberry Grove
BEACON LA
Red Barn Farm
CAX LA
B482

FRITH RD
MOOR END
MOOR END LA
Bottom Wood
Roundwood Farm
1

30 A B 81 C D 82 E F 90

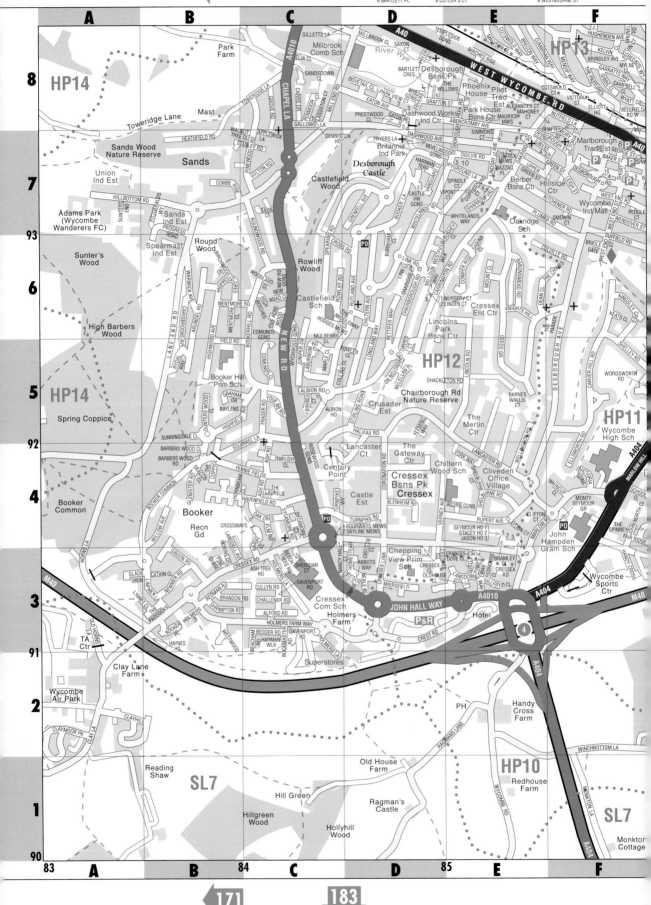

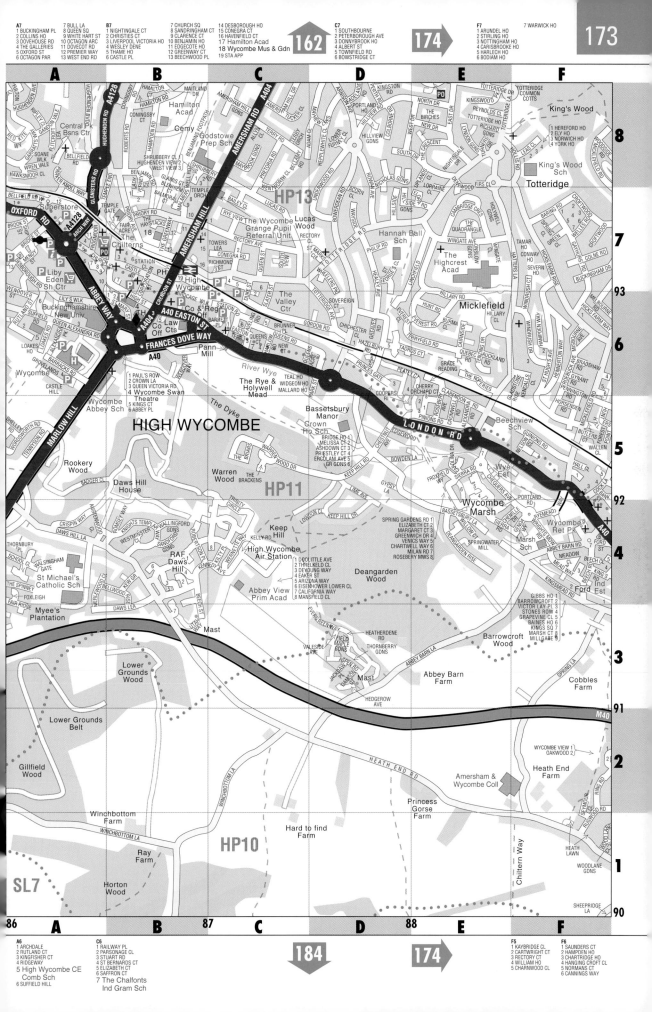

173
163

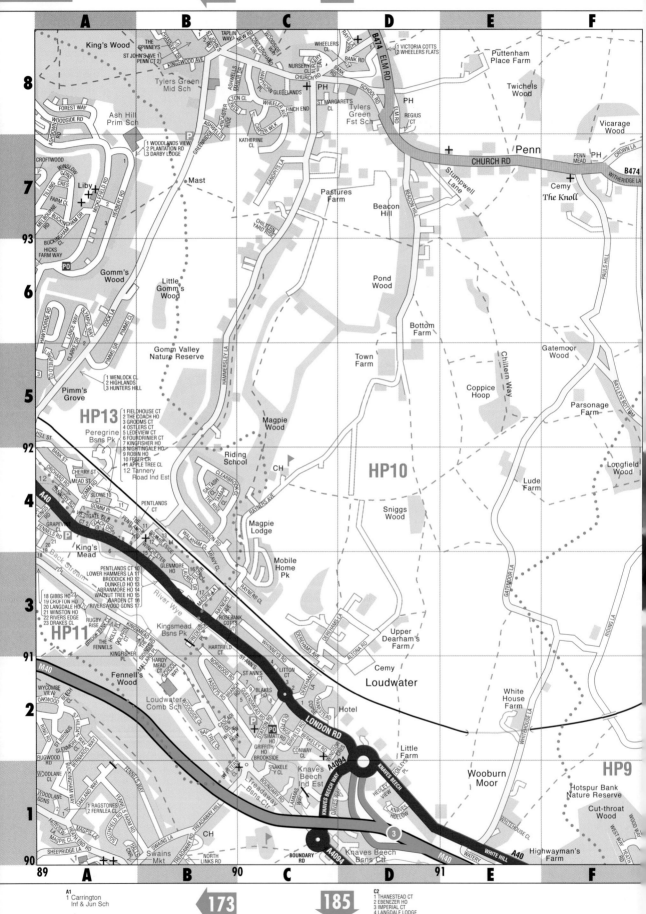

A1
1 Carrington
Inf & Jun Sch

C2
1 THANESTEAD CT
2 EBENEZER HO
3 IMPERIAL CT
4 LANGDALE LODGE
5 OVERSHOT HO
6 SEVEN ACRE HO
7 QUEENSMEAD HO
8 LOUDWATER MILL
9 MILL CL

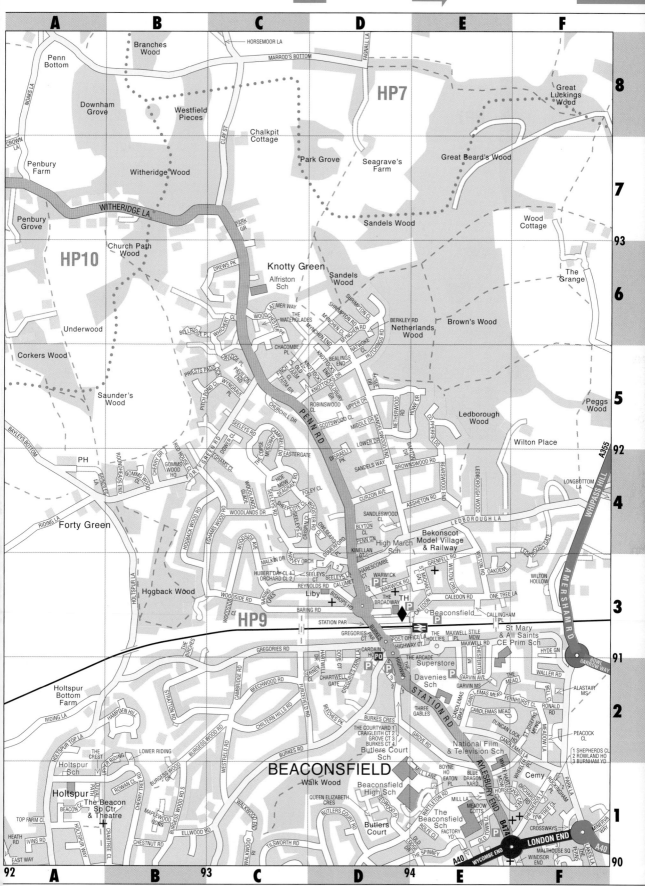

175 165

175 187

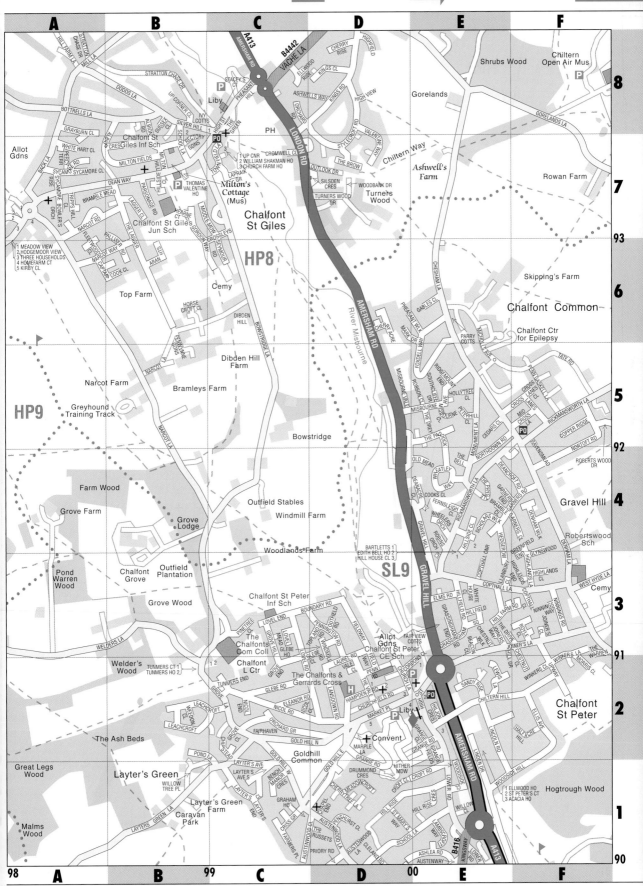

D2
1 STRINGERS COTTS
2 ADSTOCK MEWS
3 THE BROADWAY
4 BUCKINGHAM PAR
5 MARKET HO

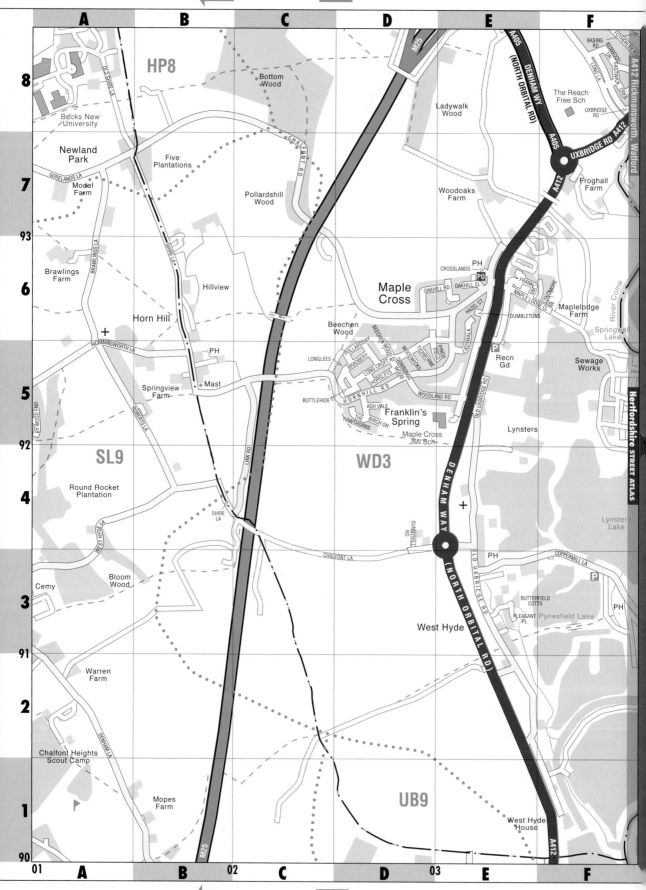

A **B** **C** **D** **E** **F**

B480
THE OLD RD.
B480
Pishill Bank
Bank Farm
Pishill
Pishill House
CHURCH HILL
Balhams Farmhouse
BALHAMS LA
BALHAMS LA
HOLLANDRIDGE LA
8

Long Wood
The Warren

Nuttall's Farm
Doyley Wood
Whitepond Farm
7

Upper Maidensgrove
Pishillbury Wood
The Round Clump
89

Russell's Water Common
Maidensgrove Farm
Stonor
6

PH
PARK LA
Little Cookley Hill
Oak Farm
Park Wood
Almshill Wood

Hatch Lane
Maidensgrove
Chiltern Way
Upper Assendon Farm
5

Big Ashes Plantation
Nature Trail
Lodge Farm
Rowdow
Great Hill
88

Warburg Nature Reserve
Maidensgrove Scrubs
RG9

Pages Bottom
Pages Farm
4

Kitesgrove Wood
P

Stockings Plantation
Soundess Wood
Freedom Wood
The Firfields

Oxfordshire Way
Warmscombe La
3
87

Soundess House
Bix Bottom

Wellgrove Wood
St James's Church (remains of)
Paradise Wood
2

Crocker End
Valley Farm
Bix Bottom

Halfridge Wood
1

CATSLIP
A4130 Wallingford
Halfridge Gate
CATSLIP
A4130
Coney Burrow
RECTORY LA
Bix
Little Bixbottom Farm
B480
86

Oxfordshire STREET ATLAS

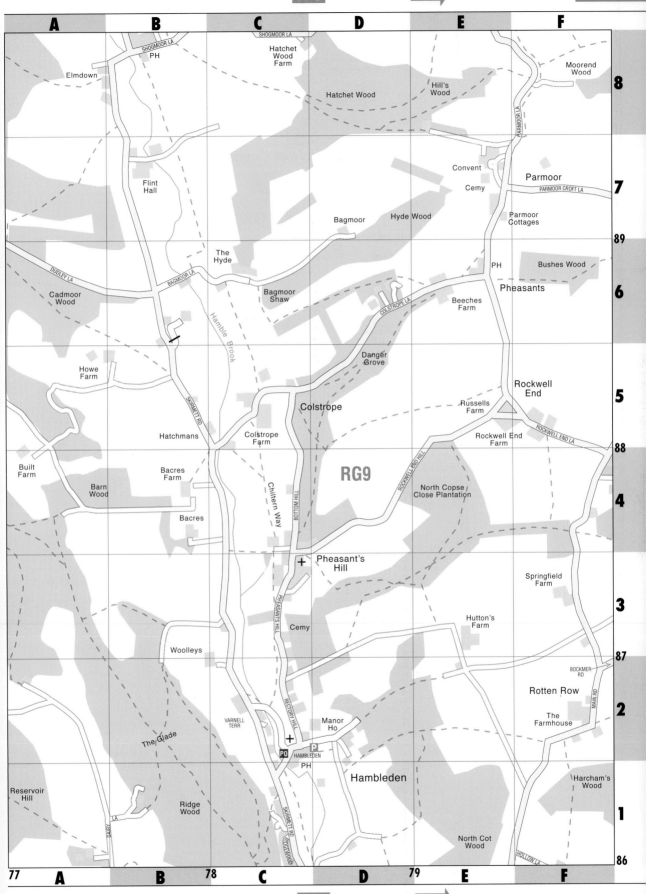

MARLOW RD
B482

A **B** **C** **D** **E** **F**

8

Moorend
Wood

HP14

Bottom Wood

Finnamore La

Beacon La
Beacon
Farm

7

Finnamore
Wood

Bluey's
Farm

Beacon La

MOOR END LA

PARMOOR CROFT LA

The Roost

89

Chisbridge

CHISBRIDGE LA

Chisbridge
Cross

Copy Green

6

Shillingridge Wood

Holme Wood
Cottage

Holme
Wood

Woodlands

MAIN RD

Kent's
Wood

Holme Wood

SHILLINGRIDGE
PK

Denelands
Farm

Oaklands
Farm

5

FRIETH RD

Bottom House

Woodend
House

Hawkins
Farm

Mundaydean
Bottom

MUNDAYDEAN LA

88

RG9

SL7

MUNDAYDEAN LA

4

Fountain's

Woodend Farm

WOODEND HOUSE RD

LOWER WOODEND RD

Arbon

Lower
Woodend

Holywick

Walnut
Tree
Farm

3

Heath Wood

Lord's
Wood

FRIETH RD

Marlow
Common

87

Homefield Wood
Nature Reserve

BOCKMER LA

MARLOW COMM LA

2

Rogues Plantation

Chiltern Way

MARLOW COMM RD

Davenport Wood

Bockmer End
Farm

BOCKMER RD

Pullingshill
Wood

1

Woodland Plain

BOCKMER LA

Bockmer
House

Bockmer End

MARLOW COMM RD

Hook's Farm

86

Widefield

HOOKS LA

A 80 **B** 81 **C** **D** 82 **E** **F**

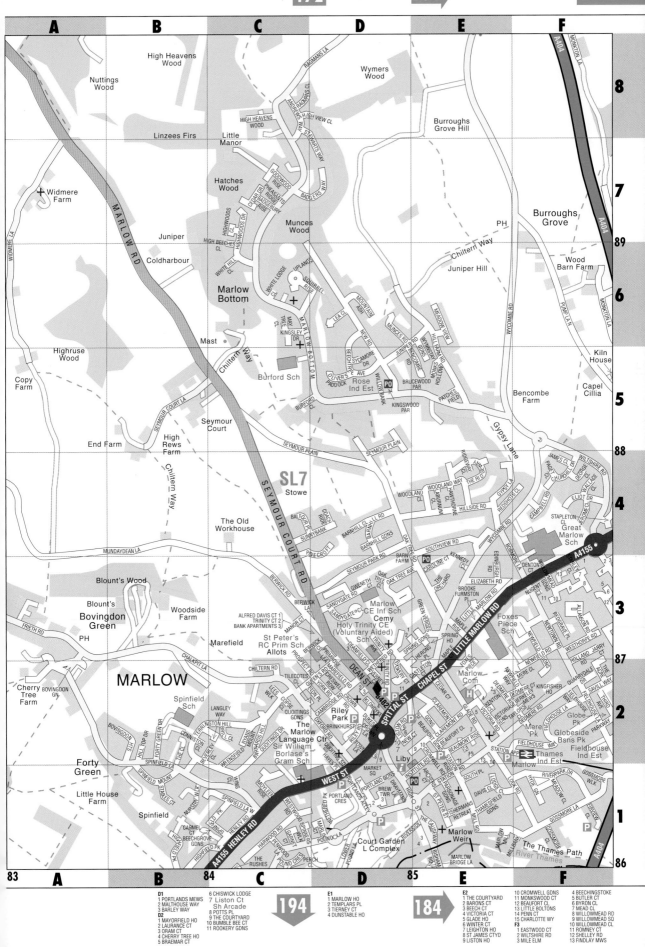

A   B   C   D   E   F

8
7
89
6
5
88
4
3
87
2
1
86

High Heavens Wood
Nuttings Wood
Linzees Firs
Little Manor
Wymers Wood
Burroughs Grove Hill
Widmere Farm
Juniper
Coldharbour
Hatches Wood
Munces Wood
Burroughs Grove
Wood Barn Farm
Marlow Bottom
Chiltern Way
Juniper Hill
Highruse Wood
Mast
Burford Sch
Kiln House
Copy Farm
Seymour Court
High Rews Farm
End Farm
Rose Ind Est
Bencombe Farm
Capel Cillia
Seymour Plain
Gypsy Lane
Kingswood Par
SL7
Stowe
The Old Workhouse
Seymour Plain
Great Marlow Sch
MUNDAYDEAN LA
Blount's Wood
Blount's Bovingdon Green
Woodside Farm
Foxes Piece Sch
Marefield
Marlow CE Inf Sch
Holy Trinity CE (Voluntary Aided) Sch
Cherry Tree Farm
MARLOW
Spinfield Sch
St Peter's RC Prim Sch Allots
Marlow Com
Forty Green
Riley Park
The Marlow Language Ctr
Sir William Borlase's Gram Sch
Liby
Globeside Bsns Pk
Fieldhouse Ind Est
Little House Farm
Spinfield
WEST ST
Market Sq
Thames Ind Est
Marlow
Court Garden L Complex
Marlow Weir
Marlow Bridge La
Marlow Mill
The Thames Path
River Thames

A   B   C   D   E   F

D1
1 PORTLANDS MEWS
2 MALTHOUSE WAY
3 BARLEY WAY
D2
1 MAYORFIELD HO
2 LAURANCE CT
3 ORAM CT
4 CHERRY TREE CT
5 BRAEMAR CT
6 CHISWICK LODGE
7 LISTON CT
   Sh Arcade
8 POTTS PL
9 THE COURTYARD
10 BUMBLE BEE CT
11 ROOKERY GDNS

E1
1 MARLOW HO
2 TEMPLARS PL
3 TIERNEY CT
4 DUNSTABLE HO

E2
1 THE COURTYARD
2 BARONS CT
3 BEECH CT
4 VICTORIA CT
5 GLADE HO
6 WINTER CT
7 LEIGHTON HO
8 ST JAMES CTYD
9 LISTON HO
10 CROMWELL GDNS
11 MONKSWOOD CT
12 BEAUFORT CL
13 LITTLE BOLTONS
14 PENN CT
15 CHARLOTTE WY
F3
1 EASTWOOD CT
2 WILTSHIRE RD
3 MILE ELM
4 BEECHINGSTOKE
5 BUTLER CT
6 BYRON CL
7 MEAD CL
8 WILLOWMEAD RD
9 WILLOWMEAD SQ
10 WILLOWMEAD CL
11 ROMNEY CT
12 SHELLEY RD
13 FINDLAY MWS

83   84   85   86

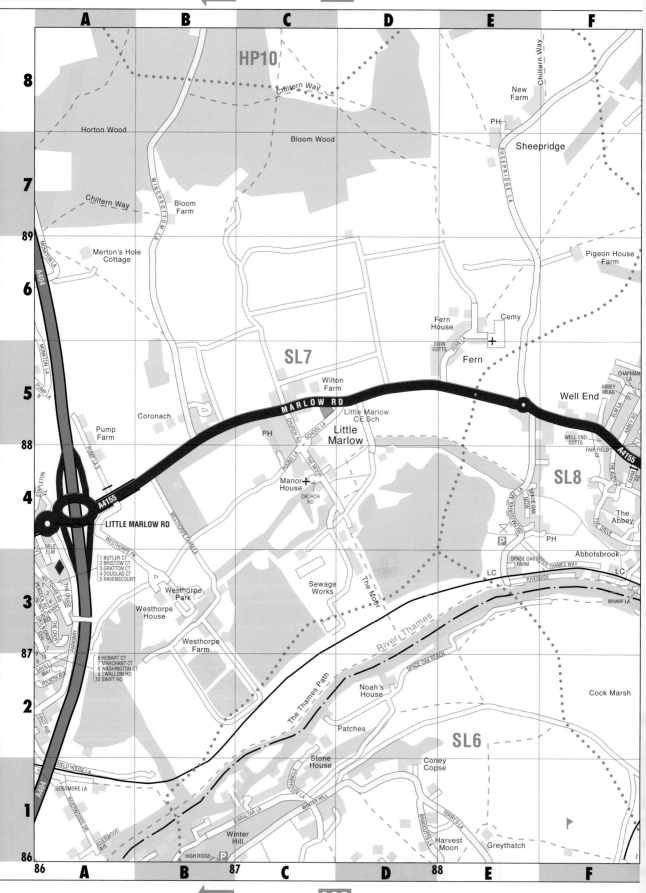

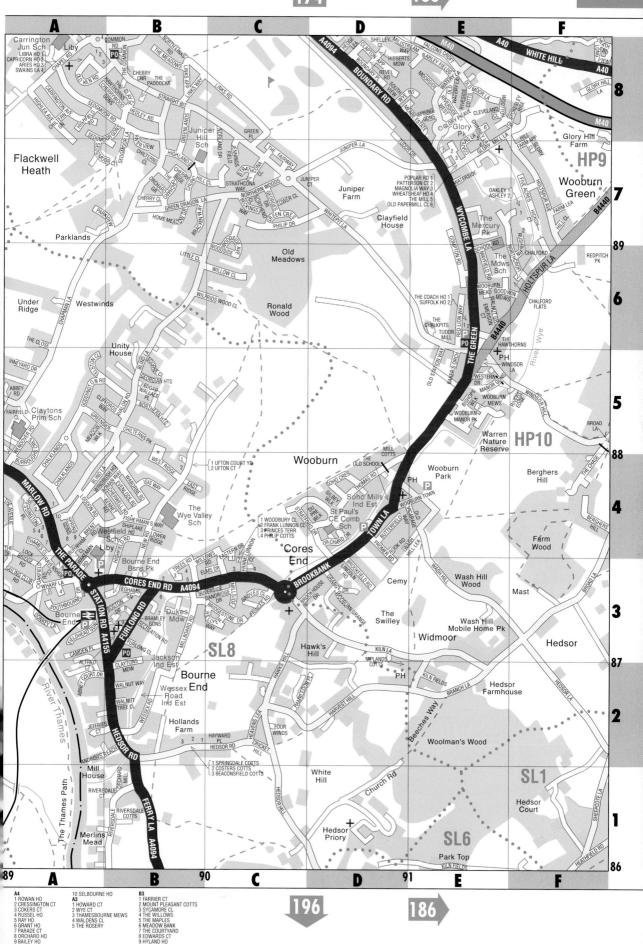

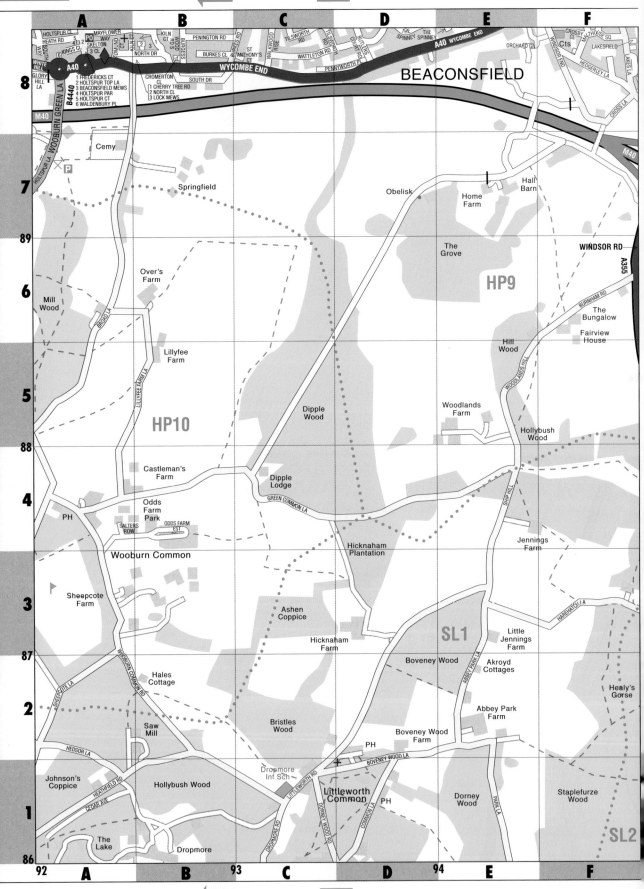

A   B   C   D   E   F

HOLTSPUR CL
HEATH RD
KINGS CL
MAYFLOWER
WAY
SKELTON
EDMUND
CT
PO
KILN
CT
KILN
RD'S
NORTH DR
KILN
BURGESS
PENINGTON RD
BURKES CL
ST ANTHONY'S
CT
WALKWOOD
RISE
TILSWORTH
RD
WATTLETON RD
BUTLERS
COURT RD
THE
SPINNEY
THE
SPINNEY
A40 WYCOMBE END
ORCHARD GN
CROSBY
CL
MALTHOUSE SQ
Cts
LAKESFIELD

WHITE
HILL
WAY
A40
B4440
CROMERTON
CL
SOUTH DR
WYCOMBE END
CHERRY TREE RD
PENNYWORTH
BEACONSFIELD

1 FREDERICKS CT
2 HOLTSPUR TOP LA
3 BEACONSFIELD MEWS
4 HOLTSPUR PAR
5 HOLTSPUR CT
6 WALDENBURY PL

1 CHERRY TREE RD
2 NORTH CL
3 LOCK MEWS

GLORY
HILL
LA

8

HEDGERLEY LA
LAKES LA
WINDSOR END
CROSS LA

M40

7
Cemy
P
Springfield
Obelisk
Home
Farm
Hall
Barn
M40

89
The
Grove
WINDSOR RD
A355

HOLTSPUR LA
WOOBURN GREEN LA

6
Mill
Wood
Over's
Farm
HP9
BURNHAM RD
The
Bungalow
Fairview
House

BROAD LA
Lillyfee
Farm
Hill
Wood
WOODLANDS HILL

5
HP10
Dipple
Wood
Woodlands
Farm
Hollybush
Wood

LILLYFEE FARM LA

88
Castleman's
Farm
Dipple
Lodge

4
PH
Odds
Farm
Park
GREEN COMMON LA
Hicknham
Plantation
SHIP HILL
Jennings
Farm

SALTERS
ROW
ODDS FARM
EST
Wooburn Common

3
Sheepcote
Farm
Ashen
Coppice
SL1
HAREHATCH LA
Little
Jennings
Farm

WOOBURN COMMON RD

87
Hales
Cottage
Hicknham
Farm
Boveney Wood
Akroyd
Cottages

SHEEPCOTE LA

2
Saw
Mill
Bristles
Wood
Boveney Wood
Farm
Abbey Park
Farm
ABBEY PARK LA
Healy's
Gorse

HEDSOR LA
Johnson's
Coppice
Dropmore
Inf Sch
PH
Littleworth
Common
PH
Dorney
Wood
Staplefurze
Wood

1
HEATHFIELD RD
CEDAR AVE
Hollybush Wood
DROPMORE RD
LITTLEWORTH RD
DORNEY WOOD RD
BOVENEY WOOD LA
COMMON LA
PARK LA
PH

The
Lake
Dropmore
SL2

86
92   A   B   93   C   D   94   E   F

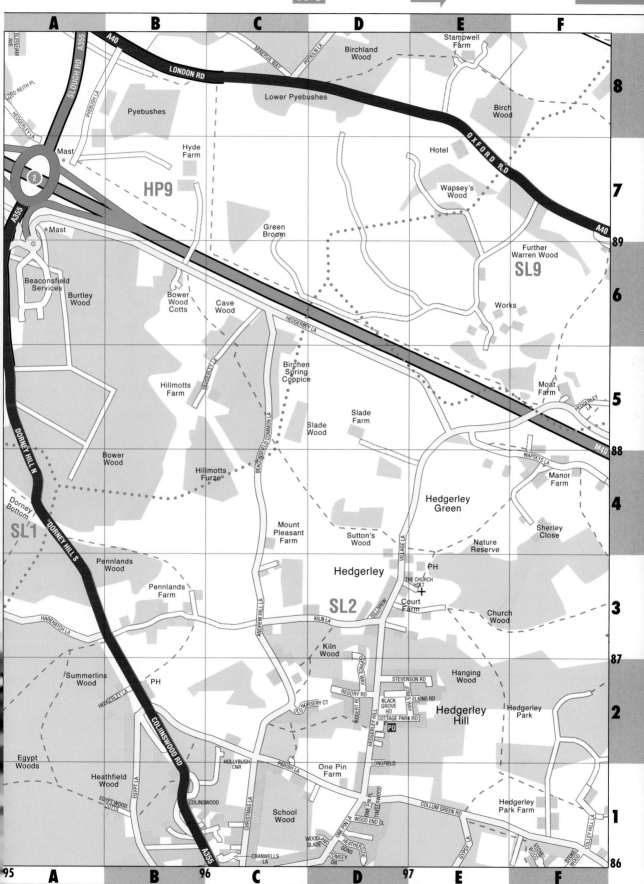

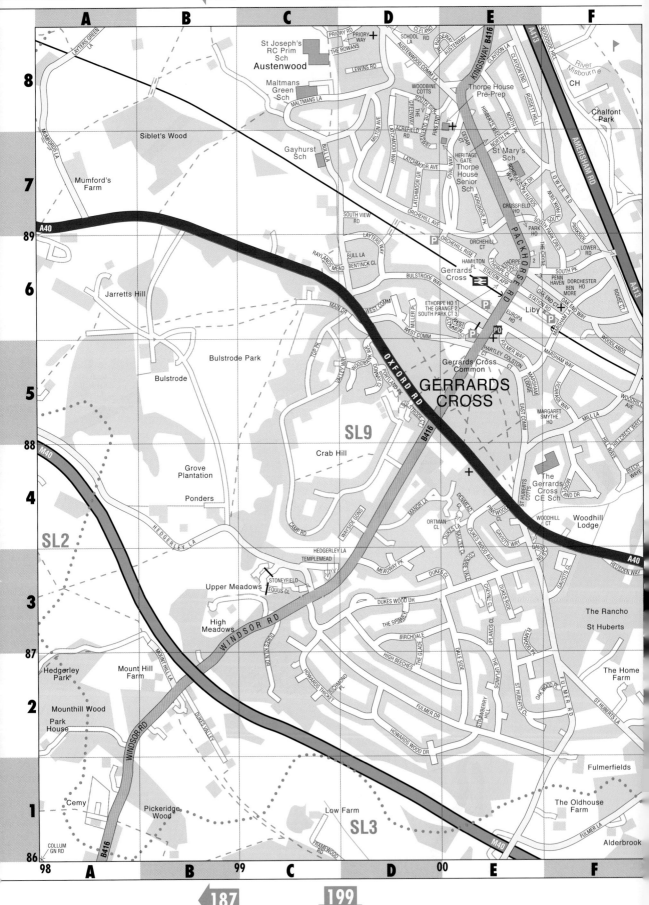

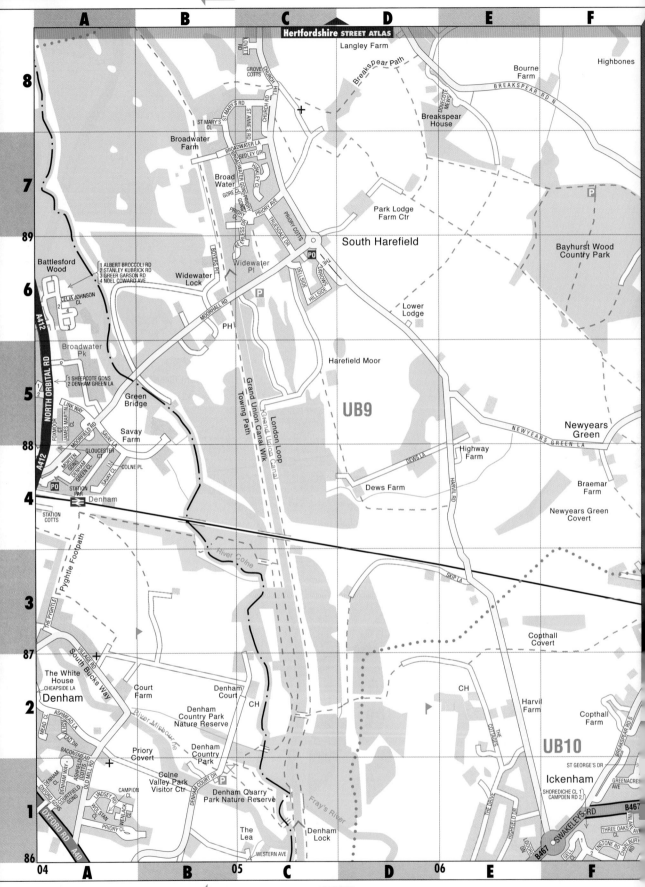

Hertfordshire STREET ATLAS

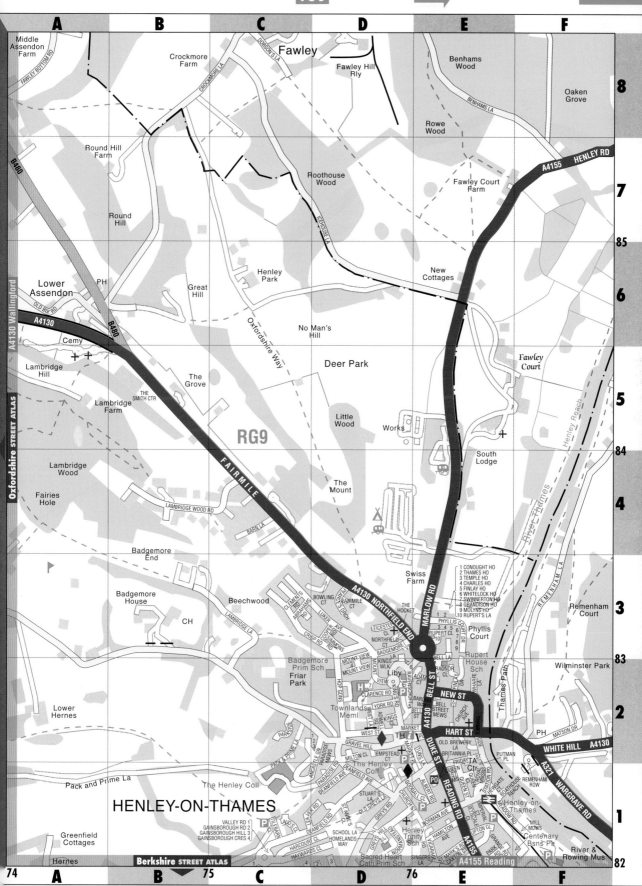

D2
1 CEDAR
2 BEECH
3 ACACIA
4 MOUNT VIEW CT
5 MARKET PLACE MEWS
6 KINGS RD UPPER
7 LAUREATE GDNS

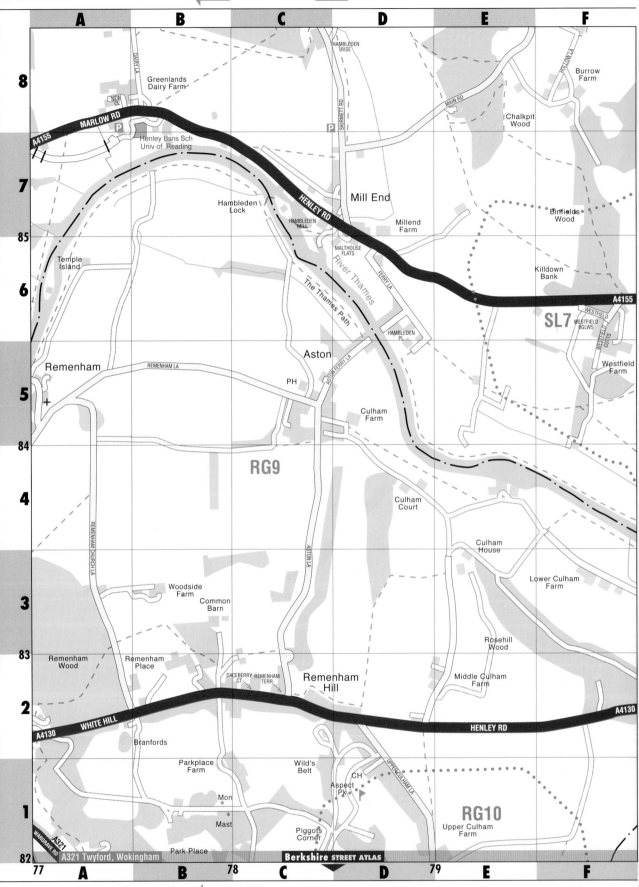

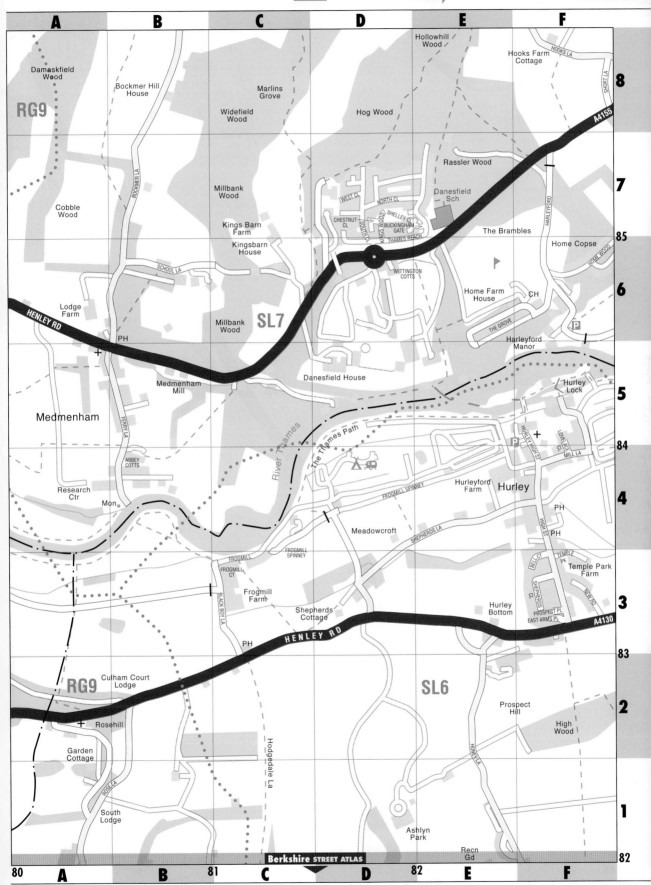

A B C D E F

8

Damaskfield
Wood

Bockmer Hill
House

Marlins
Grove

Hollowhill
Wood

Hooks Farm
Cottage

HOOKS LA

SHORT LA

RG9

Widefield
Wood

Hog Wood

A4155

7

Cobble
Wood

Millbank
Wood

Rassler Wood

Danesfield
Sch

BOCKMER LA

Kings Barn
Farm

WEST CL

NORTH CL

HARLEYFORD

The Brambles

85

Kingsbarn
House

CHESTNUT
CL

SHELLEY CT
BUCKINGHAM
GATE

SOUTH CL

KINGS WOOD

Thames Reach

Home Copse

HOME WOOD

6

Lodge
Farm

SCHOOL LA

SL7

WITTINGTON
COTTS

Home Farm
House

CH

P

HENLEY RD

PH

Millbank
Wood

Danesfield House

THE GROVE

Harleyford
Manor

5

Medmenham
Mill

FERRY LA

Medmenham

River Thames

The Thames Path

Hurley
Lock

HURLEY HIGH ST

LOVELACE CL

P

84

ABBEY
COTTS

FROGMILL SPINNEY

Hurleyford
Farm

MILL LA

Hurley

4

Research
Ctr

Mon

Meadowcroft

SHEPHERDS LA

Hurleyford
Farm

PH

HIGH ST

PH

FROGMILL

Frogmill
Spinney

BELL CT

TEMPLE
PK

Temple Park
Farm

3

FROGMILL
CT

BLACK BOY LA

Frogmill
Farm

Shepherds
Cottage

HENLEY RD

SHEPHERDS CL

Hurley
Bottom

PROSPECT PL
EAST ARMS PL

NEW RD

A4130

PH

83

RG9

Culham Court
Lodge

SL6

Prospect
Hill

2

ROSE LA

Rosehill

HODGEDALE LA

HONEY LA

High
Wood

Garden
Cottage

1

South
Lodge

Ashlyn
Park

Recn
Gd

82

80 A B 81 C D 82 E F

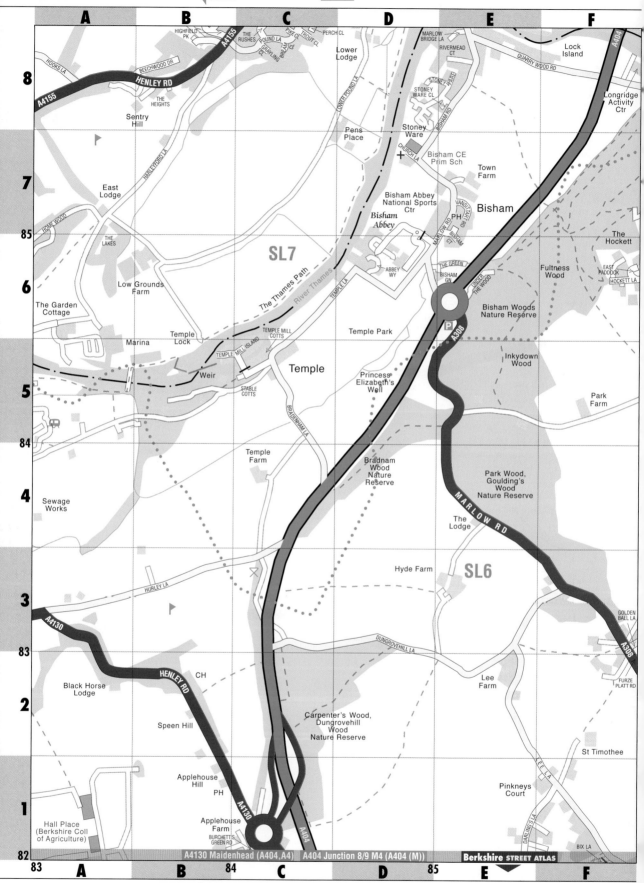

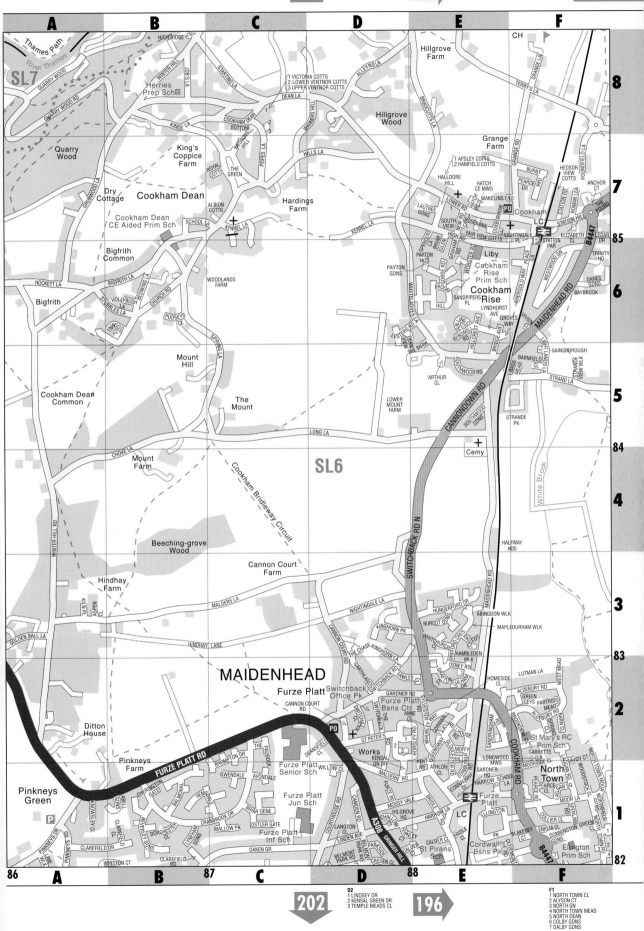

8

7

85

6

5

84

4

3

83

2

1

82

SL7

Thames Path

River Thames

Quarry Wood

Quarry Wood

Dry Cottage

Bigfrith Common

Bigfrith

Hockett La

Stubbles La

Inwood Cl

Hollybush La

Church Rd

Pudseys Cl

Spring La

Mount Hill

The Mount

Cookham Dean Common

Choke La

Mount Farm

Beeching-grove Wood

Hindhay Farm

Golden Ball La

Klnk La

Aspen Cl

Winter Hill Rd

Malders La

Hindhay Lane

Cannon Court Farm

Cannon Court Rd

MAIDENHEAD

Furze Platt

Cannon Court Rd

Ditton House

Pinkneys Farm

FURZE PLATT RD

Pinkneys Green

Pinkneys Dr

Pinkneys Rd

Winkfield Cl

Clarefield Cl

Clarefield Dr

Winston Ct

Clarefield Rd

Abell Gdns

Beverley Gdns

Cherington Gate

Dorchester Cl

Lynch Cl

Cranbrook La

Mallow Pk

Balmoral

Hemel Rd

Gwendale

Avondale

Briar Dene

Ostler Gate

Oaken Gr

Furze Platt Inf Sch

Belmont Park Rd

Parkside

Creden Cl

Courthouse Rd

Langton Cl

Linden Ave

Camden Rd

Furze Platt Jun Sch

Furze Platt Senior Sch

Willow Cl

The Paddock

Brompton Dr

High Ridge

Winter Hill

Job St La

Startins La

Herries Prep Sch

King's Coppice Farm

Cookham Dean

Cookham Dean CE Aided Prim Sch

School La

Kennel La

Woodlands Farm

Kings La

Cookham Dean Bottom

W Sisns Hill

Popes La

Royal Cotts

The Green

Albion Cotts

Groomwood La

Wagers Hill

Hills La

Dean La

1 Victoria Cotts
2 Lower Ventnor Cotts
3 Upper Ventnor Cotts

Alleyns La

Bradcotts La

Hillgrove Wood

Hillgrove Farm

Hardings Farm

Kennel La

Long La

SL6

Cookham Bridleway Circuit

Nightingale La

Malvern Rd

The Chase

Kinghorn Pk

Kinghorn La

Carthill Cl

Switchback Rd

Fawley

Burcot Gdns

Whitchurch Cl

Radcot

Hambleden Wlk

Osney Rd

Grafton Cl

Culham Dr

The Switchback

St Peter's

Gardner Rd

Anne Cl

Works

Kensal Gn

Queensway

Kent Rd

Athlone Cl

Whurley Way

Wellhouse Rd

Cornwall Cl

Moffy Hl

Harrow Cl

Gainey Rd

Connaught

Hurley

Silvester Rd

Hurley

Horsley Rd

Mossy Vale

Hilgrove Fd

Harrow La

Chapmon

Fenley

Calder Cl

Calder

Bridle Cl

Ellington

St Pirans Sch

Langhorn Hill

A308

Gringer Hill

CH

Grange La

Terry's La

Grange Rd

Grange Farm

1 Apsley Cotts
2 Hamfield Cotts

Burnt Cl

Pearce Dr

Hedsor View Cotts

Poundfield La

Anchor Ct

Hatch CE Mws

Wakelins End

Cookham

Station Hill

Station Rd

Roman Lea

Elizabeth Cl

Trinity Ho

Danes Gdns

Baybrook

Halldore Hill

Lower Rd

Southview

Rosebank

Fair View Cotts

Nightingale Pl

Cookham Rise

Cookham Rise Prim Sch

Liby

Spencers La

Briar Glen

High Rd

Graham La

Payton Hos

Gorse Cl

Broom Hill

Sandpipers Pl

Lyndhurst Ave

Groves Way

King La

Windmill La

Hillcrest Ave

Bridge Ave

Lesters Rd

Dean Cl

The Shaw

Arthur Cl

Southwood Rd

Southwood Gdns

Barnfield Cl

Strand La

Strand Rd

Gainsborough

Strande View Wlk

Strande Pk

CANNONDOWN RD

Maidenhead Rd

Whitelands La

Payton Gdns

Lautree Gdns

Webster Rd

Peace La

Shergold Way

Westwood Gn

Station Par

Cedar Dr

B4447

Lower Mount Farm

Cemy

SWITCHBACK RD N

Maidenhead Rd

Halfway Hos

Abingdon Wlk

Mapledurham Wlk

Hungerford Dr

Homeside Cl

Lutman La

West Mead

Aldebury Rd

Green Leys

Partridge Mead

Barn Cl

Longwood Mws

Gardner Rd

Moorside Cl

St Mary's RC Prim Sch

Garretts La

Savoy Cl

North Town Moor

Woodstock Cl

North Town

Cookham Rd

Pearce Rd

Moor La

Collier Cl

Donnington Gdns

Emilia Cl

Blakeney

Ellington Prim Sch

Cordwallis Bsns Pk

B4447

Furze Platt

White Brook

SWITCHBACK RD

Switchback Office Pk

Furze Platt Bsns Ctr

Deansfield Cl

D2
1 LINDSEY DR
2 KENSAL GREEN DR
3 TEMPLE MEADS CL

F1
1 NORTH TOWN CL
2 ALYSON CT
3 NORTH GN
4 NORTH TOWN MEAD
5 NORTH DEAN
6 COLBY GDNS
7 DALBY GDNS

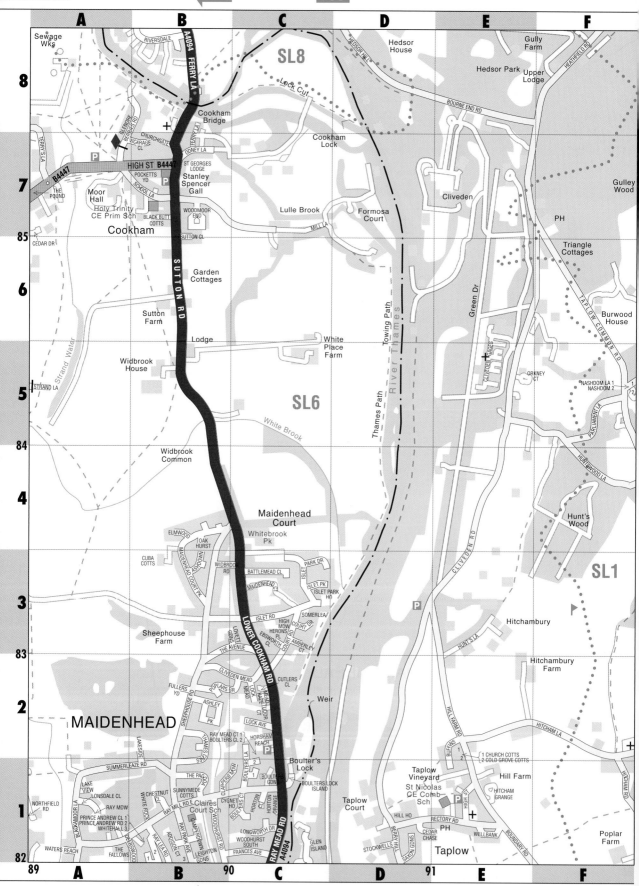

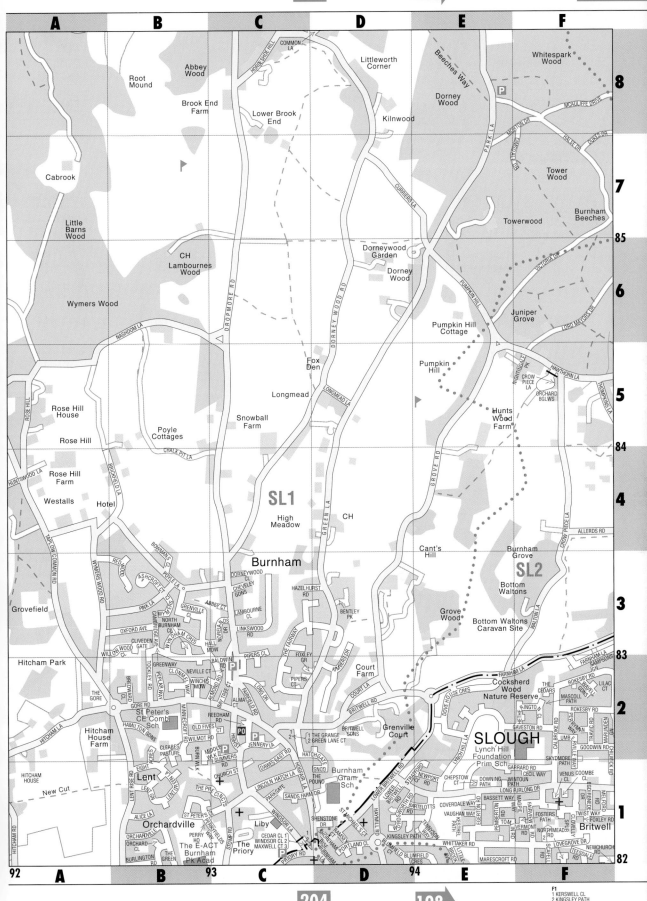

F1
1 KERSWELL CL
2 KINGSLEY PATH

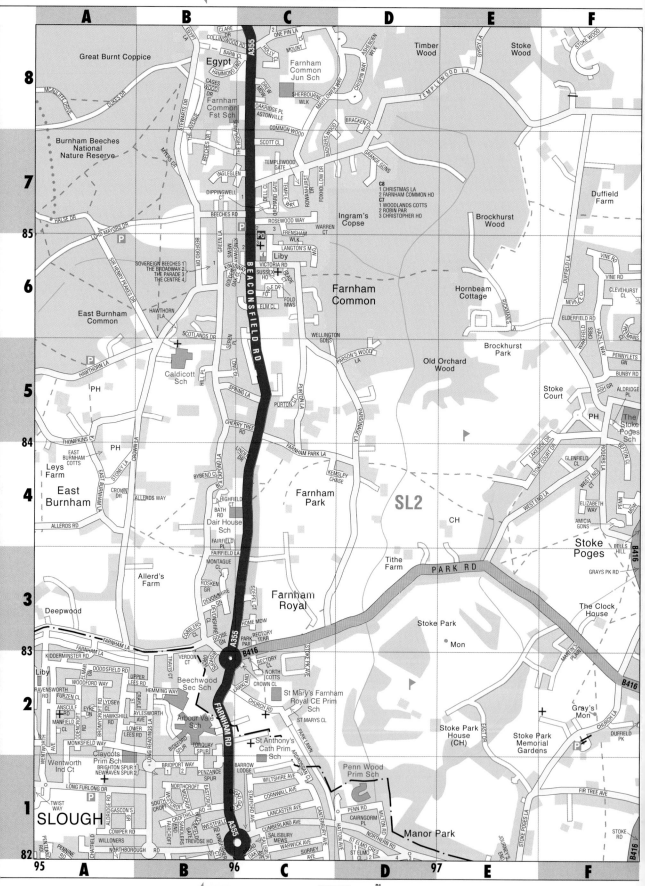

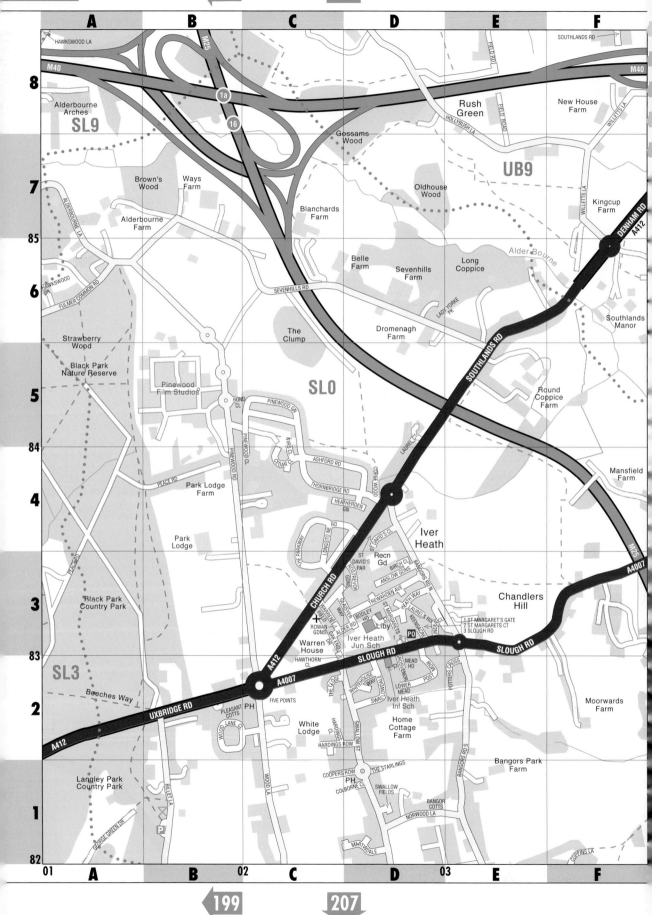

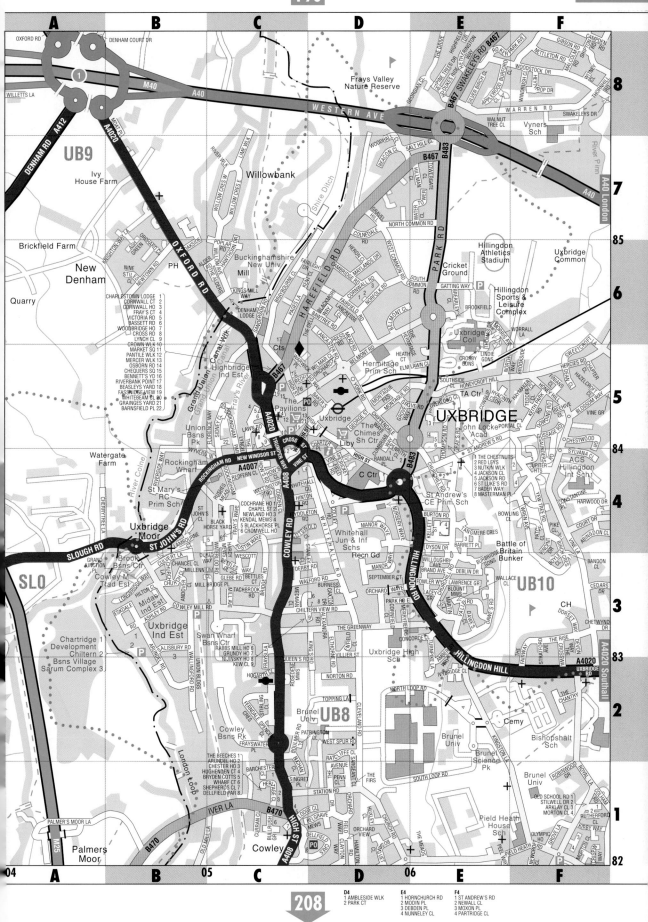

	D4	E4	F4
	1 AMBLESIDE WLK	1 HORNCHURCH RD	1 ST ANDREW'S RD
	2 PARK CT	2 MODIN PL	2 NEWALL CL
		3 DEBDEN PL	3 MOXON PL
		4 NUNNELEY CL	4 PARTRIDGE CL

B8
1 WELLINGTON CL
2 BUSHNELL PL
3 ST MATTHEWS CT
4 WOODBURY CL

D6
1 THE COURTYARD
2 VICARAGE MEWS
3 BHAMRA GDNS

E8
1 Gladstone
Ind Est

F7
1 WHITE HART RD
2 Nicholsons Sh Ctr
3 REGENT CT
4 FROGMORE CT
5 WHITCHURCH HO
6 KINGSWAY HO

7 WILBERFORCE MEWS
8 SYGNUS CT
9 PROVIDENCE PL
10 ST MARY'S WLK
11 OLD POST OFFICE LA
12 QUEEN'S LA
13 Heritage Ctr

14 KING ST
15 FOLLY HILL
GDNS

F8
1 COLBY GDNS
2 St Luke's
CE Prim Sch
3 NORTH TOWN RD

195

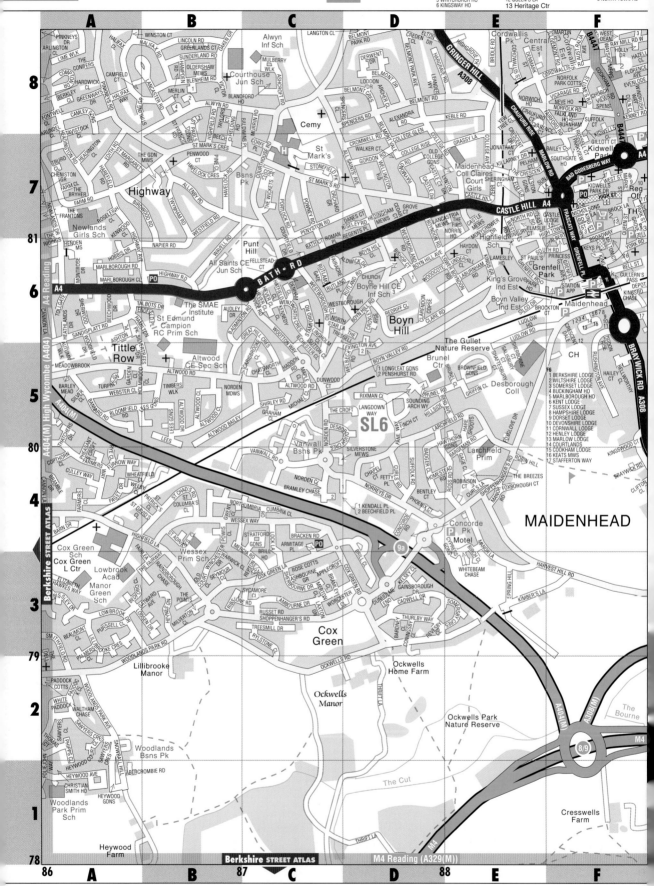

A8
1 HAZELL CL
2 FIRE STATION CT

A7
1 COLONNADE
2 GLYNWOOD HO
3 CHAPEL ARCHES
4 SWANBROOK CT
5 MOORLAND WAY

B7
1 SPRINGFIELD CT
2 WEXFORD CT
3 KINGSQUARTER

B8
1 PRINCE ANDREW CL
2 DEERSWOOD

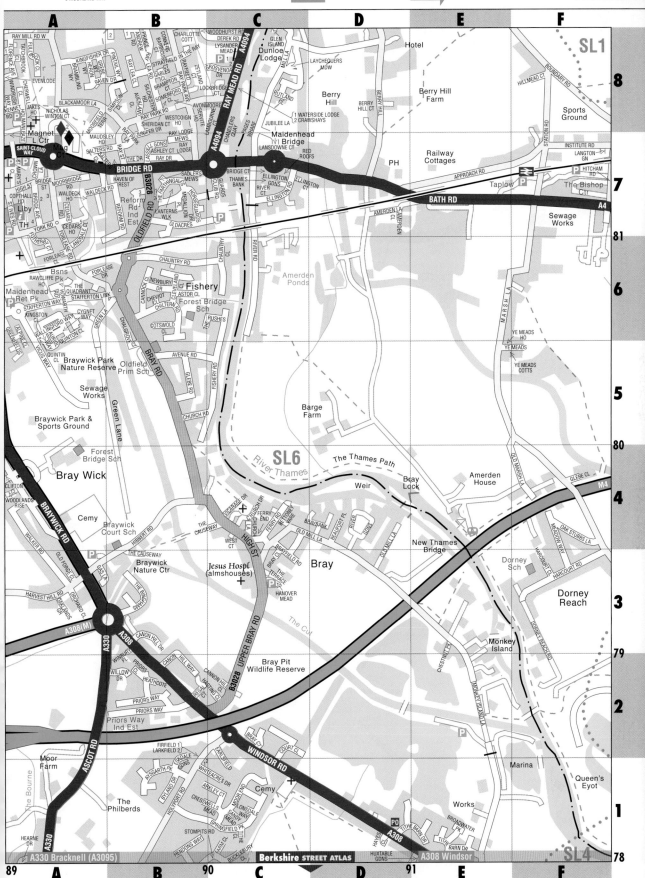

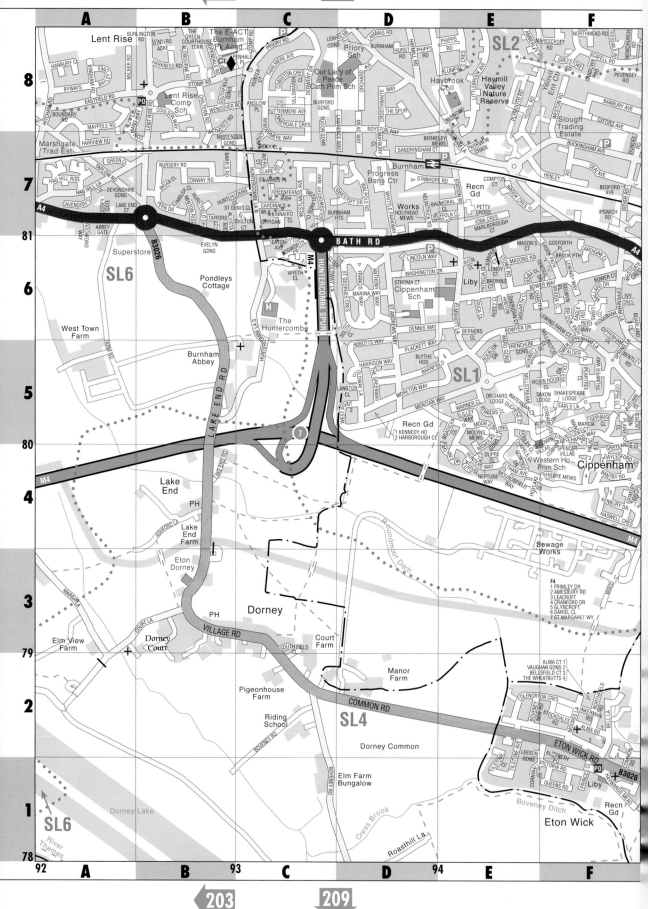

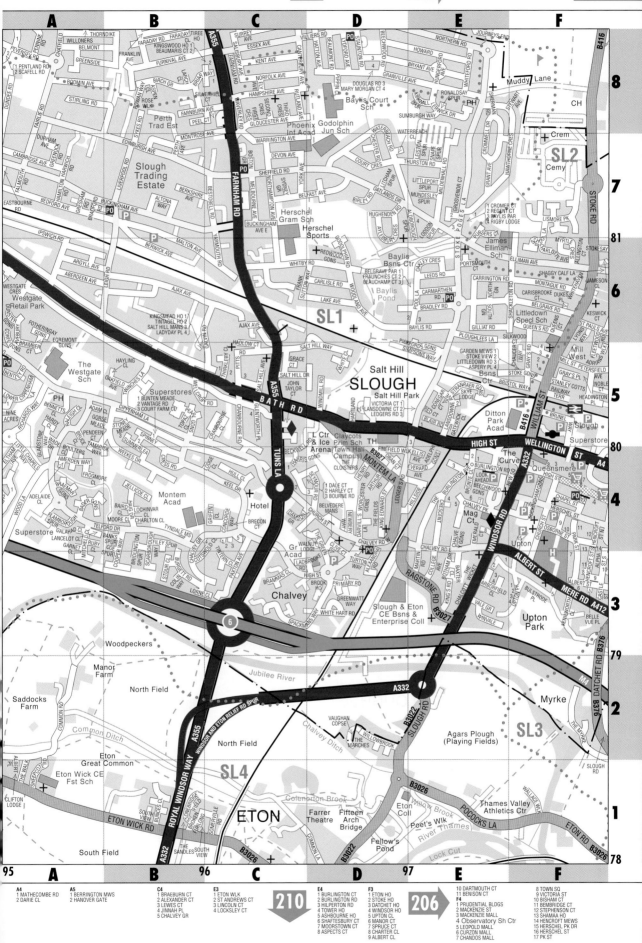

A4
1 MATHECOMBE RD
2 DARIE CL

A5
1 BERRINGTON MWS
2 HANOVER GATE

C4
1 BRAEBURN CT
2 ALEXANDER CT
3 LEWES CT
4 JINNAH PL
5 CHALVEY GR

E3
1 ETON WLK
2 ST ANDREWS CT
3 LINCOLN CT
4 LOCKSLEY CT

E4
1 BURLINGTON CT
2 BURLINGTON RD
3 HILPERTON RD
4 TOWER HO
5 ASHBOURNE HO
6 SHAFTESBURY CT
7 MOORSTOWN CT
8 ASPECTS CT

F3
1 ETON HO
2 STOKE HO
3 DATCHET HO
4 WINDSOR HO
5 UPTON CL
6 MANOR CT
7 SPRUCE CT
8 CHARTER CT
9 ALBERT CL

10 DARTMOUTH CT
11 BENISON CT
F4
1 PRUDENTIAL BLDGS
2 MACKENZIE ST
3 MACKENZIE MALL
4 OBSERVATORY SH CTR
5 LEOPOLD MALL
6 CURZON MALL
7 CHANDOS MALL

8 TOWN SQ
9 VICTORIA ST
10 BISHAM CT
11 BEMBRIDGE CT
12 STEPHENSON CT
13 SHAMAA HO
14 HENCROFT MEWS
15 HERSCHEL PK DR
16 HERSCHEL ST
17 PK ST

210   206

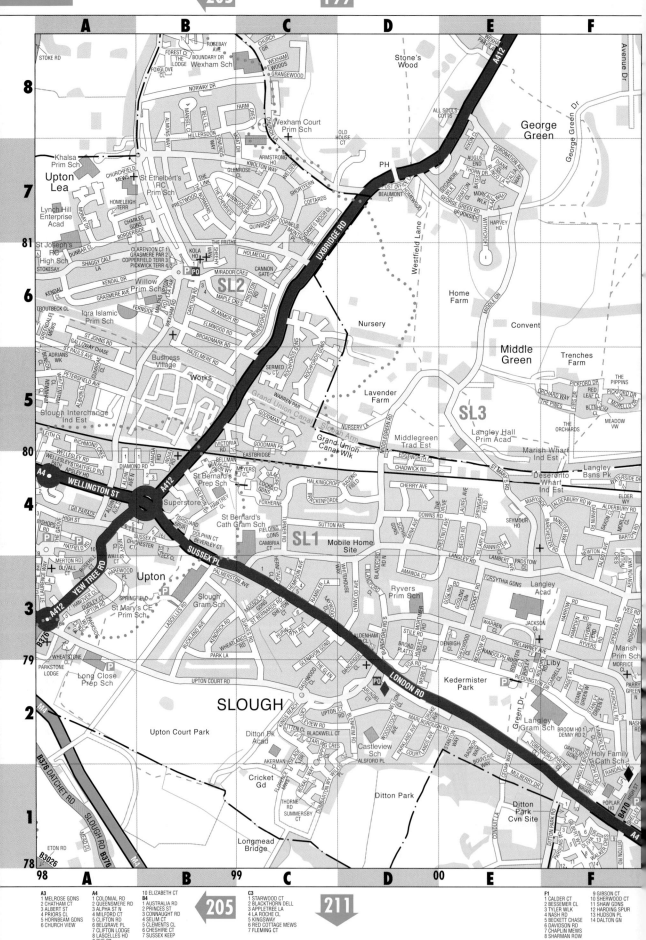

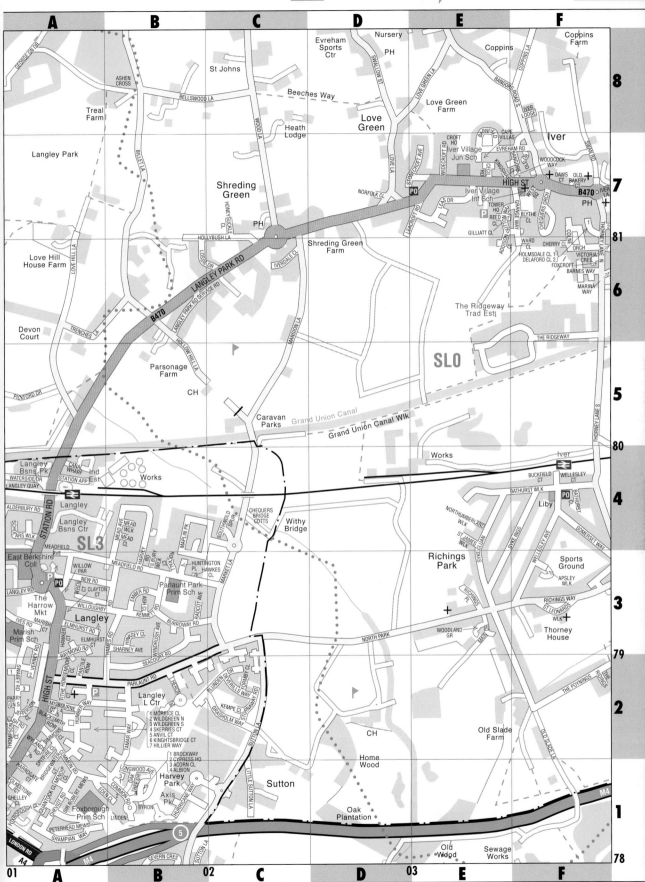

◄ 207   ▲ 201

YIEWSLEY

WEST DRAYTON

Cowley Peachey

UB8

UB7

SL0

SL3

Huntsmoor Park

Cowley Lake

Little Britain

Thorney Farm

Thorney

Mercers Farm

Thorney Country Park

Mayfield Cvn Pk

Riverside Cvn Pk

Meadow High Sch

Hillingdon

Stockley Acad

Young People's Acad

Hillingdon Tuition Ctr

West Drayton

Horton Road Ind Est

Horton Ind Pk

Recn Gnd

Cemy

Colne Brook

London Loop

Grand Union Canal Slough Arm

Grand Union Canal Walk

Frays River

River Colne

Wraysbury River

M25   M4   B470   A408   A3044

HIGH RD   FALLING LA   HOLLOWAY LA

Grand Union Office Pk

Packet Boat Marina

Tomo Ind Est

Zodiac Bsns Pk

Rainbow Ind Est

Thorney Mill Rd

Beeches Way

Trout La

◄ 207   ▲ 213

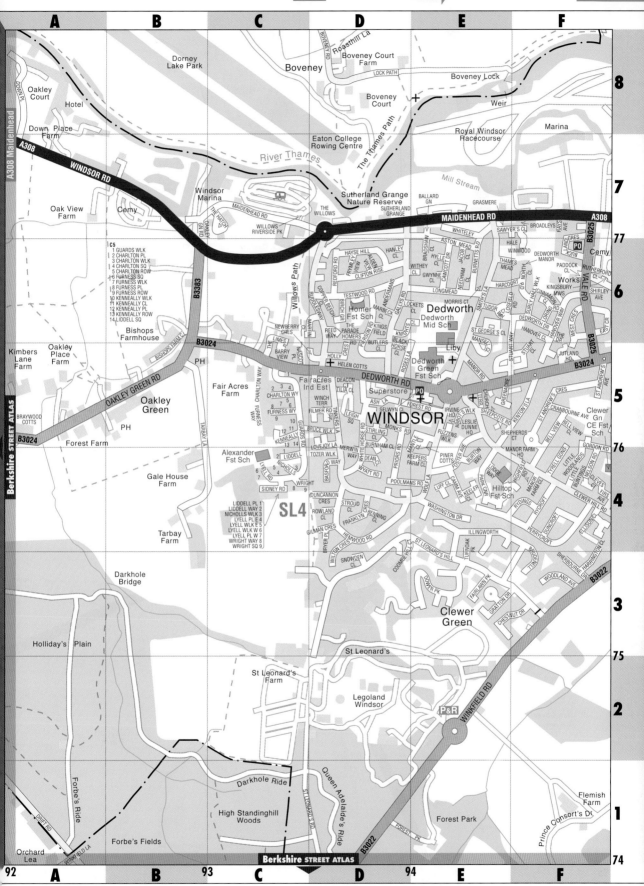

A5
1 ST ANDREWS COTTS   7 ST ANNES MWS
2 ALBION PL
3 ST CATHERINES CT
4 THE MEADS
5 BRIDGEMAN CT
6 CEDAR CT

A4
1 HUNSFORD LODGE
2 LAMBTON HO
3 PEMBERLEY LODGE
4 MERYTON HO
5 HIGHGATE
6 PINEWOOD PL

C5
1 GARFIELD PL
2 ST LEONARD'S AVE
3 ELIZABETH CT
4 CROSSWAYS CT
5 KNIGHTS PL
6 HOUSTON CT
7 WARWICK CT
8 CHELMSFORD CT
9 CAMPERDOWN HO

C6
1 BEAUMONT COTTS
2 KING EDWARD CT SERVICE RD
3 WARD ROYAL PAR
4 CHRISTIAN SQ
5 CRESCENT VILLAS
6 WARD ROYAL
7 BOWES-LYON CL

10 TRANSCEND

D6
1 WINDSOR ROYAL STA
2 THE CURFEW YD
3 HORSESHOE CLOISTERS

8 MOUNTBATTEN SQ
9 CHARLES HO
10 QUEEN ANNE'S CT
11 WESSEX CT
12 VISCOUNT CT
13 SHENSTON CT

4 LODGINGS OF THE MILITARY KNIGHTS
5 KING EDWARD CT
6 CHURCH ST
7 ST ALBANS CL
8 CHURCH LA
9 MARKET ST
10 QUEEN CHARLOTTE ST
11 AMBERLEY PL
12 PEASCOD PL
13 ROYAL FREE CT

14 ELLISON HO
15 SUN PAS
16 HIBBERT'S ALLEY
17 HENRY III TOWER
18 BURFORD HO
19 DARVILLE HO
20 RALSTON CT
21 VICTORIA CT
22 THE COURTYARD
23 MELLOR WLK

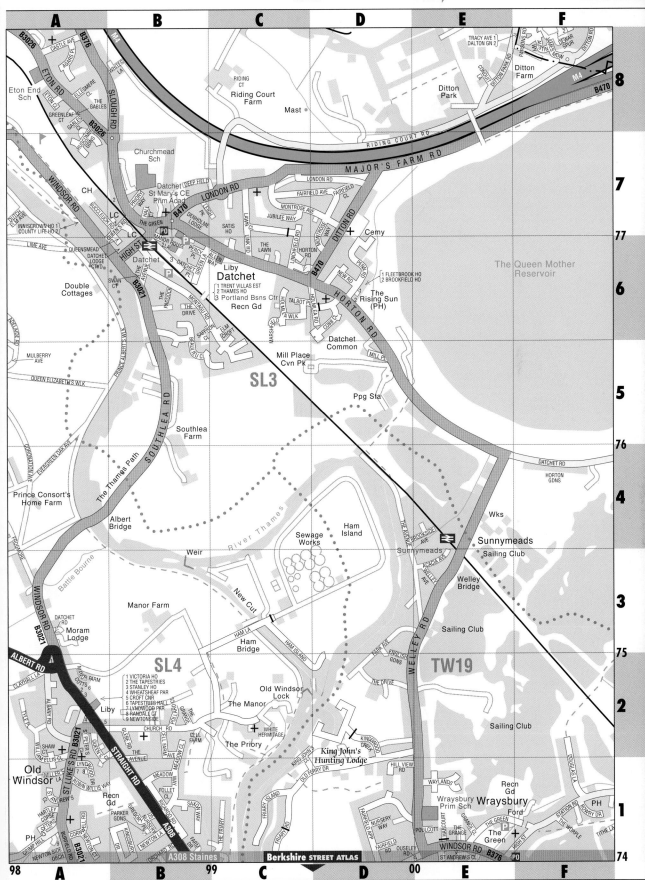

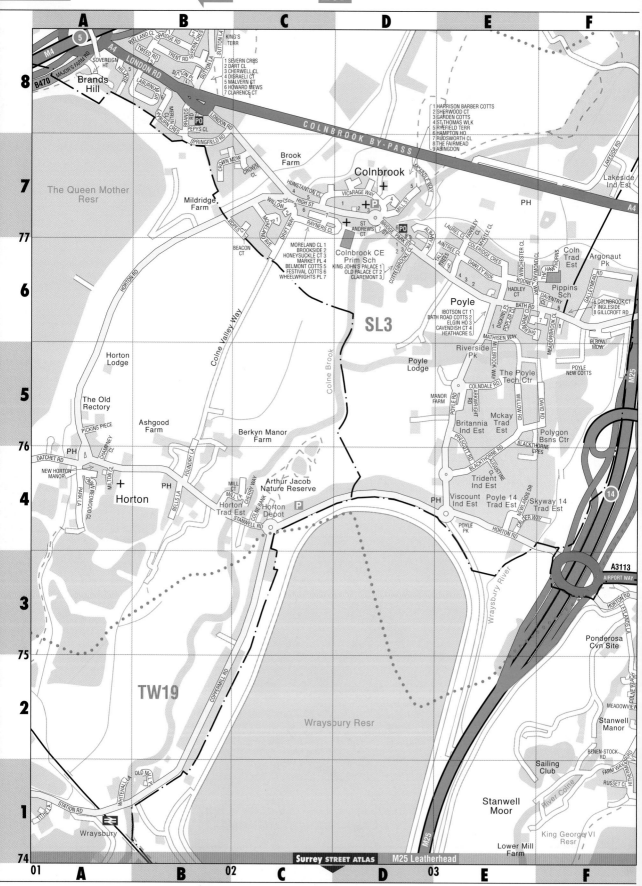

A **B** **C** **D** **E** **F**

8

Brands
Hill

1 SEVERN CRES
2 DART CL
3 CHERWELL CL
4 DISRAELI CT
5 MALVERN CT
6 HOWARD MEWS
7 CLARENCE CT

1 HARRISON BARBER COTTS
2 SHERWOOD CT
3 GARDEN COTTS
4 ST. THOMAS WLK
5 RYEFIELD TERR
6 HAMPTON HO
7 RUDSWORTH CL
8 THE FAIRMEAD
9 ABINGDON

COLNBROOK BY-PASS

Lakeside
Ind Est

7

The Queen Mother
Resr

Mildridge
Farm

Brook
Farm

Colnbrook

PH

77

MORELAND CL 1
BROOKSIDE 2
HONEYSUCKLE CT 3
MARKET PL 4
BELMONT COTTS 5
FESTIVAL COTTS 6
WHEELWRIGHTS PL 7

Colnbrook CE
Prim Sch

KING JOHN'S PALACE 1
OLD PALACE CT 2
CLAREMONT 3

Coln
Trad Est

Argonaut
Pk

6

Poyle

Pippins
Sch

SL3

1 IBOTSON CT 1
BATH ROAD COTTS 2
ELGIN HO 3
CAVENDISH CT 4
HEATHACRE 5

6 COLNBROOK CT
7 INGLESIDE
8 GILLCROFT RD

Horton
Lodge

Riverside
Pk

The Poyle
Tech Ctr

POYLE
NEW COTTS

5

The Old
Rectory

Ashgood
Farm

Berkyn Manor
Farm

Colne Valley Way

Poyle
Lodge

MANOR
FARM

Mckay
Trad Est

Polygon
Bsns Ctr

76

PH

New Horton
Manor

PH

Horton

Arthur Jacob
Nature Reserve

Britannia
Ind Est

Trident
Ind Est

4

Horton
Trad Est

Horton
Depot

Viscount
Ind Est

Poyle 14
Trad Est

Skyway 14
Trad Est

PH

POYLE
PK

14

A3113
AIRPORT WAY

3

Ponderosa
Cvn Site

75

TW19

Wraysbury Resr

2

Stanwell
Manor

Sailing
Club

1

Wraysbury

Stanwell
Moor

Lower Mill
Farm

King George VI
Resr

74

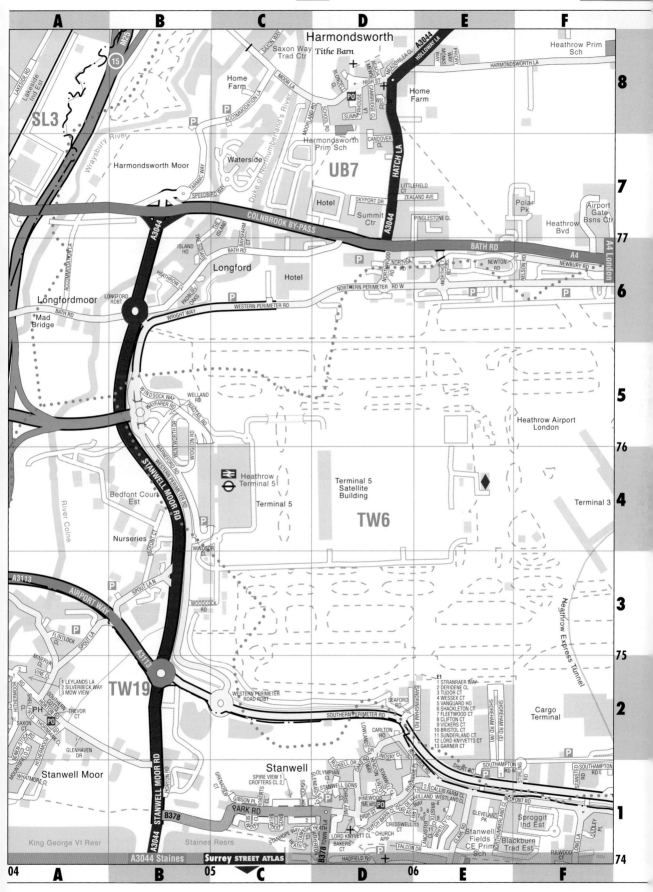

Index

Abbreviations used in the index

Acad	**Academy**	Comm	**Common**	Gd	**Ground**	L	**Leisure**	Prom	**Promenade**
App	**Approach**	Cott	**Cottage**	Gdn	**Garden**	La	**Lane**	Rd	**Road**
Arc	**Arcade**	Cres	**Crescent**	Gn	**Green**	Liby	**Library**	Recn	**Recreation**
Ave	**Avenue**	Cswy	**Causeway**	Gr	**Grove**	Mdw	**Meadow**	Ret	**Retail**
Bglw	**Bungalow**	Ct	**Court**	H	**Hall**	Meml	**Memorial**	Sh	**Shopping**
Bldg	**Building**	Ctr	**Centre**	Ho	**House**	Mkt	**Market**	Sq	**Square**
Bsns, Bus	**Business**	Ctry	**Country**	Hospl	**Hospital**	Mus	**Museum**	St	**Street**
Bvd	**Boulevard**	Cty	**County**	HQ	**Headquarters**	Orch	**Orchard**	Sta	**Station**
Cath	**Cathedral**	Dr	**Drive**	Hts	**Heights**	Pal	**Palace**	Terr	**Terrace**
Cir	**Circus**	Dro	**Drove**	Ind	**Industrial**	Par	**Parade**	TH	**Town Hall**
Cl	**Close**	Ed	**Education**	Inst	**Institute**	Pas	**Passage**	Univ	**University**
Cnr	**Corner**	Emb	**Embankment**	Int	**International**	Pk	**Park**	Wk, Wlk	**Walk**
Coll	**College**	Est	**Estate**	Intc	**Interchange**	Pl	**Place**	Wr	**Water**
Com	**Community**	Ex	**Exhibition**	Junc	**Junction**	Prec	**Precinct**	Yd	**Yard**

Index of towns, villages, streets, hospitals, industrial estates, railway stations, schools, shopping centres, universities and places of interest

Aba–Ald

A

Abacus Dr MK10 . . . . . 35 E2
Abbats Wood MK17. . 37 B1
Abbey Barn La
    HP10. . . . . 173 E3
Abbey Barn Rd
    HP11. . . . . 173 F4
Abbey Cl SL1 . . . . . . 204 E6
Abbey Cotts SL7 . . 193 B4
Abbey Ct
    Burnham SL1. . . . . . 197 C3
    Chesham HP5 . . . . . . 154 B6
Abbey Ctr The HP19 101 B2
Abbeydore Gr MK10 . 35 F1
Abbeyfield Ho HP16 152 A7
Abbey Gate SL6 . . . . 204 A7
Abbey Mead SL8 . . . 184 F5
Abbey Park La SL1 . 186 E2
Abbey Pl HP11 . . . . . 173 B6
Abbey Rd
    Aylesbury HP19. . . . . 101 B2
    Bourne End SL8. . . . . 184 F5
    Bourne End SL8. . . . . 185 A5
    Milton Keynes, Bradwell
        MK13 . . . . 34 A4
    Milton Keynes, Simpson
        MK6 . . . . 47 E5
    Syresham NN13 . . . . 27 C7
Abbey's Prim Sch
    MK3 . . . . 47 A2
Abbey Sq MK43 . . . . . . .8 E5
Abbey Terr MK16. . . . 22 D4
Abbey View Prim Acad
    HP11. . . . . 173 C4
Abbey Way
    Milton Keynes MK13 . . 34 B6
    Ravenstone MK46. . . . . 5 E2
Abbey Wlk HP16 . . . 152 B7
Abbey Wy SL7 . . . . . 194 D6
Abbot Ridge HP18. . 125 D5
Abbotsbury MK4 . . . 45 E2
Abbots Cl MK13 . . . . 34 B6
Abbotsfield MK6 . . . 47 B8
Abbots Way
    High Wycombe
        HP12. . . . . 172 D3

Abbots Way continued
    Monks Risborough
        HP27. . . . . 139 C5
Abbot's Wlk SL4 . . . 209 E5
Abbotswood HP27 . 150 C4
Abbotts Cl HP20. . . . 101 E1
Abbotts Rd HP20 . . . 101 E1
Abbotts Vale HP5 . . 144 C3
Abbotts Way
    Slough SL1 . . . . 204 D5
    Wingrave HP22. . . . . . 89 A4
Abbot Wlk HP18. . . . 125 D5
Abells Cl MK7. . . . . . . 47 F5
Abercrombie Rd
    SL6. . . . . 202 A1
Abercromby Ave
    HP12. . . . . 172 E8
Abercromby Ct 🖪
    HP12. . . . . 172 D8
Aberdeen Ave SL1. . 205 A6
Aberdeen Cl MK3 . . . 46 F2
Abigar Cl MK19 . . . . . 45 C8
Abingdon Cl
    🖪 Thame OX9. . . . . 125 F1
    Uxbridge UB10 . . . . . 201 F4
Abingdon Sch SL3. . 212 D7
Abington SL3. . . . . . . 212 D7
Abney Court Dr SL8 185 A2
Abraham Cl MK15 . . . 35 C6
Abrahams Cl MK3 . . . 46 F2
Abrahams Rd RG9. . 191 C3
Abstacle Hill HP23 . 118 F3
Acacia 🖪 RG9 . . . . . 191 D2
Acacia Ave
    West Drayton UB7. . . 208 F6
    Wraysbury TW19. . . . 211 E3
Acacia Cl HP5. . . . . . 144 A1
Acacia Gr HP4 . . . . . 135 B3
Acacia Ho SL9 . . . . . 177 E2
Acacia Mews UB7 . . 213 D8
Acacia Wlk HP23. . . 118 E3
Accommodation La
    Harmondsworth
        SL3. . . . . 213 A7
    Harmondsworth UB7 213 C8
Acker Bilk Dr 🖪
    MK17. . . . . 48 E8
Ackerman Cl MK18. . . 52 F8
Ackroyd Pl MK5. . . . . 46 B5
Acorn Bsns Ctr LU7. .78 F3

Acorn Cl
    High Wycombe
        HP13. . . . . 173 D7
    Slough SL3 . . . . 207 B1
Acorn Gdns HP12 . . 172 E4
Acorn Ho MK9 . . . . . 34 D2
Acorn Wlk MK9 . . . . . 34 E2
Acrefield Rd SL9 . . . 188 D8
Acre Pas SL4 . . . . . . 210 D6
Acres End HP7. . . . . 165 E8
Acres The HP13. . . . 161 E1
Acres Way HP19 . . . 101 C4
Acre The SL7 . . . . . . 183 F2
ACS Hillingdon Int Sch
    UB10. . . . . 201 F4
Adal Cl MK19 . . . . . . 33 C1
Adam Cl
    High Wycombe
        HP13. . . . . 173 D8
    Slough SL1 . . . . 205 A5
Adam Ct RG9 . . . . . . 191 E2
Adams Cl MK18 . . . . 41 C1
Adams Ct MK6 . . . . . 47 C8
Adams Park (Wycombe
    Wanderers FC)
        HP12. . . . . 172 A7
Adams Way HP23 . . 119 B6
Ada Wlk MK10 . . . . . 35 E2
Addenbrookes MK16 .22 F3
Addersley Mws MK46. .7 F7
ADDINGTON 65 A6
Addington Ave MK12 33 B6
Addington Cl SL4 . . 210 A4
Addington Cotts
    HP22. . . . . 131 B5
Addington Estate Rd
    MK18 . . . . 65 A6
Addington Estate Roads
    MK18 . . . . .64 F6
Addington Rd MK18 . 41 D1
Addington Terr
    MK18 . . . . 41 D1
Addison Cl SL0. . . . . 207 E6
Addison Ct SL6 . . . . 196 B1
Addison Rd
    Chesham HP5 . . . . . . 144 C2
    Steeple Claydon MK18 63 D2
Adelaide Cl SL1 . . . . 205 A4
Adelaide Rd
    High Wycombe
        HP13. . . . . 162 D1
    Windsor SL4 . . . . 210 F6
Adelaide Sq SL4 . . . 210 D5

Adelphi Gdns SL1 . . 205 E4
Adelphi St MK9 . . . . .34 F4
Adkins Cl HP19. . . . . 100 F3
Adkins Ct HP14 . . . . 158 E5
Admiralty Cl UB7. . . 208 F4
Admiral Way HP4 . . 134 F6
Adrians Wlk SL2 . . . 205 F5
ADSTOCK 53 F1
Adstock Fields
    Adstock MK17. . . . . . . 54 A1
    Adstock MK18. . . . . . . 53 F1
Adstock Mews 🗷
    SL9. . . . . 177 D2
Adstock Rd MK18 . . 53 E5
Adwell Sq RG9. . . . . 191 D2
Aerodrome Rd
    HP22. . . . . 117 B2
Aesop Rd HP22. . . . . 117 D2
Agars Pl SL3. . . . . . . 211 A8
Agase Way MK10. . . 36 D4
Agora Ctr MK12. . . . 33 D7
Agora Ctr (Sh Ctr) 🔳
    MK2. . . . . 58 C8
Aidan Cl HP21. . . . . . 116 A4
Aiken Grange MK10 . 35 E2
Ailward Rd
    Aylesbury HP19. . . . . 100 F2
    Aylesbury HP19. . . . . 101 A2
Ainsdale Cl MK3 . . . 46 D1
Aintree Cl
    Milton Keynes MK3 . . 57 C6
    Poyle SL3 . . . . 212 E6
Airport Gate Bsns Ctr
    UB7. . . . . 213 F7
Airport Way TW19. . 213 A3
Aiston Pl HP20. . . . . 101 F2
Ajax Ave
    Slough SL1 . . . . 205 B6
    Slough SL1 . . . . 205 C6
AKELEY 41 E8
Akeley Rd
    Akeley MK18. . . . . 41 D7
    Lillingstone Lovell
        MK18 . . . . 30 B8
Akeley Wood Jun Sch
    MK19 . . . . 31 A1
Akeley Wood Lodge Rd
    MK18 . . . . 41 D8
Akeley Wood Sch
    MK18 . . . . 41 C7
Akeley Wood Senior Sch
    MK18 . . . . 29 B4
Akeman Row HP22 . 116 F6

Akeman St HP23 . . . 119 A3
Akerlea Cl MK6 . . . . . 47 C6
Akerman Cl
    Milton Keynes MK12 . . 33 B5
    Slough SL1 . . . . 206 C2
Akister Cl MK18 . . . . 52 E8
Alan Ct HP14. . . . . . . 158 E4
Alan Way SL3 . . . . . . 206 E7
Alastair Mews HP9 . 175 F2
Albany Ct MK14 . . . . 34 D7
Albany Gate HP5. . . 144 B1
Albany Pk SL3 . . . . . 212 D7
Albany Pl HP19 . . . . 101 A2
Albany Rd
    Old Windsor SL4 . . . . 211 A2
    Windsor SL4 . . . . 210 D5
Albany Terr HP23 . . 119 B6
Albert Broccoli Rd
    UB9. . . . . 190 A6
Albert Cl 🖪 SL1 . . . . 205 F3
Albert Orchard
    HP22. . . . . 118 A4
Albert Pl SL4 . . . . . . 205 A1
Albert Rd
    Henley-on-Thames
        RG9. . . . . 191 E1
    West Drayton UB7. . . 208 E5
    Windsor SL4 . . . . 210 E3
Albert St
    Aylesbury HP20. . . . . 116 A8
    🖪 High Wycombe
        HP13. . . . . 173 C7
    Maidenhead SL6 . . . . 202 F7
    Milton Keynes MK2 . . 58 C8
    🖪 Slough SL1 . . . . . . 205 F3
    Tring HP23 . . . . 119 A3
    Windsor SL4 . . . . 210 B6
Albion SL3. . . . . 207 B1
Albion Cl SL2 . . . . . . 206 A5
Albion Cotts SL6 . . . 195 C7
Albion Cres SL6 . . . . 177 B7
Albion Ho HP12 . . . . 172 C5
Albion Pl
    Milton Keynes MK9 . . 35 A3
    🗷 Windsor SL4. . . . . 210 A5
Albion Rd
    Chalfont St Giles
        HP8. . . . . 177 B8
    High Wycombe HP12. 172 C5
    Pitstone LU7. . . . . . . 105 D5
Albion St HP20. . . . . 115 E8
ALBURY 136 B7
Albury Ct 🖪 MK8. . . .33 F1

Albury View
    Tiddington OX9 . . . . . 136 A6
    Tiddington OX9 . . . . . 136 A6
Albus Cl MK11 . . . . . .32 F3
Aldborough Spur
    SL1 . . . . 205 E7
Aldbourne Rd SL1. . 204 B8
ALDBURY. 120 D5
Aldbury CE Prim Sch
    HP23. . . . . 120 C6
Aldbury Gdns HP23. 119 B6
Aldbury Rd WD3 . . . 167 F2
Aldbury Rd SL6 . . . . 195 F2
Aldene Rd MK19 . . . . 11 B3
Aldenham MK6 . . . . . 47 D5
Aldenham Cl SL2. . . 206 D3
Alden View SL4 . . . . 209 D6
Alderbourne La SL3 199 E8
Alderbourne Manor
    SL9. . . . . 189 A1
Alderbury Rd SL3 . . 207 A4
Alderbury Road W
    SL3. . . . . 206 F4
Alder Cl SL1 . . . . 204 F5
Alder Ct MK14 . . . . . .21 F3
Aldergill MK13 . . . . . 34 C5
Alderley Ct HP4 . . . . 135 C3
Alderman Dr HP18 . 100 E5
Aldermead MK12. . . 33 E5
Alderney Ave MK3. . . 58 B4
Alderney Pl MK5 . . . .45 F4
Alderpark Mdw
    HP23. . . . . 104 A3
Alder Rd
    Aylesbury HP22. . . . . 116 C4
    Iver Heath SL0 . . . . . 200 D3
    New Denham UB9 . . . 201 C6
Alderson Cl 🖪
    HP19. . . . . 101 A2
Alderson Way HP17 127 B5
Alders The UB9 . . . . 201 C6
ALDERTON 9 A2
Alderton Dr HP4 . . . 121 B8
Alderton Rd NN12. . . 17 D8
Aldin Avenue
    North SL1 . . . . 206 A4
Aldin Avenue
    South SL1 . . . . 206 A4
Aldrich Dr MK15 . . . . 35 E7
Aldridge Pl SL2 . . . . 198 F5
Aldridge Rd SL2. . . . 198 A1
Aldwick Dr SL6 . . . . 202 D6
Aldwycks Cl MK5. . . .45 F4

Alexander Ct
High Wycombe
HP12 . . . . 172 E8
Slough SL1 . . . . 205 C4
Alexander Fst Sch
SL4 . . . . 209 C4
Alexander Ho 1
MK2 . . . . 58 C8
Alexander Rd HP20 101 D1
Alexander St HP5 . . 144 C1
Alexandra Ct
Leighton Buzzard LU7 . . 80 F8
4 Milton Keynes
MK13 . . . . 34 A4
Windsor SL4 . . . . 210 D5
Alexandra Dr MK16 . . 22 C2
Alexandra Pk HP11 . 173 A6
Alexandra Rd
High Wycombe
HP13 . . . . 173 E5
Maidenhead SL6 . . . . 202 D8
Slough SL1 . . . . 205 D3
Uxbridge UB8 . . . . . . 201 D3
Windsor SL4 . . . . 210 D5
Alford Pl MK3 . . . . 47 B1
Alford Rd HP12 . . . . . 172 C3
Alfred Burt Vc Cl 8
HP5 . . . . 144 C1
Alfred Ct SL8 . . . . . . 185 B3
Alfred Davis Ct SL7 183 D3
Alfred Way MK18 . . . . 52 B8
Alfriston Specl Sch
HP9 . . . . 175 C6
Alham Rd HP21 . . . . 115 C6
Alice Cl HP15 . . . . . . 163 C7
Alice La SL1 . . . . 197 B1
Alladale Pl MK12 . . . . 33 D4
Allanson Rd SL7 . . . 183 F3
Allenby Rd SL6 . . . . . 202 B7
Allen Cl MK2 . . . . 58 C5
Allen Dr HP14 . . . . . . 161 C8
Allen Way SL3 . . . . . 211 C6
Allerds Rd SL2 . . . . . 198 A4
Allerds Way SL2 . . . . 198 B4
Allerford Ct MK4 . . . . 46 C4
Alleyns La SL6 . . . . . 195 D8
Allhusen Gdns SL3 . 199 E8
Allhusen Pl SL2 . . . . 199 A5
Allington Circ MK4 . . 45 E1
Allington Ct SL2 . . . 205 F6
Allison Ct MK15 . . . . . 35 C1
Allkins Ct SL4 . . . . . . 210 D5
Allnutts Cl HP14 . . . . 158 E5
Allonby Way HP21 . . 116 B7
All Saints' Ave SL6 . 202 D7
All Saints CE Jun Sch
SL6 . . . . 202 C6
All Saints Cl MK17 . . . 44 C1
All Saints View MK5 . 46 B8
All Souls Cotts SL3 . 206 E8
Allyn Cl HP13 . . . . . 173 C8
Alma Ct
Burnham SL1 . . . . . . 197 C2
Eton Wick SL4 . . . . . 204 F2
Alma Rd
Berkhamsted HP4 . . 134 E6
Chesham HP5 . . . . . 144 C2
Eton Wick SL4 . . . . . 204 F2
Windsor SL4 . . . . . . 210 C6
Alma St HP18 . . . . . . 100 D4
Almhouses MK14 . . . . 21 E1
Almond Cl
Newport Pagnell
MK16 . . . . 22 B3
Windsor SL4 . . . . . . 210 B5
Almond Rd SL1 . . . . 197 C2
Almond Tree Dr
HP22 . . . . 116 C4
Almond Way HP27 . 139 A2
Almond Wlk HP15 . . 163 B3
Almons Way SL2 . . . 206 B8
Almshouses
Eton SL4 . . . . 210 D7
Old Windsor SL4 . . . . 210 F1
Worminghall HP18 . . 123 E5
Almshouses The MK46 5 E2
Alnwick Dr HP23 . . . 103 F7
Alpha Ct HP7 . . . . . . 165 B7
Alpha Street N 3
SL1 . . . . 206 A4
Alpha Street S SL1 . 205 F3
Alpine Cl SL6 . . . . . . 203 A6
Alpine Croft MK5 . . . . 46 A3
ALSCOT 139 A5
Alscot La HP27 . . . . 139 A5
Alsford Pl SL1 . . . . . 206 D2
Alsford Wharf HP4 . 135 C5
Alston Dr MK13 . . . . . . 33 F3
Alstonefield 1 MK4 . 46 B3
Alston Gdns SL6 . . . 202 E7
Altair Rd
7 Milton Keynes
MK10 . . . . 35 E2
Oakgrove MK10 . . . . . 35 E2
Althorpe Cres MK13 . 34 B6
Altona Rd HP10 . . . . 174 D3
Altona Way SL1 . . . . 205 B7
Alton Bsns Pk HP19 101 B1
Alton Gate MK4 . . . . . 45 F3
Altwood Bailey SL6 . 202 B5
Altwood CE Sch
SL6 . . . . 202 B5
Altwood Cl
Maidenhead SL6 . . . . 202 B5
Slough SL1 . . . . 204 E8
Altwood Dr SL6 . . . . 202 B5
Altwood Rd SL6 . . . . 202 B5
Alverton MK14 . . . . . . 34 F8
Alvista Ave SL6 . . . . 204 B7
Alvric Way 3 MK12 . . 33 A6
Alwin Cl HP21 . . . . . 115 C4
Alwins Field LU7 . . . . 80 D8
Alwyn Inf Sch SL6 . . 202 C8
Alwyn Rd SL6 . . . . . . 202 B8
Alyngton HP4 . . . . . . 134 E7
Alyson Ct 2 SL6 . . . 195 F1
Amanda Ct SL3 . . . . 206 D3
Amber Cl HP18 . . . . . 100 E5
Amber Cotts HP7 . . . 164 F3
Ambergate MK16 . . . . 36 B4
Amberley Ct SL6 . . . 196 C3
Amberley Pl 11 SL4 210 D6
Amberley Rd SL2 . . . 204 E8
Amberley Way
UB10 . . . . 201 E3
Amberley Wlk MK4 . . 45 E1
Amblers Way MK18 . . 53 A1
Ambleside
Amersham HP6 . . . . . 154 C2
Aylesbury HP21 . . . . . 116 B5
Ambleside Wlk UB8 201 D4
Ambridge Gr MK6 . . . 35 C1
Ambridge La MK17 . . . 48 F8
Ambrose Ct MK15 . . . 35 C2
Amelias La MK9 . . . . . 35 A3
Amerden Cl SL6 . . . . 203 D7
Amerden La SL6 . . . . 203 D7
Amerden Way SL1 . . 205 A4
AMERSHAM 154 B2
AMERSHAM
COMMON 165 E8
Amersham Ct HP7 . . 165 A7
Amersham Field Study
Centre HP7 . . . . 164 B6
Amersham Hill
HP13 . . . . 173 B7
Amersham Hill Dr
HP13 . . . . 173 C8
Amersham Hill Gdns
HP13 . . . . 173 C8
Amersham Hospl
HP7 . . . . 165 A6
Amersham Mus★
HP7 . . . . 165 B7
AMERSHAM OLD
TOWN 165 A7
AMERSHAM ON THE
HILL 154 D2
Amersham Pl HP7 . . 166 C8
Amersham Rd
Beaconsfield HP7 . . . 176 A6
Chalfont Common HP8,
SL9 . . . . 177 D6
Chalfont St Giles HP8 166 B2
Chalfont St Peter SL9 177 E2
Chesham HP6 . . . . . . 154 B5
Chorleywood WD3 . . . 167 C8
Denham Green SL9 . . 189 A4
Gerrards Cross SL9 . . 188 F7
Hazlemere HP15 . . . . 162 E2
High Wycombe HP13 . 173 C8
Little Chalfont HP6 . . 166 E8
Little Missenden HP7 152 F3
Little Missenden HP7 153 C2
Penn HP7 . . . . 164 B5
Amersham Sch HP7 165 E7
Amersham Sta/U Sta
HP6 . . . . 154 C1
Amersham Way
HP6 . . . . 166 E8
Amersham & Wycombe
Coll HP10 . . . . 173 E2
Amesbury Rd
Slough SL1 . . . . 204 F4
2 Slough SL1 . . . . . . 204 F4
Ames Cl MK6 . . . . 46 F8
Amherst Ct MK15 . . . 35 C7
Amicia Gdns SL2 . . . 198 F4
Amorosa Gdns
HP18 . . . . 100 E5
Amos Ct MK13 . . . . . . 34 A6
Ampleforth 2 MK10 . 36 B1
Amy La HP5 . . . . 154 B7
Ancastle Gn RG9 . . . 191 D1
Ancell Rd MK11 . . . . . 32 E5
Anchor Ct SL6 . . . . . 195 F7
Anchor La 1 HP20 . 115 E8
Ancona Gdns 1 MK5 45 F3
Andania La MK17 . . . . 36 E3
Andermans SL4 . . . . 209 D6
Andersen Gate MK4 . 57 A7
Anderson Cl HP14 . . 158 F4
Anding Cl MK46 . . . . . . 6 E4
Andover Cl UB8 . . . . 201 B3
Andrewes Croft
Great Linford MK16 . . . 21 F1
Milton Keynes MK14 . . 34 F8
Andrew Hill La SL2 . 187 C3
Andrews Cl LU7 . . . . . 69 E3
Andrews Reach SL8 185 A2
Andrews Way
Aylesbury HP19 . . . . 115 A7
Marlow Bottom SL7 . . 183 C8
Andromeda Chase
MK17 . . . . 36 E3
Anershall HP22 . . . . . 89 B3
Angdale Rd HP17 . . . 126 B1
Angel Cl MK15 . . . . . . 35 A7
Angelica Cl UB7 . . . . 208 F7
Angelica Ct MK7 . . . . 48 A5
Angels Cl MK18 . . . . . . 65 F4
Anglefield Rd HP4 . 135 B4
Anglesey Ct
Milton Keynes MK8 . . . 46 A8
Stokenchurch HP14 . . 158 E5
Anglesey View MK17 58 B3
Angling Spring Wood
Talking Trail HP16 . 151 F7
Anglo Bsns Pk
HP19 . . . . 101 A1
Angood Cl HP27 . . . . 139 A3
Angora Cl MK5 . . . . . . 46 A3
Angstrom Cl MK5 . . . 46 B5
Angus Dr MK3 . . . . 46 F2
Angus Rd HP19 . . . . 101 A3
Angus Way MK8 . . . . . 45 C7
Anjou Terr 8 MK8 . . . 45 C7
Anne Cl SL6 . . . . 195 E2
Annes Gr MK14 . . . . . . 21 D1
Annesley Rd MK16 . . 22 B3
Annet Pl MK3 . . . . 58 B4
Anns Cl
Aylesbury HP21 . . . . 116 A4
Tring HP23 . . . . 118 E3
Ansculf Rd SL2 . . . . . 198 A2
Anslow Gdns SL0 . . 200 D3
Anslow Pl SL1 . . . . . 204 C8
Anson Cl
Aylesbury HP21 . . . . 115 E4
Bovingdon HP3 . . . . . 145 F4
Anson Rd MK12 . . . . . 33 C6
Anstey Brook HP22 . 117 A3
Anstey Cl HP18 . . . . . . 99 B6
Anstey Ct HP18 . . . . . 99 B7
Anthony Cl HP13 . . . 161 F1
Anthony Ct MK11 . . . . 32 D5
Anthony Way SL1 . . 204 D6
Antigua Wy MK3 . . . . . 58 C4
Antolian Ave MK8 . . . . 33 C1
Antonia Wy 2 MK16 . 36 B5
Anton Way HP21 . . . 115 D3
Anvil Cl HP3 . . . . 146 B3
Anvil Ct SL3 . . . . 207 A2
Anxey Way HP17 . . . 126 F6
Aplin Rd HP21 . . . . . 116 C6
Apollo Ave MK11 . . . . . 32 F3
Apollo Cl HP18 . . . . . 100 D4
Appleacres MK17 . . . . 69 D8
Appleby Heath MK2 . 58 D6
Apple Cotts HP3 . . . 146 A4
Applecroft
Berkhamsted HP4 . . . 134 E6
Maidenhead SL6 . . . . 202 C3
Newton Longville
MK17 . . . . 57 D4
Appledore Gr 3
MK16 . . . . 36 B5
Applefield HP7 . . . . 166 C7
Appleton Cl HP7 . . . 166 B7
Appleton Mews 4
MK4 . . . . 46 B3
Appletree Ave UB7,
UB8 . . . . 208 F7
Appletree Cl HP22 . . 117 D5
Apple Tree Cl
Leighton Buzzard
LU7 . . . . 80 D6
Loudwater HP13 . . . . 174 A4
Appletree La 3
SL3 . . . . 206 C3
Appletree Wlk HP5 154 D5
Applewick La HP12 . 172 C8
Applewood Cl UB10 201 E8
Appleyard Pl 1 MK6 34 E1
Approach Rd SL6 . . . 203 E7
Approach The MK8 . . 33 E2
Apsley Cotts SL6 . . . 195 E7
Apsley Ho SL1 . . . . . 206 A4
Apsley Wlk SL0 . . . . 207 F3
Aqua Vale Swimming &
Fitness Ctr HP20 . . 115 F8
Aquila Gdns MK11 . . . 33 A3
Aquitania Cl MK16 . . . 36 C5
Aragon Way HP22 . . 102 E3
Aran Ct MK13 . . . . 34 B8
Aran Hts HP8 . . . . . . 177 B6
Arborfield Cl SL1 . . . 205 E3
Arbour Vale Sch
SL2 . . . . 198 B2
Arbour View HP7 . . . 166 B8
Arbroath Cl MK3 . . . . 46 E3
Arbrook Ave MK13 . . . 34 D3
Arcade The HP9 . . . . 175 E3
Archdale 1 HP11 . . 173 A6
Archer Cl SL6 . . . . . . 202 D8
Archer Ct HP6 . . . . . 154 C2
Archer Dr HP20 . . . . 102 A2
Archers Ct SL7 . . . . . 183 E1
Archers Way HP14 . 171 B5
Archers Wells MK3 . . 47 B2
Archer Terr UB7 . . . 208 E6
Archery The MK12 . . . 33 B7
Archford Croft MK4 . 46 C3
Arch Gr HP18 . . . . . . 100 E5
Archive Cl HP22 . . . . 117 D5
Archive Mews HP4 . 135 A2
Arch Way
High Wycombe
HP13 . . . . 173 A7
Speen HP27 . . . . 150 B4
Archways 14 HP20 . . 115 D8
Arden Cl HP3 . . . . . . 146 A3
Ardenham La HP19 101 D1
Ardenham St HP19 . 101 C1
Arden Park MK12 . . . . 33 B7
Ardley Mews 7
MK10 . . . . 36 B3
Ardrossan Cl SL2 . . . 198 C1
Ardwell La MK12 . . . . 33 B5
Ardwick Cl LU7 . . . . 118 E3
Ardys Ct MK5 . . . . 46 B8
Arena MK MK1 . . . . . . 47 C3
Argonaute Wharf
MK17 . . . . 36 F3
Argonaut Pk SL3 . . . 212 F6
Argus Way MK17 . . . . 36 D3
Argyle Ave HP19 . . . 101 B2
Argyll Ave SL1 . . . . . 205 A6
Argyll Ho MK3 . . . . 46 F1
Aries Ho HP10 . . . . . 185 A8
Aris Way MK18 . . . . . . 52 D6
Arkley Cl UB8 . . . . . . 201 F1
Arkley Ct SL6 . . . . . . 203 C1
Arklow Ct WD3 . . . . . 167 D5
Ark Royal MK16 . . . . . 36 B5
Arkwright Mews
MK14 . . . . 34 C8
Arkwright Rd SL3 . . 212 E5
Arlington Cl SL6 . . . 202 A8
Arlington Ct MK4 . . . . 46 E3
Arlott Cres MK6 . . . . . 46 F8
Armada Ave 3 MK16 36 C4
Armitage Pl SL6 . . . . 202 C4
Armourer Dr MK14 . . . 34 F6
Armstrong Cl MK8 . . . 45 E7
Armstrong Ho SL2 . 206 C7
Armstrongs Fields
HP22 . . . . 102 D2
Arncliffe Dr MK13 . . . 34 B5
Arncott Rd
Boarstall OX5 . . . . 94 D4
Piddington OX25 . . . . . 95 D7
Arncott Way HP19 . . 100 F1
Arncott Wood Rd
OX25 . . . . 94 E6
Arne La MK7 . . . . 48 D5
Arnison Ave HP13 . . 162 D1
Arnold Cl HP22 . . . . 116 C2
Arnold Cott MK19 . . . 32 C7
Arnold Ct HP21 . . . . 115 F6
Arnold Pl MK1 . . . . . . 47 E3
Arnolds Cl MK18 . . . . . 53 A1
Arnold's Cotts HP5 . 143 B4
Arnos Gr MK10 . . . . . . 35 F1
Arnott's Yd HP18 . . . 125 D6
Arranmore Ho
HP11 . . . . 174 B4
Arrewig La HP5 . . . . 142 E8
Arrow Pl MK2 . . . . 58 D4
Artemis Grove MK17 . 36 E3
Arthur Cl SL6 . . . . . . 195 E5
Arthur Jacob Nature
Reserve SL3 . . . . . . 212 C4
Arthur Rd
Slough SL1 . . . . 205 D4
Windsor SL4 . . . . . . 210 C6
Artichoke Dell WD3 167 E4
Aruba Cl MK3 . . . . 58 B3
Arundel Cl SL6 . . . . . 202 A8
Arundel Ct SL3 . . . . . 206 D2
Arundel Gn HP20 . . . 101 F2
Arundel Gr MK3 . . . . . 57 E7
Arundel Ho
1 High Wycombe
HP13 . . . . 173 F7
Uxbridge UB8 . . . . . . 201 C1
Arundel Rd
High Wycombe
HP12 . . . . 172 B6
Uxbridge UB8 . . . . . . 201 B2
Ascension Gdns MK3 58 B4
Ascot Dr LU7 . . . . 80 D6
Ascot Ho MK9 . . . . 34 C2
Ascot Pl MK3 . . . . 57 D7
Ascot Rd SL6 . . . . . . 203 A1
ASCOTT 80 A2
Ascott Ct HP20 . . . . 101 E1
Ascott House★ LU7 . 80 A2
Ascott Rd HP20 . . . . 101 E1
Ascough Cl HP19 . . . 101 D3
Ashbourne End
HP21 . . . . 115 D4
Ashbourne Gr SL6 . . 202 C3
Ashbourne Ho 5
SL1 . . . . 205 E4
Ashbrook Sch MK8 . . 33 E1
Ashburnham Cl 2
MK3 . . . . 46 D1
Ashburnham Cres
LU7 . . . . 80 E6
Ashburnham Dr
HP14 . . . . 150 A1
Ashby MK6 . . . . 47 A8
Ashby Rd HP4 . . . . . 134 D7
Ashby Villas LU7 . . . . 92 A1
Ash Cl
Aylesbury HP20 . . . . 102 A2
Slough SL3 . . . . 207 B3
Walter's Ash HP14 . . 161 B8
Ashcroft Ct SL1 . . . . 197 B3
Ashcroft Dr UB9 . . . 189 F4
Ashcroft Rd SL6 . . . . 202 C8
Ashcroft Terr HP23 . 119 A5
Ashdene Cl MK16 . . . . 36 E8
Ashdown SL6 . . . . . . 196 B3
Ashdown Cl MK14 . . . 35 A8
Ashdown Ct HP13 . . 173 D6
Ashdown Rd HP13 . . 174 A8
Ashdown Way HP6 . 154 D2
Ashen Cross SL3 . . . 207 B8
Ashenden Wlk SL2 . 198 D8
ASHENDON 97 F1
Ashendon Rd
Dorton HP18 . . . . 97 B2
Westcott HP18 . . . . . . 98 C6
Wotton Underwood
HP18 . . . . 97 B3
ASHERIDGE 143 C6
Asheridge Rd HP5 . . 144 A2
Asheridge Rd Ind Est
HP5 . . . . 144 A2
Ashfield MK14 . . . . . . 34 D8
Ashfield Barn Rd
RG9 . . . . 169 D4
Ashfield Cl HP15 . . . 163 B2
Ashfield Cotts UB9 . 190 A1
Ashfield Gr MK2 . . . . . 58 C7
Ashfield Rd HP5 . . . . 144 D2
Ashfield Rise HP18 109 D5
Ashfield Way HP15 . 163 B3
Ashfold Sch HP18 . . 110 F8
Ashford Cl HP21 . . . 116 A5
Ashford Cres MK8 . . . 45 D6
Ashford La SL4 . . . . . 204 B4
Ashford Rd SL0 . . . . 200 C4
Ash Furlong La
Biddlesden MK18 . . . . 27 B1
Finmere NN13 . . . . 39 F1
Ash Gn UB9 . . . . 201 B6
Ash Gr
Amersham HP6 . . . . . 154 A3
Aylesbury HP21 . . . . . 116 A7
Chesham HP5 . . . . . . 144 B2
Stoke Poges SL2 . . . . 198 F5
West Drayton UB7 . . . 208 F6
Ashgrove MK18 . . . . . 63 D2
Ashgrove Gdns HP22 86 E7
Ash Hill Prim Sch
HP13 . . . . 174 A7
Ash Hill Rd MK16 . . . . 22 B4
Ash La SL4 . . . . 209 D5
Ashland Rdbt MK1 . . 47 C5
Ashlea MK46 . . . . 6 E3
Ashlea Rd SL9 . . . . . 177 E1
Ashleigh Cl HP7 . . . . 165 E8
Ashley HP10 . . . . 185 F7
Ashley Cl LU7 . . . . . . 105 A8
Ashley Ct
15 Aylesbury HP19 . . 115 A8
Maidenhead SL6 . . . . 203 B7
Tylers Green HP10 . . 163 B1
West Drayton UB7 . . . 208 E5
Ashley Dr HP10 . . . . 163 C1
ASHLEY GREEN 144 F7
Ashley Green Rd
HP5 . . . . 144 E5
Ashley Pk SL6 . . . . . 196 B2
Ashley Rd UB8 . . . . . 201 B3
Ashley Row
Aylesbury HP20 . . . . 101 F1
Aylesbury HP20 . . . . 102 A1
Ashleys WD3 . . . . . . 167 F2
Ashlyns Ct HP4 . . . . 135 B3
Ashlyns Gr HP4 . . . . 135 B2
Ashlyns Rd HP4 . . . . 135 B3
Ashlyns Sch HP4 . . . 135 C2
Ashmead Comb Sch
HP21 . . . . 115 C5
Ash Mead Dr UB9 . . 190 A2
Ashmead La UB9 . . . 190 A2
Ashmead Pl HP7 . . . 166 C8
Ashmead St HP18 . . 100 D6
Ashmount Cres 1
SL1 . . . . 205 A4
Ashotts La
Chartridge HP5 . . . . . 143 A5
Chartridge HP5 . . . . . 143 B7
Ashover 5 MK10 . . . . 36 C4
Ashpidge Pk HP4 . . . 121 A6
Ashpole Furlong
MK5 . . . . 46 B7
Ash Rd
High Wycombe
HP12 . . . . 172 C4
Princes Risborough
HP27 . . . . 139 B3
Tring HP23 . . . . 118 F4
Tring HP23 . . . . 119 A4
Ashridge OX39 . . . . . 147 B6
Ashridge Cl
1 Bovingdon HP3 . . . 146 A3
Milton Keynes MK3 . . . 57 D7
Ashridge Coll Gdns★
HP4 . . . . 121 D5
Ashridge Cotts HP4 121 E5
Ashridge Est Visitor
Ctr★ HP4 . . . . 120 E6
Ashridge Executive
Education HP4 . . . . 121 C5
Ashridge La HP5 . . . 155 D7
Ashridge Pk HP23 . . 120 F6
Ashridge Rd
Nettleden HP1 . . . . . 121 E1
Potten End HP4 . . . . 135 F8
Ashridge Rise HP4 . 134 F5
ASHTON 9 E8
Ashton Pl SL6 . . . . . . 202 A6
Ashton Rd NN12 . . . . . . 9 D8
Ash Tree Ho HP12 . . 172 C4
Ashtree Wlk HP15 . . 163 B2
Ashurstwood 5 MK7 48 A8
Ash Vale WD3 . . . . . . 178 D5
Ashwells HP10 . . . . . 174 B8
Ashwells Manor Dr
HP10 . . . . 174 C8
Ashwell St 1 LU7 . . . . 80 F8
Ashwells Way HP8 . 177 D8
Ashwood MK13 . . . . . 34 A7
Ashwood Dr HP5 . . . 144 B1
Askerton Cres 7
MK4 . . . . 56 E8
ASKETT 139 D6
Askett La HP27 . . . . . 139 D7
Askett Village La
HP27 . . . . 139 C7
Aspen Cl
Aylesbury HP20 . . . . 102 A2
Maidenhead SL6 . . . . 195 A3
Slough SL2 . . . . 205 B8
West Drayton UB7 . . . 208 F5
Aspen Rd HP10 . . . . . 173 D3
Aspens Pl HP1 . . . . . 146 F8
Aspery Pl SL1 . . . . . . 205 F5
Asplands Cl MK17 . . . 49 B4
Aspley Ct
Aylesbury HP19 . . . . . 101 C1
Woburn Sands MK17 . . 49 C3
ASPLEY GUISE 49 F4
Aspley Guise Lower Sch
MK17 . . . . 49 F4
Aspley Guise Sta
MK17 . . . . 49 D6
ASPLEY HEATH 49 A2
Aspley Hill MK17 . . . . 49 C4
Aspley La MK17 . . . . . 49 E2
Aspley Woods View
MK17 . . . . 48 D2
Aspreys MK46 . . . . 6 E4
Assheton Rd HP9 . . . 175 E4
Astlethorpe MK8 . . . . . 33 F2
Astley Pl HP23 . . . . . 119 F5
Astley Rd OX9 . . . . . . 126 B1
ASTON 192 C5
ASTON ABBOTTS 88 D5
Aston Abbotts Rd
Cublington LU7 . . . . . . 78 C1
Cublington LU7 . . . . . . 88 C8
Weedon HP22 . . . . 87 E1
Aston Cl
Aylesbury HP19 . . . . . 101 A3
Milton Keynes MK5 . . . 46 B5
ASTON CLINTON . . . 117 D6
Aston Clinton Bypass
Aston Clinton HP22 . . 117 D7
Drayton Beauchamp
LU7 . . . . 118 B5
Aston Clinton Ragpits
Wildlife Reserve
HP22 . . . . 117 F2
Aston Clinton Rd
HP22 . . . . 116 E6
Aston Clinton Sch
HP22 . . . . 117 D5
Aston Ferry La RG9 192 D5
Aston Hill OX49 . . . . 157 E7
Aston Hill Chivery
Aston Clinton HP22 . . 117 F1
Aston Clinton HP22 . . 132 A8
Aston Clinton LU7 . . . 118 A1
Aston La RG9 . . . . . . 192 C3
Aston Mead SL4 . . . . 209 E6
Aston Rd HP17 . . . . . 127 B5
Aston Rowant National
Nature Reserve★
HP14 . . . . 157 E6
ASTON
SANDFORD 127 D4
Astonville SL2 . . . . . 198 C8
Astor Cl SL6 . . . . 203 B6
Astronomy Way 12
HP19 . . . . 115 A8
ASTROPE 104 A3
Astrope La
Long Marston HP23 . . 104 B3
Puttenham HP23 . . . . 103 F2
ASTWOOD 16 A3
Astwood Rd MK43 . . . 25 C7
Athelstan St MK18 . . . 52 B8
Athens Ave HP21 . . . 115 F3
Atherstone Ct MK8 . . 33 C2
Atherstone La
HP22 . . . . 102 D3
Atherton Cl TW19 . . 213 D1
Atherton Ct SL4 . . . . 210 D7
Athlone Cl SL6 . . . . . 195 E1
Athlone Sq SL4 . . . . 210 C5
Atkins Cl MK13 . . . . . . 34 B3
Atkinson Way MK10 . . 36 E2
Atkins Way HP22 . . . 116 E7
Atlanta Way HP21 . . 115 F3
Atlantic Ave MK10 . . . 36 D4
Atlas Ho HP5 . . . . . . 144 B1
Atlas Wy MK10 . . . . . . 35 E2
Atterbrook MK13 . . . . 34 A4
ATTERBURY 36 A4
Attika Cl MK16 . . . . . . 22 F3
Attingham Hill
5 Milton Keynes
MK8 . . . . 33 F1
Milton Keynes MK8 . . . 34 A1
Atwell Cl MK8 . . . . 45 E7
Auckland Cl SL6 . . . 203 B8
Auckland Pk MK1 . . . . 47 D4
Auckland Rd HP13 . . 173 E6
Auden Cl MK16 . . . . . . 22 A5
Audley Dr SL6 . . . . . . 202 B6
Audley Mead MK13 . . 34 B3
August End SL3 . . . . 206 E7
Augustine Cl SL3 . . . 212 E4
Augustine Mews
HP16 . . . . 152 B7
Augustus Rd MK11 . . . 32 E4
Augustus Smith Ho 2
HP4 . . . . 135 D4
Aurelia Cl MK11 . . . . . 33 A3
Aureol La MK10 . . . . . 36 B5
Auriol Way SL6 . . . . . 203 A6
Austen Ave MK46 . . . . . 7 A4
Austen Pl HP19 . . . . . 100 F2
Austenway SL9 . . . . . 188 E8
AUSTENWOOD 188 C8
Austenwood Cl
Chalfont St Peter
SL9 . . . . 177 C1
High Wycombe HP11 . 173 A4

Austenwood Comm La
SL9 . . . . 188 D8
Austenwood La SL9 177 D1
Austins Ct MK2. . . . . 47 E1
Austins Mead HP3. . 146 B3
Austin Way SL3 . . . . 211 F8
Austin Waye UB8. . . 201 C4
Australia Ave SL6 . . 202 F8
Australia Rd 🞂 SL1. 206 B4
Austwick La MK4. . . . 46 B2
Autumn Cl
Aylesbury HP19. . . . 101 A3
Slough SL1 . . . . . . 204 F5
Autumn Dr HP27 . . 138 D6
Autumn Wlk SL6 . . . 202 A5
Autumn Way UB7 . . 208 F4
Avalon Rd SL8 . . . . . 185 B5
Avalon St HP10 . . . . 185 D3
Avant Bsns Ctr MK1 . 47 C2
Avebury SL1. . . . . . . 205 A6
Avebury Bvd MK9 . . . 34 E2
Avebury Rdbt MK9 . . 34 D1
Aveling Rd HP13 . . 173 C6
Avenue Cl UB7 . . . . 208 D3
Avenue Dr
Iver Heath SL0 . . . . 199 F1
Slough SL3 . . . . . . 206 F8
Avenue Ho HP5 . . . 154 B8
Avenue Rd
Buckingham MK18 . . . 41 E3
Maidenhead SL6 . . . 203 B5
Winslow MK18 . . . . . 65 F4
Avenue The
Amersham HP7 . . . . 154 C1
Bourne End SL8 . . . 184 F4
Chinnor OX39 . . . . 147 D6
Datchet SL3. . . . . . 211 B6
Dunstable LU6. . . . . 93 E7
Farnham Common
SL2 . . . . 198 B8
Maidenhead SL6 . . . 196 C3
Old Windsor SL4 . . . 211 B2
Princes Risborough
HP27. . . . . 139 C4
Uxbridge UB8 . . . . 201 D1
Whitfield NN13 . . . . 26 D4
Worminghall HP18 . . 123 E5
Wraysbury TW19 . . 211 D4
Averdal Dr HP18 . . 100 E5
Averil Ct SL6. . . . . . 204 C7
Avery Ave HP13 . . . 161 D2
Avery Ct MK16 . . . . . 22 C2
Ave The MK17. . . . . . 49 E5
Avington MK8. . . . . . 33 E1
Avocet Way HP19 . . 101 E3
Avonbury Ct NN13. . . 38 A5
Avon Cl
Newport Pagnell
MK16 . . . . 22 D3
Slough SL1 . . . . . . 204 E6
Avondale SL6 . . . . . 195 C1
Avon Gr MK3. . . . . . . 57 E8
Avonmoore SL6. . . . 203 B8
Avon Pl HP21 . . . . . 115 D4
Axis Pk SL3 . . . . . . 207 B1
Axtell Way HP22 . . 116 D7
Aydon Ct MK3. . . . . . 57 E7
AYLESBURY 115 D7
Aylesbury Bsns Ctr
HP19. . . . . 101 B1
Aylesbury Cres
SL1 . . . . 205 D6
Aylesbury End HP9 . 175 D1
Aylesbury Gram Sch
HP21. . . . . 115 F7
Aylesbury High Sch
HP21. . . . . 115 F7
Aylesbury Ind Ctr 🞂
HP19. . . . . 101 C1
Aylesbury Rd
Aston Abbotts HP22 . . 88 E2
Aston Clinton HP22 . . 117 B5
Aston Clinton HP22 . . 117 B5
Aston Clinton HP22 . . 117 C5
Bierton HP22 . . . . . 102 B3
Blackthorn HP18. . . . 81 D4
Cuddington HP18 . . 113 A3
Fleet Marston HP19 . 100 A5
Great Missenden
HP16. . . . . 141 F2
Haddenham HP17,
OX9. . . . . 126 C6
Monks Risborough
HP27. . . . . 139 D6
Thame OX9 . . . . . . 125 F2
Tring HP23 . . . . . . 118 E2
Waddesdon HP18. . . . 99 E6
Wendover HP22 . . . 130 F7
Wendover HP22 . . . 131 B6
Wing HP22 . . . . 89 C7
Wing LU7. . . . . 79 E1
Aylesbury St
Milton Keynes, Bletchley
MK2 . . . . 58 E8
Milton Keynes, Wolverton
MK12 . . . . 33 D6
Aylesbury Sta HP20 115 D7
Aylesbury Street W
MK12 . . . . 33 C6
Aylesbury UTC
HP21. . . . . 115 C7
Aylesbury Vale Acad
HP18. . . . . 100 E4
Aylesbury Vale Parkway
Sta HP18 . . . . . . 100 D3

Aylesbury Waterside
Theatre HP20 . . . . 115 E8
Aylesford Gr MK10 . . 36 A1
Ayless Cl HP18 . . . . . 98 B7
Ayleswater HP19. . . 101 E4
Aylesworth Ave SL2 198 B2
Aylward Gdns HP5 . 144 A1
Aynho Ct MK8. . . . . . 45 F8
Ayres Cl HP21. . . . . 115 B6
Ayreshire Way MK8 . 45 C7
Ayrshire Cl HP19 . . 101 A3
Ayrton Cl MK8 . . . . . 45 D6
Ayr Way MK3 . . . . . . 46 E2
Aysgarth Pk SL6 . . . 203 B1
Azalea Cl HP15. . . . . 163 A3
Azalea Way SL3 . . . 206 E7

B
Babbage Gate MK10. 35 E2
Babington Cl MK10 . . 36 A3
Babington Rd HP22 131 D6
Babylon Gr 🔟 MK4 . . 45 F1
Baccara Gr MK2. . . . . 58 C7
Bacchus La
Milton Keynes MK11 . . 32 F3
Milton Keynes MK11 . . 33 A3
Bachelors Acre SL4 210 D6
Back La
Chalfont St Giles
HP8. . . . . 177 A7
Great Missenden
HP16. . . . . 152 B7
Tingewick MK18 . . . . 51 A6
Backleys MK7. . . . . . 48 A2
Back St
Gawcott MK18 . . . . . 51 F4
Thornborough MK18 . . 53 F8
Thornborough MK18 . . 54 A8
Wendover HP22 . . . 131 B4
Backs The HP5. . . . . 154 C8
Backwell St HP22 . . 102 D4
Bacombe Hill Nature
Reserve HP22. . . . 131 A3
Bacombe La
Wendover HP22 . . . 131 B3
Wendover HP22 . . . 131 B3
Bacon Hill MK46 . . . . 6 E3
Baconsmead UB9 . . 190 A2
Bader Gdns SL1 . . . 205 A4
Bader Way UB8 . . . 201 E5
Badgebury Rise
SL7 . . . . 183 C7
Badgemore Cl MK4. . 33 C2
Badgemore La RG9 191 D3
Badgemore Prim Sch
RG9. . . . . 191 D2
Badger Cl
Brackley NN13 . . . . . 26 A2
High Wycombe HP11. 173 A5
Maidenhead SL6 . . . 202 D4
Badgers Cl MK43. . . . 25 B2
Badgers Gate LU6. . . 93 E8
Badgers Holt 🞂
MK17. . . . . 49 A5
Badgers Mdw HP22 131 C5
Badgers Oak MK7 . . . 48 B7
Badgers Rise HP17 . 114 C5
Badgers Way
Buckingham MK18 . . . 52 E7
Marlow Bottom SL7. 183 D7
Badgers Wlk WD3. . . 167 F5
Badgers Wood SL2 . 198 C2
Badger Way HP15. . . 163 B5
Bad Godesberg Way
SL6 . . . . 202 F7
Badmington Ct 🞂
HP7. . . . . 165 B7
Badminton Ho 🞂
HP7. . . . . 165 B7
Badminton Rd SL6 . 202 B6
Badminton View
MK8 . . . . 34 A1
Badrick Rd HP19 . . . 100 F2
Baghill La HP17 . . . . 126 C6
Bagley Cl UB7. . . . . 208 E4
Bagmoor La RG9 . . . 181 B6
Bagshot Ct MK2. . . . . 58 C7
Bailey Cl
High Wycombe
HP13. . . . . 173 C7
Maidenhead SL6 . . . 202 F7
Windsor SL4 . . . . . 210 A5
Bailey Ho 🞂 SL8 . . . 185 U4
Bailey's Ct 🔟 HP20 115 D8
Baily Cl MK5. . . . . . . 46 A5
Baines Ho HP11 . . . 173 F4
Baird Cl SL1 . . . . . . 205 B4
Baird Pl 🞂 HP22 . . . 131 D6
Baisley Ho MK2 . . . . . 58 D8
Baker Gr 🞂 MK17 . . . 48 E8
Bakers Cl
Stoke Goldington
MK16 . . . . 12 B5
Turvey MK43. . . . . . . 8 E5
Bakers Ct
Stanwell TW19 . . . . 213 D1
Waddesdon HP18 . . . 99 A6
Bakers La NN12 . . . . . 9 A8
Baker's Orch HP10 . 185 E6
Baker's Piece Ho
OX39 . . . . 147 A4
Baker St
High Wycombe
HP11. . . . . 172 F7

Baker St *continued*
Waddesdon HP18. . . . 99 A6
Bakers View MK16 . . 13 F2
Bakers Wlk HP22 . . 116 F2
Bakers Wood UB9 . . 189 D3
BAKER'S WOOD . . . 189 D3
Bakery Cl
Cranfield MK43 . . . . . 25 B1
Grendon Underwood
HP18. . . . . 83 A6
Bakery Ho 🔟 HP20 . 115 D8
Bakery Mws HP16 . . 152 A7
Bala Cl MK2. . . . . . . 58 D5
Bala Lake Cres MK10 36 B4
Bala Way MK2 . . . . . . 58 C5
Balbina Way MK11. . 32 F3
Balcary Gdns MK4 . . 134 F3
Balcary Gr 🞂 MK4. . . . 56 F8
Balderstone Rd MK7 48 D7
Baldways Cl HP22 . . . 89 C3
Baldwin Cres MK16. . 22 C3
Baldwin Rd
Beaconsfield HP9 . . 176 B1
Burnham SL1. . . . . 197 C2
Baldwins Pl SL6. . . . 202 C7
Baldwin's Shore
SL4 . . . . 210 D8
Balfe Mews MK7 . . . . 48 D4
Balfour Mews 🞂
HP3. . . . . 146 A4
Balfour Pl SL7 . . . . . 183 D4
Balfour Way HP20. . 101 E2
Balham's La
Stonor RG9 . . . . . . 179 F8
Turville RG9. . . . . . 169 A1
Ballard Cl HP21 . . . . 116 B5
Ballard Gn SL4. . . . . 209 E7
Ballards Row HP22 117 D6
BALLINGER
COMMON 142 E3
Ballinger Ct HP4 . . . 135 B3
Ballinger Grange
HP16. . . . . 142 E2
Ballinger Rd HP16. . 142 E1
Ballinger Row
HP16. . . . . 142 D3
Ball Moor MK18. . . . . 52 D6
Balmer Bridge MK18 52 E5
Balmer Cut MK18. . . . 52 E6
Balmerino MK10. . . . 36 B2
Balmoral SL6. . . . . . 195 B1
Balmoral Cl SL1. . . . 204 E7
Balmoral Ct
High Wycombe
HP13. . . . . 173 B7
Newport Pagnell MK16 22 B3
Balmoral Gdns SL4 210 D4
Balsam Cl MK7. . . . . . 48 B6
Balwen Cl MK18 . . . . 41 D2
Balwen Gr MK19 . . . . 45 D8
Bamburgh Gate MK4 45 E1
Bamfords La MK43 . . . 8 E1
Bamfords Yd MK43 . . . 8 E5
Bampton Cl MK4 . . . . 46 E2
Banburies Cl MK3 . . . 47 A3
Banbury Ave SL1. . . 204 F8
Banbury Rd MK18 . . . 50 C6
Bancroft MK1. . . . . . 33 F5
Bancroft Rdbt MK13. 34 A5
Bancroft St HP23. . . 104 F7
Bandon Cl UB10. . . . 201 F3
Bangor Cotts SL0 . . 200 D1
Bangors Cl SL0 . . . . 207 F7
Bangors Road N
SL0 . . . . 200 D3
Bangors Road S
SL0 . . . . 207 E8
Bank Apartments
SL7 . . . . 183 D3
Bank Court Mews
MK12 . . . . 33 D7
Bankfield Rdbt MK9 . 35 A2
Bank Gn HP5. . . . . . 143 C8
Bank Mill HP4 . . . . . 135 E4
Bank Mill La HP4 . . . 135 E3
Bankside MK21. . . . . 131 B5
Banks Rd HP17. . . . . 127 A6
Banks Spur SL1. . . . 205 B4
Bank St HP13 . . . . . 174 A4
Banks Yd HP18 . . . . 100 D4
Banktop Pl MK4. . . . . 46 C3
Bannard Rd SL6. . . . 202 A5
Banner Ct 🞂 HP22 . . 172 D8
Bannister Cl SL3. . . . 206 E4
Banteng Terr MK8. . . 45 C7
Bantock Cl MK7. . . . . 48 C5
Bantry Rd SL1 . . . . . 204 F4
Barbados Row MK3 . 58 B4
Barber Dr MK2. . . . . . 58 F7
Barbers Mews MK14 . 34 F6
Barbers Wlk HP23. . 118 F3
Barbers Wood Cl
HP12. . . . . 172 B4
Barbers Wood Rd
HP12. . . . . 172 B4
Barbicus Ct SL6. . . . 203 B8
Barbury Ct MK14 . . . 35 A8
Barcelona Bvd
HP21. . . . . 115 F3
Barchester Cl UB8 . 201 C1
Barchester Rd SL3 . 206 F4
Barclay Cl OX27 . . . . 72 E6
Barclay Ct 🞂 HP12 . 172 E7
Bardeen Ct MK10. . . . 35 E2
Bardney Cl SL6 . . . . 202 D3
Bardolphs Cl HP27 . 139 C4
Bardon Gn HP20 . . . 101 E2

Bardsey Ct MK10 . . . 36 A2
Barford MK11. . . . . . . 32 F4
Bargeman Rd SL6 . . 202 E5
Barham Lodge 🞂
MK18. . . . . 52 C8
Baring Cres HP9 . . . 175 C3
Baring Rd
Beaconsfield HP9 . . 175 D3
High Wycombe HP13. 173 F7
Barker La HP22 . . . . 117 D6
Barkers Croft MK12 . 33 C4
Barkestone Cl MK4 . . 46 C1
Barkham Cl LU7. . . . 104 F7
Barkus Way MK14 . . 158 F5
Bar La MK27 . . . . . . 138 E7
Barland Wy HP18. . . 100 E3
Barlee Cres UB8 . . . 208 C8
Barley Cl
Hazlemere HP15. . . 163 A3
Lewknor OX49. . . . . 157 A8
Longwick HP27 . . . . 138 D6
Weston Turville HP22 116 F2
Barley Cres HP21. . . 115 D3
Barleycroft MK4 . . . . 46 E4
Barley Fields HP10 . 185 E8
Barley Hill Prim Sch
OX9. . . . . 126 A1
Barleyhurst Park Prim
Sch MK3 . . . . 46 F2
Barley Mead SL6 . . . 202 A5
Barley Rye OX39 . . . 147 C5
Barley View HP16 . . 151 D6
Barley Way 🞂 SL3. . . 183 D1
Barlow Rd HP22. . . . 131 C5
Barnabas Rd LU7. . . . 80 D6
Barnacre Cl UB21 . . 208 D7
Barnard Cres HP21. . 115 F5
Barnards Hill SL7. . . 183 C2
Barn Cl
Farnham Common
SL2 . . . . 198 B8
Maidenhead SL6 . . . 195 F2
Barncroft MK43. . . . . . 8 E6
Barncroft Rd HP4 . . 134 F3
Barn Ct HP12 . . . . . 172 C7
Barn Dr SL6. . . . . . . 202 A4
Barnes Ave HP5. . . . 144 C1
Barnes La
Hazlemere HP15. . . 162 F3
Hazlemere HP15. . . 163 A3
Barnes Mws HP22 . . 102 D2
Barnes Pl MK6 . . . . . 46 E8
Barnes Wallis Ct
HP12. . . . . 172 E5
Barnes Way SL0. . . . 207 F6
Barnet Cl MK5 . . . . . 45 D5
Barnett Way HP22 . . 102 B4
Barnfield
Iver SL0 . . . . 207 E7
Slough SL1 . . . . . . 204 D5
Barnfield Cl SL6. . . . 195 F5
Barnfield Dr MK6 . . . 47 C5
Barnhill Cl SL7. . . . . 183 D4
Barnhill Gdns SL7. . 183 D4
Barnhill Rd SL7 . . . . 183 D4
Barn La
Hazlemere HP15. . . 162 F5
Hazlemere HP15. . . 163 A5
Henley-on-Thames
RG9. . . . . 191 C4
Barn Owl La HP17 . . 127 B5
Barn Rd HP27. . . . . . 138 E6
Barnsbury Ave
HP20. . . . . 116 B8
Barnsbury Gdns
MK16 . . . . 22 C3
Barns Cl OX33. . . . . 122 B1
Barnsdale Dr MK4. . . 45 F2
Barnsfield Pl UB8 . . 201 C5
Barnstable Ct MK4 . . 46 D3
Barns The HP23 . . . 118 F1
Barn View LU6. . . . . . 92 E3
Baroma Way RG9 . . 191 E2
Barons Cl MK2 . . . . . 58 C8
Barons Ct 🞂 SL7 . . . 183 E2
Baronsmead RG9 . . 191 D2
Baronsmead Rd
HP12. . . . . 172 E6
Barrack Hill HP18 . . 112 E5
Barrack La SL4 . . . . 210 D6
Barracks Hill HP7 . . 164 F2
Barracks Rd HP11 . . 173 A6
Barracks The
Hillesden MK18. . . . 52 A1
Hillesden MK18. . . . 63 A8
Barrards Way HP9 . . 176 C4
Barrett Pl
High Wycombe
HP11. . . . . 173 C6
Milton Keynes MK5 . . 45 F6
Uxbridge UB10 . . . . 201 E4
BARRETTS END . . . 42 F7
Barrie Cl HP21 . . . . . 100 F2
Barrington Ct NN13 . 38 A5
Barrington Mews 🞂
MK6 . . . . 34 E1
Barrington Park Prim
HP8. . . . . 166 D1
Barrosa Wy
Crownhill MK19. . . . 45 D8
Two Mile Ash MK8. . 33 D1
Barrowcroft HP11. . 173 F4
Barrow Lodge SL2 . 198 C1
Barr Piece MK12 . . . 33 C6
Barr's Rd SL6. . . . . . 204 B7
Barry Ave
Eton SL4 . . . . 210 C7

Barry Ave *continued*
Milton Keynes MK14 . . 34 C7
Barry Cl HP22. . . . . . 172 C4
Barry View SL4 . . . . 209 C5
Bartelotts Rd SL2 . . 197 E1
Bartholomew Cl MK7 48 A5
Bartlett Cres HP13 . 172 D8
Bartlett Pl
Buckingham MK18 . . . 41 E1
🞂 High Wycombe
HP13. . . . . 172 D8
Bartletts SL3 . . . . . . 177 E3
Bartletts Cl HP22 . . . 89 C3
Barton Dr HP9 . . . . . 175 E4
BARTON
HARTSHORN 50 D2
Barton Hartshorn Rd
MK18 . . . . 50 D1
Barton Rd
Milton Keynes MK2 . . 58 C6
Slough SL3 . . . . . . 206 F4
Tingewick MK18 . . . . 50 F3
Tingewick MK18 . . . . 51 A4
Bartons Rd HP10 . . . 163 A1
Barton Way HP13 . . 162 E1
Bascote MK6 . . . . 47 D5
Base Cl 🞂 HP20 . . . . 101 F2
Basford Way SL4 . . . 209 D4
Basildon Ct
🞂 Leighton Buzzard
LU7. . . . . 80 F7
Milton Keynes MK8. . 45 F8
Basing Rd WD3. . . . . 167 F1
Baskerfield Gr MK6 . 47 C8
Basket St HP22. . . . . 102 C2
Basset Rd HP14. . . . 171 C4
Bassetsbury La
High Wycombe
HP11. . . . . 173 D5
High Wycombe HP11. 173 E4
Bassett Cl
Leighton Buzzard LU7 . 80 F7
Newport Pagnell MK16 22 C4
Bassett Rd
Leighton Buzzard LU7 . 80 F7
Uxbridge UB8 . . . . 201 C5
Bassett Way SL2 . . . 197 E1
Bass Mead SL6 . . . . 195 F5
Batchelor Cl HP20. . 101 F2
Batchelors Way
Amersham HP7. . . . 165 D8
Chesham HP5 . . . . 144 B2
Bateman Croft MK5 . 45 F6
Bateman Dr HP21 . . 115 E5
Bates Cl
Granborough MK18. . 75 F8
Milton Keynes MK15 . 35 D7
Slough SL3 . . . . . . 206 F7
Bates Ct HP20. . . . . . 101 F2
Bates Gdns MK17. . . 68 B6
Bates La HP22 . . . . . 116 F2
Bath Cl SL6 . . . . 202 C6
Bath La MK18 . . . . . . 52 C8
Bath Lane Terr MK18 52 C8
Bath Rd
Harmondsworth
UB7. . . . . 213 C6
Maidenhead SL6 . . . 202 C6
Poyle SL3 . . . . 212 E6
Slough SL1, SL6. . . 204 D6
Slough SL2 . . . . . . 198 B4
Taplow SL6 . . . . . . 203 E7
Bath Road Cotts
SL3 . . . . 212 E6
Bathurst Cl SL0. . . . 207 F4
Bathurst Wlk SL0 . . 207 F4
Battersby Mews
HP21. . . . . 115 C7
Batt Furlong HP21 . . 115 E3
Batting Cl HP14 . . . . 159 F8
Battings Wood Gdns
HP14. . . . . 161 C8
Battle Cl MK46 . . . . . 118 F8
Battlemead Cl SL6 . . 196 C3
Battle of Britain Bunker
UB10. . . . . 201 F4
Battoney Vare SL6 . . 203 C4
Baulk Rd HP22 . . . . . 86 D7
Baulk The
Cheddington LU7. . . 104 F7
Ivinghoe LU7. . . . . 105 F5
Bawtree Rd UB8 . . . 201 D6
Baxter Cl
Milton Keynes MK8 . . 45 E7
Slough SL1 . . . . . . 205 E3
Baybrook SL6 . . . . . 195 F6
Bay Ct HP4 . . . . 135 B4
Bayhurst Wood Ctry
Pk* UB9 . . . . 190 F6
Bay La MK46 . . . . 5 D2
Bayley Cres SL1. . . . 204 A8
Bayley Gdns HP16 . . 161 E6
Bayley Hatch HP16 . 152 D8
Bayleys Bottom
Penn HP10 . . . . . . 174 F5
Penn HP9 . . . . 175 A5
Baylis Bsns Ctr SL1 205 D6
Baylis Court Sch
SL1 . . . . 205 D8
Baylis Par SL1. . . . . 205 E7
Baylis Rd SL1 . . . . . 205 D6
Bayman Manor HP5 144 C4
Bayne Hill HP9. . . . . 176 D3
Bayne Hill Cl HP9 . . 176 D3
Baynton Rd HP21 . . 115 E4
Baysfarm Ct UB7. . . 213 C6
Bay Tree Cl
Loudwater HP11. . . 174 B2

Bay Tree Cl *continued*
Newton Longville
MK17. . . . . 57 D4
Bay Tree Ct SL1 . . . . 197 C2
BEACHAMPTON . . . 44 B6
Beachampton Bsns Pk
MK19 . . . . 44 C4
Beachampton Rd
MK19 . . . . 43 D4
Beacham Rd HP12. . 172 C3
Beachborough Sch
NN13. . . . . 39 A4
Beacon Ave LU6. . . . . 93 E7
Beacon Cl
Beaconsfield HP9 . . 175 A1
Chalfont St Peter SL9 177 E3
Stone HP17. . . . . . 114 C5
Uxbridge UB8 . . . . 201 D7
Beacon Ct
Colnbrook SL3. . . . 212 C7
Milton Keynes MK4 . . 46 D2
Pitstone LU7 . . . . . 105 D2
Beacon Hill HP10 . . 174 D7
Beacon La
Great Marlow SL7. . 182 E8
Marlow Bottom SL7. . 171 E1
Beacon Rd HP4 . . . . 106 E2
BEACON'S
BOTTOM 159 D3
Beacon Sch The
HP6. . . . . 154 B4
BEACONSFIELD . . . 175 D1
Beacons Field LU7 . . 105 A7
Beaconsfield Ave
High Wycombe
HP13. . . . . 161 F2
High Wycombe HP13. 162 A1
Beaconsfield Common
La SL2. . . . . 187 C5
Beaconsfield Cotts
SL8 . . . . 185 B2
Beaconsfield High Sch
HP9. . . . . 175 D1
Beaconsfield Mews
HP9. . . . . 186 A8
Beaconsfield Pl
MK16 . . . . 22 C4
Beaconsfield Rd
Aston Clinton HP22 . . 117 F4
Aylesbury HP21. . . 115 E8
Farnham Common
SL2 . . . . 198 C5
Tring HP23 . . . . . . 118 E3
Beaconsfield Sch The
HP9. . . . . 175 E1
Beaconsfield Sta
HP9. . . . . 175 E3
Beacon Sports Ctr &
Theatre The HP9 . . 175 A1
Beacon View
Dunstable LU6. . . . . 92 B4
Lewknor OX49. . . . 157 B8
Beacon Way HP23 . . 119 C5
Beadlemead MK6 . . . 47 C6
Beales La
Walton MK7 . . . . . . 47 F5
Walton MK7 . . . . . . 48 A5
Bealings End HP9 . . 175 E3
Beamangreen Wood Rd
Lacey Green HP27. . 149 C5
Walter's Ash HP14 . 150 A2
Beamish Way MK18 . 66 B5
BEAMOND END . . . 163 F6
Beamond End La HP7,
HP15. . . . . 163 F7
Beanfare MK6 . . . . . . 47 B4
BEANHILL 47 B4
Bearbrook Cl HP21. . 115 C7
Bearbrook Comb Sch
HP19. . . . . 115 C8
Bearswood End
HP9. . . . . 175 E4
Beasleys Yard UB8 . 201 C5
Beatrice Cl OX27 . . . . 72 C6
Beauchamp Cl MK14 34 D5
Beauchamp Ct SL1. 205 E6
Beaudesert Mews
UB7. . . . . 208 E4
Beaufort Cl
Aylesbury HP21. . . 116 D7
Marlow SL7. . . . . . 183 E2
🔟 Marlow SL7 . . . . 183 E2
Beaufort Dr MK15 . . . 35 C7
Beaufort Gdns SL7 . 183 E2
Beaufort Pl SL6. . . . 203 D4
Beaulieu Cl SL3 . . . . 211 B5
Beaumaris Ct SL1. . 205 C8
Beaumaris Gr MK5 . . 46 A6
Beaumont Cl SL6. . . 202 A3
Beaumont Cotts 🞂
SL4 . . . . 210 C6
Beaumont Ct SL3 . . 206 D7
Beaumont Gr HP15. 162 F3
Beaumont Rd
🔟 Slough SL2. . . . 198 D1
Slough SL2 . . . . . . 205 D8
Windsor SL4 . . . . . 210 C5
Beaumont Rise SL7 183 E2
Beaumont Way
HP15. . . . . 162 F3
Beaverbrook Ct MK3 46 F1
Beaver Cl MK18 . . . . 52 E7
Beckets Sq SL3 . . . . 206 F1
Beckett Chase 🞂
SL3 . . . . 206 F1
Beckett Cl 🞂 HP19 . 101 A3
Becketts La MK18 . . . 63 E3
Beckings Way HP10 185 C7

Beckinsale Gr MK8.. 45 E7
Beckton Rise MK10.. 35 E1
Beckwell Rd SL1 .... 205 C4
Bec La MK15 ...... 35 B7
Bedder Rd HP12 .. 172 C3
Beddoes Croft MK5. 45 E4
Bede Ct HP4 ...... 121 C8
Bedfont Court Est
TW19 .... 213 B4
Bedfont Rd TW19 .. 213 F1
Bedford Ave
Little Chalfont HP6 .. 166 C8
Slough SL1 ...... 204 F7
Slough SL1 ...... 205 A7
Bedford Cl
Chenies WD3....... 156 B1
Maidenhead SL6 ... 202 A3
Bedford Ct
Chorleywood WD3... 167 C5
Little Chalfont HP6 . 166 D8
Bedford Dr SL2 .. 198 B6
Bedford Rd
Aspley Guise MK17 ...49 F5
Cold Brayfield MK46 .. 8 B5
Cranfield MK43 .... 25 C2
Lavendon MK46 ..... 7 F7
Milton Keynes MK7 .. 48 B6
Sherington MK16 .... 14 A1
Sherington MK16 .... 14 E1
Turvey MK46 .... 8 F5
Walton MK7 .... 48 A6
Bedford Road E NN7 . 1 D5
Bedford Road W NN7 .1 A6
Bedford St
Berkhamsted HP4... 135 D4
Milton Keynes, Bletchley
MK2 .... 58 C8
Milton Keynes, Wolverton
MK12 .... 33 D6
Woburn MK17...... 60 F7
Woburn MK17...... 60 F7
Bedfort Rd MK16.. 15 A1
Bedgebury Pl MK7 .. 48 A8
BEDGROVE 116 C5
Bedgrove HP21 .. 116 C6
Bedgrove Inf Sch
HP21............ 116 C5
Bedgrove Jun Sch
HP21............ 116 C6
BEDLAM 14 C1
Bedlam La
Chicheley MK16 ..... 14 C1
Chicheley MK16 .... 23 C8
Bedlam Wlk MK16.. 14 C1
Bedlington Mews
HP19............ 114 E8
Bedwins La SL6 ... 195 B6
Bedwyn Wlk HP21.. 115 D4
Beech ☑ RG9 .... 191 D2
Beechams The MK17 67 D6
Beech Ave
Lane End HP14 .... 171 C5
Olney MK46........ 6 E3
Beech Cl
Bierton HP22 .... 102 B3
Buckingham MK18 ... 41 D2
Flackwell Heath
HP10.......... 174 A2
High Wycombe HP13 . 173 F4
Maidenhead SL6.... 202 B8
Stokenchurch HP14.. 158 F3
Beechcroft HP4.... 135 C3
Beechcroft Rd MK3.. 57 E6
Beech Ct
Berkhamsted HP4... 135 D4
☑ Marlow SL7 ... 183 E2
Beech Dr HP4 .... 135 C3
Beechen Wood
WD3............ 178 D5
Beeches Dr SL2 .. 198 B7
Beeches Gr HP10.. 163 A2
Beeches Pk HP9 .. 175 D2
Beeches Way SL1 .. 197 C2
Beeches The
Amersham HP6.... 154 A3
Chorleywood WD3.. 167 F4
Deanshanger MK19 .. 31 E3
Milton Keynes MK1 .. 47 E1
Tring HP23 .... 119 C4
Uxbridge UB8 ..... 201 C1
Wendover HP22 ... 131 C5
Beechfern MK7 .... 48 A5
Beechfield Pl SL6 .. 202 C4
Beechfield Way
Hazlemere HP15.... 163 B3
Hazlemere HP15.... 163 B3
Beechfield Wlk
HP15............ 163 A3
Beech Gn HP21 .... 115 D6
Beech Gr
Amersham HP7.... 165 D8
Leighton Buzzard LU7 . 80 E7
Tring HP23 .... 119 C4
Beechgrove Gdns
SL7............. 183 B1
Beech Hill Ct HP4 .. 135 D5
Beech House Dr
NN12............18 F4
Beeching Stoke ☑
SL7............. 183 F3
Beech La
Prestwood HP16.... 151 B7
Seer Green HP9 ... 176 E3
Beechlands HP5 ... 162 E2
Beech Leys MK18... 63 E3
Beech Pk
Little Chalfont HP6 . 155 B1

Beech Pk continued
Naphill HP14........ 150 A1
Wigginton HP23 ... 133 F5
Beech Rd
Aylesbury HP21..... 115 D6
Chinnor OX39...... 147 C6
High Wycombe HP11. 173 F4
Newport Pagnell MK16 22 B3
Princes Risborough
HP27........... 139 C3
Slough SL3 ...... 206 E4
Beechtree Ave SL7 183 D5
Beech Tree Cl MK19. 20 D2
Beech Tree Ct HP22. 87 A6
Beech Tree La LU7 .. 79 E2
Beech Tree Rd
HP15............ 163 C7
Beech Trees Rd
HP12............ 172 C3
Beechview Acad
HP13............ 173 E5
Beech Waye SL9 .. 189 A4
Beech Wlk HP23 .. 119 B4
Beechwood Ave
Chorleywood WD3.. 167 B5
Little Chalfont HP6 . 155 C1
☑ Uxbridge UB8.. 208 F7
Beechwood Cl HP6. 166 C8
Beechwood Cotts
WD3............ 167 B3
Beechwood Ct
Aston Clinton HP22.. 118 A3
Dunstable LU6....... 93 F7
Beechwood Dr
Aldbury HP23 ...... 120 D5
Maidenhead SL6 ... 202 A6
Marlow SL7 .... 194 B8
Beechwood Gdns
SL1............. 205 E4
Beechwood Ho
HP22............ 117 F5
Beechwood La
HP22............ 131 D5
Beechwood Pk
Chorleywood WD3.. 167 F5
Felden HP3 .... 146 F7
Beechwood Pl ☑
HP13............ 173 B7
Beechwood Rd
Beaconsfield HP9 .. 175 C2
High Wycombe HP12. 161 B2
☑ Slough SL2.... 198 D1
Slough SL2 ...... 205 D8
Beechwood Sch
SL2............. 198 B2
Beechwood View
HP27............ 149 C1
Beechwood Way
HP22............ 117 F5
BEECROFT.........93 F8
Beecroft Lower Sch
LU6.............93 F8
Beecroft Way LU6...93 F8
Beehive Cl UB10 .. 201 F5
Beel Cl HP7....... 166 C8
Beeley St HP18..... 100 F5
Beeston La HP19... 101 B4
Beethoven Cl MK4... 45 E3
Beethoven Dr HP21 115 F3
Beeward Cl MK12... 33 A5
Beggars La HP17.... 130 B8
Bekonscot Ct MK14.. 21 F1
Bekonscot Model Village
& Railway ★ HP9 . 175 D3
Belfast Ave SL1 ... 205 D7
Belgrave Mews
UB8............. 201 D1
Belgrave Par SL1.. 205 E6
Belgrave Pl ☑ SL1. 206 A4
Belgrave Rd
Aylesbury HP19..... 101 A3
Slough SL1 ...... 205 E6
Bellamy Mews ☑
MK4 .... 45 E3
Bellamy Rd HP13... 173 C8
Bell Ave UB7...... 208 F3
Bell Bsns Pk HP19... 100 F1
Bell Cl
Beaconsfield HP9 .. 175 F2
Cublington LU7..... 78 B1
Drayton Parslow MK17 68 B6
Princes Risborough
HP27........... 139 B3
Slough SL2 ...... 206 B8
Thame OX9....... 125 E1
Bellclose Rd UB7... 208 E4
Bell Cres HP27.... 138 E6
Bell Ct SL6....... 193 F3
Belle Vue HP17 .... 114 F5
Belle Vue Pl SL3 .. 205 F5
Bellfield Rd HP13 .. 173 A8
Bellfield Road W
HP11............ 172 F7
Bellfounder Ho MK13 34 B4
Bell Gn HP3....... 146 B4
Bell Gr MK17...... 37 B1
BELLINGDON 143 E7
Bellingdon Rd HP5. 144 B1
Bellingham Way
HP22............ 102 C2
Bellini Cl MK7..... 48 D5
Bellis Gr MK6..... 47 C8
Bell La
Berkhamsted HP4... 134 E5
Eton Wick SL4 .... 204 F2
Henley-on-Thames
RG9............ 191 E3
Little Chalfont HP6 . 155 C1

Bell La continued
Princes Risborough
HP27........... 139 B3
Syresham NN13 .... 27 B8
Thame OX9....... 125 F1
Bell Lane Comb Sch
HP6............. 155 B1
Bell Leys HP22..... 89 B3
Bellman Cl SL1.... 206 B4
Bellows Mill La LU6. 93 A4
Bellridge Pl HP9 .. 175 B6
Bellsfield Ct SL4... 204 F2
Bells Hill
Stoke Poges SL2 ... 198 F4
Stoke Poges SL2 ... 199 A4
Bells Hill Gn SL2 .. 199 A5
Bells La SL3 ...... 212 B4
Bells Mdw MK15 ... 35 B7
Bell St
Henley-on-Thames
RG9............ 191 E2
Henley-on-Thames
RG9............ 191 E2
Maidenhead SL6 ... 202 F6
Princes Risborough
HP27........... 139 B3
Bell Street Mews
RG9............ 191 E2
Bellswood La SL0 .. 207 B8
Bell View SL4 .... 209 F5
Bell View Cl SL4... 209 F5
Bellway MK17...... 49 A6
Bellwether MK11... 33 A4
Bell Wlk
Wingrave HP22..... 89 B3
Winslow MK18 ..... 65 F3
Bellwood Rise HP11 173 B4
Bellworthy Cl SL6 .. 202 F5
Belmers Rd HP23.. 119 D1
Belmont SL2...... 205 A8
Belmont Cl UB8.... 201 D6
Belmont Cotts SL3. 212 C7
Belmont Cres SL6 .. 202 D8
Belmont Ct MK8.... 33 C2
Belmont Dr SL6.... 202 D8
Belmont Park Ave
SL6............. 202 D8
Belmont Park Rd
SL6............. 202 D8
Belmont Rd
Chesham HP5 .... 144 B3
Maidenhead SL6 ... 202 D8
Uxbridge UB8 .... 201 D5
Belmont Vale SL6.. 202 D8
Belsham Cl HP5.... 144 B3
BELSIZE 156 F6
Belsize Ave MK16 .. 15 A3
Belsize Cotts WD3.. 156 E6
Belton Rd HP4 .... 135 A5
Belvedere Cl HP6 . 154 F2
Belvedere La HP7...58 F8
Belvedere Mans
SL1............. 205 D4
Belvedere Rdbt MK9 .34 F4
Belvoir Ave MK4 .... 46 C1
Bembridge Ct ☑
SL1............. 205 F4
Benacre Croft MK4.. 57 A8
Benbow Cl MK4 .... 46 A7
Benbow Way UB8 .. 208 C8
Bench Manor Cres
SL9............. 177 C1
Bencombe Rd SL7.. 183 E5
Benen-Stock Rd
Stanwell TW19 .... 213 A2
Stanwell Moor SL3 .. 212 F2
Bengrove MK12..... 33 A6
Benham Cl HP5.... 144 A1
Benhams La RG9... 180 D2
Benison Ct ☑ SL1.. 205 F3
Benjamin Coll HP19 114 F8
Benjamin Ho ☑
HP13............ 173 B7
Benjamin La SL3 .. 199 B1
Benjamin Rd HP13. 173 B8
Benjamins Footpath
HP13............ 173 B8
Ben More SL9..... 188 F6
Benmore Rise ☑
MK4 .... 45 E2
Bennels Ct HP17 .. 139 A8
Bennet Cl MK11.... 32 E4
Bennet's Yd UB8... 201 D5
BENNETT END 159 C7
Bennett End Rd
HP14............ 159 C7
Bennetts HP5..... 144 D1
Bennetts Cl
Padbury MK18 ..... 53 B1
Slough SL1 ...... 205 A5
Bennett's Hill
Swanbourne MK18 .. 76 C8
Winslow MK18 ..... 65 D8
Bennetts La HP22 .. 102 E8
Bennett Way ☑
HP18............ 100 D5
Benning Ave LU6...93 F8
Benning Cl SL4 ... 209 D4
Benningfield Gdns
HP4............. 135 E6
Bens Cl MK19....... 19 F5
Bensheim Way HP6 154 D1
Benson Cl
Slough SL2 ...... 206 A5
Uxbridge UB8 .... 208 E8
Bentall Cl MK15 .... 35 C7
Bentinck Cl SL9.... 188 D6
Bentinck Ct UB7... 208 D5

Bentinck Rd UB7.. 208 D5
Bentley Ct SL6 .... 202 D5
Bentley Pk SL1.... 197 D3
Bentley Rd
Slough SL1 ...... 204 F5
Slough SL1 ...... 205 A5
Benton Dr OX39... 147 C7
Benton Mews HP18 100 D4
Bentons The HP4 .. 134 F4
Benwell Cl MK13.... 33 F5
Benwells OX39.... 147 C6
Berber Bsns Ctr
HP11............ 172 E2
Berberis Cl MK7.... 48 A5
Berberis Wlk UB7 . 208 E2
Bercham MK8...... 33 C2
Beresford Cl
Aylesbury HP19..... 101 C3
Slough SL2 ...... 206 C6
Beresford Rd WD3 . 167 F1
Beretun MK8 ...... 33 E1
Bereville Ct MK10... 35 E3
Bergamot Gdns MK7 48 B5
Berghers Hill HP10. 185 B6
Bergman Cl ☑ MK4 . 45 D2
Berkeley Ave
Chesham HP5 .... 144 A1
Stoke Goldington
MK16 .... 12 B6
Berkeley Cl
Chesham HP5 .... 144 A1
Stoke Goldington
MK16 .... 12 B6
Berkeley Mews
Marlow SL7 ...... 183 F2
Slough SL1 ...... 204 E7
Berkeley Rd
Loudwater HP10... 174 C2
Thame OX9....... 126 A1
Berkeley Rise ☑
HP19............ 101 B2
Berkhampstead Rd
HP5............. 144 C2
BERKHAMSTED ... 135 C6
Berkhamsted Castle ★
HP4............. 135 C6
Berkhamsted Common
HP4............. 121 A4
Berkhamsted Girls' Sch
HP4............. 135 B4
Berkhamsted Pl
HP4............. 135 C6
Berkhamsted Pre-Prep
Sch HP4......... 135 B1
Berkhamsted Prep Sch
HP4............. 135 C4
Berkhamsted Sch ☑
HP4............. 135 C4
Berkhamsted Sta
HP4............. 135 C5
Berkhamsted Way
HP22............ 102 D3
Berkley Cl
Maidenhead SL6 ... 202 A8
Pitstone LU7 ...... 105 D3
Berkley Ct HP4 ... 135 C4
Berkley Rd HP9 ... 175 D5
Berks Hill WD3.... 167 C4
Berkshire Ave SL1.. 205 B7
Berkshire Gn ☑ MK5 .45 F3
Berkshire Lodge ☑
SL6............. 202 F6
Berling Rd MK8..... 33 F2
Bernard Cl HP18... 112 F2
Bernardines Way
MK18 .... 52 E7
Bernards Cl HP16 .. 152 A7
Bernards Way HP10 174 A2
Bernay Gdns MK15.. 35 B7
Berndene Rise
HP27............ 139 B4
Berners Cl SL1.... 204 E6
Bernewode Cl HP18 125 C7
Bernstein Cl MK7 .. 48 C4
Bernwood Mdws
Wildlife Reserve
HP18............ 108 F2
Berrells Ct
☑ Olney MK46.....6 F3
☑ Olney MK46.....7 A3
Berrenda Ave MK19 . 45 C7
Berries Rd MK4 ... 196 A8
Berrington Gr ☑
MK4 .... 45 E2
Berry Cl OX27.....71 F2
Berry Ct MK13 .... 34 B6
BERRYFIELD 100 D5
Berryfield LU7 .... 104 F7
Berry Field SL2 ... 206 C2
Berry Field Pk HP6. 154 B2
Berryfield Rd
Aylesbury HP19..... 101 B3
Princes Risborough
HP27........... 139 C4
Berryfields
Berryfields HP19.... 100 C7
Berryfields HP22.... 86 B1
Quainton HP22.....85 F2
Berryfields CE Prim Sch
HP18............ 100 E4
Berry Gr ☑ MK10... 35 D2
Berry Hill SL6..... 203 D8
Berry Hill Ct SL6 .. 203 D8
Berry La
Aspley Guise MK17...49 F6
Chorleywood WD3... 167 D3
Berrystead MK7.... 48 B3
Berry Way MK17.... 57 D4
Bertram Cl MK13... 34 B8
Berwald Cl MK7.... 48 D4

Berwick Ave SL1 .. 205 B6
Berwick Cl
Beaconsfield HP9 .. 176 B1
Marlow SL7....... 183 D3
Berwick Dr MK3.... 46 F2
Berwick La SL7 ... 183 D3
Berwick Rd SL7.... 183 C3
Bessemer Cres
HP19............ 100 E1
Bessemer Ct MK14... 22 A1
Bestobell Rd SL1... 205 C7
Betjeman Ct UB7... 208 D5
Betjeman Gdns
WD3............ 167 C5
Bettina Gr MK2.... 58 C7
Bettles Cl UB8 .... 201 C3
Bettles Ct UB8 .... 201 C3
Betty's La HP23 ... 119 A4
Beulah Gr ☑ MK8... 45 D8
Bevan Cl MK18......65 F4
Bevan Hill HP5.... 144 B2
Bevelwood Gdns
HP12............ 172 D7
Beverley Cl SL7 ... 183 B2
Beverley Ct SL1 .. 206 B4
Beverley Gdns SL6. 195 B1
Beverley Pl MK6 ... 35 B2
Beverley Rd
Chesham HP5 .... 144 A1
Stoke Goldington
MK16 .... 12 B6
Bewdley Dr LU7.... 80 C7
Bewdley Gr MK10 .. 36 A4
Bexley St SL4 .... 210 C6
Bhamra Gdns ☑
SL6............. 202 D6
Bicester Rd
Aylesbury HP19..... 101 A1
Blackthorn OX25.... 81 C5
Boarstall HP18 ..... 95 C3
Boarstall HP18 .... 109 C8
Chilton HP18....... 110 E2
Fleet Marston HP19 . 100 B4
Grendon Underwood
HP18........... 82 E4
Long Crendon HP18. 111 A1
Long Crendon HP18. 125 C6
Ludgershall HP18 ...81 F4
Ludgershall HP18 ...82 B1
Ludgershall HP18 .. 96 C8
Marsh Gibbon OX27 . 71 F2
Oakley HP18....... 109 D5
Twyford MK18...... 62 C1
Westcott HP18 .... 98 C8
Woodham HP18 .... 83 D2
Bicester Road Ind Est
HP19............ 101 A1
Bickleigh Cres MK4 . 46 D3
Biddles Cl SL1 .... 204 E5
BIDDLESDEN 27 D5
Biddlesden MK18 ... 27 C4
Biddlesden Rd
Syresham NN13 .... 27 C6
Westbury NN13..... 39 A5
Bideford Ct LU7.... 80 C8
Bideford Gn
Leighton Buzzard
LU7............ 80 C8
Leighton Buzzard LU7 . 80 D8
Bideford Spur SL2. 198 B2
BIERTON 102 A3
Bierton CE Comb Sch
HP22............ 102 B3
Bierton Rd HP20... 101 F1
Bigfrith La SL6..... 195 B6
Biggs La HP17 .... 113 E2
Bigmore La
Beacon's Bottom
HP14........... 170 B8
Stokenchurch HP14. 159 C1
Bignell Croft MK5 .. 34 B1
Bigton Chase ☑
MK10 .... 36 B2
Biko Cl UB8....... 208 D5
Bilbrook La MK4 .... 46 C4
Billet La
Berkhamsted HP4... 135 A4
Iver SL0, SL3...... 207 B7
Billings Cl HP14.... 158 F5
Billingwell Pl MK6 .. 35 B2
Billwell HP18...... 125 C6
Bilton Rd MK1 ..... 47 D2
Binder Dr HP27 ... 138 D6
Binders Ind Est
HP15............ 162 D7
Bingham Cl MK4 ... 46 C1
Bingham Rd SL1 .. 204 A8
Binghams The SL6. 203 B3
Birch Ave UB7 .... 208 F7
Birch Cl
Amersham HP6.... 154 E2
Aston Clinton HP22.. 117 E4
Bedford MK43...... 25 C3
Iver Heath SL0 .... 200 D3
Maidenhead SL6 ... 202 E3
Birch Cres UB10.... 201 F4
Birch Ct HP21..... 115 D5
Birch Dr WD3..... 178 D5
Birchen Lee MK4... 46 C4
Birches Rise HP12. 172 E8
Birches The
Beaconsfield HP9 .. 175 D3
Felden HP3 ...... 146 F8
High Wycombe HP13. 173 E8
Birchfield Gr MK2... 58 C7
Birch Gdns HP7... 165 E8
Birch Gr
Slough SL2 ...... 205 B8

Birch Gr continued
Windsor SL4 ...... 209 D6
Birchington Rd SL4 210 A5
Birch La HP3...... 156 B7
BIRCHMOOR GREEN . 60 E8
Birchmoor Green
MK17 .... 60 E8
Birchmoor La
Woburn MK17...... 49 E1
Woburn MK17......60 F8
Birch Rd HP4 .... 134 D7
Birch Tree Gr HP5.. 145 B1
Birch Way
Chesham HP5 .... 144 D2
Tylers Green HP10 . 163 B1
Birchwood Chase
HP15............ 151 D1
Birchwood Cl HP12. 172 B6
Birdcage Wlk HP13. 173 B6
Birdlip La MK7 .... 48 B7
Bird Mount Cotts
SL4............. 210 C8
Birds La MK16 .... 12 B6
Birdwood Rd SL6... 202 B7
Birfield Rd HP10 .. 174 C2
Birinus Ct HP12 ... 172 C5
Birkdale Cl MK3.... 57 D7
Birkett Way HP5... 144 D6
Birley Rd SL1 .... 205 D6
Birmingham Dr
HP19............ 102 C2
Birnbeck Ave MK3... 58 A4
Birtchnell Cl HP4... 135 A5
BISHAM 194 E7
Bisham Abbey National
Sports Ctr SL7 ... 194 D7
Bisham CE Prim Sch
SL7............. 194 D7
Bisham Ct
☑ Slough SL1.... 205 F4
Bisham Gn SL7.... 194 E6
Bisham Rd
Bisham SL7 ...... 194 E8
Marlow SL7....... 183 E1
Bisham Woods Nature
Reserve SL6 ..... 194 E6
Bishop Ct SL6..... 202 D6
Bishop Ctr The SL6. 203 F7
Bishop Parker Catholic
Sch MK2......... 58 C6
Bishops HP18 .... 123 E5
Bishops Ct MK18 .. 52 C7
Bishops Farm Cl
SL4............. 209 B6
Bishops Field HP22. 118 A4
Bishopshalt Sch
UB8............. 201 F2
Bishops Ho HP9.... 175 D3
Bishops Mdw HP22. 102 A3
Bishops Orch SL2 .. 198 B2
Bishops Rd SL1 ... 206 A4
BISHOPSTONE 115 A1
Bishopstone
Milton Keynes MK13 . 34 B5
Stone HP17....... 115 A1
Bishopstone Rd
HP17............ 114 D5
Bishops Wlk
Aylesbury HP21..... 115 F6
Woburn Sands MK17... 49 B3
Wooburn Green
HP10........... 185 E5
Bishop Wood Sch ☑
HP23............ 119 A3
Bissley Dr SL6 .... 202 A3
Bit La HP18....... 96 C8
Bittenham Cl HP17. 114 D4
Bittern Way ☑
HP20............ 101 E3
Bit The HP13...... 119 D1
BIX 179 D1
Bix La SL6........ 194 F1
Black Acre Cl HP7.. 165 E8
Blackamoor La SL6. 196 A1
Blackbeard MK16 ... 36 B5
Blackberry Ct MK7 . 48 B6
Black Boy La SL6... 193 C3
Blackburn Trad Est
TW19 .... 213 F1
Black Butt Cotts
SL6............. 196 B7
Black Ditch La HP3. 156 B6
Blacketts Wood MK11....32 F4
Blacketts Wood Dr
WD3............ 167 B5
Blackfield La HP16 . 142 E3
Blackgrove Rd
Quainton HP22.....85 D3
Waddesdon HP18 ...99 D7
Blackham Ct MK5... 46 E7
Black Horse Ave
HP5............. 154 D6
Black Horse Cl SL4 209 D5
Blackhorse Cres
HP6............. 154 E1
Blackhorse Dr MK19. 32 B7
Black Horse Pl UB8. 201 C4
Blackmoor Gate
MK4 .... 46 E2

Blackmore Gate
HP22. . . . . .118 A4
Blackmore Way
UB8. . . . . .201 D6
Black Park Ctry Pk★ SL0,
SL3 . . . . .199 F3
Black Park Ctry Pk
Visitor Ctr★ SL3 . .199 F2
Black Park Nature
Reserve SL0 . . . . . . .200 A5
Black Park Rd SL3. . .199 E4
Blackpond La SL2 . .198 B4
Black Robins La
HP3. . . . . .156 C7
Blacksmith La HP16 151 C6
Blacksmith Row
SL3 . . . . .207 A2
Blacksmith's La
UB9. . . . . .189 D2
Blacksmiths Rd
HP27. . . . . .138 D7
Blacksmiths Way
MK17 . . . . .49 B5
BLACKTHORN 81 A4
Blackthorn Cl OX25 .81 A3
Blackthorn Dell ②
SL3 . . . . .206 C3
Blackthorne Cres
SL3 . . . . .212 E5
Blackthorne Ind Pk
SL3 . . . . .212 E5
Blackthorne La
HP16. . . . . .142 E3
Blackthorne Rd SL3 212 E4
Blackthorn Gr MK17 .49 A4
Blackthorn Rd
Marsh Gibbon OX27 . .71 D1
Marsh Gibbon OX27 . .81 C8
Blackwater Dr
HP21. . . . . .115 C4
Blackwell Ct SL1 . .206 C2
Blackwell End NN12 .18 C3
Blackwellhall La
HP5. . . . . .155 C8
Blackwell Hall La
HP5. . . . . .155 C6
Blackwell Pl MK5 . . .46 A4
Blackwell Rd HP4 . .171 B5
Blackwells Yd NN7 . . .1 B6
Blackwood Cres
MK13 . . . . .33 E6
Blaine Cl HP23 . . . .119 A6
Blainways Ave LU7 .118 D3
Blairmont St MK9 . . .34 F4
Blair Rd SL1 . . . . . .205 E5
Blakedown Rd LU7 . .80 C6
BLAKELANDS 22 B1
Blakelands Hospl
(Private) MK14. . . . . .22 A2
Blakeney Ct
Maidenhead SL6 . . .195 F1
Milton Keynes MK4 . . .57 B8
Blakes Ho HP10 . . . .174 C2
Blake St ① HP19 . . .101 C1
Blake Way OX9. . . . .126 A1
Blanchland Circ
MK10 . . . . .36 A1
Blandford Cl SL3. . .206 D3
Blandford Ho SL6 . .202 C8
Blandford Rd MK13. .34 B7
Blandford Road N
SL3 . . . . .206 D3
Blandford Road S
SL3 . . . . .206 D3
Blanes Ct HP18 . . . .125 C6
Blansby Chase MK4 .46 C3
Blatherwick Ct MK5 .45 F7
Blaydon Cl MK3 . . . . .57 D6
BLEAK HALL 46 F5
Bleak Hall Rdbt MK6 .47 A5
Bleasdale MK13. . . . .34 C5
BLEDLOW 138 B1
Bledlow Cotts HP27 138 C1
Bledlow Rd HP27. . . .148 E8
BLEDLOW RIDGE . . .159 F8
Bledlow Ridge Rd
HP14. . . . . .148 C8
Bledlow Ridge Sch
HP14. . . . . .159 F8
Blegberry Gdns
HP4. . . . . .134 E4
Blencowe Cres MK18 63 E3
Blenheim MK19 . . . . .32 B7
Blenheim Ave MK11 .32 E4
Blenheim Cl
Cheddington LU7. . . .104 F8
Longwick HP27 . . . . .138 D6
Slough SL3 . . . . .206 D2
Blenheim Ct HP13. . .173 B7
Blenheim Mws MK11 32 E5
Blenheim Pl
Aylesbury HP21. . . . .115 E5
Syresham NN13 . . . . .27 C7
Blenheim Rd
High Wycombe
HP12. . . . . .172 D4
Maidenhead SL6. . . .202 B8
Slough SL3 . . . . .206 D2
Blessbury Cl HP22. .116 A1
Bletcham Rdbt MK1 .47 E3
Bletcham Way
Milton Keynes MK1 . . .47 E2
Milton Keynes MK1 . . .47 E2
Walton Park MK7 . . . .48 B4
BLETCHLEY 58 A7

Bletchley Bsns Campus
MK2. . . . . .58 C6
Bletchley Com Hospl
MK3 . . . . .47 A1
Bletchley L Ctr MK2 .58 C8
Bletchley Park★
MK3 . . . . .58 A8
Bletchley Rd
Buckingham MK18 . . .53 C7
Drayton Parslow MK17 68 F8
Great Horwood MK17 . .55 A5
Great Horwood MK17 . .55 C5
Milton Keynes MK5 . . .46 B4
Newton Longville
MK17 . . . . .57 D4
Newton Longville
MK17 . . . . .57 F1
Stewkley LU7 . . . . . . .68 D3
Stoke Hammond MK17 58 A1
Thornborough MK17. . .54 D6
Whaddon MK17. . . . . .56 A6
Whaddon MK17. . . . . .56 A6
Bletchley St HP22 . .102 E2
Bletchley Sta MK3. . .58 B8
Blinco La SL3 . . . . .206 E7
Blind La
Bourne End HP10,
SL8 . . . . .185 B5
Bourne End SL8. . . . .185 B5
South Heath HP16. . .153 B8
Blind Pond Ind Est
MK17 . . . . .48 D2
Blind Pond La MK17 .48 D2
Bliss Ave MK43. . . . .25 C2
Bliss Ct MK7 . . . . . . .48 C4
Blisworth MK6. . . . . .47 D5
Blondell Cl UB7. . . .213 D8
Bloomfield Cotts
HP5. . . . . .143 E7
Bloomfield Rd SL6. .202 A5
Bloomsbury Cl MK17 .60 F6
Blossom Way UB10. .201 F5
Blount Mws UB10 . .201 E3
Blue Albion La MK8 .45 C7
Blue Anchor Ave ①
MK10 . . . . .36 B3
Bluebell Cl MK18. . . .52 C7
Bluebell Croft MK7. .48 B6
Bluebell Gdns ⑪
MK10 . . . . .36 C4
Bluebell Terr ②
UB7. . . . . .208 F4
Blue Dragon Yard
HP9. . . . . .175 E1
Blue Funnel Grange
MK10 . . . . .36 C4
Blue Lagoon Nature
Reserve MK3. . . . . . . .58 B7
Blue Rock Dr ⑥
HP18. . . . . .100 C5
Blumfield Cres SL1. .204 E8
Blumfield Ct SL1. . .197 D1
Blundells Rd MK13 . . .34 C6
Blunden Dr SL3 . . . .207 C2
Blyth Cl MK4. . . . . . .57 A8
Blythebridge MK10. .36 C3
Blythe Cl
Aylesbury HP21. . . . .115 C5
Iver SL0 . . . . .207 F7
Newport Pagnell
MK16 . . . . .22 D3
Blythe Hos SL1 . . . . .204 D5
Blyton Cl HP9 . . . . . .175 D4
Blyton La MK4 . . . . . .56 F8
Boadicea Cl SL1. . . .204 E5
Boarlands Cl SL1. . .204 F6
BOARSTALL 95 B1
Boarstall Duck Decoy★
HP18. . . . . .95 A1
Boarstall Tower★
HP18. . . . . .95 A1
Boathouse Reach
RG9. . . . . .191 E1
Bobbins Wy MK18. . .52 F6
Bobby Rd HP22 . . . .102 C2
Bobmore La SL7 . . .183 F3
BOCKMER END. 182 C1
Bockmer La
Bockmer End SL7 . . .182 D2
Medmenham SL7. . . .193 B7
Bockmer Rd
Bockmer End SL7 . . .182 C1
Rotten Row RG9 . . . .181 F2
Boddington Rd
HP22. . . . . .131 C4
Bodenham Cl MK18 . .52 F8
Bodiam Cl
Aylesbury HP21. . . . .116 B5
Milton Keynes MK5 . . .46 A5
Bodiam Ho ⑥ HP13 173 F7
Bodiam Path ②
LU7. . . . . .105 D3
Bodle Cl MK15. . . . . .35 A7
Bodley Ho SL0 . . . . .200 D3
Bodmin Ave SL2 . . .205 A8
Bodmin Pl MK10 . . . .36 A2
Bodnant Ct MK4. . . . .45 F2
Bogart Pl MK4 . . . . . .45 C2
Bois Ave HP6. . . . . . .154 B3
Bois Hill HP5. . . . . . .154 E5
Bois La HP6. . . . . . . .154 D4
Bois Moor Rd HP5. . .154 D5
Bolan Ct MK4 . . . . . . .45 C2
BOLBECK PK. 35 A7
Boldison Cl ②
HP19. . . . . .101 C1
Bold's Ct SL2. . . . . .199 A5
Bolebec Ave MK17. . .37 B1

Bolebec End LU7. . .105 D3
BOLTER END 170 F5
Bolter End La HP14. .171 A6
Bolton Ave SL4. . . . .210 D4
Bolton Cres SL4. . . .210 C4
Bolton Rd SL4 . . . . .210 C4
Boltwood Gr MK5 . . .45 E5
Bonaire Grange MK3 58 B3
Bond Ave MK1 . . . . . .47 D3
Bond Cl
Aylesbury HP21. . . . .115 B6
Iver Heath SL0 . . . . .200 B5
West Drayton UB7. . .208 F7
Wooburn Green
HP10. . . . . .185 D8
Boundary The ①
MK6 . . . . .34 F1
Bone Hill MK18 . . . . .52 C7
Bonham Carter Rd
HP22. . . . . .131 E7
Bonham Cl HP21 . . .115 B6
Bonham Ct HP22 . . .117 D5
Bonnards Rd MK17. . .57 D4
Bonnersfield HP18 . .125 C7
BOOKER. 172 B4
Booker Ave MK18 . . .34 D4
Booker Common
HP12. . . . . .172 B4
Booker Hill Prim Sch
HP12. . . . . .172 B4
Bookerhill Rd HP12 172 C6
Booker La HP12. . . .172 D7
Booker Park Sch
HP21. . . . . .115 E3
Booker Pl HP12 . . . .172 B3
Boot Cl MK18 . . . . . . .65 F3
Booth Pl LU6. . . . . . . .92 E6
Boot La HP17 . . . . . . .94 E6
Boran Way MK8 . . . . .45 D7
Border Cl MK8 . . . . . .45 C7
Border La MK18 . . . . .52 F6
Borderside SL2 . . . .206 A7
Boreray MK18. . . . . . .41 D3
Boreray Cl MK8 . . . . .45 D7
Borodin Ct MK7 . . . . .48 D5
Boroma Way RG9 . .191 E2
Boroughbridge MK5. 45 D5
Borough Ct NN13 . . .38 A5
Borough Rd NN13 . . .38 A5
Borough Wlk MK9 . . .34 E3
Bosanquet Ct SL8. .201 D1
Bosmore La RG9 . . .180 B4
Bossiney Pl MK6 . . . .34 F1
Bossington La
Leighton Buzzard LU7 .80 E7
Leighton Buzzard LU7 .80 F8
Boss La
Great Kingshill
HP15. . . . . .162 B8
Hughenden Valley
HP14. . . . . .162 B6
Bostock Ct MK18. . . .52 C8
Boston Dr SL8 . . . . .185 B3
Boston Gr SL1 . . . . .205 C7
Boswell Cl MK18 . . . .41 E2
Boswell La MK19 . . . .31 E4
Bosworth Cl MK3. . . .46 E2
Bosworth Ct SL1 . . .204 C6
Botany Mws HP22. . .116 E6
Botham Dr SL1. . . . .205 E3
BOTLEY 145 A1
Botley La HP5. . . . . .145 A1
Botley Rd HP5 . . . . .144 E1
Botolph Mws MK18. .52 B8
Bottesford Cl MK3. . .46 D1
Bottle Dump Rdbt
MK7 . . . . .56 E6
Bottle Square La
HP14. . . . . .159 D6
Bottom Dr LU6. . . . . .93 D5
Bottom Hill RG9. . . .181 C4
Bottom House Farm La
HP8. . . . . .165 E2
Bottom House La
HP23. . . . . .120 A1
Bottom La
St Leonards HP23 . . .132 C2
Seer Green HP9 . . . .176 C5
Bottom Orch HP18 . .112 C1
Bottom Rd
Bledlow Ridge
HP14. . . . . .160 B5
Buckland Common
HP23. . . . . .132 F3
Tring LU7. . . . . .118 D1
**Bottom Waltons Caravan
Site** SL2. . . . . .197 F3
Bottrells La HP8 . . . .176 E8
Botyl Rd MK18 . . . . . .74 E6
Boughton Bsns Pk
HP6. . . . . .166 B8
Boughton Way HP6 155 C1
Boulevard The MK4 .52 F2
Boulmer Rd UB8 . . .201 C2
Boulters Cl
Maidenhead SL6 . . .196 C1
Slough SL1 . . . . .205 A4
Boulters Ct
③ Amersham HP6 . . .154 E2
Maidenhead SL6 . . .196 C1
Boulters Gdns SL6 .196 C1
Boulters La SL6 . . . .196 C1
Boulters Lock MK14 . .21 C7
Boulters Lock Island
SL6 . . . . .196 C1
Boulton Rd HP21 . . .116 D7
Bounary Rd MK18 . . .53 C2
Boundary Cotts
WD4 . . . . .146 E2
Boundary Cres MK11 32 E6

Boundary Dr SL2. . .206 B8
Boundary Pl HP10. .185 D8
Boundary Rd
Brackley NN13 . . . . . .38 A6
Chalfont St Peter SL9 177 D3
Loudwater HP10. . . .174 C1
Slough SL1 . . . . .204 A8
Taplow SL6 . . . . .203 F8
Wooburn Green
HP10. . . . . .185 D8
Boundary The ①
MK6 . . . . .34 F1
Bounds Croft MK12. .33 C4
Bounty St MK13 . . . .33 F7
Bouquet Cl HP16 . . .151 C5
Bourbon St HP20 . . .115 D8
Bourne Ave SL4. . . .210 C3
Bourne Cl SL8 . . . . .185 B5
BOURNE END 185 B2
Bourne End MK43 . . .25 C6
Bourne End Bsns Pk
SL8 . . . . .185 B3
Bourne End Mills Ind Est
HP1. . . . . .146 B8
Bourne End Rd
Bourne End SL6,
SL8 . . . . .196 E8
Cranfield MK43 . . . . .25 C4
Wootton MK43 . . . . . .25 B5
Bourne End Sta SL8 185 A3
Bourne Rd
Berkhamsted HP4. . .134 F5
Slough SL1 . . . . .205 D4
Bourne The HP3 . . . .146 A4
BOURTON 52 F8
Bourton Low MK4. . . .48 B5
Bourton Meadow Sch
MK18 . . . . .52 F8
Bourton Rd MK18 . . .52 E8
Bourtonville MK18 . .52 D8
Bouverie Way SL3. . .206 E2
BOVENEY 209 D8
Boveney Cl SL1 . . . .205 A4
Boveney New Rd
SL4 . . . . .204 E2
Boveney Rd SL4. . . .204 C1
Boveney Wood La
SL1 . . . . .186 D1
BOVINGDON. 146 B4
Bovingdon Dr SL3. . .146 A3
Bovingdon Gn SL7 . .183 A4
**BOVINGDON
GREEN** 146 A2
Bovingdon Green
HP3. . . . . .145 F2
Bovingdon Hts SL7 183 B2
Bovingdon Prim Acad
HP3. . . . . .146 B4
Bovingdon Rd
Ley Hill HP5. . . . . . . .145 C1
Ley Hill HP5. . . . . . . .155 C8
BOW BRICKHILL. 48 C1
**Bow Brickhill CE Prim
Sch** MK17 . . . . .48 D2
Bow Brickhill Rd
MK17 . . . . .48 F3
Bow Brickhill Sta
MK7 . . . . .48 B2
Bowden La HP11. . . .173 C5
Bowen Cl MK7 . . . . . .48 C5
Bowerbank Ct HP20 101 F1
Bower Cl LU6. . . . . . . .92 F5
Bower Ct SL1 . . . . . .204 F6
Bowerdean Rd
HP13. . . . . .173 D7
Bower La LU6. . . . . . . .92 F5
Bowers La HP14. . . .159 D7
Bower Way SL1 . . . . .204 E6
Bowes Cl MK16 . . . . .22 C3
Bowes-Lyon Cl ②
SL4 . . . . .210 C6
Bowhill Cl HP22 . . . .130 A8
Bowland Dr MK4 . . . .46 B1
Bowl Barrow Way
Beaconsfield HP9 . . .175 F2
Beaconsfield HP9 . . .176 A2
Bowler Lea HP13 . . . .161 D2
Bowler Rd HP21 . . . .115 E4
Bowlers Cl MK2 . . . . .47 E5
Bowlers La MK18 . . . .53 C2
Bowler's Orch HP8 . .177 A7
Bowles Pl MK6 . . . . . .47 D7
Bowling Alley HP22 . .86 D7
Bowling Cl UB10 . . .201 F4
Bowling Ct
Chesham HP5. . . . . .154 C8
Henley-on-Thames
RG9. . . . . .191 D3
Bowling Gn HP10 . . .158 D5
Bowling Gn Cl
④ Bletchley MK2. . . . .58 D8
Fenny Stratford MK2. .47 D1
Bowling Green Cl ①
MK3 . . . . .58 D8
Bowling Green Rd
MK43 . . . . .25 C1
Bowling Leys MK10. . .36 A2
Bowl Rdbt The MK4 . .46 D5
Bowmans Cl SL1. . . .197 B3
Bowmont Dr HP21. . .115 D4
Bowood
④ Great Holm MK8. . . .33 F1
⑤ Milton Keynes MK8 .33 F1
Bowood La HP22 . . . .141 E5
Bow Rd MK10 . . . . . . .36 C4
Bowry Dr TW19 . . . .211 F7
Bowstridge Ct ⑥
HP13. . . . . .173 C7

Bowstridge La HP8. .177 C5
Bowstring Link MK17 37 D7
Bowyer Cres SL1 . . .189 F5
Bowyer Dr SL1 . . . . .204 E6
Bowyers Mews MK14 34 F6
Boxall Wy SL1. . . . . .206 C1
Boxberry Gdns MK7 .48 A6
Boxer Rd MK27 . . . .138 E6
Boxgrove Ct MK10. . .36 A1
Box La HP3 . . . . .146 E7
Box Tree Cl HP5. . . .154 D6
Boxwell Rd MK4 . . . .135 B4
Boxwood Cl UB7. . . .208 F4
Boyce Cres MK7. . . . .48 E5
Boycott Ave MK6 . . . .34 E1
Boyers Pit UB9 . . . . .190 B6
Boyle Cl UB10 . . . . .201 F3
Boyndon Rd SL6. . . .202 B7
BOYNE HILL. 202 D6
Boyne Hill CE Inf Sch
SL6. . . . . .202 D6
Boyne Ho HP9 . . . . .175 E1
Boyn Hill Ave SL6 . .202 D6
Boyn Hill Cl SL6 . . . .202 C6
Boyn Hill Rd SL6 . . .202 D6
Boyn Valley Ind Est
SL6. . . . . .202 E6
Boyn Valley Rd SL6 202 D5
Bozenham Mill La
NN7. . . . . .9 F5
Bozenham Mill Rd
NN7. . . . . .9 F7
Bracken Cl SL2 . . . .198 D8
Brackenforde SL3. . .206 C4
Bracken Hill HP4. . . .135 E5
Bracken Rd SL6 . . . .202 C4
Brackens The HP11 173 C5
Bracken Way
Aylesbury HP21. . . . .115 B8
Flackwell Heath
HP10. . . . . .185 B7
Brackenwood HP14 161 C7
BRACKLEY. 38 A8
Brackley Cll HP22 . . .117 C5
**Brackley Community
Hospital** NN13 . . . . .26 A1
Brackley Dr HP15 . . .163 A6
Brackley La MK18 . . .73 B6
Brackley Rd
Chackmore MK18 . . . .41 B1
Hazelmere HP15. . . .163 A6
Shalstone MK18 . . . . .39 E5
Water Stratford MK18. .40 B4
Westbury NN13. . . . . .39 B5
Bradbery WD3 . . . . .178 D5
Bradbery Cl NN13 . . .27 B7
Bradbourne Dr MK7 .48 C3
Bradbury Cl MK13. . .34 A3
Bradbury Gdns SL3 199 D8
Bradcutts La SL6. . .195 E8
Braddenham Wlk
HP21. . . . . .115 E4
Braddens Furlong
HP18. . . . . .125 C6
Braden Cl HP21 . . . .116 A6
BRADENHAM 160 F7
Bradenham Beeches
Walter's Ash HP14 . . .150 A1
Walter's Ash HP14 . . .161 A8
Bradenham La SL7 .194 C5
Bradenham Rd
HP14. . . . . .161 A3
Bradenham Wood La
Naphill HP14. . . . . . .150 B1
Walter's Ash HP14 . . .161 A7
Bradfield Ave MK18 .41 D2
Bradford Gdns MK5 .46 B4
Bradford Rd
Heronsgate WD3. . . .167 C2
Slough SL1 . . . . .205 A7
Bradley Cl HP18. . . .109 D5
Bradley Gr MK4 . . . . .46 B2
Bradley Rd SL1 . . . . .205 E6
**Bradnam Wood Nature
Reserve** SL6 . . . . . .194 D4
Bradshaw Cl SL4 . . .209 E6
Bradshawe Waye
UB8. . . . . .208 F8
Bradshaw Rd HP13 173 F6
BRADVILLE 34 B7
Bradvue Cres MK13 .34 B6
BRADWELL 34 A4
BRADWELL ABBEY. . .33 F3
**BRADWELL
COMMON**. 34 B3
Bradwell Common Bvd
Bradwell MK9 . . . . . . .34 C3
Milton Keynes MK13 . .34 C3
Milton Keynes MK13 . .34 C3
Bradwell Pk MK8. . . . .33 E3
Bradwell Rd
Milton Keynes MK5,
MK8 . . . . .34 A1
Milton Keynes, Bradville
MK13 . . . . .34 A6
Milton Keynes, Loughton
MK5 . . . . .46 B8
Bradwell Village Sch
MK13 . . . . .34 B4
Braeburn Ct SL1 . . .205 C4
Braeburn Wy MK43. .25 B2
Brae Hill HP18 . . . . . .110 A8
Braemar Ct ⑤ SL7 .183 D2
Braemar Gdns SL1 .205 A4
Braeside HP14. . . . . .161 C6
Braford Gdns MK5 . .46 B4
BRAGENHAM. 70 C6

Bragenham La LU7,
MK17 . . . . .70 D5
Bragenham Side
MK17 . . . . .69 F7
Bragmans La
Belsize WD3 . . . . . . .156 D6
Chipperfield WD4 . . .156 E6
Brahaman Way
Whitehouse MK19. . . .33 C1
Whitehouse MK19. . . .45 C8
Brahms Cl MK7 . . . . .48 C5
Brahms La HP21 . . . .115 F3
Braid End MK18. . . . .52 F6
Braid The HP5 . . . . .144 E1
Brailsford Wy ②
MK7 . . . . .48 A5
Braken Rd OX39. . . .147 D8
Brakynbery HP4 . . . .134 E7
Bramber Cl MK3 . . . . .57 E7
Bramber Ct SL1 . . . .205 A5
Bramble Ave MK14 . .34 E4
Bramble Cl
Chalfont St Peter
SL9 . . . . .177 C4
Uxbridge UB8 . . . . . .208 F7
Bramble Cres HP15 163 C6
Bramble Dr SL6 . . . .202 A4
Bramble La HP7. . . .165 E6
Bramble Mead HP7 187 B7
Brambleside HP11. . .174 B4
Brambles The UB7 .208 E2
Brambling HP19 . . . .101 E3
Bramblings The
Little Chalfont HP6 . .155 A1
① Little Chalfont
HP6. . . . . .166 A8
Brambling Wy SL6 . .203 A8
Bramcote Cl HP20. . .116 C8
Bramley Chase SL6 .203 A8
Bramley Cl
High Wycombe
HP12. . . . . .172 E4
Maidenhead SL6 . . .202 C3
Bramley Ct MK43. . . . .3 F6
Bramley End HP14 . .151 C4
Bramley Gdns SL8. .185 B3
Bramley Grange
MK2 . . . . .58 D4
Bramley Mdws MK16 22 B3
Bramley Rd
Aylesbury HP18. . . . .100 A3
Milton Keynes MK1 . . .47 D3
Brammas Cl SL1 . . . .205 C3
Brampton Ct
Maidenhead SL6 . . .203 B8
Milton Keynes MK13 . .34 A6
Branch La
Broughton HP22. . . .102 E2
Wooburn HP10 . . . . .185 E2
Branch Rd HP10. . . .174 B2
Brand Ave UB10. . . .201 E3
Brandon Cl HP22. . . .117 E6
Brandon Ct HP23. . . .103 D7
Brandon Mead HP5 143 F2
Brandon Rd HP12 . . .172 B3
BRANDS HILL 212 A8
Brands Hill Ave
HP13. . . . . .162 C2
Brands Rd SL3 . . . . .212 B8
Brandville Rd UB7. . .208 E4
Brandy St HP18 . . . .100 E4
Bransgill Ct MK13 . . .34 B4
Bransworth Ave
MK10 . . . . .48 C8
Brantham Cl MK7 . . . .48 A3
Brantwood Cl ⑦
MK4 . . . . .45 F1
Braunston MK6 . . . . .47 D6
Bravenfield MK18 . . .53 C2
Brawlings La SL9. . . .178 A6
Brawn Gr MK17 . . . . .48 D8
BRAY 203 D3
Braybank SL6. . . . . .203 D4
Braybourne Cl UB8. .201 C6
Braybrooke Dr MK4 . .46 F2
Bray Cl SL6 . . . . .203 C3
Bray Ct
② Amersham HP6 . . .154 E2
Maidenhead SL6 . . .203 C2
Brayfield Cl HP8 . . . .166 D7
Brayfield Ho MK46 . . . .8 B5
Brayfield Rd HP8 . . .166 D7
Brayfield Rd SL6. . . .203 C4
Brayfield Way HP8. . .166 D7
Bray Pit Wildlife Reserve
SL6. . . . . .203 C2
Bray Rd SL6 . . . . . . .203 B5
Brays Cl HP6. . . . . . .153 C4
Brays Green La HP6 153 C4
Brays La HP6 . . . . . .153 C5
Brays Mdw HP6 . . . .153 C4
Brayton Ct MK5. . . . .46 C6
BRAY WICK 203 B4
Braywick Court Sch
SL6. . . . . .203 A4
Braywick Nature Ctr★
SL6. . . . . .203 B3
**Braywick Park Nature
Reserve** SL6 . . . . . .203 A5
**Braywick Park & Sports
Gd** SL6. . . . . .203 A5
Braywick Rd
Maidenhead SL6 . . .202 F4
Maidenhead SL6 . . .203 A4
Braywood Cotts
SL4 . . . . .209 A5
Braziers End HP5 . . .133 C1
Breachwell Pl LU7. . .91 A1

Breakspear Road N UB9 . . . . 190 E8
Breakspear Road S UB10 . . . . 190 F2
Bream Cl SL7 . . . . . . 194 C8
Breamore Ct MK8 . . . . 45 F8
Brearley Ave MK6 . . . . 46 E7
Brearley Cl UB8 . . . . 201 E6
Breckland MK14 . . . . 34 D6
Brecknock Chase MK19 . . . . 45 C8
Brecon Ct
Milton Keynes MK10 . . . 35 F1
Slough SL1 . . . . 205 C4
Brecon Way HP13 . . 172 E8
Bredward Cl SL1 . . . 197 B2
Breedon Dr HP18 . . 100 E5
Breezes The SL6 . . . 202 E4
Bremen Gr MK5 . . . . . 46 A4
Brenchwood Cl HP13 . . . . 161 C2
Brenda's Way HP19 101 D2
Brendon Ct MK4 . . . . 46 D2
Brent MK6 . . . . 47 D5
Brent Gr MK19 . . . . . . 10 F2
Brent Path HP21 . . . 115 D4
Brent Rd SL8 . . . . . . 185 A4
Brentwood Way HP21 . . . . 116 B6
Bretby Chase MK4 . . . . 45 F3
Breton MK11 . . . . 32 E6
Brewery La HP22 . . . 102 E3
Brewhouse La HP22 . 88 E1
Brewster Cl MK5 . . . . 45 D5
Brew Twr SL7 . . . . . . 183 D1
Briaily HP14 . . . . . . 159 C2
Briar Cl SL6 . . . . 204 B7
Briar Dene SL6 . . . . . 195 C1
Briar Glen SL6 . . . . . 195 E6
Briar Hill MK12 . . . . . . 33 E4
Briar Lodge MK12 . . . 33 D5
Briars Cl HP19 . . . . . 101 B2
Briars The
High Wycombe HP11 . . . . 173 C5
Holmer Green HP15 . 163 C7
Slough SL3 . . . . 206 F1
Briarswood HP15 . . 163 B3
Briarswood Cl HP14 158 E5
Briar Way
Berkhamsted HP4 . . . 135 D3
Slough SL2 . . . . 205 B8
Briary Ct MK18 . . . . . . 74 F8
Briary View MK17 . . . 56 C8
Brices Mdw MK5 . . . . . 46 A3
Brich La HP3 . . . . . . 156 B6
Brick Cl MK11 . . . . . . 33 C2
Brick Field MK2 . . . . . 58 E8
Brickfield La SL1 . . . 197 B4
Brickfields Way UB7 . . . . 208 F3
Brick Hill HP18 . . . . . . 97 E1
Brickhill Manor Ct MK17 . . . . 59 D5
Brickhill Rd
Bow Brickhill MK17 . . . 48 B1
Bow Brickhill MK17 . . . 59 A8
Soulbury MK17 . . . . 70 F8
Brickhill St
Giffard Park MK14 . . . . 22 A1
Milton Keynes, Monkston Park MK10 . . . . 35 E2
Milton Keynes, Willen Park MK15 . . . . 35 C6
Walton Park MK7 . . . . . 48 A4
Brickhill Way MK18 . . 73 B5
Brick Kiln La HP22 . 102 B4
Bricks La HP14 . . . . 159 C4
Brickwell Wlk HP15 163 B3
Bricstock HP22 . . . . . 88 D4
Bridens Way HP17 . . 126 F6
Bridge Acad Central MK6 . . . . 47 A6
Bridge Ave
Cookham Rise SL6 . . . 195 E6
Maidenhead SL6 . . . . 203 A7
Bridge Bank Cl HP11 . . . . 174 A3
Bridge Cl SL1 . . . . . . 204 F6
Bridge Ct
Berkhamsted HP4 . . . 135 D4
Maidenhead SL6 . . . . 203 C7
Bridge Farm Bldgs HP17 . . . . 128 B8
Bridgeford Ct MK6 . . 46 E8
Bridgegate Bsns Pk HP19 . . . . 101 B1
Bridge Ho
High Wycombe HP13 . . . . 173 D6
West Drayton UB7 . . . 208 D5
Bridge Hook Cl 4 MK12 . . . . 33 A6
Bridge Leys Mdw HP19 . . . . 101 D4
Bridgeman Ct 5 SL4 . . . . 210 A5
Bridgeman Dr SL4 . 210 A5
Bridge Pl HP6 . . . . . . 154 F1
Bridge Rd
Cosgrove MK19 . . . . . . 19 E2
Ickford HP18 . . . . 123 F2
Maidenhead SL6 . . . . 203 B7
Stoke Bruerne NN12 . . . . 9 A8
Uxbridge UB8 . . . . . . 201 C3
Bridge St
Berkhamsted HP4 . . . 135 D4
Buckingham MK18 . . . 52 D8
Bridge St *continued*
Colnbrook SL3 . . . . . . 212 D7
Great Kimble HP17 . . 129 D1
High Wycombe HP11 . 173 A7
Leighton Buzzard LU7 . . 80 F7
Maidenhead SL6 . . . . 203 A7
Milton Keynes MK13 . . . 33 F7
Olney MK46 . . . . 6 F2
Thornborough MK18 . . 54 B8
Turvey MK43 . . . . 8 D5
Bridgestone Dr SL8 185 C3
Bridgeturn Ave MK12 . . . . 33 D8
Bridgewater Cl LU6 . 93 A8
Bridgewater Ct
Little Gaddesden HP4 . . . . 121 C8
Slough SL3 . . . . 207 A2
Bridgewater Hill HP4 . . . . 134 F7
Bridgewater Ho 6 MK18 . . . . 52 C8
Bridgewater Monument★ HP4 . . . . 120 E7
Bridgewater Rd HP4 . . . . 135 B5
Bridgewater Sch HP4 . . . . 135 A6
Bridgewater Terr SL4 . . . . 210 D6
Bridgewater Way SL4 . . . . 210 D6
Bridgeway
Cuddington HP18 . . . 112 E3
Milton Keynes MK13 . . 34 A7
Bridge Wlk MK19 . . . . 31 E4
Bridgnorth Dr MK4 . . 45 E1
Bridle Cl
Maidenhead SL6 . . . . 195 E1
Milton Keynes MK13 . . 34 B6
Bridle Gate HP11 . . . 172 F6
Bridle Manor HP22 . 131 C8
Bridle Rd SL6 . . . . . . 195 E1
Bridleway
Buckland Common HP22 . . . . 132 E5
Weston Turville HP22 116 F2
Bridle Way HP4 . . . . 135 A6
Bridleways HP22 . . . 131 A5
Bridlington Cres MK10 . . . . 36 A1
Bridlington Spur SL1 . . . . 205 B4
Bridport Way SL2 . . 198 B1
Briery Way HP6 . . . . 154 E1
Brighton Spur SL2 . 198 B1
Brightwell Ave LU6 . . 93 C7
Brigidine Sch SL4 . . 210 D4
BRILL 96 B1
Brill CE Comb Sch HP18 . . . . 96 B1
Brill Cl
Maidenhead SL6 . . . . 202 D3
Marlow SL7 . . . . 183 C2
Brill Ho SL6 . . . . 202 C3
Brill Pl MK13 . . . . 34 C3
Brill Rd
Chilton HP18 . . . . 110 F3
Chilton HP18 . . . . 111 A3
Horton-cum-S OX33 . 108 C6
Ludgershall HP18 . . . . 96 B7
Oakley HP18 . . . . 109 F5
Brill Windmill HP18 . 96 A1
Brimmers Hill HP15 162 F6
Brimmers Rd HP27 139 D2
Brimmers Way HP19 . . . . 114 F8
Brimstone La HP19 . 101 C4
Brimstone Way HP4 . . . . 134 F6
Brindlebrook MK8 . . . 33 E1
Brindles Cl MK18 . . . . 73 B5
Brindles La HP9 . . . . 175 A4
Brindley Ave HP13 . 161 F1
Brindley Pl UB8 . . . . 208 C7
Brinkburn Chase MK10 . . . . 36 A1
Brinkhurst SL7 . . . . . 183 D2
Brinklow Rdbt MK10 . 36 C1
Briskman Way HP21 . . . . 115 B6
Bristle Hill MK18 . . . . 52 C8
Bristol Cl
Haddenham HP17 . . . 126 E6
Stanwell TW19 . . . . . 213 E1
Bristol Ct 10 TW19 . . 213 E1
Bristol Way SL1 . . . . 205 F5
Bristow Cl MK2 . . . . . 47 E1
Britain La HP18 . . . . . 99 B7
Britannia Ct UB7 . . . 208 D3
Britannia Ind Est High Wycombe HP12 . . . . 172 D7
Poyle SL3 . . . . 212 E5
Britannia Pl RG9 . . . 191 E1
Britannia Rd 6 HP5 . . . . 144 C2
Britannia St HP20 . . 115 E8
Britnell Ct HP14 . . . . 158 E5
Britten Cl HP21 . . . . 115 F3
Britten Gr MK7 . . . . . . 48 D5
Brittens Ct MK46 . . . . . . 7 C3
Brittens La MK17 . . . . 37 C3
BRITWELL 197 F1
Britwell Dr HP4 . . . . 135 E6
Britwell Gdns SL1 . . 197 D2
Britwell Rd SL1 . . . . 197 D2
Broad Arrow Cl MK14 . . . . 34 E7
Broad Dean MK6 . . . . 47 A8
Broadfields HP19 . . 101 A1
Broadfields Ct HP19 . . . . 101 A1
Broadfields Ret Pk HP19 . . . . 101 A1
Broad Gn MK43 . . . . . 25 C3
BROAD GREEN 25 B3
Broad Highway HP23 . . . . 103 F1
Broad La
Aylesbury HP22 . . . . . 116 D7
Beaconsfield HP9, HP10 . . . . 186 A6
Hedsor HP10 . . . . 185 F3
Broadlands MK6 . . . . 47 C5
Broadlands Ave HP5 . . . . 144 C1
Broadleys SL4 . . . . . 209 F7
Broad Leys HP27 . . . 139 A3
Broadmark Rd SL2 . 206 B6
Broad Oak SL2 . . . . . 198 C1
Broad Oak Ct SL2 . . . 198 C1
Broadpiece MK15 . . . 35 A7
Broad Platts SL3 . . . 206 D3
Broad Rush Gn LU7 . . 80 E8
Broad St
Chesham HP5 . . . . . . 144 C1
Newport Pagnell MK16 22 C4
Syresham NN13 . . . . . 27 B8
Broadview Rd HP5 . 144 B4
Broadwater
Berkhamsted HP4 . . . 135 C5
Milton Keynes MK6 . . . 47 D6
Broadwater Gdns UB9 . . . . 190 C7
Broadwater La UB9 190 C7
Broadwater Pk UB9 190 A5
Broadwater Pk SL6 . 203 E1
Broadway SL6 . . . . . . 202 F7
Broadway Ave MK14 . . 21 F2
Broadway Cl 5 HP7 . . . . 165 B7
Broadway Ct HP5 . . 154 B8
Broadway Par UB7 . 208 E4
Broadway The
Amersham HP7 . . . . . 165 B7
Beaconsfield HP9 . . . 175 D3
3 Chalfont St Peter SL9 . . . . 177 D2
Chesham HP5 . . . . . . 154 B8
Farnham Common SL2 . . . . 198 C6
Grendon Underwood HP18 . . . . 82 F6
Brocas St SL4 . . . . . . 210 D7
Brocas Terr SL4 . . . . 210 D7
Brocas Way LU7 . . . . . 91 A3
Brockhampton MK15 35 B6
Brockhurst Cl 6 MK7 . . . . 48 A8
Brockhurst Rd HP5 . 144 C2
Brock La SL6 . . . . 202 F7
Brocklehanger Edge MK43 . . . . 25 B2
Brockton Ct SL6 . . . 202 F6
Brockway SL3 . . . . . . 207 B1
Brockwell MK16 . . . . . 22 C4
Broddick Ho HP11 . . 174 B4
Brokend HP18 . . . . . 100 D4
Broken Furlong SL4 . . . . 205 B1
Broken Gate La UB9 . . . . 189 C3
Bromham Mill MK14 . . 21 F2
Bromley HP23 . . . . . 104 A4
Bromley Gr MK10 . . . 36 C3
Bromley La HP6 . . . . 153 C5
Brompton Cl 2 HP19 . . . . 101 B2
Brompton Cres HP19 . . . . 101 B2
Brompton Dr SL6 . . 195 C2
Bromycroft Rd SL2 . 198 A2
Bronsdon Way UB9 . 189 F2
Bronte Ave MK4 . . . . . . 56 F7
Bronte Cl
Aylesbury HP19 . . . . . 100 F2
Slough SL1 . . . . 205 E4
Brookbank HP10 . . . 185 D3
Brook Bsns Ctr UB8 201 B3
Brook Cl
Aston Clinton HP22 . . 117 D5
Ludgershall HP18 . . . . 96 C8
Brook Cres SL1 . . . . 204 E7
Brook Dene MK18 . . . . 65 F4
Brookdene Cl SL6 . . 195 F2
Brooke Cl MK3 . . . . . . 57 F7
Brooke Furmston Pl SL7 . . . . 183 E3
BROOK END
Ivinghoe 105 E4
North Crawley 23 F5
Weston Turville 117 A3
Brook End
North Crawley MK16 . . 24 A6
Weston Turville HP22 . . . . 117 A3
Brook End Sp Ctr MK5 . . . . 46 A3
Brooke Rd HP27 . . . . 139 B4
Brook Farm Cl MK18 . 62 C1
Brookfield UB8 . . . . . 201 E6
Brookfield Cl HP23 . 119 B4
Brookfield Ho SL3 . . 211 D6
Brookfield La MK18 . 52 D7
Brookfield Rd
Haversham MK19 . . . . 20 D2
Newton Longville MK17 . . . . 57 D3
Wooburn HP10 . . . . . 185 D3
Brookfields MK17 . . . . 69 F7
Brook Ho
Slough SL1 . . . . 205 D3
West Drayton UB7 . . . 208 D5
Brookhouse Dr HP10 . . . . 185 C3
Brook La
Berkhamsted HP4 . . . 135 B5
Harrold MK43 . . . . 3 F7
Newton Blossomville MK43 . . . . 8 B3
Thame OX9 . . . . 125 E1
Brooklands Farm Prim Sch (Countess Wy Campus) MK10 . . . . . 36 D3
Brooklands Farm Prim Sch (Fen St Campus) MK10 . . . . 36 C5
Brooklands Rd
1 Broughton MK10 . . 36 D4
Milton Keynes MK2 . . . 58 C7
Brooklyn Way UB7 . 208 D3
Brook Mdw HP17 . . . 127 B6
Brookmead Sch LU7 . . . . 105 E5
Brook Path SL1 . . . . 204 F6
Brooks Ct MK18 . . . . . 52 D8
Brookside
Colnbrook SL3 . . . . . . 212 C7
Halton HP22 . . . . 117 C1
Lillingstone Lovell MK18 . . . . 30 A6
Loudwater HP10 . . . . 174 C2
Milton Keynes MK12 . . 33 D4
Oakley HP18 . . . . 109 D5
Slough SL3 . . . . 206 E7
Thame OX9 . . . . 125 F1
Uxbridge UB10 . . . . . 201 F5
Weston Turville HP22 116 F2
Weston Turville HP22 . . . . 117 A2
Brookside Ave TW19 . . . . 211 E4
Brookside Cl
Old Stratford MK19 . . . 32 B6
Tiddington OX9 . . . . . 136 A7
Brookside La HP17 . 129 E3
Brookside Terr 5 HP21 . . . . 115 E8
Brooks Mews HP19 . 115 C8
Brook St
Aston Clinton HP22 . . 117 D5
Edlesborough LU6 . . . . . 92 F4
High Wycombe HP11 . 173 A7
Tring HP23 . . . . 119 B4
Windsor SL4 . . . . 210 D5
Brooksward Sch MK14 . . . . 34 F7
Brookway MK19 . . . . . 31 E4
Broombarn La HP16 151 E7
Broom Cl HP15 . . . . . 163 A3
Broomfield MK12 . . . 33 D4
Broomfield Cl HP16 151 E7
Broomfield Gate SL2 . . . . 198 B1
Broomfield Hill HP16 . . . . 151 E7
Broom Hill
Cookham Rise SL6 . . . 195 E6
Stoke Poges SL2 . . . . 199 A5
Broom Ho SL3 . . . . . 206 F2
Broomlee MK13 . . . . . 34 A5
Broomstick Ind Est LU6 . . . . 92 E4
Broomstick La
Botley HP5 . . . . 145 A1
Botley HP5 . . . . 154 F8
Cholesbury HP4 . . . . 133 A3
Brora Cl MK2 . . . . 58 C5
Brosse Cres MK17 . . . . 36 F1
Brotheridge Ct HP21 . . . . 115 B6
Brough Cl MK5 . . . . . . 46 A5
BROUGHTON
Aylesbury 116 D8
Milton Keynes 36 A3
Broughton Ave HP20 . . . . 116 B8
Broughton Cl HP22 . 102 B3
Broughton Com Inf Sch HP20 . . . . 116 B8
BROUGHTON CROSSING HP22 . . . . 102 C2
Broughton Fields Prim Sch MK10, MK16 . . . . 36 B4
Broughton Grounds Bsns Pk MK16 . . . . . . 37 A6
Broughton Grounds Com Woodlands★ MK16 . 36 E6
Broughton Grounds La
Atterbury MK16 . . . . . . 36 B5
Cranfield MK17 . . . . . . 37 A6
Broughton Jun Sch HP20 . . . . 116 B8
Broughton La HP20, HP22 . . . . 116 C8
Broughton Manor Bsns Pk MK16 . . . . 36 B4
Broughton Manor Prep Sch MK10 . . . . 36 C4
Broughton Rd
Milton Keynes MK10 . . . 35 F3
Milton Keynes MK10 . . 36 B4
Broughton Rd *continued*
Salford MK17 . . . . 36 F4
Salford MK17 . . . . 37 C3
Brow Bsns Ctr 10 HP11 . . . . 172 E7
Brownbaker Ct MK14 . . . . 34 F6
Browne Willis Cl MK2 . . . . 58 D8
Brownfield Gdns SL6 . . . . 202 E5
Browning Cl MK16 . . 22 A4
Browning Cres MK3 . 58 A7
Brownlow Ave LU6 . . . 92 F3
Brownlow Gate HP4 . . . . 107 A1
Brownlow La LU7 . . 105 A7
Brownlow Rd HP4 . . 135 C5
Brownlow Rise LU6 . 93 A8
Brownlow Wlk HP4 . 121 C5
Browns Cl MK18 . . . . . 65 E4
Browns Ct SL1 . . . . . 204 E6
Brownset Dr MK4 . . . 45 E1
Brownsfield Rd NN12 18 E6
Browns Hedge
Leighton Buzzard LU7 . . . . 105 D2
Pitstone LU7 . . . . 105 C3
Pitstone LU7 . . . . 105 C3
Browns La HP23 . . . . 133 A6
Browns Rd
Holmer Green HP15 . . . . 163 C6
Holmer Green HP15 . 163 C6
South Heath HP16 . . . 153 A7
Brown's Rise HP23 . 132 F3
Browns Way MK17 . . . 49 E5
BROWNS WOOD 48 C4
Brownswood Dr NN12 . . . . 18 D3
Brownswood Rd HP9 . . . . 175 E4
Browns Wood Rdbt MK7 . . . . 48 C5
Brow The HP8 . . . . . 177 D7
Broxbourne Cl MK14 . 21 F2
Brubeck Rd HP21 . . 115 F3
Brubeck Way 3 MK17 . . . . 48 E8
Bruce Cl SL1 . . . . 205 A5
Bruce Wlk SL4 . . . . . 209 D5
Brucewood Par SL7 183 E5
Bruckner Gdns MK7 . 48 D5
Brudenell SL4 . . . . . 209 F3
Brudenell Cl 5 HP6 154 F1
Brudenell Dr
Milton Keynes MK10 . . 48 C8
Stoke Mandeville HP22 . . . . 116 B1
Brunel Cl SL6 . . . . . . 202 E5
Brunel Ctr SL6 . . . . . 202 D5
Brunel Ctr (Sh Ctr) MK2 . . . . 58 C8
Brunel Gate HP19 . . 100 F1
Brunel Rd
Aylesbury HP19 . . . . . 100 F1
High Wycombe HP13 . 161 F1
Maidenhead SL6 . . . . 202 D5
Brunel Science Pk UB8 . . . . 201 E2
Brunel Univ
Uxbridge UB8 . . . . . . 201 D2
Uxbridge UB8 . . . . . . 201 E2
Uxbridge UB8 . . . . . . 201 F1
Brunel Way SL1 . . . . 205 F5
Brunleys MK11 . . . . . . 33 B3
Brunner Pl HP13 . . . 173 C6
Brunswick Cl HP19 . 101 B3
Brunswick Pl HP13 162 D2
Brushford Cl MK4 . . . 46 D3
Brushmakers Ct HP5 . . . . 144 B1
Brushwood Dr WD3 167 C5
Brushwood Jun Sch HP5 . . . . 144 E2
Brushwood Rd HP5 . 144 E2
Bryans Cres MK16 . . . 24 A6
Bryanston Ave HP20 101 F2
Bryant Ave SL2 . . . . 205 E8
Bryants Acre HP22 . 131 B6
BRYANT'S BOTTOM 150 F4
Bryants Bottom Rd HP16 . . . . 150 F4
Bryden Cotts UB8 . . 201 C1
Bryer Pl SL4 . . . . 209 D4
Bryfield Cotts HP3 . 146 C1
Bryher The SL6 . . . . 202 A7
Bryne La MK18 . . . . . . 53 B2
Bryony Cl UB8 . . . . . 208 F8
Bryony Pl MK14 . . . . . 34 E5
Buccaneer MK10 . . . . 36 B5
Buccleuch Rd SL3 . . 211 B7
Buchanan Ct OX25 . . 94 E7
Buchanan Rd OX25 . . 94 E7
Buchan Cl UB8 . . . . . 201 C2
Buckby MK6 . . . . 47 D6
Buckfast Ave MK3 . . . 47 A2
Buckfield Ct SL0 . . . 207 F4
Buckingham Ave SL1 . . . . 205 B7
Buckingham Avenue E SL1 . . . . 205 C7
Buckingham Canal Wildlife Reserve★ MK18 . . . . 42 D3
Buckingham Chantry Chapel MK18 . . . . . . 41 D1
Buckingham Cl HP13 . . . . 174 A7
BUCKINGHAM COM . . 41 D2
Buckingham Com Hospl MK18 . . . . 41 D1
Buckingham Ct
Amersham HP6 . . . . . 154 E2
Amersham HP6 . . . . . 154 E2
Brackley NN13 . . . . . . 38 A6
Newport Pagnell MK16 22 B3
Buckingham Ctr 8 MK18 . . . . 41 D1
Buckingham Dr HP13 . . . . 174 A7
Buckingham Gate
Medmenham SL7 . . . . 193 D7
Milton Keynes MK6 . . . 35 B1
Buckingham Gdns SL1 . . . . 205 F4
Buckingham Ho
Amersham HP6 . . . . . 154 D3
4 Maidenhead SL6 . 202 F6
Buckingham Ind Pk MK18 . . . . 52 D5
Buckingham Par 4 SL9 . . . . 177 D2
Buckingham Park CE Prim Sch HP19 . . . . 101 C5
Buckingham Pl 1 HP13 . . . . 173 A7
Buckingham Prim Sch MK18 . . . . 41 E2
Buckingham Rd
Adstock MK18 . . . . 64 F8
Aylesbury HP19, HP20 . . . . 101 D3
Biddlesden MK18 . . . . 27 C2
Brackley NN13 . . . . . . 38 A6
Chackmore MK18 . . . . 40 E3
Chackmore MK18 . . . . 41 A2
Deanshanger MK19 . . 31 E2
Deanshanger MK19 . . . 31 F3
Edgcott HP18 . . . . 72 F2
Gawcott MK18 . . . . . . 52 A5
Lillingstone Lovell MK18 . . . . 29 E8
Maids Moreton MK18 . 41 E6
Milton Keynes MK3 . . . 57 D7
Milton Keynes, Church Hill MK17 . . . . 56 E6
Newton Purcell MK18 . 50 B2
Padbury MK18 . . . . 53 A3
Shalstone MK18 . . . . . . 39 F8
Steeple Claydon MK18 63 E3
Tingewick MK18 . . . . . 51 D7
Tring HP23 . . . . 118 E3
Water Stratford MK18 . 40 A7
Weedon HP22 . . . . . . 101 C7
Westbury NN13 . . . . . . 39 B5
Whitchurch HP22 . . . . 77 A1
Whitchurch HP22 . . . . . 86 F7
Wicken MK19 . . . . 43 B7
Winslow MK18 . . . . 65 F5
Buckingham Ring Rd
Buckingham MK18 . . . 52 B7
Buckingham MK18 . . . 53 A7
Buckingham Ring Rd East MK18 . . . . 52 F8
Buckingham Road Ind Est NN13 . . . . 38 A6
Buckingham Sch MK18 . . . . 52 D7
Buckinghamshire Coll Group Amersham Campus HP7 . . . . . . 165 F8
Buckinghamshire County Mus★ HP20 . . . . 115 D8
Buckinghamshire New Univ
Chalfont St Peter HP8 . . . . 178 A8
High Wycombe HP11 . 173 A6
Uxbridge UB8 . . . . . . 201 C6
Buckinghamshire Railway Ctr★ HP22 . 84 F2
Buckingham Sq 1 MK9 . . . . 34 C2
Buckingham St
8 Aylesbury HP20 . . 101 D1
Milton Keynes MK12 . . 33 D7
Tingewick MK18 . . . . . 51 B6
Buckingham View HP5 . . . . 144 C1
Buckingham Way HP10 . . . . 174 A1
BUCKLAND 117 F6
Buckland Ave SL3 . . 206 B3
BUCKLAND COMMON 133 A3
Buckland Cres SL4 . 209 F6
Buckland Dr MK6 . . . . 47 C6
Buckland Gate SL3 . 199 B2
Buckland Lodge MK6 47 B6
Buckland Rd
Aston Clinton HP22 . . 117 F5
Aston Clinton HP22 . . 118 A4
Aston Clinton LU7 . . . 118 A4
Bucklands Croft HP23 . . . . 118 C8
BUCKLANDWHARF . 118 B4
Bucklebury Cl SL6 . . 203 C1
Buckle Cl HP22 . . . . 102 B1
Buckley Ct MK11 . . . . . 32 F4
Buckman Cl MK12 . . . 33 B5

Buckmaster Rd
  HP12 . . . . .172 C3
BUCKMOOREND 140 D6
Buckmoorend La
  HP17 . . . . .140 D6
**Bucks Goat Ctr & Animal
Farm The**★ HP22 . .130 A7
Buckthorn MK12 . . . . . 33 E5
Buckthorn Mws
  HP22 . . . . .116 D6
Budge Rd NN12 . . . . . . .18 F5
Buffins SL6 . . . . .196 E2
BUFFLER'S HALT 40 C3
Bufflers Holt Rd
  Chackmore MK18 . . . . 40 E4
  Chackmore MK18 . . . . 41 A4
BULBOURNE 119 C8
Bulbourne Cl HP4 . . .134 F6
Bulbourne Ct HP23 . .119 B7
Bulbourne Rd HP23 .119 B7
Bulkeley Ave SL4 . . . .210 B4
Bullbaiters La HP6 . .153 B5
Bullbeggars La HP4 .135 F3
Bullfinch Gdns 8
  HP19 . . . . .101 F3
BULLINGTON END . . . 20 C7
Bullington End MK16 20 C7
Bullington End Rd
  MK19 . . . . 20 A6
Bull La
  Gerrards Cross SL9 . .188 C7
  Gerrards Cross SL9 . .188 D6
  7 High Wycombe
   HP11 . . . . .173 A7
  Milton Keynes MK2 . . 58 D8
Bullocks Farm La
  HP14 . . . . .171 B7
Bullrush Gr UB8 . . . .201 C1
Bulls La HP18 . . . . . .124 A3
Bullsland Gdns
  WD3 . . . . .167 B3
Bullsland La WD3 . . .167 B3
Bulmer Cl MK10 . . . . . 36 B3
Bulrush Rd HP22 . . . .102 D3
BULSTRODE 146 E3
Bulstrode Cl WD4 . . .146 E2
Bulstrode Ct SL9 . . . .188 D5
Bulstrode WD4 . . . . .146 F3
Bulstrode Pl SL1 . . . .205 F3
Bulstrode Way SL9 . .188 D6
Bulwrk Way MK10 . . . 36 D3
Bumble Bee Ct 10
  SL7 . . . . .183 D2
Bunby Rd SL2 . . . . . .198 F5
Bunces Cl SL4 . . . . . .205 B1
Bunces Ct HP20 . . . . .101 D1
Bungalows The
  MK18 . . . . 51 A6
Bunhill Cl LU6 . . . . . . .93 F8
Bunkers Cres MK3 . . . 47 B2
Bunkers La LU7 . . . . . 80 D6
Bunstrux HP23 . . . . . .119 A4
Bunsty Ct MK11 . . . . . .32 F5
Bunten Meade SL1 . .205 B5
Bunyan Ct HP23 . . . . .119 B5
Burano Cl MK7 . . . . . . 48 C6
Burbridge Gdns
  UB10 . . . . .201 E3
Burchard Cres MK5 . . 46 A6
Burchett's Green Rd
  SL6 . . . . .194 C1
Burcot Gdns SL6 . . . .195 E3
BURCOTT 79 E4
Burcott Cl HP22 . . . . .102 B3
Burcott La HP22 . . . . .102 C2
Burdeleys La MK5 . . . 46 A4
Burdett Cl HP20 . . . . .101 C1
Burdett Dr HP14 . . . .161 B8
Burdett Rd 18 SL4 . .210 D6
Burdock Cl MK16 . . . . .21 F4
Bure Valley 5 MK10. 36 C3
Burewelle MK8 . . . . . 33 D1
Burfield Rd
  Chorleywood WD3 . . .167 A4
  Old Windsor SL4 . . . .211 A1
Burford Cl
  Ickenham UB10 . . . . .201 E8
  Marlow Bottom SL7 . .183 C5
Burford Gdns SL1 . . .204 C8
Burford Ho 18 SL4 . .210 D6
Burford Sch SL7 . . . .183 C5
Burgess Ave MK17 . . . 59 A7
Burgess Gdns MK16 . . 22 B2
Burgess La HP17 . . . .128 B7
Burgess Wood Gr
  HP9 . . . . .175 B1
Burgess Wood Rd
  HP9 . . . . .175 B2
Burgess Wood Road S
  HP9 . . . . .175 B1
Burgett Rd SL1 . . . . . .205 B3
Burgh Dr MK3 . . . . . . 58 A4
Burghley Ct MK8 . . . . .45 F8
Burgidge Way OX39 147 C7
Burholme MK4 . . . . . . 46 C4
Burke Rd
  Wendover HP22 . . . . .131 C4
  Wendover HP22 . . . . .131 C5
Burkes Cl HP9 . . . . . .186 B8
Burkes Cres HP9 . . . .175 D2
Burkes Ct HP9 . . . . . .175 D2
Burkes Par HP9 . . . . .175 D2
Burkes Rd HP9 . . . . . .175 D2
Burleigh Ct MK18 . . . .52 E8
Burleigh Piece MK18 .41 F1

Burleys Rd MK18 . . . . .65 F4
Burlington Ave SL1 . .205 E4
Burlington Ct 1
  SL1 . . . . .205 E4
Burlington Rd
  Burnham SL1 . . . . . . .197 B1
  Slough SL1 . . . . .204 B8
  Slough SL1 . . . . .205 E4
  2 Slough SL1 . . . . . .205 E4
Burma Cl HP13 . . . . . .173 E6
Burners La MK11 . . . . 33 B4
Burners Lane Ind Pk
  MK11 . . . . 33 B4
Burners Lane S
  MK11 . . . . 33 B3
Burness Cl UB8 . . . . .201 D3
Burnet MK14 . . . . 34 C7
Burnet La HP22 . . . . .102 D2
Burnetts Ct HP16 . . . .151 C5
Burnetts Rd SL4 . . . . .209 E6
Burney Dr
  Wavendon MK17 . . . . . 36 F1
  Wavendon MK17 . . . . . 37 A1
  Wavendon MK17 . . . . . 37 A1
  Wavendon MK17 . . . . . 48 E8
BURNHAM 197 C3
Burnham SL1 . . . . . . .204 D8
Burnham Ave HP9 . . .176 A1
**Burnham Beeches
National Nature
Reserve**★ SL2 . . . .198 A7
Burnham Cl
  Bourne End SL8 . . . . .185 A4
  High Wycombe HP12 .172 D6
  Windsor SL4 . . . . . . .209 D5
Burnham Ct SL6 . . . . .202 F8
Burnham Dr MK13 . . . .34 C3
Burnham Gram Sch
  SL1 . . . . .197 D1
Burnham Hts SL1 . . . .204 C7
Burnham La SL1 . . . . .204 E7
Burnham Pl NN13 . . . .27 B8
Burnham Rd
  Beaconsfield HP9 . . . .186 F6
  Hughenden Valley
   HP14 . . . . .162 A6
  Westcott HP18 . . . . . . .98 B7
Burnhams Field
  HP22 . . . . .116 E7
Burnham Sta SL1 . . . .204 D7
Burnhams The
  Aston Clinton HP22 . .117 C5
  Shabbington HP18 . . .124 D3
Burnham Yd HP9 . . . .175 F1
Burnmoor MK2 . . . . . 58 D4
Burnmoor Cl MK2 . . . 58 D4
Burns Cl
  Long Crendon
   HP18 . . . . .125 D7
  Newport Pagnell MK16 22 A4
Burns Ct HP21 . . . . . .115 F6
Burns Rd MK3 . . . . . . 58 A7
Burnt Oak SL6 . . . . . .195 F7
Burnt Wlk SL1 . . . . . .197 B1
Burrell Ct HP21 . . . . .115 C6
Burren The HP6 . . . . .154 D2
Burroughs Cres
  SL8 . . . . .185 A4
Burrow Ash Cl MK19 . .10 F2
Burroway Rd SL3 . . . .207 B5
Burrows Cl
  Tylers Green HP10 . . .163 C2
  Woburn Sands MK17 . .49 B5
Burrows Ho HP13 . . . .161 E2
Burr Wood Ct HP22 . .116 F3
Burton La HP27 . . . . .139 C5
Burton Rd UB10 . . . . .201 E4
Burtons La
  Chorleywood WD3 . . .167 A4
  Little Chalfont HP8 . .166 E5
Burton's Way HP8 . . .166 C7
Burton Way
  Oxley Park MK4 . . . . . 45 E3
  Windsor SL4 . . . . . . .209 E4
Burtree Cl MK12 . . . . . 33 D5
Burt's La HP27 . . . . . .125 D6
Burwell Hill NN13 . . . .26 A1
Bury Ave MK16 . . . . . . 22 C4
Bury Cl MK16 . . . . 22 C4
BURY END 165 D6
Bury Farm HP7 . . . . . .165 C7
Bury Farm Cl LU7 . . . .91 C6
Buryfield La HP16 . . . .152 B7
Buryhook Cnr OX33 . .122 C2
Bury La HP5 . . . . .154 B8
Bury Rise HP3 . . . . . .146 D6
Bury St MK16 . . . . 22 C4
Busby Cl MK18 . . . . . .41 F1
Buscot Pl MK8 . . . . . . .45 F8
Bushel Wharf HP23 . .119 A6
Bushey Bartrams
  MK5 . . . . 46 A3
Bushey Cl
  Buckingham MK18 . . . .41 F1
  High Wycombe HP12 .172 E7
  Whipsnade LU6 . . . . . .93 F1
  Whipsnade LU6 . . . . .107 F8
Bushey La MK18 . . . . . 51 C1
Bushfield Rd HP3 . . . .146 C6
Bushfields MK12 . . . . . 33 D6
Bushfield Sch MK12 . 33 D6
Bushmead MK10 . . . . .35 F1
Bushmead Cl HP22 . . . 87 B5
Bushmead Rd HP22 . . 87 B5
Bushnell Pl 2 SL6 . .202 B8
Bush The HP17 . . . . . .126 F5
Bushy La MK18 . . . . . .47 A3
Business Ctr The
  HP6 . . . . .154 F1

Business Village
  SL2 . . . . .206 B5
Buslins La HP5 . . . . . .143 E3
Butcher Cres MK17 . . 48 D8
Butcher La 7 MK5 . . .45 F3
Bute Brae MK3 . . . . . . 46 E2
Butler Ct 5 SL7 . . . . .183 F3
Butlers Cl
  Amersham HP6 . . . . .154 A2
  Windsor SL4 . . . . . . .209 D6
Butlers Court Rd
  HP9 . . . . .175 D1
Butlers Court Sch
  HP9 . . . . .175 D1
BUTLERS CROSS 176 F6
BUTLER'S CROSS 130 C3
Butlers Ct HP13 . . . . .173 F5
Butlers Gr MK14 . . . . . 34 D8
Butler Wlk HP19 . . . . .115 A7
Butterfield HP10 . . . .185 D4
Butterfield Cl MK15 . . 35 C2
Butterfield Cotts
  WD3 . . . . .178 E3
Butterfly Cl MK18 . . . .52 F6
Butterfly Gate 5
  MK10 . . . . 36 B3
Butterly Rd
  High Wycombe
   HP14 . . . . .158 B6
  Stokenchurch HP14. . .158 F4
Buttermere HP21 . . . .116 B7
Buttermere Ave
  SL1 . . . . .204 C8
Buttermere Cl MK2. . . 58 D6
Butter Row MK12. . . . 33 B6
Butterton Gdns
  MK10 . . . . 36 C3
Buttfurlong HP17 . . . .127 A7
Buttlehide WD3 . . . . .178 D5
**Buttler's Hanging
Wildlife Reserve**
  HP14 . . . . .160 D5
Button Gr MK5 . . . . . . 47 A7
Buxton Cl MK17 . . . . . 48 D8
Buzzacott La MK4 . . . 46 C3
Bybend Cl SL2 . . . . . .198 B4
Bycell Rd MK18 . . . . . 41 C6
Bye Gn HP22 . . . . . . .117 A3
BYE GREEN 117 A3
Byerly Ho MK14 . . . . . .34 F5
Byerly Pl MK14 . . . . . .34 F5
Byford Way MK18 . . . .65 F4
Byland Dr SL6 . . . . . .203 B1
Byrd Cres MK7 . . . . . . 48 D6
Byres The HP17 . . . . .126 F6
Byron SL3 . . . . .207 B1
Byron Cl
  6 Marlow SL7 . . . . . .183 F3
  Milton Keynes MK3 . . .57 F7
Byron Ct SL4 . . . . . . .210 A4
Byron Dr MK16 . . . . . . 22 A4
Byron Rd HP21 . . . . . .115 F6
Byron Way UB7 . . . . .208 F2
Byward Cl MK14 . . . . . 34 E7
Byways
  Berkhamsted HP4 . . .135 E5
  Burnham SL1 . . . . . . .204 A8
Bywell Ct 6 MK4 . . . . 56 E8
By-Wood End SL9 . . .178 A5

C

Cable Cres MK17 . . . . 49 B5
Cable Gr MK13 . . . . . . 34 C8
Cadeby St MK10 . . . . . 36 B3
Cadman Sq MK5 . . . . . 46 C5
CADMORE END
  170 C6
  Cadmore End HP14 . .170 D6
Cadmore End Ce Sch
  HP14 . . . . .170 C6
Cadmore End Comm Rd
  HP14 . . . . .170 F7
Cadsdean Rd
  Askett HP27 . . . . . . .139 E6
  Princes Risborough
   HP27 . . . . .139 F5
Cadwell Dr SL4 . . . . . .202 D3
Caernarvon Cres
  MK3 . . . . 57 E7
Caesars Cl MK3 . . . . . 34 A5
Caesars Gate NN13 . . 38 A6
Cages Wood Dr SL2 .198 B8
Cagney Cres 1 MK4. 45 E3
Cairngorm Gate MK6 46 D8
Cairngorm Pl SL2 . . .198 D1
Cairnside HP13 . . . . .173 E6
Caister Ct 2 MK4 . . . 56 E8
Caithness Ct MK3 . . . 46 E2
Calamus MK7 . . . . 48 B6
Calbroke Rd SL2 . . . .197 F2
CALDECOTE 22 E1
Caldecote La MK16 . . .22 F2
Caldecote St MK16 . . 22 C4
CALDECOTTE 48 A2
Caldecotte La MK7 . . 48 A3
Caldecotte Lake Dr
  MK7 . . . . 48 A2
Caldecotte Rdbt MK7 47 F3
Calder Cl SL6 . . . . . . .195 E1
Calder Ct
  Maidenhead SL6 . . . .195 D1
  1 Slough SL3 . . . . . .206 F1
Calder Gdns LU7 . . . . 80 B7
Calder Vale MK3 . . . . . 46 E1
Calder Way SL3 . . . . .212 E4
Caldwell MK8 . . . . 33 D1

Caldicot Cl HP21 . . . .116 B6
Caldicott Sch SL2 . . .198 B5
Caledon Cl HP9 . . . . .175 C3
Caledon Rd HP9 . . . . .175 C3
Calewen MK8 . . . . 33 E1
CALIFORNIA
  Aylesbury 115 C7
  Dunstable 93 F6
Callaghan Ct HP4 . . .135 D4
Callingham Pl HP9 . . .175 C3
Callis Farm Cl
  TW19 . . . . .213 E1
Calluna Dr MK3 . . . . . 47 A3
Calshot Dr 19 MK4 . . 56 E8
Calumet HP9 . . . . . . .175 B3
Calvards Croft MK12. . 33 C4
Calverleigh Cres
  MK4 . . . . 46 D3
Calverley Cres HP13 161 F2
CALVERT 73 B6
Calvert Cotts MK18 . . 73 D7
Calverton 32 E5
Calverton La MK19 . . 33 B1
Calverton Lane Rdbt
  MK11 . . . . 33 B2
Calverton Rd
  Middle Claydon
   MK18 . . . . .74 B6
  Steeple Claydon HP18. 73 D7
Calves Cl MK5 . . . . . . .46 A3
Calvie Croft MK12 . . . 33 D4
Calville Gdns HP18 . .100 E5
Cambell Sq MK9 . . . . 35 A3
Camber Cl MK3 . . . . . .57 F7
Camberton Rd LU7 . . 80 E6
**Cambian Bletchley Pk
Sch** 1 MK3 . . . . . . .57 F8
Cambidge Ave
  HP21 . . . . .116 B5
Cambria Ct SL3 . . . . .206 C4
Cambridge Ave
  Burnham SL1 . . . . . . .197 B3
  Slough SL1 . . . . .205 A7
Cambridge Cl
  5 Aylesbury HP20 . .101 E1
  Aylesbury HP20 . . . . .101 E1
  Harmondsworth UB7 .213 D8
Cambridge Close Ret Pk
  6 HP20 . . . . .101 E1
Cambridge Cres
  HP13 . . . . .173 E7
Cambridge Pl HP19 101 D1
Cambridge Rd
  Beaconsfield HP9 . . .175 C2
  Marlow SL7 . . . . .183 D2
  Uxbridge UB8 . . . . . .201 C1
Cambridge St
  Aylesbury HP20 . . . . .101 E1
  Milton Keynes, Bletchley
   MK2 . . . . 58 C8
  Milton Keynes, Wolverton
   MK12 . . . . 33 C6
Cambridge Terr 13
  HP4 . . . . .135 D4
Cambron MK8 . . . . . . 33 D2
Cam Ct MK3 . . . . 57 E8
Camden Ct HP19 . . . .101 C1
Camden Pl SL8 . . . . . .185 A4
Camden Rd SL6 . . . . .195 D1
Cameron Rd 6
  HP5 . . . . .144 C1
Camfield Ct SL6 . . . . .202 A8
Camilla Pl MK11 . . . . . .32 F3
Camlet Gr MK14 . . . . .34 D7
Camley Gdns SL6 . . . .202 A8
Camm Ave SL4 . . . . .209 E4
Cam Mead HP21 . . . . .116 B6
Camomile Ct MK7 . . . 48 C5
Camomile Way UB7 208 E6
Campania Cl MK10 . . . 36 A2
Campbell Cl
  Buckingham MK18 . . .52 E8
  High Wycombe HP13 .172 F8
Campbell Dr HP9 . . . .175 C5
Campbell La LU7 . . . .105 D3
CAMPBELL PARK . . . 35 A3
Campbell Park Rdbt
  MK9 . . . . .34 F7
Campbell Rd SL7 . . . .183 F4
Campbells Ride
  HP15 . . . . .163 D7
Campden Rd UB10 . . .190 F1
Camperdown SL6 . . . .196 B1
Camperdown Ho 9
  SL4 . . . . .210 C5
Camp Ind Est OX9 . .136 B4
Campion MK14 . . . . . . 21 E2
Campion Cl
  Aylesbury HP20 . . . . .116 C8
  Denham UB9 . . . . . . .190 A1
  Uxbridge UB8 . . . . . .208 F8
  Wavendon MK17 . . . . . 37 A1
Campion Rd HP15 . . . .162 F6
Campions Ct HP4 . . . .135 B3
Camp Rd SL9 . . . . . . .188 C4
Canada Rd SL1 . . . . . .206 B4
Canal Ct HP4 . . . . . . .135 D4
Canal La MK19 . . . . . . .31 F4
Canal Mus The★
  NN12 . . . . .9 A8
Canal Mws LU7 . . . . . 80 E7
Canalside
  Berkhamsted HP4 . . .134 C6
  Old Stratford MK19 . . .32 C7

Canalside continued
  Stoke Bruerne NN12 . . .9 A8
Canalside Rdbt MK9 . 35 B4
Canal St MK6 . . . . 35 B3
Canal Wharf SL3 . . . .207 A4
Canaria Cl 9 MK8 . . . 45 D8
Canberra Chase 5
  MK16 . . . . 36 B5
Candleford MK18 . . . . 52 D8
Candlemas La HP9 . . .175 E2
Candlemas Mead
  HP9 . . . . .175 E2
Candlemas Oaks
  HP9 . . . . .175 E2
Candover Cl UB7 . . . .213 D7
Candy La MK5 . . . . 46 B4
Candytuft Gn HP15 . .162 F6
Cane End Ct HP27 . . .139 A3
Cane End La
  Bierton HP22 . . . . . . .102 C6
  Bierton HP22 . . . . . . .102 C6
Canford Ct HP21 . . . .115 F5
Cannings Way 6
  HP13 . . . . .173 F6
Cannock Cl SL6 . . . . .203 B6
Cannock Rd HP20 . . . .101 E3
Cannon Court Rd
  SL6 . . . . .195 D3
Cannon Ct MK16 . . . . 22 D6
Cannondown Rd
  SL6 . . . . .195 E5
Cannon Gate SL2 . . . .206 C6
Cannon Hill Cl SL6 . .203 C2
Cannon Hill Way SL6 203 B2
Cannon La SL6 . . . . . .202 A6
Cannon Mill Ave
  HP5 . . . . .154 E5
Cannon Pl HP27 . . . . .139 B4
Cannons Hill HP18 . . .112 C5
Cannons Orch HP22 . 85 B4
Canonbury MK10 . . . . 35 E1
Canon Harnett Ct
  MK12 . . . . .32 F6
Canon Hill Dr SL6 . . .203 B3
Canon Ind Pk MK12. . 33 C7
Canon's Cloisters
  SL4 . . . . .210 D7
Canons Rd MK12 . . . . 33 C7
Canons The MK16 . . . 22 E3
Cantell Cl MK18 . . . . . 41 D1
Canterbury Cl
  Amersham HP7 . . . . .165 E8
  Monks Risborough
   HP27 . . . . .139 B5
Canterbury Ave SL2 198 C1
Canterbury Cl
  Aylesbury HP21. . . . . .115 D6
  High Wycombe HP12 172 D6
  Newport Pagnell MK16 22 E3
  Slough SL1 . . . . .205 E6
Cantilupe Cl LU6 . . . . 92 D6
Cantle Ave MK14 . . . . 35 A5
Cantley Cl HP20 . . . . .101 E2
Canvey Way MK3 . . . . 58 A4
Cape End MK14 . . . . . .21 F3
Capek Rd MK10 . . . . . 35 E2
Capel Cl MK18 . . . . . . .41 F7
Capel Dr MK14 . . . . . .34 F5
Capell Ave WD3 . . . . .167 C4
Capell Rd WD3 . . . . . .167 D4
Capell Way WD3 . . . . .167 D4
Cape Villas SL0 . . . . .207 E7
Capian Wlk MK8 . . . . 33 E1
Capital Dr MK14 . . . . . 34 E6
Capps La HP5 . . . . . . .143 A5
Capricorn Ho HP10 . .185 A8
Capron MK6 . . . . 47 B5
Capswood Bsns Ctr
  UB9 . . . . .189 C3
Captain Cook Cl
  HP8 . . . . .177 B6
Captain's Cl HP5 . . . .144 A4
Captain's Wlk HP4 . . .135 D3
**Captain's Wood Nature
Reserve** HP5 . . . . . .143 F4
Caraway Cl MK7 . . . . . 48 B4
Cardain Ho HP9 . . . . .175 D3
Cardigan Cl
  Milton Keynes MK3 . . .46 F1
  Slough SL1 . . . . .204 F6
Cardinal Dr HP18. . . . .100 E5
Cardinals Wlk SL6. . . .204 F7
Carding Pl MK13 . . . . 34 B8
Cardno Ave
  Wavendon MK17. . . . . .36 F1
  Wavendon MK17. . . . . .37 A1
Cardwell Cl MK4 . . . . 46 C2
Carew Ct
  16 Shenley Brook End
   MK4 . . . . 56 E8
  4 Shenley Brook End
   MK4 . . . . .56 E8
Carey Cl
  Aylesbury HP21. . . . . .115 D4
  Windsor SL4 . . . . . . .210 B4
Careys Croft HP4 . . . .135 A7
Careys Rd NN12 . . . . . 17 A8
Carey Way MK46. . . . . .7 A4
Carhampton Ct MK4 . 46 D3
Carisbrooke Ave
  HP12 . . . . .172 A5
Carisbrooke Cl SL6 . .202 C6
Carisbrooke Ct
  Buckingham MK18 . . . 41 E2
  Slough SL1 . . . . .205 F6
Carisbrooke Ho 4
  HP13 . . . . .173 F7
Carisbrooke Way
  MK4 . . . . 45 E1
Carleton Gate MK15 . 35 E7
Carlina Pl MK14 . . . . . 34 D3

Carlisle Rd SL1 . . . . .205 D6
Carlton Cl
  Aylesbury HP19 . . . . .101 A2
  Newport Pagnell MK16 22 E4
Carlton Ct HP27 . . . . .139 B3
Carlton Ho TW19 . . . .213 D2
Carlton Rd
  Slough SL2 . . . . .206 B6
  Turvey MK43 . . . . .8 E7
Carlyle Ave HP21. . . . .115 F7
Carlyle Cl MK16 . . . . . 22 A4
Carman Ct HP23 . . . .118 F3
Carmania Circle
  MK10 . . . . 36 C5
Carmarthen Rd SL1 .205 D5
Carmel Cl SL7 . . . . . .183 B1
Carnation Way
  HP21 . . . . .115 E5
Carne The MK11 . . . . . 32 E5
Carnot Cl MK5 . . . . . . 46 C4
Carnoustie Cl MK3 . . 57 C7
Carnweather Ct MK4 57 B8
Carolina Dr HP11 . . . .173 E5
Caroline Cl UB7 . . . . .208 D4
Caroline Ct SL7 . . . . .183 E5
Carolus Creek MK5 . . 35 A4
Carpenter Ct MK14 . . .34 F6
Carpenters Wood Dr
  WD3 . . . . .167 B5
**Carpenter's Wood,
Dungrove Wood Nature
Reserve** SL6 . . . . . .194 C2
Carpenters Yd
  HP23 . . . . .119 B3
Carradine Cres MK4 . 45 E3
Carr Cl HP19 . . . . .101 A2
Carriage Pl UB8 . . . . .208 D8
Carriage Rd HP22 . . . .102 C2
Carrick Rd MK6 . . . . . .34 F1
Carrick St
  Aylesbury HP18 . . . . .100 F4
  Berryfields HP18 . . . .100 E4
Carriers Cl MK19 . . . . 11 A2
Carrington Ave
  HP10 . . . . .185 C8
Carrington Cl MK18 . 77 E5
Carrington Cres
  HP22 . . . . .131 A7
Carrington Ct 9
  HP12 . . . . .172 E7
Carrington Hall Rd
  MK17 . . . . 68 C5
Carrington Inf & Jun Sch
  1 Flackwell Heath
   HP10 . . . . .174 A1
  Flackwell Heath
   HP10 . . . . .185 A8
Carrington Pl
  Holmer Green
   HP15 . . . . .163 C7
  Tring HP23 . . . . .119 B5
Carrington Rd
  Aylesbury HP21. . . . . .115 D6
  High Wycombe HP12 172 D6
  High Wycombe HP12 172 D6
  Newport Pagnell MK16 22 E3
  Slough SL1 . . . . .205 E6
Carrington Way
  HP16 . . . . .151 C5
Carroll Cl MK16 . . . . . 22 A5
Carron Cl LU7 . . . . . . 80 B7
Carron Ct MK2 . . . . . . 58 C4
Carrs Dr HP12 . . . . . .172 C8
Carter Cl SL4 . . . . . . .210 A5
Carteret MK15 . . . . . . 35 E7
Carters Cl MK16 . . . . . 13 F1
Carters Gate MK18 . . 65 F5
Carters La
  Long Crendon HP18. . 125 B7
  Milton Keynes MK11 . . 33 A3
  North Marston MK18. . 75 E1
  Quainton MK22, MK18 . 85 E6
Carters Mdw MK18 . . 76 A2
Carters Ride HP22 . . .116 B2
Carter Wlk HP10 . . . .174 E8
Carthovel La HP18 . . . 83 A6
Cartington Gdns 8
  MK4 . . . . 56 E8
Cartmel Cl MK3 . . . . . 57 C6
Cartwright Ct 2
  HP13 . . . . .173 F5
Cartwright Pl MK6 . . . 46 E8
Carver Hill Rd HP11 . 172 F5
Carvers Mews MK14 . 34 E7
Carwithen Cl HP17 . . .126 F7
Cascadia Cl HP11 . . . .174 B2
Cashmere Cl MK5 . . . 46 A4
Cassius Cl MK11. . . . . 33 A3
Castell Gr MK11 . . . . . 33 A3
Casterton Cl MK13 . . 34 C4
Castle Acre MK10 . . . .35 F1
Castle Ashbyrd NN7 . .1 B7
Castle Ashby Rd NN7 . .1 B7
Castle Ave
  Datchet SL3 . . . . . . .211 D4
  West Drayton UB7. . . .208 F6
Castle Cl
  Marsh Gibbon OX6 . . .72 A3
  Pitstone LU7 . . . . . . .105 D3
  Totternhoe LU6 . . . . . .93 A8
  Wing LU7 . . . . 79 E3
Castle Ct
  13 Aylesbury HP20 . .115 D8
  Buckingham MK18 . . . 52 D8
  Maidenhead SL6 . . . .202 D7
Castle Dr SL6 . . . . . . .202 D7
Castle Est HP12 . . . . .172 D4
Castlefields HP22 . . . .116 C3

Castlefield Sch HP12 172 C6
Castle Gate Way HP4 135 C6
Castle Hill
Berkhamsted HP4 135 C5
High Wycombe HP11 173 A6
Maidenhead SL6 202 E7
Windsor SL4 210 D6
Castle Hill Ave HP4 135 C5
Castle Hill Cl HP4 135 C5
Castle Hill Ct HP4 135 C6
Castle Hill Rd LU6 93 A8
Castle Hill Terr SL6 202 E7
Castle Ho 5 LU7 80 E7
Castle La HP22 86 F6
Castle Lodge SL6 202 F7
Castlemead Cotts SL4 210 C3
Castle Meadow Cl MK16 22 E4
Castle Mews
Berkhamsted HP4 135 C4
Maidenhead SL6 202 E7
Castlemilk 2 MK18 41 D3
Castle Park Rd HP22 131 B6
Castle Pl 6 HP13 173 B7
Castle Rd MK46 2 F1
Castle Rose MK6 47 D6
Castle Row 16 HP23 119 A3
Castle St
Aylesbury HP20 115 D8
Berkhamsted HP4 135 C4
Buckingham MK18 52 D8
High Wycombe HP13 173 B7
Marsh Gibbon OX27 72 A3
Slough SL1 205 F3
Wingrave HP22 89 B3
Castlesteads MK13 33 F5
CASTLETHORPE 19 E5
Castlethorpe Fst Sch MK19 19 F5
Castlethorpe Rd
Hanslope MK19 11 A2
Hanslope NN12 19 F8
Castleton Ct SL7 183 E2
Castle View Gdns HP12 172 D7
Castleview Ho SL4 210 D7
Castleview Rd SL3 206 C2
Castleview Sch SL3 206 D2
Caswell La MK17 60 F7
Catchpin St MK8 52 F6
Catchpole Cl MK12 33 B5
Cater Rd HP14 171 C4
Catesby Croft MK5 46 C8
Cathay Cl MK3 58 B7
Cathedral of Trees MK15 35 C5
Catherine Cotts HP23 133 E8
Catherine Ct MK18 41 E2
Catherines Cl UB7 208 D4
Catkin Cl HP12 172 B3
Catslip RG9 179 A1
Caudery Pl 4 HP22 131 D6
Causeway Cl HP23 125 D1
Causeway The
Bray SL6 203 B3
Bray SL6 203 C4
Marlow SL7 183 E1
Causey Arch MK10 36 C3
Cautley Cl HP22 85 A5
Cavalier Ct HP4 135 C4
Cavalier Rd OX9 126 A1
Cavalry Cres SL4 210 C4
Cavan Way MK10 36 A4
Cavendish Cl
Burnham SL6 204 A7
Little Chalfont HP6 166 B8
Wendover HP22 131 B6
Cavendish Ct
Milton Keynes MK5 46 A7
Poyle SL3 212 E6
Cavendish Rd HP5 154 D7
Cavendish Way
9 Aylesbury HP19 100 F1
Aylesbury HP19 114 F8
Cavendish Wlk OX9 126 B1
Cavenham MK8 33 F2
Caversham Gn 1 HP20 101 D1
Cawardon MK14 34 C7
Cawcott Dr SL4 209 E6
Cawdor Rise MK4 45 E2
Cawkwell Way
Bletchley MK2 58 D8
Milton Keynes MK2 58 C8
Caxton Ct RG9 191 E1
Caxton Dr UB8 201 D3
Caxton Rd MK12 33 B7
Cayman Wk MK3 58 B3
Cecil Rd SL0 207 E7
Cecils Yd 7 MK18 41 D1
Cecil Way SL2 197 F1
Cecily Cl HP4 134 E4
Cecily Ct MK5 46 A5
Cedar 1 RG9 191 D2
Cedar Ave
Hazelmere HP15 163 A5
Hedsor SL1 186 A1
West Drayton UB7 208 F6
Cedar Chase SL6 196 D1
Cedar Cl
Aylesbury HP20 102 A2
Burnham SL1 197 C1
Chesham HP5 144 E1
Cedar Cl *continued*
Iver Heath SL0 200 C4
Milton Keynes MK19 32 B7
Cedar Ct
Gerrards Cross SL9 188 E7
High Wycombe HP13 173 B7
Maidenhead SL6 202 D7
Marlow SL7 183 E2
6 Windsor SL4 210 A5
Cedar Dr
Chesham HP5 144 A1
Cookham SL6 196 A7
Cookham Rise SL6 195 F7
Marlow Bottom SL7 183 C7
Cedar Gr
Amersham HP7 165 D8
Bellingdon HP5 143 D8
Cedar Lodge Dr MK12 33 D7
Cedar Park Sch HP15 162 F5
Cedar Rd HP4 135 D3
Cedar Ridge HP6 153 C5
Cedars Cl
Akeley MK18 41 F8
Chalfont St Peter SL9 177 E5
Cedars Dr UB10 201 F3
Cedars Ho SL6 203 A7
Cedars Prim Sch MK16 22 C4
Cedars Rd SL6 203 A7
Cedars The
Berkhamsted HP4 135 E4
Slough SL2 197 F2
Tring HP23 119 B4
Wendover HP22 131 A5
Cedars Upper Sch LU7 80 E5
Cedars Village WD3 167 F5
Cedars Way
Leighton Buzzard LU7 80 E5
Newport Pagnell MK16 22 C4
Cedars Wlk WD3 167 F5
Cedar Terr 1 HP11 172 F7
Cedar Way
Berkhamsted HP4 135 D3
Slough SL3 206 E2
Ceely Ho HP21 115 D6
Ceely Rd HP21 115 D6
Celandine Ct MK7 48 A5
Celia Johnson Cl UB9 190 A6
Celina Cl MK2 58 C7
Cell Farm SL4 211 B2
Cell Farm Ave SL4 211 B2
Centaur Ct MK10 36 D3
Centenary Bsns Pk RG9 191 F1
Centenary Cotts HP27 138 D7
Centenary Way 2 HP6 154 F1
Central Ave
Cranfield MK43 24 E2
Whipsnade LU6 107 E8
Central Dr SL1 204 F6
Central Est SL6 202 E7
Central Est SL6 202 E8
CENTRAL MILTON KEYNES 34 D1
Central Park Bsns Ctr HP13 173 A8
centre:mk (Sh Ctr) MK9 34 E3
Centre Par HP27 139 C5
Centre The SL2 198 C6
Centre Wlk HP15 163 A3
Centurion Ct MK11 33 C2
Centurion Rdbt MK1 47 C2
Century Ave
Milton Keynes MK6 46 E7
Oldbrook MK6 46 E8
Century La SL2 199 B1
Century Point HP12 172 C4
Ceres Gr MK11 32 F4
Cestreham Cres HP5 144 D2
CHACKMORE 41 B4
Chackmore Rd MK18 40 F3
Chacombe Pl HP9 175 D5
Chadbone Cl 9 HP20 115 D8
Chadds La MK6 47 C8
Chadwell Path HP21 116 C6
Chadwick Dr MK6 47 B7
Chadwick Rd SL1 206 D4
Chadwick St HP13 162 D2
Chaffinch HP19 101 F4
Chaff Rd HP22 102 B2
Chaffron Way
Leadenhall MK6 46 F7
Milton Keynes, Oakgrove MK6, MK10, MK15 35 D1
Milton Keynes, Shenley Lodge MK4, MK5, MK6 46 C5
Shenley Brook End MK4 56 E8
Chairborough Rd HP12 172 D6
Chairborough Rd Nature Reserve HP12 172 D5
Chairmakers Cl HP27 139 A1
Chairmakers Way RG9 170 F1
Chairmans Wlk UB9 189 F6
Chalcot Pl MK8 45 F8
Chalcott SL1 205 E3
Chalet Cl HP4 134 F4
Chalfont Ave HP6 166 D8
Chalfont Cl MK13 34 A6
CHALFONT COMMON 177 F6
Chalfont & Gerrards Cross Com Hospl SL9 177 D2
Chalfont Ho HP7 166 D7
Chalfont La
Chorleywood WD3 167 B4
Maple Cross WD3 178 D3
Chalfont & Latimer Sta/U Sta HP7 166 C8
Chalfont L Ctr SL9 177 C2
Chalfont Rd
Maple Cross SL9 178 C7
Seer Green HP9 176 D5
Seer Green HP9 176 D5
CHALFONT ST GILES 177 C7
Chalfont St Giles Inf Sch HP8 177 B7
Chalfont St Giles Jun Sch HP8 177 B7
CHALFONT ST PETER 177 F2
Chalfont St Peter CE Academy SL9 177 D2
Chalfont St Peter Inf Sch SL9 177 C3
Chalfonts Com Coll The SL9 177 C3
Chalfont Station Rd HP7 166 C7
Chalford HP10 185 F6
Chalford Flats HP10 185 F6
Chalford Way HP19 114 F8
Chalgrove Cl SL6 203 B6
Chalgrove End HP22 116 B1
Chalgrove Field MK5 45 D4
Chalgrove Rd OX9 126 A1
Chalgrove Wlk HP21 115 C6
Chalkdell Dr MK5 45 F4
Chalk Farm Rd HP14 158 D5
Chalk Hill
Chesham HP5 144 B2
Coleshill HP7 164 F2
Windsor SL4 210 F6
Chalkhill Blue Cl HP19 101 C4
Chalk La HP6, HP7 153 B4
Chalklands SL8 185 A4
Chalkpit La
Chinnor OX39 147 C5
Marlow SL7 183 B3
Chalk Pit La SL1 197 B4
Chalkpits The HP10 185 E6
CHALKSHIRE 130 C4
Chalkshire Cotts HP17 130 C4
Chalkshire Rd HP17 130 C4
Chalk Stream Rise HP6 155 A1
Chalkstream Way HP10 185 E7
Chalky Field HP14 171 C3
Challacombe MK4 46 D2
Challener Rd HP12 172 C3
Challenge Ho MK3 47 B1
Challow Ct SL6 195 D1
Chalmers Ave MK19 20 D2
Chaloner Pl HP21 115 D6
Chaloner Rd HP21 115 D6
Chaloners Hill MK18 63 D3
CHALVEY 205 C3
Chalvey Gdns SL1 205 E4
Chalvey Gr
Slough SL1 205 B4
5 Slough SL1 205 C4
Chalvey Pk SL1 205 E4
Chalvey Road E SL1 205 E4
Chalvey Road W SL1 205 D4
Chalwell Ridge MK5 46 B4
Chamberlain Rd HP19 101 B1
Chambers Cl 2 MK17 48 F8
Champflower MK4 46 D3
Champney Cl SL3 212 A4
Champneys Beauty Coll HP23 133 E6
Chancel Cl UB8 201 B3
Chancellors HP7 164 B5
Chancellors Cnr HP7 164 B5
Chancellors Rd HP19 101 C4
Chancery Cl MK13 34 A6
Chancerygate Bsns Ctr MK1 47 B3
Chancery Pl SL4 210 D7
Chandler Mws HP4 134 E6
Chandlers Ct MK6 47 E5
CHANDLERS HILL 200 E3
Chandlers Quay SL6 203 C8
Chandos Cl
Buckingham MK18 52 D7
Little Chalfont HP6 155 C1
Chandos Croft MK18 65 E5
Chandos Ct MK18 52 D7
Chandos Mall 7 SL1 205 F4
Chandos Pl
Milton Keynes MK2 58 B8
Wendover HP22 131 B4
Chandos Rd MK18 52 D8
Channer Dr HP10 163 B1
Channory Cl MK4 46 A1
Chantry Cl
Windsor SL4 210 A6
Woburn Sands MK17 49 A6
3 Yiewsley UB8 208 D6
Chantry Rd HP19 101 C3
Chantry Rise 8 MK46 6 F3
Chantry The
15 Aylesbury HP20 115 D8
Uxbridge UB8 201 F2
Chapel Arches SL6 203 A7
Chapel Cl
Blackthorn OX25 81 A3
Deanshanger MK19 31 E4
Little Gaddesden HP4 121 D6
Chapel Cotts SL2 199 B5
Chapel Crofts HP4 134 E6
Chapel Ct SL6 202 D4
Chapel Dr HP22 117 E5
CHAPEL END 118 C8
Chapel End SL9 177 D1
Chapel End La HP23 118 C8
Chapel Farm NN7 10 C6
Chapel Fields HP23 118 C8
Chapel Hill
Soulbury LU7 69 E3
Speen HP27 150 C4
Windsor SL4 210 D6
Chapel Ho HP6 153 C5
Chapel La
Akeley MK18 41 F8
Chilton HP18 111 B3
Drayton Parslow MK17 68 B5
High Wycombe HP12 172 C8
Ivinghoe Aston LU7 92 A1
Long Marston HP23 104 B4
Northall LU6 92 A5
Pitch Green HP27 138 B3
Rout's Green HP14 148 E2
St Leonards HP23 132 D3
St Leonards HP23 132 D3
Stoke Bruerne NN12 9 A8
Stoke Mandeville HP22 116 A1
Stoke Poges SL2 199 B5
Thornborough MK18 54 B8
Totternhoe LU6 92 F8
Turweston NN13 38 B7
Walter's Ash HP14 161 C7
Wendover HP22 131 B4
Weston Underwood MK46 6 B2
Whitfield NN13 26 D3
Chapel Rd
Flackwell Heath HP10 185 A8
Ford HP17 128 A7
Chapel Row HP14 171 A7
Chapels Cl SL1 204 E5
Chapel Sq LU7 68 E1
Chapel St
Berkhamsted HP4 135 D4
High Wycombe HP13 161 D3
Marlow SL7 183 E2
Slough SL1 205 F4
Tring HP23 118 F3
Uxbridge UB8 201 C4
Woburn Sands MK17 49 B4
Chaplin Gr MK8 45 D7
Chaplin Mews 7 SL3 206 F1
Chapman Ave MK14 35 A6
Chapman Cl
Aylesbury HP21 115 B6
West Drayton UB7 208 F3
Chapman La
Bourne End HP8, HP10 185 A6
Little Marlow SL8 184 F5
Chapmans Cres HP5 144 A2
Chapmans Dr MK19 32 B7
Chapmans La
Brill HP18 95 F2
Brill HP18 96 A2
Chapmans Lea HP22 88 D5
Chappell Cl HP19 101 D2
Chappell Way LU7 78 F8
Chappel Mdw HP23 119 B6
Chapter
Milton Keynes MK6 46 F5
Milton Keynes MK6 47 A5
Chapter Cl UB10 201 F5
Chapter Ho MK6 47 A5
Chapter Mews SL4 210 D7
Charbray Cres MK5 46 A4
Chardacre MK8 33 E1
Charisse Gdns MK4 45 D3
Charlbury Rd UB10 190 F1
Charles Cl HP21 116 B4
Charles Dr OX9 126 A1
Charles Gdns SL2 206 A7
Charles Ho
Henley-on-Thames RG9 191 E3
9 Windsor SL4 210 C6
Charles Kidnee Way HP22 116 A2
Charlespym Rd HP19 101 C4
Charles St
Berkhamsted HP4 135 B4
Tring HP23 119 A3
Windsor SL4 210 C6
Charlestown Lodge UB8 201 D6
Charles Warren Acad MK6 47 D5
Charles Way MK16 22 C4
Charle Wood MK17 60 C7
Charlewood Ho MK17 49 B3
Charlock Ct MK16 21 F4
Charlotte Ave SL2 205 F6
Charlotte Cl
Berkhamsted HP4 134 E4
Wing LU7 79 F2
Charlotte Cott SL6 203 B8
Charlotte Way 12 SL7 183 E2
Charlton SL4 209 C5
Charlton Cl
Slough SL1 205 B4
Swanbourne MK17 66 F3
Charlton Pl 2 SL4 209 C5
Charlton Row 5 SL4 209 C5
Charlton Sq 4 SL4 209 C5
Charlton Way SL4 209 C5
Charlton Wlk 3 SL4 209 C5
Charmfield Rd HP21 116 A5
CHARNDON 72 E6
Charnwood Cl 5 HP13 173 F5
Charsley Cl HP6 166 C8
Charter Cl 3 SL1 205 F3
Charter Dr 4 HP6 154 F1
Charter Pl UB8 201 D5
Charter Rd SL1 204 E6
Chartley Ct MK5 46 B4
CHARTRIDGE 143 C4
Chartridge Comb Sch HP5 143 C4
Chartridge Development UB8 201 B3
Chartridge Grange Dr HP5 143 D4
Chartridge Ho 3 HP13 173 F6
Chartridge La
Chartridge HP5 143 A6
Chesham HP5 143 F1
Chesham HP5 143 F2
The Lee HP16 142 F6
Chartridge Park Mobile Home Pk HP5 143 D4
Chartwell Gate HP9 175 D2
Chartwell Rd MK16 22 E4
Chartwell Way 6 HP11 173 E5
Chase Ave MK7 48 A4
Chase Cl HP7 165 A4
Chase Farm Barns MK17 56 C4
Chase Park Rd NN7 1 A5
Chaseport Cl MK46 5 D2
Chase Rd HP22 102 D2
Chaseside Cl LU7 105 A7
Chase The
1 Chesham HP5 144 B2
Maidenhead SL6 195 D3
Marlow SL7 184 A3
Newton Longville MK17 57 D4
Tylers Green HP10 163 C1
Wooburn HP10 185 F4
Chasewater Cres MK10 36 B3
Chater Dr MK46 7 A4
Chatfield SL2 205 A8
Chatham Ct 2 SL1 206 A3
Chatsworth MK8 33 F1
Chatsworth Cl SL6 202 C5
Chaucer Cl
Berkhamsted HP4 134 F5
Newport Pagnell MK16 22 A4
Windsor SL4 210 D4
Chaucer Dr HP21 115 F6
Chaucer Rd MK3 58 A7
Chaucer Way SL1 205 F5
Chaundler Dr HP19 101 B4
Chauntry Cl SL6 203 C6
Chauntry Rd SL6 203 B6
Chawton Cres MK8 33 F1
Cheapside La
Denham UB9 189 F2
Denham UB9 190 A2
CHEARSLEY 112 A2
Chearsley Rd
Chilton HP18 111 D3
Long Crendon HP18 125 E7
CHEDDINGTON 105 B7
Cheddington Comb Sch LU7 105 A7
Cheddington Gr HP22 102 B2
Cheddington La HP23 104 C5
Cheddington Rd
Mentmore LU7 90 A5
Mentmore LU7 90 C4
Pitstone LU7 105 C4
Cheddington Sta LU7 91 A2
Chelmsford Ct 8 SL4 210 C5
Chelsea Gn LU7 80 D6
Chelsea Ho 6 LU7 80 E7
Chelsea Rd HP19 100 E1
Cheltenham Gdns MK3 57 D6
Cheney Cl LU7 78 B1
Cheneys Wlk MK3 47 A2
Cheney Way HP20 101 E1
Cheney Wlk 3 HP20 101 F2
CHENIES 156 B2
Chenies Ave HP6 166 D8
CHENIES BOTTOM 156 B2
Chenies Hill
Chenies WD3 156 A2
Flaunden HP5 156 B4
Chenies Manor Ho* WD3 156 A1
Chenies Par HP7 166 C7
Chenies Parade HP7 166 C7
Chenies Rd
Chorleywood WD3 167 D7
Chorleywood WD3 167 E6
Chenies Sch WD3 156 B1
Chenille Dr HP11 173 E4
Cheniston Gr SL6 202 A7
Chepping Cl HP10 163 A1
Chepping View Prim Sch HP12 172 D3
Chepstow Ct SL2 197 E1
Chepstow Dr MK3 57 D6
Chequers
Ellesborough HP17 140 C7
Ellesborough HP17 140 C8
Princes Risborough HP17 139 F8
Chequers Ave HP11 173 E5
Chequers Bridge Cotts SL0 207 C4
Chequers Cl LU7 105 C4
Chequers Ct HP21 115 E4
Chequers Dr HP16 151 C6
Chequers End MK18 66 A4
Chequers Hill HP7 165 D7
Chequers La
Ibstone HP14, RG9 170 A5
North Crawley MK16 24 B6
Pitstone LU7 105 C5
Prestwood HP16 151 C7
Chequers Orch SL0 207 F7
Chequers Sq UB8 201 C5
Chequers The
Castlethorpe MK19 19 F5
Eaton Bray LU6 92 F5
Cherington Gate SL6 195 B1
Cheriton MK4 46 E3
Cherleton MK8 33 E1
Cherries The SL2 206 B7
Cherry Acre SL9 177 D6
Cherry Ave SL3 206 D4
Cherry Cl
Flackwell Heath HP10 185 B7
Iver SL0 207 F6
Prestwood HP16 151 D6
Cherry Cnr HP10 185 B8
Cherrycroft Dr HP14 161 D6
Cherry Dr HP9 175 B4
Cherryfields HP6 155 B1
Cherry Gdns HP23 118 F3
Cherry Gr HP15 163 C6
Cherry La
Amersham HP7 165 A7
West Drayton UB7 208 F2
Woodrow HP7 164 D6
Cherry Lane Prim Sch UB7 208 F2
Cherry Leas MK17 55 B3
Cherry Leys MK18 63 E3
Cherry Orch
Amersham HP6 154 E2
Olney MK46 6 E4
Prestwood HP16 151 C6
Stoke Poges SL2 199 A5
West Drayton UB7 208 E4
Cherry Orchard Ct HP13 173 E6
Cherry Pit The HP13 161 E2
Cherry Rd MK16 22 B3
Cherry Rise
Chalfont St Giles HP8 177 D8
Flackwell Heath HP10 185 B7
Cherry St HP13 174 A4
Cherry Tree Ave UB7 208 F7
Cherrytree Cl HP15 163 C6
Cherry Tree Cl
Great Kingshill HP15 151 D1
Hughenden Valley HP14 162 A7
Speen HP27 150 B5
Cherry Tree Ho 4 SL7 183 D2
Cherrytree La
Chalfont St Peter SL9 177 D1

Cherrytree La continued
Iver Heath SL0 . . . . . **201** A4
Cherry Tree La
Buckland Common
HP23 . . . . **133** A3
Fulmer SL3 . . . . **199** F6
Heronsgate WD3 . . . . . **167** C1
Lee Common HP16 . . . **142** E4
Cherry Tree Rd
Beaconsfield HP9 . . . . **175** B1
Chinnor OX39 . . . . . . **147** C6
Farnham Common
SL2 . . . . **198** C5
Cherry Tree Way
HP10 . . . . **163** C1
Cherry Tree Wlk
Chesham HP5 . . . . **144** D2
Leighton Buzzard LU7 . . **80** E7
Wendover HP22 . . . . . **131** A5
Cherry Way
Hazelmere HP15 . . . . . **163** A6
Horton SL3 . . . . **212** C4
Cherrywood Cl HP9 **176** D5
Cherrywood Gdns
HP10 . . . . **185** B8
Chertsey Cl MK3 . . . . **47** B3
Chervil MK6 . . . . **47** B5
Cherwell Cl
Maidenhead SL6 . . . . . **203** A8
Slough SL3 . . . . **212** B8
Cherwell Ho MK3 . . . **57** E8
Cherwell Rd
Aylesbury HP21 . . . . . **115** C6
Bourne End SL8 . . . . . **185** B4
CHESHAM **154** C8
Chesham Ave MK13 . . **34** C3
CHESHAM BOIS **154** C3
Chesham Bois CE Comb
Sch HP6 . . . . **154** D4
Chesham Grammar Sch
HP5 . . . . **144** D1
Chesham Gram Sch
HP5 . . . . **154** D8
Chesham La
Chalfont St Peter
SL9 . . . . **177** E6
The Lee HP16 . . . . **142** A8
Chesham Mus HP5 . . **154** B8
Chesham Prep Sch
HP5 . . . . **145** A4
Chesham Rd
Amersham HP6 . . . . . . **154** C2
Ashley Green HP4 . . . . **135** A1
Ashley Green PH4,
PH5 . . . . **144** F8
Bellingdon HP5 . . . . . **143** E7
Berkhamsted HP4 . . . . **135** B2
Bovingdon HP3, HP5 . . **145** E4
Hyde Heath HP16 . . . . **153** C7
Wigginton HP23 . . . . . **133** D7
Chesham U Sta
HP5 . . . . **154** C8
Cheshire Cotts OX27 . **72** F6
Cheshire Ct 6 SL1 . **206** B4
Cheshire Rise MK3 . . **46** E1
Chesly Gdns MK14 . . **35** A8
Chesney Wold MK6. . . **46** F5
Chessbury Cl HP5 . . . **154** A7
Chessbury Rd HP5 . . **154** A7
Chess Cl
Aylesbury HP21 . . . . . **115** D3
Latimer HP5 . . . . **155** D3
Chessfield Pk HP6 . . **166** E8
CHESSMOUNT **154** E7
Chessmount Rise
HP5 . . . . **154** D6
Chester Cl MK3 . . . . . **57** D7
Chesterfield Cl
HP17 . . . . **114** C5
Chesterfield Cres
LU7 . . . . **79** E3
Chesterfield Pl
HP19 . . . . **115** B8
Chester Ho UB8 . . . . **201** C1
Chesterholm MK13 . . **33** F5
Chester Rd SL1 . . . . **205** D7
Chesterton Cl HP5 . **142** B2
Chesterton Gn HP9. **175** E2
Chestnut Ave
Chesham HP5 . . . . **144** E2
Halton HP22 . . . . **131** D8
High Wycombe HP11 . **173** D5
Slough SL3 . . . . **206** E4
West Drayton UB7 . . . . **208** F6
Chestnut Cl
Amersham HP6 . . . . . . **154** D2
Aston Clinton HP22 . . . **117** F5
Chalfont St Peter SL9 . **177** F2
Dagnall HP4 . . . . **107** C5
Maidenhead SL6 . . . . . **196** B1
Medmenham SL7. . . . . **193** D7
Milton Keynes MK11 . . **32** D5
Monks Risborough
HP27 . . . . **139** C5
Newton Longville
MK17 . . . . **57** D7
Waddesdon HP18 . . . . . **99** A6
Chestnut Cotts MK18 **52** C7
Chestnut Cres
Aylesbury HP21 . . . . . **115** D6
Milton Keynes MK2 . . . **58** D7
Chestnut Ct HP6 . . . **154** D2
Chestnut Dr
Berkhamsted HP4 . . . . **135** D3

Chestnut Dr continued
Windsor SL4 . . . . **209** F3
Chestnut End HP22 . **117** C1
Chestnut Gn NN13 . . **26** E4
Chestnut Hill LU7 . . **80** D8
Chestnut La
Amersham HP6 . . . . . . **154** E2
Hazelmere HP15 . . . . . **163** B5
Chestnut Lane Sch
HP6 . . . . **154** E2
Chestnut Leys MK18 **63** C3
Chestnut Pk SL6 . . . **203** E3
Chestnut Rd
Beaconsfield HP9 . . . . **175** B1
Princes Risborough
HP27 . . . . **139** C3
Yardley Gobion NN12 . . **18** F6
Chestnut Rise LU7 . . **80** D8
**Chestnuts Mill Farm
Courtyard** The M19. . **32** B1
Chestnuts Prim Sch
MK3 . . . . **57** E7
Chestnuts The
Castlethorpe MK19. . . . **19** F5
Felden HP3 . . . . **146** F7
Uxbridge UB10 . . . . . . **201** E5
Chestnut View MK18 **.74** F7
Chestnut Way
Longwick HP27 . . . . . . **138** E6
Stoke Mandeville
HP22. . . . . **116** C1
Chestnut Wlk SL9 . . **177** E3
Chestwood Gr
UB10. . . . . **201** F5
Chettle Pl NN12 . . . . **18** E2
CHETWODE
61 E8
Barton Hartshorn
MK18 . . . . **50** F1
Chetwode Ave MK10. **51** A2
Chetwode Cl MK18 . . **36** B1
Chetwode Ct MK18 . . **41** E2
Chetwode Grange Rd
MK18 . . . . **61** D7
Chetwynd Dr UB10 . **201** F3
Chevalier Gr MK8 . . . **45** D7
Cheveley Gdns SL1 . **197** C3
Cheverton Ave
HP27 . . . . **139** A4
Cheverton Gdns
HP27 . . . . **139** A4
Cheverton Mws
HP27 . . . . **139** A4
Cheviot Cl
High Wycombe
HP13 . . . . **161** E1
Leighton Buzzard LU7 . **80** C8
Maidenhead SL6 . . . . . **203** B6
Cheviot Cres MK15 . **45** C7
Cheviot Gdns MK14. . **21** C1
Cheviot Rd SL3 . . . . **207** A1
Chevry CI MK17 . . . . **.48** F8
Cheyne Cl
Amersham HP6 . . . . . **154** D3
Buckingham MK18 . . . **41** F1
Gerrards Cross SL9. . . **188** E3
Pitstone LU7 . . . . **105** D4
Cheyne Mews HP5 . **154** D3
Cheyne Wlk HP5 . . . **154** D8
CHICHELEY **23** C8
Chicheley Hall MK16 **23** D8
Chicheley Hill MK16 **23** A8
Chicheley Rd MK16 . **23** E7
Chicheley St MK16 . . **22** E4
Chichester Cl HP13 **173** D6
Chichester Ct SL1 . **206** A4
Chichester Row 7
HP6. . . . . **154** D1
Chicksands Ave
MK10 . . . . **36** A2
Chievely Ct MK4 . . . . **46** C1
Chilcote La HP7. . . . **166** A8
Childs Way
Kingsmead MK4 . . . . . **45** E1
Milton Keynes MK4,
MK5, MK6, MK10. . . . **46** C7
Shenley Church End
MK4 . . . . **45** F4
Chilley Leys MK15 . . **35** E7
Chillingham Ct MK5. **46** A4
Chiltern Ave
Amersham HP6 . . . . . **154** D1
Edlesborough LU6. . . . **92** E3
High Wycombe HP12 **172** D6
Stone HP17. . . . . **114** D5
Chiltern Brewery The
HP17. . . . . **130** C5
Chiltern Bsns Village
UB8. . . . . **201** B3
Chiltern Cl
Berkhamsted HP4 . . . **134** F5
1 Berkhamsted HP4 **135** A5
Princes Risborough
HP27 . . . . **139** A3
Stone HP17 . . . . **114** D5
Wendover HP22 . . . . . **131** B5
Chiltern Cnr HP4 . . . **135** A5
Chiltern Commerce Ctr
HP5. . . . . **144** A2
Chiltern Cotts
Buckland Common
HP23 . . . . **133** A2
Ibstone HP14 . . . . . . **169** D7
Chiltern Court Mews
SL4 . . . . **210** B6
Chiltern Ct
Amersham HP6 . . . . . **154** C2
Chesham HP5 . . . . . . **144** A2

Chiltern Ct continued
5 High Wycombe
HP12. . . . . **172** E2
Wendover HP22 . . . . . **131** B4
Windsor SL4 . . . . **210** B6
Winslow MK18 . . . .**65** F3
Chiltern Dr
Rickmansworth
WD3 . . . . **167** F2
Stokenchurch HP14. . . **158** F4
Chiltern Gn HP10 . . **185** A8
Chiltern Hill SL9 . . . **177** E2
Chiltern Hills Acad
Chesham HP5 . . . . **144** A1
Chesham HP5 . . . . **154** A8
Chiltern Hills Cl
HP23 . . . . **120** A2
Chiltern Hills Rd
HP9 . . . . **175** C2
Chiltern Ho HP5. . . . **154** C7
Chiltern Hospital The
(private) HP16 . . . . . . **152** C4
Chiltern Hts HP7 . . . **166** A8
Chiltern La HP15 . . . **162** F4
Chiltern Manor Pk
HP16. . . . . **152** A7
Chiltern Open Air Mus★
HP8. . . . . **177** F8
Chiltern Par HP6 . . . **154** C2
Chiltern Park Ave
HP4. . . . . **135** A6
Chiltern Pools The
HP6. . . . . **154** D1
Chiltern Rd
Amersham HP6 . . . . . **154** B4
Ballinger Common
HP16. . . . . **142** E3
Burnham SL1. . . . . . . **204** B8
Maidenhead SL6 . . . . **203** B6
Marlow SL7 . . . . **183** C2
Wendover HP22 . . . . . **131** B5
Wingrave HP22 . . . . . **89** A3
Chiltern Ridge
HP14 . . . . **158** C4
Chilterns
Berkhamsted HP4 . . . **134** F6
World's End HP22 . . . **130** F7
Chilterns Cl HP10 . . **185** B7
Chilterns Gateway Ctr
LU6 . . . .**93** F4
Chilterns Pk SL8 . . . **185** B5
Chiltern St HP22 . . . **115** E6
Chilterns The (Sh Ctr)
HP13 . . . . **173** B7
**Chiltern Valley Winery &
Brewery**★ RG9. . . . **180** F7
Chiltern View
Chinnor OX39 . . . . . . **147** C4
Chinnor OX39 . . . . . . **147** D5
Northall LU6 . . . . **92** C5
Saunderton HP14 . . . **149** C1
Chiltern View Cl
HP27 . . . . **149** D5
Chiltern View Rd
UB8. . . . . **201** D3
Chiltern Villas HP23 **118** E2
Chiltern Way
Aston Clinton HP22 . . **117** C2
Tring HP23 . . . . **119** C5
Chiltern Way Acad
HP22. . . . . **131** C3
**Chiltern Way Acad
(Prestwood Campus)**
HP16. . . . . **151** D5
Chiltern Wood Sch
High Wycombe
HP12. . . . . **172** E1
High Wycombe HP13 **161** D3
Chiltern Yard Rise
HP10. . . . . **174** C7
CHILTON **111** A4
Chilton Cl
Holmer Green
HP15. . . . . **163** C7
Tylers Green HP10 . . . **163** C2
Chilton Ct
Burnham SL6. . . . . . . **204** C7
Stantonbury MK14 . . . **34** E6
Chilton Pl HP20 . . . . **101** E1
Chilton Rd
Chearsley HP18 . . . . . **111** F3
Chearsley HP18 . . . . . **112** A2
Chesham HP5 . . . . . . **144** C2
Long Crendon HP18. . **125** C7
Chilwick Rd SL2. . . . **197** F1
Chimes Sh Ctr The
UB8. . . . . **201** D5
Chimes The HP12 . . **172** E6
Chimney La HP10 . . **185** E8
Chimney Mdws
MK18 . . . . **73** B5
Chinalls Cl MK18. . . . **50** D6
Chingle Croft MK4 . . **46** C2
Chinneck Ho HP4 . . **135** C4
CHINNOR **147** D7
Chinnor Hill OX39 . . **147** E4
**Chinnor Hill Wildlife
Reserve**★ OX39. . . **147** F5
**Chinnor & Princes
Risborough Rly**★
OX39. . . . . **147** E7
Chinnor Rd
Bledlow HP27 . . . . . . **138** A2
Bledlow Ridge HP14 . **148** C3
Chinnor OX39 . . . . . . **147** A4
Crowell OX39 . . . . . . **147** B4
Henton HP27. . . . . . . **137** F1
Chinnor Sta★ OX39 **147** D5

Chippendale Cl
HP13. . . . . **162** D1
Chippendale Waye
UB8. . . . . **201** D5
Chippenham Dr
MK10 . . . . **36** C1
CHIPPERFIELD **156** F8
Chipperfield Cl MK13 **34** A7
Chipperfield Rd
HP3 . . . . **146** C3
Chipping Vale MK4 . . **46** C2
Chipps Hill HP14 . . . **171** B8
Chipstead SL6 . . . . . **203** A2
Chirbury Cl MK10 . . . .**35** F1
Chirk Cl SL6 . . . . **177** C2
**CHISBRIDGE
CROSS** **182** D6
Chisbridge La SL7. . **182** B6
Chislehampton MK15 **35** C3
Chiswick Cl MK4 . . . . .**45** F2
Chiswick Lodge **6**
SL7 . . . . **183** D2
**CHIVERY
132** C4
Aston Clinton HP23 . . **132** B6
Chivery Rd HP23 . . . **132** C3
Choke La SL6 . . . . . . **195** B4
Cholesbury Rd
HP23 . . . . **133** E5
CHOLESBURY **133** C3
Cholesbury La
HP23 . . . . **133** A2
Cholesbury Rd
HP23 . . . . **133** D5
Chorley Rd HP14 . . . **160** E3
CHORLEYWOOD **167** D5
**CHORLEYWOOD
BOTTOM** **167** C3
Chorleywood Bottom
Chorleywood WD3. . . **167** C4
Chorleywood WD3. . . **167** D4
**Chorleywood Comm
Nature Reserve**
WD3 . . . . **167** E5
Chorleywood Ho
WD3 . . . . **167** E6
Chorleywood House Dr
WD3 . . . . **167** E6
**Chorleywood House Est
Nature Reserve**
WD3 . . . . **167** F6
Chorleywood Lodge La
WD3 . . . . **167** F6
Chorleywood Prim Sch
WD3 . . . . **167** C3
Chorleywood Sta/U Sta
WD3 . . . . **167** D5
**CHORLEYWOOD
WEST** **167** A4
Chrislaine Cl TW19 **213** D1
**Christ Church
Chorleywood** CE Sch
WD3 . . . . **167** F6
Christchurch Gr
MK12 . . . . **33** B6
Christchurch Ho **15**
HP23 . . . . **119** A3
Christchurch Rd
HP23 . . . . **118** F4
Christian Ct MK15 . . **35** D7
Christian Smith Ho
SL6 . . . . **202** A1
Christian Sq **4** SL4. **210** C6
Christie Cl
High Wycombe
HP12. . . . . **172** D3
Newport Pagnell MK16 **22** A5
Christies Cl **2**
HP13. . . . . **173** B7
Christine Ho **3** MK2. **58** C8
**CHRISTMAS
COMMON** **168** B7
Christmas Gorse La
MK18 . . . . **76** C7
Christmas La **1**
SL2 . . . . **198** C8
Christopher Cl
HP18 . . . . **161** D7
Christopher Ho **3**
SL2 . . . . **198** C7
**Christ the Sower
Ecumenical Prim Sch**
MK8 . . . . **45** D4
Chrysalis Theatre The
MK15 . . . . **35** C6
Chuech La MK17 . . . . **56** B8
Church App TW19. . **213** D1
Church Ave RG9. . . . **191** E2
Church Cl
Aston Clinton HP22 . . **117** D5
Cuddington HP18 . . . . **112** F3
Eton SL4 . . . . **210** D8
Maidenhead SL6 . . . . **202** D6
Loughton MK5. . . . . . . **46** B8
West Drayton UB7 . . . **208** E3
Wicken MK19 . . . . **31** B3
Church Cotts SL6 . . **196** E2
Church Croft LU6 . . . **92** E3
Church Ct
Aylesbury HP22. . . . . **116** B2
High Wycombe HP13 **162** D1
Church Dr SL6 . . . . . **203** C4
CHURCH END
Chorleywood. **156** F1
Drayton Parslow. **68** B5
Haddenham **127** A5
Haddenham HP17. . . . **127** A5

CHURCH END continued
Hanslope **11** A2
Long Crendon **125** C7
Pitstone **105** D3
Steeple Claydon **63** E2
Totternhoe **93** B7
Church End
Adstock MK18. . . . .**53** F1
Bledlow HP27 . . . . . . **138** B1
Drayton Parslow MK17 **68** B5
Edlesborough LU6. . . . **92** E3
Haddenham HP17. . . . **127** A5
Hillesden MK18. . . . . . **63** B6
Leckhampstead MK18. **30** C1
Leckhampstead MK18. **42** D8
Newton Longville
MK17 . . . . **57** D3
Sherington MK16 . . . . **14** A2
Syresham NN13 . . . . . **27** C8
Wavendon MK17. . . . . **48** E7
Yardley Gobion NN12 . **19** A5
Church End Cotts
WD3 . . . . **156** F1
Church End Farm
LU6 . . . . **93** B7
Church End Rd MK5. **46** A4
Church Farm Cl
HP22 . . . . **102** B3
Church Farm Cres
MK14 . . . . **34** E8
Church Farm Ho
HP8. . . . . **177** C7
Church Farm La
HP23 . . . . **104** F3
Churchfield Mews
SL2 . . . . **206** A7
Churchfield Rd SL9 **177** D2
Churchgate SL6 . . . **196** B7
Churchgates **3**
HP4. . . . . **135** C4
Church Gn
Long Crendon
HP18. . . . . **125** D7
Totternhoe LU6. . . . . . **93** B7
Church Gr
Little Chalfont HP6 . . **166** E8
Slough SL3 . . . . **206** C8
Church Green Rd
MK3 . . . . **58** A8
Church Headland La
HP22 . . . . **87** A6
CHURCH HILL **56** A8
Church Hill
Akeley MK18 . . . .**41** F8
Aspley Guise MK17 . . **49** E5
Cheddington LU7. . . . **105** A8
Ellesborough HP17 . . **130** E3
Milton Keynes MK8 . . **33** F2
Pishill RG9. . . . . **179** E8
South Harefield UB9 . **190** C8
Whaddon MK17. . . . . . **45** B1
Church Holt The
SL2 . . . . **187** E3
Churchill Ave HP21 **115** E7
Churchill Cl HP10 . . **185** B7
Churchill Ct **1**
HP21 . . . . **115** E7
Churchill Dr
Beaconsfield HP9 . . . **175** C5
Marlow SL7 . . . . **183** F4
Churchill Ho UB7 . . **208** D6
Churchill Rd
Slough SL3 . . . . **206** F2
Uxbridge UB10 . . . . . **201** E4
Church La
Alderton NN12 . . . .**9** A2
Aston Clinton HP22 . . **117** D4
Bellingdon HP5 . . . . . **143** F8
Berkhamsted HP4 . . . **135** C4
Bisham SL7 . . . . **194** D7
Bledlow HP27 . . . . . . **148** E8
Bledlow Ridge HP14 . **159** F8
Bovingdon HP3 . . . . . **146** B4
Bray SL6 . . . . **203** C4
Chalfont St Peter SL9 **177** D2
Chearsley HP18 . . . . . **112** B1
Cheddington LU7. . . . **105** A8
Chinnor OX39 . . . . . . **147** D6
Cholesbury HP5 . . . . **144** A8
Clifton Reynes MK46. . **.7** C3
Cryers Hill HP15 . . . . **162** C4
Deanshanger MK19 . . **31** E4
Drayton Beauchamp
LU7. . . . . **118** C5
Eaton Bray LU6 . . . . . . **92** E6
Edgcott HP18 . . . . . . **72** F2
Emberton MK46 . . . . . .**13** F7
Fawley RG9. . . . . **180** C2
Grafton Regis NN12 . . **9** D2
Granborough MK18. . . **75** F6
Great Brickhill MK17. . **59** C2
Great Horwood MK17. **55** A3
Great Kimble HP17 . . **129** E1
Great Missenden
HP16. . . . . **152** B7
Hastoe HP23. . . . . . . **132** F7
Hastoe HP23. . . . . . . **132** F7
Horton-cum-S OX33. **128** F7
Lacey Green HP27. . . **149** E4
Latimer HP5 . . . . **155** D4
Lillingstone Lovell
MK18 . . . . **30** A6
Ludgershall HP18 . . . **96** C7
Marsworth HP23. . . . **104** F1
Marsworth HP23. . . . **105** A1
Milton Keynes MK5 . . **46** B8
Mixbury NN13 . . . . . . **38** D1
Mursley MK17. . . . . . . **67** D5

Church La continued
Newport Pagnell
MK16 . . . . **22** D7
Oving HP22 . . . . **86** C7
Padbury MK18. . . . . . . **53** C2
Potsgrove MK17 . . . . . .**60** F2
Pottersbury NN12. . . . **18** E3
Princes Risborough
HP27 . . . . **139** B4
Radnage HP14 . . . . . . **159** B8
Sarratt WD3 . . . . **156** F1
Slough SL2, SL3. . . . . **206** C8
Soulbury LU7 . . . . **69** E2
Stoke Bruerne NN12. . . **.9** A8
Stoke Goldington
MK16 . . . . **12** A7
Stoke Poges SL2 . . . . **198** F2
Thornborough MK18. . **54** A8
Tingewick MK18 . . . . . **40** C1
Tingewick MK18 . . . . . **51** B7
Tring HP23 . . . . **133** A7
Upper Winchendon
HP18. . . . . **99** B1
Uxbridge UB8 . . . . . . **201** B3
Waddesdon HP18 . . . . **98** B7
Walter's Ash HP14 . . **151** B7
Walton MK7. . . . .**47** F6
Wendover HP22 . . . . . **131** C3
Weston Turville HP22 **116** F1
West Wycombe
HP14. . . . . **161** A2
Whaddon MK17. . . . . . **45** B1
Whitchurch HP22 . . . . **86** A4
Wicken MK19 . . . . **31** B3
8 Windsor SL4. . . . . **210** D6
Yardley Hastings NN7. . **.1** D1
Church Lees MK16 . . **21** D1
Churchmead Sch
SL3 . . . . **211** B7
Churchmere Wlk
HP21. . . . . **115** C6
Church Pas MK16 . . **22** D4
Church Path
Cheddington LU7. . . . . **91** A1
Cublington LU7 . . . . . . **78** B1
Hardwick HP22. . . . . . **87** A2
Lane End HP14 . . . . . **171** B4
Prestwood HP16. . . . . **151** D5
Stokenchurch HP14. . **158** D5
Church Rd
Aspley Heath MK17. . . **49** B3
Aspley Heath MK17. . . **59** B8
Bow Brickhill MK17. . . **48** D1
Bow Brickhill MK17. . . **59** F8
Brackley NN13 . . . . . . **38** A7
Cadmore End HP14 . . **170** C6
Chackmore MK18 . . . . **40** F1
Chinnor OX39 . . . . . . **147** D6
Cookham Dean SL6 . . **195** B6
Farnham Royal SL2 . . **198** C4
Ickford HP18 . . . . **123** F3
Iver Heath SL0 . . . . . **200** C3
Ivinghoe LU7 . . . . **105** F5
Lane End HP14 . . . . . **171** B3
Leighton Buzzard LU7 . **80** E6
Lewknor OX49. . . . . . **157** B8
Little Gaddesden
HP4. . . . . **121** C8
Little Marlow SL7 . . . **184** C5
Maidenhead SL6. . . . **203** B5
Old Windsor SL4 . . . . **211** B2
Penn HP10 . . . . **174** E7
Pitstone LU7 . . . . **105** E3
Puttenham HP23. . . . **103** F2
Radclive MK18 . . . . . . **51** F8
Seer Green HP9 . . . . . **176** D4
Sherington MK16 . . . . **13** F2
Slapton LU7. . . . . **91** D6
South Harefield UB9 . **190** C8
Stoke Hammond MK17 **69** E8
Stokenchurch HP14. . **158** D5
Thame OX9 . . . . **125** E1
Totternhoe LU6. . . . . . **93** B6
Tylers Green HP10 . . **174** C8
Uxbridge UB8 . . . . . . **201** B7
West Drayton UB7. . . **208** E3
Church Row SL3 . . . **199** D8
Churchside HP15 . . **163** D7
Church Sq
7 High Wycombe
HP11. . . . . **173** B7
Leighton Buzzard LU7 **.80** F4
Church St
Amersham HP7. . . . . **165** B7
Aspley Guise MK17 . . **49** E5
16 Aylesbury HP20 . . **115** D8
Bovingdon HP3 . . . . . **146** B4
Brill HP18 . . . . **110** B8
Buckingham MK18 . . . **52** C8
Burnham SL1. . . . . . . **197** C1
Chesham HP5 . . . . . . **154** B7
Gawcott MK18 . . . . . . **52** A4
Great Missenden
HP16. . . . . **152** B7
Henley-on-Thames
RG9. . . . . **191** D1
High Wycombe HP11. **173** B7
Little Horwood MK17 . **55** C2
Maids Moreton MK18 . **41** F3
Marsh Gibbon OX27 . .**71** F3
Milton Keynes, Fenny
Stratford MK2. . . . . . . **47** E1
Milton Keynes, New
Bradwell MK13 . . . . . .**33** F7
Milton Keynes, Stony
Stratford MK11. . . . . . **32** D5
Milton Keynes, Wolverton
MK12 . . . . **33** D7

Church St *continued*
North Marston MK18 ... 76 B2
6 Olney MK46 ... 6 F3
Olney MK46 ... 7 A3
Princes Risborough HP27 ... 139 B3
Quainton HP22 ... 85 B5
Slough, Chalvey SL1 ... 205 D4
Slough, Upton Park SL1 ... 205 F4
Stokenchurch HP14 ... 158 D5
Twyford MK18 ... 62 C2
6 Windsor SL4 ... 210 D6
Wing LU7 ... 79 E2
Wingrave HP22 ... 89 B2
Winslow MK18 ... 65 F4
Wolverton MK12 ... 33 E7
Church Terr
Turvey MK43 ... 8 E5
Windsor SL4 ... 209 E5
Church View
Brackley NN13 ... 38 A7
Edlesborough LU6 ... 92 D3
Halton HP22 ... 117 C1
Long Marston HP23 ... 104 A4
Newport Pagnell MK16 ... 22 D4
6 Slough SL1 ... 206 A3
Steeple Claydon MK18 63 E2
Church View Ct LU7 . 80 E6
Church Views SL6 .. 202 F8
Churchway HP17 ... 127 A6
Church Way
East Claydon MK18 ... 74 F8
Haddenham HP17 ... 127 A8
Stone HP17 ... 114 C5
Church Wlk
Milton Keynes MK3 ... 57 F7
North Crawley MK16 .. 24 B6
Weston Turville HP22 116 F1
Wing LU7 ... 79 E2
Winslow MK18 ... 65 F4
Church Yd HP23 ... 119 A3
Churston 1 MK10 ... 36 C3
Chyne The SL9 ... 188 F6
Cicero Cres
Fairfields MK11 ... 32 F3
Milton Keynes MK11 .. 32 F3
Cincukair HP14 ... 150 A2
Cinnamon Cl SL4 ... 209 F6
Cinnamon Gr MK7 ... 48 A5
CIPPENHAM ... 204 F4
Cippenham Cl SL1 . 204 F6
Cippenham La SL1 . 205 B5
Cippenham Sch SL1 ... 204 D6
City Rd HP14 ... 159 D6
CITY THE ... 159 D6
City The HP14 ... 160 A7
Clailey Ct MK11 ... 32 F5
Claires Court Girls Schs SL6 ... 202 E7
Claires Court Sch SL6 ... 196 B1
Clammas Way UB8 . 208 D8
Clapham Pl MK13 ... 34 C2
Clappers Mdw SL6 . 196 B1
Clappins La
Naphill HP14 ... 150 D1
Walter's Ash HP14 .. 161 C8
Clapton App HP10 .. 185 D8
Clare Croft MK10 ... 36 A3
Clare Dr SL2 ... 198 B8
Clarefield Cl SL6 ... 195 B1
Clarefield Dr SL6 ... 195 A1
Clarefield Rd SL6 .. 195 A1
Claremont SL3 ... 212 D6
Claremont Ave MK11 32 E4
Claremont Cl HP21 . 115 F5
Claremont Gdns SL7 ... 183 E2
Claremont Rd
Marlow SL7 ... 183 E2
Windsor SL4 ... 210 C5
Clarence Cres SL4 . 210 C6
Clarence Ct
Colnbrook SL3 ... 212 C8
9 High Wycombe HP13 ... 173 B7
Maidenhead SL6 ... 202 E8
Windsor SL4 ... 210 B6
Clarence Ho 2 MK9 . 34 C2
Clarence Rd
Berkhamsted HP4 ... 135 C4
Henley-on-Thames RG9 ... 191 D2
Milton Keynes MK11 .. 32 E5
Windsor SL4 ... 210 B6
Clarendon Copse SL6 ... 202 D6
Clarendon Ct
Slough SL2 ... 206 B6
Windsor SL4 ... 210 B6
Clarendon Dr
Milton Keynes MK8 ... 33 F2
Thame OX9 ... 126 A1
Clarendon Ind Pk MK8 ... 33 F2
Clarendon Rd
High Wycombe HP13 ... 173 E5
Prestwood HP16 ... 151 B6
Clare Park HP7 ... 165 E7
Clare Rd
Maidenhead SL6 ... 202 D6
Prestwood HP16 ... 151 C6
Slough SL6 ... 204 C7
Stanwell TW19 ... 213 E1
Claridge Cres MK17 . 37 A1
Claridge Dr MK10 ... 36 A2
Clarke Ct HP20 ... 101 F2
Clarke Dr HP13 ... 174 A6
Clarke Mws 10 MK17 58 B2
Clarke Rd MK1 ... 47 D4
Clarkes Dr UB8 ... 208 E8
Clarkes Field Cl HP18 ... 110 B8
Clarkes Orch
Newport Pagnell MK16 ... 12 B5
Stoke Goldington MK16 ... 12 B5
Clarke's Spring HP23 ... 119 F5
Clarke Wlk 2 HP20 101 F2
Clarks Cotts HP16 .. 151 C7
Classon Cl UB7 ... 208 E4
Claudius Wy MK11 .. 33 A3
Clauds Cl HP15 ... 163 A5
Claverton Cl HP3 ... 146 A3
Clay Acre HP5 ... 144 D1
Clay Cl HP10 ... 185 B8
Claycots Prim Sch SL2 ... 198 A1
Claycots Prim Sch (Town Hall Campus) SL1 ... 205 D5
Claycutters MK18 ... 66 A4
Claydon Cl HP21 ... 115 D6
Claydon Ct HP12 ... 172 E4
Claydon End SL9 ... 188 E8
Claydon Hill MK18 ... 64 C4
Claydon Ho★ MK18 . 74 C7
Claydon La SL9 ... 188 E8
Claydon Path HP21 . 115 E3
Claydon Rd
Hogshaw HP22 ... 74 F1
Quainton MK18 ... 84 E8
Claydons Pl HP27 .. 138 D7
Clayfields HP10 ... 163 C2
Clay Gdns 5 MK17 .. 49 A5
Clayhall La SL4 ... 210 F2
Clayhill
Marlow Bottom SL7 .. 172 A2
Wigginton HP23 ... 133 E7
Clay Hill MK8 ... 33 E2
Clay La
Calvert MK18 ... 73 A5
Marlow Bottom SL7 .. 172 A2
Wendover HP22 ... 131 C5
Claymoor Pk SL7 ... 172 A2
Clay Pit La 9 MK46 ... 6 F3
Clays La MK17 ... 55 E2
Clay St HP7, HP9 ... 175 C7
Clays The HP17 ... 127 A7
Clayton Ct SL3 ... 207 A3
Clayton Gate MK14 .. 35 A8
Clayton Rd HP14 ... 171 B4
Claytons Mdw SL8 .. 185 B2
Claytons Prim Sch SL8 ... 185 A5
Clayton Way UB8 ... 201 D1
Clayton Wlk HP7 ... 166 C8
Clearbrook Cl HP13 174 B4
Cleares Pasture SL1 ... 197 B2
Cleavers OX39 ... 147 B6
Cleavers Ave MK14 .. 34 E3
Cleeve Cres MK3 ... 47 A2
Clegg Sq MK5 ... 46 B5
Cleland Rd SL9 ... 177 D1
Clemens Rd
Berryfields HP19 ... 100 E5
Berryfields HP19 ... 100 F5
Clementi Ave HP15 163 D7
Clement Pl 5 HP23 119 A3
Clements Cl 5 SL1 . 206 B4
Clements Dr MK2 ... 58 F7
Clements La OX27 ... 71 F2
Clements Rd
Chorleywood WD3 .. 167 D4
Henley-on-Thames RG9 ... 191 C3
Clerkenwell Cotts HP17 ... 126 F5
Clerkenwell Pl MK6 . 35 B2
Clerk St HP22 ... 102 C2
Clevehurstcl SL2 ... 198 F6
Clevehurst Cl SL2 .. 199 A6
Cleveland MK13 ... 34 B6
Cleveland Cl
Maidenhead SL6 ... 203 B6
Wooburn Green HP10 ... 185 E8
Cleveland Dr LU7 ... 80 C8
Cleveland Pk
Aylesbury HP20 ... 101 F3
Stanwell TW19 ... 213 E1
Cleveland Pl 13 HP20 ... 101 F3
Cleveland Rd
Aylesbury HP20 ... 101 E3
Uxbridge UB8 ... 201 D2
Cleves Ct SL4 ... 209 F4
Clewer Ave SL4 ... 210 A5
Clewer Court Rd SL4 ... 210 B7
Clewer Fields SL4 .. 210 C6
Clewer Gn Ce Fst Sch SL4 ... 209 F4
CLEWER GREEN ... 209 E3
Clewer Green CE Fst Sch SL4 ... 210 A4
Clewer Hill Rd SL4 . 209 F4
CLEWER NEW TOWN ... 210 A5
Clewer New Town SL4 ... 210 A5
Clewer Pk SL4 ... 210 A7
CLEWER VILLAGE ... 210 A7
Clickers Yd Ct MK46 ... 6 F4
Clifden Rd HP18 ... 123 E5
Clifford Ave MK2 ... 58 C7
Clifford Rd
Princes Risborough HP27 ... 139 B3
Quainton HP22 ... 84 F3
Cliffords Way SL8 .. 185 B5
Clifton Bsns Pk HP19 ... 101 B1
Clifton Cl SL6 ... 203 A4
Clifton Ct
High Wycombe HP11 ... 172 E4
Olney MK46 ... 7 A3
8 Stanwell TW19 ... 213 E1
Clifton Gn HP19 ... 101 B2
Clifton Lawns HP6 . 154 C4
Clifton Lodge
Eton Wick SL4 ... 205 A1
7 Slough SL1 ... 206 A4
Clifton Moor MK5 ... 45 D5
Clifton Rd
Amersham HP6 ... 154 C4
Newton Blossomville MK43 ... 8 A4
5 Slough SL1 ... 206 A4
CLIFTON REYNES ... 7 C3
Clifton Rise SL4 ... 209 D6
Cline Ct MK8 ... 45 E6
Clinkard Pl HP14 ... 171 A3
Clinton Cres HP21 .. 116 A8
Clipstone Brook Way 4 MK10 ... 36 B3
Clitheroe Croft MK4 . 45 D1
Clive Ct SL1 ... 205 D4
Cliveden★ SL6 ... 196 E7
Cliveden Gages SL6 196 E5
Cliveden Gate SL1 .. 197 B3
Cliveden Mead SL6 . 196 C2
Cliveden Office Village HP12 ... 172 E4
Cliveden Pl MK4 ... 45 F2
Cliveden Rd SL6 ... 196 E4
Clivedon Way HP19 101 D4
Clivemont Rd SL6 .. 202 F8
Clock Ho The MK17 .. 59 D6
Clockhouse Mews WD3 ... 167 E6
Cloebury Paddock MK15 ... 35 C3
Cloister Garth HP4 . 135 C4
Cloisters The
High Wycombe HP13 ... 162 D2
Slough SL1 ... 205 D4
Clonmel Way SL1 .. 197 B2
Closes The
Haddenham HP17 ... 126 F7
Haddenham HP17 ... 127 A7
Close The
Akeley MK18 ... 42 A8
Ashendon HP18 ... 97 F1
Bierton HP22 ... 102 A4
Bourne End SL8 ... 185 A6
Great Horwood MK17 . 55 B3
Hardmead MK16 ... 15 D4
Hardwick HP22 ... 87 B3
Iver Heath SL0 ... 200 C2
Lathbury MK16 ... 22 D7
Marlow SL7 ... 183 B2
Milton Keynes, Bradwell MK13 ... 34 A4
Milton Keynes, The Green MK6 ... 47 D7
Newton Blossomville MK43 ... 7 F3
Ravenstone MK46 ... 5 E2
Slough SL1 ... 204 D6
Weston Underwood MK46 ... 6 A1
Woburn Sands MK17 .. 49 B4
Cloudberry MK7 ... 48 A6
Cloutsham Cl MK4 .. 46 D3
Clovelly Spur SL2 .. 197 F1
Clover Cl MK5 ... 46 B8
Clover End MK18 ... 52 C7
Clover La HP21 ... 115 E5
Clovers Ct WD3 ... 167 C3
Club Cotts MK17 ... 49 B4
Club La MK17 ... 49 C4
Clun Forest Way MK8 ... 33 C1
Cluny Ct MK7 ... 48 D6
Clyde Cl SL2 ... 206 A3
Clyde Pl MK3 ... 46 E1
Clydesdale Pl MK14 .. 34 F4
Coach Ho The
Loudwater HP11 ... 174 A4
Wooburn Green HP10 ... 185 E6
Coachmaker Ct MK14 ... 34 F6
Coachman's Lodge SL4 ... 210 D5
Coach Ride SL7 ... 183 D4
Coachway Rd MK10 . 36 A5
Coach Yd NN12 ... 18 E3
Coaley Dr MK17 ... 37 A1
Coalmans Way SL1 . 204 A8
Coal Mws HP22 ... 102 D3
Coaters La HP10 ... 185 E7
Coates La HP13 ... 162 A1
Coat Wicks HP9 ... 176 C4
Cobb Cl SL3 ... 211 D6
Cobbetts Mount MK18 ... 63 D2
Cobbetts Ride HP23 118 F3
Cobb Hall Rd MK17 .. 57 C3
Cobblers Cl SL2 ... 198 B3
Cobblers Hill HP22 . 141 D6
Cobblershill La HP16 ... 141 B4
Cobblers Wick HP22 . 89 B3
Cobb Rd HP4 ... 134 F4
Cobbs Gdn MK46 ... 6 F4
Cobden Cl UB8 ... 201 C4
Coberley Cl MK15 ... 35 B6
Cobham Cl
Buckingham MK18 ... 41 C1
Slough SL1 ... 204 F5
Cochran Cl MK8 ... 45 E7
Cochrane Ho UB8 .. 201 C4
Cockerell Gr MK5 ... 46 C5
Cockett Rd SL3 ... 206 E3
Cock Gr HP4 ... 134 D4
Cock La HP10 ... 174 A6
Cock La or Lucky La HP20 ... 101 D1
Cockpit Cl HP15 ... 151 E1
Cockpit Rd HP15 ... 162 D8
Cocksherd Wood Nature Reserve SL2 ... 197 E2
Cockslease La RG9 . 180 A5
Cockton Rd HP19 .. 101 C1
Coddimoor La MK17 . 56 B7
CODMORE ... 144 E1
Codmore Cres HP5 . 144 E1
Codmore Cross HP5 ... 144 D1
Codmore Wood Rd HP5 ... 155 D6
Coe Spur SL1 ... 205 B3
COFFEE HALL ... 46 F7
Coffee Hall Rdbt MK6 ... 47 B6
Cofferidge Cl MK11 . 32 D5
Coftards SL2 ... 206 C7
Cogan Ct MK8 ... 45 E7
Cogdells Cl HP5 ... 143 B4
Cogdells La HP5 ... 143 B4
Coggeshall Gr MK7 .. 48 C7
Coin Cl MK10 ... 35 F3
Cokers Ct 3 SL8 ... 185 A4
Cokes Farm La HP8 166 B6
Coke's La HP8 ... 166 B6
Colborne Cl SL0 ... 200 D1
Colborne Rd HP13 .. 173 D8
Colby Gdns 1 SL6 .. 202 F8
Colchester Ct MK3 .. 57 E7
Colchester Wlk MK3 . 57 E7
COLD BRAYFIELD ... 8 B5
Cold Brayfield Rd MK46 ... 7 F6
Coldeaton La MK4 ... 46 B3
Cold Grove Cotts SL6 ... 196 E2
Coldharbour HP22 . 131 C4
Cold Harbour CE Prim Sch MK3 ... 46 F3
Coldharbour Way HP19 ... 115 A7
Coldmoorholme La SL8 ... 184 E4
Coldmoreham Yd HP7 ... 165 A8
Coleheath Bottom HP27 ... 150 C5
Coleman Rd MK17 ... 58 B2
Colenorton Cres SL4 ... 204 E2
Cole Rd HP21 ... 115 C5
Coleridge Cl
Milton Keynes MK3 ... 58 A7
Newport Pagnell MK16 21 F4
Coleridge Cres SL3 . 212 E6
Coleridge Way UB7 208 F2
Coles Ave MK6 ... 46 F6
Colesbourne Dr MK15 ... 35 B6
COLESHILL ... 164 F3
Coles Hill HP18 ... 111 B3
Coleshill CE Inf Sch HP7 ... 164 F3
Coleshill Ho HP7 ... 165 A4
Coleshill La HP7 ... 164 D2
Coleshill Pl MK13 ... 34 C3
Colet Rd HP22 ... 131 C5
Colgrain St MK9 ... 35 A4
Colham Ave UB7 ... 208 E5
Colham Mill Rd UB7 ... 208 D5
Colham Rd UB8 ... 201 F1
Colindale St MK10 ... 35 E1
Colinswood SL2 ... 187 B1
Colin Way SL1 ... 205 B3
College Ave
Maidenhead SL6 ... 202 E7
Slough SL1 ... 205 E3
College Bsns Pk HP22 ... 103 C1
College Cl
Holton OX33 ... 122 C1
Thame OX9 ... 125 E1
College Cres
Oakley HP18 ... 109 E4
Windsor SL4 ... 210 B5
College Farm Rd
Hillesden MK18 ... 51 D1
Maids Moreton MK18 .. 41 F3
Maids Moreton MK18 . 42 A2
Preston Bissett MK18 . 62 D8
College Glen SL6 ... 202 D7
College La MK19 ... 43 C5
College Lake Wildlife Reserve★ HP23 ... 105 C1
College Rd
Cranfield MK17 ... 37 C8
Cranfield MK43 ... 24 E2
Little Gaddesden HP4 ... 121 C4
Little Gaddesden HP4 ... 121 C5
Maidenhead SL6 ... 202 E7
Slough SL1 ... 204 F5
College Rd South HP22 ... 117 B6
College Rise SL6 ... 202 D7
College Road N HP22 ... 117 C6
College The OX27 ... 71 F3
Colley Cl
Brill HP18 ... 96 A1
Brill HP18 ... 110 A8
Colley Hill MK13 ... 34 A4
Colley Hill La SL2 .. 187 F1
Colley Ho UB8 ... 201 D4
Colleyland WD3 ... 167 D5
Collier Cl SL6 ... 195 F1
Collier's La HP16 ... 159 A7
Colliers Wood MK10 . 35 E8
Collings Walk HP16 151 C5
Collington Rd HP19 100 E5
Collins Cl
High Wycombe HP12 ... 172 C5
Walton MK17 ... 48 D8
Collins Ho 2 HP11 . 173 A7
Collins Wlk MK16 ... 22 A4
Collinswood Rd
Egypt SL2 ... 198 B8
Farnham Common SL2 ... 187 B2
Collum Gn Rd SL9 .. 199 A8
Collum Green Rd SL2 ... 187 E1
Collyer Rd HP14 ... 158 E4
COLNBROOK ... 212 D7
Colnbrook By-Pass
Colnbrook SL3 ... 212 D7
Harmondsworth UB7 213 C7
Colnbrook CE Prim Sch SL3 ... 212 D6
Colnbrook Ct SL3 .. 212 F6
Coln Cl SL6 ... 202 F8
Colndale Rd SL3 ... 212 E5
Colne MK6 ... 47 D6
Colne Ave UB7 ... 208 C4
Colne Bank SL3 ... 212 C4
Colnedale Rd UB8 .. 201 D7
Colne Orch SL0 ... 207 F6
Colne Park Cvn Site UB7 ... 208 C2
Colne Pl UB9 ... 190 A4
Colne Rd HP13 ... 173 F7
Colne Reach TW19 . 212 F2
Colne Valley Park Visitor Ctr★ UB9 ... 190 B1
Colney Rd HP18 ... 100 D4
Coln Trad Est SL3 ... 212 F6
Colonel Grantham Ave HP19 ... 101 D4
Colonial Rd 1 SL1 . 206 A4
Colonnade SL6 ... 203 A7
Colossus Way MK3 .. 47 A1
Colsons Way MK46 ... 6 F5
Colston Bassett MK4 46 C1
Colston Ct SL9 ... 188 E5
COLSTROPE ... 181 D5
Colstrope La RG9 .. 181 D6
Coltman Ave HP18 .. 125 C6
Coltsfoot Dr UB7 ... 208 E7
Coltsfoot Pl MK14 ... 34 D3
Colts Holm Rd MK12 . 33 C8
Columbia Dr MK19 .. 33 C1
Columbia Pl MK9 ... 35 A3
Columbine Rd HP15 162 F6
Colville Ct HP16 ... 152 B7
Colville Rd HP11 ... 172 F6
COMBE ... 130 C1
Combe Martin MK4 . 46 D3
Combe Rise HP12 .. 172 B7
Combermere Cl SL4 ... 210 B5
Combes Cres MK6 ... 46 F6
Comerford Way MK18 ... 66 A5
Comet Way HP18 ... 100 C4
Comfrey Cl MK7 ... 48 A5
Comfrey The 2 HP19 ... 101 E4
Commodore Cl MK10 ... 36 B5
Common Field HP23 ... 119 D1
Common Gate Rd WD3 ... 167 E4
Common La
Eton SL4 ... 205 D1
Hedgerley SL1 ... 186 D1
Littleworth Corner SL1 ... 197 C8
Milton Keynes MK5 ... 46 C8
Milton Keynes, Bradwell MK13 ... 34 A4
Common Rd
Chorleywood WD3 ... 167 D5
Dagnall LU6 ... 107 F3
Dorney SL4 ... 204 D2
Eton Wick SL4 ... 205 A2
Common Rd *continued*
Flackwell Heath HP10 ... 185 B8
Great Kingshill HP15 151 D1
Slough SL3 ... 207 A1
Commonside HP13 . 161 E3
Common St
Ravenstone MK46 ... 5 D1
Ravenstone MK46 ... 12 E8
COMMON THE ... 55 B4
Common The
Berkhamsted HP4 ... 135 F6
Chipperfield WD4 ... 156 F7
Flackwell Heath HP10 ... 185 B8
Great Kingshill HP15 151 D1
Holmer Green HP15 . 163 D7
Potten End HP4 ... 135 F6
Stokenchurch HP14 .. 158 E5
West Drayton UB7 ... 208 C2
Common Wood SL2 198 C8
Common Wood La HP10 ... 163 E1
Comm The
Preston Bissett MK18 ... 51 C1
Stokenchurch HP14 .. 158 E5
Tylers Green HP10 .. 163 D1
Winchmore Hill HP7 . 164 C3
Como Rd HP20 ... 116 B8
Comp Gate LU6 ... 92 E6
Comp The LU6 ... 92 E6
Compton Ct
Moulsoe MK16 ... 36 D8
Slough SL1 ... 204 E7
Compton Dr SL6 ... 202 A8
Compton Rd
Wendover HP22 ... 131 D5
Wooburn Green HP10 ... 185 E6
Concorde Cl UB10 .. 201 E3
Concorde Pk SL6 ... 202 D4
Concorde Rd SL6 ... 202 D4
Concorde Sq HP18 .. 100 E4
Concorde Way SL1 .. 205 C4
Concourse The 6 MK2 ... 58 C8
Concra Pk MK17 ... 49 C4
Concrete Cows★ MK13 ... 33 F4
Condor Cl MK6 ... 47 A8
Conduit La
Datchet SL3 ... 211 F8
Slough SL3 ... 206 E1
Conegar Ct SL1 ... 205 E5
Conegra Ct 15 HP13 173 B7
Conegra Rd HP13 .. 173 C7
Coneygere MK46 ... 7 A3
Conference Rd HP18 ... 100 E4
Congreve MK6 ... 47 D5
Conifer Rise HP12 .. 172 E6
Conifers The
Felden HP3 ... 146 F8
Maidenhead SL6 ... 202 A8
Conigre OX39 ... 147 B6
Coningsby Cl SL6 .. 202 D3
Coningsby Ct HP13 . 173 B8
Coningsby Rd HP13 162 B1
Coniston Cres SL1 . 204 C8
Coniston Gn HP20 .. 101 D3
Coniston Rd LU7 ... 80 C7
Coniston Way MK2 .. 58 D6
Conkers SL6 ... 203 B8
Connaught Cl SL6 .. 195 E1
Connaught Gdns HP4 ... 134 F7
Connaught Rd
Aylesbury HP20 ... 116 C8
3 Slough SL1 ... 206 B4
CONNIBURROW ... 34 E4
Conniburrow Bvd MK14 ... 34 E4
Conniston Cl SL7 ... 183 B2
Conought Ho RG9 .. 191 E3
Constable Cl 2 MK14 ... 34 F7
Constable Pl HP19 . 100 F2
Constable's Croft OX25 ... 94 E7
Constabulary Cl UB7 ... 208 E3
Constabulary Pl UB7 ... 208 E3
Constance St MK18 .. 52 E6
Constantine Pl UB10 ... 201 E4
Constantine Way MK13 ... 33 F5
Convent Ct HP23 ... 118 F3
Convent Rd SL4 ... 210 A5
Conway Cl
Aylesbury HP21 ... 115 F7
Loudwater HP10 ... 174 C2
Milton Keynes MK3 ... 57 F8
Conway Cres MK3 ... 57 E8
Conway Ct SL9 ... 189 B3
Conway Ho HP13 ... 173 F7
Conway Rd SL6 ... 204 B7
Conwy Pl 1 LU7 ... 105 D3
Cook Cl MK7 ... 48 B4
Cookfield Cl LU6 ... 93 E8
COOKHAM ... 196 A7
Cookham Ct 1 HP6 154 E2
COOKHAM DEAN ... 195 B7

Cookham Dean Bottom
 SL6 . . . . 195 C8
Cookham Dean CE Prim
 Sch SL6 . . . . 195 B7
Cookham Lodge 15
 SL6 . . . . 202 F6
Cookham Rd SL6 . . 195 F1
COOKHAM RISE . . 195 E6
Cookham Rise Prim Sch
 SL6 . . . . 195 E6
Cookham Sta SL6 . . 195 F7
Cooks Cl
 Ashton NN7 . . . . .9 F8
 Chalfont St Peter SL9 177 E4
Cookshall La
 High Wycombe
 HP12. . . . . 161 A2
 Naphill HP12. . . . . . 161 C5
Cooks La MK17. . . . 67 E6
Cooks Rd HP19. . . . 114 F8
Cook's Mdw LU6 . . . 92 E4
Cooks Yd 1 HP15. . 154 E7
Coombe Ave HP22. . 131 B4
Coombe Cl
 Slough SL2 . . . . 197 F1
 Stoke Mandeville
 HP22. . . . . 116 C2
Coombe Dr LU6 . . . . 93 E7
Coombe Gdns
 Berkhamsted HP4 . . . 134 F5
 Hughenden Valley
 HP14. . . . . 162 A6
Coombe Hill Ct SL4 209 D4
Coombe La
 Aylesbury HP20. . . . 100 F1
 Walter's Ash HP14 . . 161 F6
Coombes Quarry Nature
 Reserve MK18 . . . . 53 E6
Coombe Vale SL9 . . 188 E3
Cooper Croft MK19. . 10 F2
Cooper Ct MK4. . . . . 45 E3
Cooper Rd RG9 . . . . 191 D3
Coopers Court Rd
 HP14. . . . . 158 D5
Coopers Ct MK16. . . 22 C4
Coopers Hill MK43 . . 25 B3
Coopers Mews MK14 .34 F6
Coopers Rise HP13 173 D5
Coopers Row SL0 . . 200 D1
Cooper's Yd HP15. . 101 D1
Cooper Way
 3 Berkhamsted
 HP4 . . . . 135 D4
 Slough SL1 . . . . . . 205 B3
Coots Cl MK18. . . . . 52 E7
Cop Cl HP23 . . . . . . 125 D7
Cope Ct SL6 . . . . . . 202 C7
Copeland Cl MK7. . . 48 C5
Copes Haven MK5. . . 46 B3
Copes Rd HP15. . . . 151 E1
Copes Shroves
 HP15. . . . . 162 F5
Copmans Wick
 WD3 . . . . 167 D4
Copners Dr HP15. . . 163 C6
Copners Way HP15. 163 B6
Copper Beech Cl
 Felden HP4 . . . . . . 146 F8
 Windsor SL4 . . . . . 209 D6
Copperfields
 Beaconsfield HP9 . . . 175 E6
 High Wycombe HP11. 161 B1
Copperfield Terr
 SL2 . . . . 206 B6
Copper Horse Ct
 SL4 . . . . 210 A5
Copperhouse Ct
 MK7 . . . . 48 A2
Copperkins Gr HP6. 154 B3
Copperkins La HP6. 154 A3
Coppermill La WD3 178 F3
Coppermill Rd
 TW19. . . . . 212 B2
Copper Ridge SL9. . 177 F5
Coppice Cl
 Aylesbury HP20. . . . 102 A2
 Hudnall HP4 . . . . . 121 F6
Coppice Farm Pk
 HP23. . . . . 132 D3
Coppice Farm Rd
 HP10. . . . . 163 C2
Coppice The
 Great Kingshill
 HP15. . . . . 151 E1
 High Wycombe HP12. 172 B4
 Seer Green HP9 . . . 176 D4
 Stokenchurch HP14. 158 E5
 Walter's Ash HP14 . . 161 B8
 West Drayton UB7. . 208 E7
 Wigginton HP23 . . . 119 C1
Coppice Way
 Aylesbury HP20. . . . 102 A2
 Hedgerley SL2. . . . . 187 D2
Coppidwell Dr
 HP21. . . . . 115 E8
Coppinger Ct UB7. . 208 E4
Coppin La MK13. . . . 34 A3
Coppins Cl HP4 . . . . 134 F4
Coppins La SL0 . . . 207 F8
Copse Cl
 Marlow SL7. . . . . . 183 C2
 Slough SL1. . . . . . . 205 B3
 West Drayton UB7. . 208 D3
Copse Gate MK18. . . 66 A4
Copse La HP9. . . . . 176 E3

Copse The
 Amersham HP7 . . . . 154 C1
 Beaconsfield HP9 . . . 175 C4
Copse Way HP5 . . . 144 A4
Copse Wood SL0 . . . 200 D4
Copthall Cl SL9 . . . . 177 F3
Copthall Cnr SL9 . . . 177 E3
Copthall Ho SL6. . . . 203 A7
Copthall La SL9 . . . . 177 F3
Copthorn Cl SL6. . . 202 A4
Copthorne Pl MK7. . 48 B8
Copyground Ct
 HP12. . . . . 172 E7
Copyground La
 HP12. . . . . 172 E7
Coral Cl LU6 . . . . 92 E6
Coram Cl HP4. . . . . 135 C3
Corbet Ride LU7 . . . . 80 D8
Corbet Sq LU7 . . . . . 80 D8
Corbett Cl MK15 . . . . 35 D7
Cordons Cl SL9 . . . . 177 D2
Cordwainer St MK14 .34 F6
Cordwallis Bsns Pk
 SL6 . . . . 195 E1
Cordwallis Est SL6 . 202 E8
Cordwallis Pk SL6 . 202 E8
Cordwallis Rd SL6. . 202 E8
Cordwallis St SL6 . . 202 E8
CORES END 185 C4
Cores End Rd SL8 . 185 B3
Corfe Cl HP21. . . . . 116 B5
Corfe Cres MK3. . . . .57 F8
Corfe Gdns SL1 . . . 205 A6
Corfe Mdws 10 MK10 36 B3
Corfe Pl SL6 . . . . . . 202 C7
Corfe Rd LU7 . . . . . 105 C3
Coriander Ct MK7. . . 48 B5
Corin Cl MK2 . . . . . . 58 D5
Corinium Ind Est
 HP6. . . . . 154 F1
Corin Way MK2 . . . . . 58 D5
Cork Pl MK3. . . . . . . 46 E2
Cornbrook Rd HP21 115 C5
Cornbury Cres MK15 35 A6
Corn Cl HP17 . . . . . 114 D5
Corncrake 9 HP19. 101 F3
Cornel Cl MK15. . . . 163 B3
Cornel Ho 1 SL4. . 210 D4
Cornelia Cl MK2. . . . 58 C6
Cornelius Cres MK1 .32 F3
Cornerways HP27. . 150 C5
Cornfield Cl UB8 . . 201 D6
Cornfield Cres HP4 134 D7
Cornfields OX39 . . . 147 C5
Cornflower Pl MK18. 52 C7
Corn Hill MK8. . . . . . 33 E1
Corn Mill Cl LU7 . . . . 79 E2
Corn Mkt HP11. . . . 173 B7
Cornwall Ave SL2 . . 198 C1
Cornwall Cl
 Eton Wick SL4 . . . . 204 E1
 Maidenhead SL6. . . . 195 E2
Cornwall Ct UB8 . . 201 D6
Cornwall Gr MK3. . . .46 F1
Cornwall Ho UB8. . 201 D6
Cornwall Lodge 11
 SL6 . . . . 202 F6
Cornwall Pl MK18 . . .41 D1
Cornwall Rd UB8 . . 201 D6
Cornwalls Mdw 3
 MK18. . . . . 41 D1
Cornwell Rd SL4 . . . 211 A1
Coronation Ave
 Slough SL3 . . . . . . 206 E7
 Windsor SL4 . . . . . 211 A4
Coronation Cotts
 MK18. . . . . .41 F8
Coronation Cres
 HP14. . . . . 171 C5
Coronation Mews
 LU7. . . . . .80 F8
Coronation Pl MK18. 63 D2
Coronation Rd
 Cranfield MK43. . . . . 25 B1
 High Wycombe HP12 172 D4
 Milton Keynes MK11. . 32 E5
Coronation Villas
 HP21. . . . . 115 E8
Coronet Rd HP22. . 102 D2
Corporation St
 HP13. . . . . 173 B7
Corrib Ind Est HP19 101 B1
Corrid Ind Pk HP19. 101 B1
Corrigan Cl MK3. . . . 58 A8
Corris Ct 3 MK10 . . 36 A3
Corsewall Pl MK4 . .45 F1
Cosford Mews 2
 HP22. . . . . 131 E6
COSGROVE 19 D2
Cosgrove Rd
 Old Stratford MK19. . 32 C7
 Old Stratford MK19. . 32 C8
Cosgrove Village Prim
 Sch MK19. . . . . . . 19 E2
Costers Cotts SL8 . 185 B2
Costins Wlk 7 HP4 135 D4
Cosway Pl MK8 . . . . 45 D6
Cosy Corner HP22. . 117 D5
Cotes Way LU7. . . . . 79 F3
Cotman Cl
 Milton Keynes MK12 . .33 B5
 Wolverton MK12. . . . 33 B5
Cotswold Cl
 Maidenhead SL6. . . . 203 B6
 Slough SL3. . . . . . . 205 B3
 Uxbridge UB8 . . . . 201 C4
Cotswold Ct HP12. . 172 F8
Cotswold Dr LU7. . . . 80 C8

Cotswold Gn HP20. . 101 E2
Cotswolds Way MK18 73 B5
Cotswold Way HP13 172 E8
Cottage Comm MK5. . 46 B8
Cottage Farm Way
 HP27. . . . . 150 C4
Cottage Grounds
 HP17. . . . . 114 D5
Cottage Park Rd
 SL2 . . . . 187 D2
Cottages The
 Ickenham UB10. . . . 190 E2
 Syresham NN13 . . . . 27 C5
Cottesbrooke Cl
 SL3 . . . . 212 D6
Cottesloe Cl LU7. . . . 79 E3
Cottesloe Ct MK11. . 32 F5
Cottesloe Rd HP21 . 115 E5
Cottesloe Sch The
 LU7. . . . . 79 D1
Cottingham Gr MK3. . 58 A7
Cottisford Cres
 MK14. . . . . 21 F1
Cottland Clay HP17 127 A7
Cotton End MK18. . . . 52 E6
Cotts Field 1 HP17. 126 E6
Cotts The
 Long Crendon HP18. 125 C6
 Longwick HP27 . . . . 138 E5
Coubert Cres 1
 MK17. . . . . 48 F8
Coulson Ave MK8,
 MK5 . . . . 45 E6
Coulson Ct HP16 . . 151 D6
Coulson Way SL1 . . 204 B8
Council Hos LU7 . . . 92 A1
Countess Wy MK10. . 36 D3
Countisbury MK4 . . . 46 D2
Country La HP15 . . . 151 E1
Country Life Ho SL3 211 B7
County Rd NN13. . . . 38 A6
Courageous Wy 6
 MK10 . . . . 36 C4
Cours La Ville Cl
 MK18. . . . . 65 E3
Court Cl
 Aylesbury HP21. . . . 115 E7
 High Wycombe HP13 161 D1
 Maidenhead SL6. . . . 203 C2
 Princes Risborough
 HP27. . . . . 139 A3
Court Cnr MK46. . . . .6 E3
Court Cres SL1. . . . 205 D7
Court Dr
 Maidenhead SL6 . . . 196 C3
 Uxbridge UB10 . . . . 201 F4
Courtenay Croft
 MK17 . . . . 37 B1
Courteneys Lodge
 MK4 . . . . 46 E3
Court Farm Cl MK5. . 205 B5
Courtfield Dr SL6 . . 202 C6
Courtfield Gdns
 UB9. . . . . 190 A1
Court Garden L Complex
 SL7 . . . . 183 D1
Courthouse Cl MK18. .65 F5
Courthouse Jun Sch
 SL6. . . . . 202 B8
Courthouse Mews
 MK16. . . . . 22 C4
Courthouse Rd SL6. 202 C8
Courthouse Terr
 SL1. . . . . 204 B8
Court La
 Burnham SL1. . . . . 197 D2
 Dorney SL4 . . . . . 204 B3
 Iver SL0 . . . . 208 A5
Courtlands
 Leighton Buzzard LU7 . 80 E6
 14 Maidenhead SL6 . 202 F6
Courtlands Ave SL3 206 D2
Court Lawns HP10. . 163 C1
Courtmoor Cl HP27. 139 C6
Courtneidge Cl LU7. . 78 E8
Courtney Ho UB9. . 189 F5
Court Rd
 Cranfield MK43. . . . . 25 B1
 Maidenhead SL6. . . . 196 C3
Court The MK17. . . . . 37 C3
Courtyard Cl HP6 . . 154 C1
Courtyards The
 HP22. . . . . 117 E4
Courtyard The 7
 HP19. . . . . 101 C1
Courtyard The
 Beaconsfield HP9 . . . 175 D2
 7 Bourne End SL8 . 185 B3
 1 Maidenhead SL6 . 202 D6
 9 Marlow SL7 . . . . 183 D2
 1 Marlow SL7 . . . . 183 E2
 22 Windsor SL4. . . 210 D6
Cousins Cl UB7 . . . 208 E6
Cousins Dr HP20. . . 101 F2
Coventon Rd HP19 . 101 C2
Coverack Pl MK4. . . 57 B8
Coverdale MK13 . . . 34 C5
Coverdale Way SL2. 197 E1
Covert Cl HP4. . . . . 134 D6
Covert Rd HP14 . . . 134 D6
Cowdray Cl MK15. . . 35 C3
Cow Ground HP18. 100 D4
Cow La
 Edlesborough LU6. . . 92 E4
 Gawcott MK18 . . . . .51 F4
 Tring HP23 . . . . . 119 D4
Cowleaze OX39 . . . 147 B6
COWLEY 201 C1

Cowley Bsns Pk
 UB8. . . . . 201 C2
Cowley Cl HP22. . . . 102 B3
Cowley Cotts HP7. . 164 C3
Cowley Cres UB8. . 208 C8
Cowley Mill Rd UB8 201 B3
Cowley Mill Trad Est
 UB8. . . . . 201 B3
COWLEY PEACHEY . 208 D8
Cowley Rd
 Preston Bissett
 MK18. . . . . 62 C6
 Uxbridge UB8. . . . . 201 C4
Cowley St Laurence CE
 Prim Sch UB8. . . . 208 D8
Cowpasture La MK17 57 C1
Cowper Cl MK46. . . . 6 F3
Cowper & Newton Mus
 The * MK46. . . . . . 6 F3
Cowper Rd
 Berkhamsted HP4. . 135 B4
 Chesham HP5 . . . . 144 B2
 High Wycombe HP13 173 E8
 Slough SL2 . . . . . . 198 A1
Cowpers Orch MK46. . 6 A1
Cowper St MK46 . . . 7 A5
COW ROAST 120 B1
Cowslip Cl UB10 . . 201 E5
Cowslip Rd HP15. . . 162 F6
Coxborrow Cl SL6. . 195 E7
Coxfield Cl HP14 . . 158 F5
COX GREEN 202 C3
Cox Green La SL6 . 202 A3
Cox Green L Ctr
 SL6. . . . . 202 A3
Cox Green Rd SL6. . 202 D3
Cox Green Sch SL6 202 A4
Coxhill Way HP21. . 115 C7
Coxon Cl HP17 . . . 126 E7
Coxwell Cl MK18 . . .41 F1
Coy Ct HP20 . . . . . 116 A8
Cozens Cl HP18 . . . 125 B7
Crabbe Cres HP5. . 144 D2
Crabs Gr HP22 . . . . .86 F7
Crabtree Cl
 Beaconsfield HP9 . . . 175 B1
 Great Horwood MK17 55 B3
Crab Tree Cl MK46. . .6 E5
Crabtree Cotts
 HP27. . . . . 139 A1
Crabtree La HP17 . . 49 C8
Crabtree Rd HP17. . 127 A5
Craddocks Cl MK13. 34 B3
Cradley Wlk HP20. . 101 C3
CRAFTON 89 F3
Crafton
 Mentmore LU7. . . . . 89 F4
 Mentmore LU7 . . . . 90 A4
Crafton La LU7. . . . . 90 A3
Crafton Lodge Rd
 LU7. . . . . 90 A3
Crafton Pl 4 HP19. 100 F1
Craigleith Ct HP9 . . 175 D2
Craigmore Ave MK3. .57 F8
Craigwell Ave HP21 116 C7
Cranborne Ave MK4. 45 E2
Cranbourne Ave
 SL4 . . . . 209 F5
Cranbourne Cl SL1 205 C5
Cranbourne Rd SL1 205 C5
Cranbrook MK17. . . . 49 B5
Cranbrook Dr SL6. . 195 C1
Crane Ct MK5 . . . . . 34 B1
Cranesbill Pl MK14 . 34 E4
Cranesbill Way
 HP22. . . . . 102 C3
Cranes Cl MK43 . . . .8 C5
Crane Way MK43 . . . 25 C2
CRANFIELD 25 B1
Cranfield Airport
 MK43 . . . . 24 F1
Cranfield CE Acad (St
 Paul Site) MK43. . . 25 B2
Cranfield CE Acad (St
 Peter Site) MK43. . 25 B1
Cranfield Innovation Ctr
 MK43 . . . . 37 D8
Cranfield Rd
 Astwood MK16 . . . . 16 A3
 Astwood MK16, MK43. 16 B3
 Cranfield MK43 . . . . 37 E6
 Cranfield MK43 . . . . 25 F3
 Moulsoe MK16 . . . . 36 E8
 Moulsoe MK17 . . . . 37 A8
 Salford MK17 . . . . . 37 D5
 Sherington MK16 . . . 14 E5
 Wavendon MK17 . . . 49 B7
Cranfield Tech Pk
 MK43 . . . . 37 C8
Cranfield Univ MK43. 24 E2
Cranford Dr 4 SL1. 204 F4
Cranley Cres HP19. 101 C4
Cranmore Circ MK10 36 D3
Cranwell Cl MK5 . . . 46 B3
Cranwell Cres MK2. .58 F7
Cranwells La SL2. . 187 C1
Cratel MK10. . . . . . . 36 A3
Craufurd Ct SL6. . . 202 E8
Craufurd Rise SL6. 202 E8
Craven The MK13 . . 34 C4
Crawford Rd HP19 . 100 F4
Crawford Way 3
 MK4 . . . . 45 D2
Crawley Rd
 Cranfield MK43. . . . . 25 A5
 Cranfield MK43. . . . . 25 A5
 Sherington MK16 . . . 14 F4
 Woburn MK17 . . . . .60 F8
 Woburn MK17. . . . . .60 F8

Crawley's La HP23 . 133 F7
Crawshays SL6. . . . 203 C8
Crayle St SL2 . . . . . 198 E2
CR Bates Ind Est
 HP14. . . . . 158 E5
Creden Cl
 Maidenhead SL6 . . . 195 D1
 Maidenhead SL6 . . . 202 D8
Creed St MK12 . . . . 33 D7
Creighton Rd HP18. .83 F1
Crendon Rd
 Chearsley HP18 . . . 112 A1
 Shabbington OX9 . . 124 D3
Crendon St HP13. . 173 B7
Creran Wlk LU7 . . . . 80 C7
Crescent Cotts HP18 83 A6
Crescent Dale SL6. 202 F6
Crescent The
 Cranfield MK43 . . . . 24 C2
 Haversham MK19 . . . 20 C2
 High Wycombe HP13 173 E8
 Maidenhead SL6 . . . 202 E7
 Marsworth HP23. . . 105 A1
 Milton Keynes, Fenny
 Stratford MK2 . . . . 47 E1
 Milton Keynes, Giffard Park
 MK14 . . . . 21 E2
 Pitstone LU7 . . . . . 105 C4
 Princes Risborough
 HP27. . . . . 139 C3
 Slough SL1 . . . . . . 205 E3
Crescent Villas 5
 SL4 . . . . 210 C6
CRESLOW 87 B8
Creslow HP22. . . . . . 77 B1
Creslow Ct MK11. . . .32 F5
Creslow Way HP17 . 114 B5
CRESSEX 172 C4
Cressex Bsns Pk
 HP12. . . . . 172 C3
Cressex Cl HP12. . . 172 D3
Cressex Com Sch
 HP12. . . . . 172 C3
Cressex Ent Ctr
 HP12. . . . . 172 C6
Cressex Link HP11 . 172 D3
Cressex Rd
 High Wycombe
 HP12. . . . . 172 C3
 High Wycombe HP12. 172 E4
Cressex Sq HP12 . . 172 D3
Cressey Ave MK5. . . 46 B4
Cressington Ct 2
 SL8. . . . . 185 A4
Cressington Pl SL8. 185 A4
Cress Rd SL1. . . . . 205 B4
Cresswell La MK9 . . 34 D1
Cresswell Rd HP5 . 154 D3
Cresswells Mead
 SL6. . . . . 203 C1
Cresswell Way
 HP15. . . . . 163 D7
Crest Rd HP11 . . . . 172 C3
Crest The
 Beaconsfield HP9 . . 175 A1
 Bledlow Ridge HP14 159 F8
Creswell Row SL7. . 183 D2
Creswick Mdw
 HP21. . . . . 116 A5
Crew Curve HP4 . . 134 F7
Cricketers Cl LU7 . . 68 E2
Cricketers Row
 MK18 . . . . 66 A4
Cricketers Wy HP17 127 B6
Cricketfield Rd UB7 208 C2
Cricket Field Rd
 UB8. . . . . 201 D4
Cricket Green Rdbt
 MK9 . . . . 35 B4
Cricket Ground
 HP14. . . . . 158 D5
Cricket Hill SL8 . . . 185 C2
Cricklebeck MK13. . 34 B5
Crimp Hill SL4 . . . . 211 A1
Crispin Cl HP9 . . . . 175 C4
Crispin Field LU7 . . 105 C4
Crispin Rd MK13 . . . 34 B7
Crispin St HP19 . . . 100 E6
Crispin Way
 Farnham Common
 SL2 . . . . 198 D8
 High Wycombe HP11. 173 A4
 Uxbridge UB8 . . . . 208 F8
Crisp Rd RG9 . . . . 191 C3
Criss Gr SL9 . . . . . 177 C1
Crocketts La HP16. . 142 D5
Crockmore La
 Fawley RG9. . . . . . 180 C1
 Fawley RG9. . . . . . 191 C8
Crocus Dr HP21 . . . 115 B5
Croft Cl SL9. . . . . . 177 D1
Croft Cnr SL4 . . . . 211 A2
Croft Ct 5 HP21 . . 115 E7
Croft Ctyd HP17. . . 126 F6
Crofters SL4 . . . . . 211 A1
Crofters Cl TW19 . . 213 E1
Croft Gn LU6. . . . . . .93 F8
Crofthill Rd SL2. . . 198 B1
Crofton Cl MK3 . . . . 46 E1
Crofton Ho HP11 . . 174 A4
Croft Rd
 Aylesbury HP21. . . . 115 D7
 Chalfont St Peter SL9 177 E4
CROFTS END. 14 A1

Crofts End MK16 . . . 14 A1
Crofts La MK17. . . . . 57 D3
Croft The
 Haddenham HP17. . 126 F5
 Maidenhead SL6 . . . 202 C5
 Marlow SL7. . . . . . 184 A3
 Soulbury LU7. . . . . .79 F6
Croftwood
 High Wycombe
 HP13. . . . . 173 F7
 High Wycombe HP13. 173 F7
Cromarty Ct MK3. . . 46 E3
Cromer Cl HP4. . . . 121 E5
Cromer Ct SL1 . . . . 205 E7
Cromerton Cl HP9. . 186 B8
Cromhamstone
 HP17. . . . . 114 C8
Cromwell Ave
 Aylesbury HP19. . . 101 D2
 Newport Pagnell MK16 22 A3
 Thame OX9 . . . . . . 126 A1
Cromwell Cl HP8. . 177 C7
Cromwell Ct MK18 . . 41 E2
Cromwell Dr SL1. . 205 E7
Cromwell Gdns 10
 SL7 . . . . 183 E2
Cromwell Ho
 Chesham HP5 . . . . 144 B1
 Uxbridge UB8 . . . . 201 C4
Cromwell Mews 1
 HP19. . . . . 115 A8
Cromwell Rd
 High Wycombe
 HP13. . . . . 173 E5
 Maidenhead SL6 . . . 202 D7
 Marlow SL7. . . . . . 183 E2
Cropredy Ct MK18 . . 41 E2
Cropton Rise MK4. . 46 A2
Cropwell Bishop
 MK4 . . . . 46 C1
Crosby Cl HP9 . . . . 186 F8
Crosby Ct MK8 . . . . 45 E6
Crosby Gdns UB10. 201 E5
Crosland Rd HP21. . 116 B6
Cross Cl HP13. . . . . 161 D2
Cross End MK17. . . . .48 F7
Cross Farm Mews
 HP3. . . . . 146 D2
Crossfield Cl HP4 . . 134 F4
Crossfield Ho SL9 . 188 E7
Crossfield Rd HP27. 139 C4
Crosshills MK11. . . . 32 C4
Crossinglands Business
 Pk MK17. . . . . . . 49 D6
Cross La
 Beaconsfield HP9 . . 186 F8
 Tingewick MK18 . . . . 51 B6
 Weston Underwood
 MK46. . . . . .6 B2
Crosslands
 Maple Cross WD3 . . 178 E6
 Milton Keynes MK14 . 34 E8
Cross Lanes
 Bledlow HP27 . . . . 138 A2
 Chalfont St Peter SL9 177 F5
Cross Lanes Cl SL9 177 F5
Crossleys HP8 . . . . 177 C7
Crosslow Bank MK4. 46 C3
Cross Mdw HP5 . . . 143 F2
Cross Oak SL4 . . . . 210 A5
Cross Oak Rd HP4. 135 A4
Cross Rd
 High Wycombe
 HP12. . . . . 172 C6
 Uxbridge UB8 . . . . 201 C5
Cross St
 Newport Pagnell
 MK16 . . . . 22 C4
 Uxbridge UB8 . . . . 201 C5
Cross Tree Rd MK19. 31 B3
Crossway HP5 . . . . 144 E1
Crossways
 Beaconsfield HP9 . . 175 F1
 Berkhamsted HP4. . 134 F3
 High Wycombe HP12. 172 C4
Crossways Bsns Pk
 HP18. . . . . 83 C3
Crossways Ct 4
 SL4 . . . . 210 C5
Crossway The UB10 201 F3
Crosthwaite Way
 SL1. . . . . 204 D8
Crowborough La
 HP27. . . . . 139 C6
Crowbrook Rd
 HP27. . . . . 139 C6
CROWELL 147 B4
CROWELL HILL. . . 147 D2
Crowell Mews HP19 115 A8
Crowell Rd
 Chinnor OX39 . . . . 147 B5
 Crowell OX39 . . . . 147 A4
CROWFIELD 26 F8
Crow La MK17 . . . . . 49 B8
Crown Bsns Est
 HP5. . . . . 144 C1
Crown Cl SL3 . . . . 212 C7
Crown Cotts
 Botley HP5 . . . . . . 155 B8
 Windsor SL4 . . . . . 210 D3
Crown Ct HP14. . . . 161 A2
Crown Dr SL2. . . . . 198 A4
Crown Mdws LU7. . 105 A7
CROWNFIELD HP27 149 C3
CROWNHILL 45 E7
Crownhill Bsns Pk
 MK8. . . . . 45 E8
Crownhill Rdbt MK8. 45 E8

Crown House Sch
High Wycombe HP11 173 C6
High Wycombe HP11 173 C6
Crown La
East Burnham SL2 198 A4
High Wycombe HP11 173 B6
Maidenhead SL6 203 A7
Marlow SL7 183 D2
Penn HP10 174 F7
Crown Leys HP20 101 E1
Crown Mdw SL3 212 B7
Crown Rd SL7 183 D2
Crown Rose Ct HP23 119 A3
Crown Way UB7 208 F5
Crown Wlk
Milton Keynes MK9 34 E3
Uxbridge UB8 201 C5
Crow Piece La
Burnham SL1 197 F5
East Burnham SL2 197 F4
Crowther Ct MK5 46 C5
Croxley Ct 3 LU7 80 F8
Croxley Rise SL6 202 D6
Croydon Cl MK4 46 C3
Cruickshank Dr
1 Wendover HP22 131 D6
Wendover HP22 131 D6
Cruickshank Gr MK8 45 E7
Crummock Cl SL1 204 C7
Crummock Pl MK2 58 D6
Crusader Est HP12 172 D5
Crutches La HP9 176 E4
CRYERS HILL 162 D6
Cryers Hill La HP15 162 D6
Cryers Hill Rd HP15 162 C6
Ct Cft MK10 35 F1
Cuba Cotts SL6 196 B3
Cuba Cres MK3 58 B4
Cubb Field HP19 115 B7
Cubitt St HP19 101 C1
CUBLINGTON 78 B1
Cublington Rd
Aston Abbotts HP22 88 D6
Stewkley LU7 78 F7
Wing LU7 79 B2
Cuckoo Hill Rise MK19 10 F2
Cuckoo Way HP19 114 F8
CUDDINGTON 113 A2
Cuddington & Dinton CE Sch HP17 113 F3
Cuddington & Dinton CE Sch (Inf) HP18 112 F3
Cuddington Hill HP18 112 E3
Cuddington Rd HP17, HP18 113 E3
Cudsdens Ct HP16 152 D7
Cuff La
Great Brickhill MK17 59 D1
Soulbury MK17 70 D8
Culbertson La MK13 33 E6
Culham Dr SL6 195 E2
Cullen Pl MK2 58 D5
Cullern's Pass SL6 202 F6
Culley Way SL6 202 A4
Cullyn Rd HP12 172 C3
Culmstock Cl MK4 46 D2
Culpepper Cl HP19 101 C4
Culrain Pl MK12 33 D4
Culross Gr MK10 36 A2
Culver Ave 11 MK10 36 B3
Culverhouse Wy HP5 144 D3
Culvers Croft HP9 176 C4
Culvert La UB8 201 B3
Culverton Hill HP27 139 B3
Culverton La HP27 139 B1
Cumberland Ave SL2 198 C1
Cumberland Cl
Aylesbury HP21 116 B7
Little Chalfont HP7 166 B8
Cumbrae Cl SL2 206 A5
Cumbria Cl
Maidenhead SL6 202 C4
Milton Keynes MK3 46 F1
Cumbrian Way
High Wycombe HP13 161 E1
High Wycombe HP13 172 F8
Uxbridge UB8 201 D5
Curfew Yd The 2 SL4 210 D6
Curlew HP19 101 F3
Curlew Cl
Berkhamsted HP4 135 C3
High Wycombe HP13 161 C2
Curls La SL6 202 E4
Curls Rd SL6 202 D4
Curran Cl UB8 201 C1
Currier Dr MK14 34 F6
Curriers La SL1 197 D7
Cursley Path 11 HP19 115 A8
Curtis Cotts HP5 144 F7
Curtis Croft MK5 46 B3
Curtiss La HP22 116 D7
Curtis Way HP4 135 D3
Curve The SL1 205 F4
Curzon Ave
Beaconsfield HP9 175 D4
Tylers Green HP15 163 C2
Curzon CE Comb Sch HP7 164 A5
Curzon Cl HP15 163 C2
Curzon Gate Ct HP14 158 E5
Curzon Mall 6 SL1 205 F4
Curzon Pl MK7 48 E4
Cushing Dr 7 MK4 45 E2
Cutlers Cl SL6 196 C2
Cutler's Ct 6 HP12 172 E7
Cutlers Mews MK14 34 F6
Cut Throat Ave HP4 107 E7
Cut Throat Way LU6 107 E8
Cuttle Brook Gdns OX9 125 E1
Cuttli Mill La NN12 17 B8
Cyber Ave MK10 35 E2
Cyclamen Pl HP21 115 B5
Cygnet Cl MK2 58 E8
Cygnet Ho SL6 196 C1
Cygnet Way SL6 203 A6
Cypress MK16 22 A3
Cypress Gdns SL6 202 E4
Cypress Ho SL3 207 B1
Cypress Wlk HP15 163 B3
Cyprus Wy MK3 58 B3

D

Daceberry Ct RG9 192 C2
Dacre Rd HP22 131 E7
Dadbrook
Cuddington HP18 112 F2
Cuddington HP18 113 A1
Dadbrook Cl HP18 112 F2
Dadfield Cl HP18 112 F2
DADFORD 28 D1
Dadford Rd
Chackmore MK18 41 A4
Dadford MK18 28 D5
Stowe MK18 40 D5
Dag La MK16 12 A7
Dagmar Rd SL4 210 D5
DAGNALL 107 C6
Dagnall Cres UB8 208 C8
Dagnall Rd
Olney MK46 6 E3
Studham HP4 107 E1
Whipsnade LU6 93 D2
Whipsnade LU6 107 D8
Dagnall Sch HP4 107 C5
Dair House Sch SL2 198 B4
Dairy La RG9 192 B8
Dairymede HP27 150 C4
Daisy Cotts HP14 171 B4
Dalby Cl 10 MK12 33 A6
Dalby Gdns 7 SL6 195 F1
Dale Cl NN13 38 A7
Dale Ct SL1 205 C4
Dalegarth Way MK10 36 C3
Dalegarth Wy MK10 36 C3
Dalesbredgr 1 MK19 45 D8
Dalesbred Gr MK19 45 C8
Dalesford Rd HP21 116 A4
Dale Side SL9 188 E2
Dalgin Pl MK9 35 A3
Dalston Cl HP20 101 F2
Dalston End MK10 35 E1
Dalton Gate MK10 35 F4
Dalton Gn 14 SL3 206 F1
Dalvina Pl MK12 33 D4
Dalwood Mews 3 HP19 115 A8
Daly Way HP20 116 B7
Damask Cl HP23 119 C4
Damson Ct HP10 173 D3
Damson Gr SL1 205 C4
Damson Rd 6 HP18 100 D5
Damson Way LU6 92 E4
Danbury Ct MK14 34 E5
Dancers End La HP22, HP23 118 C2
Dancersend Wildlife Reserve HP23 132 C8
Dancers Pl MK18 41 E4
Dandridge Cl SL3 206 D2
Dandridge Ct MK8 45 C6
Dandridge Dr SL8 185 C3
Dane Cl HP7 165 F6
Dane Ct HP21 115 D4
Dane Rd MK1 47 E2
Danesborough Dr MK17 49 A2
Danes Ct SL6 202 D7
Danesfield Sch SL7 193 E7
Danes Gdns SL6 195 F6
Daneswood MK17 49 A1
Daniels Welch MK6 47 A6
Dankworth Way MK17 48 E8
Dansteed Way
Great Linford MK14 34 F5
Milton Keynes, Bradwell Common MK8, MK13, MK14, MK15 34 C4
Milton Keynes, Crownhill MK8 45 D7
Danvers Croft HP23 119 C5
Darby Cl
Milton Keynes MK13 34 C2
Milton Keynes MK5 46 B5
Darby Lodge HP13 174 A7
D'arcy Cl HP19 100 E6
Darie Cl 3 SL1 205 A4
Dariel Cl 6 SL1 204 F4
Darin Ct MK8 45 F8
Dark La
Oving HP22 86 C7
Wingrave HP22 89 C2
Darlash Rd HP22 116 E6
Darley Cl HP21 116 B6
Darley Gate MK14 35 A5
Darleys Cl HP18 83 A6
Darling's La SL6 194 E1
Darlington Cl 2 HP6 154 D1
Darnel Cl MK6 47 A5
Darrell Cl SL3 206 F2
Darr's La HP4 134 D6
Darsham Wlk HP5 154 B8
Dart Cl
Aylesbury HP21 115 C5
Newport Pagnell MK16 22 D4
Slough SL3 212 B8
Darter St HP22 102 D2
Dartmouth Ct 10 SL1 205 F3
Dartmouth Dr
2 Milton Keynes MK10 35 F4
Milton Keynes MK10 36 A4
Dartmouth Rd MK46 6 F4
Darvell Dr HP5 144 A2
Darvells Yd WD3 167 D5
Darville Ho 19 SL4 210 D6
Darvill Rd HP17 114 B5
DARVILLSHILL 150 A4
Darvill's La SL1 205 D4
Darvills Mdw HP15 163 C7
Darwin Cl MK5 45 E5
Darwin Rd SL3 206 F4
Dashfield Gr HP15 162 F6
Dashwood Ave HP12 172 D7
Dashwood Cl SL3 206 C2
Dashwood Works Ind Est HP12 172 D7
DATCHET 211 C6
Datchet Ho 3 SL1 205 F3
Datchet Lodge Ctyd SL3 211 B6
Datchet Pl SL3 211 B6
Datchet Rd
Eton SL4 205 F2
Horton SL3 211 F4
Old Windsor SL4 211 A3
Old Windsor SL4 211 A3
Windsor SL4 210 D7
Datchet St Mary's CE Prim Acad SL3 211 B6
Datchet Sta SL3 211 B6
Daubeney Gate MK5 45 F6
Daunt Cl HP19 101 D4
Davenies Sch HP9 175 E2
Davenport Lea MK7 48 E5
Davenport Rd
High Wycombe HP12 172 C3
High Wycombe HP12 172 D3
Daventry Cl SL3 212 F6
David Bishop Ct HP5 154 D5
David Cl HP21 116 A4
Davidge Pl HP9 175 C5
David Rd SL3 212 F5
Davidson Rd 6 SL3 206 F1
Davies Cl HP20 115 D8
Davies Ct HP12 172 D5
Davies Way HP10 174 C1
Davis Cl SL7 183 E1
Davis Gr MK4 45 E3
Davis Ho 3 HP4 135 C3
Davison Ct MK8 45 D6
Davy Ave MK5 46 D6
Dawes Cl HP5 154 B7
Dawe's Cl UB10 201 E3
Dawes East Rd SL1 197 C2
Dawes La WD3 156 F3
Dawes Moor Cl SL2 206 C7
Dawe's Rd UB10 201 E3
Dawley Ride SL3 212 E6
Dawney Cl HP19 101 C2
Dawn Redwood Cl SL3 212 A4
Daws Ct SL0 207 F7
Daws Hill La
High Wycombe HP11 173 A4
High Wycombe HP11 173 A4
Daws Lea HP11 173 B3
Dawson Cl SL4 210 A5
Dawson Rd MK1 47 D3
Daylesford Ct MK15 35 B5
Daylesford Gr SL1 204 F4
Deacon Cl HP12 172 B4
Deacon Ct SL4 209 D5
Deacon Pl MK10 35 F3
Deadhearn La HP8 166 E1
Deal Ave SL1 204 F7
Deanacre Cl SL9 177 E4
Dean Cl
Aylesbury HP21 116 A5
High Wycombe HP12 172 E6
Uxbridge UB10 201 F5
Windsor SL4 209 D4
Deancroft Rd SL9 177 E4
Dean Farm La LU7 69 E4
Deanfield
Bledlow Ridge HP14 160 B8
Lacey Green HP27 149 F4
Dean Field HP3 146 A4
Deanfield Ave RG9 191 D1
Deanfield Cl
Marlow SL7 183 D2
Saunderton HP14 149 C1
Deanfield Rd RG9 191 D1
Dean Forest Way MK10 36 A5
Deangarden Rise HP11 173 E4
De Angeli Cl 4 MK18 41 E3
Dean La SL6 195 C8
Dean Rd
Dunton LU7 77 F8
Stewkley LU7 68 B2
Deans Cl
Amersham HP6 154 F2
Tring HP23 119 A4
Wexham Street SL2 199 B4
Dean's Cloisters SL4 210 D7
Deansfield Cl SL6 195 D2
Deans Furlong HP23 119 A4
DEANSHANGER 31 D4
Deanshanger Dr NN12 17 F1
Deanshanger Prim Sch MK19 31 E3
Deanshanger Rd
Deanshanger NN12 18 B1
Lillingstone Lovell MK18 17 A1
Lillingstone Lovell MK18 29 F6
Lillingstone Lovell MK18 30 A6
Old Stratford MK19 32 B6
Wicken MK19 31 B3
Wicken MK19 31 C3
Deans Lawn HP4 135 C4
Deans Mdw HP4 107 C5
Dean's Rd MK12 33 C7
Dean St SL7 183 D2
Deansway HP5 144 B2
Dean The HP22 89 B3
Dean View SL6 195 D6
Dean Way
Aston Clinton HP22 117 F4
Chalfont St Giles HP8 177 B7
Holmer Green HP15 163 B6
Dean Wood Rd HP9 176 D2
Dearing Cl 10 HP20 101 F2
Debbs Cl MK11 32 E5
Debden Pl 3 UB10 201 E4
De Beauchamp Ave MK19 10 F3
Deben Cl MK16 22 E3
Deblin Dr UB10 201 E3
Decies Way SL2 199 A4
De Clare Ct MK18 41 E1
Dedmere Ct SL7 183 F2
Dedmere Rd SL7 183 F2
Dedmere Rise SL7 183 E2
DEDWORTH 209 E6
Dedworth Dr SL4 209 F6
Dedworth Green Fst Sch SL4 209 E5
Dedworth Manor SL4 209 F6
Dedworth Mid Sch SL4 209 E6
Dedworth Rd SL4 209 D5
Deeds Gr HP12 172 E5
Deena Cl SL1 204 E6
Deep Acres HP6 154 A3
Deepdale MK13 34 C5
Deep Field SL3 211 B7
Deep Mill La HP16 152 D3
Deerfern Cl MK14 21 E1
Deerfield Cl MK18 52 E7
Deermead HP16 152 B4
Deer Park Wlk HP5 144 E3
Deerswood 2 SL6 203 B8
Deer Wlk MK9 34 F3
Deethe Cl MK17 49 B6
Defiance Ave MK17 36 E4
De Havilland Ct HP13 162 D2
De Havilland Dr HP15 162 E2
De Havilland Way TW19 213 E1
Delafield Cl HP14 158 F4
Delaford Cl
Iver SL0 207 F7
Iver UB8 208 A7
Delaford Ho UB7 208 D5
Delahay Rise HP4 135 B6
Delamere Cl HP20 101 F2
Delamere Gdns LU7 80 C7
Delaware Dr
Milton Keynes MK15 35 B8
Tongwell MK15, MK16 22 B1
Delius Cl MK7 48 C4
Dell Cl
Chesham HP5 143 F2
Farnham Common SL2 198 C7
Dellfield HP5 144 A2
Dell Field HP16 151 C5
Dell Field Ave HP4 135 B6
Dellfield Cl HP4 135 A6
Dellfield Cres UB8 201 C1
Dellfield Par UB8 201 C1
Dell Lees HP9 176 C4
Dell Orch HP7 164 C2
Dell Rd
Berkhamsted HP4 134 D7
Dell Rd *continued*
West Drayton UB7 208 F3
Dells MK46 6 F4
Dells Comm HP14 159 C1
Dellside UB9 190 C6
Dell The
Aylesbury HP20 102 A2
Chalfont St Peter SL9 177 E4
Maidenhead SL6 202 A2
Stokenchurch HP14 158 F3
Tylers Green HP10 163 C1
Uxbridge UB8 201 C6
Delmeade Rd HP5 154 A7
Delorean Wy NN13 26 A1
Deltic Ave MK13 34 B2
Deltic Trade Pk MK9 34 B2
Demoram Cl MK18 65 F3
Dempster Ct 13 MK10 36 C4
Denbigh Cl
4 Berryfields HP18 100 C5
Slough SL2 206 E3
Denbigh East Ind Est MK1 47 D2
Denbigh Hall MK3 46 F3
Denbigh Hall Dr MK3 46 F3
Denbigh Hall Ind Est MK3 46 F3
Denbigh Rd
Milton Keynes MK1 47 B2
Thame OX9 126 A1
Denbigh Rdbt MK1 47 C2
Denbigh Sch MK5 46 A6
Denbigh Way MK2 47 C1
Denbigh West Ind Est MK1 47 B2
Denby Cl HP20 116 A8
Denby Walk HP20 116 A8
Denchworth Ct 2 MK4 46 C2
Dene Cl
Winslow MK18 66 A3
Woburn Sands MK17 49 C4
Dene The
Steeple Claydon MK18 63 D3
Woburn Sands MK17 49 C4
Denewood HP13 173 E8
DENHAM
Denham Green 190 A2
Quainton 85 D5
Denham HP22 85 C5
Denham Aerodrome UB9 189 E6
Denham Ave UB9 189 F3
Denham Cl
Denham UB9 190 A1
Maidenhead SL6 202 C6
Milton Keynes MK3 57 D8
Denham Court Dr UB9 190 B1
Denham Ctry Park Nature Reserve UB9 190 B2
Denham Ctry Pk* UB9 190 B2
Denham Garden Village UB9 189 F5
Denham Golf Club Sta UB9 189 D4
DENHAM GREEN 189 E5
Denham Green Cl UB9 190 A4
Denham Green La UB9 189 F5
Denham La SL9 178 A2
Denham Lodge UB9 201 C6
Denham Quarry Park Nature Reserve UB9 190 C1
Denham Rd
Denham SL0 200 F7
Iver Heath SL0 200 E5
Lane End HP14 171 C5
Denham Sta UB9 190 A4
Denham View MK18 75 F6
Denham Village Inf Sch UB9 189 F2
Denham Way UB9 190 A1
Denham Way (North Orbital Rd) WD3 178 E4
Denham Wlk SL9 177 F4
Denholme Lodge SL3 211 B7
Denison Ct MK7 48 D6
Denmark St
Maidenhead SL6 202 E8
Milton Keynes MK2 58 E8
Denmead MK8 33 E2
Denmead Cl SL9 188 E4
DENNER HILL 150 E4
Denner Hill Farm Rd HP16 150 F5
Denner Hill Rd HP16 151 E5
Dennis Cl HP22 118 A4
Denniston Ho HP12 172 C8
Dennis Way SL1 204 D6
Denny La MK3 58 A4
Denny Rd SL3 206 F2
Denny's La HP4 134 F2
Denton Ct SL7 183 F3
Denton Dr MK19 10 F1
Denton Wy SL1 206 B4
De Pirenore HP15 162 E2
Depot Rd SL6 203 A6
Derby Arms 2 HP20 115 D8
Derby Pl HP18 100 E5
Derby Rd UB8 201 D3
Derbyshire Cl 2 MK3 46 F2
Derehams Ave HP10 174 C3
Derehams La HP10 174 C2
Derek Rd SL6 203 C8
Dere Pl MK2 58 E4
Deridene Cl 2 TW19 213 E1
Derwent Cl
Little Chalfont HP7 166 B8
Newport Pagnell MK16 22 D4
Derwent Dr
Maidenhead SL6 202 D8
Milton Keynes MK3 57 E8
Slough SL1 204 C8
Derwent Rd
Aylesbury HP21 116 B6
Leighton Buzzard LU7 80 B7
Desborough Ave
High Wycombe HP11 172 F6
9 High Wycombe HP11 172 F7
Desborough Bsns Pk HP12 172 E8
Desborough Coll SL6 202 E5
Desborough Cres SL6 202 D5
Desborough Gn 1 HP20 101 D2
Desborough Ho 14 HP13 173 B7
Desborough Park Rd HP12 172 E8
Desborough Rd HP11 172 F7
Desborough St HP11 172 F7
Deseronto Wharf Ind Est SL3 206 E4
Develin Cl MK14 34 F7
De Vere Cl HP5 143 F2
Devereux Ct MK17 48 E8
Devereux Pl
Aylesbury HP19 101 A2
Milton Keynes MK6 46 F7
Devereux Rd SL4 210 D5
Deverill Rd HP21 115 C3
Deverills Way SL3 207 C2
Devon Ave SL1 205 C7
Devon Cl MK3 46 F1
Devon Rd HP19 101 A3
Devonshire Ave HP6 154 B2
Devonshire Cl
Amersham HP6 154 C2
Farnham Royal SL2 198 B3
Devonshire Gdns SL6 204 A7
Devonshire Gn SL2 198 B3
Devonshire Lodge 10 SL6 202 F6
Devon Way UB10 201 F3
Dewar Spur SL3 211 F8
Dewberry St HP22 102 D2
Dewsbury MK14 34 C8
Dews La UB9 190 E4
Dexter Ave MK6 46 F8
Dexter Dr MK19 45 D8
Dexter Ho MK6 46 F8
Dhoon Rise SL6 202 F6
Diamond Ct HP7 165 B7
Diamond Rd SL1 206 A4
Diana Cl SL3 206 E7
Diana Way MK11 32 F3
Diane Cl HP21 116 A4
Diane Wlk HP21 116 A4
Dibden Hill HP8 177 C6
Dickens Cl MK43 3 F6
Dickens Dr MK19 32 B6
Dickens La MK17 58 B2
Dickens Pl SL3 212 E6
Dickens Rd MK12 33 C8
Dickens Spinney MK46 6 E4
Dickens Way HP19 100 F2
Dickens Yd LU7 80 E6
Dickins Pl SL3 212 E6
Dicks Way HP19 100 F3
Diddington Cl MK2 58 C3
Digby Cl OX9 126 B1
Digby Croft MK10 35 E3
DIGGS 126 F5
Dilwyn Ct 1 HP12 172 E7
Dimbles Gate OX39 147 C7
Dimmock Cl MK17 58 B3
Dimsdale Dr SL1 197 F7
Diners Hill
Dunsmore HP22 141 A7
Ellesborough HP22 140 F7
Dingle Dell LU7 70 F2
Dingledery MK46 6 F4
Dinmore 2 HP3 145 F3
DINTON 113 F2
Dippingwell Ct SL2 198 B7
Discovery St HP18 100 E5
Disraeli Cres HP13 161 F1
Disraeli Ct SL3 212 B8

Disraeli Pk HP9 175 D4
Disraeli Sch and Children's Centre The HP13 161 F1
Disraeli Sq 4 HP19 115 A8
Diswell Brook Way MK19 31 E5
DITCHFIELD 171 A3
Ditchfield Cotts HP14 171 A3
Ditchingham Cl HP19 115 B7
Ditton Park Acad SL1 205 E5
Ditton Park Cvn Site SL3 206 F1
Ditton Park Rd SL3 211 E8
Ditton Pk Acad SL1 206 C2
Ditton Rd
Datchet SL3 211 D7
Slough SL3 211 F8
Dixie Ct HP20 116 A8
Dixie La MK7 48 C6
Dixon Cl HP21 115 B6
Dixon's Wharf HP23 104 D2
Dobbins La HP22 131 B5
Dobson's La RG9 191 C8
Docton Mill 3 MK4 45 E2
Doctor's Commons Rd HP4 135 B4
Doctors Spinney NN13 39 B4
Doddershall
Quainton HP22 84 E5
Quainton MK18 84 B5
Dodds Cl HP22 117 E6
Doddsfield Rd SL2 198 A2
Dodds La HP8 177 B8
Dodkin MK6 47 B5
Dodman Gn MK4 57 B8
Doggetts Farm Rd UB9 189 C4
Doggett St LU7 80 F7
Doggetts Wood Cl HP8 166 B6
Doggetts Wood La HP8 166 B5
Dog Kennel La WD3 167 F5
Dolben Ct MK15 35 D8
Dolesden La
Turville RG9 169 D1
Turville Heath RG9 169 C2
Dollicot HP17 126 F6
Dolphin Ct
Loudwater HP11 174 A3
Slough SL1 206 B4
Dolphin Pl HP21 115 E6
Dolphin Rd SL1 206 B4
Dolphin Sq 2 HP23 119 A3
Dominica Gr MK3 58 B3
Domino Wy HP18 100 E5
Donegan Cl 1 MK17 48 E8
Donkey Dr SL8 185 A3
Donkey La
Bourne End SL8 185 A3
Tring HP23 118 E2
West Drayton UB7 208 C2
Donnay Cl SL9 188 D5
Donnington MK13 34 B6
Donnington Gdns SL6 195 F1
Donnington Row HP17 113 E2
Donnybrook Ho 3 HP13 173 C7
Don The MK3 46 D1
Doolittle Ave HP11 173 B4
Doolittle La LU6 93 B5
Doonican Dr MK17 48 E8
Doon Way MK2 58 C5
Doppler Gr 2 MK10 35 D2
Dorcas Farm La MK17 69 B7
Dorchester Ave MK3 47 A2
Dorchester Cl
Maidenhead SL6 195 B1
Stoke Mandeville HP22 116 B2
Dorchester Ho SL9 188 F6
Doreen Cl MK2 58 C7
Dorian Cl HP23 119 D4
Dorking Pl MK5 46 B4
Dormans Cl MK10 36 A2
Dormer Ave LU7 79 E3
Dormer Cl HP21 115 B6
Dormer Ct 4 HP20 101 F2
Dormer La HP15 163 B7
Dornels SL2 206 C7
DORNEY 204 C3
Dorney Court* SL4 204 B3
Dorney End HP5 144 A1
Dorney Hill N SL1, HP9 187 A4
Dorney Hill S SL2 187 A4
Dorney Lake Pk* SL4 209 B8
Dorney Pl MK13 34 C3
DORNEY REACH 203 F3
Dorney Reach Rd SL6 203 F3
Dorney Sch SL6 203 F3
Dorneywood Cl SL1 197 C3
Dorneywood Gdn* SL1 197 D6
Dorney Wood Rd
Burnham SL1 197 D6
Littleworth Common SL1 186 C1
Dorothy La HP22 102 D2
Dorper Dr MK8 33 C1
Dorrells Rd HP27 138 D6
Dorriens Cft HP4 134 F6
Dorrien's Croft HP4 134 F7
Dorset Cl
Berkhamsted HP4 134 F5
Milton Keynes MK3 46 F1
Dorset Lodge 9 SL6 202 F6
Dorset Pl HP21 116 C6
Dorset Rd SL4 210 C6
Dorset Way
Uxbridge UB10 201 F3
Whitehouse MK19 45 C8
Dorsey Cl MK8 45 E6
DORTON 96 F1
Dorton HP18 97 B1
Dorton Cl MK8 33 F1
Dorton Hill
Dorton HP18 97 A1
Dorton HP18 111 A7
Dorton Rd HP18 111 B4
Douglas Ct SL7 184 A3
Douglas Gdns HP4 135 A5
Douglas La TW19 211 F1
Douglas Pl MK6 46 E8
Douglas Rd
Aylesbury HP20 102 A1
Slough SL2 205 D8
Stanwell TW19 213 D1
Douglas Wlk 6 MK10 36 C3
Doune Ho MK3 46 F2
Dove Cl
Aylesbury HP21 115 C5
Buckingham MK18 52 E7
Newport Pagnell MK16 22 D4
Dovecote
Haddenham HP17 126 F6
Newport Pagnell MK16 22 C4
Dove Cote HP22 117 B6
Dovecote Cft MK14 21 E1
Dovecote Cl
Haddenham HP17 126 F6
Monks Risborough HP27 139 C5
Dovecote Cotts MK5 46 A4
Dovecote Mews UB9 190 E8
Dovecot Rd 11 HP13 173 A7
Dove Ct HP9 175 D3
Dove Ho HP19 101 F4
Dove House Cl
Edlesborough LU6 92 F4
Winslow MK18 66 A4
Dove House Cres SL2 197 E2
Dovehouse Mews MK16 12 B6
Dovehouse Rd 3 HP11 173 A7
Doveleat OX39 147 D7
Dove Pk WD3 167 B4
Dover Cl LU7 105 D2
Dover Gate MK3 57 F8
Dover Hedge HP21 116 C7
Dover Rd SL1 204 F7
Dove St LU7 78 E8
Dovetail Cl HP12 172 D8
Dowding Rd UB10 201 F5
Dower Cl HP9 175 C5
Dower Mews 5 HP4 135 C4
Dower Pk SL4 209 E3
Downdean MK6 47 A8
Downderry Croft MK4 57 B8
Downer Cl MK18 52 F8
Downer Dr WD3 156 F3
Downham Rd MK17 49 C4
DOWNHEAD PARK 35 B5
Downhill Cl MK5 46 B6
Downing Cl MK3 58 B8
Downing Path SL2 197 E1
Downings Wood WD3 178 D5
Downland MK8 33 E2
DOWNLEY 161 C3
Downley Ave MK13 34 C3
Downley Ct HP13 161 D2
Downley Rd HP14 161 D6
Downley Sch The HP13 161 D3
Down Pl SL4 209 A8
DOWNS BARN 35 A5
Downs Barn Bvd MK14 34 F5
Downs Barn Rdbt MK14 34 F5
Downs Barn Sch MK14 34 F5
Downs Field MK16 22 F3
Downs Pk HP13 161 E2
Downs Rd SL3 206 D4
Downs View MK17 48 C2
Downs Villas 17 HP23 119 A3
Doxford Heath 1 MK10 36 C4
Dragon Tail HP17 127 A5
Drake Ave SL3 206 D2
Drake Cl HP21 115 B6
Drakeloe Cl MK17 60 F8
Drakes Dr HP18 125 E5
Drakes Farm HP18 125 E5
Drakes Mews MK8 45 F7
Drakes Mews Bsns Ctr MK8 45 F7
Drakes Rd HP7 165 E8
Drakewell Rd MK17 48 D1
Drayhorse Cres MK17 49 A5
Draymans La SL7 183 D1
DRAYTON BEAUCHAMP 118 B5
Drayton Cl LU7 118 E3
Drayton Ct UB7 208 F2
Drayton Gdns UB7 208 E4
Draytonmead Farm Rd HP23 103 D1
Drayton Park Sch MK2 58 D5
DRAYTON PARSLOW 68 C6
Drayton Parslow Village Sch MK17 68 C6
Drayton Rd
Aylesbury HP20 101 D2
Milton Keynes MK2 58 C5
Newton Longville MK17 57 C2
Stoke Hammond MK17 58 B2
Dr Challoner's Gram Sch HP6 154 C1
Dr Challoner's High Sch HP7 166 B7
Dresser Rd HP16 151 C5
Drew Ct MK3 47 A4
Drewitt Pl HP21 115 F5
Drew Mdw SL2 198 C8
Drews Pk HP9 175 C6
Drey The SL9 177 E5
Drift Rd SL4 209 A1
Drift Way
Colnbrook SL3 212 C7
Olney MK46 6 F5
Drinkwater Cl OX25 95 D7
Drive The
Amersham HP7 154 D1
Bourne End SL8 184 F4
Bourne End SL8 185 A4
Chalfont St Peter SL9 177 F3
Cranfield MK43 24 D2
Datchet SL3 211 B6
Ickenham UB10 190 E1
Ivinghoe Aston LU7 92 A1
Maidenhead SL6 203 B8
Slough SL3 206 E4
Windsor SL4 209 F6
Wraysbury TW19 211 D2
Drlycott OX33 123 F2
Dropmore Inf Sch SL1 186 C1
Dropmore Rd
Burnham SL1 197 C5
Littleworth Common SL1 186 C1
Drovers Cres HP23 125 D1
Drovers Croft MK12 33 B4
Drovers La
Amersham HP7 165 F5
Turville Heath RG9 169 B2
Drovers Way
Dunstable LU6 93 F8
Newton Longville MK17 57 D2
Seer Green HP9 176 C4
Drovers Wy NN12 18 E2
Druce End NN12 18 E6
Druids Wlk OX39 147 C6
Drummond Cres SL9 177 D1
Drummond Ho 4 SL4 210 D4
Drummond Ride HP23 119 A5
Drummond Hay MK15 35 C7
Drydell La HP5 153 F8
Dryden Cl
Aylesbury HP20 101 E2
Newport Pagnell MK16 22 A4
Dubery Cl HP17 114 D5
Dublois Cl LU7 118 E3
Duchess Gdns NN12 18 D3
Duchess Gr MK7 48 C7
Duchess St SL1 204 E5
DUCK END
Akeley 42 A8
Swanbourne 66 F4
Duck End
Aylesbury HP20 115 C8
Great Brickhill MK17 59 D1
Duck La
Ludgershall HP18 96 C8
Woburn MK17 60 F7
Duck Lake MK18 41 E3
Duck Lake Cl MK18 41 E4
Duckmore La HP23 118 E2
Duck Sq OX39 147 C6
Duckworth Ct MK6 46 E7
Dudley Cl MK18 76 A2
Dudley Ct SL1 206 A3
Dudley Hill MK5 46 A6
Dudley Ho 1 HP3 146 A4
Dudley La RG9 181 A6
Dudley Pl TW19 213 F1
DUDSWELL 134 D8
Dudswell La HP4 134 D7
Duffield Bank 8 MK10 36 B3
Duffield La SL2 198 F6
Duffield Pk
Stoke Poges SL2 198 F2
Stoke Poges SL2 199 A2
Dugdale MK46 6 E6
Dukes Ave LU6 107 E8
Dukes Cl
Gerrards Cross SL9 188 E3
Shabbington HP18 124 D2
Dukes Dr
Farnham Common SL2 198 A8
Milton Keynes MK2 47 C1
Dukes Kiln Dr SL9 188 C3
Dukes La SL9 188 E4
Dukes Mdw SL8 185 B3
Dukes Mws HP27 139 B4
Dukes Piece MK18 52 F8
Dukes Pl
Marlow SL7 183 D2
Slough SL1 205 F6
Dukes Ride
Gerrards Cross SL9 188 E3
Ickenham UB10 201 E8
Leighton Buzzard LU7 70 F3
Dukes Row HP18 99 A1
Duke St
Aspley Guise MK17 49 D4
Eton SL4 210 C7
Henley-on-Thames RG9 191 E2
High Wycombe HP13 173 C6
Princes Risborough HP27 139 B4
Dukes Valley SL9 188 B2
Dukes Way
Berkhamsted HP4 135 A6
Uxbridge UB8 201 C4
Dukes Wood Ave SL9 188 E3
Dukes Wood Dr SL9 188 D3
Dulverton Ct LU7 80 C8
Dulverton Dr MK4 46 D3
Dulwich Cl MK16 22 C2
Dumbarton Wy SL1 206 C1
Dumbletons WD3 178 E6
Dumfries Cl MK3 46 F3
Dunbar Cl
Milton Keynes MK3 57 D8
Slough SL2 206 A6
Dunbar Dr OX9 126 A1
Duncan Gr MK5 45 F6
Duncan Lock Ho HP9 175 F2
Duncannon Cres SL4 209 D4
Duncan Rd MK43 24 E2
Dunchurch Dale MK7 48 B5
Duncombe Cl HP6 154 E1
Duncombe Rd HP4 134 E6
Duncombe St MK2 58 C7
Duncroft SL4 209 F4
Dundale Prim Sch HP23 119 A5
Dundale Rd HP23 119 A4
Dundee Rd SL1 205 A8
Dungeness Ct MK4 46 A1
Dungrovehill La SL7 194 D3
Dunholme End SL6 202 D3
Dunkeld Ho HP11 174 B4
Dunkery Beacon MK4 46 D3
Dunkley Ct 7 MK18 52 C8
Dunnet Cl MK4 57 A8
Dunny La WD4 156 F7
Dunsby Rd MK6 47 A4
Dunsham La HP20 101 E2
Dunsley Pl HP23 119 B3
DUNSMORE 141 A7
Dunsmore HP22 141 A6
Dunsmore Ave HP27 139 C5
Dunsmore La HP22 141 B7
Dunsmore Rd HP22 141 C8
Dunsmore Ride HP27 139 C5
DUNSTABLE 93 E8
Dunstable Downs* LU6 93 E4
Dunstable Ho 4 SL7 183 E1
Dunstable Rd
Dagnall HP4 107 C7
Eaton Bray LU6 93 A5
Ivinghoe LU7 105 F4
Ivinghoe LU7 106 A6
Totternhoe LU6 93 D7
Whipsnade LU6 93 F3
Dunstanburgh Cl 13 MK4 56 E8
Dunstan St MK18 52 B8
Dunster Ct MK4 46 E3
Dunster Gdns SL1 205 A6
Dunston Hill HP23 119 A4
Dunthorne Way MK8 45 D6
DUNTON 77 E5
Dunton Rd
Cublington LU7 78 A3
Hoggeston HP22 77 B2
Littlecote MK18 78 C5
Stewkley LU7 78 D6
Dunvedin Pl MK12 33 D4
Dunvegan Cl MK2 58 D4
Dunwood Ct SL6 202 C5
Dunwood Rise HP13 162 B1
Duparc Cl MK7 48 C5
Dupre Cl SL1 204 E4
Dupre Cres HP9 176 B1
Du Pre Wlk HP10 185 D4
Durgate MK7 48 A8
Durham Ave SL1 205 A7
Durham Farm La HP22 141 E6
Durham Ho 1 MK3 46 F1
Durham Rd LU7 105 C3
Durley Hollow HP13 162 B1
Durlston End MK4 57 A8
Durrans Ct MK2 47 E1
Durrans Ho MK2 47 E1
Durrants La HP4 134 F5
Durrants Path HP5 144 A4
Durrants Rd
Berkhamsted HP4 134 F5
2 Berkhamsted HP4 135 A5
Durrell Cl LU7 80 E7
Dutch Barn Cl TW19 213 D1
Dutch Elm Ave
Datchet SL3 211 A7
Windsor SL4 210 F7
Dutton Way SL0 207 E7
Duvall Ct SL1 206 A3
Dwight Cl HP16 151 C5
Dwights Yd 6 HP4 135 C4
Dyersdale MK13 34 C5
Dyers Mews MK14 34 F6
Dyers Rd LU6 92 D7
Dymchurch Cl 2 MK10 36 B4
Dymock Ct HP22 85 B4
Dynasty Dr MK2 47 C1
Dyson Cl SL4 210 B4
Dyson Dr UB8 201 E4

E

E-ACT Burnham Pk Acad The SL1 204 B8
Eagle Cl HP6 154 F2
Eagle Rd SL1 204 F6
Eagles Rd HP20 116 A8
EAGLESTONE 47 B7
Eaglestone Rdbt MK6 47 A8
Eagle Way MK43 3 F6
Eagle Wlk MK9 34 F3
EAKLEY LANES 4 D2
Eakley Lanes
Stoke Goldington MK16 5 A1
Stoke Goldington MK16 12 A8
Ealing Chase MK10 47 F8
Eames Cl HP20 101 F3
Eardley Pl MK8 45 D6
Earl Cl HP13 162 A1
Earl Howe Rd HP15 163 D6
Earls Cl MK2 58 C8
Earlsfield SL6 203 C2
Earls Gdns HP7 165 D7
Earlshall Pl 2 MK4 45 F1
Earls La SL1 204 F5
Earls Willow MK13 34 A8
Earlswood Cl HP21 116 A5
Easby Gr MK10 36 A1
Eascote Rd HP21 116 B4
EASINGTON 111 B1
Easington HP18 111 B1
Easington La HP18 111 B1
Easington Terr HP18 111 B1
Eastaff Croft 6 MK17 49 A5
East Arms Pl SL7 193 F3
East Berkshire Coll
Slough SL3 207 A3
Windsor SL4 210 C5
Eastbourne Rd SL1 205 A7
Eastbridge SL2 206 B5
Eastbrook Cl OX25 95 E7
EAST BURNHAM 198 A4
East Burnham Cotts SL2 198 A4
East Burnham La SL2 198 A4
Eastbury Ct MK4 46 D1
East Chapel MK4 57 B8
EAST CLAYDON 74 E8
East Claydon Rd MK18 65 D2
East Claydon Sch MK18 74 E7
East Comm SL9 188 E5
East Cres SL4 209 F6
Eastcroft SL2 198 B1
East Dales MK13 34 C5
East Dr
High Wycombe HP13 173 E8
Stoke Poges SL2 198 E2
EAST END
Cranfield 25 C1
North Crawley 24 F6
East End
Sherington MK16 14 E6
Weedon HP22 87 D1
Weedon HP22 101 D8
Eastergate HP9 175 C4
Eastern Dene HP15 163 B5
Eastern Dr SL8 185 C4
Eastern St HP20 101 E1
Eastfield MK17 55 B3
Eastfield Cl 3 SL1 206 A3
Eastfield Cres NN12 18 F5
Eastfield Dr MK19 11 A3
Eastfield Rd
Aylesbury HP20 116 B8
Burnham SL1 204 A8
Princes Risborough HP27 139 C3
East Green Cl MK5 45 F6
East Hills MK43 25 B1
East La
Great Hampden HP16 150 E7
Walton MK7 47 F7
Eastlands HP27 149 E5
Eastmoor Dr 8 MK12 33 A6
Eastnor HP3 146 A3
Eastoke Pl MK4 57 A8
Easton St HP11 173 B6
Easton Terr HP13 173 C6
East Paddock SL6 194 F6
East Rd
Cranfield MK43 24 E2
Maidenhead SL6 202 E7
West Drayton UB7 208 F2
East Richardson St 5 HP11 172 F7
East Ridge SL8 185 B4
East Spur MK7 47 F6
East St
Adstock MK18 53 F1
Chesham HP5 154 B8
Olney MK46 7 A4
East Terr SL4 210 E7
East View OX25 81 A3
East Walk N MK9 34 E2
East Walk S MK9 34 E2
East Way HP9 175 A1
Eastwick Cres WD3 178 F8
Eastwood Ct 1 SL7 183 F3
Eastwood Rd HP14 158 F3
Eaton Ave
High Wycombe HP12 172 D8
Milton Keynes MK2 58 D7
Slough SL1 204 C6
EATON BRAY 92 F6
Eaton Bray Acad LU6 92 F6
Eaton Bray Rd
Edlesborough LU6 92 C5
Honeywick LU6 92 E8
Eaton Cl HP22 116 F2
Eatongate Cl LU6 92 E5
EATON GREEN 92 C7
Eaton Hall Cres MK10 36 C3
Eaton Pk LU6 92 F6
Eaton Pl
Beaconsfield HP9 175 E1
High Wycombe HP12 172 D8
Eaton Rd HP21 115 D7
Ebble Cl HP21 115 C4
Ebbsgrove MK5 34 B1
Ebenezer Ho HP10 174 C2
Ebsworth Cl SL6 196 C3
Eclipse Ave MK10 35 E2
Edburg St MK18 52 B8
Eddington Ct MK4 46 D1
Eddy St HP4 135 A5
Eden Cl
Aylesbury HP21 115 D4
Slough SL3 207 A1
Eden Ct MK2 58 E8
Eden Sh Ctr HP11 173 A7
Eden Wlk MK3 46 E1
Edgar Rd UB7 208 E5
Edgar Wallace Pl SL8 185 B5
EDGCOTT 72 F2
Edgcott Rd
Calvert MK18 73 A4
Hillesden MK18 51 F1
Little Marsh OX27 72 B2
Marsh Gibbon OX27 71 F2
Preston Bissett MK18 62 D6
Steeple Claydon MK18 62 F2
Edgecombe Rd HP21 116 B5
Edgecote MK8 46 A8
Edgecote Ho 11 HP13 173 B7
Edgecott Rd HP18 82 F7
Edgehill OX9 125 F2
Edge Hill Ct MK18 41 E2
Edge St HP19 101 C1
Edgewood HP11 173 D5
Edgeworth Cl SL1 206 D4
Edging La MK18 52 F6
Edinburgh Ave SL1 205 B7
Edinburgh Gate UB9 189 F5
Edinburgh Gdns SL4 210 D5
Edinburgh Ho MK3 57 D7
Edinburgh Pl HP21 115 C6
Edinburgh Rd
Maidenhead SL6 195 E1
Marlow SL7 183 E3
Edison Cl UB7 208 F4
Edison Rd HP19 100 E1
Edison Sq MK5 46 C5
Edith Bell Ho SL9 177 E4
Edith Rd SL6 202 A7
EDLESBOROUGH 92 E4

Edlesborough Sch LU6 92 E3
Edlyn Cl HP4 134 F5
Edmonds Cl MK18 41 F1
Edmondson St HP22 102 D3
Edmonds Rd HP14 171 B4
Edmund Ct
Beaconsfield HP9 186 A8
Milton Keynes MK5 45 F7
Edmund La MK18 51 B6
Edmunds Cl HP12 172 C5
Edmunds Gdns HP12 172 C5
Edmunds Way SL2 206 B7
Edrich Ave MK6 46 F8
Edstone Pl MK4 46 C3
Edward Cl HP21 116 A4
Edward Rd MK18 52 B8
Edwards Croft MK13 34 A7
Edwards Ct [8] SL8 185 B3
Edward Wlk HP21 116 A4
Edwin Allman Pl HP15 162 E2
Edwin Cl MK17 48 D2
Edy Ct MK5 34 A1
Edzell Cres MK4 45 E2
Eelbrook Ave MK13 34 C2
Eeles Cl HP19 100 F3
Egdirbnede Dr SL2 197 F1
Egerton Cl NN13 38 A7
Egerton Gate MK5 46 B4
Egerton Rd
Berkhamsted HP4 135 B6
Slough SL2 197 E1
Egerton-Rothesay Sch HP4 134 E4
Egglesfield Cl HP4 134 E6
Eggleton Cl [2] HP21 115 E5
Eggleton Dr HP23 119 A5
Eghams Cl HP9 175 C4
Eghams Gn SL8 185 B3
Eghams Wood Rd HP9 175 C4
Egmont Ave MK11 32 E4
Egremont Gdns SL1 205 A5
EGYPT 198 B8
Egypt La SL2 187 B1
Egypt Way HP19 115 A8
Egypt Wood Cotts SL2 187 B1
Eider Cl MK18 52 E8
Eight Acres
Burnham SL1 197 B1
East End MK43 25 B2
Tring HP23 119 A4
Elangeni Sch HP6 154 E3
Elba Gate MK3 58 C4
Elbow Mdw SL3 212 F6
Elderberry Rd HP18 100 D5
Elder Cl
Loudwater HP11 174 B3
West Drayton UB7 208 E6
Elderdene OX39 147 D8
Elderfield Rd SL2 198 F6
Elder Gate
Milton Keynes, Rooksley MK9 34 C1
Milton Keynes, Winterhill MK9 46 C8
Elder Way HP15 163 B3
Elder Wy SL3 206 F4
Eldridge La HP17 130 C3
Eleanor Cl MK17 60 F7
Eleanor Gdns HP21 115 F6
Eleanor Rd SL9 177 C2
Eleanor Wlk MK17 60 F7
Elfords MK6 47 A6
Elgar Gr MK7 48 C4
Elgar Mws HP21 115 F3
Elgin Ho SL3 212 E6
Elgiva La HP5 154 B8
Elgiva Theatre HP5 154 B8
Elham Way HP21 116 A4
Elia Cl HP12 172 C8
Eliot Cl
Aylesbury HP19 100 F2
Newport Pagnell MK16 21 F5
Eliot Dr SL7 183 F4
Elizabeth Ave HP6 166 C8
Elizabeth Cl
Aylesbury HP21 116 B4
Cookham Rise SL6 195 F7
Elizabeth Ct
High Wycombe HP13 173 C6
High Wycombe, Wycombe Marsh HP13 173 E5
[10] Slough SL1 206 A4
[3] Windsor SL4 210 C5
Elizabeth Dr HP23 119 B6
Elizabeth Hawkes Way SL6 202 A3
Elizabeth Ii Ave HP4 134 E4
Elizabeth Rd
Marlow SL7 183 E3
Stokenchurch HP14 158 F4
Elizabeth Sq MK2 58 C8
Elizabeth Way SL2 198 F4
Elizabeth Woodville Sch The MK19 31 F4
Elkins Rd SL2 187 E2
Ellen Pl HP21 115 C5
Ellen Rd HP21 115 C5
Ellenstow MK13 34 A4
Ellen Wlk HP21 115 B6
Ellerburn Pl MK4 46 B3
Ellerman Sq [15] MK10 36 C4
Ellery Rise RG9 170 F1
ELLESBOROUGH 130 B2
Ellesborough Gr MK8 33 D3
Ellesborough Rd
Butler's Cross HP17 130 C2
Ellesborough HP17 130 A2
Wendover HP22 131 A3
Ellesmere Cl
Datchet SL3 211 A8
Totternhoe LU6 93 C6
Ellesmere Rd HP4 135 D4
Elliman Ave SL2 205 F6
Ellington Ct SL6 203 C7
Ellington Gdns SL6 203 C7
Ellington Pk SL6 195 E1
Ellington Prim Sch SL6 195 F1
Ellington Rd SL6 203 C7
Elliots Cl UB8 208 C8
Elliott Ho HP11 172 F8
Ellis Ave
Chalfont St Peter SL9 177 F2
Slough SL1 205 E4
Ellisgill Ct MK13 34 B4
Ellison Cl SL4 209 F4
Ellison Ct HP23 118 F3
Ellison Ho [14] SL4 210 D6
Ellis Way HP14 171 B4
Ellsworth Rd HP11 172 F4
Ellwood Ho SL9 177 E2
Ellwood Rd HP9 175 B1
Ellwood Rise HP8 177 C8
Ellwood Terr WD3 167 D4
Elmar Gn SL2 198 A2
Elm Brook Cl HP18 112 C1
Elm Cl
Amersham HP6 154 C1
Butler's Cross HP17 130 C3
Chinnor OX39 147 C5
Farnham Common SL2 198 C6
Hazelmere HP15 163 A3
Newton Longville MK17 57 C2
Weston Turville HP22 116 F2
Elm Croft SL3 211 C6
Elm Ct
Berkhamsted HP4 135 B4
Butler's Cross HP17 130 C3
Elmdale Gdns HP27 139 B3
Elm Dr
Chinnor OX39 147 C5
Deanshanger MK19 31 D5
Elmers Cl MK19 44 A6
Elmers Mdw MK18 76 A2
Elmers Pk MK3 58 A8
Elm Farm Rd HP21 116 A5
Elmfield Cl NN12 18 D3
Elmfields Gate MK18 66 A4
Elm Gn HP21 115 D7
Elm Gr
Berkhamsted HP4 135 C4
Maidenhead SL6 202 E7
West Drayton UB7 208 F6
Woburn Sands MK17 49 B4
ELMHURST 101 E3
Elmhurst [5] HP16 152 A8
Elmhurst Cl
High Wycombe HP13 162 D1
Milton Keynes MK4 46 F4
Elmhurst Ct SL3 207 A3
Elmhurst Rd
Aylesbury HP20 101 E2
Slough SL3 207 A3
Elmhurst Sch HP20 101 E2
Elm La SL8 184 F5
Elm Lawn Cl UB8 201 E5
Elmlea Dr MK46 6 E3
Elm Leys HP22 89 C3
Elmodesham Ho [7] HP7 165 B7
Elmore St HP18 100 E5
Elm Rd
High Wycombe HP12 172 C4
Princes Risborough HP27 139 C3
Tylers Green HP10 174 D8
Windsor SL4 210 B4
Elmridge Ct MK4 46 C2
Elms Dr SL8 185 C3
Elmshott Cl HP10 163 A1
Elmshott La SL1 204 E6
Elmside MK18 66 A4
Elmslie Ct SL6 202 E7
Elms Rd SL9 177 E3
Elm St MK18 52 D8
Elms The
Leighton Buzzard LU7 80 E7
Milton Keynes MK3 57 F8
Preston Bissett MK18 51 B1
Elmswell Gate MK10 48 D8
Elmswell Rd MK17 48 D8
Elm Tree Cl OX25 81 A4
Elm Tree Cotts HP7 164 C2
Elmtree Ct [6] HP16 152 A8
Elmtree Gn HP16 152 A8
Elmtree Hill HP5 144 B1
Elm Trees HP18 125 B7
Elmtree Sch HP5 144 B1
Elm Tree Wlk
Chorleywood WD3 167 F5
Elm Tree Wlk *continued*
Tring HP23 119 A5
Elmwood
Maidenhead SL6 196 B4
Turvey MK43 8 E6
Elmwood Cl HP18 109 D5
Elmwood Pk SL9 188 E3
Elmwood Rd SL2 206 B6
Elora Rd HP13 173 E7
Elruge Cl UB7 208 D3
Elsage Ct LU7 105 B8
Elsmore Cl HP21 116 A4
Eltham Ave SL1 204 E4
Elthorne Rd UB8 201 D3
Elthorne Way MK16 22 C2
Elton MK6 47 D7
Elton Cl HP18 100 E4
Elton Dr SL6 202 D8
Elwes Rd HP14 171 C4
Ely Ave SL1 205 C8
Ely Cl HP7 165 E8
Ely Ho HP13 173 F8
Ely Rd [3] HP22 131 E6
Ember Path HP21 115 C4
Ember Rd SL3 207 B3
EMBERTON 13 E8
Emberton Ctry Pk★ MK46 6 E1
Emberton Sch MK46 13 F8
Embleton Way MK18 52 C7
Emerald Cl MK18 74 F8
Emerald Ct SL1 205 E4
Emerald Gate MK15 35 E5
Emerald Way HP22 102 D2
Emerson Ct HP10 185 E6
EMERSON VALLEY 46 B2
Emerson Valley Sch MK4 46 C2
Emerton Ct HP4 134 F7
Emerton Garth HP4 134 E7
Emerton Gdns MK11 32 E5
Emilia Cl SL6 195 F1
Emlyns Bldgs SL4 210 D7
Emma Rothschild Ct HP23 119 A5
Emmett Cl MK4 46 C1
Emmett Dr HP21 115 E5
EMMINGTON 137 A1
Emmington View OX39 147 C7
Emperor Cl HP4 134 F7
Emperor Dr MK8 45 D6
Emperor La HP22 102 E2
Empingham Cl MK2 58 D4
Empire Cl HP19 100 E6
Empress Matilda Gdns MK12 33 B7
Empstead Ct RG9 191 D2
Enborne Cl HP21 115 D4
Enders Ct MK5 45 E5
Endfield Pl SL6 202 B6
Enfield Chase MK14 34 D5
Enfield Cl UB8 201 D3
Engaine Dr MK5 45 F7
Engine La HP22 102 C2
English Gdns TW19 211 D2
Enigma Ctr The MK1 47 E2
Enigma Pl MK3 47 A1
Enmore Gate MK9 35 A3
Enmore Rdbt MK9 35 A3
Ennell Gr MK2 58 C5
Ennerdale Cl MK2 58 D6
Ennerdale Cres SL1 204 C8
Ensbury Path HP20 101 E2
Enstone Rd UB10 190 F1
Enterprise La MK9 35 A3
Epsom Cl LU7 80 D6
Epsom Gr MK3 57 D6
Equine Way OX39 147 B7
Equus Cl SL9 188 C3
Ercolani Ave HP13 173 D6
Eriboll Cl LU7 80 B6
Erica Cl SL1 204 E6
Erica Rd MK12 33 E4
Eridge Gn MK7 48 A8
Erle Rd HP22 102 B2
Errington Dr SL4 210 A6
Escarpment Ave LU6 107 D8
Eskan Ct MK9 35 B4
Eskdale Ave HP5 144 D1
Eskdale Gdns SL6 203 B2
Eskdale Lodge HP6 154 C2
Eskdale Rd
Stoke Mandeville HP22 116 B2
Uxbridge UB8 201 B3
Eskdale Way MK10 36 B3
Esk Way MK3 46 E1
Essenden Ct MK11 32 F5
Essex Ave SL2 205 C8
Essex Cl MK3 46 F1
Essex Ho [5] HP20 101 D1
Essex Pl HP19 101 A3
Essex Rd HP5 144 C2
Essex Yd HP22 89 C2
Estcourt Dr HP15 162 F6
Esther Cl MK13 34 A6
Eston Ct MK13 34 A5
Estover Way OX39 147 B6
Etheridge Ave MK10 48 C8
Ethorpe MK8 33 E1
Ethorpe Cl SL9 188 E6
Ethorpe Cres SL9 188 E6
Ethorpe Ho SL9 188 E6
ETON 210 C8
Eton Cl SL3 211 A8
Eton Coll
Eton SL4 205 D1
Eton SL4 210 D8
Eton College Rowing Ctr★ SL4 204 D7
Eton Cres MK12 33 C6
Eton Ct SL4 210 D7
Eton Dorney Sch SL4 204 B3
Eton End Sch SL3 211 A8
Eton Ho [1] SL1 205 F3
Eton Pl SL7 183 D2
Eton Porny CE Fst Sch SL4 210 D8
Eton Rd
Datchet SL1 206 A1
Datchet SL3 211 A8
Eton Riverside SL4 210 D7
Eton Sq SL4 210 D7
ETON WICK 204 F1
Eton Wick CE Fst Sch SL4 205 A1
Eton Wick Rd SL4 205 B1
Eton Wlk [1] SL1 205 E3
Eunice Gr HP5 154 D7
Europa Bsns Pk MK10 36 C2
Europa Ho SL9 188 E6
Evans Cl HP21 116 A4
Evans Gate MK6 46 E8
Evans Way HP23 119 B4
Evelyn Cl LU7 79 E1
Evelyn Gdns SL6 204 B6
Evelyn Pl MK13 34 A7
Evelyns Cl [2] UB8 208 F7
Evenley Rd
Mixbury NN13 38 C1
Mixbury NN13 38 D1
Evenlode SL6 202 F8
Evenlode Cl HP21 115 C5
Evenlode Rd SL8 185 B4
Everard Ave SL1 205 E4
Everest Cl HP13 173 D6
Everest Rd HP13 173 E6
Evergreen Dr [3] UB7 208 F4
Evergreen Oak Ave SL4 211 A4
Evergreen Way HP10 173 D3
Everley Cl MK4 46 C3
Eversden Cl MK17 59 E5
Evesham Gn HP19 101 C3
Evesham Way MK5 45 D5
Evreham Rd SL0 207 E7
Evreham Sp Ctr SL0 207 D8
Exbury La MK4 45 F1
Excalibur Rd HP18 100 E3
Exchange Ho MK9 34 E2
Exchange St HP20 115 E8
Exebridge MK4 46 C3
Exhims Mews HP4 134 E6
Exmoor Gate MK4 46 E2
Eynesford Rd HP22 116 B2
Eynsford Terr UB7 208 F7
Eynsham Ct MK15 35 C2
Eyre Cl HP19 114 F8
Eyre Gn SL2 198 A2
EYTHROPE 113 F8
Eythrope Rd
Eythrope HP18 100 A1
Stone HP17 114 C6

F

Fabius Dr MK11 32 E3
Factory Yd HP9 175 E1
Fadmoor Pl [3] MK4 46 B3
Fagnall La HP7 164 D2
Fairacre SL6 202 C6
Fair Acre HP13 173 B7
Fair Acres HP16 151 D5
Fairacres Ind Est SL4 209 D5
Fairchild End HP17 126 F7
Faircroft SL2 198 B1
Fairface Wy [4] MK17 49 A5
Fairfax MK13 34 C6
Fairfax Cres HP20 101 E2
Fairfax Mews HP7 165 A7
Fairfield HP6 154 B3
Fairfield App TW19 211 D1
Fairfield Ave SL3 211 D7
Fairfield Cl
Bourne End SL8 185 A5
Datchet SL3 211 D7
Haddenham HP17 127 B5
Olney MK46 7 A3
Fair Field Cl SL8 184 F5
Fairfield La SL2 198 B3
Fairfield Pl SL2 198 B4
Fairfield Rd
Burnham SL1 197 C2
Paulerspury NN12 17 B7
Uxbridge UB8 201 D6
West Drayton UB7 208 E6
Wraysbury TW19 211 D1
Fairfields HP15 151 E1
Fairfields Prim Sch MK11 33 A2
Fairford Cres MK15 35 B6
Fairford Leys Way HP19 115 A7
Fairford Rd SL6 202 F8
Fairhaven SL9 177 C2
Fair Isle Vw MK14 21 B1
Fairlawn Pk SL4 209 E3
Fairlawns HP13 162 C1
Fairlea SL6 202 B3
Fair Leas HP5 144 A2
Fairlie Rd SL1 205 A8
Fairlight Ave SL4 210 D5
Fairlight Dr UB8 201 D6
Fair Mdw MK18 66 A4
Fairmead The SL3 212 D7
Fairmile RG9 191 C4
Fair Mile HP21 116 A7
Fairmile Ct RG9 191 D3
Fair Ridge HP11 172 F4
Fairthorn Cl HP23 118 E3
Fair View Cotts
Chalfont St Peter SL9 177 E3
Cookham Rise SL6 195 E7
Fairview Ind Est
Amersham HP6 154 F1
High Wycombe HP11 173 F4
Fairview La HP10 174 A1
Fairview Rd
Burnham SL6 204 A7
Slough SL2 197 F1
Fairway HP27 139 A3
Fairway Ave UB7 208 D5
Fairway Cl UB7 208 D5
Fairways MK8 33 C2
Fairways Rdbt MK8 33 C2
Fairway The
Burnham SL1 197 C3
Flackwell Heath HP10 185 C7
Maidenhead SL6 202 B3
Uxbridge UB10 201 F3
Faithfull Cl HP17 114 B5
Faithorn Cl HP5 144 A1
Faith Terr MK19 11 A2
Falaise MK15 35 B7
Falcon Ave MK6 35 B2
Falcon Dr
Milton Keynes MK19 32 B7
Stanwell TW19 213 E1
Falconhurst Sch MK6 47 B8
Falcon Ridge HP4 135 C3
Falcon Rise HP13 161 C1
Falcons Croft HP10 185 E8
Falcon The HP19 101 F4
Falkland Gr MK17 58 B3
Falkland Ho SL6 202 F8
Falklands Cl MK18 63 D2
Fall Cl HP19 101 D3
Falling La UB7 208 E6
Fallow Field HP15 163 B3
Fallows The SL6 196 A1
Falmouth Pl MK6 34 F1
Falmouth Rd SL1 205 A7
Fane Way SL6 202 D5
Fantail La HP23 118 F4
Faraday Cl SL2 205 B8
Faraday Dr MK5 46 C5
Faraday Rd
Aylesbury HP19 101 A1
Slough SL2 205 B8
FAR BLETCHLEY 57 D7
Far Furlong Cl HP21 115 D3
Far Holme MK10 35 F2
Farinton MK8 33 F2
Farjeon Ct MK7 48 D4
Farleigh Dr [7] HP18 100 D5
Farmborough MK6 47 C6
Farmbrough Cl HP20 102 A1
Farm Cl
High Wycombe HP13 174 A7
Ickford HP18 123 F3
Little Chalfont HP6 166 D8
Maidenhead SL6 203 C1
Maidenhead, Highway SL6 202 A7
Stewkley LU7 78 E7
Farm Cres SL2 206 C8
Farm Ct [3] MK5 46 A3
Farm Dr SL4 211 B1
Farmers Cl SL6 202 A4
Farmers Pl SL9 177 C1
Farmers Way
Longwick HP27 138 D6
Maidenhead SL6 202 A4
Seer Green HP9 176 C4
Farmery Ct HP4 135 E6
Farm Gr HP9 175 C5
Farm La HP9 176 D3
Farm Lea HP10 185 F7
Farm Pl
Berkhamsted HP4 134 F5
Henton OX39 137 E1
Farm Rd
Bourne End SL8 184 F4
Brackley NN13 38 A6
Burnham SL6 204 A5
Chorleywood WD3 167 A5
Maidenhead SL6 202 A7
Farm Way TW19 212 F1
Farm Yd SL4 210 D7
Farnburn Ave SL1 205 B8
Farndale Gdns HP15 163 A6
Farnell Ct MK5 46 C8
Farnham Cl HP3 146 A3
FARNHAM COMMON 198 D6
Farnham Common Ho [2] SL2 198 C8
Farnham Common Inf Sch SL2 198 B8
Farnham Common Jun Sch SL2 198 C8
Farnham Ct MK8 33 F1
Farnham La SL2 198 A2
FARNHAM PARK 198 C4
Farnham Park La SL2 198 C4
Farnham Rd
Slough SL1 205 C8
Slough SL1, SL2 205 C7
FARNHAM ROYAL 198 C3
Farnley Rd HP20 101 E2
Farrer Cl NN13 26 D4
Farrer Theatre Eton SL4 205 C1
Farrier Ct [1] SL8 185 B3
Farrier Pl MK14 35 A5
Farriers Cl HP3 146 B3
Farriers Corner LU7 105 D4
Farriers Way HP5 144 A3
Farringdon St MK10 35 F1
Farr Mdw MK17 37 B1
Farthingales The SL6 203 B7
Farthing Ent Ctr The MK6 47 C6
Farthing Gr MK6 47 C6
Farthing Green La SL2 199 B4
Farthings The HP6 154 A3
Fassets Rd HP10 174 B2
Fassnidge View UB8 201 C5
Faulkner Dr MK3 47 B1
Faulkner's Way LU7 80 E7
Faulkner Way HP13 161 D3
Favell Dr MK4 46 F4
Faversham Cl HP23 119 A4
Fawcett Mws HP19 101 D2
Fawcett Rd SL4 210 B6
FAWLEY 191 C8
FAWLEY BOTTOM 180 B2
Fawley Bottom La RG9 180 B1
Fawley Cl SL6 195 D2
Fawley Court★ RG9 191 E5
Fawley Gn RG9 180 D2
Fawley Hill Rly★ RG9 191 D8
Fawsley Cl SL3 212 E7
Fearney Field Cl HP5 154 D7
Fearnley Cl MK17 48 D8
Featherbed Cl MK18 65 E4
Featherbed La HP15 163 D8
Featherstone Rd MK12 33 A5
Fedden Ho MK43 24 D3
Fegans Ct MK11 32 D6
Felbridge MK7 48 A7
FELDEN 146 F7
Felden La HP3 146 F8
Fells Cl HP18 125 D6
Fellstead Ct SL6 202 C6
Felstar Wlk [2] MK6 47 C4
Felsted MK7 48 A3
Fences La MK16 13 A2
Fenlandia [6] MK6 47 C4
Fennel Dr MK14 34 E4
Fennell Dr LU7 78 F8
Fennels Farm Rd HP10 174 A1
Fennels Rd HP11 174 A4
Fennels The HP11 174 A3
Fennels Way HP10 174 A1
Fennemore Cl HP18 109 D4
Fennings The HP6 154 D3
FENNY LOCK 47 E2
Fennymere MK8 33 D1
Fenny Rd
Stoke Hammond MK17 58 E1
Stoke Hammond MK17 69 E8
FENNY STRATFORD 47 D1
Fenny Stratford Sta MK1 47 E1
Fensom Pl [4] MK10 35 D2
Fen St
Atterbury MK10 36 B5
Broughton MK17 36 F3
Milton Keynes MK17 36 F1
Fenton Ct MK8 45 F8
FERN 184 E5
Fernan Dell MK8 45 D7
Fernborough Haven [4] MK4 46 C2
Fern Cotts SL7 184 E5
Fern Ct HP4 135 B4
Fern Dale MK6 35 B1
Ferndale Cl HP14 158 F4
Ferndale Cres UB8 201 C2
Fern Dr SL6 204 B7
Ferne Furlong MK46 6 F5
Fernes Cl UB8 208 C7
Fernfield MK17 56 A5
Fern Gr MK2 58 D5
Fernhill Cl OX9 136 A6
Fernhurst Cl HP9 175 F2
Fernie Fields HP12 172 C4

Fern La
Fern SL7 184 E5
Haddenham HP17 127 A6
Fernlea Cl HP10 174 A1
Fernley Ct SL6 195 D1
Fernside
Great Kingshill HP15 151 E1
Hazelmere HP15 163 A6
Slough SL2 206 B6
Fernsleigh Cl SL9 177 E4
Ferns The HP9 175 F1
Fern Wlk HP15 163 B3
Fernwood Sch MK17 49 B2
Ferranti Pl MK10 35 E2
Ferrers Ave UB7 208 D4
Ferrers Cl SL1 204 E5
Ferry End SL6 203 C4
Ferry La
Bourne End SL8 196 B8
Medmenham SL7 193 B5
Mill End RG9 192 D6
Ferry Mdws Cl MK10 36 A4
Ferry Rd SL6 203 C4
Festival Cotts SL3 212 C7
Fetty Pl SL6 202 D4
Fidlers Field HP22 84 E4
Field Cl
Aylesbury HP20 102 A2
Buckingham MK18 51 B6
Chesham HP5 144 E3
Ickford HP18 124 A3
Sherington MK16 14 A2
Field Ct MK5 46 B8
Field End HP18 125 F5
Field End Cl HP23 119 D1
Fieldfare HP19 101 E4
Field Farm Bsns Ctr OX26 71 A5
Fieldhead Gdns SL8 185 A3
Fieldhouse Ct HP13 174 A4
Fieldhouse Ind Est SL7 183 F2
Fieldhouse La SL7 183 F2
Field House La SL7 184 A1
Fieldhouse Way SL7 183 F2
Field Hurst SL3 206 F1
Fielding Gdns SL3 206 C4
Fielding Rd SL6 202 B8
Field La MK12 33 B5
Field Maple Gdns HP10 173 D3
Field Rd
Denham UB9 189 E1
Denham, Rush Green UB9 200 E8
High Wycombe HP12 172 B5
Murcott OX5 94 A5
Field Rose HP21 116 D6
Fields End HP23 119 A6
Fields The SL1 205 D4
Fieldway
Amersham HP7 165 B6
Berkhamsted HP4 135 E2
Chalfont St Peter SL9 177 D3
Wigginton HP23 119 D1
Field Way
Aylesbury HP20 102 A2
Bovingdon HP3 146 A4
Chalfont St Peter SL9 177 D2
Uxbridge UB8 201 D1
Field Wlk MK9 34 F3
Fiesta End HP18 100 E5
Fife Ct MK4 57 A8
Fife Ho MK3 46 F1
Filey Spur SL1 205 B4
FILGRAVE 13 C5
Filgrave Sch MK16 13 C5
Filmer Rd SL4 209 D5
Finch Cl MK10 35 F3
Finch Cres LU7 80 E5
Finch Ct SL6 202 D5
Finch End HP10 174 C8
Finch Gn WD3 167 F5
Finch La
Amersham HP7 165 F5
Beaconsfield HP9 175 C5
Little Chalfont HP7 166 B7
Finch Rd HP4 135 A4
Finch St HP22 102 E3
Findlay Mws 13 SL7 183 F3
Findlay Way MK2 58 C8
Finefield Wlk SL1 205 D4
Finemere Wood Wildlife Reserve HP22 84 B8
Fingest La RG9 170 D4
Fingest Rd RG9 170 A2
Fingle Dr MK13 33 E7
Finians Cl UB10 201 F5
Finings Rd HP14 171 A4
Finlay Dr RG9 191 E2
Finlay Ho RG9 191 E3
FINMERE 50 D7
Finmere CE Prim Sch MK18 50 D6
Finmere Cres HP21 116 C5
Finmere Rd
Finmere MK18 39 F1
Shalstone MK18 39 D4
Water Stratford MK18 40 A1
Finsbury Chase MK10 47 F8
Fircroft Cl SL2 199 A6
Fircroft Ct SL2 199 A6
Firecrest Way HP19 100 F1
Fire La MK17 57 D4
Firemans Run MK17 49 B5
Fire Station Ct 2 SL6 203 A8
Fire Station Rd MK18 52 E8
Firfield SL6 203 B1
Firs Ave SL4 209 F4
Firs Cl
Hazelmere HP15 163 B2
High Wycombe HP13 173 E8
Iver Heath SL0 200 C4
Lane End HP14 171 C5
Whitchurch HP22 87 A5
Firs Ct
Amersham HP6 154 C2
Bierton HP22 102 C4
Princes Risborough HP27 138 F3
Firs Dr SL3 206 F5
Firs End SL9 188 D8
Firs Rise HP16 151 E7
First Ave
Amersham HP7 165 D7
Marlow SL7 184 A2
Milton Keynes MK1 47 C1
First Cres SL1 205 C8
Firs The
Bierton HP22 102 C4
Brill HP18 96 B1
Brill HP18 110 B8
Grendon Underwood HP18 83 A6
Maidenhead SL6 202 E7
Uxbridge UB8 201 D1
Wigginton HP23 119 D1
Firs View Rd HP15 163 B2
Firs Wlk HP15 163 B2
Firth St HP22 102 E3
Fir Tree Ave
Stoke Poges SL2 198 F1
Stoke Poges SL2 199 A1
Fir Tree Cotts HP14 161 B8
Firview Cl SL7 183 F1
Fisher Gr MK46 7 A4
Fishermans Cl MK46 6 E4
Fishermans Retreat SL7 183 E1
Fisherman's Way SL8 185 B4
FISHERMEAD 35 A1
Fishermead Bvd
5 Central Milton Keynes MK6 34 F1
2 Milton Keynes MK6 34 F1
Fishermead Rdbt MK1 47 B2
Fishers Field MK18 52 C8
Fishery Rd SL6 203 C5
Fishguard Spur SL1 206 B4
Fish Ponds La OX9 125 E1
Fishweir LU7 68 D1
Fitkins Mdw HP22 116 F3
Fitzgerald Gr MK4 56 E8
Fitzgeralds Way HP12 172 B7
Fitzhamon Ct MK12 33 A5
Fitz Hugh Cres MK17 49 A8
Fitzwilliam St MK3 58 B8
Five Acres
Chesham HP5 154 D6
Wooburn Green HP10 185 F7
Five Acre Wood HP12 172 C6
Five Points SL0 200 C2
FLACKWELL HEATH 185 A7
Flaggs Mdw MK46 6 E4
Flambard Cl MK15 35 A7
Flamborough Spur SL1 205 A4
Flamstead Gate MK5 45 E5
Flanders Way NN13 26 A2
FLAUNDEN 156 A6
Flaunden Bottom HP5 155 E4
Flaunden Hill HP3 156 A6
Flaunden La
Bovingdon HP3 146 D3
Chipperfield WD3 156 E6
Flaunden HP3 156 C6
Flavius Gate NN13 38 A7
Flavius Gdns MK11 33 A2
Flaxbourne Ct MK7 48 C7
Flaxen Field HP22 116 F2
Flaxley Gate MK10 36 A2
Fledgelings Wlk MK18 66 A5
Fleetbrook Ho SL3 211 D6
Fleet Cl
Buckingham MK18 41 F2
Walter's Ash HP14 161 F7
FLEET MARSTON 100 B4
Fleet St HP20 101 D1
Fleet The MK6 35 B2
Fleetwood Cl HP8 177 A6
Fleetwood Ct 7 TW19 213 E1
Fleetwood Rd SL2 205 F6
Fleetwood Way OX9 125 F2
Fleming Ct 7 SL3 206 C3
Fleming Dr MK6 47 B6
Fleming Rd 7 HP22 131 D6
Fleming Way HP12 172 D5
Fletcher Cl HP19 100 F3
Fletchers Mews MK14 34 F6
Fletton Dell MK17 49 A5
Fletton End MK18 73 B5
Flexerne Cres MK6 47 D5
Flintergill Ct MK13 34 B4
Flint Ho 7 MK3 46 F1
Flint Hollow OX39 147 B6
Flintlock Cl TW19 213 A3
Flint St HP17 127 A5
Flint Way HP16 151 C7
Flitcroft Lea HP13 173 A8
Flitt Cl HP22 117 E6
Flitt Leys Cl MK43 25 B2
Flitton Ct MK11 32 F5
Flora Ave HP22 117 F4
Flora Gdn MK11 32 F3
Flora Thompson Dr MK16 21 F6
Florence Ave SL6 203 A8
Florence Ct HP19 101 D1
Florence Mws SL1 206 C1
Florence Way UB8 201 C5
Florey Gdns HP20 115 F8
Florin Cl MK15 35 A7
FLOWERS BOTTOM 150 A4
Flowers Bottom La HP27 150 B4
Flowers Mws MK10 35 D2
Flynn Croft MK4 45 D1
Focus Sch Stoke Poges Campus SL2 199 B5
Fog Cotts HP23 120 A5
Folding Cl LU7 78 E8
Fold Mws SL2 198 C6
Foley Cl HP9 175 C4
Foliejohn Way SL6 202 A1
Folkestone Ct SL3 207 A1
Follet Cl SL4 211 B1
Folleys Pl HP10 174 D1
Folly Farm Rd
Hardwick HP22 86 F3
Hardwick HP22 87 A3
Folly La
Hartwell NN7 10 C8
North Crawley MK16 24 B5
Folly Rd MK19 31 D4
Fonda Mdws MK4 45 D3
Fontaines Rd
Wavendon MK17 36 F1
4 Wavendon MK17 48 F8
Fontwell Cl SL6 202 A8
Fontwell Dr MK3 57 C6
Forbes Pl MK5 45 E4
Forches Cl MK4 46 D2
FORD 128 B7
Fordcombe Lea MK7 48 B8
Ford End UB9 189 F2
Ford La SL0 208 A7
Ford Rd HP17 113 F3
Ford's Cl HP14 159 F8
Ford St
Buckingham MK18 52 D8
High Wycombe HP11 173 F4
Ford Way HP13 161 E3
Forelands Way HP5 154 C7
Forest Bridge Sch
Maidenhead SL6 203 A4
Slough SL6 203 B6
Forest Cl
Princes Risborough HP27 139 B3
Slough SL2 206 B8
Wendover HP22 131 B4
Foresters
Beacon's Bottom HP14 159 C5
Chinnor OX39 147 B6
Oakley HP18 109 D6
Forest Pk SL4 209 E1
Forest Point HP13 173 F5
Forest Rd
Hanslope MK19 10 F5
Piddington (Northants) NN7 4 A8
Windsor SL4 209 E5
Forest Rise MK6 47 B8
Forestry Hos OX49 168 A7
Forest Way HP13 174 A8
Forfar Dr MK3 46 F2
Forge Cl
Ashendon HP18 97 E1
Holmer Green HP15 163 C6
Horton-cum-S OX33 108 B5
Marsh Gibbon OX27 71 F3
Oakley HP18 109 D4
Steeple Claydon MK18 63 E2
Forge Ct HP22 117 D5
Forge Dr SL2 198 C6
Forge End HP7 165 B7
Forge Rd HP14 161 C8
Forge The MK46 13 F8
Forgetts Rd HP14 171 C4
Forlease Cl SL6 203 A6
Forlease Dr SL6 203 A6
Forlease Rd SL6 203 A6
Formby Cl
Milton Keynes MK3 57 C7
Slough SL3 207 C2
Forrabury Ave MK13 34 C3
Forrester Gdns MK4 56 F7
Forrester Wlk MK10 35 E2
Forsyth Cl 2 MK17 48 D8
Forsythia Gdns SL3 206 E3
Fort End HP17 127 A6
Fortescue Dr MK5 46 B6
Forthill Pl MK5 45 F7
Fortuna Ct MK7 48 C6
Fortune St
Aylesbury HP18 100 E5
Broughton MK10 36 D4
Forty Gn HP27 137 F3
FORTY GREEN
Beaconsfield 175 A4
Princes Risborough 137 F3
Forty Green Dr SL7 183 B2
Forty Green Rd HP9 175 C4
Forum The MK14 34 E5
FOSCOTE 42 B4
Foscote Cotts MK18 42 B4
Foscote La MK18 42 B5
Foscote Rd MK18 41 F3
Foscott Rd MK18 42 A4
Foscot Way MK18 41 E2
Foskett Way HP21 115 E5
Fossey Cl MK5 45 F3
Foster Ave SL4 209 E4
Foster Cl HP20 101 F3
Fosters La MK13 34 A3
Fosters Path SL2 197 F1
Fotherby Ct SL6 203 A6
Fotheringay Gdns SL1 205 A6
Fotherley Rd WD3 178 F8
Founders Mews MK14 34 F6
Foundry Dr MK18 52 C8
Foundry La
Horton SL3 212 B4
Lacey Green HP27 149 C5
Fountain Ct
6 Aylesbury HP20 115 D8
1 Olney MK46 6 F3
Fountaine Cl MK14 34 E7
Fountain Gdns SL4 210 D4
Four Acres HP22 86 D8
FOUR ASHES 162 D4
Four Ashes Rd HP15 162 C5
Fourdrinier Ct HP11 174 A4
Four Marks Cl
4 Milton Keynes MK10 35 F4
Milton Keynes MK10 36 A4
Four Oaks HP5 144 A4
Four Seasons Terr 5 UB7 208 F4
Fourth Ave SL7 184 A2
Fourways Mews HP12 172 C4
Four Winds SL8 185 C2
Fowler MK14 34 C7
Fowler Cl HP12 172 D5
Fowler Rd HP19 115 B8
Fowlers Farm Rd HP14 158 E4
Fowler Wy UB10 201 E3
Foxborough Cl SL3 207 A1
Foxborough Ct SL6 202 E4
Foxborough Prim Sch SL3 207 A1
Fox Cl
Wigginton HP23 119 D1
Woburn ML17 60 F7
Fox Cover OX39 147 C6
Fox Covert La MK19 20 A5
Foxcovert Rd MK5 45 F4
Foxcroft SL0 207 F6
Foxdell Way SL9 177 E5
Foxes Piece SL7 183 E2
Foxes Piece Sch SL7 183 E3
Fox Farm Rd MK17 59 D6
Foxfield MK10 36 B3
Fox Field HP15 162 F5
Foxgate MK16 22 B4
Foxglove HP21 115 B5
Foxglove Cl
Buckingham MK18 52 C7
Slough SL2 206 B8
West Drayton UB7 208 F4
Foxglove Ct MK16 21 F4
Foxglove Dr SL6 202 E5
Foxgoles Cl MK19 31 F5
Foxherne SL3 206 C4
Foxhill
Olney MK46 6 E4
Olney MK46 6 E5
Foxhill Cl HP13 162 B1
Foxhills Way NN13 26 A1
Foxhollow Dr SL2 198 C7
Foxhunter Dr MK14 34 E6
Fox La
Drayton Parslow MK17 68 C6
Dunsmore HP22 141 A6
Holmer Green HP15 163 B6
Foxleigh HP11 173 A4
Foxley Gr SL1 197 C2
Foxley Pl MK5 46 C8
FOX MILNE 35 F4
Fox Milne Rdbt MK10 35 F4
Foxmoor Ct UB9 190 A5
Fox Rd
Holmer Green HP15 163 B6
Slough SL3 206 D2
Wigginton HP23 119 C2
Foxtail Cl HP22 102 D2
Foxton MK6 47 D6
Fox Way MK18 52 E7
Fraderica Cotts MK16 22 C3
Framers Ct HP14 171 B4
Framewood Manor SL2 199 C6
Framewood Rd
Slough SL3 188 C1
Wexham Street SL2, SL3 199 C6
Framlingham Ct MK5 46 A5
Frampton Gr 11 MK4 45 F1
France Furlong MK14 34 F8
Frances Ave SL6 196 C1
Frances Ct LU7 80 E7
Frances Dove Cl HP12 172 E3
Frances Dove Way HP11 173 A6
Frances Rd SL4 210 D5
Frances St HP5 144 C2
Franchise St 3 HP5 144 C1
Francis Ct MK5 46 B6
Francis Way SL1 204 D6
Francis Yd 2 HP5 154 B8
Frank Atter Croft MK12 33 C5
Frank Howe Ct MK6 35 A1
Franklin Ave SL2 205 B8
Franklin Cl
Chesham HP5 143 F2
Haddenham HP17 127 A7
Franklin Ct
Amersham HP7 154 C1
Yardley Gobion NN12 18 E6
Franklin Rd
Dunstable LU6 93 F8
Haddenham HP17 127 A7
Franklins Croft MK12 33 C5
FRANKLIN'S SPRING 178 D5
Frank Lunnon Cl
Bourne End SL8 185 C3
Bourne End SL8 185 C3
Franklyn Cres SL4 209 D4
Frankston Ave MK11 32 E5
Frank Sutton Way SL1 205 D6
Frankswood Ave UB7 208 F7
Frantons The SL6 202 A7
Frascati Way SL6 202 F7
Fraser Rd HP12 172 C5
Fraucup Cl HP17 128 B7
Fraunchies Ct SL1 205 E6
Frays Ave UB7 208 D4
Frays Cl UB7 208 D3
Fray's Ct UB8 201 C5
Frayslea UB8 201 C3
Frays Valley Nature Reserve UB10 201 D8
Frayswater Pl UB8 201 C2
Fray's Waye UB8 201 C4
Frederick Pl HP11 174 B3
Fredericks Ct HP9 186 A8
Frederick Smith Ct MK12 33 D4
Frederick St HP18 99 A7
Freeman Cl MK12 33 B5
Freeman Ct HP5 144 C1
Freemans Cl SL2 199 A6
Freemans Gdns MK46 7 A3
Freer Cres
High Wycombe HP11 174 A4
Loudwater HP13 174 A4
Fremantle Rd
Aylesbury HP21 115 E5
High Wycombe HP13 162 E2
Frenchum Gdns SL1 204 E5
Frensham Dr MK2 58 C7
Frensham Wlk SL2 198 C6
Freshfield Ave 1 MK10 36 A3
Freyberg Dr
Aylesbury HP18 100 D5
3 Berryfields HP18 100 D5
Friarage Rd HP20 115 D8
Friarscroft Way HP20 115 C8
Friars Field HP4 134 E7
Friars Furlong HP18 125 B7
Friars Gdns HP14 162 A7
Friars Walk HP16 151 D5
Friars Wlk HP23 119 A4
Friary Gdns MK16 22 C2
Friary Island TW19 211 C1
Friary Rd TW19 211 C1
Friary The SL4 211 C1
Friday Ct OX9 125 F1
Friday St
Henley-on-Thames RG9 191 E2
Leighton Buzzard LU7 80 F7
Frideswide St MK18 52 B8
Friendship La LU7 79 E3
Friesland Ave MK19 45 C8
FRIETH 170 F1
Frieth CE Comb Sch RG9 170 F1
Frieth Hill RG9 170 F1
Frieth Rd
Frieth RG9 170 E3
Marlow SL7 182 E5
Marlow Common SL7 182 F3
Moor End RG9 171 A1
Frimley Dr
Slough SL1 204 F4
1 Slough SL1 204 F4
Fripp Gdns MK8 45 D6
Frithe The SL2 206 B7
FRITH-HILL 152 C7
Frith Hill
Great Missenden HP16 152 B7
South Heath HP16 152 C8
Frithsden Copse HP4 135 F8
Frithsden La HP1 121 F1
Frithsden Rise HP4 121 D3
Frithwood Cres MK7 48 B7
Fritillary Ave OX39 147 C5
Frobisher Gate MK15 35 C4
Froggy La UB9 189 D1
Frog La HP18 112 F3
Frogmill SL6 193 C3
Frogmill Ct SL6 193 C3
Frogmill Spinney
Hurley SL6 193 C4
Hurley SL6 193 D4
Frogmoor HP13 173 A7
Frogmore Cl
Hughenden Valley HP14 162 A7
Slough SL1 205 A4
Frogmore Cotts SL4 210 E5
Frogmore Ct 4 SL6 202 F7
Frogmore Dr SL4 210 F5
Frogmore Flats SL4 210 F5
Frogmore Ho SL4 210 F5
Frogmore La HP18 125 C5
Frogmore Pl 9 MK4 45 E2
Frogmore St HP23 119 A3
Frome Cl HP21 115 C5
Fromer Rd HP10 185 D4
Frost Ho 4 HP4 135 C3
Frost Rd HP9 176 B1
Froxfield Ct MK4 46 C1
Froxfield Wy HP11 173 E5
Fryday St MK6 46 E7
Fryer Cl HP5 154 D6
Fryers Ct 3 HP12 172 D8
Fryers Farm La HP14 171 E5
Fryers La HP12 172 D8
Frymley View SL4 209 D6
Fuggle Dr HP21 115 E5
Fulbrook Mid Sch MK17 49 B5
Fullbrook Cl SL6 203 A8
Fuller's Cl HP5 154 B6
Fullers Ground MK17 37 B1
Fuller's Hill HP5, HP6 154 A6
FULLERS SLADE 33 A4
Fullers Yd SL6 196 B2
Fulmar Pl 1 HP19 101 F3
FULMER 199 C8
Fulmer Chase SL3 199 C8
Fulmer Common Rd SL3, SL0 199 E6
Fulmer Dr SL9 188 D2
Fulmer Inf Sch SL3 199 E8
Fulmer La SL9 189 A2
Fulmer Rd SL3 188 F2
Fulmer St
Milton Keynes, Emerson Valley MK4 46 C3
Milton Keynes, Medbourne MK8, MK5 45 E6
Fulmer Way SL9 188 E5
Fulton Cl
High Wycombe HP13 161 F1
High Wycombe HP13 173 A8
FULWELL 39 A2
Fulwell Ct MK14 34 E8
Fulwell Rd
Finmere MK18 50 C7
Westbury NN13 39 A4
Westbury NN13 39 B3
Fulwood Ct TW19 213 F1
Fulwoods Dr
Milton Keynes MK6 46 F8
Milton Keynes MK6 47 A8
Furlong Cl SL8 185 B3
Furlong Cres HP17 115 A1
Furlong La LU6 93 C7
Furlong Rd SL8 185 B3
Furlong The 12 HP23 119 A3
Furness SL4 209 C5
Furness Cres
8 Bletchley MK3 46 F1
Bletchley MK3 47 A1
Furness Pl 8 SL4 209 C5
Furness Row 9 SL4 209 C5
Furness Sq 6 SL4 209 C5
Furness Way SL4 209 C5
Furness Wlk 7 SL4 209 C5
Furnival Ave SL2 205 B8
Furrow Cl HP21 115 D4
Furrow Dr HP27 138 D6
Furrows The UB9 190 C6
Furrow Way SL6 202 A4
FURTHO 19 A3
Furtho Ct MK19 32 B7
Furtho La NN12 18 E3
Fury Ct MK8 45 F7
Furze Down Sch MK18 65 E4
Furze Field La HP16 142 B8

Furzefield Rd HP9.. **175** C2
Furzeham Rd UB7.. **208** E4
Furze La MK18.... **65** E5
Furzen Cl SL2.... **198** A2
FURZE PLATT.... **195** C2
Furze Platt Bsns Ctr
  SL6.... **195** D2
Furze Platt Inf Sch
  SL6.... **195** C1
Furze Platt Jun Sch
  SL6.... **195** C1
Furze Platt Rd
  Maidenhead SL6.... **194** F2
  Maidenhead SL6.... **195** B1
Furze Platt Senior Sch
  SL6.... **195** C2
Furze Platt Sta SL6. **195** E1
Furze Rd SL6.... **195** D1
Furze View WD3.... **167** C4
Furze Way MK12.... **33** C6
Furzey Way MK3.... **58** C4
FURZTON.... **46** C4
Furzton Rdbt MK4.... **46** C4
Fuzzens Wlk SL3.... **199** C2
Fyfield Barrow MK7. **48** C6
Fyne Dr LU7.... **80** C8

G

Gables Cl
  Chalfont St Peter
  SL9.... **177** E6
  Datchet SL3.... **211** A8
  Maidenhead SL6.... **203** B8
  Wendover HP22.... **131** A4
Gables Dr HP14.... **149** C1
Gables Mdw HP15. **163** C6
Gables The
  Datchet SL3.... **211** A8
  Haddenham HP17.... **127** A5
  Leighton Buzzard LU7. **80** E6
Gable Thorne MK7 .. **48** D8
Gabriel Cl MK7.... **48** C5
Gaddesden Cres
  MK7.... **48** C6
Gadge Cl OX9.... **125** E1
Gadmore La HP23.. **132** F7
Gadsden Cl MK43.... **25** D3
Gadsden Ct MK17.... **69** E8
Gage Cl SL6.... **202** E4
Gaia Dr MK11.... **32** F4
Gainsborough SL6. **195** F5
Gainsborough Cl
  MK8.... **45** D6
Gainsborough Dr
  SL6.... **202** D3
Gainsborough Hill
  RG9.... **191** D1
Gainsborough Pl
  HP19.... **100** F3
Gainsborough Rd
  Aylesbury HP21.... **115** E4
  Henley-on-Thames
  RG9.... **191** D1
Gairloch Ave MK2.. **58** D5
Gaius Cft MK11....**32** F2
Galahad Cl SL1.... **205** A4
Galapagos Gr MK3.. **58** B4
Gala Rd HP18.... **100** E5
Gallagher Cl MK8 .. **45** E8
Gallant Way MK16.... **36** D4
Galleons La SL3.... **199** C2
Galleries The
  4 High Wycombe
  HP13.... **173** A7
  13 Olney MK46.... **6** F3
Galley Hill MK11....**32** F5
Galley La
  Fenny Stratford
  MK17.... **59** A7
  Great Brickhill MK17.. **59** A4
  Great Brickhill MK17.. **59** A6
Galleymead Rd SL3. **212** F6
Galloway HP19.... **101** A3
Galloway Chase
  SL2.... **206** A6
Galloway Cl MK3.... **46** E2
Gallows La HP12.... **172** C8
Gallys Rd SL4.... **209** D6
Galsworthy HP19 **100** F2
Galvin Rd SL1.... **205** D6
Galway Gr **4** MK19.. **33** D1
Gambit Ave **6**
  MK10.... **35** E2
Gamnel HP23.... **119** A6
Gamnel Mews HP23 **119** B7
Gamnel Terr HP23.. **119** A6
Gandon Vale HP13. **173** A8
Ganton Cl MK3.... **46** D1
Garamonde Dr MK8 **33** F2
Garbo Cl MK8.... **45** D7
Garden Cl
  Halton HP22.... **131** C8
  Maidenhead SL6.... **202** A5
Garden Cotts SL3.. **212** D7
Garden Ct HP11.... **174** B3
Garden End HP4.... **140** F1
Gardener Wlk HP15 **163** C6
Garden Field La
  HP4.... **135** F2
Garden Mews SL1.. **205** F5
Garden Mews The
  SL6.... **202** B7
Garden Reach HP8 **166** D6
Gardens Cl HP14.... **158** F4
Gardens The MK18..**53** F1
Gardiner Ct MK13... **33** E6

Gardner Cl
  Aylesbury HP19.... **101** A3
  Great Kingshill HP15 **151** D1
Gardner Ho SL6.... **195** C1
Gardner Rd SL6.... **195** D2
Gardner's Cl LU6.... **93** E7
Garfield Pl **1** SL4. **210** C5
Garforth Pl MK5.... **46** D6
Garland Ct MK8.... **45** E8
Garland Way HP22. **117** E5
Garner Ct **13** TW19 **213** E1
Garner La MK7.... **48** D7
Garners Cl SL9.... **177** E4
Garners End SL9.... **177** E4
Garners Rd SL9.... **177** E4
Garnet Cl SL1.... **205** A4
Garnet Ct SL1.... **183** C1
Garnet Pl UB7.... **208** D5
Garnett Wy MK14.... **21** C1
Garrard Rd SL2.... **197** F1
Garratt Cl MK19....**10** F1
Garratt Dr MK9.... **34** A2
Garraways MK6.... **47** A6
Garrett Cl HP5.... **154** D6
Garretts La SL6.... **195** F2
Garrick Wlk MK9 .... **34** F3
Garron Cl HP21.... **115** D3
Garrowmore Gr MK2 **58** D5
Garry Cl MK2.... **58** E5
Garside Way HP20.. **102** A1
Garson Gr HP5.... **144** A2
Garston MK8....**33** F1
Garthlands SL6.... **195** D2
Garthwaite Cres
  MK5.... **46** A4
Garvin Ave HP9.... **175** E2
Garvin Mews HP9.. **175** E2
Garwood Cres MK8.. **45** C6
Gascon's Gr SL2.... **198** A1
Gaskin Ct MK14.... **35** A5
Gas La SL6.... **203** A3
Gatcombe MK8....**33** F1
Gatehouse Cl
  Aylesbury HP19.... **115** C8
  Windsor SL4.... **210** B4
Gatehouse Way
  HP19.... **101** B1
Gatemoor La HP10. **174** E3
Gatensbury Pl HP27 **139** B3
Gatesdene Cl HP4.. **121** E8
Gates Orch HP22.... **117** D5
Gateway Ctr The
  HP12.... **172** D4
Gateway Sch The
  HP16.... **152** A8
Gatewick Cl SL1.... **205** E5
Gatewick La MK7.... **48** A3
Gatting Way UB8.... **201** E6
Gatward Ave SL6.... **202** A3
Gaveston Dr HP4.... **135** B6
Gaveston Rd SL2.... **197** F2
Gaviots Cl SL9.... **188** F3
Gaviots Gn SL9.... **188** F3
Gaviots Way SL9 .... **188** E4
GAWCOTT....**51** F4
Gawcott Fields
  MK18.... **52** B7
Gawcott Rd
  Buckingham MK18 .... **52** B6
  Steeple Claydon MK18 **73** A8
  Tingewick MK18 .... **51** D6
  Twyford MK18....**62** F1
Gawcott Road Ind Pk
  MK18.... **52** B7
Gawdrey Cl HP5.... **154** D6
Gayal Croft MK5.... **46** B4
Gayhurst Ho MK16 .. **12** D1
Gayhurst Rd HP13.. **173** B8
Gayhurst Sch SL9 .. **188** C7
Gayton Cl HP6.... **154** E4
Gdn La MK16....**12** F3
Geary Mews MK17... **58** B2
Gees Farm Cl NN7....**1** A5
Gell Cl UB10.... **190** F1
Genesis Gn **4** MK6.. **47** C4
Genoa Wy HP11.... **173** F4
Geoffrey Keen Rd
  HP5.... **144** A3
George Ave MK17....**36** F1
George Cl
  Marlow SL7.... **183** F4
  Wavendon MK10.... **36** E1
George Ct HP18.... **83** B5
George Farm Cl
  MK17.... **59** D5
George Gn Dr SL3.. **207** A1
GEORGE GREEN **206** E8
George Green Dr
  Iver Heath SL0.... **200** A1
  Slough SL3.... **206** F7
George Green Rd
  SL3.... **206** E7
George Grenville Acad
  MK18.... **52** D7
George Hammond Cl
  HP18.... **100** D4
George Inn Pl MK16 .. **12** B6
George Lee Ct
  HP14.... **160** C1
George Pass Ave
  MK18.... **65** F5
George Rd HP14.... **158** E5
Georges Dr HP10.. **185** C7
George's Hill HP15. **162** F6

George St
  18 Aylesbury HP20.... **115** D8
  Berkhamsted HP4.... **135** B7
  5 Chesham HP5.... **144** C1
  High Wycombe HP11. **172** F7
  Milton Keynes MK2.... **47** E1
  Uxbridge UB8.... **201** D5
  Wing LU7....**79** E2
  Woburn MK17....**60** F7
George V Pl SL4.... **210** D7
George Yd MK11.... **32** D5
Georgian Cl UB10.. **201** E8
Georgian Hts SL8 .. **185** B5
Geralds Ct HP13.... **162** D1
Geralds Rd HP13.... **162** D1
Gerard Cl MK13.... **34** A7
Germains Cl HP5.... **154** B7
Germain St HP5.... **154** B7
Germander Park First
  Sch MK14.... **34** D4
Germander Pl MK14. **34** D4
GERRARDS CROSS. **188** E5
Gerrards Cross CE Sch
  The SL9.... **188** F4
Gerrards Cross Rd
  SL2.... **199** A6
Gerrards Cross Sta
  SL9.... **188** E6
Gershwin Ct MK7.... **48** C4
Gershwin Rd HP21.. **115** F3
Gervaise Cl SL1.... **204** F5
Ghyll Gdns HP4.... **134** D7
Gibbings Cl MK18.... **76** A3
Gibbs Cl
  High Wycombe
  HP13.... **172** F8
  Winslow MK18....**65** F4
Gibbs Ho HP11.... **173** F4
Gibbwin MK14.... **34** E8
Gib La HP22.... **102** D4
Gibraltar HP17.... **113** D2
Gibraltar La SL6.... **184** C1
Gibson Ct **9** SL3.. **206** F1
Gibson La HP17.... **127** A5
Gibson Pl TW19.... **213** C1
Gibson Rd
  High Wycombe
  HP12.... **172** B3
  Ickenham UB10.... **201** F8
Gibsons Gn MK13 .... **34** C4
Gibsons Green MK13 **34** C4
GIFFARD PARK....**22** A2
Giffard Park Prim Sch
  MK14.... **22** A2
Giffard Park Rdbt
  MK14.... **21** F3
Giffard Way MK2.... **58** C6
Gifford Gate MK14 .. **34** E7
Gifford Pl MK18.... **41** E1
Gilbert Cl MK3.... **58** B7
Gilbert Ho **4** HP11. **172** E1
Gilbert Scott Ct **9**
  HP7.... **165** B7
Gilbert Scott Gdns
  MK18.... **52** A4
Gilbert Scott Rd
  MK18.... **41** D2
Gilbert's Hill HP23. **132** E3
Gilbert Way
  Berkhamsted HP4.... **135** A4
  Slough SL3.... **206** F1
Gilbey Wlk HP10.. **185** D4
Gilders Mews MK14. **34** F6
Giles Brook Prim Sch
  MK4.... **57** A7
Giles Gate HP16.... **151** B6
Giles Gr MK17.... **37** A1
Gillamoor Cl **2**
  MK4.... **46** B3
Gillcroft Rd SL3.... **212** F6
Gilletts La HP12.... **161** C1
Gillfield Cl HP11.... **172** E2
Gilliat Rd SL1.... **205** E6
Gilliatt Cl SL1.... **205** A4
Gilliflower St HP18. **100** E5
Gillions Pl HP21.... **116** B7
Gillott Cl SL6.... **202** F8
Gilman Cres SL4 .... **209** F4
Gilmore Cl SL3.... **206** C4
Gilmore Rd HP20.... **101** E3
Gilpin's Ride HP4.. **135** E5
Gilpin Way MK46.... **7** A4
Ginger Row **6** MK17 **58** B7
Gingers Cl HP22.... **117** E5
Ginsberg Cres MK10. **35** E2
Gipsy La
  Prestwood HP16.... **151** F4
  Slapton LU7....**91** D8
Girton Way MK3.... **58** B8
Gisburn Cl MK13 .... **34** B5
Glade Ho **5** SL7.. **183** E2
Glade Rd
  Hampden Bottom
  HP16.... **141** A1
  Little Hampden HP16 **141** F1
  Marlow SL7.... **183** E2
Glade The
  Gerrards Cross SL9.. **188** D2
  Tylers Green HP10 .. **163** A1
Glade View HP12.... **172** A3
Gladius Gr MK11.... **32** F5
Gladstone Ind Est **1**
  SL6.... **202** E8
Gladstone Pl HP5.. **144** C1

Gladstone Rise
  HP13.... **173** F6
Gladstone Way SL1. **205** A5
Glaisyer Way SL0.. **200** D3
Glamis Ct HP13.... **173** B8
Glamis Ho MK3.... **57** E7
Glamorgan Cl MK3.. **46** F1
Glanmor Rd SL2.... **206** B6
Glassmill Ho **4**
  HP4.... **135** D4
Glastonbury Cl MK3 **47** A2
Glastonbury Thorn Fst
  Sch MK5.... **46** B6
Glaven Rd HP21.... **115** C4
Glazier Dr MK14....**34** F6
Glebe Cl
  Chalfont St Peter
  SL9.... **177** D3
  Dorney SL6.... **203** F4
  Holmer Green HP15 . **163** B7
  Maids Moreton MK18 .**41** F3
  Pitstone LU7.... **105** D5
Glebe Cotts HP14 .. **169** C7
Glebe Dr NN13.... **38** A7
Glebe Ho **5** SL9.. **177** D3
Glebe House Dr
  MK18.... **39** E6
Glebe La MK19.... **10** E5
Glebelands HP10.. **174** C8
Glebelands Cl HP16 **151** E4
Glebe Rd
  Chalfont St Peter
  SL9.... **177** C2
  Deanshanger MK19 .. **31** E5
  Maidenhead SL6.... **203** B5
  Old Windsor SL4.... **211** B2
  Uxbridge UB8.... **201** C3
Glebe Rdbt MK9.... **35** B4
Glebe Terr
  Buckingham MK18 ....**41** F3
  Maids Moreton MK18. **41** E3
Glebe The
  Lavendon MK46....**7** F8
  Lewknor OX49.... **157** B8
  Prestwood HP16.... **151** C7
  Stone HP17.... **114** D5
  Walter's Ash HP14 .. **161** D6
  West Drayton UB7.... **208** F2
  Weston Turville HP22 **116** F2
Glebe Way HP6.... **154** D3
Gledfield Pl MK12.... **33** D4
Gleeman Cl MK12.... **33** A5
Glenavon Gdns SL3. **206** C4
Glenduragan Ct **9**
  MK4.... **45** F1
Gleneagles Cl
  Milton Keynes MK3.. **57** D7
  Stanwell TW19 .... **213** D1
Glenfield Cl MK22.. **22** D1
Glenfield Cl
  Aylesbury HP21.... **116** A5
  Stoke Poges SL2.... **198** F4
Glenham Rd OX9.... **126** B1
Glenhaven Dr TW19 **213** A2
Glen Island
  Taplow SL6.... **196** C1
  Taplow SL6.... **203** C8
Glenister Rd
  Chesham HP5.... **144** C3
  High Wycombe HP12. **172** B4
Glenisters Rd HP13. **173** A8
Glenmore Cl HP10.. **174** A2
Glenmore Ho HP11. **174** A3
Glenore SL6.... **196** A8
Glenrose Cl SL2.... **206** C7
Glenstal Pl MK9.... **35** A3
Glen The SL3.... **206** C2
Glenton Gn HP19.... **100** D5
Glentworth Pl SL1.. **205** C5
Glenwater Ho HP15 **163** A5
Glenwoods MK16.... **22** C3
Glimbers Gr OX39.. **147** C5
Globe Ho UB7.... **208** D5
Globe La LU7....**70** E1
Globe Pk (Bsns Ctr)
  SL7.... **183** F2
Globeside Bsns Pk
  SL7.... **183** F2
Glory Cl HP10.... **185** F7
Glory Hill La HP9 .. **185** F8
Glory Mill La HP10. **185** E7
Glory Pk HP10.... **185** E8
Glory Pk Ave HP10. **185** E8
Gloucester Ave SL1 **205** C5
Gloucester Cl SL9 .. **188** A4
Gloucester Gate **9**
  MK10.... **36** C3
Gloucester Pl SL4.. **210** D5
Gloucester Rd
  Maidenhead SL6.... **195** E2
  Milton Keynes MK12. **33** D5
Glovers Cl **2** HP20. **101** E1
Glovers La
  Milton Keynes MK13 .. **34** B4
  2 Tring HP23.... **119** A3
Glyncroft **5** SL1.. **204** F4
Glyn Mews HP22.... **102** C2
Glyn Sq MK12.... **33** D7
Glyn St MK13.... **34** A7
Glynswood
  Chalfont St Peter
  SL9.... **177** F3
  Chinnor OX39.... **147** C6
  High Wycombe HP13. **162** B1
Glynswood Ho
  OX39.... **147** C6
Glynswood Rd MK18. **41** C1

Glyn Valley Pl **4**
  MK10.... **36** C3
Glynwood Ho SL6 .. **203** A7
Gn St **19** HP15.... **163** A4
Goathland Croft **2**
  MK4.... **46** B2
Goddards Croft
  MK12.... **33** C5
Goddington Rd SL8. **185** A5
Godfreys Cl HP18 .... **96** E1
GODLINGTON.... **61** E3
Godolphin Inf & Jun
  Schs SL1.... **205** D7
Godolphin Inf Sch
  SL1.... **205** C7
Godolphin Rd
  Seer Green HP9.... **176** C4
  Slough SL1.... **205** D6
Godrevy Gr MK4.... **57** B8
Godstowe Sch
  HP13.... **173** B8
Godwin Cl MK7.... **48** C7
Gogh Rd HP19.... **100** F2
Gog La MK16.... **15** A1
Gold Crest HP19.... **101** F4
Golden Ball La
  Maidenhead SL6.... **194** F3
  Maidenhead SL6.... **195** A3
Golden Dr MK6.... **47** B8
Golden Hills OX39 . **147** D6
Golden Hinde Gdns
  MK16.... **36** D4
Golden Mede HP18. **99** B6
Golden Miller Ct LU7 **79** E2
Golden Oak Cl SL2 . **198** C6
Golden Riddy LU7... **80** E8
Golder's Cl HP18.. **123** F3
Goldfield Inf Sch
  HP23.... **118** F3
Goldfield Rd HP23.. **118** F3
Goldhawk Rd MK10.. **47** E8
Gold Hill E SL9.... **177** D1
Gold Hill N SL9.... **177** C2
Gold Hill W SL9.... **177** C1
Goldilocks MK7.... **48** B6
Goldmark Cl MK7.... **48** D5
Goldney Ct **8** MK4.. **45** E2
Gold Oak Wlk MK9 .. **34** F3
Goldsmith Cl **3**
  HP21.... **115** E5
Goldsmith Dr MK16.. **21** F4
Gold St MK19.... **11** A2
Goldsworth Rd
  HP23.... **119** B7
Goldsworthy Way
  SL1.... **204** C7
Golf Club La HP27.. **139** E5
Golf Club Rd HP4.. **121** A8
Golspie Croft MK12.. **33** C4
Gomez Cl MK4.... **45** D3
Gomm Pl MK13.... **174** A4
Gomm Rd HP13.... **174** A3
Gomms Wood Cl
  HP9.... **175** B4
Gomms Wood Ho
  HP9.... **175** B4
Gomm Valley Nature
  Reserve HP13.... **174** B5
Goodacres La HP27 **149** E6
Goodall Cl RG9.... **191** E1
Goodearl Pl HP27 .. **139** A1
Goodlake Ct MK18.. **52** B3
Goodman Gdns MK6. **47** D8
Goodman Pk SL2.... **206** C5
Goodrich Gn **5** MK4. **56** E8
Goodrington Pl **2**
  MK10.... **36** A4
Goodwick Gr MK4.. **57** B8
Goodwin Mdws
  HP10.... **185** E6
Goodwin Rd
  Aylesbury HP19.... **115** C8
  Slough SL2.... **197** F2
Goodwins Mead
  LU7.... **105** A7
Goodwin Villas SL1. **204** F5
Goodwood MK8....**45** F8
Goodwood Rise
  SL7.... **183** C7
Goose Acre
  Botley HP5.... **145** A1
  Cheddington LU7.... **105** A7
Goose Gn SL2.... **198** B3
Goosemere MK19.... **31** E4
Goosen Gn HP21.... **116** C6
Goran Ave MK11.... **32** E4
Gordale MK13.... **34** C5
Gordon Rd
  Chesham HP5.... **154** C7
  High Wycombe HP13 **173** B8
  Maidenhead SL6.... **202** D7
  West Drayton UB7... **208** E6
  Windsor SL4.... **209** F5
Gordon Smith Cl
  HP22.... **117** E5
Gordon Way HP8.... **177** B7
Gore Cl UB9.... **190** C7
Gore Hill
  Amersham HP7.... **165** B5
  Amersham HP7.... **165** C5
Gorelands La HP8 .. **177** F8
Gorell Rd HP9.... **176** B1
Gore Rd SL1.... **197** B2
Gore Rd SL1.... **197** A2
Goring MK14.... **34** C7
Gorman Pl MK2.... **58** E4
Gorregan Ave MK3.. **58** B4

Fur–Gra **229**

Gorrella La MK18.... **40** C8
Gorrell Cl MK18.... **51** B6
Gorrell La
  Dadford MK18.... **28** C1
  Tingewick MK18.... **51** B6
  Tingewick MK18.... **51** B6
Gorricks MK18.... **32** D4
Gorse Croft MK18....**65** F4
Gorse Meade SL1 .. **205** B5
Gorse Rd SL6.... **195** E6
Gorse Wlk
  Hazelmere HP15.... **163** A3
  West Drayton UB7... **208** E7
Gosforth Cl SL1.... **204** F6
Goslar Way SL4.... **210** B5
Gosling Gn SL3.... **206** E3
Gosling Gr HP13.... **161** D2
Gosling Rd SL3.... **206** E3
Gossage Rd UB10 .. **201** F5
GOSSARD'S GREEN. **25** C4
Goss Ave HP10....**99** B6
Gossmore Cl SL7... **183** F1
Gossmore La
  Marlow SL7.... **183** F1
  Marlow SL7.... **184** A1
Gossmore Wlk SL7. **183** F1
Gossoms Ryde HP4. **135** A5
Goswell Hill SL4.... **210** D6
Goswell Rd SL4.... **210** D6
Gotland Ave **6** MK8. **45** D8
Goudhurst Ct MK7.. **48** B7
Governors Cl HP6 .. **154** F1
Gower Ho HP6.... **154** E3
Gowers Field HP19,
  HP20.... **101** D3
Gowers The HP6.... **154** E4
Gowers Yard LU7 .. **118** F3
Gowings Gn SL1.... **204** E4
Goya Pl HP19.... **100** F2
Grable Ave MK4.... **45** E3
Grace Ave MK6.... **46** E8
Grace Cl SL1.... **205** C5
Grace Gdns MK17... **59** A7
Grace Reading
  HP13.... **173** E6
Grace Reading Cl
  HP13.... **173** E6
Graces Cl MK43.... **25** C3
Graces Maltings **4**
  HP23.... **119** A3
Graeme Ave HP16 . **151** C6
Grafham Cl MK14 .... **35** A8
Grafton Cl
  Maidenhead SL6.... **195** E2
  Potterspury NN12.... **18** E3
  Slough SL3.... **206** E7
Grafton Ct NN7....**4** A8
Grafton Gate MK9.. **34** C1
Grafton Ho OX39.. **147** C2
Grafton Orch OX39 **147** D7
Grafton Park MK3.. **34** D1
Grafton Rd
  Alderton NN12....**9** B3
  Aylesbury HP19.... **101** A2
  Yardley Gobion NN12 ..**18** F6
GRAFTON REGIS....**9** D2
Grafton St
  High Wycombe
  HP12.... **172** D8
  Milton Keynes, Bradwell
  MK13.... **34** B4
  Milton Keynes, Granby
  MK1.... **47** B3
  Milton Keynes, New
  Bradwell MK12, MK13,
  MK19.... **33** E8
  Milton Keynes, Winterhill
  MK6.... **46** E7
Graham Cl SL6.... **202** C5
Graham Dr HP12.... **172** B5
Graham Ho SL9 .... **177** C1
Graham Rd SL6.... **195** E6
Grainge Chase MK17 **55** A3
Grainge Cl NN13.... **39** A5
Grainges Yard UB8. **201** C5
Grain Mws HP22.... **102** C1
Grampian Gate MK6. **46** E7
Grampian Way SL3. **207** A1
Gramwell MK5....**45** F7
Granary Cl
  Haversham MK19....**20** F3
  Haversham MK19....**21** A3
GRANBOROUGH....**75** E7
Granborough Rd
  East Claydon MK18... **74** F5
  East Claydon MK18... **75** B5
  North Marston MK18.. **76** A2
  Winslow MK18.... **65** E2
GRANBY....**47** B3
Granby Cl MK1.... **47** A3
Granby Ind Est MK1. **47** B3
Granby Rdbt MK1.... **47** C3
Grandison Ho RG9 . **191** E3
Grand Junction
  HP22.... **102** D2
Grand Junction Pl
  SL0.... **201** A3
Grand Union Office Pk
  The UB8.... **208** C2
Granes End MK14.... **34** E8
Grange Chase MK17. **55** A3
Grange Cl
  Chalfont St Peter
  SL9.... **177** E2
  Leighton Buzzard LU7 . **80** D6

Grange Cl continued
Maids Moreton MK18 . **41** E3
Newton Longville
MK17 . . . . **57** D3
Twyford MK18 . . . . . . **62** D2
Wraysbury TW19 . . . **211** E1
Grange Cotts HP16 . **152** A3
Grange Dr
Terriers HP13 . . . . . . **162** D3
Wooburn HP10 . . **185** D3
Grange Farm Rd
HP14 . . . . **159** B7
Grange Farm Rdbt
MK8 . . . . **45** D7
Grange Fields SL9 . . **177** E2
Grange Gdn HP18 . . . **83** A6
Grange Gdns
Farnham Common
SL2 . . . . **198** D7
Wendover HP22 . . . . **131** B5
Grange La SL6 . . . . . **195** F8
**Grangelands & Pulpit
Hill Reserve**★ **139** F6
Grange Rd
Chalfont St Peter
SL9 . . . . **177** D2
Chalfont St Peter SL9 **177** D2
Cookham Rise SL6. . **195** F7
Hazlemere HP15 . . . **162** F4
Hazlemere, Widmer End
HP15 . . . . **162** E5
Henley-on-Thames
RG9 . . . . **191** E1
Milton Keynes MK3 . . **57** F7
Pitstone LU7 . . . . . . **105** D5
Terriers HP13 . . . . . . **162** D3
Tring HP23 . . . . **119** C4
Wilstone HP23 . . . . . **104** D1
Grangers Croft MK12 **33** C4
Grange Sch The
HP21 . . . . **115** F6
Grange Sch The
HP21 . . . . **116** A6
Grange The
Burnham SL1 . . . . . **197** C2
Gerrards Cross SL9 . **188** E6
Old Windsor SL4 . . . . **211** B2
Wraysbury TW19 . . . **211** E1
Grange View
Askett HP27 . . . . . . **139** E7
Hazlemere HP15 . . . **163** A4
Grange Way SL0 . . . . **207** F7
Grangewood SL3. . **206** C8
Grant Ave SL1. . . . . **205** E7
Grant Gdns MK4 . . . . **45** D3
Grantham Ct MK5 . . . **46** C5
Grantham Mews
HP4 . . . . **135** D4
Grant Ho 6 SL6 . . . **185** A4
Granville Ave SL2 . . **205** D8
Granville Dene HP3 **146** A4
Granville Pl 5
HP20 . . . . **115** D8
Granville Rd HP11 . **174** A4
Granville Sq MK15. . . **35** C7
Grapevine Cl
High Wycombe
HP11 . . . . **173** F4
High Wycombe HP11 . **174** A4
Grasholm Way SL3 . **207** C2
Grasmere
Aylesbury HP21 . . . . **116** B5
Windsor SL4 . . . . . . **209** E7
Grasmere Ave SL2 . **206** A6
Grasmere Par SL2. . **206** B6
Grasmere Way
Leighton Buzzard
LU7 . . . . **80** D7
Milton Keynes MK2 . . **58** D6
Grasscroft MK4 . . . . **46** C4
Grass Hays HP21 . . . **116** C7
Grassingham End
SL9 . . . . **177** E3
Grassingham Rd
SL9 . . . . **177** E3
Grassington MK13. . . **34** A5
Grasslands HP20 . . . **102** A1
Grassy La SL6. . . . . **202** E7
Grattan Ct SL7 . . . . **184** A3
Gratton Ct MK4 . . . . **46** C3
Gratton Dr SL4. . . . **209** E3
Gravel Dr HP23 . . . . **118** B3
GRAVEL HILL **177** F4
Gravel Hill
Chalfont St Peter
SL9 . . . . **177** E3
Henley-on-Thames
RG9 . . . . **191** D2
Uxbridge UB8 . . . . . **201** D7
Gravel Path
Berkhamsted HP4. . . **135** E5
Berkhamsted HP4. . . **135** E6
Gravel Wlk MK46 . . . . **13** F7
Graveney Pl MK6. . . . **35** B2
Gravett MK46 . . . . **6** E6
Grayburn Cl HP8 . . **177** A8
Graylands Cl SL1. . **204** F5
Grayling Cl SL7 . . **194** C8
Grayling Ct HP4. . . **134** F6
Grays Cl NN12 . . . . . **17** D8
Grays La
Ibstone HP14 . . . . . **169** C7
Paulerspury NN12. . . **17** D8
Yardley Gobion NN12 . **18** E6

Gray's La HP13 . . . . **161** D2
Gray's Mon★ SL2 . . **198** F2
Grays Park Rd SL2. . **199** A3
Grays Pk Rd SL2. . . **199** A3
Gray's Pl SL2 . . . . . **205** F5
Gray's Rd
Slough SL1 . . . . . . **205** F5
Uxbridge UB10 . . . . **201** E5
Grays Wlk HP5 . . . . **144** B2
Gr Corner MK14. . . . . **21** F3
Greamesdyke Rd
HP4. . . . . **135** C4
Greatacre 7 HP5 . . **144** C1
Great Benty UB7 . . **208** E2
Great Bois Wood
HP6 . . . . **154** B3
GREAT BRICKHILL . . **59** D2
Great Brickhill La
MK17 . . . . **59** D5
Great Brickhill Rd
Soulbury LU7. . . . . . **69** F4
Soulbury MK17 . . . . . **70** A5
Greatchesters MK13. . **33** F5
Great Denson
Milton Keynes MK6 . . **47** A8
Milton Keynes MK6 . . **47** A8
GREATGAP **105** D6
Great Ground
Berryfields HP18. . . **100** D4
Milton Keynes MK14 . **34** E7
GREAT HAMPDEN . . **150** D7
Greatheed Dell MK7. **48** D4
Great Hill Cres SL6 **202** C6
GREAT HIVINGS . . . **144** A3
Great Hivings HP5. . **144** A4
GREAT HOLM **45** E8
GREAT HORWOOD . . . **55** A1
**Great Horwood CE
Comb Sch**
Great Horwood
MK17 . . . . **54** F3
Great Horwood MK17. . **55** A3
Great Horwood Rd
Great Horwood
MK18. . . . . **65** F7
Little Horwood MK17. . **55** D3
GREAT KIMBLE. . . . **139** E8
Great Kimble CE Sch
HP17. . . . . **129** E1
GREAT KINGSHILL . . **162** E8
**Great Kingshill CE Comb
Sch** HP15. . . . . . **162** C6
Great La
Bierton HP22 . . . . . **102** A4
Wendover HP22 . . . . **131** B4
Great Linch MK10 . . . **36** A2
GREAT LINFORD **34** E8
Great Linford Comb Sch
MK14 . . . . **34** E8
Great Linford Lakes★
MK14 . . . . **21** D3
Great Marlow Sch
SL7 . . . . **183** F4
Great Meadow Way
HP19 . . . . **114** F8
**GREAT
MISSENDEN** **152** A6
**Great Missenden CE
Comb Sch** HP16. . **152** B7
Great Missenden Sta
HP16. . . . . **152** A7
Great Monks St
Milton Keynes, Wolverton
MK12 . . . . **33** C5
Milton Keynes, Wymbush
MK8 . . . . **33** E2
Wolverton MK12 . . . . **33** A6
Greatmoor Rd
Grendon Underwood
HP18. . . . . **73** E1
Grendon Underwood
HP18. . . . . **83** F8
Kingswood HP18. . . . **83** B2
Quainton MK18. . . . . **84** A6
Great Ormes MK4 . . . **56** F8
Great Pasture MK10. . **35** F3
Great Slade MK16 . . . **52** D6
Great Stone HP18 . . **112** F3
Great Western St 22
HP20. . . . . **115** D8
Greaves Rd HP13 . . **173** D6
Grebe Cl
Aylesbury HP19 . . . . **101** F3
Calvert MK18 . . . . . . **73** B5
Grebe Wy SL6. . . . . **203** A8
Grecian St HP20 . . . **116** A8
Greenacre SL4. . . . **209** E5
Green Acre HP21. . . **116** A7
Greenacres
Aylesbury HP22 . . . . . **89** B2
Holmer Green HP15 . **163** D5
Northall LU6 . . . . . . **92** A6
Pitstone LU7 . . . . . **105** C4
Slapton LU7. . . . . . . **91** D8
Greenacres Ave
UB10. . . . . **190** F1
Green Acres Cl HP22 **86** E7
Greenacres La
HP10. . . . . **163** A1
Greenacres The
HP13. . . . . **162** C1
Greenbury Cl WD3 . **167** C5
Green Cl
Burnham SL6. . . . . . **204** A7
High Wycombe HP13. . **173** F4
Maidenhead SL6. . . . **195** F1
Green Common La HP10,
HP9, SL1. . . . . **186** C4

Green Cres HP10 . . . **185** C7
Greendale Mews
SL2. . . . . **206** A6
Green Dragon La
HP10. . . . . **185** B7
Green East Rd HP9 . **176** E3
Greene Field Rd
HP4. . . . . **135** C4
Greenell Cl MK19. . . . **31** F4
GREEN END
Granborough **76** A7
High Wycombe **160** A4
Green End
Aylesbury HP20 . . . **115** D8
Granborough MK18. . . **76** A7
Great Brickhill MK17. . **59** D2
Green End La MK16 . . **22** C4
Green End Rd HP14. **159** E5
Green End St HP22 . . **117** E5
Greenes Ct HP4 . . . **135** C5
Greene Wlk HP4 . . . **135** D3
Green Farm Rd
MK16 . . . . **22** C4
Greenfern Ave SL1 . **204** D7
GREENFIELD **168** A4
Greenfield OX49 . . **168** A6
Greenfield End SL9. **177** E3
Greenfield Rd MK16 . **22** C4
Greenfields
Adstock MK18. . . . . . **53** F1
Maidenhead SL6. . . . **202** A6
Upper Arncott OX6 . . . **94** D7
Greenford Cres
MK10 . . . . **47** E8
Green Ground OX33 **123** A2
Green Hailey HP27 . **139** F3
Greenhalch Cl 6
HP22 . . . . **117** D5
Green Hill HP13 . . . **162** B1
Green Hill HP13 . . . **162** C1
Green Hill Gate
HP13. . . . . **162** B1
Greenings Mead
HP23 . . . . **125** D7
Green La
Amersham HP6. . . . . **154** E2
Aspley Guise MK17 . . **49** E4
Botley HP5 . . . . **155** B6
Bovingdon HP3 . . . . **146** A3
Burnham SL1. . . . . . **197** D4
Chesham Bois HP6 . . **154** D3
Datchet SL3. . . . . . . **211** B6
Eaton Bray LU6 . . . . . **92** D7
Farnham Common
SL2 . . . . **198** B6
Ivinghoe LU7. . . . . . **105** E5
Maidenhead SL6. . . . **203** A6
Milton Keynes MK12 . . **33** D6
Owlswick HP27 . . . . **128** B1
Prestwood HP16 . . . **151** E6
Radnage HP14 . . . . **159** D5
Stokenchurch HP14. . **158** C5
Upper Arncott OX6 . . . **94** E7
Windsor SL4 . . . . . . **210** B5
Greenlands
Flackwell Heath
HP10. . . . . **185** B8
Lacey Green HP27 . . **150** A4
Greenlands Cl MK16. . **22** A3
Greenlands Ct SL6 . **202** B8
Greenlands La
HP16. . . . . **151** B7
Green Lane Cl HP6 . **154** D3
Green Lane Cl SL1 . **197** C2
Green Lane Rdbt
MK9 . . . . **35** B5
Greenlaw HP5 . . . . . **144** B1
Greenleaf Ct SL3. . . **211** A8
Greenleas Lower Sch
LU7 . . . . **80** C7
GREENLEYS **33** B5
Green Leys
High Wycombe
HP13. . . . . **161** C2
Maidenhead SL6 . . . **195** F2
Greenleys Fst Sch
MK12 . . . . **33** C5
Greenleys Jun Sch
MK12 . . . . **33** C5
Greenleys La MK12. . **33** C4
Greenleys Rdbt
MK12 . . . . **33** B6
Green North Rd
HP9. . . . . **176** E4
Greenock Rd SL1. . . **205** A7
Green Park Dr MK16. **22** C3
Green Park Sch
MK16 . . . . **22** B3
Green Path HP22,
HP23. . . . . **118** D4
Green Pk
Amersham HP6. . . . . **153** F4
Prestwood HP16. . . . **151** E6
Green Pl HP10 . . . . **185** C8
Green Rd HP13. . . . **162** C2
Greenridge HP10. . . **174** B8
Green Ridge Prim Acad
HP19. . . . . **100** D6
Greensand View
MK17 . . . . **49** B5
Greenside
Bourne End SL8. . . . **185** A5
Prestwood HP16. . . . **151** C5
Slough SL2 . . . . . . **205** A8
Greenside Hill MK4. . **46** F2
Greens Keep HP17 . **126** F6
Greensleeves Dr 14
HP19. . . . . **100** E5

Green St
Chorleywood WD3. . . **167** C6
Hazlemere HP15 . . . **162** F4
High Wycombe HP11. . **172** F7
GREEN THE
Milton Keynes **47** D8
Newport Pagnell **22** C3
Whipsnade **107** F8
Green The
Aldbury HP23 . . . . . **120** D5
Amersham HP7. . . . . **154** C1
Aston Abbotts HP22 . . **88** F5
Belsize WD3 . . . . . . **156** F5
Brill HP18 . . . . **110** B8
Burnham SL1. . . . . . **197** B1
Chalfont St Giles HP8 **177** C8
Cheddington LU7. . . **105** A7
Chetwode MK18 . . . . **61** E8
Cosgrove MK19. . . . . **19** F2
Cranfield MK43. . . . . **24** E2
Cuddington HP18 . . . **112** F3
Deanshanger MK19 . . **31** E4
Dinton HP17 . . . . . . **113** E2
Edlesborough LU6. . . **92** F4
Great Horwood MK17. . **55** A3
Hanslope MK19. . . . . **11** A2
Hardwick HP22. . . . . **87** A3
Horton-cum-S OX33 . **108** A5
Hulcott HP22. . . . . . **102** E6
Hyde Heath HP6 . . . **153** C5
Ley Hill HP3. . . . . . . **145** B1
Little Horwood MK17. . **55** E2
Little Missenden HP7 **153** A2
Longwick HP27 . . . . **138** D6
Maidenhead SL6 . . . **195** C7
Marlow SL7. . . . . . . **194** A8
Mentmore LU7 . . . . . **90** D4
Milton Keynes, Loughton
MK5 . . . . **46** A8
Milton Keynes, The Green
MK6 . . . . **47** C8
Nash MK17 . . . . **55** C8
Newport Pagnell MK16 **22** C4
Paulerspury NN12. . . **17** B7
Pitstone LU7 . . . . . **105** D4
Quainton HP22 . . . . . **85** B5
Slough SL1 . . . . . . **205** D4
Soulbury LU7. . . . . . . **69** E3
Steeple Claydon MK18 **63** D3
Stoke Bruerne NN12 . . . **9** A8
Stoke Hammond MK17 **69** E2
Thornborough MK18. . **54** A8
Turvey MK43. . . . . **8** E5
Turweston NN13 . . . . **38** C8
West Drayton UB7. . . **208** D3
Whipsnade LU6. . . . . **93** D1
Whipsnade LU6. . . . **107** F8
Wingrave HP22. . . . . **89** B2
Wooburn Green
HP10. . . . . **185** E5
Wraysbury TW19 . . . **211** E1
Green Tiles UB9. . . **189** F4
Green Tiles La UB9 . **189** F5
Green Verges SL7. . **183** E3
Green View HP20 . . **102** A2
Green View HP3 . . . **146** A2
Greenwatt Wy SL1 . **205** D3
Greenway
Berkhamsted HP4. . . **135** A4
Burnham SL1. . . . . . **197** B3
Chesham HP5. . . . . **144** B3
Great Horwood MK17 . **55** A2
Haddenham HP17 . . **126** F5
Milton Keynes MK10 . . **36** C3
2 Thame OX9. . . . . **125** F1
Green Way MK17 . . . **57** D4
Greenway Bsns Pk
MK17 . . . . **55** A1
Greenway Ct 12
HP13 . . . . **173** B7
Greenway Par HP5 . **144** B3
Greenway Prim Sch
HP4. . . . . **134** F4
Greenway Prim Sch
HP4. . . . . **134** F4
Greenways
Bow Brickhill MK17. . . **48** C2
Eaton Bray LU6. . . . . **92** D7
Greenways Dr SL6. . **202** A8
Greenway The
Gerrards Cross SL9. . **188** D8
High Wycombe HP13. . **173** B7
Slough SL1 . . . . . . **204** D5
Stoke Bruerne NN12. . . **9** B8
Tring HP23 . . . . **118** F5
Tylers Green HP10 . . **163** B1
Uxbridge UB8 . . . . . **201** D3
Greenway Wlk MK18 . **41** C1
Green West Rd HP9 **176** E3
Greenwich Dr 4
HP11. . . . . **173** C5
Greenwich Gdns
MK16 . . . . **22** C2
Greenwood HP14 . . **150** A2
Greenwood Ave
OX39 . . . . **147** C5
Greenwood Cl
Amersham HP6. . . . . **154** E1
Seer Green HP9 . . . . **176** D4
Greenwood Mdw
OX39 . . . . **147** D6
Greenwood Pl MK18. **63** D3
Greenwood The
HP22 . . . . **117** D5
Greenyard The NN7 . . . **1** B7
Greer Garson Rd
UB9 . . . . **190** A6
Greetham Rd HP21. **116** C6

Gregories Ct HP9 . . **175** D3
Gregories Dr MK7. . . **48** D6
Gregories Farm La
HP9. . . . . **175** D2
Gregories Rd HP9 . . **175** C3
Gregory Ct 2 MK46 . . . **7** D3
Gregory Dr SL4 . . . **211** B1
Gregorys Field
HP23. . . . . **104** A3
Grenada Cres MK3 . . **58** B3
Grenadier Ct TW19 . **213** C1
Grenadine Way
HP23. . . . . **119** A5
Grendon Hill HP22 . **102** A5
Grendon Rd
Edgcott HP18 . . . . . . **72** C1
Edgcott HP18 . . . . . . **82** F8
Kingswood HP18. . . . **83** C3
Yardley Hastings NN7. . **1** B8
**GRENDON
UNDERWOOD** **83** A6
**Grendon Underwood
Comb Sch** HP18. . . **83** A6
Grendon Way HP22. **102** A4
Grenfell Ave
High Wycombe
HP12. . . . . **172** D7
Maidenhead SL6. . . . **202** F6
Grenfell Pl SL6. . . . **202** F6
Grenfell Rd
Beaconsfield HP9 . . **175** E3
Maidenhead SL6. . . . **202** E6
Grenville Ave HP22 **131** A2
Grenville Cl SL1. . . **197** B3
Grenville Ct WD3. . . **167** C5
Grenville Gn HP21. . **115** D4
Grenville Rd
Aylesbury HP21. . . . **115** D5
Buckingham MK18 . . . **41** C1
Grenville Way OX9 . **126** B1
Gresham Ct HP4 . . . **135** B3
Gresham Rd SL1. . . **205** A7
Greyfriars Ct MK10 . . **36** B2
Greyhound Ct MK18 . **66** A4
Greyhound La
Thame OX9 . . . . . . **125** F1
Winslow MK18 . . . . . **66** A4
Greyhound Wlk
OX9. . . . . **125** F1
Greylag Gdns MK5 . . **46** A3
Greys Hill RG9 . . . . **191** D1
Greys Rd RG9 . . . . **191** D1
Greys The MK6. . . . . **47** C8
Greystoke Ct HP4 . . **135** A3
Greystoke Rd SL2. . **204** F8
Greystonley 1 MK4 . . **46** C2
Gr Gdns 6 HP23 . . **173** D6
Griffin Cl
Maidenhead SL6. . . . **202** E5
Slough SL1 . . . . . . **205** C4
Griffin Field LU7 . . . . **78** E8
Griffin House Prep Sch
HP17 . . . . **129** E1
Griffin Ind Mall
HP19. . . . . **101** B1
Griffin La
Aylesbury HP19. . . . **101** B1
6 Aylesbury HP19. . **115** A8
Griffin Lane Ind Est
HP19. . . . . **101** B1
Griffith Gate MK10 . . **36** A1
Griffith Gate Rdbt
MK10 . . . . **36** A2
Griffith Ho HP10 . . . **174** C2
Griffiths Acre HP17. **114** E5
Griffiths Yd HP5 . . . **144** B1
Griffon Cl MK6 . . . . . **47** A7
Grigby Rise MK6 . . . . **47** A7
Griggs Orch MK16. . . **14** A2
Grimbold Ct MK15. . . **35** C7
Grimmer Cl HP19 . . **100** F3
Grimms Hill HP16 . . **151** F7
Grimms Mdw HP14. . **150** B1
Grimsby Rd SL1. . . **204** F4
Grimsdell's La HP6 . **154** D2
Grimsdyke Rd HP23 **119** D1
Gringer Hill SL6. . . **202** E8
Grizedale MK13. . . . . **34** B5
Groombridge MK7 . . **48** A7
Groom Rd HP16 . . . **151** C5
Groomsby Dr LU7 . . **105** E5
Grooms Cotts HP5 . **145** B1
Grooms Ct HP11 . . . **174** A4
Grosmont 7 MK4. . . **46** B2
Grosmont Cl 1 MK4. **46** B2
Grosvenor Cl SL0 . . **200** D2
Grosvenor Ct SL1 . . **205** E7
Grosvenor Dr SL6 . . **203** C8
Grosvenor Way
HP19. . . . . **114** E8
Groundsel Cl MK7. . . **48** B6
Grove LU7 . . . . **80** C7
Grove Acad SL1 . . . **205** C4
Grove Ash MK1 . . . . . **47** D3
Grovebury Rd LU7. . . **80** F7
Grove Cl
Chalfont St Peter
SL9 . . . . **177** C2
1 Slough SL1 . . . . . **206** A3
Grove Cotts UB9 . . **190** C8
Grove Ct
Beaconsfield HP9 . . **175** D2
Bierton HP22 . . . . . **102** C5
Maidenhead SL6. . . . **202** D7
Turvey MK43. . . . . **8** E6
Grove End SL9 . . . . **177** C2
Grove End Barns
OX9. . . . . **126** B4

Grove Farm La LU7. . **69** E2
Grove Gdns HP23 . . **119** B5
Grove Hill SL7 . . . . **177** C3
Grove Ind Sch The
MK5 . . . . **46** C7
Grove La
Ashley Green HP5. . . **145** C5
Chalfont St Peter SL9 **177** C2
Little Kimble HP17. . . **129** E2
Uxbridge UB8 . . . . . **201** F1
Grovelands HP11. . . **173** A6
Grove Leys HP23 . . . **119** C5
Grovels The HP4 . . . **121** F7
Grove Pk HP23 . . . . **119** C5
Grove Rd
Amersham HP6. . . . . **154** F1
Beaconsfield HP9 . . **175** E2
Burnham SL1, SL2. . . **197** E4
Hazlemere HP15 . . . **162** F3
High Wycombe HP12. . **172** C8
Maidenhead SL6 . . . **202** F7
Tring HP23 . . . . **119** C5
Turvey MK43. . . . . **8** E6
Uxbridge UB8 . . . . . **201** D5
Windsor SL4 . . . . . . **210** D5
Grove Road Prim Sch
HP23. . . . . **119** C5
Grovers Ct HP27 . . . **139** A2
Grovesbrook MK17. . **48** D2
Groves Cl SL8. . . . . **185** C3
Groves Rd HP22 . . . **131** E7
Groves Way
Chesham HP5 . . . . . **143** F2
Cookham Rise SL6. . **195** F4
Grove The
Amersham HP6. . . . . **154** F1
Latimer HP5 . . . . . . **155** D3
Medmenham SL7. . . **193** E6
Milton Keynes, Bradwell
MK13 . . . . **34** A4
Milton Keynes, Rickley Park
MK3 . . . . **57** F7
Newport Pagnell MK16 **22** B3
Slough SL1 . . . . . . **206** A4
Tring HP23 . . . . **119** C5
Waddesdon HP18. . . . **99** A6
Groveway
Bow Brickhill MK7. . . . **48** B7
Brinklow MK10 . . . . . **48** C8
Milton Keynes, Redmoor
MK3 . . . . **47** A3
Milton Keynes, Simpson
MK6 . . . . **47** D5
Grove Way
Chorleywood WD3. . . **167** B4
Uxbridge UB8 . . . . . **201** D5
Waddesdon HP18 . . . . **99** A6
Grovewood Cl WD3 **167** B4
Gr Parade SL2 . . . . **206** A4
Grubbins La HP27. . **150** B5
Grubbs Cl LU7 . . . . . **68** D2
Grubwood La SL6. . **195** C4
Grundy Ho UB8 . . . **201** D3
Gryms Dyke HP16 . . **151** D6
Guards Club Rd SL6 **203** C7
Guards Rd SL4 . . . . **209** C5
Guards View SL4. . . **210** D6
Guards Wlk 1 SL4. . **209** C5
GUBBLECOTE **104** D3
Gubblegore MK18. . . **65** E5
Guernsey Cl HP19 . . **101** A3
Guernsey Cres MK8 . . **45** C7
Guernsey Rd MK3 . . . **58** C5
Guest Gdns MK13 . . . **34** B8
Guildford Ave MK4. . **56** E8
Guildford Cl MK18. . **52** A4
Guillemot Way
HP19 . . . . **101** E3
Guinea Orch MK46 . . . **6** E4
Guinions Rd HP13. . **173** F5
Guise Ct MK17 . . . . . **49** F4
**Gullet Nature Reserve
The** SL6 . . . . **202** E5
Gullicot Way LU7. . . **105** C4
Gulliver's SL4. . . . **210** D8
Gulliver's Land★
MK15. . . . . **35** C4
Gull Way 4 HP19 . . **101** F3
Gundale Ct MK4. . . . **46** B2
Gun La MK16. . . . . . **14** A2
Gunmaker Ct MK14. . **34** F6
Gunthorpe Rd SL7. . **184** A3
Gunver La MK4. . . . . **57** B8
Gurnard Cl UB7 . . . **208** D4
Gurnards Ave
6 Central Milton Keynes
MK6 . . . . **34** F1
Milton Keynes MK6 . . **35** A2
Gurnells Rd HP9 . . . **176** C5
Gurney Cl
9 Aylesbury HP20. . **101** F2
Beaconsfield HP9 . . **175** D2
Milton Keynes MK5. . . **46** A7
Gurney Ct LU6 . . . . . **92** F6
Gurneys Mdw HP15 **163** D5
Guttmann Rd HP21. . **115** F5
Guyana La MK17 . . . . **58** A3
Guy Mws 5 HP22 . . **117** D5
Gwendale SL6 . . . . . **195** F1
Gwendolyn Buck Dr 2
HP21. . . . . **115** E4
Gweneth Ct SL7. . . **183** D3
Gwent Cl SL6 . . . . . **202** B5
Gwynant Ct MK2 . . . . **58** C3
Gwynne Cl
Tring HP23 . . . . **119** A5
Windsor SL4 . . . . . . **209** E6

Gynant Rd HP13 173 F6
Gyosei Gdns MK15 35 B5
Gypsy La
Aspley Guise MK17 49 F3
High Wycombe HP11 173 D5
Marlow SL7 183 E4
Stoke Poges SL2 187 E1

H

Haberley Mead MK13 34 B3
Hackett Pl MK16 24 A6
HADDENHAM 127 B5
Haddenham Airfield HP17 126 E7
Haddenham Bsns Pk HP17 126 F7
Haddenham Cty Fst Sch HP17 127 A6
Haddenham Jun Sch HP17 127 A6
Haddenham Mus★ HP17 126 F6
Haddenham Rd HP17 127 A3
Haddenham St Mary's CE Sch HP17 127 A4
Haddenham & Thame Parkway Sta HP17 126 E6
Haddington Cl
Milton Keynes MK3 46 E2
Wendover HP22 131 D6
Haddington Way HP20 102 A1
Haddon MK8 45 F8
Haddon Rd
Chorleywood WD3 167 C4
Maidenhead SL6 202 C5
Hadfield Rd TW19 213 D1
Hadland Cl HP3 146 A4
Hadley Ct SL3 212 E6
Hadley Pl MK13 34 C3
Hadlow Ct SL1 205 C5
Hadrians Dr MK13 34 A5
Hadrian's Gate NN13 38 A7
Hagdale La HP4 134 A4
Haggar St HP17 114 B5
Hag Hill La SL6 204 A7
Hag Hill Rise SL6 204 A7
Haglis Dr HP22 131 B6
Haig Dr SL1 205 B4
Haileybury Ct SL4 210 A4
Hailey Croft OX39 147 B6
Hailey Ct SL6 202 F5
Hainan Dr MK3 58 B3
Hainault Ave MK14 22 A1
Haines Cl HP19 100 F2
Haines Rd HP15 162 F6
Haithewaite MK8 33 D1
Haldene MK8 33 E2
Hale SL4 209 F6
Hale Ave MK11 32 E5
Hale La HP22 131 E3
Hale Leys Sh Ctr 23 HP20 115 D8
Hale Rd HP22 131 C3
Hales Croft HP21 116 B4
Hale St HP20 115 E8
Halesworth Ave 1 MK10 36 B4
Halfacre Hill SL9 177 F2
Halfway Hos
Hanslope MK19 10 F4
Maidenhead SL6 195 E4
Halfway House La HP5 153 F7
Halifax Cl SL6 202 A8
Halifax Gn HP17 126 E6
Halifax Ho HP7 166 C8
Halifax Rd
Heronsgate WD3 167 C2
High Wycombe HP12 172 D5
Maidenhead SL6 202 A8
Halifax Way SL6 202 A8
Halings La UB9 189 E7
Halkingcroft SL3 206 C4
Hall Cl
High Wycombe HP13 173 F5
Maids Moreton MK18 41 F3
Old Stratford MK19 32 B6
Hall Cotts HP18 82 F7
Hall Ct SL3 211 B7
Halldore Hill SL6 195 E7
Hall Green MK17 58 B2
Hall La MK16 23 C8
Hall Mdw SL1 197 C3
Hall Park Gate HP4 135 E3
Hall Park Hill HP4 135 E3
Hall Pk HP4 135 E3
Hall Place (Berkshire Coll of Agriculture) SL6 194 A1
Halls Cnr HP10 174 A1
Halse Dr SL1 197 F7
Halswell Pl MK10 36 A3
HALTON 117 D1
Haltonchesters MK13 33 F6
Halton Com Comb Sch HP22 131 D7
Halton La
Halton HP22 131 B8
Halton HP22 131 C8
Halton Village HP22 131 C8
Halton Wood Forest Wlks★ HP23 132 A5
Halton Wood Rd HP22 131 D5
Haly Cl MK13 34 B4
Hamberlins La HP4, HP23 134 B7
HAMBLEDEN 181 D1
Hambleden RG9 181 C2
Hambleden Mill RG9 192 C7
Hambleden Pl RG9 192 D6
Hambleden Rise RG9 192 D8
Hambleden Wlk SL6 195 E3
Hambledines MK14 21 F3
Hambledon Cl HP21 116 B5
Hambledon Pl SL8 185 C2
Hamble Dr HP21 115 C6
Hambleton Gr MK4 46 B2
Hambling Pl LU6 93 F8
Hamburg Croft MK5 46 B3
Hambye Cl HP27 149 E4
Hamer Cl HP3 146 A3
Hamfield Cotts SL6 195 E7
HAM GREEN 83 D2
Hamilton Acad (annexe) HP13 173 B8
Hamilton Acad (main site) 17 HP13 173 B7
Hamilton Ave RG9 191 E1
Hamilton Cl
Buckingham MK18 52 C8
Dagnall HP4 107 C5
Hamilton Ct
Aylesbury HP19 101 D1
High Wycombe HP13 173 B8
Hamilton Gdns SL1 197 B2
Hamilton La MK3 57 C6
Hamilton Mead 5 HP3 146 A4
Hamilton Pk SL6 202 A6
Hamilton Pl SL9 188 E6
Hamilton Rd
Berkhamsted HP4 135 B4
High Wycombe HP13 162 C1
Slough SL1 205 A7
Thame OX9 126 A1
Uxbridge UB8 201 D1
Ham Island SL4 211 C3
Ham La SL4 211 C3
Hamlins MK6 47 A6
Hammersley La HP10, HP11 174 B5
Hammerwood Gate MK7 48 A7
Hammond Cres MK15 35 B6
Hammond End SL2 198 B8
Hammond St HP22 117 B5
Hamon Way 2 MK12 33 A6
Hampden Ave HP5 144 A1
HAMPDEN BOTTOM 141 B2
Hampden Bottom HP16 140 B4
Hampden Cl
Aylesbury HP21 115 D6
Stoke Mandeville HP22 116 B1
Stoke Poges SL2 199 A2
Hampden Gate HP27 150 C5
Hampden Gdns HP21 115 D6
Hampden Hill
Beaconsfield HP9 175 B2
Charndon OX27 72 E6
Hampden Ho 2 HP13 173 F6
Hampden Rd
Aylesbury HP21 115 D6
Chalfont St Peter SL9 177 D2
High Wycombe HP13 173 B8
Hughenden Valley HP16 151 B3
Little Hampden HP16 140 E1
Maidenhead SL6 202 B8
Slough SL3 206 F3
Speen HP27 150 C5
Stoke Mandeville HP22 116 B1
Wendover HP22 131 C5
Hampden Sq 2 HP19 115 A8
Hampden Villas OX27 71 F7
Hampden Way HP13 173 F6
Hampshire Ave SL1 205 C8
Hampshire Ct MK3 46 F2
Hampshire Lodge 8 SL6 202 F6
Hampson Cl MK13 34 A5
Hampstead Cl 7 HP19 100 F1
Hampstead Gate MK13 34 C3
Hampton 5 MK8 45 F8
Hampton Ho SL3 212 D7
Hanbury Cl SL1 204 A8
Hancock Cl HP21 115 E5
Handel Gr HP21 115 F3
Handel Mead MK7 48 E5
Handleton Comm HP14 171 B5
Handley Dr HP17 126 E7
Handley Page Cl MK43 24 E2
Handy Cross HP11 172 F3
Hangar Rd UB9 189 E7
Hanging Croft Cl 4 HP13 173 F6
Hangings La HP16 151 A6
Hanley Cl SL4 209 D6
Hanmer Rd MK6 47 E5
Hannah Ball Sch HP13 173 D7
Hannon Rd HP21 115 C5
Hanover Cl
3 Aylesbury HP19 101 A2
Slough SL1 206 A3
Windsor SL4 209 F6
Hanover Ct
2 Aylesbury HP21 115 E7
Hazelmere HP15 163 B3
Leighton Buzzard LU7 80 D7
Milton Keynes MK14 34 D7
Hanover Mead SL6 203 C3
Hanover Way SL4 209 F6
Hanscomb Cl MK15 35 C2
Hansen Croft MK5 46 B5
HANSLOPE 11 B3
Hanslope Pk Rd
Bullington End MK16 20 C8
Hanslope MK19 11 D1
Hanslope MK19 11 D1
Hanslope Prim Sch MK19 11 A3
Hanslope Rd
Castlethorpe MK19 19 F6
Gayhurst MK16 12 C2
Hanslope MK19 11 F2
Hanslope MK19 11 F2
Hartwell NN7 10 D7
Hanson Ave MK10 35 E2
Hanson Cl UB7 208 F3
Hanson Way HP21 116 A4
Hanwell Ct 1 MK14 35 A5
Harborne Ct MK8 33 C2
Harborough Cl SL1 204 D5
Harbourne Cl HP21 115 C3
Harby Cl MK4 46 C1
Harcourt
Milton Keynes MK13 34 A3
Wraysbury TW19 211 E1
Harcourt Cl
Dorney SL6 203 F3
Henley-on-Thames RG9 191 C1
Leighton Buzzard LU7 80 E7
Harcourt Gn HP19 101 B2
Harcourt Rd
Dorney SL4 203 F3
Tring HP23 119 C4
Windsor SL4 209 F6
Har Ct MK43 25 B2
Hardenwaye HP13 162 E1
Harding Rd
Chesham HP5 144 D1
Milton Keynes MK10 48 C8
Hardings Cl SL0 200 C2
Harding Spur 12 SL3 206 F1
Hardings Row SL0 200 D2
HARDMEAD 15 D3
Hardmead Rd
Clifton Reynes MK43 15 C8
Newton Blossomville MK43 8 A3
HARDWICK 87 B3
Hardwick Cl SL6 202 A8
Hardwicke Gdns HP6 154 E1
Hardwick Mews MK17 49 B3
Hardwick Pl MK17 49 B4
Hardwick Rd MK17 49 B4
Hardy Cl
Aylesbury HP21 115 F7
Slough SL1 205 A5
1 Walton MK17 48 D8
Hardy Mead Ct HP11 174 B2
Hardy Mews UB8 201 C3
Harebell Cl MK7 48 B5
Harebell Wlk HP15 162 F6
Harebridge La HP22 117 E1
Hare Cl MK18 52 E7
Hareden Croft MK4 46 B2
Harefield Rd
Maidenhead SL6 202 A7
Uxbridge UB8 201 D6
Harehatch La SL1 186 F3
Hare La HP16 152 B3
Hare Lane End HP16 152 A3
Harescombe Ct HP9 175 D3
Hare Shoots SL6 202 E5
Harewood Pl SL1 206 A3
Harewood Rd HP8 166 C6
Hargrave Rd SL6 202 D8
Hargreaves Nook MK14 22 B2
Hariana Cl MK8 45 C7
Harkness Cl MK2 58 D6
Harkness Rd SL1 204 B8
Harlans Cl MK6 47 B8
Harlech Ho 5 HP13 173 F7
Harlech Pl MK3 57 E7
Harlech Rd LU7 105 C3
Harlequin La MK43 25 C2
Harlequin Pl 3 MK5 45 F3
Harlesden Cl MK10 35 E1
Harle Stone Ct MK14 22 A1
Harley Ct SL1 205 C4
Harley Dr
Walton MK7 47 F5
Walton MK7 48 A5
Harleyford SL7 193 F7
Harleyford La SL7 194 B7
Harling Rd LU6 93 B4
Harlow Cres 6 MK4 45 E2
Harlow Rd HP13 173 C6
Harmans Cross MK10 36 B3
Harman Terr HP12 172 D7
Harman Wlk HP12 172 C3
HARMONDSWORTH 213 D8
Harmondsworth La UB7 213 E8
Harmondsworth Prim Sch UB7 213 D8
Harmondsworth Rd UB7 208 E2
Harnett Dr MK12 32 F6
Harper Cl OX25 94 D7
Harpers La MK14 34 F8
Harrier Cl HP20 101 F3
Harrier Ct MK6 47 A8
Harrier Dr MK6 47 A8
Harries Cl HP5 144 B1
Harries Way HP15 163 B6
Harriet Walker Way WD3 167 F2
Harrington Cl SL4 209 F3
Harriotsend La HP4 135 B1
Harriots End La HP4 145 B8
Harris Cl
Brill HP18 110 A8
Milton Keynes MK17 58 B2
Harris Gdns SL1 205 C4
Harrison Barber Cotts SL3 212 D7
Harrison Cl MK5 46 D6
Harrison Pl OX9 125 F1
Harrisons Wy 3 HP13 162 A1
Harrison Way SL1 204 D5
Harris Rd HP14 171 B5
Harris Way 3 MK17 48 D8
Harroell
Long Crendon HP18 125 D5
Long Crendon, Church End HP18 125 D6
Harrogate Ct SL3 207 A1
HARROLD 3 F6
Harrold Prim Acad MK43 3 F6
Harrold Rd MK46 3 B1
Harrow Cl
4 Aylesbury HP21 115 E4
Maidenhead SL6 195 E1
Harrowden MK13 34 B7
Harrow La SL6 195 E1
Harrow Mkt The SL3 207 A3
Harrow Rd
Longwick HP27 138 D6
Slough SL3 206 F3
Harrow Yd 6 HP23 119 A3
Harrup Cl MK17 69 E7
Harry Mews HP22 102 C2
Hartdames MK5 46 A3
Hartfield Cl MK7 48 A7
Hartington Gr 5 MK4 46 B3
Hartland Ave MK4 57 B8
Hartland Cl SL1 205 D5
Hartley MK14 34 E8
Hartley Cl SL3 199 C4
Hartley Copse SL4 211 A1
Hartley Ct SL9 188 E5
Hart Moor Cl HP14 158 E4
Hartop Cl LU7 91 F2
Harts Rd HP17 127 B6
Hart St RG9 191 E2
HARTWELL 10 D8
Hartwell Cl HP10 163 C2
Hartwell Dr HP9 175 D3
Hartwell End HP21 115 B7
Hartwell Rd
Ashton NN7 9 F8
Hanslope MK19 10 E5
Hartwell View HP19 100 E1
Hartwort Cl MK7 48 B5
Harvard Cl MK14 21 F2
Harvard Way MK10 35 D2
Harvest Bank HP6 153 C4
Harvest Cl HP21 115 D3
Harvester Cl MK12 33 B5
Harvest Hill HP10 185 D2
Harvest Hill Rd SL6 202 F3
Harvest Pl HP15 163 B6
Harvey Dr MK46 6 F1
Harvey Ho SL3 206 E7
Harvey Orch HP9 175 C3
Harvey Rd
Aylesbury HP21 115 E5
Dunstable LU6 93 D7
Slough SL3 207 B4
Harvie Card Way MK17 37 B2
Harvil Rd
Ickenham UB9, UB10 190 E4
South Harefield UB9 190 E4
Harvington Cres MK19 10 F3
Harvington Pk LU7 105 D3
Harwich Rd SL1 205 A7
Harwood Dr UB10 201 F4
Harwood Rd SL7 183 C1
Harwood St MK13 34 A7
Hasgill Ct MK13 34 B4
Haslemere Rd SL4 210 A6
Haslerig Cl HP21 115 F5
Haslow Ct MK8 33 E3
Hasting Cl SL6 203 C2
Hastings MK11 32 E5
Hastings Mdw SL2 199 A4
HASTOE 132 F7
Hastoe Cross HP23 133 A7
Hastoe Farm Barns HP23 132 F7
Hastoe Hill HP23 132 F8
Hastoe La HP23 119 A2
Hastoe Pk HP20 101 F2
Hastoe Row HP23 133 A7
Haswell Cres SL1 204 F4
Hatch Ce Mws SL6 195 E7
Hatches La
Great Kingshill HP15 151 C1
Hughenden Valley HP15 162 B8
Hatchet Leys La MK18 53 F8
Hatchgate Gdns SL1 197 D1
Hatch La
Hackleton NN7 4 D6
Harmondsworth UB7 213 D7
Radnage HP14 160 B4
Windsor SL4 210 A5
Hatchlands MK8 33 F1
Hatch Pl SL6 195 E7
Hatch The SL4 209 C7
Hatfield Cl SL6 202 C6
Hatfield Rd SL1 206 A4
Hathaway Ct MK8 45 E8
Hatters La HP13 173 F7
Hatter's La HP13 173 F6
Hatton MK6 47 D6
Hatton Ave SL2 198 D1
Hatton Ct SL4 210 C5
Hatton Gr UB7 208 D4
Hatton St HP22 102 C2
Hauksbee Gdns MK5 46 D5
Havelock Ave MK17 36 E4
Havelock Bsns Pk SL6 202 C7
Havelock Cres SL6 202 B7
Havelock Ct HP20 101 D1
Havelock Rd SL6 202 B7
Havelock St HP20 101 D1
Havenfield Ct 16 HP13 173 B7
Havenfield Rd HP12 172 C4
Haven of Rest SL6 203 B7
Haven Shaw Cl HP21 116 A5
Haven St MK10 36 C3
Haven The HP14 158 C4
Havergate Rise MK3 58 A4
HAVERSHAM 20 E2
Haversham Rd
Gayhurst MK16 12 E1
Gayhurst MK16 21 D7
Haversham MK19 20 D1
Haversham Village Sch MK19 20 E2
Haverthwaite View MK10 36 C3
Hawfinch 1 HP19 101 E3
Hawker Ct SL3 207 A3
Hawker Rd 4 HP17 126 E6
Hawkes Cl SL3 207 B3
Hawkhurst Gate MK7 47 F7
Hawkings Way HP3 146 A5
Hawkins Cl MK11 32 D5
Hawkins Mws HP22 117 C5
Hawkmoor Cl MK6 47 B8
Hawkridge MK4 46 E3
Hawkshead Dr MK4 46 C3
Hawks Hill SL8 185 C3
Hawkshill Dr HP3 146 F8
Hawkshill Rd SL2 198 A2
Hawkslade Furlong HP21 115 D3
Hawksmoor Cl HP13 173 A8
Hawkswood MK46 6 F5
Hawkswood Gr SL3 199 F6
Hawkswood La SL3, SL9 199 F8
Hawkwell Dr HP23 119 C4
Hawkwell Est MK19 32 B7
Haw La HP14 149 A2
Hawleys La HP22 87 A6
Haworth Croft 2 MK10 36 B3
HAWRIDGE 133 E1
Hawridge & Cholesbury CE Sch HP5 133 E2
HAWRIDGE COMMON 133 E2
Hawridge Common HP5 133 E2
Hawridge Hill
Cholesbury HP5 133 F1
Heath End HP5 134 A1
Hawridge La HP5 143 E8
Hawridge Vale
Cholesbury HP5 133 F1
Heath End HP5 134 A1
Hawthorn Ave MK2 58 E8
Hawthorn Cl
Aylesbury HP20 101 F2
Aylesbury HP20 102 A1
Hawthorn Cl *continued*
Chinnor OX39 147 E7
Iver Heath SL0 200 C2
Turvey MK43 8 E6
Hawthorn Cres HP15 163 B2
Hawthorn Dr UB9 201 C6
Hawthorne Cl
Leighton Buzzard LU7 80 E8
Marlow SL7 183 E4
Hawthorne Cres
Slough SL1 205 F7
West Drayton UB7 208 F4
Hawthorne Gdns HP10 174 A2
Hawthorne Rd HP13 174 A6
Hawthorn Gdns SL6 202 E5
Hawthorn Gr 6 MK16 36 B5
Hawthorn La SL2 198 A5
Hawthorn Pl HP10 174 C8
Hawthorn Rd HP27 139 C3
Hawthorns The
Berkhamsted HP4 135 A5
Cranfield MK43 25 B1
Felden HP3 146 F7
Little Chalfont HP8 166 C7
Maple Cross WD3 178 D5
Monks Risborough HP27 139 C6
Poyle SL3 212 F6
Wooburn Green HP10 185 E6
Hawthorn Way
Chesham HP5 144 D2
Wing LU7 79 E3
Wing LU7 79 F3
Hawthorn Wlk HP15 163 B2
Hawtrey Cl SL1 206 B4
Hawtrey Rd SL4 210 C5
Haxters End HP4 134 E4
Hay Barn Bsns Pk The HP22 88 C6
Haybrook Coll SL1 204 E8
Hayden Ho 3 HP11 172 F7
Haydock Cl MK3 57 C6
Haydon Abbey Sch HP19 101 C2
Haydon Ct SL6 202 E6
HAYDON HILL 100 E2
Haydon Rd HP19 101 C2
Hayes Cl SL6 203 D1
Hayes Pl SL7 183 D1
Hayes Rd
Deanshanger MK19 31 F4
Deanshanger MK19 31 F5
Deanshanger MK19 31 F5
Hayfield Dr HP15 163 B2
Hay La
Fulmer SL3 199 D8
Stagsden MK43 16 F5
Hayles Field RG9 170 E1
Hayley Ct MK14 34 D6
Hayling Cl SL1 205 B5
Haymaker Cl UB10 201 F5
Hayman Rise MK8 45 D6
Haymill Rd SL1, SL2 197 D1
Haymill Valley Nature Reserve SL2 204 E8
Haynes Cl
Bow Brickhill MK17 48 D2
Slough SL3 206 F1
Haynes Ho HP12 172 B3
Haynes Mead HP4 135 A6
Hayse Hill SL4 209 D6
Haystacks The HP13 173 B7
Hayter Cl HP19 101 C4
Haythrop Cl MK15 35 B6
Hayton Way MK4 56 E8
Hayward Pl SL8 185 C2
Haywards Cl RG9 191 C1
Haywards Croft MK12 33 B5
Haywards Mead SL4 204 F1
Haywood Dr WD3 167 F4
Haywood Pk
Chorleywood WD3 167 F4
Stewkley LU7 68 C3
Haywoods Dr HP3 146 F8
Haywood Way HP19 100 F3
Hayworth Pl 2 MK4 45 D2
Hazelbury Rd HP13 173 D6
Hazel Cl SL7 183 C6
Hazelcroft Cl UB10 201 F5
Hazel Ct WD3 178 E5
Hazeldene HP22 131 C4
HAZELEY 45 D5
Hazeley Acad The MK8 45 D5
Hazel Gr MK2 58 D7
Hazelhurst 7 MK4 46 B2
Hazelhurst Rd SL1 197 D3
Hazell Ave HP21 116 A7
Hazell Cl
Maidenhead SL6 202 F8
1 Maidenhead SL6 203 A8
Hazell Pk HP7 165 D8
Hazell Rd HP16 151 C5
Hazell Way SL2 198 F6
Hazelmead Dr MK16 13 F2
HAZELMERE 163 B4

Hazel Rd HP4 . . . . . . 135 D3
Hazelwood MK14. . . . . 34 F8
Hazelwood Cl HP5 . 144 D2
Hazely HP23 . . . . . . 119 C4
Hazlehurst Dr HP21 116 A5
Hazlemere CE Comb Sch
HP15. . . . . 163 B5
Hazlemere Ct HP15. 163 A4
Hazlemere Rd
Slough SL2 . . . . 206 B5
Tylers Green HP10 . 163 C2
Hazlemere View
HP15. . . . . 163 B5
Hazleton MK18. . . . . . 65 F5
Hazley Wlk MK18. . . . .41 F1
Headington Cl SL6 202 D7
Headington Pl SL2. 205 F5
Headington Rd SL6. 202 A7
Headland Cl **1**
HP16. . . . . 152 A8
Headland End HP17 138 D6
Headlands Dr HP4. . 135 E5
Healey Ave HP13 . . 173 D7
Heals Cl MK3 . . . . 57 E6
Heaney Cl MK16. . . . . 22 A5
Hearn Cl HP10 . . . . . 162 F2
Hearne Ct HP8 . . . . 177 B7
Hearne Dr SL6 . . . . . 203 A1
Hearnes Cl HP9 . . . . 176 D5
Hearnes Mdw HP9 . 176 D5
Hearn Gn HP22. . . . . 102 E3
Hearns Yard HP5. . . 144 C2
Heathacre SL3. . . . . 212 E6
Heath Cl
Aylesbury HP21. . . . 116 B5
Holmer Green HP15 . 163 B6
Stanwell TW19 . . . . 213 C1
Woburn Sands MK17. . 49 C3
Heathcote SL6 . . . . 203 B2
Heathcote Ct **2**
SL4 . . . . 210 D4
Heathcote Way
UB7. . . . . 208 D5
Heath Ct
Leighton Buzzard LU7 . 70 E3
Uxbridge UB8 . . . . . 201 D5
HEATH END
Cholesbury 134 A2
Prestwood 151 E1
Heath End HP5. . . . . 144 A2
Heath End Cl HP15 . 151 E1
Heath End Rd
Flackwell Heath
HP10. . . . . 174 A1
Great Kingshill HP15,
HP16. . . . . 151 E2
Little Missenden HP10 . 173 D2
Heather Cl
Buckingham MK18 . . . 52 C7
Uxbridge UB8 . . . . . 208 F8
Heathercroft MK14. . 34 E7
Heatherdene Rd
HP10. . . . . 173 D3
Heatherden Gn SL0 200 D4
Heather La UB7 . . . . 208 C7
Heather Mead LU6 . . 92 E5
Heathers Cl MK18 . . . 73 B5
Heatherside Gdns
SL2. . . . . 187 D1
Heatherton House Sch
HP6. . . . . 154 C3
Heatherton Pk HP6. 154 B3
Heather Wlk
Aylesbury HP21. . . . 115 B6
Hazlemere HP15. . . . 163 A3
Heathfield MK12 . . . . 33 E4
Heathfield Ind Est
MK12 . . . . 33 E4
Heathfield Rd
High Wycombe
HP12. . . . . 172 B7
Taplow SL1 . . . . . . 186 A1
Heath La MK17. . . . . . 49 A2
Heathlands Dr SL6. 202 A6
Heath Lawn HP10 . . 173 F1
Heath Rd
Beaconsfield HP9 . . 186 A8
Great Brickhill MK17. . 59 C1
Great Brickhill MK17,
LU7. . . . . 59 E1
Hyde Heath HP6 . . . 153 C5
Soulbury MK17 . . . . . 70 E8
Heathrow Bvd UB7 . 213 F7
Heathrow Cl UB7 . . 213 B6
Heathrow Prim Sch
UB7. . . . . 213 F8
Heathrow T5 Sta/U Sta
TW6 . . . . 213 C4
Heath The LU7 . . . . . 70 E4
Heath Way SL0 . . . . 200 D3
Heavens Lea SL8. . . 185 C2
Hebridean **2** MK18. . 41 D2
Hebridean Cl MK8. . . 45 B7
Hebrides Gate
Bletchley MK17. . . . . 58 C3
Milton Keynes MK3 . . 58 C3
Hedge Furlong
HP17. . . . . 127 A6
Hedgehog Way HP4 134 E4
Hedge Lea HP10 . . . 185 D6
HEDGERLEY 187 D3
Hedgerley OX39. . . . 147 B6
HEDGERLEY
GREEN 187 E4

HEDGERLEY HILL . . . 187 E2
Hedgerley Hill SL2. 187 D2
Hedgerley La
Beaconsfield HP9 . . 186 F8
Gerrards Cross SL9. 188 B4
Gerrards Cross SL9. 188 C3
Hedgerley HP9 . . . . 187 F5
Hedgerley SL2. . . . . 187 D6
Hedgerow The MK4 46 B4
Hedgerow SL9 . . . . 177 E4
Hedgerow Ave
HP10. . . . . 173 D3
Hedgerows The MK4 46 A4
Hedgerows Wlk
HP27. . . . . 138 D6
Hedges Ct MK5 . . . . 46 B6
Hedges Way HP20. . 101 F1
Hedingham St MK5. . 46 A5
Hedingham Mews
SL6. . . . . 202 D7
Hedley Cl HP22 . . . . 118 A4
Hedley Rd HP10. . . . 185 B8
Hedley View HP13. . 174 D1
HEDSOR. 185 F3
Hedsor Hill SL8 . . . 185 C1
Hedsor La
Hedsor HP10. . . . . . 185 F2
Taplow SL1 . . . . . . 186 A2
Hedsor Rd SL8 . . . . 185 B2
Hedsor View Cotts
SL6. . . . . 195 F7
HEELANDS. 34 C4
Heelands Sch MK13. 34 B4
Heet Rd OX27. . . . . . 81 E6
Heights The SL7 . . . 194 B8
Hele Ct MK7 . . . . 48 B3
Helena Rd SL4 . . . . 210 D5
Helen Cotts SL4 . . . 209 D5
Helford Cl HP21. . . . 115 C4
Helford Pl MK6 . . . . . 35 A1
Heligan Pl MK4. . . . . .45 F1
Hellfire Caves★
HP14. . . . . 160 F2
Hellyer Way SL8 . . . 185 C3
Helmsley Rise MK4. . 45 E1
Helston La SL4 . . . . 210 A1
Helston Pl **3** MK6. . .34 F1
Helvellyn Ct MK6. . . . 46 D7
Hemel Hempstead Rd
HP4. . . . . 107 F1
Hemingway Cl MK16. .21 F5
Hemingway Rd
HP19. . . . . 100 F2
Hemlock Cl HP22. . . 116 C4
Hemmings The HP4 134 F3
Hemming Way SL2 . 198 B2
Hemp Hill **10** HP19 . 115 A8
Hemp La HP23 . . . . . 119 F1
Hempson Ave SL3. . 206 C3
Hempstead Rd HP3. 146 B5
HEMPTON
WAINHILL 147 F7
Hemsdale SL6 . . . . . 195 B1
Hemwood Rd SL4 . . 209 D4
Hencroft Mews **14**
SL1 . . . . 205 F4
Hencroft Street N
SL1 . . . . 205 F4
Hencroft Street S
SL1 . . . . 205 F3
Henden Mews SL6 . . 202 A6
Henders MK11. . . . . . 32 E5
Hendon Ct **5** MK10. . .35 F1
Hendons Way SL6 . . 203 B1
Hendon Way TW19 . 213 D1
Hendrix Dr
Aston Clinton HP22. . 117 B5
Milton Keynes MK8. . . 45 D7
Henge Ct HP23. . . . . 125 D1
Hengistbury La MK4. 46 A1
Henley Business Sch
Univ of Reading
RG9. . . . . 192 B7
Henley Coll (Rotherfield
Bldgs) The RG9 . . 191 D1
Henley Coll The
(Rotherfield Bldgs)
RG9. . . . . 191 C1
Henley Lodge **12**
SL6. . . . . 202 F6
HENLEY-ON-
THAMES 191 B1
Henley-on-Thames Sta
RG9. . . . . 191 E1
Henley Rd
Hambleden RG9 . . . 191 F7
Hurley SL6. . . . . . . 193 F1
Maidenhead SL6, SL7 194 B2
Marlow SL7 . . . . . . 194 B8
Medmenham SL7. . . 193 A6
Mill End RG10 . . . . . 192 C7
Remenham Hill RG10. 192 E2
Slough SL1 . . . . . . 204 F7
Henley Trinity Sch
RG9. . . . . 191 B1
Hennerton Way
HP13. . . . . 173 F6
Henrietta Rd OX9 . . 126 A1
Henrietta Way HP9. . 35 A3
Henry Hoare Dr
MK10. . . . . 48 D8
Henry III Tower **17**
SL4 . . . . 210 D6
Henry Mash Ct HP5. 144 E3
Henry Rd
Aylesbury HP20. . . . 116 B8
Slough SL1 . . . . . . 205 D4
Henry St HP23 . . . . 119 A3
Hensman Gate MK10 .35 F4

Henson Cl MK43. . . . 24 E3
HENTON 137 E2
Henton Mews **5**
HP19. . . . . 115 A8
Hepburn Cres MK4 . 45 E3
Hepleswell MK8. . . . . 33 C1
Hepplewhite Cl
HP13. . . . . 173 D8
Herald St HP22. . . . . 102 D2
Herbert Rd HP13 . . . 174 A7
Herberts Hole
Chesham HP5. . . . . . 143 C1
South Heath HP5,
HP16. . . . . 142 F1
Hercies Rd UB10 . . 201 F5
Herdman Cl MK12. . . 33 B5
Herds Hill
Steeple Claydon
MK18. . . . . .63 F4
Steeple Claydon MK18 64 A6
Herd's Hill MK18. . . . 64 A4
Hereford Ho HP13. . 173 F8
Hereford Way HP19 101 A3
Hereford Wy
Crownhill MK8. . . . . . 45 D8
4 Whitehouse MK19 . 45 D8
Heren La MK19. . . . . . 45 C8
Heritage Cl UB8. . . . 201 C1
Heritage Gate SL9. . 188 E7
Heritage House Sch
Chesham HP5. . . . . . 144 D1
Chesham HP5. . . . . . 144 D1
Heritage Wlk WD3 . 167 E6
Herman St **10** HP18 100 D5
Hermes Row MK10 . . 36 D4
Hermitage Cl SL3 . . 206 C3
Hermitage La SL4 . . 210 A4
Hermitage Prim Sch
UB8. . . . . 201 D5
Hermitage The
Great Missenden
HP16. . . . . 152 A7
Uxbridge UB8 . . . . . 201 D6
Hernes Oak OX39. . . 147 D8
Heron Cl
Aylesbury HP20. . . . 116 C8
Uxbridge UB8 . . . . . 201 D6
Heron Dr SL3 . . . . . 207 B2
Heron Lodge MK14. . 34 C6
Heron Path HP22. . . 131 C3
Herons Elm HP4 . . . 134 E7
Heronsfield Ho
WD3 . . . . 167 B3
HERONSGATE 167 D2
Heronsgate Rd
WD3 . . . . 167 B3
Heronsgate Sch MK7 48 B5
Heronshaw Sch MK7 48 B5
Herons Pl
Maidenhead SL6 . . . 196 C3
Marlow SL7. . . . . . . 183 E3
Heron The HP19 . . . 101 E4
Heron Wy SL6. . . . . 203 A8
Herries Prep Sch
SL6. . . . . 195 B8
Herriot Cl MK16. . . . 22 A5
Herschel Gram Sch
SL1 . . . . 205 C7
Herschel Pk Dr **15**
SL1 . . . . 205 F4
Herschel Sports
SL1 . . . . 205 C7
Herschel St
16 Slough SL1 . . . . 205 F4
Slough SL1. . . . . . . 205 F4
Herston Cl HP21. . . 116 B5
Hertford La HP18. . . 100 D4
Hertford Pl MK3 . . . . 46 F2
Hervines Ct HP6 . . . 154 C2
Hervines Rd HP6 . . . 154 C2
Hesketh Rd NN12 . . 18 E6
Hesselby View MK10 36 C2
Heston Wk MK4. . . . 45 D3
Hetherington Cl
SL2. . . . . 197 F2
Hetherington Way
UB10. . . . . 201 E8
Het's Orch HP27 . . . 149 E5
Hetton Cl MK13 . . . . 34 C4
Heusden Way
Gerrards Cross SL9. . 188 F3
Tatling End SL9 . . . . 189 A3
Hever Cl
Maidenhead SL6 . . . 202 C6
Pitstone LU7 . . . . . 105 D2
12 Shenley Brook End
MK4 . . . . 56 E8
Hewgal Way HP22. . 117 C5
Hewgate Ct RG9 . . . 191 E1
Hexham Gdns MK3 . . 57 D6
Heybridge Cres MK7 48 B3
Heydon Ct MK13. . . . 34 A7
Heynes Gn SL6. . . . 202 B3
Heythrop Dr UB10. . 201 F8
Heyward Gate MK6. . 47 C5
Heywood Ave SL6. . 202 A1
Heywood Court Cl
SL6. . . . . 202 A2
Heywood Gdns SL6. 202 A1
Hibbert Rd SL6. . . . 203 B4
Hibbert's Alley **16**
SL4 . . . . 210 D6
Hibberts Mdw HP10 185 D8
Hibberts Way SL9. . 188 E8
Hickey La HP9 . . . . 176 B1
Hickmans Cl MK18 . . 51 B6
Hickman St HP19. . . 114 F8
Hickox Ct HP10 . . . 185 F7

Hicks Farm Rise
HP13. . . . . 173 F7
Hicks Farm Way
HP13. . . . . 174 A6
Hidcote Dr MK4. . . . . 45 F1
Hide The MK6. . . . . . 47 C6
Higgs Ct MK5 . . . . . 46 A8
HIGHAM CROSS . . . 10 D3
Higham Cross Rd
MK19 . . . . 10 E4
Higham Mead HP5. . 144 A3
Higham Rd HP15. . . 144 A3
High Ash CE Prim Sch
MK17 . . . . 59 D2
High Beeches
Gerrards Cross SL9. . 188 D3
High Wycombe HP12. 172 C6
High Beeches Cl
SL7 . . . . 183 C7
High Bois La HP6. . . 154 C4
Highbridge Ind Est
UB8. . . . . 201 C5
Highbridge Rd
HP21. . . . . 115 E8
Highbridge Wlk **4**
HP21. . . . . 115 E8
Highbury La MK9. . . . 35 C3
High Coppice HP7. . 165 C8
Highcrest Acad The
HP13. . . . . 173 E7
Highcroft Cl NN12. . 18 E6
High Cross
Syresham NN13 . . . . 26 F6
Syresham NN13 . . . . 27 A6
HIGHER DENHAM. . 189 C4
Highfield
Chalfont St Giles
HP8. . . . . 177 D8
Long Crendon HP18. 125 C7
Highfield Ave HP12. 172 B5
Highfield Cl
Amersham HP6 . . . . 154 D2
Milton Keynes MK3 . . 47 B2
Newport Pagnell MK16 22 E4
Highfield Dr
Farnham Royal SL2 . 198 A4
Hazlemere HP15. . . 163 A3
Highfield Dr UB10. . 190 E1
Highfield La SL4 . . . 202 A4
Highfield Pk SL7 . . . 183 B1
Highfield Rd
Berkhamsted HP4. . . 135 D4
Bourne End SL8. . . . 185 B4
Chesham HP5 . . . . . 144 B2
Flackwell Heath
HP10. . . . . 185 A8
Maidenhead SL6 . . . 202 B8
Princes Risborough
HP27. . . . . 139 C4
Tring HP23 . . . . . . 118 E3
Wigginton HP23 . . . 119 D1
Windsor SL4 . . . . . 209 F4
Winslow MK18 . . . . . 65 F5
Highfield Sch SL6. . 202 E7
Highfield Way
Hazlemere HP15. . . 163 A3
Yardley Hastings NN7. .1 B6
Highgate **5** SL4 . . . 210 A4
Highgate Mews **2**
HP19. . . . . 100 F1
Highgate Over MK7 . 48 B6
Highgrove Pk SL6. . 202 E8
Highgrove Hill MK8. 45 F3
High Halden MK7. . . 48 B8
High Heavens Wood
SL7 . . . . 183 C8
Highland Cl MK3. . . . 46 F3
High Land Cl HP18 . 96 A1
Highland Dr MK10. . 36 C3
Highland Rd HP7. . . 165 D8
Highlands
Flackwell Heath
HP10. . . . . 185 B7
High Wycombe HP13. 174 A5
Highlands Cl SL9. . . 177 F3
Highlands End SL9. 177 F3
Highlands La SL9 . . 177 F3
Highlands Rd
Buckingham MK18 . . 41 E2
Seer Green HP9 . . . . 176 C5
Highlands The SL2. 198 C7
Highlea Ave HP10. . 185 A8
Highley Gr MK10 . . . 36 B3
High March Sch
HP9. . . . . 175 D4
High Mdw SL6. . . . . 196 C3
Highmoor HP7. . . . . 165 D8
Highmoors HP22. . . 131 B8
Highmore Cotts
HP7. . . . . 152 F3
Highmore Croft MK8 45 D6
Highover Pk HP7. . . 165 C7
High Park Dr MK12 . . 33 A6
High Rd
Cookham Rise SL6. . 195 E2
Soulbury LU7. . . . . . 69 E2
Uxbridge UB8 . . . . . 208 C7
High St South HP4 . 134 E6
High St The MK8 . . . 33 E1
High St
Amersham HP7 . . . . 164 F8
Amersham HP7 . . . . 165 A7
Aylesbury HP20. . . . 115 E8
Berkhamsted HP4. . . 135 A5
Berkhamsted HP4. . . 135 C4
Bovingdon HP3 . . . . 146 A4
Bray SL6. . . . . 203 C4
Brill HP18. . . . . . . 110 A8

High St continued
Buckingham MK18 . . 28 D1
Buckingham MK18 . . 41 D1
Burcott LU7. . . . . . 79 D4
Burnham SL1. . . . . 197 C2
Chalfont St Giles HP8 177 C8
Chalfont St Peter SL9 177 E2
Chalvey SL1. . . . . . 205 D3
Cheddington LU7. . . 105 A7
Chesham HP5. . . . . 154 B8
Chinnor OX39 . . . . 147 D7
Chinnor, Kingston Blount
OX39. . . . . 147 A4
Colnbrook SL3. . . . 212 C7
Cookham SL6 . . . . . 196 B7
Cranfield MK43 . . . . 25 B1
Creslow LU7 . . . . . . 87 F8
Cublington LU7 . . . . 78 B1
Datchet SL3. . . . . . 211 B6
Deanshanger MK19 . . 31 E4
Dinton HP17 . . . . . 113 C2
Dinton HP17 . . . . . 113 E2
Downley HP13 . . . . 161 D3
Eaton Bray LU6 . . . . 92 E6
Edlesborough LU6. . . 92 E3
Emberton MK46 . . . . 13 F7
Eton SL4 . . . . 210 D8
Great Horwood MK17. 55 A3
Great Missenden
HP16. . . . . 152 A7
Haddenham HP17 . . 126 F6
Hanslope MK19. . . . . 11 A2
Harmondsworth UB7 213 D8
Harrold MK43 . . . . . . 3 F6
Haversham MK19 . . . 21 A3
High Wycombe HP11 . 173 B6
High Wycombe HP13. 161 A2
Hurley SL6. . . . . . . 193 F4
Iver SL0 . . . . 207 F7
Ivinghoe LU7. . . . . 105 E5
Lane End HP14 . . . . 171 B4
Lavendon MK46 . . . . 7 F8
Leighton Buzzard LU7 .80 F6
Lewknor OX49. . . . . 157 B8
Long Crendon HP18. 125 D6
Ludgershall HP18 . . . 96 B8
14 Maidenhead SL6 202 F7
Marlow SL7 . . . . . . 183 E1
Milton Keynes MK2 . . 47 E3
Milton Keynes, Great Linford
MK14 . . . . 21 E1
Milton Keynes, New
Bradwell MK13 . . . . 34 A7
Milton Keynes, Stony
Stratford MK11. . . . 32 D6
Nash MK17 . . . . . . 44 C1
Newport Pagnell
MK16 . . . . 22 D4
North Crawley MK16. 24 B6
North Marston MK18. . 76 A2
Olney MK46. . . . . . . 6 F3
Paulerspury NN12. . . 17 C8
Potterspury NN12. . 18 D3
Prestwood HP16. . . 151 D6
Princes Risborough
HP27. . . . . 139 B3
Sherington MK16 . . . 13 F7
Slough SL3 . . . . . . 207 A2
Slough, Upton SL1. . 205 F4
Stagsden MK43. . . . 16 F6
Stanwell TW19 . . . . 213 D1
Stoke Goldington
MK16 . . . . 12 B6
Syresham NN13 . . . . 27 B7
Taplow SL6 . . . . . . 196 E1
Thame OX9 . . . . . . 125 E1
Thornborough MK18. 53 F7
Thornborough MK18. 54 A8
Tring HP23 . . . . . . 119 A3
Turvey MK43 . . . . . . 8 E5
Uxbridge UB8 . . . . . 201 D5
Uxbridge, Cowley
UB8. . . . . 201 C1
Waddesdon HP18 . . . 99 A6
Weedon HP22. . . . . . 87 C1
Wendover HP22 . . . 131 B4
Westcott HP18 . . . . . 98 B7
West Drayton UB7. . 208 E6
Weston Underwood
MK46 . . . . 6 B2
West Wycombe HP14 160 F2
Whaddon MK17. . . . . 45 B1
Whitchurch HP22. . . 87 A6
Windsor SL4 . . . . . 210 D6
Wing LU7 . . . . 79 E2
Winslow MK18 . . . . . 65 F4
Woburn MK17 . . . . . 60 F7
Woburn Sands MK17. . 49 B4
Wraysbury TW19 . . 211 F1
Yardley Gobion NN12. .18 F6
Yardley Hastings NN7. .1 B6
High Street N LU7. . . 68 D2
High Street S
Olney MK46. . . . . . . 6 F3
Stewkley LU7 . . . . . 78 E4
High Thorn Piece
MK14 . . . . 21 F3
High Town Rd SL6. . 202 F7
High Trees MK6. . . . 47 B8
Highveer Croft MK4. 46 B1
High View
Chalfont St Giles
HP8. . . . . 177 D8
Deanshanger MK19 . . 31 E5
Little Brickhill MK17 . 59 E5
High View Cl SL7. . . 183 C6
High View Pl HP7. . . 165 C7
HIGHWAY 202 B7

Highway MK17. . . . . 68 C6
Highway Ave SL6. . . 202 A6
Highway Ct
Beaconsfield HP9 . . 175 D3
Chesham HP5 . . . . . 144 D1
Highway Rd SL6. . . . 202 B6
Highway The HP9 . . 175 D2
Highwood Ave
HP12. . . . . 172 B5
Highwood Bottom
HP27. . . . . 150 A5
Highwood Cres
HP12. . . . . 172 B6
Highwoods Cl SL7. . 183 C7
Highwoods Dr SL7 . 183 C7
Highworth Cl HP13. 162 E1
Highworth Comb Sch
HP13. . . . . 162 E1
HIGH WYCOMBE. . . 173 B7
High Wycombe CE Comb
Sch **5** HP11 . . . . 173 A6
High Wycombe Sta
HP13. . . . . 173 B7
Hikers Way HP18. . . 125 F4
Hilbre Ct **5** MK4 . . . .45 F1
Hilbury Cl HP5 . . . . 154 C3
Hilbury Rd HP20 . . . 115 F8
Hilda Wharf HP20 . . 115 F8
Hildreth Rd HP16. . . 151 C5
Hilgrove Ho SL6. . . 195 D1
Hiljon Cres SL9 . . . 177 E2
Hillary Cl
Aylesbury HP21. . . 116 A5
High Wycombe HP13. 173 E1
Hillary Rd
High Wycombe
HP13. . . . . 173 E6
Slough SL3 . . . . . . 206 E4
Hill Ave
Amersham HP6 . . . 154 C1
Hazelmere HP15. . . 163 B5
Hillbeck Gr MK10. . . 35 E3
Hillbottom Rd HP12 172 B7
Hill Cl HP10. . . . . . 185 F7
Hillcott MK18. . . . . . 63 E2
Hill Cotts HP18. . . . 97 E1
Hillcrest MK43 . . . . 25 C2
Hillcrest Ave SL6. . 195 E6
Hillcrest Cl MK5. . . . 46 B6
Hillcrest Ct HP6. . . 154 C1
Hillcrest Rise MK18 . 52 E6
Hillcrest Way MK18 . 52 E5
Hillcrest Waye SL9 . 188 E5
Hillcroft Rd
Chesham HP5 . . . . . 144 D2
Tylers Green HP10 . 163 C1
Hillersdon SL2. . . . 206 B8
Hillersdon Chase
MK17 . . . . 69 D8
HILLESDEN 63 A4
Hillesden Hamlet
MK18 . . . . 51 F1
Hillesden Rd
Gawcott MK18 . . . . . .51 F2
Gawcott with Lenborough
MK18 . . . . 52 A3
Hillesden Way MK18. 41 E1
Hill Farm MK18 . . . . 76 A2
Hill Farm App HP10 185 F7
Hill Farm Ct OX39 . . 147 D6
Hill Farm La
Chalfont St Giles
HP8. . . . . 166 A1
Dunsmore HP17 . . . 140 F8
Ellesborough HP22 . 130 E1
Little Horwood MK17. . 55 E2
Hill Farm Rd
Chalfont St Peter
SL9 . . . . 177 E3
Chesham HP5 . . . . . 154 D5
Lewknor HP14. . . . . 157 F5
Marlow Bottom SL7. 183 E5
Stagsden MK43. . . . 16 D5
Stokenchurch HP14. 158 A4
Taplow SL6 . . . . . . 196 E2
Hill Farm Way HP15 163 B2
Hillfield Cl HP13 . . . 161 E2
Hillfield Rd SL7 . . . 177 E3
Hillfield Sq SL9 . . . 177 E3
Hill Foot View HP22. 89 A3
Hill Gr SL9. . . . . . . 177 E2
Hill Green La HP23 . 119 F1
Hill Ho SL6 . . . . . . 196 D1
Hill House Cl SL9. . 177 E3
Hilliard Dr
Bradwell MK13 . . . . 34 A3
Milton Keynes MK13 . 34 A3
Hilliards Rd UB8 . . . 208 D7
Hillier Rd HP21 . . . 115 D3
Hillier Way **7** SL3. . 207 A2
Hillingdon Athletics
Stadium UB10 . . . . 201 E6
Hillingdon Hill
UB10. . . . . 201 C2
Hillingdon Hospl
UB8. . . . . 208 F8
Hillingdon Rd UB10 201 E5
Hillingdon Sports &
Leisure Complex
UB10. . . . . 201 E6
Hillingdon Tuition Ctr
UB7. . . . . 208 E5
Hillington Cl HP19 . 115 B7
Hillman Cl UB8. . . . 201 E7
Hill Mdw HP7. . . . . 164 F4
Hill Mdw HP4 . . . . 135 A3
Hillmead Ct SL6. . . 203 F8
Hill Pl SL2. . . . . . . 198 B5

Hill Radnor 1 MK18. 41 D2
Hill Rd
Chinnor OX39 . . . . . . 147 D5
Christmas Common
OX49. . . . . 168 A8
Lewknor OX49. . . . . . 157 C6
Hillrise SL3. . . . . 212 A8
Hill Rise SL9. . . . . . . 177 D1
Hill Rise Cres SL9 . . 177 E1
Hills Cl MK14 . . . . 34 E7
Hillside
Chesham HP5 . . . . . . 144 A3
Gawcott MK18 . . . . . . .51 F4
High Wycombe HP13 173 D7
Maidenhead SL6. . . . 202 D5
Slough SL1 . . . . 205 E4
South Harefield UB9 . 190 C6
Tingewick MK18 . . . . . 51 B6
Hill Side LU7. . . . . . . 104 F7
Hillside Cl
Chalfont St Giles
HP8. . . . . 177 B7
Chalfont St Peter SL9 177 E4
Upper Arncott OX25 . . 94 E7
Hillside Cotts HP18. 112 F2
Hillside Ct SL0 . . . . . . 208 B4
Hillside Ctr HP11. . . 172 F7
Hillside Gdns
Amersham HP7. . . . . 165 E7
Berkhamsted HP4. . . 135 D3
High Wycombe HP13 173 D7
Hillside Rd
Chorleywood WD3. . . 167 C4
Marlow SL7. . . . . 183 E4
Tylers Green HP10 . . 163 A2
Hillside View OX39 147 D5
Hills La SL6. . . . . 195 D7
Hill St HP13. . . . . 174 A5
Hill The
Syresham NN13 . . . . . 27 B8
Winchmore Hill HP7 . 164 C3
HILLTOP 144 D2
Hilltop HP18 . . . . 125 D5
Hilltop Ave MK18. . . . . 41 E2
Hill Top Dr SL7. . . . . 183 B2
Hilltop Fst Sch SL4 . 209 E4
Hill Top La OX39 . . . 147 F4
Hilltop Rd HP4 . . . . . 135 C3
Hillview
Saunderton HP14 . . . 149 C1
Sherington MK16 . . . . 14 A1
Hill View
Berkhamsted HP4. . . 135 A6
Great Kimble HP17 . . 129 D1
Hedgerley SL2. . . . . . 187 D3
Newport Pagnell MK16 22 A3
Oakley HP18 . . . . 109 D5
Hillview Gdns HP13 173 D8
Hillview Rd HP13. . . 173 D8
Hill View Rd TW19. . 211 D1
Hillway MK17 . . . . 49 A6
Hill Way HP7. . . . . . . 165 B6
Hill Waye SL9. . . . . . . 188 F4
Hillwerke OX39 . . . . 147 C6
Hillyer Ct MK6 . . . . . . 35 C1
Hilperton Rd 3 SL1 205 E4
Hilton Ave HP20. . . . 101 E2
Hilton Cl UB8 . . . . . . 201 B3
Himley Gn LU7 . . . . . . 80 D6
Hindemith Gdns
MK7 . . . . 48 D5
Hinde Way MK46 . . . . . .6 E6
Hindhay La SL6 . . . . . 195 B3
Hindhead Knoll MK7 48 B6
Hinds Way HP21 . . . 115 B6
Hinkley Cl UB9. . . . . 190 C7
Hinksey Cl SL3. . . . . . 207 B3
Hinton Cl
East Claydon MK18 . . . .74 F8
High Wycombe HP13 . 162 A1
Hinton Crossing
OX39. . . . . 137 E4
Hinton Ct MK3 . . . . . . .46 F1
Hinton Rd
Slough SL1 . . . . 204 E6
Uxbridge UB8 . . . . . . 201 C4
Hipwell Ct MK46 . . . . . .6 F3
Hitcham Grange
SL6 . . . . 196 E1
Hitcham House SL1 197 A1
Hitcham La SL6, SL1 196 F2
Hitcham Rd SL1,
SL6 . . . . 204 A8
Hithercroft Rd
HP13. . . . . 161 E1
Hither Mdw SL9. . . . 177 E1
Hithermoor Rd
TW19 . . . . 213 A2
Hiving's Hill HP5 . . . 144 A2
Hivings Pk HP5 . . . . 144 B4
Hoathly Mews MK7. . 48 B8
Hobart Cl HP13 . . . . 162 E1
Hobart Cotts HP16 . 150 D8
Hobart Cres MK15. . . 35 B7
Hobart Ct SL7. . . . . . . 184 A3
Hobart Rd HP13. . . . 162 D1
Hobbis Dr SL6 . . . . . 202 A6
Hobbs Cl MK18. . . . . . 63 E3
Hobbshill Rd HP16 . 152 B6
Hobbs Rd HP14 . . . . 171 C4
Hobsons Wlk HP23 . 118 F5
Hockeridge View
HP4. . . . . 134 F3
Hocket The RG9. . . . 191 D3
Hockett La SL6. . . . . 195 A6
Hockley Bottom
HP3. . . . . 155 E6
Hockley La SL2 . . . . 199 B4
Hockliffe Brae MK7 . 48 C5
Hodder La MK4 . . . . . 46 C2
Hodds Wood Rd
HP5. . . . . 154 C6
Hodge Lea La MK12 . 33 D4
Hodgemoor View
Chalfont St Giles
HP8. . . . . 176 F7
Chalfont St Giles HP8 177 A7
Hodgemore Ct
MK14 . . . . .21 F2
Hodges Cl HP14. . . . 158 F4
Hodges Mews HP12 172 C6
Hoe Mdw HP9 . . . . . 175 C4
Hogarth Cl
Slough SL1 . . . . 204 E6
Uxbridge UB8 . . . . . . 201 C2
Hogback Wood Rd
HP9. . . . . 175 B4
Hogfair La SL1. . . . . . 197 C1
Hoggeston Rd MK18. 77 C6
Hogg La HP15. . . . . . 163 D6
Hog Hall La HP4. . . . 107 A5
Hog La
Ashley Green HP5 . . . 144 D8
Berkhamsted HP5. . . 134 C2
HOGPITS BOTTOM. . 156 B7
Hogpits Bottom
HP3. . . . . 156 B7
HOGSHAW HP22 . . . . . .74 F2
Hogshaw MK18 . . . . . 75 D1
Hogshaw Farm & Wildlife Centre*
MK18 . . . . 74 F3
Hogshaw Rd MK18 . . 75 E6
Hogtrough La
Great Missenden
HP16. . . . . 141 F8
Wendover HP22 . . . . 131 D2
Holborn Cres MK4. . . 57 A8
Holden Ave MK4 . . . . 45 E3
Holdom Ave MK1. . . . 47 D2
Holes La MK46 . . . . .6 F4
Holiday La MK19 . . . . .10 F4
Holland Cl
Chinnor OX39 . . . . . . 147 D7
Wendover HP22 . . . . 131 B4
Holland Rd
Aylesbury HP19. . . . . 101 B2
Marlow SL7. . . . . 183 F3
Hollandridge La
Christmas Common
OX49. . . . . 168 A8
Christmas Common
OX49, RG9. . . . . 168 D4
Holland Way MK16 . . 22 C3
Holland Wy 1 MK7. . 48 A5
Hollerith Cl MK10 . . . 35 D2
Holliday Cl MK8. . . . . 45 E7
Holliday St HP4 . . . . 135 D4
Hollies Ct LU7 . . . . . . 80 E7
Hollies The
Beaconsfield HP9 . . . 175 E3
Bovingdon HP3 . . . . . 146 A2
Tring HP23 . . . . 119 D1
HOLLINGDON 69 C3
Hollingdon Depot
LU7 . . . . 69 D3
Hollingdon Rd
Hollingdon LU7 . . . . . . 69 C3
Stewkley LU7 . . . . .68 F4
Hollington HP18 . . . . 125 B7
Hollin La MK12 . . . . . 33 E4
Hollinwell Cl 3 MK4 46 D1
Hollis Rd HP13 . . . . . 173 F8
Hollister Chase MK5. 46 B4
Holloway Cl UB7 . . . 208 E1
Holloway Dr MK18. . . 41 E2
Holloway La
Chenies WD3. . . . . . . 156 C2
Turville RG9. . . . . 169 F3
Turville Heath RG9 . . 169 C4
West Drayton UB7. . . 208 F1
Holloway The
Monks Risborough
HP27. . . . . 139 D5
Tring HP22, HP23 . . . 118 C4
Hollow Hill End
MK18 . . . . .75 F7
Hollow Hill La SL0. . 207 C5
Hollow La
Hambleden RG9 . . . . 181 F1
Mill End RG10 . . . . . . 192 F8
Hollow Rise HP13 . . . 162 B1
Hollow Way HP5 . . . 143 E1
Hollow Way La HP5,
HP6. . . . . 154 E4
Hollow Wood MK46 . . .6 E3
Hollyberry Gr HP15. 163 C7
Holly Blue Mws
HP19. . . . . 101 B4
Hollybrook Way
HP13. . . . . 162 F1
Hollybush Cnr SL2 . 187 C2
Hollybush Hill SL2. . 199 B5
Hollybush La
Amersham HP6. . . . . 154 D3
Cookham Dean SL6. . 195 B6
Denham UB9. . . . . . . 200 E8
Iver SL0, SL3. . . . . . . 207 B7
Hollybush Rd HP5. . 144 A4
Hollybush Row
HP23. . . . . 133 D8
Holly Cl
Farnham Common
SL2 . . . . 198 C8
Milton Keynes MK8 . . . 45 E6
Holly Cres SL4 . . . . . 209 D5
Holly Dr
Aylesbury HP21. . . . . 115 E6
Berkhamsted HP4. . . 135 D3
Maidenhead SL6. . . . 202 F8
Windsor SL4 . . . . 210 E2
Holly End HP14 . . . . 161 C8
Hollyfield HP23 . . . . 119 C5
Hollyfield Cl HP23. . 119 C5
Holly Gdns UB7 . . . . 208 F4
HOLLY GREEN. 138 A3
Holly Green La
HP27. . . . . 138 A3
Holly Hedges La
HP3. . . . . 156 C8
Holly Pl HP11 . . . . . . 174 A3
Hollytree Cl
Botley HP5 . . . . 155 B8
Chalfont St Peter SL9 177 E5
Holly Tree La HP18 . 112 F3
Holly Wlk MK17 . . . . . 49 B2
Holmanleaze SL6 . . 203 A8
Holman St HP19. . . . 101 C2
Holmedale SL2 . . . . 206 C6
HOLMER GREEN. . . . 163 D6
Holmer Green Fst Sch
HP15. . . . . 163 B7
Holmer Green Jun Sch
HP15. . . . . 163 D7
Holmer Green Rd
HP15. . . . . 163 A4
Holmer Green Senior
Sch HP15. . . . . 163 B7
Holmer Pl HP15. . . . 163 C7
Holmers Ct HP12. . . 172 B3
Holmers Farm Way
HP12. . . . . 172 C3
Holmers La HP12. . . 172 C3
Holmes Mdw MK14. . .21 F3
Holmewood MK4. . . . 46 E4
Holmfield Cl MK6 . . . 47 D5
Holmgate MK5. . . . . . 46 A8
Holmlea Rd SL3. . . . 211 D6
Holmlea Wlk SL3. . . 211 C6
Holmoak Wlk HP15. 163 B3
Holmsdale Cl SL0 . . 207 F7
Holmwood Cl SL6 . . 202 B5
Holmwood Sch 8
MK8 . . . . .33 F1
Holne Chase Prim Sch
MK3 . . . . 58 A7
Holsey La MK2 . . . . . . 58 E6
Holst Cres MK7 . . . . . 48 D4
Holstein Cres MK19 . 45 C7
Holt Ave MK10 . . . . . . 36 C4
Holt Gr MK5 . . . . 46 A8
HOLTON. 122 C2
Holton Hill MK4. . . . . 46 C2
Holton Rd MK18. . . . . 41 D2
Holts Gn MK17 . . . . . . 59 C1
HOLTSPUR 175 A1
Holtspur Ave HP10 . 185 F7
Holtspur Cl HP9. . . . 186 A8
Holtspur Ct HP9. . . . 186 A8
Holtspur La
Beaconsfield HP9 . . . 175 B3
Wooburn Green
HP10. . . . . 185 F6
Holtspur Par HP9 . . 186 A8
Holtspur Sch HP9 . . 175 A1
Holtspur Top La
HP9. . . . . 175 A2
Holtspur Way HP9. . 175 A1
Holt The MK18 . . . . . . 52 E7
Holy Family RC Sch
SL3 . . . . 206 F1
Holyhead Cres MK3 . 57 C8
Holyhead Mews
SL1 . . . . 204 D7
Holyport Rd SL6 . . . 203 B1
Holyrood MK8 . . . . . . 45 E8
Holy Thorn La MK5 . . 46 A5
Holy Trinity CE Prim Sch
SL6 . . . . 196 B7
Holy Trinity CE Sch
SL7 . . . . 183 D3
Holywell Ce(Va) Middle
Sch MK43. . . . . 25 B1
Holywell Gdns
HP13. . . . . 173 E7
Holywell Pl MK6 . . . . 35 C2
Holywell Rd MK43. . . 25 C1
Home Cl
Holton OX33 . . . . 122 B2
Milton Keynes MK3 . . . 47 B2
Shabbington HP18 . . 124 D3
Weston Turville HP22 116 F2
Home Ct MK10. . . . . . 36 A3
Home Farm
Newton Longville
MK17 . . . . 57 D4
Northchurch HP4 . . . 134 D7
Tring HP23 . . . . 118 F2
Home Farm Cl MK19. 31 E4
Homefarm Ct HP8. . 177 A7
Home Farm Ct
Bovingdon HP3 . . . . . 145 F1
Emberton MK46 . . . . . 13 E8
Home Farm La MK17 59 D2
Home Farm Rd
HP4. . . . . 134 D7
Home Farm Way
SL3 . . . . 199 C4
Homefield HP3 . . . . 146 B3
Home Field
Aylesbury HP19. . . . . 115 A7
Bow Brickhill MK7. . . . 48 B3
Homefield Cl HP14 . 158 E4
Homefield Rd WD3 . 167 D5
Homefield Wood Nature
Reserve SL7 . . . . . . 182 C2
Homeground MK18. . 52 E6
Homelands Gdns
HP15. . . . . 162 D8
Homelands Way
RG9. . . . . 191 D1
Homeleigh Terr
SL2 . . . . 206 A7
Home Mdw SL2 . . . . 198 C3
Home Meadow Dr
HP10. . . . . 185 B7
Homer Fst Sch SL4 209 D6
Homeridings Ho
MK13 . . . . 34 B4
Homers Rd SL4 . . . . 209 D6
Homerton St 1 MK3 58 B8
Homeside Cl SL6. . . . 195 E2
Homestall MK18 . . . . 52 D6
Homestall Cl MK5. . . 46 A7
Homestead Cl HP17 114 A4
Homestead La MK18. 63 C2
Homestead Pl 14
HP19. . . . . 115 A8
Homestead Rd SL6 202 D4
Homestead The
Great Kingshill
HP15. . . . . 151 D1
High Wycombe HP12 172 D3
Milton Keynes MK5 . . . 46 A6
Thame OX9 . . . . 125 E1
Homestead Way
NN12. . . . . 18 E3
Homeward Ct MK5 . . 46 B7
Home Way WD3. . . . 167 F1
Homewood SL3. . . . 206 D7
Home Wood SL7 . . . 193 F6
Homewood Ct WD3 167 F5
Honduras Gdns MK3. 58 B3
Honey Banks HP22 . 131 C4
HONEYBURGE
HP18. . . . . 109 A7
Honeycomb Wy
MK18 . . . . .52 F6
Honeycroft Hill
UB10. . . . . 201 E5
Honey Hill
Emberton MK46 . . . . . .13 F7
Uxbridge UB10 . . . . . 201 F5
Honey Hill Dr MK19. . 31 E5
Honey La SL6 . . . . . . 193 E2
Honeypin Dr 11
HP18. . . . . 100 D5
Honeypot Cl MK13. . . 34 B4
Honeysuckle Cl SL0 207 C7
Honeysuckle Ct SL3 212 C7
Honeysuckle Field
HP5. . . . . 144 C2
Honeysuckle Pl
HP22. . . . . 116 C3
Honeysuckle Rd
HP15. . . . . 162 F7
Honey Way HP14. . . 161 B8
HONEYWICK. 92 E8
Honeywick La LU6 . . 92 E8
Honiton Ct MK7 . . . . . 48 C7
Honor End La
Little Hampden
HP16. . . . . 140 F1
Prestwood HP16. . . . 151 A7
Honor Rd HP16 . . . . 151 D6
Honorwood Cl
HP16. . . . . 151 B6
Honour Cl HP20. . . . 102 A2
Honours Mead 4
HP3. . . . . 146 A4
Hoods Farm Cl
HP22. . . . . 102 C4
Hookes Mdw MK43. . 25 B2
Hooke The MK15. . . . 35 D7
Hooks La
Great Marlow SL7. . . 182 E1
Great Marlow SL7. . . 193 F8
Marlow SL7. . . . . 194 A8
Hooper Gate MK15 . . 35 C7
Hopcraft Cl OX25. . . . 94 E7
Hopcrofts Mdw
MK14 . . . . .21 F3
Hope Brook Cotts
LU7 . . . . .91 F2
Hop Gdns RG9 . . . . . 191 D2
Hopkins Cl MK10. . . . 36 A2
Hopkins Ct HP20. . . . 101 F2
Hopkins Rd MK17 . . . 58 B2
Hoppers Hill MK46 . . . .6 F5
Hoppers Mdw MK5. . 46 A8
Hoppers Way HP15 162 D8
Hops Rd HP22. . . . . . 102 D4
Hopton Gr MK16 . . . . .22 F3
Hopton Rd OX9 . . . . 126 A1
Hordern Cl HP17. . . 126 F6
Hornbeam MK16 . . . . 22 A3
Hornbeam Cl
Frieth RG9. . . . . 170 F1
High Wycombe HP12. 172 B4
Hornbeam Gdns 5
SL1 . . . . 206 A3
Hornbeam Way
HP22. . . . . 116 C4
Hornbeam Wlk
HP15. . . . . 163 A3
Hornbill Cl UB8 . . . . 208 D7
Hornby Chase MK4. . 46 B2
Hornchurch Rd 1
UB10. . . . . 201 E4
Horners Croft MK12 . 33 C5
HORN HILL 178 B6
Hornhill Rd WD3 . . . 178 D5
Horn La MK11. . . . . . . 32 D5
Horns La
High Wycombe
HP12. . . . . 172 A3
Princes Risborough
HP27. . . . . 139 B3
Horn St MK18 . . . . .65 F4
Horseblock La HP4. 133 E2
Horsebuck La HP23 133 E3
Horse Croft Cl SL9 . 177 B6
Horsefair Gn MK11 . . 32 D5
Horseguards Dr
SL6 . . . . 203 B7
Horse Hill HP5 . . . . . 155 D7
Horsemead Piece
MK18 . . . . .65 F4
Horsemoor Cl SL3. . 207 A2
Horsemoor La
Winchmore Hill
HP7. . . . . 164 B3
Winchmore Hill HP7 . 164 C2
HORSENDEN. 138 E2
Horsenden La HP27 138 F2
Horsenden Rd HP13 173 F5
Horsepond MK17. . . . 59 C2
Horsepool La MK17. . .49 F4
Horseshoe Cl
Cheddington HP23 . . 104 F8
Cheddington LU7. . . . 105 A7
Horseshoe Cloisters 3
SL4 . . . . 210 D6
Horseshoe Cres
HP9. . . . . 175 F1
Horseshoe Hill SL1. 197 C8
Horseshoe Rd HP14 159 C7
Horseshoes Cl HP18. 83 A6
Horsetone Bglws
HP17. . . . . 129 D2
Horsham Reach
SL6 . . . . 196 C2
Horsley Rd SL6. . . . . 195 E2
Horsleys WD3. . . . . . 178 D5
HORSLEYS GREEN . . 159 C3
Horsleys Green Rd
HP14. . . . . 159 C3
HORTON
Cheddington 91 B3
Wraysbury 212 A4
Horton Bridge Rd
UB7. . . . . 208 F5
Horton Cl
Aylesbury HP19. . . . . 115 A7
Maidenhead SL6. . . . 196 C1
West Drayton UB7. . . 208 F5
HORTON-CUM-
STUDLEY. 108 B6
Horton Depot SL3 . . 212 C4
Horton Gate MK14. . . .21 F2
Horton Gdns SL3. . . 211 F4
Horton Grange SL6. 196 C1
Horton Ind Pk UB7 . 208 F5
Horton Par UB7 . . . . 208 E5
Horton Rd
Datchet SL3. . . . . 211 C6
Datchet SL3. . . . . 211 D6
Horton SL3 . . . . 212 A6
Ivinghoe LU7. . . . . 91 A2
Ivinghoe LU7. . . . . . . 105 D7
Poyle SL3 . . . . 212 E4
Slapton LU7. . . . . 91 C6
Stanwell TW19 . . . . . 213 A2
West Drayton UB7. . . 208 F5
Horton Road Ind Est
UB7. . . . . 208 F5
Hortonsfield Rd
NN12. . . . . .18 F5
Horton Trad Est
SL3 . . . . 212 B4
HORTON WHARF 91 C4
Horton Wharf Rd
LU7 . . . . 91 C3
Horwood Cl HP22 . . 117 B5
Horwood Ct MK1. . . . 47 D2
Horwood Mill MK17 . 55 A3
Hospital Hill HP5 . . . 154 C7
Hospital Rdbt MK6 . . 47 B6
Hotch Croft MK43 . . . 25 C3
HOTLEY BOTTOM. . . 151 C8
Hotley Bottom La
HP16. . . . . 151 C8
Hotspur Bank Nature
Reserve HP9. . . . . . 174 F1
Hotspur Cl HP17 . . . 126 E6
Houghton Ct 3 MK8. .45 F8
Hounslow Cl LU7 . . 118 E3
Housman Cl MK16. . . 22 A5
Houston Ct 6 SL4. . 210 C5
Howard Agne Cl
HP3. . . . . 146 A4
Howard Ave
Aylesbury HP21. . . . . 116 B6
Slough SL2 . . . . 205 E8
Howard Cres HP9 . . 176 D5
Howard Ct 1 SL8 . . 185 A3
Howard Ind Est
HP5. . . . . 144 C2
Howard Mews SL3 . 212 B8
Howard Rd
Chesham HP5 . . . . . . 144 B3
Seer Green HP9 . . . . 176 D5
Howards Thicket
SL9 . . . . 188 C2
Howards Wood Dr
SL9 . . . . 188 D2
Howard Way MK16 . . 23 A3
Howarth Rd SL6. . . . 203 A6
Howcutt La NN7. . . . . . .1 A5
Howe Ct MK10 . . . . . . 36 A3
Howe Dr HP9 . . . . . . 175 E5
Howe Hill La HP15. . 163 B8
Howell Hill Cl LU7. . . 90 D5
Howe Mews MK17. . . 58 B2
Howe Park Sch MK4. 46 B1
Howe Rock Pl MK4 . 46 B1
Howe St HP22. . . . . . 116 D7
Howgate St HP18 . . 100 E4
Howitt Dr MK13 . . . . . 34 B8
Howland Pl MK17 . . . .60 F7
Howletts Cl HP19. . . 115 A7
How's Cl UB8 . . . . . . 201 C4
How's Rd UB8. . . . . . 201 C4
Hoylake Cl
Milton Keynes MK3 . . . 57 D7
Slough SL1 . . . . 204 E4
Hoyton Gate MK8 . . . 45 D6
Hubbard Cl MK18 . . . .41 F1
Hubbards Ct WD3 . . 167 D4
Hubbards Rd WD3. . 167 D4
Hubert Day Cl HP9 . 175 D3
Hubert Rd SL3 . . . . . 206 D3
Huckleberry Cl MK7. 48 B6
Hudge Furlong MK18 65 E5
Hudnall Common
HP4. . . . . 121 F7
Hudnall La HP4 . . . . 121 E7
Hudson La MK8 . . . . . 45 D7
Hudson Mews HP19 100 E1
Hudson Pl 13 SL3. . . 206 F1
Hughenden Ave
High Wycombe
HP13. . . . . 161 F1
High Wycombe HP13. 173 A8
Hughenden Bvd
High Wycombe
HP13. . . . . 162 A1
High Wycombe HP13 173 A8
Hughenden Cl SL6 . 202 C6
Hughenden Ct UB8. 201 C1
Hughenden Gn 2
HP21. . . . . 115 E4
Hughenden Manor*
HP14. . . . . 162 A3
Hughenden Pl HP15 151 F1
Hughenden Prim Sch
HP14. . . . . 162 A7
Hughenden Rd
High Wycombe
HP13. . . . . 162 B1
Slough SL1 . . . . 205 D7
HUGHENDEN
VALLEY 162 B7
Hughenden View
HP13. . . . . 173 B8
Hughes Croft 3 MK3 57 F7
Hugh Park Cl MK5. . . 46 C8
Hulbert End HP21 . . 116 D5
Hulcombe Wlk
HP20. . . . . 101 E2
HULCOTE. 37 E2
HULCOTT
102 E6
Hulcott HP22. . . . . . . 102 D6
Hulcott La HP22. . . . 102 D5
Hull Cl
Aylesbury HP21. . . . . 115 E6
Slough SL1 . . . . 205 C4
Hullwell Gate
Walton MK7 . . . . .47 F5
Walton MK7 . . . . 48 A5
Hulme End 3 MK10 . 36 C3
Hulse Cl MK46 . . . . .7 F7
Hulton Dr MK46 . . . . . .13 F8
Humber Cl UB7 . . . . 208 D5
Humber Dr HP21 . . . 115 C5
Humber Way
Milton Keynes MK3 . . . 46 E1
Slough SL3 . . . . 207 A2
Hume Cl MK13 . . . . . . 34 B7
Humphreys Cl HP22 . 88 D5
Humphrey Talbot Ave
LU6 . . . . 107 F7
Hundred Acres La
HP7. . . . . 165 D8
Hungerford Ave
SL2 . . . . 205 E8
Hungerford Dr SL6. 195 E3
Hungerford Ho 1
MK4 . . . . 46 D1
Hunsbury Chase
MK10 . . . . 36 A3
Hunsdon Cl MK14 . . . 34 D6
Hunsford Lodge
SL4 . . . . 210 A4
Hunstanton Cl SL3 . 212 C7
Hunstanton Way
MK3 . . . . 57 D8
Hunt Ct HP14 . . . . . . 158 F4
Huntercombe Cl
SL1 . . . . 204 C7
Huntercombe Hospl The
SL6 . . . . 204 C6
Huntercombe Lane N
SL6 . . . . 204 C7
Huntercombe Lane S
SL6 . . . . 204 C6
Huntercombe Spur
SL6 . . . . 204 C6
Hunter Ct SL1. . . . . . 204 C8
Hunter Dr MK2. . . . . . 58 C6
Hunters Cl
Bovingdon HP3 . . . . . 146 A2
Chesham HP5 . . . . . . 144 A1
Tring HP23 . . . . 119 B5

Hunters Farm Ind Est
HP18 . . . . 100 B5
Hunters Hill HP13 . . . 173 F5
Hunters Mews SL4 . . 210 C6
Hunters Pk HP4 . . . . 135 E5
Hunters Point OX39 147 C6
Hunters Reach MK13 34 A3
Hunter St MK18 . . . . . 52 C8
Hunters Way
  Aston Abbotts LU7 . . . 88 D4
  Slough SL1 . . . . 204 E4
HUNTGATE END 10 D2
Huntingbrooke **6**
  MK8 . . . . .45 F8
Huntingdon Cres
  MK3 . . . . 57 D6
Huntington Pl SL3 . . . 207 B3
Huntley Cl HP13 . . . . 162 C2
Huntley Cres MK9 . . . 35 A3
Hunt Rd HP13 . . . . . . 173 E6
HUNT'S HILL 161 D5
Hunts Hill La HP14 . . 161 E5
Hunt's La SL6 . . . . . . 196 E3
Huntsman Gr MK14. . . 22 A2
Huntsmans Cl HP4 . . 107 C5
Huntswood La SL6,
  SL1 . . . . 196 F4
Hurdlesgrove Hill
  HP22. . . . . 77 A3
HURLEY 193 E4
Hurley Croft MK10 . . . 36 B1
Hurley La SL1 . . . . . . 194 B3
Hurlstone Gr MK4. . . . 46 D3
Hurricane Way SL3. . 207 B1
HURST END 24 A3
Hurstfield Dr SL6 . . . 204 B7
Hurstleigh WD3. . . . . 167 C4
Hurst Rd SL1. . . . . . . 204 D8
Hurworth Ave SL3. . . 206 C3
Hutchings Cl MK5. . . . 46 A8
Hutchings Rd HP9. . . 175 D5
Hutton Ave MK6. . . . . 34 F1
Hutton Ct MK17. . . . . . 49 B5
Hutton Way MK17 . . . . 49 B5
Huxley Cl
  Newport Pagnell
  MK16 . . . . 21 F4
  Slough SL3 . . . . 199 B1
  Uxbridge UB8 . . . . . . 201 D1
Huxtable Gdns SL6 . . 203 E1
Hyacinth Dr UB10 . . . 201 E5
Hychenden Cl HP14 . 161 E6
Hyde Cl MK16. . . . . . . 22 C2
HYDE END 152 F7
Hyde Gn
  Beaconsfield HP9 . . . 175 F3
  Marlow SL7. . . . . 183 F1
HYDE HEATH. 153 C5
Hyde Heath Inf Sch
  HP6. . . . . 153 C5
Hyde Heath Rd HP6,
  HP10. . . . . 153 A6
Hyde La
  Bovingdon HP3 . . . . . 146 A3
  South Heath HP16. . . 152 E5
Hyde Mdws HP3. . . . . 146 A4
Hyde St HP22 . . . . . . 117 C5
Hyde The HP22. . . . . . 116 F2
Hyland Ho **9** SL8 . . . 185 B3
Hylle Cl SL4 . . . . 209 E6
Hylton Rd HP12 . . . . . 172 C7
Hyrons Cl HP6 . . . . . 154 E1
Hyrons La HP6 . . . . . 154 D1
Hythe The MK8. . . . . . 33 E3
Hyton Sq HP19 . . . . . 101 D4

I

Ibotson Ct SL3 . . . . . 212 E6
IBSTONE 169 D7
Ibstone Ave MK13 . . . 34 D4
Ibstone Ce Prim Sch
  HP14. . . . . 169 D6
Ibstone Rd
  Fingest RG9 . . . . 170 A3
  Ibstone HP14 . . . . . . 169 E5
  Stokenchurch HP14. . 158 C3
Icehouse La RG9 . . . 191 D7
ICKENHAM 190 F1
ICKFORD 124 A3
Ickford Rd
  Shabbington HP18 . . 124 C2
  Tiddington-with-Albury
  OX33. . . . . 123 F1
  Worminghall HP18 . . . 123 E6
Ickford Sch HP18. . . . 124 A3
Icknield Cl
  Chinnor OX39 . . . . . . 147 A4
  Wendover HP22 . . . . 131 C5
Icknield Cotts HP17 129 F2
Icknield Gdns **6**
  LU7 . . . . 105 C4
Icknield Gn HP23. . . . 119 A6
Icknield Way
  Dunstable LU6. . . . . . 93 D4
  Edlesborough LU6. . . 106 F8
  Tring HP23 . . . . 118 E4
Icknield Way Farm Cotts
  LU6 . . . . 93 C3
Icknield Way Ind Est
  HP23. . . . . 118 E4
Idaho Pk HP16 . . . . . 151 B6
Idaho St HP18. . . . . . 100 E4

Ideal Ho **3** HP20. . . . 115 E8
Iffley Cl UB8 . . . . . . 201 D5
Ilchester Cl SL6. . . . 202 C5
Ilex Cl HP15. . . . . 163 B3
Ilex Ct HP4 . . . . 135 B4
Illingworth SL4 . . . . 209 E4
Illingworth Pl MK6 . . 46 F8
Illustrious MK10 . . . . 36 B5
ILMER 137 F8
Ilmer La
  Bledlow HP27 . . . . . 138 D1
  Ilmer HP17 . . . . 137 F8
  Owlswick HP27 . . . . 138 B1
Imperial Ct
  Henley-on-Thames
  RG9 . . . . 191 E1
  Loudwater HP10 . . . . 174 C2
  Windsor SL4 . . . . . . 210 A4
Imperial Rd SL4. . . . 210 A5
Ince Wy MK4. . . . . 56 E8
Independent Bsns Pk
  HP14. . . . . 158 C5
India Rd SL1 . . . . . . 206 B4
Ingleglen SL2 . . . . . . 198 B7
Ingleside SL3 . . . . . . 212 F6
Ingleton Cl MK13. . . . 34 C4
Ingram Ave HP21. . . . 116 C5
Inkerman Dr HP15. . . 163 B5
Inkerman Rd SL4. . . . 204 F2
Inkerman Terr HP5. . 154 C6
Innes Ct MK8. . . . . . . 45 D6
Inn Farm Ct MK16 . . . 22 D7
Innholder Ct MK14. . . 34 F6
Innings Gate RG9 . . . 170 E1
Innings Rd RG9 . . . . 170 E1
Inniscrown Ho SL3 . 211 B7
Innkeepers Ct HP27 138 D7
Inns Cl MK18. . . . . . . 63 E3
Institute Rd
  Marlow SL7. . . . . 183 E1
  Taplow SL6 . . . . 203 F7
Intalbury Ave HP17 . . 101 A2
Interchange Pk MK16 22 F3
In the Ray SL6. . . . . 203 B8
Inverness Cl MK3. . . . 46 F2
Invicta Rd HP18. . . . . 100 C5
Inwood Cl SL6 . . . . . 195 B6
Iona Cres SL1 . . . . . 204 E7
Ipswich Rd
  Slough SL1 . . . . 204 F7
  Slough SL1 . . . . 205 A7
Iqra Islamic Prim Sch
  SL2 . . . . 206 B6
Ireland Cl MK7. . . . . . 48 D4
Ireton Ct OX9 . . . . . . 125 F1
Iris Cl HP21 . . . . 115 B5
Iris Ct HP20. . . . . 116 B8
Ironmonger Ct MK14 .34 F6
Irvine Dr HP22 . . . . . 116 A2
Irvine Ho SL4 . . . . . . 209 E5
Irving Cres LU7 . . . . 105 A8
Irving Dale MK7. . . . . 48 E5
Isaacson Dr MK7. . . . 48 C7
Isis Cl HP21 . . . . 115 D3
Isis Way SL8 . . . . . . 185 B4
Isis Wlk MK3. . . . . . . 46 E1
Island Ho UB7. . . . . . 213 B6
Island The
  Harmondsworth
  TW6 . . . . 213 C7
  Steeple Claydon MK18 63 D2
Islay Ct MK17 . . . . . . 58 C3
Isle of Wight La LU6 .93 F4
Islet Park Dr SL6 . . . 196 C3
Islet Park Ho SL6. . . 196 C3
Islet Pk SL6. . . . . . . 196 C3
Islet Rd SL6. . . . . . . 196 C3
Isling Brook MK5. . . . 46 B3
Islington Gr **6** MK10 .35 F1
Itter La MK18 . . . . . . 73 B5
Ivanhoe Cl UB8 . . . . 208 D8
IVER 207 F7
Iver Ct MK18. . . . . 52 C7
Iverdale Cl SL0. . . . . 207 C6
IVER HEATH 200 D4
Iver Heath Inf Sch
  SL0 . . . . 200 D2
Iver Heath Jun Sch
  SL0 . . . . 200 D3
Iver La SL0. . . . . 208 A8
Iver Lodge SL0. . . . . 207 F8
Ivernia Ave MK10. . . . 36 B6
Iver Sta SL0. . . . . . . 207 F7
Iver Village Inf Sch
  SL0 . . . . 207 F7
Iver Village Jun Sch
  SL0 . . . . 207 E7
Ives Rd SL3 . . . . 207 A3
Ivester Ct LU7. . . . . . 80 E6
Ivin Cl HP17. . . . . . . 127 B5
IVINGHOE 105 F5
Ivinghoe Aston
  Ivinghoe LU7. . . . . . . .91 F1
  Ivinghoe LU7. . . . . . 106 B8
  Northall LU6. . . . . 92 A6
Ivinghoe Aston Rd
  LU7. . . . . 91 D4
Ivinghoe View HP20 101 F1
Ivinghoe Way LU6. . . 92 E1
Ivingswood Acad
  HP5. . . . . 144 B3
Ivins Rd HP9 . . . . . . 175 A1
Ivybridge Cl UB8 . . . 201 E2
Ivy Cl
  Buckingham MK18 . . .41 E8
  Chesham HP5 . . . . . . 144 A1
  Longwick HP27 . . . . 138 E5

Ivy Cl continued
  Newport Pagnell MK16 22 E4
Ivy Cotts HP8 . . . . . . 177 B8
Ivy Cres SL1 . . . . . . 204 F6
Ivyhill Ct HP27 . . . . . 139 B3
Ivy House La HP4 . . . 135 E5
Ivy La
  Bierton HP22 . . . . . . 102 D1
  Burcott LU7. . . . . 79 D4
  Great Brickhill MK17. . 70 C8
  Newton Longville
  MK17 . . . . 57 C3
  Stewkley LU7 . . . . . . 68 E1
Ivy Pl HP14 . . . . 171 C5

J

Jackdaw Pl HP10. . . . 173 D3
Jacks Cl MK46 . . . . . . .7 E7
Jack's La MK43 . . . . . . 8 E5
Jackson Cl
  Slough SL3 . . . . 206 E3
  Uxbridge UB10 . . . . 201 E5
Jackson Ct HP15. . . . 163 A3
Jackson Ind Est SL8 185 B2
Jackson Pl **6** HP22 131 D6
Jackson Rd
  Aylesbury HP19 . . . . 101 A3
  Uxbridge UB10 . . . . 201 E5
Jacksons Cl LU6 . . . . 92 E4
Jacob MK18 . . . . 41 E2
Jacob Cl SL4 . . . . . . 209 E6
Jacob Gr **5** MK19 . . . 45 D8
Jacobs Cl MK14 . . . . 34 D7
Jakeman Way HP21 115 B6
Jakes Ho SL6 . . . . . . 203 A8
Jamaica MK6 . . . . 47 A6
James Cl
  Hazlemere HP15. . . . 163 A6
  Marlow SL7. . . . . 183 F4
James Elliman Sch
  SL2 . . . . 205 E2
James Martin Cl
  UB9. . . . . 190 A5
James Mdw SL3. . . . 211 F8
Jameson Cl SL2. . . . 205 F6
James Rd HP14 . . . . 171 B4
James St SL4 . . . . . . 210 D6
James Way MK1. . . . . 47 B1
Jane Cl HP21 . . . . . . 116 A4
Janes Way HP14 . . . 161 C8
Jannetta Cl HP20. . . 116 B7
Jansel Sq HP21 . . . . 116 B6
Japonica La MK15. . . 35 C6
Jardine Cotts SL2 . . 199 A8
Jarman Cl MK18 . . . . .52 F8
Jarrett Ho SL4 . . . . . 210 B4
Jarry Ct SL7 . . . . 183 F3
Jarvis Cl HP21 . . . . . 116 A4
Jasmine Cl HP21. . . . 116 A4
Jasmine Cres HP27. 139 B3
Jasmine Wlk HP5 . . . 144 A1
Jason Ho SL2. . . . . . 172 E4
Jasons Hill HP5. . . . 145 B2
Jazz Rd HP19 . . . . . . 100 E6
Jeannie Arm Rd **2**
  HP22. . . . . 131 D6
Jeeves Cl MK6. . . . . . 47 C7
Jefferies Rd HP17. . . 114 B5
Jefferson Cl SL3 . . . 207 A2
Jeffrey Wlk HP19. . . . 115 A7
Jeffries Cl SL8 . . . . . 185 B2
Jellicoe Cl SL1. . . . . 205 B4
Jemima Way SL3. . . . 58 B8
Jenkins Cl MK5. . . . . .45 F5
Jenkins Ct HP22 . . . . 89 C3
Jenkins La HP23 . . . 132 E3
Jenna Way MK16. . . . 23 A3
Jenner Rd HP21. . . . 115 E5
Jennery La SL1 . . . . 197 C2
Jenney Cres LU7 . . . 118 E3
Jennings MK14 . . . . . 34 C7
Jennings Field
  HP10. . . . . 185 C7
Jennings Wharf
  SL4 . . . . 210 D7
Jennys La HP4 . . . . . 134 D8
Jerome Cl SL7. . . . . . 183 F4
Jerome Wy
  Shenley Brook End
  MK4 . . . . 56 E8
  3 Shenley Brook End
  MK4 . . . . .56 F8
Jersey Dr MK17 . . . . 58 C3
Jersey Rd MK12 . . . . 33 C6
Jersey Way MK19 . . . 33 C1
Jesse's La HP18. . . . 125 D6
Job's La SL6. . . . . . . 195 B8
John Bradbury La
  HP22. . . . . 116 A2
John Colet Sch
  HP22. . . . . 131 C5
John Fitzjohn Ave
  HP18. . . . . 100 D4
John Hall Way
  HP11. . . . . 172 D3
John Hampden
  Grammar Sch
  HP11. . . . . 172 F4
John Hampden Sch
  HP21. . . . . 131 B5
John Hampden Way
  HP16. . . . . 151 B7
John Hellins Prim Sch
  NN12. . . . . 18 D3
John Horncapps La
  MK17 . . . . 59 C3

John Locke Acad
  UB10. . . . . 201 E5
John Mills Cl UB9 . . 189 F5
John North Cl HP11 172 F4
John Rawbone Cl
  MK18 . . . . .65 F5
Johns La HP5 . . . . . . 134 E1
Johnson Field MK46. . .6 E4
Johnson St HP22. . . . 102 D2
Johnston Pl MK6. . . . 46 E4
John Taylor Cl SL1. . 205 C5
John Watson Sch
  OX33. . . . . 122 B1
Joiner's Cl
  Botley HP5 . . . . 145 B1
  Chalfont St Peter SL9 177 F3
Joiners La SL9 . . . . . 177 F3
Joiners La SL9 . . . . . 177 E3
Joiners Way
  Chalfont St Peter
  SL9. . . . . 177 E3
  Lavendon MK46 . . . . . .7 F8
Jonathan Ct SL6 . . . 202 E7
Jonathans Cl MK6. . . 47 A6
Jonathans Ct MK6. . . 47 A6
Jones Way
  Beacon's Bottom
  HP14. . . . . 159 C2
  Hedgerley SL2. . . . . 187 E2
Joplin Ct MK8. . . . . . .45 F7
JORDANS 176 F3
Jordans La HP9 . . . . 176 E3
Jordans Sch HP9. . . . 176 F4
Jordans Way HP9. . . 176 F3
Joseph Seamon Scl
  HP22. . . . . 116 A2
Joules Cl MK5 . . . . . . 46 C5
Jourdelay's Pas
  SL4 . . . . 210 D8
Journeys End SL2. . . 205 E8
Jubilee Cotts MK18. . .64 F3
Jubilee Farm Rd
  Hillesden MK18 . . . . . 62 E7
  Hillesden MK18 . . . . . 63 A8
Jubilee Gdns LU7 . . . 118 F3
Jubilee La SL6 . . . . . 203 C8
Jubilee Rd
  High Wycombe
  HP11. . . . . 172 E7
  High Wycombe, Downley
  HP13. . . . . 161 E2
  Stokenchurch HP14. . 158 F3
Jubilee Terr MK11 . . . 32 E5
Jubilee Way
  Datchet SL3. . . . . . . 211 C7
  Holmer Green HP15 . 163 D6
Jubilee Wood Prim Sch
  MK6 . . . . 34 F1
Judge's La LU7. . . . . .80 F6
Julius Pl MK11 . . . . . 33 A2
Jumelle Mews **4**
  HP13. . . . . 162 A1
Juniper Cl
  Chesham HP5 . . . . . . 144 B1
  Hazlemere HP15. . . . 163 B3
Juniper Ct
  Flackwell Heath
  HP10. . . . . 185 C7
  Rickmansworth WD3. 167 C3
  Slough SL1 . . . . 204 E6
  Slough SL1 . . . . 206 B4
Juniper Dr
  Aylesbury HP22. . . . . 116 C4
  High Wycombe HP12 172 C5
  Maidenhead SL6. . . . 203 B8
Juniper Gdns MK7 . . 48 B7
Juniper Hill Sch
  HP10. . . . . 185 B7
Juniper La HP10 . . . . 185 D7
Juniper Rd SL7. . . . . 183 D5
Juno La MK11. . . . . . . 33 A2
Jupiter Cl HP19 . . . . 100 E6
Jupiter Gdns MK17. . 36 E3
Jupiter Hts UB10. . . . 201 F4
Jura Way MK3 . . . . . . 58 B4
Juson's Glebe HP22 131 C5
Jutland Ho SL4 . . . . . 209 F5

K

Kalman Gdns MK7. . . 48 D5
Kaplan Cl MK5 . . . . . 46 B5
Karenza HP14. . . . . . 158 E5
Katherine Cl
  Tylers Green HP10 . . 174 C8
  Walton MK7 . . . . 48 A4
Katrine Pl MK2. . . . . . 58 D7
Kaybridge Cl **1**
  HP13. . . . . 173 F5
Kay Cl HP23 . . . . 119 A5
Kay Gr MK14 . . . . 34 C8
Kaywood Cl SL3. . . . 206 C3
Keach Cl MK18. . . . . . 66 A5
Keasden Ct MK4 . . . . 46 B2
Keaton Cl MK8 . . . . . 45 D7
Keats Cl
  Aylesbury HP21. . . . . 115 F6
  High Wycombe HP11. 172 F6
  Newport Pagnell MK16 22 A4
Keats La SL4 . . . . . . 210 C8
Keats Mws **16** SL6. . 202 F6
Keats Way
  Bletchley MK3. . . . . . 58 A7
  2 Milton Keynes MK3 .57 F7
  West Drayton UB7. . . 208 F2
Keble Cl HP19 . . . . . 115 B8

Keble Rd SL6 . . . . . . 202 E8
Keeler Cl SL4 . . . . . . 209 E4
Keel Dr SL1 . . . . 205 C4
Keele Cl SL4 . . . . . . 209 E4
Keel Way MK4 . . . . . . 45 D3
Keen Cl HP19 . . . . . . 115 A8
Keen Pl HP22 . . . . . . 117 E6
Keensacre SL0. . . . . 200 D3
Keen's Acre SL2 . . . 199 A5
Keen's Cl HP13. . . . . 162 E1
Keens
  Chinnor OX39 . . . . . . 147 D6
  Chinnor OX39 . . . . . . 147 E6
Keepers Cl LU7 . . . . 105 A7
Keepers Farm Cl
  SL4 . . . . 209 E5
Keepers La HP6,
  HP7. . . . . 153 C3
Keepers St HP22 . . . 102 C2
Keep Hill Dr HP11 . . 173 D5
Keep Hill Rd HP11. . . 173 D5
Keepsake Way **3**
  HP18. . . . . 100 C5
Keighley Cl **3** MK10. .35 F4
Keightley Gate MK17 .36 F1
Keinches La HP22 . . . 87 A6
Keith Park Rd UB10 201 F5
Kellan Dr MK6 . . . . . . 35 A1
Keller Cl MK11. . . . . . 33 B2
Kellett St UB10. . . . . 201 E4
Kelling Way **3** MK10 36 A4
Kelly Gdns MK4 . . . . 45 E3
Kelly Rd HP11. . . . . . 173 C4
Kelpatrick Rd SL1. . . 204 D7
Kelsale Chase **5**
  MK6 . . . . 47 C4
Kelsey Cl
  Maidenhead SL6. . . . 202 D3
  Milton Keynes MK4. . .56 F8
Kelso Cl MK3 . . . . 57 D6
Kelvin Cl HP13 . . . . . 172 F8
Kelvin Ct HP13 . . . . . 172 F8
Kelvin Dr MK5 . . . . . . 46 D6
Kemble Cl MK15 . . . . 35 B6
Kempe Cl SL3. . . . . . 207 C2
Kempson Cl
  Aylesbury HP19 . . . . 101 B1
  Aylesbury HP19 . . . . 115 B8
Kemps Piece **2**
  HP17. . . . . 127 A6
Kempster Way
  HP20. . . . . 116 D7
Kempton Gdns MK3 52 D6
Kemsall Rise LU7 . . . 79 E2
Kemsley Chase SL2 198 D4
Kemsley Cres MK10. 36 A4
Kenbury Dr SL1 . . . . 204 F4
Kenchester MK13 . . . 33 F5
Kendal Cl
  Aylesbury HP21. . . . . 116 B6
  Slough SL2 . . . . 206 A6
Kendal Dr SL2 . . . . . 206 A6
Kendal Gdns LU7. . . . 80 C7
Kendal Green Dr **2**
  SL9 . . . . 195 D2
Kendall Pl
  Maidenhead SL6. . . . 202 C4
  Milton Keynes MK5 . . 45 E5
Kendalls Cl HP13. . . . 173 F6
Kendal Mews UB8. . . 201 C4
Kendrick Ave HP9. . . 176 B1
Kendrick Rd SL3 . . . 207 B3
Kenelm St MK18 . . . . 52 B8
Kenilworth Cl SL1. . . 205 F3
Kenilworth Dr
  Aylesbury HP19. . . . . 101 D2
  Milton Keynes MK3. . . 57 E8
Kennards Ct HP6. . . 154 E1
Kenneally SL4 . . . . . 209 C5
Kenneally Cl **11** SL4 209 C5
Kenneally Pl **9** SL4 209 C5
Kenneally Row **13**
  SL4 . . . . 209 C5
Kenneally Wlk **10**
  SL4 . . . . 209 C5
Kennedy Ave HP11 173 B5
Kennedy Cl
  Farnham Common
  SL2 . . . . 198 C6
  Maidenhead SL6. . . . 202 C6
  Marlow SL7. . . . . 183 E3
Kennedy Ct LU7. . . . .80 F7
Kennedy Ho SL1 . . . 204 D5
Kennel La
  Cookham SL6 . . . . . . 195 D7
  Cookham Dean SL6. . 195 C7
  Whaddon MK17. . . . . 56 B8
  Whaddon MK4. . . . . . 45 B1
Kennels Dr
  Paulerspury NN12. . . 17 D3
  Potterspury NN12. . . 17 E3
Kennet Cl
  Aylesbury HP21. . . . . 115 C4
  High Wycombe HP13 162 D2
Kennet Dr MK3. . . . . . 57 E2
Kennet Pl MK3. . . . . . .57 F7
Kennet Rd
  Bourne End SL8. . . . 185 B4
  Bourne End SL8. . . . 202 F8
Kennett Rd SL3 . . . . 207 B3
Kennington Cl
  MK16 . . . . 22 C3
Kennish Cl MK18. . . . .65 F4
Kenny Ball Ave MK17 48 E8
Kensal Gn MK10. . . . 35 E1
Kensal Gn Dr SL9. . . 195 D1
Kensington Dr
  Great Holm MK8 . . . . 46 A8
  Milton Keynes MK8. . 33 F1

Kensington Mws
  SL4 . . . . 210 C4
Kensington Path **3**
  HP19. . . . . 100 F1
Kensington Pl MK46. .6 F5
Kent Ave SL1 . . . . . . 205 C8
Kent Cl UB8. . . . . 201 C6
Kent Ho MK3. . . . . . . .46 F2
Kentish St HP18. . . . 100 E4
Kent Lodge **6** SL6 . 202 F6
Kentmere Rd HP21. . 116 B7
Kenton Cl SL7. . . . . . 183 E2
Kenton Ct HP19 . . . . 101 C2
Kenton's La SL4. . . . 209 F5
KENTS HILL. 48 A7
Kents Hill Park Rdbt
  MK10 . . . . 47 E8
Kents Hill Park Sch
  MK7 . . . . 48 A7
Kents Hill Rdbt MK10 47 F8
Kents Hill Sch MK7. . 48 A7
Kents Rd MK14 . . . . . 34 D8
Kent Way SL6. . . . . . 195 E1
Kenway Dr HP7 . . . . 166 B8
Kenwell Ct MK15. . . . 35 C3
Kenwood Cl SL6 . . . 202 A7
Kenwood Dr WD3. . . 178 F8
Kenwood Gate MK6. . 35 B2
Kenyon Way SL2 . . . 206 F3
Keppel Ave MK19 . . . 20 D2
Keppel St SL4 . . . . . 210 D5
Kepwick MK8. . . . . . . 33 E1
Kercroft MK8 . . . . 33 E2
Kernal Cl MK10 . . . . . 35 E2
Kernow Cres MK6. . . 35 A1
Kerria Pl MK3. . . . . . . 47 A3
Kerr Pl HP21 . . . . . . 115 E7
Kerry Cl HP19 . . . . . 101 A3
Kerry Hill MK14 . . . . . 21 C1
Kersey MK14. . . . . . . 34 C8
Kerswell Cl **1** SL2 . 197 F1
Kessler Cl MK17. . . . 69 E7
Kesters Rd HP5 . . . . 154 D7
Kestrel Cl
  2 Berkhamsted
  HP4. . . . . 135 C3
  High Wycombe HP13. 161 C5
Kestrel Dr HP15. . . . 163 B5
Kestrel Path SL2 . . . 197 E1
Kestrel Way
  Aylesbury HP19. . . . . 101 E4
  Buckingham MK18 . . .52 F7
Keswick Ct SL2 . . . . 205 F6
Keswick Rd MK19 . . . 11 B2
Keswick St HP18. . . . 100 E5
Ketchmere Cl HP18 125 C6
Ketelbey Nook MK7 . 48 E5
Ketton Cl MK15. . . . . 35 D7
Kew Cl MK8. . . . . .33 F1
Kew Gr HP11. . . . . . . 173 B4
Kew Pl HP11 . . . . 173 B4
Keyes Way MK18 . . . 41 E2
Keynes Cl MK16 . . . . 22 E4
Keys Pl SL6. . . . . 202 F6
Khalsa Prim Sch
  SL2 . . . . 206 A7
Khasiaberry MK7. . . . 48 B5
Kidd Cl MK8 . . . . 45 E6
Kidderminster Rd
  SL2 . . . . 198 A2
Kidderminster Wlk **3**
  MK10 . . . . 36 B2
Kidwells Cl SL6. . . . . 202 F8
Kidwells Park Dr
  SL6. . . . . 202 F7
Kildonan Pl MK12. . . 33 D4
Kilfillan Gdns HP4. . 135 A3
Kilfillan Pk HP4 . . . . 135 A3
Kilgour Ct **2** LU7 . . .80 F7
Kilkenny Ho MK4. . . . 45 E2
Killarney Dr SL6 . . . 202 E7
Killerton Cl MK4 . . . . .45 F7
Kiln Ave
  Chinnor OX39 . . . . . . 147 D5
  Little Chalfont HP6 . . 155 C1
Kiln Cl
  Calvert MK18 . . . . . . 73 B5
  Prestwood HP16. . . . 151 C7
KILN COMMON 151 B8
Kiln Croft Cl SL7 . . . 184 A3
Kiln Ct HP9 . . . . 186 B8
Kiln Dr MK17. . . . . . . 49 A5
Kilner Cl HP21 . . . . . 115 E5
Kilner Rd HP21. . . . . 115 E5
KILN FARM 33 B3
Kiln Farm Ind Est
  MK11 . . . . 33 B3
Kiln Farm Rdbt MK11 33 A3
Kiln Fields
  Bourne End SL6. . . . 185 E1
  Wooburn HP10 . . . . . 185 E2
Kiln La
  Botley HP5 . . . . 155 B8
  Cores End SL8, HP10 185 D3
  Hedgerley SL2. . . . . 187 D8
  Lacey Green HP27. . 149 F5
  Lacey Green HP27. . 150 A4
Kiln Pl SL6. . . . . 195 A3
Kiln Pond La HP13. . 161 D3
Kiln Rd
  Aldbury HP23 . . . . . . 120 E4
  Hastoe HP23. . . . . . . 133 B6
  Prestwood HP16. . . . 151 B7
Kiln The HP5. . . . . . . 144 C1
Kilnwood HP14 . . . . . 150 B1

Kilpin Gn MK16 . . . . . 24 B6
Kilty Pl HP11 . . . . . 173 C4
Kilwinning Dr MK10 . .35 F1
Kimbells Cl HP18 . .124 D2
Kimber Cl SL4 . . . . .210 A4
Kimberley Cl SL3 . .206 F4
Kimbers Dr SL1 . . . .197 D2
Kimber's La SL6 . . . .202 E3
Kimble Ct HP22 . . . .129 E3
Kimble Park Rd
HP17 . . . . .129 E3
Kimblewick Rd
Great Kimble HP17 . .129 C5
Owlswick HP27 . . . . .128 F2
Kimbolton Ct MK14. . .35 A8
Kincardine Dr MK3 . .46 F3
Kindermann Ct MK5. .46 B5
Kindleton MK14. . . . .34 F4
Kinellan Ct HP9 . . . .175 D3
King Charles Cl
MK18 . . . . .41 E2
King Cl MK17 . . . . . .58 B2
King Edward Ave
HP21 . . . . .116 A7
King Edward Ct 5
SL4 . . . . .210 D6
King Edward Ct Service
Rd 2 SL4. . . . . . . .210 C6
King Edward Gdns
HP23. . . . . .119 B4
King Edward St
Milton Keynes MK13 . .33 F7
Slough SL1 . . . . .205 D4
King Edward VII Ave
SL4 . . . . .210 E8
King Edward VII Hospl
SL4 . . . . .210 C4
Kingfisher HP19 . . . .101 E4
Kingfisher Cl 10
HP16. . . . . .151 C5
Kingfisher Ct
3 High Wycombe
HP11. . . . . .173 A6
Slough SL2 . . . . .198 B1
Kingfisher Ctr The
MK16 . . . . .22 C3
Kingfisher Dr SL6. . .203 A8
Kingfisher Ho
Loudwater HP11 . . . .174 A4
Marlow SL7 . . . . . . .183 F2
Kingfisher Pl HP11 . .174 B3
Kingfisher Rd MK18 . .52 F7
King George Cres
MK11 . . . . .32 E6
King George V Rd
HP6 . . . . .154 D1
Kinghorn La SL6 . . . .195 D3
Kinghorn Pk SL6. . . .195 D3
King John's Cl
TW19 . . . . .211 C2
King Johns Palace
SL3 . . . . .212 D6
Kingsash Rd HP19. . .114 F8
Kingsbridge MK4 . . . .46 D2
Kingsbridge Farm La
MK18 . . . . .64 A5
Kingsbrook Basin
HP22. . . . . .102 D2
Kingsbrook View Prim
Acad HP22. . . . . . . .102 D2
Kingsbury HP20. . . . .115 D8
Kingsbury Dr SL4 . . .211 B1
Kingsbury Mws SL4 .209 F6
Kings Chase SL6 . . . .202 F6
Kings Cl
Beaconsfield HP9 . . . .186 A8
Chalfont St Giles HP8 .177 D8
Henley-on-Thames
RG9. . . . . .191 D2
Kings Ct
Berkhamsted HP4 . . .135 C5
Fenny Stratford MK2. .47 E1
Kingsdale Rd HP4 . . .135 A3
KINGSEY 127 B2
Kingsey Rd OX9 . . . .126 D1
Kings Farm Rd
WD3 . . . . .167 D3
Kingsfield SL4 . . . . .209 D6
Kingsfold MK13 . . . . .34 B7
Kingsgate HP15 . . . .119 B8
Kings Gr
Cranfield MK43. . . . . .25 B2
Maidenhead SL6 . . . .202 E6
King's Gr SL6 . . . . . .202 E6
King's Grove Ind Est
SL6 . . . . .202 E6
Kings Hall Par HP22 131 B4
Kingshill Ct HP13 . . .162 C3
Kingshill Dr
Deanshanger MK19 . . .31 E5
Terriers HP13 . . . . . .162 D3
Kingshill Rd HP13,
HP15. . . . . .162 D3
Kingshill Way HP4 . .135 B2
Kings La
Cookham Dean SL6. . .195 B8
Great Missenden
HP16. . . . . .141 C2
Hampden Bottom
HP16. . . . . .141 D1
Lee Common HP16,
HP22. . . . . .141 F7
King's La
South Heath HP16 . . .152 E8

King's La continued
The Lee HP16 . . . . . .142 A4
Kingsland Est HP18 . .21 F4
Kingsley Cl MK16. . . .21 F4
Kingsley Cres HP11 172 F6
Kingsley Dr SL7 . . . .183 C6
Kingsley Path
Slough SL2 . . . . .197 D1
2 Slough SL2. . . . . .197 F1
Kingsley Wlk HP23 . .119 A4
Kings Lodge
1 Amersham HP6 . . .154 D1
Finmere MK18. . . . . .50 D6
Kings Mdw
Bierton HP22 . . . . . .102 C4
Holmer Green HP15 . .163 B6
Kingsmead
Kingsmead MK4 . . . . .45 E1
Monks Risborough
HP27. . . . . .139 B6
Kings Mead LU6. . . . .92 E3
Kingsmead Bsns Pk
HP11. . . . . .174 B3
Kingsmead Ho SL1 . .205 C5
Kingsmead Rd
High Wycombe
HP11. . . . . .174 B3
Loudwater HP11 . . . .174 B3
Kingsmead Rdbt
MK4 . . . . .56 F8
Kings Mill Way UB8 201 A6
Kings Oak Cl HP27 . .139 C5
Kingsoe Leys MK16. . .36 A2
Kingsquarter 3
SL6 . . . . .203 B7
Kings Rd
Berkhamsted HP4 . . .135 B3
Chalfont St Giles HP8 177 D8
Henley-on-Thames
RG9. . . . . .191 D2
West Drayton UB7. . .208 F4
King's Rd
Aylesbury HP21 . . . .115 F8
Henley-on-Thames
RG9. . . . . .191 D2
High Wycombe HP11. .173 F4
Loudwater HP11 . . . .174 A4
Slough SL1 . . . . .205 E3
Uxbridge UB8 . . . . . .201 D3
Windsor SL4 . . . . . .210 D3
Windsor SL4 . . . . . .210 D5
Kings Rd Upper 6
RG9. . . . . .191 D2
Kings Reach SL1 . . . .206 C2
Kings Ride HP10 . . . .163 B1
King's Road Ho
SL4 . . . . .210 D5
Kings Sq HP11 . . . . .173 F4
Kings St LU7 . . . . . . .78 E7
Kings Sutton Sq
MK18 . . . . .52 B8
King St
Chesham HP5 . . . . . .154 B7
Maidenhead SL6 . . . .202 F6
Maidenhead SL6 . . . .202 F7
Milton Keynes MK11 . .32 E6
Piddington HP14. . . .160 C1
Tring HP23 . . . . . . .119 A3
Tring LU7. . . . . .118 F2
Wavendon MK17 . . . .48 B8
King Stable St SL4 . .210 D7
King Stephen Mdws
MK12 . . . . .33 B7
King's Terr SL3 . . . .212 B8
KINGSTON. 36 C2
Kingston Ave
Milton Keynes MK11 . .32 E5
West Drayton UB7. . .208 F6
KINGSTON
BLOUNT. 147 A3
Kingston Blount Rd
HP14. . . . . .158 B7
Kingston Bsns Pk
MK10 . . . . .36 D2
Kingston Cl SL6. . . . .203 A6
Kingston Gymnastics &
Fitness Ctr MK10. . .36 C1
Kingston Hill OX39,
HP14. . . . . .158 B8
Kingston La
Uxbridge UB8 . . . . . .201 E2
West Drayton UB7. . .208 F4
Kingston Rd HP13. . .162 D1
Kingston Rdbt MK10. .36 D1
Kingstons Yd NN12. . .17 B7
Kingsway
Farnham Common
SL2 . . . . .198 C6
Gerrards Cross SL9. . .188 E8
Iver SL0 . . . . .207 E7
5 Slough SL3. . . . . .206 C3
Kingsway Ho 6
SL6 . . . . .202 F7
Kingsway Mews
SL2 . . . . .198 C6
Kingswear Dr MK10 . .36 B4
Kings Wlk RG9 . . . . .191 D2
KINGSWOOD 83 B3
Kings Wood SL7 . . . .193 D7
Kingswood Ave
HP10. . . . . .174 B8
Kingswood Creek
TW19 . . . . .211 D2
Kingswood Ct SL6. . .202 F5
Kingswood Ho SL2 . .205 C8
Kingswood La
Kingswood HP18. . . . .83 B2
Ludgershall HP18 . . . .96 F6

Kings Wood National
Nature Reserve
MK17 . . . . .60 B1
Kingswood Par SL7 183 D5
Kingswood Park
HP13. . . . . .173 E8
Kingswood Pl HP13 162 E1
King's Wood Sch
HP13. . . . . .173 F8
Kingswood View
HP13. . . . . .162 E1
Kinloch HP11 . . . . . . .58 E5
Kinnaird Cl SL1 . . . .204 C7
Kinnear Cl MK8 . . . . .45 E7
Kinross Dr MK3 . . . . .46 E2
Kinson Gn HP20. . . .101 E3
Kipling Ct SL4 . . . . .210 B5
Kipling Dr MK16. . . . .21 F4
Kipling Rd MK3 . . . . .58 A7
Kippell Hill MK46. . . . .6 F5
Kirby Cl HP8 . . . . . .177 A7
Kirby Est UB7. . . . . .208 D6
Kirby Way UB8 . . . .201 F1
Kircutt Farm Cl LU6 .91 F5
Kirkeby Cl
Milton Keynes MK14. .34 D6
Stoke Mandeville
HP22. . . . . .116 B2
Kirke Cl MK5. . . . . . .46 A5
Kirkes Way 4
HP18. . . . . .100 D5
Kirkham Ct MK5. . . . .46 C8
Kirkham Way HP6. . .154 E2
Kirkstall Pl MK5. . . . .46 D8
Kirkwall Spur SL1,
SL2. . . . . .205 E8
Kirkwood Gr MK5 . . .45 D5
Kirtle Rd HP5 . . . . . .144 C1
Kirtlington MK15. . . . .35 B5
Kitchener Cl MK46 . . .7 A3
Kitchener Dr
Bletchley MK17 . . . . .58 F7
Fenny Stratford MK17. .59 A7
Kitchener Rd HP11 . .172 F7
Kite Cl HP22. . . . . . .131 C5
Kite Cres HP27 . . . . .139 A4
Kite Field HP4 . . . . .134 E7
Kite Hill MK6. . . . . . .47 B8
Kitelee Cl MK19 . . . . .11 A3
Kite Wood Rd HP10. .163 B1
Kitsbury Ct HP4. . . . .135 B4
Kitsbury Rd HP4 . . . .135 B4
Kitsbury Terr HP4. . .135 B4
Kittiwake HP19 . . . . .101 E4
Klee Cl HP22. . . . . . . .85 A5
Klondyke SL7 . . . . . .183 D2
Knapp Gate MK5. . . . .45 F7
Knaresborough Ct
MK3 . . . . .57 D7
Knaves Beech HP10 174 D1
Knaves Beech Bsns Ctr
HP10. . . . . .174 D1
Knaves Beech Ind Est
HP10. . . . . .174 C1
Knaves Beech Way
HP10. . . . . .174 C1
Knaves Hill LU7. . . . .80 D8
Knaves Hollow
HP10. . . . . .174 D1
Knebworth Gate
MK14 . . . . .22 A1
Knibb Dr MK19. . . . . .10 F2
Knighton-Way La
UB9. . . . . .201 B6
Knightsbridge Ct
SL3 . . . . .207 A2
Knightsbridge Pl 16
HP19. . . . . .115 A4
Knights Cl
Eaton Bray LU6. . . . . .92 E5
Great Brickhill MK17. .59 D1
4 Olney MK46 . . . . . .7 A3
Windsor SL4 . . . . . .209 D6
Knights Cres 2 MK3 58 D8
Knights Ct LU6. . . . . .92 E5
Knights Gn WD3 . . . .167 E6
Knights Hill HP11 . . .172 E6
Knights Pl 5 SL4 . . .210 C5
Knights Templar Way
HP11. . . . . .173 B4
Knoll Cl MK16. . . . . . .13 F2
Knolls Cl
Wingrave HP22. . . . . .89 B3
Wingrave HP22. . . . . .89 B3
Knolls View LU6. . . . .93 B8
Knoll The
Aspley Heath MK17. . .49 A1
Sherington MK16. . . . .13 F2
Knolton Way SL2. . . .206 C7
Knottocks Cl HP9 . . .175 D5
Knottocks Dr HP9 . . .175 D5
Knottocks End HP9 175 D5
KNOTTY GREEN 175 C6
Knowles Cl UB7. . . . .208 E5
Knowles Gn MK2. . . . .58 C8
Knowles Prim Sch
MK2. . . . . .58 D8
Knowl Gate MK5. . . . .46 C7
KNOWLHILL 46 B6
Knowlhill Rdbt MK5 . .46 C6
Knowsley Cl SL6. . . .195 A1
Knox Bridge MK7. . . . .48 B8
Knyghton Cl LU7. . . . .91 D2
Kola Ho SL2. . . . . . .206 B3
Kop Hill HP27 . . . . . .139 D3
Kramer Ct MK8 . . . . .45 D6

Krohn Cl MK18. . . . . .52 F8
Krypton Cl MK5 . . . . .46 C6
Kyle End 5 HP21. . . .115 E5
Kynaston Ave HP21. .115 E4

L

Laburnham Cotts
LU7 . . . . .69 E3
Laburnham Rd SL6 . .202 E6
Laburnum Ave UB7. .208 F6
Laburnum Cl SL7. . . .183 E4
Laburnum Gr
Milton Keynes MK2. . .58 E7
Slough SL3. . . . . . . .207 A3
Laburnum Rd HP12. .172 C5
Lace Hill Acad MK18. .52 F6
Lace La MK18 . . . . . .52 F6
Lacemakers
Chinnor OX39 . . . . .147 C6
Long Crendon HP18. .125 C7
Winslow MK18 . . . . . .65 E5
Lace Mews MK46. . . . .7 A4
Lacey Dr HP14 . . . . .161 C7
Lacey Gr UB10 . . . . .201 E3
LACEY GREEN. 149 E5
Laceys Dr HP15 . . . .163 B5
Laconia La MK10 . . . .36 C4
Ladbroke Cl MK10 . . .101 C2
Ladbroke Gr MK10 . . .47 F8
Ladbrooke Rd SL1. . .205 D3
Ladybridge Terr MK43 8 E5
Lady Cooper Ct
HP4. . . . . .135 C6
Ladyday Pl SL1. . . . .205 C5
Lady Dr MK15. . . . . . .35 A8
Lady Ela Dr WD3 . . .167 A2
Ladymead Cl MK17. . .56 B8
Ladymeadow Ct
MK10 . . . . .35 C7
Ladysmith Rd LU7. . .105 E5
Lady Verney Cl
HP13. . . . . .173 B8
Ladywalk WD3 . . . . .178 E6
Lady Yorke Pk SL0 . .200 D6
Laelia Dr MK11. . . . . .32 F3
Laggan Ct MK2. . . . . .58 D4
Laggan Rd SL6. . . . .195 F1
Laggan Sq SL6 . . . . .195 F1
Lagger Cl HP8 . . . . . .177 B7
Lagger The HP8. . . . .177 B7
Lagley Ho HP4 . . . . .135 A5
Lagonda Cl MK16. . . . .22 E4
Laidler Cres HP27. . .139 A4
Laidler Gdns HP27 . .139 A4
Laidon Cl MK2 . . . . . .58 D4
Lake Ave SL1 . . . . . .205 D6
Lake Cl MK18 . . . . . .66 B6
LAKE END 204 B4
Lake End Cl SL6. . . . .204 A7
Lake End Rd SL4,
SL6 . . . . .204 B5
Lakeland Dr HP19 . . .100 E6
Laker Cl MK6. . . . . . .46 E7
Laker St HP22. . . . . .117 D6
Lakes Cotts LU7. . . . .90 C8
Lakesfield HP9. . . . . .186 F8
Lakeside
Aylesbury HP19. . . . .101 E4
Maidenhead SL6 . . . .196 B1
Tring HP23 . . . . . . .119 A5
Lakeside Dr SL2. . . . .198 F4
Lakeside Est SL3 . . .212 F7
Lakeside Rd
Chinnor OX39 . . . . .147 D5
Poyle SL3 . . . . .212 F7
Lakes La
Beaconsfield HP9 . . .186 F8
Newport Pagnell MK16 22 B5
Lakes The SL7 . . . . .194 A6
Lake View SL6 . . . . .196 A1
Lamb Cl MK16 . . . . . .22 A4
Lambe Rd HP22 . . . .131 C5
Lamberhurst Gr MK7 48 A8
Lambert Ave SL3 . . .206 E3
Lambert Ct MK16. . . . .22 F7
Lambert Rd HP18 . . .100 D5
Lamberts Croft MK12 33 C5
Lambert Wlk OX9 . . .125 F1
Lambourn Ct MK4. . . .46 D2
Lambourne Ave
HP21. . . . . .115 D5
Lambourne Cl SL1 . .197 C3
Lambourne Ct
Maidenhead SL6 . . . .203 C8
Uxbridge UB8 . . . . . .201 B4
Lambourne Dr SL6 . .202 E3
Lambridge La RG9 . . .191 D3
Lambridge Wood Rd
RG9. . . . . .191 B4
Lambscroft Way
SL9 . . . . .177 E1
Lamb Sidings MK2. . .58 C7
Lambton Ho SL4 . . . .210 A4
Lambtons Way MK18 66 B5
Lamesley Ho SL6. . . .202 E6
Lammas MK6 . . . . . .47 A5
Lammas Ave SL4. . . .210 D5
Lammas Cl HP27 . . . .138 E6
Lammas Ct SL4 . . . . .210 C5
Lammas Rd
Cheddington LU7. . . .105 A7
Slough SL1 . . . . .204 D5
Lammas Way
Lane End HP14 . . . . .171 A4

Lammas Way continued
Loudwater HP11 . . . .174 C1
Lamour La MK4 . . . . .45 E3
Lampitts Cross MK6. .47 B6
Lamport Cres MK10 . .36 C4
Lamport Ct MK8. . . . .46 A8
Lamva SL1 . . . . .32 F5
Lancaster Ave SL4 . .210 E4
Lancaster Cl HP12. . .172 D4
Lancaster Dr HP3 . . .145 C4
Lancaster Gate MK3. .57 E7
Lancaster Rd
Aylesbury HP21. . . . .116 B6
High Wycombe HP12 172 E4
Maidenhead SL6 . . . .202 B8
Uxbridge UB8 . . . . . .201 D5
Lancaster Ride
HP10. . . . . .174 B8
Lancaster Wy LU7 . .105 C3
Lancastria La 2
SL6 . . . . .202 D7
Lancastria Mews
SL6 . . . . .202 D7
Lancelot Cl SL1 . . . .205 A4
Lance Way HP13 . . . .174 A6
Lanchester Rd MK43. .24 D2
Lancot Ave LU6 . . . . .93 C7
Lancotbury Cl LU6 . . .93 C7
Lancot Dr LU6 . . . . . .93 E8
Lancot Pl LU6 . . . . . .93 C6
Lancot Prim Sch LU6 93 E8
Lancresse Cl UB8 . . .201 D6
Lander Rd HP19. . . . .100 F3
Landon Ct HP21 . . . .115 F7
Landrace Ct 6 MK5. .45 F3
Lands End MK4. . . . . .56 F8
Lands The LU7 . . . . . .79 D3
LANE END 171 C4
Lane End HP4 . . . . . .134 F4
Lane End Ind Est
HP14. . . . . .171 B4
Lane End Prim Sch
HP14. . . . . .171 B4
Lane End Rd HP12. . .172 B6
Lanercost Cres MK10 36 B1
LANES END 132 C4
Lane The
Chinnor OX39 . . . . .147 D7
Grafton Regis NN12 . .9 D2
Mursley MK17. . . . . . .67 D6
Lane Wood Rd HP7 . .165 B3
Lanfranc Gdns MK15 35 B7
Langcliffe Dr
Bradwell MK13 . . . . . .34 C5
Milton Keynes MK13 . .34 C5
Langdale Cl
Maidenhead SL6 . . . .203 A6
Milton Keynes MK2. . .58 D4
Langdale Lodge
HP11. . . . . .174 A4
Langdale Ho MK6 . . . .47 C6
Langdon Ave HP21 . .116 B5
Langdon St HP23. . . .119 A3
Langdown Way SL6 202 D5
Langerstone La MK4 .46 B1
Langford Pl MK7 . . . .48 A3
Langham Way MK6. . .47 C6
Langkawi La MK17. . .58 A3
Langland Cl MK18 . . .51 B6
Langland Com Sch
MK6 . . . . .47 C6
Langland Ho MK6 . . . .47 C6
Langland Rd MK6 . . . .47 C6
Langlands MK46. . . . . .7 E7
LANGLEY 207 A3
Langley Acad SL3 . . .206 E3
Langley Ave MK17. . .59 A6
Langley Broom SL3 206 F1
Langley Bsns Ctr
SL3 . . . . .207 A4
Langley Bsns Pk
SL3 . . . . .207 A4
Langley Cl
Downley HP13. . . . . .161 D2
Winslow MK18 . . . . . .65 E4
Langley Cnr SL3. . . . .199 F6
Langley Gram Sch
SL3 . . . . .206 F2
Langley Hall Prim Acad
SL3 . . . . .206 D5
Langley Heritage Prim
Sch The SL3. . . . . .207 B3
Langley L Ctr SL3 . . .207 B2
Langley Park Ctry Pk★
SL0, SL3 . . . . .200 A1
Langley Park Rd Service
Rd SL3 . . . . .207 B2
Langley Quay SL3 . . .207 A4
Langley Rd SL3 . . . . .206 E3
Langley Sta SL3 . . . .207 A4
Langley Way SL7 . . .183 C2
Langmuir Ct MK5 . . . .46 C4
Langney Gn MK4. . . . .57 A8
Langport Cres MK5. . .45 D5
Langston Ct HP12 . . .172 C8
Langston Ho HP20. . .101 E3
Langstone Ct 11
HP20. . . . . .101 F3
Langton Cl
Maidenhead SL6 . . . .203 C8
Slough SL1 . . . . .204 D5
Langton Dr MK8. . . . .33 E2
Langton Gn SL6 . . . .203 F1
Langton's Mdw SL2 198 C6

Langtree Ave SL1 . . .204 C6
Lanner Wlk MK6 . . . . .47 B8
Lanolin Cl MK14. . . . .21 C1
Lanrick Copse HP4 . .135 C5
Lansbury Rd MK17. . .58 B2
Lansdales Rd 10
HP11. . . . . .172 F7
Lansdell Ave HP12 . .172 B3
Lansdowne Ave SL1 205 E5
Lansdowne Ct
Maidenhead SL6 . . . .203 C7
Slough SL1 . . . . .205 E5
Lansdowne Rd
Aylesbury HP20. . . . .101 D2
Chesham HP5 . . . . . .144 C2
Lansdowne Way
HP11. . . . . .172 E3
Lansdown Rd SL9 . . .177 D2
Lanterns Wlk SL6 . . .203 B7
Lantern Way SL7 . . .202 E4
Lanthorn Cl MK14. . . .34 E6
Lappetts La HP16 . . .152 E8
Lapula Wy MK17 . . . .58 A3
Lapwing Mws HP17 127 A5
Larch Cl
Aylesbury HP20. . . . .102 A2
Slough SL2 . . . . .205 B8
Tylers Green HP10 . .163 C2
Larches The
Berkhamsted HP4 . . .134 D5
Holmer Green HP15 . .163 D4
Little Chalfont HP6 . .155 B1
Larchfield Prim Sch
SL6 . . . . .202 E5
Larchfield Rd SL6. . . .202 E5
Larch Gr MK2 . . . . . .58 E7
Larchlands The
HP10. . . . . .163 D1
Larchmoor Gdns
HP4. . . . . .135 A3
Larchmoor Pk SL2 . .199 A4
Larch Rise HP4 . . . . .135 A5
Larchwood HP16. . . .152 B4
Lark Cl MK18. . . . . . .52 E7
Larkings La 2 . . . . . .199 B4
Lark Rise HP15. . . . .163 B5
Larkspur Ave MK14. .34 E5
Larkspur Way HP15 162 F6
Larks Rise HP5. . . . .154 D6
Lark Vale HP19 . . . . .101 E3
Larner Ct MK17 . . . . .58 B2
La Roche Cl 4 SL3. .206 C3
Larson Ct MK4 . . . . .35 E2
Larwood Pl MK6 . . . .34 F1
Lasborough Rd MK10 36 C1
Lascelles Cl MK15 . . .35 B7
Lascelles Ho 8 SL1 206 A4
Lascelles Rd SL3 . . .206 B3
Laser Cl MK5. . . . . . .46 C6
Lashlake Rd OX9 . . .125 F1
Lassell Gdns SL6 . . .203 B7
Lastingham Gr MK4 .46 B2
Latchmoor Ave SL9 188 D7
Latchmoor Gr SL9. . .188 D7
Latchmoor Way
SL9 . . . . .188 D7
LATHBURY 22 C7
LATIMER 155 E3
Latimer HP5 . . . . . . .155 E2
Latimer Milton Keynes MK11 . .32 E4
Latimer Bottom
HP5. . . . . .155 E2
Latimer Chase WD3 167 C7
Latimer Cl HP6. . . . .166 C8
Latimer Ct HP20 . . . .116 A8
Latimer Rd
Chenies WD3. . . . . . .156 B2
Chesham HP5 . . . . . .154 E5
Little Chalfont HP5 . .155 C2
Latimer Way HP9. . . .175 C6
Laud's Cl RG9 . . . . .191 C1
Lauds Mws MK16. . . .13 F2
Launceston Ct MK5. . .46 B6
Launceston Dr MK10. .36 C5
Launde 1 MK10. . . . .36 B1
Laurance Ct 2 SL7 183 C7
Laureate Gdns 7
RG9. . . . . .191 D2
Laurel Ave SL3 . . . . .206 E4
Laurel Bank HP3 . . . .146 F8
Laurel Cl
Milton Keynes MK8 . . .45 D7
Poyle SL3 . . . . .212 E7
Prestwood HP16. . . . .151 B7
Speen HP27. . . . . . .150 C4
Laurel Dr
Amersham HP6. . . . .154 C3
Iver Heath SL0. . . . .200 D5
Laurel Ho
Loudwater HP11 . . . .174 B3
Walter's Ash HP14. . .150 C4
Laurel La UB7. . . . . .208 E2
Laurel Lane Prim Sch
UB7. . . . . .208 D2
Laurel Rd SL9 . . . . .177 D2
Laurels Rd SL0. . . . .200 D4
Laurels The
High Wycombe
HP12. . . . . .172 C4
Milton Keynes MK1. . .47 D1

Laurel Way 4 HP21 115 E7
Lautrec Way HP19 100 F2
Lautree Gdns SL6 195 E7
Lavender Cl HP21 115 B5
Lavender Gr MK7 48 A5
Lavender Hill MK10 36 C4
Lavender Rd UB8 208 F8
Lavender Way HP15 162 F7
Lavender Wlk HP21 115 B6
LAVENDON 7 F7
Lavendon Grange
MK46 7 C7
Lavendon Rd
Harrold MK43 3 D4
Olney MK46 7 A5
Lavendon Sch MK46 7 F8
Laverde Wlk MK10 35 E2
Lavric Rd HP21 115 C6
Lawford Ave WD3 167 C3
Lawford Cl WD3 167 C3
Lawkland SL2 198 C2
Lawn Ave UB7 208 D4
Lawn Cl SL3 211 C7
Lawn Farm Bsns Ctr
HP18 83 D4
Lawn Hill HP18 73 A2
Lawn House La HP18 72 F1
Lawn Rd UB8 201 C5
Lawnsmead Gdns
MK16 22 D5
Lawns The
Brill HP18 96 B1
Tylers Green HP10 163 B2
Lawn The SL3 211 C6
Lawrence Cl
12 Aylesbury HP20 101 F2
Aylesbury HP20 102 A2
Lawrence Ct SL4 210 C5
Lawrence Gr
Prestwood HP16 151 D5
Uxbridge UB10 201 E3
Lawrence Way SL1 204 D8
Lawrence Wlk MK16 21 F5
Laws Cl MK43 8 E6
Lawsone Rise HP13 162 B1
Lawson Pl MK5 46 B5
Lawson Wy HP18 100 E4
Laxfield Dr MK10 36 A4
Laxton Gn SL6 202 C3
Laxton Rd HP19 100 D5
Layburn Cres SL3 212 B8
Laychequers Mdw
SL6 203 D8
Lay Rd HP19 101 B2
Layter's Ave SL9 177 C1
Layter's Avenue S
SL9 177 C1
Layter's Cl SL9 177 C1
Layter's End SL9 177 C1
LAYTER'S GREEN 177 B1
Layters Green La
SL9 177 B1
Layters Way SL9 188 D6
Layton Cres SL2 206 F3
Leaberry MK13 34 A8
Leachcroft SL9 177 B2
Leaches Farm Bsns Ctr
HP18 81 F4
Leach Rd HP21 115 C7
Lea Cl SL7 183 D6
Leacroft 3 SL1 204 F4
Leacroft Cl UB7 208 E6
Leacroft Rd SL0 207 E7
Lea Ct HP7 165 F8
LEADENHALL 47 A8
Leadenhall Rdbt
MK6 46 E7
Leaders Cl HP22 89 B3
Leafield Rise MK8 33 D2
Leafy La HP23 118 E1
Leaholme Gdns SL1 204 D8
Lea La HP18 125 F4
Leander Wy SL6 202 D3
Leapingwell La MK18 66 B5
Lear La HP18 82 F6
Leary Cres MK16 22 E4
Leas Cl HP13 173 F8
Leas Dr SL0 207 E7
Leaside MK16 12 B6
Leasowe Pl MK13 34 C3
Leather La HP16 142 A3
Leaver Rd RG9 191 C1
Leblanc Cl 3 MK17 48 F8
LECKHAMPSTEAD 42 E7
Leckhampstead Rd
Akeley MK18 42 A8
Wicken MK18 30 F2
Leckhampstead Wharf
La
Thornborough MK18 42 F3
Thornborough MK18 43 A2
Leckhamstead Rd
MK19 31 A3
Ledborough Gate
HP9 175 F4
Ledborough La HP9 175 E4
Ledborough Wood
HP9 175 E4
LEDBURN 90 D8
Ledburn
Ledburn LU7 90 A6
Ledburn LU7 90 C8
Ledburn Gr LU7 80 E6
Ledburn Rd
Mentmore LU7 90 D5
Ledburn Rd *continued*
Slapton LU7 80 D2
Ledbury MK14 21 E1
Ledeview Ct HP11 174 A4
Ledgers Rd SL1 205 E5
Ledger's Rd SL1 205 D4
Leeches Way LU7 105 A7
Lee Clump Rd HP16 142 C5
LEE COMMON 142 D5
Lee Common CE Sch
HP16 142 D5
Lee Cotts
Buckmoorend HP17 140 D6
Lacey Green HP27 149 A4
Lee Cres HP17 114 D5
Lee Ct 7 HP12 172 E7
Leeds Rd SL1 205 E6
Lee Farm Cl HP5 145 A1
LEE GATE 142 A7
Lee Ho 2 MK2 58 C8
Lee La SL6 194 F1
Lee Rd
Aylesbury HP21 115 D6
Quainton HP22 84 F5
Saunderton HP27 148 F6
Lees Cl SL6 202 B5
Lees Gdns SL6 202 B5
Leeson Gdns SL4 204 E2
Lees Wlk SL7 183 C2
Le Flaive Bsns Pk
HP14 161 E6
Legion Cl MK11 32 E3
Legionfield Cres
LU7 118 E3
Legoland Windsor★
SL4 209 D2
Leicester Cl RG9 191 D3
Leigh Hill MK4 46 D2
Leigh Pk SL3 211 B7
Leigh Rd SL1 205 B6
Leigh Sq SL4 209 D5
Leigh St HP11 172 F7
LEIGHTON
BUZZARD 80 F6
Leighton Buzzard Bypass
LU7 80 D4
Leighton Buzzard Sta
LU7 80 E7
Leighton Gdns SL6 196 B1
Leighton Ho 7 SL7 183 E2
Leighton Mid Sch
LU7 80 F6
Leighton Rd
Ascott LU7 80 E2
Edlesborough LU6 92 D4
Leighton Buzzard LU7 80 F7
Mentmore HP22 89 E5
Mentmore LU7 90 F7
Northall LU6 92 B5
Slapton LU7 91 A5
Soulbury LU7 70 B1
Soulbury MK17 70 C2
Stoke Hammond MK17 69 E7
Stoke Hammond MK17 69 F6
Wing LU7 80 A3
Wingrave HP22 89 C3
Woburn MK17 60 D5
Leighton St MK17 60 E6
Leiston Spur SL1 205 E7
Leisure Plaza★ MK9 46 C8
Leith Cl SL1 206 A5
Leith Rd HP19 115 A8
Lembrook Wlk
HP21 115 C6
Lemmon Wlk 5 MK4 45 E2
LENBOROUGH 52 D3
Lenborough Cl MK18 52 C7
Lenborough Ct MK15 35 C2
Lenborough Farm La
MK18 52 F1
Lenborough Rd
Buckingham MK18 52 C7
Buckingham MK18 52 D6
Gawcott MK18 52 D4
Padbury MK18 53 A4
Lendon Gr HP23 104 D3
Lennon Dr MK8 45 E7
Lennon Way HP21 115 E3
Lennox Rd MK2 58 D7
LENT 197 B1
Lent Gn SL1 197 B1
Lent Green La SL1 197 B1
Lenthall Cl MK13 34 A5
LENT RISE 204 A8
Lent Rise Comb Sch
SL1 204 B8
Lent Rise Rd SL1 204 B8
Leo Cres HP27 139 A4
Leominster Gate 4
MK10 36 A1
Leonard Mdw OX27 72 A3
Leonards Cl HP18 72 F2
Leonardslee MK4 45 F2
Leon Ave MK2 58 D8
Leon L Ctr MK2 58 C4
Leopard Dr MK15 35 A7
Leopold Mall 5
SL1 205 F4
Leopold Rd LU7 80 D7
Leopold Way HP22 102 E2
Lerwick Dr SL1 205 E8
Leslie Dunne Ho
SL4 209 E5
Lester Gr HP15 163 A4
Lester Rd
Aylesbury HP20 115 F8
Aylesbury HP20 116 A8
Lesters Rd SL6 195 D6
Letchfield
Botley HP5 155 B8
Ley Hill HP5 145 B1
Letter Box La HP27 139 D7
Leveller Way 15
HP18 100 D5
Leven Cl
Leighton Buzzard LU7 80 B7
Milton Keynes MK2 58 D5
Levens Hall Dr MK4 45 F1
Leverkus Ct OX39 147 C6
Leverkus Ho OX39 147 C6
Levings Cl HP19 101 A3
Lewens Croft MK16 16 A3
Lewes Ct SL1 205 C4
Lewes Ho MK3 57 D7
Lewins Farm Ct SL1 204 F6
Lewins Rd SL9 188 D8
Lewins Way SL1 204 F6
Lewins Yd HP5 154 B8
Lewis Cl MK16 21 F5
Lewis La SL9 177 E2
LEWKNOR 157 B8
Lewknor CE Prim Sch
OX49 157 B8
Lewknor Cl OX49 157 A7
Lexham Gdns HP6 154 C2
Lexham Rd MK6 47 C4
Lexington Ave SL6 202 D5
Leybourne Gdns
OX39 147 C7
Leyburn Ct MK13 34 C5
Leyburne Cl LU7 90 C8
Ley Field Rd HP21 115 E6
LEY HILL 145 B1
Leyhill Rd HP3 145 E3
Ley Hill Sch HP5 145 B1
Leyland Cl MK18 51 F4
Leyland Pl 3 MK6 34 E1
Leylands La TW19 213 A2
Leys Cl HP19 101 C4
Leys Ct MK5 46 B8
Leys La MK18 62 B8
Leys Rd MK5 46 B8
Leys The
Amersham HP6 154 B4
Buckingham MK18 41 F3
Halton HP22 117 C1
Tring HP23 119 B4
Woburn Sands MK17 49 B4
Yardley Hastings NN7 1 A6
Leys View MK16 13 F1
Leywood Cl HP7 165 E7
Libra Ho HP10 185 A8
Lichfield Down MK7 48 B5
Lichfield Ho HP21 115 F6
Lidcote LU7 78 A5
Liddall Way UB7 208 F5
Liddell SL4 209 C4
Liddell Pl SL4 209 C4
Liddell Sq 14 SL4 209 C5
Liddell Way SL4 209 C4
Liden Way MK17 55 B3
Liffre Dr HP22 131 B6
Lightfoot Ct MK7 47 F5
Lightlands La SL6 195 F5
Ligo Ave HP22 116 C2
Lilac Cl MK17 57 C3
Lilac Ct SL2 197 F2
Lilac Pl UB7 208 F6
Lilies The HP22 87 C1
Lilleshall Ave MK10 35 F1
Lilley Way SL1 204 E5
Lillibrooke Cres
SL6 202 A3
LILLINGSTONE
DAYRELL 29 F4
LILLINGSTONE
LOVELL 30 B5
Lillingstone Lovell Rd
Lillingstone Lovell
MK18 30 C4
Wicken NN12 30 E7
Lillingstone Rd MK18 41 F8
Lillyfee Farm La
HP10 186 B5
Lilly Hill MK46 6 F5
Lily Bottom La
HP27 149 F8
Lily Dr UB7 208 D2
Lily's Wlk HP11 173 A6
Limbaud Cl MK7 48 A5
Limbrey Dr MK46 6 E5
Lime Ave
Buckingham MK18 52 F7
High Wycombe HP11 173 D5
West Drayton UB7 208 F6
Windsor SL4 210 F7
Lime Cl
Hazelmere HP15 163 A3
Newport Pagnell MK16 22 B3
Lime Gr
Chinnor OX39 147 D6
Leighton Buzzard LU7 80 E8
Woburn Sands MK17 49 B4
Limehouse Rd
HP22 102 D2
Limelight Ave HP18 100 E6
Lime Rd
Princes Risborough
HP27 139 B3
Yardley Gobion NN12 18 E6
Limerick La MK9 35 B3
Limes Ave HP21 116 B7
Lime St MK46 6 F3
Limes The
Amersham HP6 154 B3
Chesham HP5 144 E1
Limes The *continued*
Milton Keynes MK11 32 E5
Milton Keynes, Fenny
Stratford MK2 58 E8
Tring HP23 119 C4
Windsor SL4 209 C6
Limes Way HP18 124 D2
Lime Tree Cl HP15 162 D8
Lime Tree Wlk HP7 165 F8
Lime Wlk
Maidenhead SL6 202 A8
New Denham UB9 201 C7
Limit Home Pk HP4 134 D7
Limmer La HP12 172 B3
Limmers Mead
HP15 162 D8
Limousin Ave MK8 45 D8
Linceslade Gr MK5 34 B1
Linchfield HP13 173 E7
Linchfield Rd SL3 211 C6
Lincoln
Buckingham MK18 41 D2
Milton Keynes MK14 34 C8
Lincoln Cl HP22 116 B2
Lincoln Ct
Berkhamsted HP4 135 B4
3 Slough SL1 205 E3
Lincoln Hatch La
SL1 197 C1
Lincoln Ho HP10 185 D3
Lincoln Park Bsns Ctr
HP12 172 D6
Lincoln Pk
Amersham HP7 165 E8
Brackley NN13 38 A5
Lincoln Rd
Chalfont St Peter
SL9 177 E2
High Wycombe HP12 172 E5
Maidenhead SL6 202 B8
Lincolnshire Cl MK3 46 E1
Lincolns The HP16 152 A3
Lincoln Way SL1 204 D6
Lincombe Slade LU7 80 E8
Lincroft MK43 25 B1
Linden SL3 207 B1
Linden Ave SL6 195 D1
Linden Cl SL0 200 D3
Linden Ct HP12 172 D6
Linden Dr
Chalfont St Peter
SL9 177 E1
Farnham Royal SL2 198 C4
Linden End HP21 115 F6
Linden Gr MK14 34 E8
Linden Lea HP22 131 B6
Lindens The HP3 146 F8
Linden Way HP17 128 B7
Linden Wlk HP15 163 B3
Lindie Gdns UB10 201 E6
Lindisfarne Dr MK10 36 A1
Lindo Cl HP5 144 B1
Lindores Croft MK10 36 B1
Lindsay Ave HP12 172 E7
Lindsay Cl TW19 213 D2
Lindsey Dr 1 SL9 195 D2
Lindsey Rd UB9 190 A1
Linehams Pightle
MK43 25 B2
Linen La MK18 52 F6
Lines Hill HP22 88 B3
Lines Rd HP14 171 B5
Lines The HP22 88 C4
Linfields HP7 166 C7
Linford Ave MK16 22 A4
Linford La
Milton Keynes, Willen
MK15 35 D7
Milton Keynes, Woolstone
MK15 35 C3
Linford Lakes Nature
Reserve MK14 21 C2
Lingfield MK12 33 E4
Lingfield Cl HP13 174 A5
Lingholm Cl SL6 202 C6
Lingwell Cl OX39 147 C5
Linington Ave HP5 145 A1
Link Cl HP12 172 D6
Link Rd
Chalfont St Peter
WD3 178 C4
Datchet SL3 211 C6
Great Missenden
HP16 152 A7
High Wycombe HP12 172 D6
Links App HP10 185 B8
Links Rd HP10 185 C8
Links Way HP10 185 B8
Linkswood Rd
Burnham SL1 197 C3
Burnham SL1 197 C3
Link The
Hazelmere HP15 163 A5
Slough SL2 206 B7
Link Way UB9 190 A5
Linnet Ave HP7 155 A1
Linnet Cl HP12 172 B3
Linnet Dr HP18 98 C5
Linney Ct MK4 46 A1
LINSLADE 80 D7
Linslade Lower Sch
LU7 80 D7
Linslade Mid Sch
LU7 80 E5
Linslade Rd LU7 70 F4
Linslade Western Bypass
Leighton Buzzard LU7 80 B7
Soulbury MK17 70 B2
Lintlaw Pl MK3 47 A3
Linton Cl MK13 34 C4
Lintott Ct TW19 213 D1
Linx The MK3 47 A2
Lionel Ave HP22 131 A6
Lionel Cl HP22 131 A5
Lipscombe Dr MK18 41 E1
Lipscomb La MK5 46 A7
Lisburn Path 1
HP20 101 F2
Liscombe Park LU7 79 F8
Liscombe Pk
Soulbury LU7 69 E1
Soulbury LU7 79 E8
Lisle Rd HP13 162 A1
Lisleys Field HP15 162 D7
Lismore Pk SL2 205 F7
Lissel Rd MK6 47 E5
Lisset Rd SL6 203 A6
Lister Cl MK6 47 B6
Lister Gn HP21 115 E5
Liston Ct (Sh Arcade) 7
SL7 183 D2
Liston Ho 9 SL7 183 E2
Liston Rd SL7 183 D2
Litcham Spur SL1 205 D7
Lithgows Ave 16
MK10 36 C4
Little Balmer MK18 52 E6
Little Benty UB7 208 D1
Little Boltons 13
SL7 183 E2
LITTLE BOYS
HEATH 152 C3
LITTLE BRICKHILL 59 E5
Little Brickhill La
MK17 59 D4
Little Bridge Rd
HP4 135 D4
LITTLE BRITAIN 208 C7
Littlebrook Ave SL2 204 E8
Little Buntings SL4 209 F4
LITTLE CHALFONT 155 B1
Little Chalfont Prim Sch
HP6 166 E8
Little Chapels Way
SL1 205 A4
Little Chartridge Ct
HP5 144 A1
Little Cl
Aylesbury HP20 101 D1
Flackwell Heath
HP10 185 B6
High Wycombe HP12 172 E3
LITTLECOTE 78 A5
Littlecote
Littlecote MK18 78 A5
Milton Keynes MK8 34 A1
Littledown Rd SL1 205 F5
Littledown Specl Sch
SL1 205 F6
Little Dunmow MK10 36 A1
LITTLE END 23 B8
Littlefield Ct UB7 213 D7
LITTLE FRIETH 170 E2
LITTLE
GADDESDEN 121 D7
Little Gaddesden CE
Prim Sch HP4 121 C8
Little Gaddesden Ho
HP4 121 E5
Little Gaddesden Rd
HP4 107 A2
Little Gibbs HP27 138 A2
Little Greencroft
HP5 144 A4
Little Habton 3 MK4 46 B2
Little Hame MK10 35 F3
Little Ham La HP27 139 B5
LITTLE HAMPDEN 140 F4
Little Hampden Cl
HP22 131 B4
Little Hampden Rd
Hampden Bottom
HP16 141 A2
Little Hampden HP16 140 F4
Little Hill
Chorleywood WD3 167 C3
Winslow MK18 65 E5
Little Hivings HP5 144 A4
Little Hollis HP16 151 E7
Little Hoo HP23 118 F4
LITTLE HORWOOD 55 F2
Little Horwood Manor
MK17 55 E4
Little Horwood Rd
Great Horwood
MK17 55 C3
Great Horwood MK17 55 D7
Winslow MK17 66 B5
Little Hundridge La
HP16 153 A8
Little Ickford OX9 124 A3
LITTLE KIMBLE 129 E2
Little Kimble Sta
HP17 129 E2
LITTLE KINGSHILL 152 B3
Little Kingshill Comb
Sch HP16 152 B2
Little La
Lacey Green HP27 149 C4
Yardley Hastings NN7 1 A7
LITTLE LINFORD 21 C5
Little Linford La MK16,
MK19 21 E4
Little Linford Wood
Wildlife Reserve
MK16 21 B8
LITTLE LONDON
Oakley 109 F5
Wendover 141 C7
Little London
Deanshanger MK19 31 E4
Dunsmore HP22 141 B7
Whitchurch HP22 87 A5
Little London Gn
HP18 109 F5
LITTLE MARLOW 184 D5
Little Marlow CE Sch
SL7 184 C5
Little Marlow Rd
Marlow SL7 183 E3
Marlow SL7 184 A4
Littlemarsh MK7 48 A5
LITTLE MARSH 72 A3
Little Marsh Rd OX27 72 A3
Little Mdw MK5 46 C7
Littlemere MK8 33 D1
LITTLE
MISSENDEN 153 A2
Little Missenden CE Inf
Sch HP7 153 A2
Little Mollards HP22 89 A3
Littlemoor Field
OX39 147 C5
Little Orchard Cl
HP27 138 E5
Little Orchs HP20 101 F3
Little Pk
Bovingdon HP3 146 A3
Princes Risborough
HP27 139 C3
Littleport Spur SL1 205 E7
Little Reeves Ave
HP7 165 F8
LITTLE ROW 202 A5
Little Shardeloes
HP7 165 A8
Little Spinney MK43 25 C3
Little Spring HP5 144 B3
Little St NN7 1 B6
Little Stanton MK14 34 D8
Little Stocking MK5 46 A3
Littlestone Gate
MK10 36 B3
Little Sutton La SL3 207 C1
LITTLE TINGEWICK 50 E6
LITTLE TRING 118 F6
Little Tring Rd
HP23 118 F6
Little Twye HP23 132 F3
Little Twye Rd HP23 132 F3
Little Windmill Hill
WD4 156 F7
Little Wood HP14 158 E5
Little Woodlands
SL4 209 F4
Littleworth LU7 79 E3
LITTLEWORTH
COMMON 186 D1
Littleworth Rd
Hedgerley SL1 186 C1
High Wycombe HP13 161 E2
Litton Ct HP10 174 C2
Liverdy Gr MK17 36 F1
Liverpool Rd SL1 205 B7
Liverpool Victoria Ho 3
HP13 173 B7
Livesey Hill MK5 46 B5
Living Furniture Making
Mus HP11 172 F7
Livingstone Dr MK15 35 C5
Llanbury Cl SL9 177 E3
Llewellyn Chase
MK12 33 B7
Lloyds MK6 47 A7
Loakes Ho HP11 173 A6
Loakes Rd HP11 173 A6
Lochinvar Cl SL1 205 B4
Lochnell Rd HP4 134 F6
Lochy Dr LU7 80 C7
Lock Ave SL6 196 C2
Lockbridge Ct SL6 203 C8
Lock Bridge Rd SL8 185 A3
Locke Cl HP19 101 A2
Locke Gdns SL3 206 C4
Locke Rd MK2 58 C8
Lockets Cl SL4 209 D6
Lockhart Ave MK4 45 D2
Lockharts Yard HP4 135 B5
Lock La
Cosgrove MK19 19 E2
Maidenhead SL6 202 C4
Lock Mead SL6 196 C2
Lock Mews HP9 186 B8
Lock Path SL4 209 D8
Lock Rd SL7 183 F1
Locksley Ct 4 SL1 205 E3
Lockton Ct MK4 46 B3
Lockview Cotts MK1 47 E1
Lock View La MK1 47 E1
Lodden Cl HP21 115 D3
Loddon Dr SL6 202 B8
Loddon Rd SL8 185 A4
Loddon Spur SL1 205 E7
Lodge Cl
Cheddington LU7 105 A7
Marlow SL7 183 E1
Padbury MK18 53 C2
Slough SL1 205 C4
Uxbridge UB8 201 C1
Lodge Farm Bsns Ctr
MK19 20 C3
Lodge Farm Cl
HP22 116 E2
Lodge Farm Ct MK19 19 F6

Lodge Gate MK14 34 E7
Lodge Hill HP17 140 D8
Lodge La
Little Chalfont HP8 166 F6
Prestwood HP16 151 D5
Stoke Hammond MK17 69 E7
Lodge Park The MK16 22 C4
Lodge Pk The MK16 22 B4
Lodge Rd
Cranfield MK17 37 F7
Cranfield MK43 37 F8
Lodge The
Aylesbury HP19 115 A7
Slough SL2 206 B8
Lodge Way SL4 209 E4
Lodgings of the Military Knights 4 SL4 210 D6
Lodore Gn UB10 190 E1
Logan Rock MK4 57 B8
Lollards Cl HP6 154 C2
Lombardy Dr HP4 135 D3
Lomond Dr
Leighton Buzzard LU7 80 C7
Milton Keynes MK2 58 D4
London Cl HP19 100 E1
London End
Beaconsfield HP9 175 F1
Newton Longville MK17 57 D4
Woburn MK17 60 F6
London End La MK17 48 D1
London Ho MK11 32 D5
London Rd
Aston Clinton HP22 117 E4
Beaconsfield HP9 187 B8
Berkhamsted HP4 135 E3
Bozeat NN29 2 C5
Bozeat NN29 2 C8
Buckingham MK18 52 E6
Chalfont St Giles HP8 177 C7
Datchet SL3 211 C7
Felden HP3 146 F8
High Wycombe HP11 173 E5
Little Kingshill HP16 152 B5
Loughton MK5 46 B7
Milton Common OX9 136 B3
Milton Keynes MK16 36 B5
Milton Keynes, Stony Stratford MK11 32 E5
Moulsoe MK16 23 A1
Moulsoe MK16 36 A8
Newport Pagnell MK16 22 F3
Old Stratford MK19 32 C7
Slough, Brands Hill SL3 212 B8
Slough, Langley SL3 206 D2
Wendover HP22 131 C3
Wendover HP22 141 D6
Wheatley OX33 122 A1
Wheatley OX33 122 B1
London Road E HP7 165 E6
London Road W HP7 165 C7
Londrina Ct 9 HP4 135 D4
Londrina Terr 10 HP4 135 D4
Longacre MK17 49 B8
Long Acre HP15 163 C7
Long Ayres MK7 48 A3
Longborns MK43 25 C2
Longbottom La
Beaconsfield HP9 175 F4
Seer Green HP9 176 C3
Longbourn SL4 210 A4
Longbridge Cl HP23 119 A6
Longbridge Way UB8 201 B3
Long Cl SL2 198 B5
Long Close Sch SL3 206 A2
LONG CRENDON 125 B6
Long Crendon Courthouse* HP18 125 D7
Long Crendon Ind Est HP18 125 E5
Long Crendon Rd
Long Crendon HP23 125 E3
Shabbington HP18 124 D3
Long Crendon Sch HP18 125 C7
Longcroft HP22 117 F5
Longcroft Ave HP22 131 D6
Longcroft La
Bovingdon HP3 146 D5
Paulerspury NN12 17 C8
Long Croft Rd WD3 178 D5
Longcross MK15 35 A6
Longdown Hill
Monks Risborough HP27 139 F5
Princes Risborough HP27 140 B5
Longdown Mews HP19 114 F8
Long Dr SL1 197 C2
Longfellow Dr MK16 22 A4
Longfield
Hedgerley SL2 187 D1
Little Kingshill HP16 152 B4
Longfield Dr HP6 154 B1
Longfield Gdns HP23 118 E3
Longfield Rd
Chesham HP5 143 F2
Tring HP23 118 F3
LONGFORD 213 C6
LONGFORDMOOR 213 A6
Longford Rdbt UB7 213 B6
Long Furlong
Haddenham HP17 126 F6
Stone HP17 114 B5
Long Furlong Dr SL2 197 E1
Long Gr HP9 176 C4
Long Grove Cl HP5 143 F2
Long Grove Wood Nature Reserve HP9 176 C4
Long Hale LU7 105 C3
Longhedge MK7 48 A2
Long Hedge LU7 105 C4
Long Hide HP27 139 C4
Longhorn Dr
Crownhill MK8 45 D7
Whitehouse MK8 45 C7
Long La
Bovingdon HP3 145 F1
Bovingdon HP3 155 F8
Cookham Rise SL6 195 D5
Heronsgate WD3 167 D2
Olney MK46 6 F4
Rickmansworth WD3 167 F1
Stanwell TW19 213 F1
Longland Rd 3 MK18 41 E3
Longlands Ct MK18 66 A5
Longlands Wlk MK18 66 A5
Longleat Way HP12 172 D5
Longleat Ct 6 MK8 33 F1
Longleat Gdns SL6 202 D6
Longlees WD3 178 D5
Long Ley LU7 105 A7
Long Leys HP19 115 A8
Long Lional HP20 115 D8
LONG MARSTON 104 B3
Long Marston CE Prim Sch HP23 104 B4
Long Marston Ce Prim Sch HP23 104 B4
Long Marston Rd
Cheddington LU7 104 E7
Marsworth LU7 104 F2
Long Massey MK46 6 E5
Long Mdw
Aylesbury HP21 116 B6
Chesham HP5 144 C3
Longmead SL4 209 E6
Longmead La SL1 197 D5
Long Meadow Cl
Amersham HP7 164 C3
Monks Risborough HP27 139 C5
Long Meadow Sch MK5 45 F3
Longmire MK46 7 F8
Longmore Cl WD3 178 F6
Long Orchard Dr HP10 174 C8
Long Park Cl HP6 154 C3
Long Park Way HP6 154 C3
Longpeak Cl MK4 46 B1
Long Pk HP6 154 C3
Long Plough HP22 117 D5
Long Readings La SL2 198 B2
Long Ride HP27 139 C3
Longridge (Activity Ctr)* SL7 194 F8
Long Row
Leckhampstead MK18 30 E1
Prestwood HP16 151 D6
Longships Dr MK3 58 B4
Longslade La
Aspley Guise MK17 49 D1
Aspley Heath MK17 60 B8
Longstone Rd SL0 200 C4
LONG STREET 10 F4
Longview HP9 185 F8
Long View HP4 135 A6
Longville MK12 33 B7
Long Walk The* SL4 210 D4
Long Wall HP17 126 F5
LONGWICK 138 D7
Longwick CE Combined Sch HP27 138 D6
Longwick Rd
Longwick HP27 138 F6
Monks Risborough HP27 139 A5
Long Wlk HP8 166 E6
Longwood Ave SL3 207 B1
Long Wood Dr HP9 176 F4
Longwood La HP7 165 D8
Longwood Mws SL6 195 E2
Longworth Dr SL6 196 C1
Lonsdale MK12 33 D7
Lonsdale Cl SL6 196 A1
Lonsdale Way SL6 203 C1
Look Ahead SL1 205 E4
Loosen Dr SL6 202 A3
Loose Path HP19 114 F8
Loosley Green 3 HP21 115 F4
Loosley Hill HP27 149 D6
LOOSLEY ROW 149 C6
Lord Grey Acad
Bletchley MK3 47 A1
Milton Keynes MK3 46 F1
Milton Keynes MK3 46 F1
Milton Keynes MK3 46 F1
Lord Grey Sch The MK3 46 F1
Lord Knyvett Cl TW19 213 D1
Lord Knyvetts Ct 12 TW19 213 E1
Lord Mayors Dr SL2 198 A7
Lord Raglan Ho SL4 210 C4
Lord Reith Pl HP9 187 A8
Lords Cl MK2 47 C1
Lordsmead MK43 25 C2
Lords Mead LU6 92 E6
Lords Mill Ct HP5 154 C7
Lords Terr LU6 92 E6
Loriner Pl MK14 35 A6
Loring Rd
Berkhamsted HP4 135 C3
Dunstable LU6 93 F8
Windsor SL4 209 F6
Lormay Pl NN13 39 A4
Lorne Cl SL1 205 C3
Lorraine Cl HP13 173 E8
Lorre Mews MK4 45 E3
Loseley Ct MK8 33 F1
Losfield Rd SL4 209 E6
Lossie Dr SL3 207 B6
Lothersdale MK13 34 B5
Lothian Cl MK3 46 E2
Lott Mdw HP21 115 D3
Lott Wlk HP21 115 D3
Louches La HP14 161 E6
Loudhams Rd HP7 166 C8
Loudhams Wood La HP8 166 D7
LOUDWATER 174 D2
Loudwater Comb Sch HP11 174 B2
Loudwater Mill 8 HP10 174 C2
Loughborough Dr 4 MK10 36 C4
LOUGHTON 46 A8
Loughton Manor First Sch MK5 46 A8
Loughton Rd MK13 34 A3
Loughton Rdbt MK8 45 F8
Loughton Sch MK5 46 A7
Loughton Valley Pk MK5 46 D7
Louisa Cotts 10 HP23 119 A3
Louise Wlk HP3 146 A3
Lovat Fields Village MK15 35 C5
Lovat Meadow Cl MK16 22 E3
Lovat St MK16 22 D4
Lovatt Dr MK3 57 E8
LOVE GREEN 207 D8
Love Green La SL0 207 E8
Lovegrove Dr SL2 197 F1
Love Hill La SL3 207 A6
Lovejoy La SL4 209 D5
Love La SL0 207 D7
Lovelace Cl SL6 193 F4
Lovel End SL9 177 C3
Lovell Way HP17 126 E6
Lovel Mead SL9 177 C3
Lovel Rd SL9 177 C2
Love Row MK17 68 D6
Lovett Gdns SL6 196 C3
Lovett Rd UB9 190 C8
Lovetts End LU7 78 E8
Lovibonds Ave UB7 208 F7
Lowbrook Acad SL6 202 A3
Lowbrook Cl HP21 116 A4
Lowbrook Dr SL6 202 A3
Lowdell Cl UB7 208 E7
Lowdon Cl HP11 173 D4
LOWER ASCOTT 79 F1
Lower Ascott LU7 80 A1
Lower Ash Yard MK17 67 F8
LOWER ASSENDON 191 A6
LOWER BOIS 154 C5
Lower Boyndon Rd SL6 202 E6
Lower Breaches Gdns MK43 25 B3
Lower Britwell Rd SL2 197 D1
LOWER CADSDEN 139 E5
Lower Church St
Cuddington HP18 112 F3
Stokenchurch HP14 158 E5
Lower Cippenham La SL1 204 F6
Lower Cl HP19 115 B7
Lower Cookham Rd SL6 196 C3
Lower Dr HP9 175 D5
Lower Eighth St MK9 34 E2
LOWER END
Long Crendon 125 B7
Marsworth 104 F3
Marsworth HP23 104 F2
Thornborough 53 F8
Woburn Sands 49 C8
Lower End
Ashendon HP18 97 E1
Lower End MK18 53 F8
Newton Longville MK17 57 C3
Piddington OX25 81 D1
Piddington OX25 95 E8
Wingrave HP22 89 B2
Lower End Rd MK17 49 A8
Lower Farm Cl HP18 124 D3
Lower Farm Gate HP17 114 A3
Lower Farm La MK18 63 B7
Lower Fourth St MK9 34 D1
Lower Furney Cl HP13 173 D8
Lower Gn
Cuddington HP18 112 F3
Westcott HP18 98 C7
Weston Turville HP22 117 A3
Lower Green La HP18 112 C2
Lower Hammersley La HP13 174 B4
LOWER HARTWELL 114 E6
Lower Hartwell HP17 114 E5
Lower Icknield Way
Chinnor OX39 147 D8
Great Kimble HP17 129 D1
Marsworth HP23 105 B1
Monks Risborough HP17 139 B8
Pitch Green HP27 138 C3
Wilstone HP22, HP23 118 C7
Lower Kings Rd HP4 135 C5
Lower Lees Rd SL2 198 B2
Lower Lodge La HP15 163 A5
Lower Mead SL0 200 D2
Lower Mount Farm SL6 195 D5
Lower Ninth St MK9 34 E2
LOWER NORTH DEAN 150 E1
LOWER POLLICOTT 111 F7
Lower Pound La SL7 194 D8
Lower Rd
Aylesbury HP21, HP22 115 F3
Blackthorn OX25 81 A4
Blackthorn OX25 81 A4
Chinnor OX39 147 C7
Chorleywood WD3 167 D5
Cookham Rise SL6 195 E7
Denham UB9 189 D4
Ford HP17 128 A8
Gerrards Cross SL9 188 F6
Gerrards Cross SL9 188 F7
Haddenham HP17 127 D7
Hardwick HP22 87 B3
Lacey Green HP27 149 D6
Stone HP17 114 C3
Lower Ridge SL8 185 B4
Lower Riding HP9 175 B2
Lower Second St MK9 34 D1
Lower St
Pury End NN12 17 A7
Quainton HP22 85 A5
Lower Stonehayes MK14 34 F7
Lower Tenth St MK9 34 F2
Lower Third St MK9 34 D1
Lower Twelfth St MK9 34 F3
Lower Ventnor Cotts SL6 195 C8
LOWER WAINHILL 147 E7
Lower Ward SL4 210 D7
Lower Way
Great Brickhill MK17 59 C1
Padbury MK18 53 C2
LOWER WEALD 32 E2
Lower Weald MK19 32 E2
Lower Wharf MK18 41 E1
LOWER WOODEND 182 D4
Lower Woodend Rd SL7 182 D4
Lowes Cl HP14 158 C5
Lowestoft Dr SL1 204 D7
Lowfield Cl HP15 163 B3
Lowfield Way HP15 163 B3
Lowick Pl 4 MK4 46 B2
Low La HP17 113 B2
Lowland Rd MK3 57 C8
Lowlands Cres HP15 151 D1
Lowlands Dr TW19 213 D2
Lowlands Rd TW19 213 D2
Lowman Way HP21 115 D4
Low Mdw HP22 116 F3
Lowndes Ave HP5 144 B1
Lowndes Gr MK5 45 F7
Lowndes Way MK18 66 A5
Lownes Path HP19 114 F8
Loxbeare Dr MK4 46 C4
Loxboro Hill HP14 160 D4
Loxley Rd HP4 134 F6
Loxley Stables HP23 104 B3
Loxwood Cl HP3 146 F8
Loyne Cl LU7 80 C8
Lucas Pl MK6 47 D8
Lucas Rd HP13 173 C7
Luccombe MK4 46 D3
Lucius La MK11 33 A3
Lucky La or Cock La HP20 101 D1
Lucy La MK5 46 B8
Ludgate
Milton Keynes MK6 46 E7
Ludgate *continued*
Tring HP23 118 F4
LUDGERSHALL 96 D8
Ludgershall Rd
Brill HP18 96 B4
Brill HP18 96 E4
Piddington OX25 95 E7
Ludlow Cl MK3 57 F7
Ludlow Dr OX9 126 A1
Ludlow Ho SL6 202 E6
Ludlow Mews HP11 174 A4
Ludlow Pl HP20 116 B8
Ludlow Rd SL6 202 E6
Luff Cl SL4 209 E4
Lufford Pk
Great Linford MK16 21 F1
Milton Keynes MK14 34 F8
Luggershall Rd OX25 95 E7
Luke Pl MK10 35 F3
Luker Ave RG9 191 D3
Lukes La HP23 104 D3
Lukes Lea
Marsworth HP23 104 F1
Marsworth HP23 105 A1
Lullingstone Dr MK13 33 F5
Lumber La NN12 17 B7
Lummas Mead OX39 147 C5
Lundholme MK13 34 B5
Lundy Ct SL1 204 E6
Lundy Wk MK3 58 C3
Lupin Cl UB7 208 D1
Lupin Ct HP21 115 B5
Lupin Wlk HP21 115 B5
Lutman La SL6 195 F2
Lutyens Gr MK7 48 D5
Luxborough Gr MK4 46 C4
Lychgate Cotts HP3 146 B4
Lycrome La HP5 144 D3
Lycrome Rd HP5 144 E3
Lydbrook La MK17 49 B5
Lyde End HP27 138 B1
Lydford Ave
2 Slough SL2 198 D1
Slough SL2 205 D8
Lydiard MK8 33 E1
Lydiard Cl HP21 116 A4
Lydsey Cl SL2 198 A2
LYE GREEN 144 F4
Lye Green Cotts HP5 144 E3
Lye Green Rd HP5 144 E2
Lyell Place E SL4 209 C4
Lyell Place W SL4 209 C4
Lyell Rd SL4 209 C4
Lyell Walk E SL4 209 C4
Lyell Walk W SL4 209 C4
Lye The HP4 121 D6
Lyme Ave HP4 134 D7
Lynch Cl UB8 201 C5
Lynch Hill Enterprise Acad SL2 206 A7
Lynch Hill La SL2 197 E2
Lynch Hill Sch SL2 197 F2
Lynch The UB8 201 C5
Lyndhurst Ave SL6 195 E6
Lyndhurst Cl HP13 161 D1
Lyndhurst Rd HP5 144 B2
Lyndon Cl HP16 151 C7
Lyndon Gdns HP13 173 E8
Lyndwood Dr SL4 211 A1
Lyndwood Par SL4 211 A2
Lyneham Gdns SL6 195 B1
Lynher Cl HP21 115 C4
Lynmouth Cres
Milton Keynes MK4 46 D4
Shenley Brook End MK4 46 C4
Lynnens View HP18 109 D5
Lynott Cl MK8 45 E6
Lynton Gn SL6 202 E7
Lynton Rd HP5 144 C3
Lynwood Ave SL3 206 D3
Lynwood Rd HP21 116 A5
Lyon Rd MK1 47 B2
Lyons Way SL2 205 F6
Lysander Cl HP3 146 A4
Lysander Mead SL6 203 C8

M

Macdonald Cl HP6 154 D4
MacIntyre Sch HP22 89 C3
Mackenzie Mall 3 SL1 205 F4
Mackenzie St 2 SL1 205 F4
Maconi Croft MK5 46 C5
Madeira Mdws MK3 58 B4
Madeira Wlk SL4 210 D6
Madeley Cl HP6 154 D3
Madeley Rd HP21 115 E6
Madura Gdns MK8 45 C7
Magdalen Cl
Milton Keynes MK11 32 D6
Syresham NN13 27 C8
Magdalen Ho MK11 32 D6
Magenta Cl MK2 58 D6
Magna Pk MK17 36 F1
Magnet L Ctr SL6 203 A8
Magnolia Dene HP15 162 F2
Magnolia Gdns SL3 206 C3
Magnolia St UB7 208 D2
Magnolia Way HP10 185 E7
Magnus Gr MK11 32 E3
Magpie Cl HP10 174 A1
Magpie La
Coleshill HP7 165 A1
Flackwell Heath HP10 174 A1
Loudwater HP13 174 B3
Magpie Way
Slough SL2 197 F1
Winslow MK18 66 B6
Mahler Cl MK7 48 C5
Mahoney Ct
High Wycombe HP11 172 F8
Milton Keynes MK8 45 D6
Maia Way MK11 32 F4
Maida Vale 3 MK10 35 F1
MAIDENHEAD 202 F4
Maidenhead Ave MK13 34 C3
MAIDENHEAD COURT 196 C4
Maidenhead Court Pk SL6 196 B3
Maidenhead Ct SL6 196 C3
Maidenhead Heritage Ctr 13 SL6 202 F7
Maidenhead Rd
Cookham Rise SL6 195 F6
Windsor SL4 209 E7
Maidenhead Ret Pk SL6 203 A6
Maidenhead Sta SL6 202 F6
MAIDENSGROVE 179 C5
Maids Cl MK17 67 D6
MAIDS MORETON 41 E4
Maids Moreton CE Sch MK18 41 E3
Maids Moreton Rd MK18 42 B6
Maidstone Rd MK10 36 C2
Maigno Way 1 MK12 33 A6
Main Dr
Gerrards Cross SL9 188 C6
Iver SL0 207 E3
Potterspury NN12 18 B2
Main Par WD3 167 C5
Main Rd
Aston Clinton HP22 117 E7
Astwood MK16 16 B3
Boarstall HP18 95 B2
Dinton HP17 113 F2
Dinton HP17 114 A1
Drayton Parslow MK17 68 B5
Ford HP17 128 B7
Hambleden RG9 182 A5
Lacey Green HP27 149 E5
Littlecote MK18 78 A5
Mill End RG10 192 E8
Puttenham HP23 103 D1
Rotten Row RG9 181 F2
Syresham NN13 27 C7
Upper Winchendon HP18 99 A1
Walter's Ash HP14 161 C7
Main Road N HP4 107 A6
Main Road S HP4 107 D4
Main St
Adstock MK18 53 F1
Akeley MK18 41 F8
Ashendon HP18 97 F1
Barton Hartshorn MK18 50 D1
Beachampton MK19 44 A6
Boarstall HP18 109 A8
Buckingham MK18 41 F3
Chackmore MK18 40 F1
Chackmore MK18 41 B4
Charndon OX27 72 E5
Chetwode MK18 61 E8
Cosgrove MK19 19 E2
Dadford MK18 28 D1
Dunton HP22 77 C4
Finmere MK18 50 D6
Gawcott MK18 51 F4
Grendon Underwood HP18 83 B5
Hoggeston MK18 76 F6
Hoggeston MK18 77 A6
Mursley MK17 67 D6
Padbury MK18 53 B1
Poundon OX27 71 F7
Preston Bissett MK18 62 B8
Radclive MK18 51 F8
Shalstone MK18 39 E6
Stowe MK18 40 D8
Tingewick MK18 51 B6
Turweston NN13 38 C8
Twyford MK18 62 C1
Westbury NN13 39 A4
Weston Turville HP22 116 E2
Mainst South MK18 52 A2
Maitland Dr HP13 173 B8
Maitland Rd HP22 131 D7
Major's Farm Rd
Datchet SL3 211 E8
Slough SL3 212 A8
Malbons Ct MK6 46 E7
Malborough Ho HP4 135 A3
Malborough Way NN12 18 F5
Malcolm Rd UB10 201 F8

Malden Cl HP6 . . . . . **154** F1
Malders La SL6 . . . . . **195** C3
Maldives Terr MK3 . . **58** B4
Malet Cl HP14 . . . . . . **158** F5
Malins Gate MK14 . . . **34** E8
Mallard Cl HP19 . . . . **101** E4
Mallard Croft HP17. **127** A7
Mallard Dr
  Buckingham MK18 . . . **52** E8
  Slough SL1 . . . . **204** F6
Mallard Ho HP11 . . . **173** C6
Mallard Pl HP11 . . . . **174** B3
Mallets End HP22 . . . **85** B4
Malletts Cl MK11 . . . . **32** E5
Mallow Gate MK14 . . . **34** E4
Mallow Pk SL6 . . . . . **195** C1
Malmers Well Rd
  HP13 . . . . **173** B7
Malpas Rd SL2 . . . . . **206** B6
Malthouse Flats
  RG9 . . . . **192** D6
Malthouse Sq
  Beaconsfield HP9 . . . **186** F8
  Princes Risborough
  HP27 . . . . **139** B4
Malthouse Way 2
  SL7 . . . . **183** D1
Malting Cl MK16 . . . . **12** B6
Malting La
  Aldbury HP23 . . . . . . **120** D5
  Dagnall HP4 . . . . . . **107** C5
Maltings Cl
  Cranfield MK43 . . . . . **25** A1
  Stewkley LU7 . . . . . . **78** E8
Maltings Ct MK19 . . . . **20** A5
Maltings Field HP19 . **19** F5
Maltings Row MK18 . . **31** E4
Maltings The
  Chackmore MK18 . . . . **41** B4
  3 Olney MK46 . . . . . . **7** A3
  Tingewick MK18 . . . . . **51** B6
Malt La NN13 . . . . . . **27** C8
Maltmans Green Sch
  SL9 . . . . **188** C8
Maltmans La SL9. . . . **188** C8
Malton Ave SL1 . . . . **205** B6
Malton Cl MK10 . . . . . **35** F1
Malvern Cl HP13 . . . . **172** E4
Malvern Ct SL3 . . . . **212** A7
Malvern Dr
  Leighton Buzzard
  LU7 . . . . **80** C8
  Milton Keynes MK11 . . **33** A4
Malvern Rd
  Aylesbury HP20. . . . . **116** C8
  Maidenhead SL6 . . . . **195** D1
Malyns Cl OX39 . . . . . **147** C7
Manchester Terr
  HP14 . . . . **171** B4
Mandela Ct UB8 . . . . **208** C7
Mandelyns HP4 . . . . **134** E2
Mandeville Dr MK10 . . **36** C2
Mandeville Mews 9
  HP21 . . . . **115** E4
Mandeville Rd
  Aylesbury HP21 . . . . . **115** E5
  Prestwood HP16 . . . . **151** B7
Mandeville Sch The
  HP21 . . . . **115** D4
Manfield Cl SL2 . . . . **198** A2
Manifold La MK4,
  MK5 . . . . **46** B3
Mann Way MK46 . . . . . **6** E6
Manor Cl
  Berkhamsted HP4 . . . **135** C4
  Bledlow HP27 . . . . . . **138** B1
  Buckingham MK18 . . . **53** C2
  Cosgrove MK19. . . . . . **19** E2
  Deanshanger MK19 . . . **31** F3
  Hanslope MK19 . . . . . . **11** A2
  Lewknor OX49 . . . . . **157** A8
  Milton Keynes MK10 . . **35** F1
  Milton Keynes MK17 . . **67** D6
  Prestwood HP16 . . . . **151** D4
  Salford MK17 . . . . **37** D3
  Stoke Hammond MK17 . **69** E7
  Tylers Green HP10 . . . **163** A2
Manor Cotts
  Chorleywood WD3 . . . **167** B3
  Milton Keynes MK12 . . **33** B7
Manor Court Yd
  HP13 . . . . **162** A1
Manor Court Yd
  OX33 . . . . **123** B2
Manor Cres
  Seer Green HP9 . . . . **176** D5
  Wendover HP22 . . . . **131** C5
Manor Ct
  Emberton MK46 . . . . . **13** F8
  Leighton Buzzard LU7 . . **70** E2
  Marlow SL7 . . . . **183** C3
  Slough, Cippenham
  SL1 . . . . **204** F5
  6 Slough, Upton Park
  SL1 . . . . **205** F3
  Twyford MK18 . . . . . . **62** C1
Manor Ctyd
  Haddenham HP17 . . . **127** D4
  Sherington MK16 . . . . **13** F1
Manor Dr
  Amersham HP6 . . . . . **154** B3
  Aylesbury HP20 . . . . **101** E2
  Haversham MK19 . . . . **20** E2
  Stewkley LU7 . . . . . . **78** E8

Manor Farm SL3 . . . **212** E5
Manor Farm Cl
  Edlesborough LU6. . . . **92** F3
  Soulbury LU7 . . . . **69** E2
  Stone HP17 . . . . **114** C5
  Weston Turville
  HP22 . . . . **116** E2
  Windsor SL4 . . . . . . **209** F4
Manor Farm Com Inf
  Sch HP15 . . . . **163** B2
Manor Farm Cotts
  SL4 . . . . **211** A2
Manor Farm Ct HP22 **87** B2
Manor Farm Ctyd
  HP22 . . . . **102** D8
Manor Farm Ho SL4 **209** F4
Manor Farm La
  Gawcott MK18 . . . . . . **52** C4
  Ledburn LU7 . . . . **90** C8
Manor Farm Rd
  Barton Hartshorn
  MK18 . . . . **50** D2
  Henton OX39 . . . . . . **137** E2
Manor Farm Way
  HP9 . . . . **176** D4
Manorfields Rd
  MK19 . . . . **32** B6
Manor Gdns
  Grendon Underwood
  HP18 . . . . **83** A6
  High Wycombe HP13 . . **162** A1
  Maids Moreton MK18 . . **41** E2
  Wooburn Green
  HP10 . . . . **185** E5
Manor Green Sch
  SL6 . . . . **202** A3
Manor Ho
  Brill HP18 . . . . **110** A8
  Hambleden RG9 . . . . **181** D2
Manor House Cl
  HP20 . . . . **101** F1
Manor House La
  Datchet SL3 . . . . . . **211** B6
  Lillingstone Lovell
  MK18 . . . . **30** A4
Manor La
  Gerrards Cross SL9 . . **188** D4
  Maidenhead SL6 . . . . **202** E4
MANOR PARK
  Aylesbury **101** E2
  Slough **198** D1
Manor Park Ave
  HP27 . . . . **139** A3
Manor Pk MK18 . . . . . **41** F4
Manor Pound Rd
  LU7 . . . . **105** A7
Manor Rd
  Akeley MK18 . . . . **41** F7
  Aylesbury HP20. . . . . **101** E1
  Cheddington LU7. . . . **104** F7
  Chesham HP5 . . . . . **144** C2
  Emmington OX9 . . . . **137** B6
  Hughenden HP14 . . . **162** A4
  Maidenhead SL6 . . . . **202** E4
  Milton Keynes, Bletchley
  MK2 . . . . **58** E8
  Milton Keynes, Wolverton
  MK12 . . . . **33** B7
  Newport Pagnell
  MK16 . . . . **22** A4
  Newton Longville
  MK17 . . . . **57** D3
  Oakley HP18 . . . . . . **109** D5
  Oving HP22 . . . . **86** C7
  Princes Risborough
  HP27 . . . . **139** A2
  Rowsham HP22. . . . . **102** D8
  Seer Green HP9 . . . . **176** D5
  Towersey OX9 . . . . . **137** B6
  Tring HP23 . . . . **119** A5
  Tylers Green HP10 . . . **163** A2
  Wendover HP22 . . . . **131** C5
  Windsor SL4 . . . . . . **209** E5
Manor St
  Berkhamsted HP4 . . . **135** D4
  Buckingham MK18 . . . **52** C8
Manor View
  Hazelmere HP15 . . . . **163** B2
  Steeple Claydon MK18 **63** E3
Manor View Ho
  HP13 . . . . **161** E2
Manor Way
  Chesham HP5 . . . . . **144** D1
  Coleshill HP7 . . . . . . **164** F3
  Yardley Gobion NN12 . **18** E2
Manor Waye UB7 . . . **201** D4
Mansard Cl 8
  HP23 . . . . **119** A3
Manse Cl MK11 . . . . . **32** D6
Mansell Cl
  Cosgrove MK19. . . . . . **19** E2
  Slough SL2 . . . . **206** B8
Manshead Ct MK11. . **32** F5
Mansion Dr HP23 . . . **119** B3
Mansion Gdns NN12. **18** E2
Mansion Hill HP22 . . **131** E8
Mansion La
  Harrold MK43 . . . . **3** F6
  Iver SL0 . . . . **207** C6
Mansion The HP4 . . **135** E6
Mantle Cl SL4 . . . . . **209** D4
MANTLES GN **165** A8
Manton Rd LU6 . . . . . **93** D5
Manx Rd MK8 . . . . **45** C7
Maple Ave UB7 . . . . **208** F5

Manor Farm Cl . . .
Maple Cl
  Hazelmere HP15 . . . . **163** A3
  High Wycombe HP12 . . **172** C5
  Maidenhead SL6 . . . . **202** C5
Maple Cres SL2 . . . . **206** B6
MAPLE CROSS **178** D6
Maple Cross JMI Sch
  WD3 . . . . **178** E5
Maple Ct
  Marlow SL7 . . . . **183** E3
  Windsor SL4 . . . . . . **210** C4
Mapledean MK12 . . . **33** E4
Mapledurham MK7 . . **48** B3
Mapledurham Wlk
  SL6 . . . . **195** E3
Maple End
  Aylesbury HP22. . . . . **116** C4
  Stoke Mandeville
  HP22 . . . . **116** C4
Maplefield La HP8 . . **166** B6
Maple Gr
  Milton Keynes MK2 . . . **58** E8
  Woburn Sands MK17. . . **49** B4
Maple Hill HP3 . . . . . **145** D1
Maple Leys MK18 . . . . **63** E3
Maple Lodge Cl
  WD3 . . . . **178** E6
Maple Pl UB7 . . . . . **208** F5
Maple Rise SL7 . . . . **183** E3
Maples The
  5 Bourne End SL8 . . **185** B3
  Wendover HP22 . . . . **131** C5
Maplewood Gdns
  HP9 . . . . **175** B1
Maplin Pk SL3 . . . . . **207** B4
Mapperton Cl 3
  MK4 . . . . **45** F1
Mapridge Green La
  HP16 . . . . **141** D1
Marand Ct HP21 . . . . **115** F8
Mara Pl MK9 . . . . **35** A3
Marbeck Cl SL4 . . . . **209** D6
Marcellus Wlk MK11 **32** F3
Marcellus Wy MK11 . **33** A3
Marchant Ct SL7 . . . **184** A3
March Edge MK18. . . . **41** E1
Marches The SL4 . . . **205** D2
March Mdw MK7 . . . . **48** D7
March Pl HP19 . . . . . **115** B8
Marcia Ct SL1 . . . . . **204** F5
Mardle Rd LU7 . . . . . **80** E6
Maree Cl
  Leighton Buzzard
  LU7 . . . . **80** C7
  Milton Keynes MK2 . . . **58** C5
Marefield Rd SL7. . . . **183** D2
Mare Leys MK18 . . . . . **52** F8
Marescroft Rd SL2 . **197** E1
Margam Cres MK10 . . **36** A1
Margaret Ct HP13 . . **173** E5
Margaret Lowe Pl
  HP22 . . . . **117** E4
Margaret Powell Sq
  MK9 . . . . **34** F3
Margaret Smythe Ho
  SL9 . . . . **188** F5
Margarita Gdns
  MK17 . . . . **58** B2
Marie Cl OX27 . . . . . . **71** F7
Marigold Pl MK14 . . . **34** E4
Marigold Wlk HP15. . **162** F6
Marina Dr
  Dunstable LU6. . . . . . **93** E7
  Milton Keynes MK12 . . **33** D6
Marina Rdbt MK6 . . . **47** C7
Marina Way
  Iver SL0 . . . . **208** A6
  Slough SL1 . . . . **204** D6
Marine Ct MK6. . . . . . **46** F6
Mariner Pl UB7 . . . . **208** F2
Marino Blvd MK19 . . . **33** D1
Marion Cres MK17. . . . **48** E8
Marish Ct SL3 . . . . . **207** A3
Marish La UB9 . . . . . **189** D7
Marish Primary Sch
  SL2 . . . . **206** F3
Marish Prim Sch
  SL3 . . . . **207** A3
Marish Wharf Ind Est
  SL3 . . . . **206** E4
Maritime Wy MK16. . . **36** B5
Marius Gr MK11 . . . . . **32** E3
Marjoram Pl MK14 . . **34** E4
Marjorie Cl 9
  HP18 . . . . **100** D5
Mark Dr SL9 . . . . **177** E6
Market Hill
  Buckingham MK18 . . . **41** D1
  Milton Keynes MK6 . . . **47** B8
  Whitchurch HP22 . . . . **86** F6
Market Ho 5 SL9 . . **177** D2
Market La SL3 . . . . **207** C3
Market Par HP15 . . . **163** A4
Market Pl
  Chalfont St Peter
  SL9 . . . . **177** D2
  Colnbrook SL3 . . . . . **212** C7
  Henley-on-Thames
  RG9 . . . . **191** D2
  4 Olney MK46 . . . . . . **6** F3
  Woburn MK17 . . . . **60** F7
Market Place Mews 5
  RG9 . . . . **191** D2
Market Sq
  Amersham HP7 . . . . . **165** B7
  Aylesbury HP20. . . . . **115** D8
  5 Buckingham MK18 . . **41** D1

Market Sq continued
  Chesham HP5 . . . . . **154** B8
  Eaton Bray LU6 . . . . . . **92** D6
  Hanslope MK19 . . . . . . **11** A2
  Marlow SL7 . . . . **183** D2
  Milton Keynes MK11 . . **32** D5
  Princes Risborough
  HP27 . . . . **139** B3
  Uxbridge UB8 . . . . . . **201** C5
  Winslow MK18 . . . . . . **65** F4
Market St
  Maidenhead SL6 . . . . **202** F7
  9 Windsor SL4 . . . . . **210** D6
Markham Cl HP19 . . . **115** A7
Markhams Cl MK18. . . **52** D8
Marks Orch MK18 . . . **75** F7
Marlborough Cl
  SL6 . . . . **202** A6
Marlborough Ct
  SL1 . . . . **204** D7
Marlborough Gate
  MK9 . . . . **34** F3
Marlborough Ho 5
  SL6 . . . . **202** F6
Marlborough Rd
  Aylesbury HP21 . . . . . **115** E4
  Maidenhead SL6 . . . . **202** A6
  Slough SL3 . . . . **206** D2
Marlborough St
  Milton Keynes, Neath Hill
  MK14 . . . . **34** E6
  Milton Keynes, Tinkers
  Bridge MK6. . . . . **47** D6
  Stantonbury MK13 . . . **34** D8
  Woughton on the Green
  MK6 . . . . **47** B8
Marlborough Trad Est
  HP11 . . . . **172** F7
Marley Gr MK8 . . . . . . **45** E7
Marley Wlk MK10. . . . . **36** D3
Marlin Chapel La
  HP4 . . . . **134** C2
Marlin Cl HP4 . . . . . **134** F5
Marlin Copse HP4 . . **135** A3
Marlin Ct SL7 . . . . . **183** D1
Marlin Hill HP23 . . . **133** A8
Marlins Cl WD3 . . . . **167** E7
Marlins End HP4 . . . **134** F3
Marlins End HP4 . . . **134** F3
MARLOW **183** B2
MARLOW BOTTOM . . **183** C6
Marlow Bottom
  SL7 . . . . **183** D6
Marlow Bridge La
  Bisham SL7 . . . . **194** E8
  Marlow SL7 . . . . **183** E1
Marlow CE Inf Sch
  SL7 . . . . **183** D3
Marlow Com Hospl
  SL7 . . . . **183** E2
Marlow Comm SL7 . **182** F3
MARLOW
  COMMON **182** F3
Marlow Comm Rd
  Great Marlow SL7. . . . **182** E1
  Great Marlow SL7. . . . **182** E2
Marlow Dr MK16 . . . . **22** A4
Marlow Hill HP11 . . . **173** A5
Marlow Lodge 13
  SL6 . . . . **202** F6
Marlow Mill SL7 . . . . **183** E1
Marlow Rd
  Bisham SL7 . . . . **194** E7
  Great Marlow SL7. . . . **182** F8
  Hambleden RG9 . . . . **192** A8
  Henley-on-Thames
  RG9 . . . . **191** E3
  High Wycombe HP11 . . **172** E4
  Lane End HP14, SL7. . . **171** E2
  Little Marlow SL7 . . . **184** C5
  Maidenhead SL6 . . . . **202** F7
  Maidenhead, Furze Platt
  SL6 . . . . **194** E4
  Stokenchurch HP14 . . **170** B6
Marlow Sta SL7 . . . . **183** E2
Marple La SL9 . . . . . **177** D2
Marquess Dr 3 MK3 **58** D8
Marquis Ct MK17. . . . . **60** F7
Marram Cl MK6 . . . . . . **47** A5
Marriotts Ave HP16. **142** E4
Marriott's Cl HP17 . . **126** F5
Marriott's La HP17 . . **126** F6
Marriott's Way
  HP7 . . . . **175** C8
Marron La MK12 . . . . **33** C5
Marroway HP22 . . . . **116** D2
MARSH **129** C7
Marsham Cl HP21 . . . **116** A4
Marshalls La MK15. . . **35** C2
Marshalls Lea HP22 **102** C5
Marsham Cl HP21 . . . **116** A4
Marshaw Pl 3 MK4 . . **46** C2
Marshcroft La
  HP23 . . . . **119** D6
Marsh Dr MK14 . . . . . **21** E1
Marsh End Rd MK16. . **22** D3
Marshfield SL3 . . . . **211** C6

Marshgate Trad Est
  SL6 . . . . **204** A7
MARSH GIBBON CE Sch
  OX27. . . . . **71** F3
Marsh Gibbon Rd
  Edgcott OX27 . . . . **72** D1
  Furze Ground OX27 . . . **81** B6
  Grendon Underwood
  HP18 . . . . **82** E8
  Marsh Gibbon OX27. . . **81** C8
  Piddington OX25. . . . . **81** D3
  Piddington OX25. . . . . **95** C8
Marsh Inf Sch HP11 **173** F4
Marsh La
  Little Kimble HP17. . . **129** C5
  Marsh HP17 . . . . **129** D8
  Stoke Mandeville
  HP22 . . . . **129** F8
  Taplow SL6 . . . . **203** E6
Marshment Cl HP22 **117** D5
Marsh Rd
  Great Kimble HP22 . . . **129** D4
  Shabbington HP18 . . . **124** D3
Marsh The MK43 . . . . **3** F3
Marshworth MK6 . . . . **47** D6
Marston Cl HP5 . . . . **144** A4
Marston Cl HP23 . . . . **104** B4
Marston Gate HP22. **102** B1
Marston Hill
  Cranfield MK43 . . . . . . **25** F2
  Oving HP22 . . . . **86** C8
Marston Rd
  Granborough MK18. . . . **75** F6
  Thame OX9 . . . . **126** A1
MARSWORTH **105** A1
Marsworth CE Inf Sch
  HP23 . . . . **105** A4
Marsworth Rd LU7 . . **105** D4
Marsworth Reservoir *
  HP23 . . . . **119** A3
Marsworth Wharf
  HP23 . . . . **104** F1
Martell Cl MK7 . . . . . . **48** A3
Martha La HP22 . . . . **102** D3
Martina Cl MK11 . . . . . **32** F3
Martin Ave MK17 . . . . **48** E8
Martin Cl
  Buckingham MK18 . . . **52** F7
  Milton Keynes MK14 . . **34** E6
  Uxbridge UB10 . . . . . **201** E3
  Windsor SL4 . . . . . . **209** D6
Martin Dalby Wy
  Aylesbury HP18. . . . . **100** F5
  Aylesbury HP19. . . . . **101** B5
Martindale SL0 . . . . **200** D1
Martin Dell Cotts
  HP16 . . . . **142** E4
Martingale Pl MK14 . . **34** F5
Martinique Mdws
  MK17 . . . . **58** B2
Martin Rd
  Maidenhead SL6 . . . . **202** F8
  Slough SL1 . . . . **205** E3
Martins Dr The LU7 . . **80** F8
Martinsend La
  HP16 . . . . **151** E7
Martin's Plain SL2 . . **198** F3
Martlet The 1 MK6 . . **47** C4
Martlet Way HP19. . . **100** D5
Martyrs Ct HP7. . . . . **165** C8
Marunden Gn SL2 . . **197** F2
Marwood Cl MK4. . . . . **46** D3
Mary Bassett Lower Sch
  The LU7 . . . . **80** F7
Mary Cross Cl HP23 **119** D1
Marygold Wlk HP6 . . **166** C8
Maryland ML17 . . . . . **60** E6
Maryland Rd MK15 . . **35** B8
Mary MacManus Dr
  MK18 . . . . **41** D1
Mary Morgan Ct
  SL2 . . . . **205** D8
Maryot Cl MK16 . . . . . **13** F2
Mary Rose MK16 . . . . **36** B5
Maryside SL3 . . . . . **206** E4
Marys Mead HP15 . . **163** A4
Mary Towerton Sch The
  HP14 . . . . **159** D3
Mascoll Path SL2 . . **197** F2
Masefield Cl
  Chesham HP5 . . . . . **144** B3
  Newport Pagnell MK16 **22** A4
Masefield Gr MK3 . . . **58** A7
Maslin Dr MK6 . . . . . . **47** B5
Maslin Elms HP17 . . **127** A5
Mason Cl MK14 . . . . . **34** C8
Masons Cl HP16. . . . **151** C5
Masons Ct HP5. . . . . **144** C1
Mason's Ct
  Aylesbury HP19. . . . . **115** B7
  Slough SL1 . . . . **204** E6
Masons Rd SL1 . . . . **204** E6
Masons Yd HP4 . . . . **135** D4
Massie Cl MK15 . . . . . **35** B6
Masterman Pl UB8 . . **201** E5
Mathecombe Rd 1
  SL1 . . . . **205** A4
Mathias La MK17 . . . . **36** F3
Mathiesen Rd MK13. . **34** A6
Mathisen Way SL3 . . **212** E6
Matilda Gdns MK5. . . . **46** B5
Matlock Rd MK10 . . . **101** F2
Matson Dr RG9. . . . . **191** D2
Matthau La MK4 . . . . . **45** D3
Matthew Ct MK5 . . . . . **46** B6

Matthews Cl 11
  HP20 . . . . **101** F2
Maude Cl HP9 . . . . . **176** A1
Maude Rd HP9 . . . . . **176** A1
Maud Jane's Cl LU7 **105** E5
Maudsley Cl MK5. . . . . **46** C6
Maudsley Ho SL6. . . . **203** A7
Mauduit Cl MK19. . . . . **11** A3
Maulden Gdns MK14 **35** A8
Mauretania Wy
  MK10 . . . . **36** D3
Maurice Mount
  HP15 . . . . **162** F5
Maurice Mws HP12. **172** E8
Mavoncliff Dr
  Milton Keynes MK4 . . . **57** A8
  Shenley Brook End
  MK4 . . . . **57** A8
Maxham MK5 . . . . **46** A3
Maximus Ct MK11 . . . **32** F2
Maxstoke Gr 17 MK4. **56** E8
Maxwell Ct SL1 . . . . **197** C1
Maxwell Dr HP15 . . . **163** B5
Maxwell Pl HP9 . . . . **175** E3
Maxwell Rd
  Beaconsfield HP9 . . . **175** E3
  West Drayton UB7. . . . **208** F2
Maybach Ct MK5 . . . . **46** B5
Maybrick Rd HP22. . . **102** C2
Maybrook Gdns
  HP13 . . . . **173** C8
Maybury Cl SL1 . . . . **204** D7
Maybush Gdns
  HP16 . . . . **151** C6
Maybush Wlk MK46 . . **6** E5
May Cl LU6 . . . . **92** E6
Mayditch Pl MK13 . . . **34** C3
Mayer Gdns MK5. . . . . **46** C5
Mayfield Dr SL4. . . . . **210** A4
Mayfield Rd HP10 . . . **185** E6
Mayflower St MK18. . . **52** F6
Mayflower Wy
  Beaconsfield HP9 . . . **186** A8
  Farnham Common
  SL2 . . . . **198** C8
Mayfly La HP22 . . . . . **102** E5
Maygoods Cl UB8 . . **208** D8
Maygoods Gn UB8 . . **208** D8
Maygoods La UB8. . . **208** D8
Maygoods View
  UB8. . . . . **208** C8
Mayhall Farm HP6 . . **154** A4
Mayhall La HP6 . . . . **154** B4
Mayhew Cres HP13 **173** D8
Maylands Dr UB8. . . . **201** D6
Maynard Cl MK13 . . . . **34** A3
Maynard Ct SL4. . . . . **210** A6
Mayne Terr MK19 . . . . **10** F3
Mayorfield Ho 1
  SL7 . . . . **183** D2
Maypole Rd SL6. . . . . **204** A8
Maypool Way 1
  MK10 . . . . **36** B2
May Rd MK43 . . . . **8** E6
Mays Way NN12 . . . . . **18** E3
May Tree Cl SL7. . . . . **183** C6
McArdle Way SL3 . . **212** D7
McAuliffe Dr SL1,
  SL2 . . . . **197** F8
McConnell Dr MK12 . **33** E6
McCorquodale Rd
  MK12 . . . . **33** C7
McDougall Rd 8
  HP4 . . . . **135** D4
McEwen Ride HP22 **117** D1
Mcindoe Dr HP22 . . . **131** D6
Mc Kay Dr MK19 . . . . . **10** F3
McKay Trad Est SL3. **212** E5
McKenzie Cl MK18 . . **52** D8
McLellan Pl HP12 . . **172** D5
McLernon Way MK18 **66** A5
Mdw Dr HP3 . . . . **145** F3
Mdw View TW19 . . . **213** A2
Mead Acre SL3 . . . . **207** B4
Mead Ave SL3 . . . . . **207** B4
Mead Cl
  Datchet SL1 . . . . . . **206** A1
  Denham UB9 . . . . . . **190** A2
  7 Marlow SL7 . . . . . **183** F3
  Monks Risborough
  HP27 . . . . **139** B6
  Slough SL3 . . . . **207** B4
Mead Cres MK14 . . . . **21** F3
Meades La HP5 . . . . **154** B7
Meadfield Ave SL3 . **207** A3
Meadfield Rd SL3 . . **207** B3
Mead Furlong HP17 **127** B6
Mead Haze SL6 . . . . **196** C2
Mead Ho SL0 . . . . . . **200** D2
MEADLE **139** B8
Meadle Village Rd
  Longwick HP17 . . . . . **139** A8
  Smokey Row HP17 . . . **129** B1
Meadoway
  Steeple Claydon
  MK18 . . . . **63** E3
  Stone HP17 . . . . **114** F5
Meadow Bank 6
  SL8 . . . . **185** B3
Meadowbank Cl
  Bovingdon HP3 . . . . **146** B3
  Long Crendon HP18. . **125** C2
Meadow Bank Cl
  HP7 . . . . **154** E1
Meadowbrook
  Maidenhead SL6 . . . . **202** A5
  Tring HP23 . . . . **119** B6

Meadow Brook MK17 . 69 E7
Meadowbrook Cl
SL3 . . . . 212 F6
Meadow Cl
Aylesbury HP20. . . . . 102 A1
Berkhamsted HP4. . . . 135 A2
Chesham HP5 . . . . . . 144 A4
Cublington LU7 . . . . . 78 C1
High Wycombe HP11. . 173 F4
Marlow SL7. . . . . 183 F1
Oakley HP18 . . . . 109 D4
Old Windsor SL4 . . . . 211 B2
Tring HP23 . . . . 119 A4
Meadowcott La HP7 164 F3
Meadow Cotts
Beaconsfield HP9 . . . 175 E1
Little Kingshill HP16 . 152 B3
Stone HP17. . . . . 114 D3
Meadowcroft
Aylesbury HP19. . . . . 101 B3
Berkhamsted HP4. . . . 134 D7
Chalfont St Peter SL9 177 D1
Meadow Ct MK46 . . . . 5 D2
Meadow Dr
Amersham HP6. . . . . 154 E2
4 Bovingdon HP3. . . 146 A3
Longwick HP27. . . . . 138 D6
Meadow Farm Rd
MK43 . . . . 16 F1
Meadow Gate
Padbury MK18. . . . . . 53 B2
Prestwood HP16. . . . . 151 C3
Meadow Gdns MK18. 52 E6
Meadow High Sch
UB8. . . . . 208 E8
Meadow La
Beaconsfield HP9 . . . 175 F2
Eton SL4 . . . . 210 C7
Long Crendon HP18. . 125 E4
Milton Keynes MK10 . 36 A3
Pitstone LU7 . . . . 105 A3
South Heath HP16. . . 152 E8
Meadowlea Cl UB7 213 D8
Meadow Pk HP22 . . 116 C2
Meadow Rd
Berkhamsted HP4. . . . 135 B6
Chinnor OX39 . . . . . . 147 D6
Henley-on-Thames
RG9. . . . . 191 E1
Slough SL3 . . . . 206 E3
Meadow Rise HP27. 149 E5
Meadow Row MK18 . . 41 D1
Meadow Sh Ctr 4
MK18 . . . . 41 D1
Meadowside HP9 . . 176 F4
Meadows Sch The
HP10. . . . . 185 E7
Meadows The
1 Amersham HP7 . . 154 E1
Flackwell Heath
HP10. . . . . 185 B8
Old Stratford MK19. . . 32 B6
Whitchurch HP22 . . . . 86 F7
Meadowsweet MK7 . 48 B5
Meadowview TW19 212 F2
Meadow View
Aspley Guise MK17. . . 49 D6
Chalfont St Giles HP8 177 A7
2 Little Chalfont
HP6. . . . . 166 A8
Long Crendon HP18. . 125 E4
Marlow Bottom SL7. . 183 E6
Potterspury NN12. . . . 18 D3
Slough SL3 . . . . 206 F5
Stanwell TW19 . . . . . 213 A2
Upper Arncott OX25 . . 94 E8
Uxbridge UB8 . . . . . . 208 C8
Meadow Vw MK7 . . . 155 A1
Meadow Way
Aylesbury HP20. . . . . 102 A1
Dorney SL6 . . . . 203 F4
Felden HP3 . . . . 146 F7
Hyde Heath HP6 . . . . 153 C4
Old Windsor SL4 . . . . 211 B1
1 Thame OX9. . . . . . 125 F1
Wing LU7 . . . . 79 E3
Wing LU7 . . . . 79 F3
Meadow Wlk
Bourne End SL8. . . . . 185 A5
Buckingham MK18 . . . 41 D1
Tylers Green HP10 . . 163 C1
Mead Pk HP15 . . . . . 163 C7
Mead Platt HP14 . . . 158 D5
Mead Rd UB8 . . . . . . 201 D5
Meads Cl MK13 . . . . . 34 B8
Mead St HP13 . . . . . 174 A4
Meads The
Berkhamsted HP4. . . 134 F6
Eaton Bray LU6. . . . . 92 E5
Stoke Poges SL2 . . . 199 A2
Tring HP23 . . . . 119 B4
Uxbridge UB8 . . . . . . 201 E1
4 Windsor SL4. . . . . 210 A5
Mead The
Beaconsfield HP9 . . . 175 E2
Soulbury LU7. . . . . . . 69 E3
Meadway
Berkhamsted HP4. . . . 135 E5
Buckingham MK18 . . . 52 D6
Dunstable LU6. . . . . . 93 F7
Oving HP22. . . . . 76 E1
Mead Way
High Wycombe
HP11. . . . . 173 F4
Slough SL1 . . . . 204 D8
Meadway Ct LU6. . . . 93 F7
Meadway Pk SL9. . . 188 D3
Meadway The MK5 . 46 A7

Mead Wlk SL3 . . . . . 207 A4
Meare Estate HP10 . 185 E8
Meavy Cl HP13 . . . . . 174 B3
Medale Rd MK6. . . . . 47 B5
Medallion Pl SL6. . . 203 B7
MEDBOURNE. 45 E5
Medbourne Rdbt
MK8. . . . . 45 E6
Medeswell MK4. . . . . 46 E3
Medhurst MK8 . . . . . 33 E2
Medland MK6. . . . . . 47 D7
Medlar St HP22 . . . . 116 D6
Medley Cl LU6. . . . . . 92 F5
Medman Cl UB8. . . . 201 C3
MEDMENHAM. 193 A5
Medway Cl MK16. . . . 22 C1
Medway Ct MK4. . . . . 37 D8
Meeting Oak La
MK18. . . . . 66 B5
Megdale Pl HP20. . . 101 D2
Melba St HP19 . . . . . 100 E5
Melbourne Ave SL1 205 C7
Melbourne Cl HP21. 115 C5
Melbourne Rd HP13 173 F6
Melbourne Terr
MK13 . . . . 34 A7
Melford Gn HP19. . . 101 C3
Melford Rd SL2 . . . . 197 F1
Melfort Dr
Leighton Buzzard LU7 . 80 B6
Milton Keynes MK2 . . 58 D4
Melick Rd MK6. . . . . 47 B4
Melissa Ct HP13. . . . 173 D6
Mellish Ct MK3. . . . . 47 A2
Mellor Wlk 23 SL4. . 210 D6
Mellroc kd HP21. . . 115 F5
Melrose Ave MK3 . . . 47 A3
Melrose Ct HP13. . . . 162 B1
Melrose Gdns 1
SL2 . . . . 206 A3
Melrose Wlk HP21 . . 115 F5
Melton MK14 . . . . 34 C8
Melton Ct
Dunstable LU6. . . . . . 93 F7
Maidenhead SL6 . . . 202 F7
Melville Dr MK3 . . . . 58 A4
Melville St MK9 . . . . 35 A4
Memorial Rd HP16 . 150 D7
Menday Gdns MK17 . 48 F6
Mendelssohn Gr
MK7 . . . . 48 C4
Mendip Cl SL3 . . . . . 207 A1
Mendip St HP18. . . . 100 D5
Mendip Way HP13. . 172 F8
Mendy St HP11. . . . . 173 A7
Menmarsh Rd
Horton-Cum-Studley
HP18. . . . . 108 D1
Waterperry Common
HP18. . . . . 122 F8
Worminghall HP18 . . 123 A8
Worminghall HP18 . . 123 E6
Menteith Cl MK2 . . . . 58 C5
MENTMORE 90 D4
Mentmore LU7. . . . . . 90 D3
Mentmore Cl HP12 . 172 D8
Mentmore Cross Rds
LU7. . . . . 89 F6
Mentmore Ct
Mentmore LU7 . . . . . 90 D5
2 Milton Keynes MK8 .45 E8
Mentmore Gdns LU7 80 E5
Mentmore Gn 3
HP21. . . . . 115 E3
Mentmore Rd
Cheddington LU7. . . . 90 E1
Cheddington LU7. . . 104 F8
High Wycombe HP12. 172 B4
Leighton Buzzard LU7. 80 E5
Mentmore Towers ★
LU7. . . . . 90 C4
Mentmore View
HP23. . . . . 118 F5
Mentone Ave MK17. . 49 D4
Menzies Ct MK5. . . . 46 B4
Mercers Dr MK13 . . . 34 B6
Mercers Mdw MK22 131 B6
Mercer Wlk UB8 . . . 201 C5
Merchant La
Cranfield MK43. . . . . 25 A1
Cranfield, Wharley End
MK43 . . . . 24 F2
Merchant Pl MK10. . . 35 E3
Mercian Rd HP23. . . 125 F5
Mercian Way SL1 . . 204 D5
Mercia Rd SL4. . . . . 202 C4
Mercury Gr MK8 . . . . 45 E7
Mercury Pk The
HP10. . . . . 185 E7
Merebrook Inf Sch
MK4 . . . . 46 C3
Mere Cl SL7 . . . . 183 F2
Meredith Dr HP19. . 100 F2
Mere La MK18 . . . . . . 50 E6
Mere Pk SL7. . . . . . . 183 F2
Mere Rd
Finmere MK18. . . . . . 50 D6
Slough SL1 . . . . 205 F3
Merhonour Ct 5
MK10 . . . . 36 D4
Meriland Ct MK2. . . . 58 E4
Merino Cl MK2. . . . . . 58 C8
Merino Gn MK14. . . . 34 C8
Merlebank HP5 . . . . 154 C7
Merlewood Cl HP11 173 E4
Merlewood Dr MK5 . 45 F4
Merlin Cl SL3 . . . . . . 212 B8
Merlin Ctr SL6 . . . . . 202 B8

Merlin Ctr HP19. . . . 101 C1
Merlin Ctr The
HP12. . . . . 172 E5
Merling Croft HP4. . 134 D7
Merlin Wlk MK1. . . . . 47 B8
Merman Rise MK4. . . 45 D2
Merrivale Mews
MK7. . . . . 208 D5
Merrydown HP13 . . . 161 E1
Merryfields UB8 . . . 201 D3
Merry Leys HP23. . . 104 F8
Merryweather St 5
HP18. . . . . 100 D5
Mersey Cl MK3. . . . . 46 E1
Mersey Way MK3. . . . 46 E1
Merthen Gr MK4 . . . . 57 B8
Merton Cl
Aylesbury HP18. . . . . 100 D5
Maidenhead SL6 . . . 202 C3
Merton Dr MK6 . . . . . 47 A4
Merton Rd
Princes Risborough
HP27. . . . . 139 B2
Slough SL1 . . . . 206 A3
Merwin Way SL4 . . . 209 D4
Meryton Ho SL4. . . . 210 A4
Messenger Ct HP21 116 A6
Metcalfe Gn MK14 . . . 22 B2
Mews Cotts HP15 . . 162 D7
Mews Gamnel HP23 119 B6
Mews The
Amersham HP6 . . . . 154 D3
Amersham HP6 . . . . 154 D3
Meyers Cl SL1 . . . . . 206 C4
Michael Cl SL6. . . . . 202 C5
Michaelis Rd OX9 . . 125 E1
Michigan Dr
Milton Keynes MK15 . . 35 C8
Newport Pagnell MK15 22 C1
Nicholls Ave SL9. . . . 177 E5
Micklefield Rd
HP13. . . . . 174 A7
Mickleton MK15. . . . . 35 A4
Midas Ind Est UB8. . 201 B3
Midbrook Cl MK14 . . 22 A2
Midcot Way HP4 . . . 134 F6
Midcroft SL2. . . . . . . 198 B1
Mid Cross La SL9. . . 177 F5
Middlebrook Rd
HP13. . . . . 161 E1
Middle Cl HP6 . . . . . 154 F2
Middle Dr HP9 . . . . . 175 D5
MIDDLE CLAYDON . . 74 C8
Middle Claydon
MK18. . . . . 64 D1
Middle Cres UB9 . . . 189 D4
Middle Dr HP9 . . . . . 175 D5
MIDDLE END
Leckhampstead. 42 D8
Tottenhoe 93 A8
Middle End MK18 . . . 42 D8
Middle Farm Cl
OX39. . . . . 147 C5
Middle Field HP22 . . 116 F3
Middlefield Cl MK18. .41 F1
Middle Gn SL3 . . . . . 206 E6
MIDDLE GREEN 206 E5
Middlegreen Rd
SL3 . . . . 206 D5
Middlegreen Trad Est
SL3 . . . . 206 D4
Middle La
Aylesbury HP19. . . . . 101 C1
Bovingdon HP3. . . . . 146 A1
Middle Mdw HP8. . . 177 C7
Middle Rd
Aylesbury HP21. . . . . 116 B7
Berkhamsted HP4. . . 135 B4
Denham UB9. . . . . . . 189 D4
Ley Hill HP5. . . . . 155 C8
Middlesex Dr MK3. . .46 F1
Middle Slade MK18. . 52 D6
MIDDLETON 35 E3
Middleton MK14 . . . . 34 E7
Middleton Prim Sch
MK10 . . . . 35 E3
Middleton Swimming
Pool MK16. . . . . 22 E3
Middle Way OX39 . . 147 B6
Middleway The
HP12. . . . . 172 C6
MIDDLE WEALD 32 E1
Middle Weald MK19 . 32 E2
Middle Wlk SL1 . . . . 197 C2
Midhurst Cl HP21 . . 116 B5
Midland Dr MK10. . . . 36 C3
Midland Rd MK46 . . . .7 A5
Midshires Bsns Pk
HP19. . . . . 101 A1
Midsumer Ct HP15 . 163 A3
Midsumer Arc MK9 34 E3
Midsummer Bvd
MK9 . . . . 34 E2
Midsummer Dr HP18 .82 F6
Midsummer Pl (Sh Ctr)
MK9 . . . . 34 E2
Midsummer Rdbt
MK9 . . . . 34 C1
Miersfield HP11. . . . 172 D3
Mike Griffin Way
HP22. . . . . 102 D4
Mikern Cl MK2. . . . . . 58 C8
Milan Rd 7 HP11. . . 173 E5
Milburn Ave MK6. . . . 46 E8
Milburn Dr UB7. . . . 208 E6
Mildenhall Rd SL1. . 205 E7
Mildmay Link MK12 . 33 B6

Mill La continued
Thornborough MK18. .42 F3
Turvey MK43 . . . . 8 D5
Twyford MK18. . . . . . 62 C1
Upper Arncott OX25 . . 94 E7
Westbury NN13. . . . . . 39 A4
Weston Turville
HP22. . . . . 117 A2
Windsor SL4 . . . . 210 A7
Wingrave HP22. . . . . 89 C2
Miles Cl
Aylesbury HP21. . . . . 116 A7
Milton Keynes MK14 . . 22 A3
Miles Ct HP22 . . . . . 102 B3
Miles End HP21 . . . . 115 B6
Milesmere MK8. . . . . 33 D1
Milestone Cl HP14 . 158 E5
Milfoil Ave MK4. . . . . 34 E4
Milford Ave MK11. . . 32 E4
Milford Ct 4 SL1. . . 206 A4
Milk Hall Barns HP5 154 F5
Milland Way
Milton Keynes MK4. . 45 D3
Oxley Park MK4. . . . . 45 E3
Millards Cl MK4. . . . . 25 C2
Millards Pl MK43 . . . 25 C2
Mill Ave UB8 . . . . . . 201 C3
Millbank
Leighton Buzzard LU7 . 80 F8
Marlow SL7. . . . . 183 F1
Millbank Pl MK7 . . . . 48 B8
Millboard Rd SL8 . . 185 B3
Mill Bridge Pl SL8. . 201 C3
Millbrook Cl HP12. . 172 D8
Millbrook Comb Sch
HP12. . . . . 172 D8
Millbrook Way SL3 . 212 E5
Mill Cl
Buckingham MK18 . . . .65 F5
Chesham HP5 . . . . . 154 E5
9 Loudwater HP10 . 174 C2
West Drayton UB7. . . 208 D3
Wingrave HP22. . . . . 89 A3
Mill Cnr HP18. . . . . . 83 A8
Mill Cotts HP10 . . . . 185 D4
Mill Ct
Horton SL3 . . . . 212 C3
Milton Keynes MK2 . . 33 A5
Waddesdon HP18 . . . 99 A7
West Drayton UB7. . . 208 D3
Milldun Way HP12. . 172 D6
MILL END
Henley-on-Thames . 192 D7
Little Missenden . . . 153 A3
Rickmansworth. . . . 167 F1
Mill End La HP22. . . . 33 A7
Mill End Cl
Edlesborough LU6. . . .92 F4
Prestwood HP16. . . . 151 B5
Mill End Rd HP12. . . 172 C8
Millennium Cl UB8. . 201 C3
Millennium Point
HP19. . . . . 101 C1
Miller Pl SL1 . . . . . . 188 D6
Millers Cl HP18 . . . . .82 F6
Miller's La SL4 . . . . 211 A1
Millers Turn OX39. . 147 B6
Millers Way
Aylesbury HP19. . . . . 115 A8
Milton Keynes MK12 . 33 D5
Millfield HP4 . . . . . . 135 D5
Millfield Ave
Little Marsh OX27 . . . 72 A3
Marsh Gibbon OX27 . . 71 F3
Millfield Cl
Cranfield MK43. . . . . 25 B2
Marsh Gibbon OX27 . . 71 F3
Millfield Gdns MK14. .21 F3
Millfields HP5 . . . . . 154 C6
Millfield Wood Wildlife
Reserve HP14. . . . . 162 B3
Millgate 9 HP11. . . 173 F4
Mill Gdns HP23 . . . . 119 B4
Mill Gn MK43 . . . . 8 D5
Millground Field
MK18 . . . . 65 E4
Millhayes MK14 . . . . .34 F8
Mill Ho
4 Buckingham
MK18 . . . . 52 C8
West Drayton UB7. . . 208 D5
Millholm Rise MK6 . . 47 B5
Milliners The 1
HP20. . . . . 101 E1
Millington Gate
MK15 . . . . 35 D7
Mill La
Amersham HP7. . . . . 165 A8
Aspley Guise MK17. . 49 C5
Beaconsfield HP9 . . . 175 E1
Brackley NN13. . . . . . 38 A6
Buckingham MK18 . . . .52 F6
Chalfont St Giles HP8 166 B1
Chinnor OX39 . . . . . . 147 B7
Cookham SL6 . . . . . . 196 C5
Cuddington SL6 . . . . 112 D3
Gerrards Cross SL9. . 188 F5
Great Brickhill MK17. . 59 A3
Horton SL3 . . . . 212 C4
Horton-cum-S OX33 . 108 A6
Hulcote MK17 . . . . . . 37 E1
Hurley SL6. . . . . 193 F4
Milton Keynes, Bradville
MK13 . . . . 34 A7
Milton Keynes, Stony
Stratford MK11. . . . . 32 C5
Milton Keynes, Woolstone
MK15 . . . . 35 C3
Monks Risborough
HP27. . . . . 139 B6
Salford MK17 . . . . . . 37 C3
South Heath HP16. . . 152 C7
Stokenchurch HP14. . 158 C5
Stratton Audley MK18. 61 A5
Taplow SL6 . . . . 203 C8
Thame OX9 . . . . 126 B3

Milton's Cottage (Mus) ★
HP8. . . . . 177 B7
Milton Way UB7. . . . 208 F2
Milverton Cl SL6 . . . 202 B3
Milward Dr MK2. . . . . 47 E1
Mimosa Cl HP21. . . . 115 B6
Mina Ave SL3 . . . . . . 206 D4
Minall Cl
Tring HP23 . . . . 119 A4
Tring LU7. . . . . 118 F2
Mineral La HP5 . . . . 154 C7
Minerva Cl TW19. . . 213 A2
Minerva Gdns MK7 . 48 C7
Minerva Rd MK11 . . . 32 F3
Minerva Way HP9 . . 176 A1
Mines Cl HP13 . . . . . 161 D3
Ministry Wharf
HP14. . . . . 149 C1
Minniecroft Rd SL1. 197 B3
Minorca Gr MK5 . . . . 46 A4
Minshull Cl MK18 . . . 41 D1
Minster Way SL3 . . . 206 F4
Minstrel Ct MK13. . . . 34 B7
Minter Rise MK18. . . 65 E8
Minton Cl MK14 . . . . 22 A1
Minton Rise SL6. . . . 204 B7
Mirabelle Cl 8
HP18. . . . . 100 D5
Mirador Cres SL2 . . 206 B6
Mirrie La UB9 . . . . . . 189 C6
Misbourne Ave
Chalfont St Peter
SL9. . . . . 177 E5
High Wycombe HP13. 173 F6
Misbourne Cl
Aylesbury HP21. . . . . 115 D3
Chalfont St Peter SL9 177 E5
Misbourne Ct SL3. . 207 A2
Misbourne Dr HP16 152 B6
Misbourne Ho HP8. 166 C1
Misbourne Mdws
UB9. . . . . 189 D3
Misbourne Sch The
HP16. . . . . 152 B6
Misbourne Vale
SL9. . . . . 177 D5
Miserden Cres MK4 . .45 F1
Missenden Abbey Adult
Ed Coll HP16. . . . . 152 B8
Missenden MK18 . . . .65 F4
Missenden Gdns
SL1. . . . . 204 B7
Missenden Rd
Amersham HP7. . . . . 153 F1
Amersham HP7. . . . . 164 E8
Chesham HP5 . . . . . 154 E7
Ellesborough HP17. . 130 C2
Ellesborough HP17. . 130 C2
Great Kingshill HP15 151 D2
Winslow MK18 . . . . . .65 F4
Missenden St MK17 . 58 B2
Miss Joans Ride
MK4 . . . . 107 D7
Mitcham Pl MK13 . . 118 F3
Mitcham Wlk HP19. 101 A2
Mitchell Cl
Aylesbury HP19. . . . . 115 C8
Bovingdon HP3. . . . . 145 F4
Slough SL1 . . . . 205 A4
Mitchell Rd MK43 . . . 24 E2
Mitchell Wlk HP6 . . 154 E1
Mitchell Wy MK4 . . . 56 E8
Mitchinson St MK18. 63 A3
Mithras Gdns MK7 . . 48 C6
Mitre Ct MK18 . . . . . 52 C7
Mitre St MK18. . . . . . 52 C7
MIXBURY. 38 D1
Mixbury Rd NN13. . . 38 B2
MK1 Shopping & Leisure
Pk MK1. . . . . 47 B3
Moat Cl
Prestwood HP16. . . . 151 C6
Wendover HP22. . . . 131 B6
Moat Dr
Prestwood HP16. . . . 151 C7
Slough SL2 . . . . 206 C8
Moat End HP22 . . . . . 22 E6
Moat Farm Rd MK43. 25 D3
Moat House The
MK18 . . . . 52 D8
Moat La
Aston Abbotts HP22 . . 88 D4
Marsh Gibbon OX27 . . 71 F2
Prestwood HP16. . . . 151 C7
Wingrave HP22. . . . . 89 B2
Moat Pl UB8 . . . . 201 B8
Moat Reach LU6 . . . 92 E3
Moat View HP18. . . . .82 F8
Mobbs Cl
Olney MK46. . . . . .7 A4
Stoke Poges SL2 . . . 199 A1
MOBWELL. 152 A8
Mobwell Terr 3
HP16. . . . . 152 A8
Model Row HP22. . . 117 F6
Modin Pl 2 UB10 . . 201 E4
Moeran Cl MK7 . . . . 48 C5
Moffy Hill SL6. . . . . . 195 E2
Mole Run HP19 . . . . 161 C1
Molyneaux Ave HP3 145 F4
Molyns Ho RG9 . . . . 191 E3
Molyns Mews SL1. . 204 E5
Monarch St HP18 . . 100 E6
Monarch Wy 4 LU7 . .80 F8

Monellan Cres MK7 . 48 A3
Monellan Gr MK7 . 48 A2
Monet Pl HP19 . . . . 100 E2
Money La UB7 . . . . . 208 D3
Monkey Island La
  SL6 . . . . 203 E2
Monks Ct HP23. . . . 103 D1
Monksfield Way
  SL2 . . . . 198 A2
Monks Hollow SL7 . 183 E5
Monks Path 9
  HP19. . . . . 115 A8
Monks Rd SL4 . . . . 209 D5
MONKS
  RISBOROUGH 139 C6
Monks Risborough CE
  Prim Sch HP27. . . 139 D5
Monks Risborough Sta
  HP27. . . . . 139 B6
Monks Stone Cl
  HP5. . . . . 154 D7
MONKSTON. 36 A1
MONKSTON PARK . . . 35 E1
Monkston Prim Sch
  MK10 . . . . 36 B1
Monkston Rdbt MK10 36 B2
Monks Way
  Harmondsworth
  UB7. . . . . 213 E8
  Milton Keynes MK12, MK13,
  MK14, MK15 . . . . . 34 C6
Monkswood Ct 11
  SL7 . . . . 183 E2
Monkton La SL7. . . 172 F1
Monkton Way HP27 150 C5
Monmouth Cl HP19. 101 A2
Monmouth Gr MK4 . 45 E1
Monro Ave MK8 . . . 45 E7
Montabaur Rd NN13. 38 A7
Montagu Dr MK6. . . 47 B8
Montague Cl SL2. . . 198 B3
Montague Cres
  MK10 . . . . 36 D3
Montague Pas UB8 201 D5
Montague Rd
  Aylesbury HP21. . . 115 D7
  Berkhamsted HP4. . 135 B4
  Slough SL1 . . . . . . 205 F6
  Uxbridge UB8 . . . . 201 D5
Montagu Rd SL3 . . . 211 B6
Montem Acad SL1. . 205 B4
Montem La SL1 . . . . 205 B4
Montem L Ctr SL1. . 205 D4
Montford Mews
  HP15. . . . . 162 E2
Montgomerie Cl
  HP4. . . . . 135 A6
Montgomery Cres
  MK15 . . . . 35 B7
Montgomery Pl SL2 206 C7
Montgomery Way
  MK17 . . . . 48 E8
Montpellier Ct SL4 . 210 C5
Montrose Ave
  Datchet SL3. . . . . . 211 C7
  Slough SL1 . . . . . . 205 B7
Montrose Dr SL6. . . 202 A6
Montrose St MK9. . . 35 A4
Montrose Way SL3 . 211 C7
Montserrat Ct MK3 . 58 A3
Monty Seymour Gr
  HP11. . . . . 172 F4
Monument La SL9. . 177 E5
Monycrower Dr SL6 202 E7
Moon St MK12 . . . . 33 D6
Moonstone Ct 5
  HP12. . . . . 172 D8
Moorbridge Rd SL6 203 A7
Moor Cl OX39 . . . . 147 C5
Moor Comm HP14. . 171 A2
MOOR COMMON . . . 171 A2
Moorcroft La HP18 . 100 E4
Moorcroft Sch 3
  UB8. . . . . 208 F7
Moore Cl SL1 . . . . . 205 B4
Moore Cres 12
  HP18. . . . . 100 D5
MOOR END
  Eaton Bray 92 E5
  Yardley Gobion 18 D6
Moor End La
  Eaton Bray LU6 . . . 92 F5
  Frieth RG9. . . . . . . 171 A1
  Maidenhead SL6. . . 203 C1
Moor End Cl LU6 . . 92 F4
Moorend Comm
  Frieth RG9. . . . . . . 170 F1
  Lane End RG9 . . . . 171 A2
Moorend La OX9 . . 125 F1
Moor End La
  Eaton Bray LU6 . . . 92 F5
  Hambleden RG9 . . . 182 A7
  Moor End RG9. . . . . 171 A1
Moorend Rd NN12. . 18 E6
Moore Rd MK4 . . . . 134 F6
Moores Hill MK46. . . 6 F5
Moores La SL4 . . . . 207 D2
Moorfield MK17. . . . 57 D3
Moorfield Rd
  Denham Green UB9. 190 A5
  Uxbridge UB8 . . . . 208 D7
Moorfield Terr SL6. 203 A8
Moorfoot MK11. . . . 33 A4
Moor Furlong SL1. . 204 E5
Moorgate MK6. . . . . 46 F7

Moorhall Rd UB9. . 190 B6
Moorhen Cl OX27 . . 71 F3
Moorhen Ct 2
  HP20. . . . . 101 E3
Moorhen Way
  Buckingham MK18 . 41 E1
  Buckingham MK18 . 52 E8
Moorhills Cres LU7. . 79 F3
Moorhills Rd LU7. . . 79 F3
Mooring St HP22. . . 102 D2
Moorings The
  2 Buckingham
  MK18 . . . . 52 C8
  Windsor SL4 . . . . . 210 A7
Moor La
  Harmondsworth
  UB7. . . . . 213 C8
  High Wycombe HP13 161 D3
  Maidenhead SL6. . . 195 F1
  Sarratt WD3 . . . . . 156 E3
Moorland Prim Sch
  MK6 . . . . 47 B5
Moorland Rd UB7. . 213 C8
Moorlands LU7 . . . . 79 E3
Moorlands Rd LU7. . 79 F3
Moorland Way 5
  SL6 . . . . 203 A7
Moor Pk
  Milton Keynes MK3 . 57 D8
  Wendover HP22 . . . 131 B7
Moor Rd HP5 . . . . . 154 C6
Moors Cl MK19. . . . 31 E5
Moor's Farm Cotts
  HP5. . . . . 145 B4
Moorside HP10 . . . . 185 E8
Moorside Cl SL6 . . . 195 F1
Moors La HP5. . . . . 145 B3
Moorstown Ct 7
  SL1 . . . . 205 E4
Moor The SL7. . . . . 184 C4
MOP END. 164 B7
Mop End La HP7 . . . 164 B6
Morar Cl LU7 . . . . . 80 C7
Moray Dr SL2 . . . . . 206 A7
Moray Pl MK3. . . . . 46 F2
Mordaunt Cl MK43 . . 8 E6
Mordaunts Ct MK15 . 35 C2
Moreau Wlk SL3 . . . 206 F2
More Ave HP21 . . . . 115 D7
Morebath Gr MK4 . . 46 C4
Morefields HP23 . . . 119 A6
Moreland Ave SL3 . . 212 C7
Moreland Cl SL3 . . . 212 C7
Moreland Dr SL9. . . 188 F4
Morello Cl HP18. . . 100 D4
Morello Dr SL3. . . . 206 F5
Morello Wy MK16 . . 22 F3
Moreton Dr MK18 . . 41 E2
Moreton La
  Stone HP17. . . . . . 114 F1
  Stone HP17. . . . . . 115 A1
Moreton Rd
  10 Buckingham
  MK18 . . . . 41 D1
  Buckingham MK18 . 41 D2
  Little Kimble HP17. . 129 A4
  Owlswick HP17. . . . 128 E5
Moreton Way SL1 . . 204 D5
Morgan Dr
  Aylesbury HP18. . . 100 E5
  2 Berryfields HP18 100 D5
Morgan Way 6
  MK12 . . . . 33 A6
Morland Dr MK8 . . . 45 D6
Morley Cl SL3. . . . . 206 F4
Morley Cres MK7. . . 48 D4
Morrell Cl MK5. . . . 46 B5
Morrice Cl
  Slough SL1 . . . . . . 206 F2
  Slough SL3 . . . . . . 207 A2
Morris Ave UB10 . . 201 E6
Morris Cl SL9 . . . . . 177 F2
Morris Ct
  Aylesbury HP21. . . 115 D4
  Windsor SL4 . . . . . 209 E6
Morris Gr MK17 . . . 58 F7
Morrison Ct MK8. . . 45 E6
Morris Wlk MK16. . . 22 A4
Mortain Cl MK7 . . . 48 B3
Mortain Dr MK4 . . . 134 F6
Morten Gdns HP9 . . 190 A4
Mortens Wood HP9 165 E7
Mortimer Hill HP23. 119 B4
Mortimer Rd SL3. . . 206 D3
Mortimer Rise
  HP23. . . . . 119 B4
Morton Cl
  North Marston HP18. 76 B2
  Pitstone LU7. . . . . . 105 C4
  Uxbridge UB8 . . . . 201 F1
Morton Dr SL1 . . . . 197 E8
Morton King Cl
  HP18. . . . . 124 D3
Morton Mws HP22. . 102 B1
Morton Rd MK17 . . . 37 A1
Mortons Fork MK13. 33 F6
Moseley Rd HP14 . . 161 C7
Moses Plat La HP27 150 B5
Moss Cl HP9. . . . . . 176 D4
Mossdale MK13 . . . . 34 B5
Mossmans Cl MK2. . 58 D7
Mossway HP9. . . . . 175 C5
Mossy Vale SL6 . . . 195 D1
MOULSOE. 36 D8
Moulsoe Rd MK17 . . 37 C8
Moundsfield Way
  SL1 . . . . 204 E4
Mountain Ash SL7. . 183 D6

Mount Ave MK1 . . . 47 E3
Mountbatten Sq 8
  SL4 . . . . 210 C6
Mount Cl
  Aston Clinton HP22. 117 F4
  Farnham Common
  SL2 . . . . 198 C8
  High Wycombe HP12. 172 E6
Mount Farm Ind Est
  MK1 . . . . 47 D4
Mount Farm Rdbt
  2 Buckingham
  MK18 . . . . 52 C8
Mounthill Ave MK19 . 32 B7
Mount Hill La SL9 . . 188 B2
Mount La UB9. . . . . 189 D7
Mount Nugent HP5. 144 A4
MOUNT PLEASANT
  Buckingham 52 D7
  Stoke Goldington. . . 12 B7
Mount Pleasant
  Aspley Guise MK17 . . 49 F4
  Aylesbury HP19. . . 101 D1
  Lane End HP14 . . . . 171 D5
  Milton Keynes MK6 . 47 E4
  Soulbury LU7. . . . . 69 E3
  Steeple Claydon MK18 .63 F2
  Stoke Goldington
  MK16 . . . . 12 B7
  Stoke Hammond MK17 69 E7
  Whitchurch HP22 . . 86 F7
  Yardley Gobion NN12 .18 F6
Mount Pleasant Cl
  MK18 . . . . 52 C8
Mount Pleasant Cotts 2
  SL8 . . . . 185 B3
Mountsfield Cl
  Newport Pagnell
  MK16 . . . . 22 C3
  Stanwell TW19 . . . 213 A2
Mount St HP20 . . . . 115 D8
Mount The
  Aspley Guise MK17 . . 49 D4
  Milton Keynes MK6 . 47 E4
Mount View RG9 . . . 191 D2
Mount View Ct 4
  RG9. . . . . 191 D2
Mount Way HP27. . . 139 A3
Mowbray Dr LU7. . . 80 D7
Mowbray Rd HP20. . 101 D2
Mowhills MK43 . . . . 3 F6
Moxon Pl 3 SL10 . . 204 F4
Moyleen Rise SL7. . 183 C1
Mozart Cl MK7 . . . . 48 C4
Mozart End HP21. . . 115 E3
Muddiford La MK4 . . 46 D4
Muirfield Dr
  Milton Keynes MK3 . 46 D1
  Newton Longville
  MK17 . . . . 57 C1
Mulberry Ave SL4 . . 210 F5
Mulberry Cl
  High Wycombe
  HP12. . . . . 172 C5
  Tring HP23 . . . . . . 119 A5
Mulberry Ct HP15 . . 163 D7
Mulberry Dr SL3 . . . 206 E1
Mulberry Wlk SL6 . . 202 C8
Mullen Ave MK14. . . 34 F4
Mullins Way HP19. . 100 E2
Mullion Pl MK6 . . . . 35 A1
Mull La MK17 . . . . . 58 A3
Mumfords La SL9 . . 188 A7
Muncaster Gr 5
  MK10 . . . . 36 A4
Munces Rd MK7 . . . 183 D6
MUNDAYDEAN
  BOTTOM 182 E5
Mundaydean La
  Marlow SL7. . . . . . 183 B4
  Mundaydean Bottom
  SL7. . . . . 182 E4
Munday's Farm
  HP21. . . . . 116 B7
Mundesley Spur
  SL1 . . . . 205 E7
Mundy Ct SL4. . . . . 210 C8
Munger St HP22. . . 116 D7
MURCOTT 94 A4
Murcott Rd
  Boarstall OX5 . . . . 94 C3
  Upper Arncott OX6 . 94 D6
Murdoch Ct MK5. . . 46 C6
Murphy Rd MK4. . . 45 E3
Murray Rd HP4. . . . 135 C6
Murrey Cl MK5. . . . 46 C5
Murrin Rd SL6 . . . . 202 C8
MURSLEY. 67 D6
Mursley CE Sch
  MK17 . . . . 67 D6
Mursley Ct MK11 . . . 32 F1
Mursley Rd
  Drayton Parslow LU7 . 68 B4
  Little Horwood MK17 . 55 E2
  Little Horwood MK17 . 56 B4
  Little Horwood MK17 . 66 F8
  Swanbourne MK17 . 67 A5
  Swanbourne MK17 . 67 B3
Museum Ct 9
  HP23. . . . . 119 A3
Musgrave Ct OX39 147 D7
Musgrove Pl MK5. . 45 F6
Mus of Eton Life The*
  SL4 . . . . 210 D8
Muswell Hill
  Brill HP18 . . . . 95 F2
  Brill HP18 . . . . 96 A1

Myddleton Rd UB8 . 201 C4
Myers Dr SL2 . . . . . 198 B7
Mylne Ct HP13 . . . . 172 F8
Mynchen Cl HP9 . . . 175 D6
Mynchen End HP9. . 175 D6
Mynchen Rd HP9. . . 175 D6
MYRKE. 205 F2
Myrke The SL3. . . . 205 F2
Myrtle Bank MK12. . 33 E5
Myrtle Cl
  Poyle SL3 . . . . 212 E6
  Uxbridge UB8 . . . . 208 F8
  West Drayton UB7. . 208 F8
Myrtle Cres SL2. . . 205 F6

N

Nag's Head La HP16 152 A4
Nailzee Cl SL9 . . . . 188 E4
Nairdwood Cl HP16 151 E4
Nairdwood La HP16 151 D5
Nairdwood Way
  HP16. . . . . 151 E4
Nairn Ct MK3 . . . . . 46 E2
Nairn Gr MK10 . . . . 36 D3
Naisby Dr MK17 . . . 59 C1
Nalders Rd HP5 . . . 144 D2
Nan Aires HP22 . . . 89 A3
Nancy Hall Ct HP12 172 D3
Nans Gdn MK17. . . 57 C4
NAPHILL. 161 D7
Naphill Pl MK13 . . . 34 C3
Naphill & Walters Ash
  Sch HP14. . . . . . . 150 B1
Napier Cl SL4 . . . . 208 F3
Napier Rd
  Aylesbury HP19. . . 114 F8
  Harmondsworth
  TW6. . . . . 213 D6
  Maidenhead SL6. . . 202 B6
Napier St MK2 . . . . 58 D8
Nappin Cl HP19 . . . 101 A3
Nappins Cl HP18 . . 125 D5
Nap The HP15 . . . . 109 E5
Narbeth Dr HP20 . . 116 B8
Narcot La HP8 . . . . 177 B5
Narcot Rd HP8 . . . . 177 A7
Narcot Way HP8 . . . 177 B6
Narrow La HP13 . . . 161 E3
Narrow Path MK17 . 49 B3
Nascot Pl SL4. . . . . 209 C5
Naseby Cl
  Newport Pagnell
  MK16 . . . . 22 A3
  Thame OX9 . . . . . . 126 B1
Naseby Ct
  Buckingham MK18 . 41 E2
  Milton Keynes MK13 . 34 B6
NASH 44 C1
Nash Cl
  Aylesbury HP21. . . 116 A3
  Berkhamsted HP4. . 135 A5
  Quainton HP22 . . . 85 A5
Nash Croft MK4 . . . 57 B8
Nashdom SL1. . . . . 196 F5
Nashdom La SL1 . . . 197 B6
NASH LEE 130 C5
Nash Lee End
  HP22. . . . . 130 F6
Nash Lee La HP22 . 130 E6
Nash Lee Rd
  Nash Lee HP17 . . . 130 D6
  World's End HP22. . 130 F7
Nashleigh Hill HP5 144 D3
Nashleigh Ho HP5. 144 E3
Nash Pl HP10 . . . . 163 B1
Nash Rd
  Beachampton MK19 . 44 B5
  Great Horwood MK17 . 55 A4
  Great Horwood MK17 . 55 C6
  4 Slough SL3 . . . . 206 F1
  Thornborough MK18 . 54 B8
  Thornton MK17. . . . 43 D3
  Whaddon MK17. . . . 45 A1
Nashs Farm HP22 . . 88 D4
Nathaniel Cl MK5 . . 46 B5
Nathaniel Wlk
  Tring HP23 . . . . . . 119 A5
  HP23. . . . . 118 F3
National Badminton
  Ctr MK8 . . . . 34 A1
National Bowl The*
  MK6 . . . . 46 E5
National Film &
  Television Sch
  HP9. . . . . 175 E1
National Mus of
  Computing MK3 . . 47 A1
Natural History Mus at
  Tring* HP23. . . . . 119 A3
Natwoke Cl HP9. . . 175 D5
Nawab Ct HP5 . . . . 144 B2
Neal Cl SL9 . . . . . . 189 B3
Neale Cl HP12. . . . . 172 D3
Neapland MK6 . . . . 47 B5
NEARTON END 67 A3
Nearton End MK7 . . 67 A3
Near Town MK46 . . . 7 A3
Near Town Gdns
  MK46 . . . . 7 A3
NEAR GROUND 120 A2
Neath Cres MK3. . . 47 A2
NEATH HILL. 34 F6
Neath Hill MK13. . . 34 F7
Neath Hill Rdbt
  MK15 . . . . 35 A6
Needham Cl SL4 . . 209 E6

Needham Ct 4
  HP11. . . . . 172 F7
Needlemakers
  HP13. . . . . 125 C7
Needlepin Wy MK18 .52 F6
Neild Way WD3 . . . 167 F2
Neilson Ct MK7 . . . 48 C5
Nelson Cl
  High Wycombe
  HP13. . . . . 173 F5
  Milton Keynes MK8 . 45 E6
  Slough SL2 . . . . . . 206 D2
  Winchmore Hill HP7 164 C3
Nelson Ct MK18 . . . 52 C8
Nelson Rd
  Dagnall HP4 . . . . . 107 C5
  Harmondsworth TW6 213 D6
  Windsor SL4 . . . . . 209 F4
Nelson Terr HP20 . . 115 D8
Nene Cl
  Aylesbury HP21. . . 115 C4
  Newport Pagnell
  MK16 . . . . 22 D3
Nene Dr MK3 . . . . . 57 E8
Neptune Cres MK10 . 36 C5
Neptune Way SL1 . . 204 E4
Nero Gr MK11. . . . . 33 A3
Ness Way MK2 . . . . 58 D5
Netherby Cl HP23 . . 119 C6
Nethercote La
  OX49. . . . . 157 A8
Netherfield 47 C6
Netherfield Rdbt
  MK6 . . . . 47 C7
Nether Gr MK5. . . . 46 B3
Nether Winchendon
  HP18. . . . . 112 C4
Nether Winchendon
  Ho* HP18. . . . . . . 112 E1
Netherwood Rd
  HP9. . . . . 175 D5
Netley Ct MK10 . . . 36 A1
Nettlecombe MK4. . 46 C3
Nettleden Rd
  Berkhamsted HP4. . 135 F6
  Little Gaddesden HP4 121 E4
Nettleden Rd N
  HP4. . . . . 121 C7
Nettleden Rd North
  HP4. . . . . 107 B1
Nettleton Rd UB10 . 201 F8
Neve Ho SL6 . . . . . 202 F8
Nevill Cl MK19 . . . . 11 B2
Neville Cl SL2 . . . . 198 F6
Neville Ct SL1 . . . . 197 C2
Nevis Cl LU7 . . . . . 80 C7
Nevis Gr MK4 . . . . . 58 E4
Newall Cl 2 UB10 . 201 F4
Newbarn La HP9 . . 176 E6
Newberry Cres SL4 209 D5
Newbery Way SL1. . 205 D4
Newbolt Cl
  Newport Pagnell
  MK16 . . . . 21 F5
  Paulerspury NN12. . 17 B8
NEW BRADWELL. . . 33 F8
New Bradwell Sch
  MK13 . . . . 33 F7
Newbridge Oval MK4 46 B3
Newbury Ct MK3 . . 57 D6
Newbury Dr SL6. . . 203 B6
Newbury Rd HP4 . . 213 F6
Newby Pl MK4 . . . . 46 B2
New Chapter Prim sch
  MK6 . . . . 47 A5
New Chilterns HP7. 165 E8
Newchurch Rd SL2. 204 F8
New Cl RG9 . . . . . . 192 A8
New CI Farm Rd
  OX39. . . . . 137 C3
New College MK18 . 51 F8
New College Ct
  MK18 . . . . 41 B4
New Coll Rd HP19 . 101 C4
Newcombe Cres 8
  MK18 . . . . 52 C8
Newcombe Rise
  UB7. . . . . 208 E2
Newcome St MK19 . 10 F3
Newcourt UB8 . . . . 208 C8
Newcroft Cl UB8 . . 208 F8
New Ct
  High Wycombe
  HP13. . . . . 173 C6
  Marlow SL7. . . . . . 183 D2
NEW DENHAM 201 A6
New Dr HP13 . . . . . 173 F8
Neweham Rd MK17. 37 A1
Newells Hedge LU7 105 C5
Newfield Gdns SL7 . 183 F3
Newfield Rd SL7. . . 183 F3
Newfield Way SL7. . 183 F2
New Garden Dr
  UB7. . . . . 208 E4
New Gound Rd
  HP23. . . . . 120 C4
NEW GROUND. 120 A2
New Ground Rd
  HP23. . . . . 120 B3
New Hall Ct HP3. . . 146 A4
Newhaven Spur SL2 198 B1
New Horton Manor
  SL3 . . . . 212 A4

New House Farm La
  HP5. . . . . 145 C3
Newhouse Rd HP3 . 146 A4
Newington Gate
  MK6 . . . . 47 D5
New Inn La MK18. . .51 F1
New Inn Stowe, Visitor
  Ctr MK18 . . . . 41 A6
Newland Ho UB8 . . 201 C4
NEWLAND PARK . . . 178 A7
Newlands Dr
  Maidenhead SL6. . . 202 A7
  Poyle SL3 . . . . 212 E4
Newlands Girls Sch
  SL6 . . . . 202 A7
Newlyn Pl MK6. . . . 35 A2
Newman Cl HP22. . . 86 E7
New Manor Cft 2
  MK4 . . . . 135 C4
Newmanry The 1
  MK15 . . . . 35 D2
Newmans Cl MK14 . . 21 E1
Newmans Ctyd MK17 68 C6
Newmarket Cl MK10. 36 C2
New Mdw MK21 . . . 116 C7
Newmer Rd HP12 . . 172 B3
NEW MILL 119 B6
New Mill Terr HP23. 119 B6
Newnham Cl SL2. . 206 A5
New Par
  Chorleywood WD3. . 167 C5
  West Drayton UB7. . 208 E5
New Peachey La
  UB8. . . . . 208 D8
New Pond Rd HP15. 163 C7
NEWPORT PAGNELL . 22 B5
Newport Pagnell Rd
  Hackleton MK16 . . . 4 D4
  Stagsden West End
  MK43 . . . . 16 C4
Newport Rd
  Aspley Guise MK17 . 49 D1
  Astwood MK16 . . . . 15 C2
  Astwood MK16 . . . . 16 B4
  Broughton MK10 . . . 36 A5
  Emberton NN7 . . . . 6 F1
  Gayhurst MK16 . . . 12 D3
  Hanslope MK19. . . . 11 C3
  Milton Keynes MK10 . 36 D1
  Milton Keynes, New
  Bradwell MK13 . . . 34 A8
  Milton Keynes, Oakgrove
  MK15 . . . . 35 C2
  Milton Keynes, Willen
  MK15 . . . . 35 D7
  Milton Keynes, Woughton on
  the Green MK6 . . . 35 D1
  Moulsoe MK16 . . . . 36 C7
  Sherington MK16 . . 14 A5
  Sherington MK16 . . 22 F8
  Slough SL2 . . . . . . 197 E1
  Wavendon MK17. . . 48 E7
  Woburn MK17. . . . . 60 F8
  Woughton on the Green
  MK6 . . . . 47 D8
New Providnt Pl 5
  HP4. . . . . 135 D4
Newquay Cl 4 MK4 .45 F1
New Rd
  Aldbury HP23 . . . . 120 F3
  Amersham HP6. . . . 154 E2
  Aston Clinton HP22. 117 E5
  Berkhamsted HP4. . 135 D6
  Berkhamsted, Northchurch
  HP4. . . . . 134 F7
  Bolter End HP14 . . . 170 F6
  Bourne End SL8. . . 185 B4
  Castlethorpe MK19. . 19 F5
  Chipperfield WD4 . . 146 F1
  Coleshill HP7. . . . . 164 F4
  Cookham Rise SL6. . 195 F7
  Datchet SL3. . . . . . 211 D6
  Dinton HP17 . . . . . 113 C2
  Drayton Parslow
  MK17 . . . . 68 C5
  Great Kingshill HP15 162 D8
  Harrold MK43 . . . . . 3 E6
  High Wycombe HP12. 172 C5
  Hurley SL6. . . . . . . 193 F3
  Leighton Buzzard LU7 . 80 E7
  Little Chalfont HP8 . 166 F6
  Little Kingshill HP16 152 B4
  Marlow Bottom SL7. 183 D6
  Naphill HP14. . . . . 150 A2
  Prestwood HP16. . . 151 D6
  Princes Risborough
  HP27. . . . . 139 C3
  Sarratt HP8. . . . . . 156 F1
  Slough SL3 . . . . . . 207 A3
  Stokenchurch HP14. 158 F4
  Tring HP23 . . . . . . 119 B6
  Tylers Green HP10 . 163 E1
  Tylers Green HP10 . 163 F2
  Weedon HP22. . . . . 101 B8
  Weston Turville
  HP22. . . . . 116 E5
  Wilstone HP23 . . . . 119 B8
  Winchmore Hill HP7 164 A4
New Road Ct HP12 172 C6
New Road Gdns
  HP12. . . . . 172 C6
New Row MK46 . . . . 7 E8
New Sq SL1 . . . . . . 205 F4
New St
  Aylesbury HP20. . . 101 D1
  Berkhamsted HP4. . 135 D4
  Cheddington LU7. . 104 F7

New St continued
Henley-on-Thames
RG9 . . . . 191 E2
Milton Keynes MK11 . . 32 D5
Tingewick MK18 . . . . 51 B6
Waddesdon HP18 . . . . 99 A7
Newstead Copse
UB9 . . . . 189 F5
NEWTON 144 C1
NEWTON
BLOSSOMVILLE 8 A4
Newton Blossomville CE
Sch MK43 . . . . 8 B4
Newton Cl
Chinnor OX39 . . . . 147 C5
Slough SL3 . . . . . . 206 F4
Newton Ct SL4 . . . . 211 A1
Newton La
Old Windsor SL4 . . . 211 B1
Turvey MK43 . . . . . . 8 D4
Newton Leys Prim Sch
MK17 . . . . 58 B3
NEWTON
LONGVILLE 57 D3
Newton Longville CE
Comb Sch MK17 . . . 57 D3
NEWTON PURCELL . . 50 B2
Newton Rd
Clifton Reynes MK46 . . 7 C2
Clifton Reynes MK46 . . 7 D3
Drayton Parslow
MK17 . . . . 68 D8
Emberton MK46 . . . . 14 A8
Milton Keynes MK3 . . 57 E6
Newton Longville
MK17 . . . . 57 D1
Stoke Hammond MK17 69 D8
Turvey MK43 . . . . . . 8 D5
West Drayton UB7 . . 213 F6
Newtonside SL4 . . . . 211 A1
Newtons La HP18 . . . 110 A5
Newton St MK46 . . . . 7 A4
Newtown Rd
Marlow SL7 . . . . . . 183 F3
New Denham UB9 . . . 201 B6
Newtown Sch HP5 . . 144 C2
Newville HP22 . . . . . 87 C1
New Windsor St
UB8 . . . . 201 C4
NEWYEARS GREEN . 190 F5
Newyears Green La
UB9 . . . . 190 F5
New Zealand Cotts
HP22 . . . . 88 E4
New Zealand Gdns
LU7 . . . . 79 E2
Neyland Dr HP19 . . . 101 D3
Nicholas Charles Cres
HP18 . . . . 100 D4
Nicholas Gdns
High Wycombe
HP13 . . . . 173 D8
Slough SL1 . . . . . . 204 E5
Nicholas Mead MK14 . 34 F8
Nicholas Winton Ct
SL6 . . . . 203 A8
Nicholls SL4 . . . . . . 209 C4
Nicholls Terr MK17 . . . 37 A1
Nicholls Wlk SL4 . . . 209 C4
Nicholson Gr MK8 . . . 45 E6
Nicholson Rd HP17 . 127 B5
Nicholsons La SL6 . . 202 F7
Nicholsons Sh Ctr 2
SL6 . . . . 202 F7
Nickson Ct HP15 . . 163 A3
Nicol Cl SL9 . . . . . 177 C2
Nicol End SL9 . . . . 177 C2
Nicol Rd SL9 . . . . . 177 C2
Nielson Ct MK7 . . . . 48 D5
Nigel Ct NN13 . . . . . 38 A5
Nightingale Cl
Hazelmere HP15 . . . 163 B6
Steeple Claydon MK18 63 E3
Tring HP23 . . . . . . 119 B4
Nightingale Cres
Milton Keynes MK13 . . 34 A7
New Bradwell MK12 . . 33 F7
Nightingale Ct 1
HP13 . . . . 173 B7
Nightingale Ho
HP11 . . . . 174 A4
Nightingale La HP15 195 D3
Nightingale Lodge
HP4 . . . . 135 B4
Nightingale Pk SL2 . 197 F5
Nightingale Pl
Buckingham MK18 . . . 41 E1
Cookham Rise SL6 . . 195 F7
Nightingale Rd
Aylesbury HP21 . . . 115 E6
2 Chesham HP5 . . . 144 B2
Wendover HP22 . . . 131 B5
Nightingales Cnr
HP7 . . . . 166 C7
Nightingales Ct
HP8 . . . . 166 C7
Nightingales La
HP8 . . . . 166 D4
Nightingale Way
UB9 . . . . 189 F5
Nightingale Wlk
SL4 . . . . 210 C4
Nijinsky Ho UB8 . . . 201 D3
Nimrod St HP18 . . . 100 E4
Nine Acres
6 Chesham HP5 . . . 144 B3

Nine Acres continued
Slough SL1 . . . . . . 204 F5
Nine Elms Ave UB8 208 D8
Nine Elms Cl UB8 . . 208 D8
Nine Lands Cl HP22 116 E1
Nine Stiles Cl UB9 . 201 B6
Ninnings Rd SL9 . . 177 F3
Ninnings Way SL9 . . 177 F3
Niplands Cotts
HP10 . . . . 185 D2
Niven La MK4 . . . . . 45 E3
Nixey Cl SL1 . . . . . 206 A4
Nixey La RG9 . . . . 170 F1
Nixons Cl MK6 . . . . 46 E6
Noaks La HP10 . . . 175 A8
Noble Cl MK15 . . . . 35 A7
Noble Cres HP18 . . 100 D4
Noble Ct SL2 . . . . 205 F5
Nocton Hall Dr
HP22 . . . . 131 E6
Noel Coward Ave
UB9 . . . . 190 A6
Noon Layer Dr
Milton Keynes MK10 . . 35 E3
Milton Keynes MK10 . . 35 E3
Norbrek MK8 . . . . . 33 E2
Norcott Farm La
HP4 . . . . 120 C1
NORCOTT HILL . . . 120 D2
Norcott Hill
Cow Roast HP4 . . . 120 D1
Dudswell HP4 . . . . 134 D4
Norcotts Kiln Cotts
HP18 . . . . 96 A1
Norden Cl SL6 . . . . 202 C4
Norden Mdws SL6 . . 202 C5
Norden Mead MK7 . . 48 A5
Norden Rd SL6 . . . 202 C5
Norelands Dr SL1 . . 197 C3
Norfolk Ave SL1 . . . 205 C8
Norfolk Ho 6 MK3 . . 46 F1
Norfolk Park Cotts
SL6 . . . . 202 F8
Norfolk Rd
Maidenhead SL6 . . . 202 F8
Turvey MK43 . . . . . . 8 E1
Uxbridge UB8 . . . . 201 D6
Norfolk Terr HP20 . . 101 E1
Norgrove Pk SL9 . . 188 E7
Norjo-An Villas
HP5 . . . . 154 C6
Norland Dr HP10 . . 185 C8
Norman Ave RG9 . . 191 E1
Norman Cres MK10 . . 35 E3
Normandy Dr HP4 . . 135 B6
Normandy Way MK3 . 46 E2
Normans Cl UB8 . . 208 F8
Normans Ct 5
HP13 . . . . 173 F6
Normanstead RG9 . . 191 D1
Normans The SL2 . . 206 B7
Norman Way LU6 . . . 93 E8
Normill Terr HP22 . . 117 A6
Norreys Dr SL6 . . . 202 D4
Norris Ho SL6 . . . . 202 E7
Norris Rd OX6 . . . . 94 E8
NORTHALL 92 B5
Northall Cl LU6 . . . . 92 C6
Northall Rd LU6 . . . 92 D6
Northampton Ave
SL1 . . . . 205 C7
Northampton Ct 1
MK3 . . . . 46 F3
Northampton Rd
Brackley NN13 . . . . 26 A1
Cosgrove MK19 . . . . 19 C1
Cosgrove MK19 . . . . 32 C8
Grafton Regis NN12 . . 9 C3
Lathbury MK16 . . . . 12 F1
Lathbury MK16 . . . . 22 D6
Lavendon MK46 . . . . 7 F8
Old Stratford MK19 . . 32 B8
Stoke Bruerne NN12 . . 9 C8
Tyringham and Filgrave
MK16 . . . . 13 A1
Warrington MK46 . . . . 2 A3
Warrington MK46 . . . . 2 C1
Warrington NN7 . . . . 1 F3
Yardley Hastings NN7 . 1 A4
Northborough Rd
SL2 . . . . 198 B1
Northbridge Rd
HP4 . . . . 135 A6
North Burnham Cl
SL1 . . . . 197 B3
NORTHCHURCH . . . 134 E5
Northchurch Common
Berkhamsted HP4 . . 134 F7
Berkhamsted HP4 . . 135 A7
Northchurch La
HP5 . . . . 134 D2
North Cl
Beaconsfield HP9 . . 186 B8
Drayton Parslow
MK17 . . . . 68 C5
Medmenham SL7 . . . 193 D7
Windsor SL4 . . . . . 209 F6
Northcliffe LU6 . . . . 92 E6
Northcliffe Wy
Aylesbury HP18 . . . 100 D5
1 Berryfields HP18 . . 100 D5
North Common Rd
UB8 . . . . 201 D7
North Cotts SL2 . . . 198 D1
NORTH CRAWLEY . . 24 A6
North Crawley CE Sch
MK16 . . . . 24 B6

North Crawley Rd
MK16 . . . . 23 C4
Northcroft
Milton Keynes MK5 . . 46 C6
Slough SL2 . . . . . . 198 B1
Weedon HP22 . . . . . 87 C1
Wooburn Green
HP10 . . . . 185 F6
North Croft MK18 . . . 66 A4
North Dean 5 SL6 . 195 F1
Northdown Rd SL9 . 177 E4
North Dr
Aylesbury HP21 . . . 115 E5
Beaconsfield HP9 . . 186 B8
High Wycombe HP13 173 E8
North Eastern Rd
HP19 . . . . 101 C2
North Eighth St MK9 34 E3
North Elder Rdbt
MK9 . . . . 34 C1
North Eleventh St
MK9 . . . . 34 E3
NORTHEND 168 E6
Northend MK46 . . . . 5 E3
NORTH END
Stagsden 16 E8
Steeple Claydon . . . 63 D3
Stewkley 68 D3
Northend Cl HP10 . 185 C7
Northend Ct 1
MK18 . . . . 41 D1
Northend Rd
Northend HP10 . . . 168 F5
Turville Heath RG9 . 169 A3
North End Rd
Quainton HP22 . . . . 85 A5
Steeple Claydon MK18 63 D3
Northend Sq 2
MK18 . . . . 41 D1
Northend Workshops
RG9 . . . . 168 E5
Northern Hts SL8 . . 185 B5
Northern Perimeter Rd
(W) TW6 . . . . 213 D6
Northern Rd
Aylesbury HP19 . . . 101 C2
Slough SL1 . . . . . . 198 D1
Northern Woods
HP10 . . . . 185 C7
Northey Ave MK3 . . . 58 B4
North Farm La
Grendon Underwood
HP18 . . . . 83 E4
Quainton MK18 . . . . 84 A6
NORTHFIELD 35 F5
Northfield Barns Dr
MK19 . . . . 31 F4
Northfield Cl MK19 . . 31 F4
Northfield Cl RG9 . . 183 D3
Northfield Dr MK15 . . 35 F5
Northfield End RG9 191 D3
Northfield Rd
Aylesbury HP20 . . . 116 B8
Eton Wick SL4 . . . . 204 F2
Maidenhead SL6 . . . 195 F1
Maidenhead SL6 . . . 196 A1
Princes Risborough
HP27 . . . . 139 C4
Tring HP23 . . . . . . 119 F7
Northfield Rdbt
MK10 . . . . 36 A5
North Fifth St MK9 . . 34 D2
North Fourteenth St
MK9 . . . . 34 F4
North Fourth St MK9 34 D2
North Gate MK2 . . . . 47 C1
North Gn
3 Maidenhead SL6 . . 195 F1
Slough SL1 . . . . . . 205 E6
North Grafton Rdbt
MK13 . . . . 34 C2
North Hill
Dadford MK18 . . . . 28 D2
Sarratt WD3 . . . . . 167 E8
North Hills HP18 . . . 96 A1
North La MK7 . . . . . 47 C7
Northlands Rd MK18 . 53 F1
NORTH LEE 130 A7
North Lee La
North Lee HP22 . . . 130 A6
Stoke Mandeville
HP22 . . . . 129 F7
Northleigh MK4 . . . . 46 B2
North Links Rd
HP10 . . . . 174 B1
North Loop Rd UB8 201 D2
NORTH MARSTON . . 76 A2
North Marston CE Sch
MK18 . . . . 76 B2
North Marston La
HP22 . . . . 86 E7
Northmead Rd SL2 . 204 F8
Northmill HP27 . . . . 138 F3
North Mill Rd HP27 . 138 C1
Northmoor Hill Wood
Nature Reserve
UB9 . . . . 189 F7
North Ninth St MK9 . 34 E3
Northolt Rd TW6 . . 213 E6
North Orbital Rd
Denham Green UB9 . 189 F4
Denham Green UB9 . 189 F4
Rickmansworth WD3 178 E1
North Overgate Rdbt
MK15 . . . . 35 B5
North Pk
Gerrards Cross SL9 . 188 E8
Iver SL0 . . . . 207 D3

North Rd
Amersham HP6 . . . 154 C3
Berkhamsted HP4 . . 135 B4
Chorleywood WD3 . . 167 D4
Cryers Hill HP15 . . . 162 D5
Maidenhead SL6 . . . 202 E7
West Drayton UB7 . . 208 F3
North Ridge MK6 . . . 35 B1
North Row
Fulmer SL3 . . . . . . 199 E8
Milton Keynes MK9 . . 34 C2
North Saxon Rdbt
MK14 . . . . 34 D3
North Secklow Rdbt
MK14 . . . . 34 E3
North Second St
MK9 . . . . 34 C2
North Seventh St
MK9 . . . . 34 D2
North Sixth St MK9 . . 34 D2
North Skeldon Rdbt
MK9 . . . . 35 A4
North Sq MK16 . . . . 22 D5
North St
Castlethorpe MK19 . . 19 F5
Milton Keynes, Bradville
MK13 . . . . 34 A7
Milton Keynes, Fenny
Stratford MK2 . . . . 47 C1
Thame OX9 . . . . . . 125 F1
North Star La SL6 . . 202 C6
North Tenth St MK9 . 34 E3
North Terr SL4 . . . . 210 E7
North Third St MK9 . . 34 C2
North Thirteenth St
MK9 . . . . 34 F3
NORTH TOWN 195 F1
North Town Cl 1
SL6 . . . . 195 F1
North Town Mead 4
SL6 . . . . 195 F1
North Town Moor
SL6 . . . . 195 F1
North Town Rd
Maidenhead SL6 . . . 195 F1
Maidenhead SL6 . . . 202 F8
North Twelfth St
MK9 . . . . 34 F3
Northumberland Ave
HP21 . . . . 116 B6
Northumberland Cl
TW19 . . . . 213 E1
Northumberland Wlk
SL0 . . . . 207 A4
Northumbria Rd
SL6 . . . . 202 B4
North View HP22 . . . 87 B3
North Way
Deanshanger NN12 . . 31 E5
Potterspury NN12 . . . 18 E2
Uxbridge UB10 . . . . 201 E5
NORTH WESTON . . 136 F8
Northwich MK6 . . . . 47 D7
Northwick Rd MK10 . 35 F1
North Witan Rdbt
MK13 . . . . 34 D2
Northwood Rd TW6 213 D6
Nortoft Rd SL9 . . . . 177 F5
Norton Leys MK7 . . . 48 C7
Norton Rd UB8 . . . . 201 D2
Nortons Pl MK18 . . . 52 C8
Nortons The MK7 . . . 48 B3
Norvic Rd HP23 . . . 105 A1
Norway Dr SL2 . . . . 206 B8
Norwich Ho
High Wycombe
HP13 . . . . 173 F8
Maidenhead SL6 . . . 202 E8
Norwood Cl HP20 . . 101 F2
Norwood Ct 4 HP7 165 B7
Norwood La
Newport Pagnell
MK16 . . . . 22 C3
Uxbridge SL0 . . . . 200 D1
Norwood Rd HP10 . 174 B2
Notley Farm HP18 . 126 A7
Nottingham Ave MK3 . 46 E2
Nottingham Ho 3
HP13 . . . . 173 F7
Nottingham Rd
WD3 . . . . 167 C1
Nova Lodge MK4 . . . 46 B2
Novello Croft MK7 . . 48 D4
Nugent Cl HP19 . . . 101 D4
Nugent Ct
Chesham HP5 . . . . 144 A3
Marlow SL7 . . . . . . 183 F3
Nuneham Gr MK4 . . . 45 F2
Nunneley Ct 4
UB10 . . . . 201 E4
NUP END 89 B3
Nup End Cl HP22 . . . 89 B3
Nup End La HP22 . . . 89 B3
Nurseries The LU6 . . 92 E6
Nursery Cl
2 Amersham HP7 . . 165 E8
Aylesbury HP21 . . . 115 C5
Chinnor OX39 . . . . 147 C7
Tylers Green HP10 . . 174 C8
Nursery Ct MK7 . . . 172 D6
Nursery Dr HP14 . . 171 B5
Nursery Gdns
Milton Keynes MK13 . . 34 A4
Tring HP23 . . . . . . 119 B4
Nursery La
Slough SL3 . . . . . . 206 D5
Tylers Green HP10 . . 174 C8
Nursery Pl SL4 . . . . 211 B1

Nursery Rd SL6 . . . 204 B7
Nursery Way TW19 211 D1
Nursery Waye UB8 201 D4
Nursery Wlk SL7 . . 183 B5
Nutfield La HP11 . . 172 F8
Nuthatch 10 HP19 . 101 F3
Nutkins Way HP5 . . 144 C2
Nutmeg Cl MK7 . . . . 48 B5
Nye Way HP3 . . . . 146 A3
Nymans Gate 8 MK4 45 F1

O

Oak Barn Cl MK43 . . 25 A1
Oak Cres HP12 . . . 172 C4
Oak Ct MK9 . . . . . . 34 E2
Oakdene HP9 . . . . 175 E3
Oakdown Cres MK46 . . 6 F3
Oak Dr HP4 . . . . . . 135 D3
Oak End Cl SL9 . . . 188 F6
Oak End Dr SL0 . . . 200 C3
Oak End Way
Chinnor OX39 . . . . 147 D5
Gerrards Cross SL9 . 188 F6
Oaken Gr
Maidenhead SL6 . . . 195 C1
Milton Keynes MK2 . . 58 E7
Oakengrove Cl
Holmer Green
HP15 . . . . 163 C6
Holmer Green HP15 . 163 C6
Oakengrove La
HP15 . . . . 163 B3
Oakengrove Rd
HP15 . . . . 163 A3
Oaken Head MK4 . . . 46 C2
Oakeshott Ave
HP14 . . . . 161 D6
Oakfield WD3 . . . . 167 F2
Oak Field HP5 . . . . 144 B1
Oakfield Ave SL1 . . 205 B5
Oakfield Cl HP6 . . . 154 C2
Oakfield Cnr HP6 . . 154 C2
Oakfield Fst Sch
SL4 . . . . 210 B5
Oakfield Rd
Aylesbury HP20 . . . 116 A8
Bourne End SL8 . . . 185 A3
Oakfield View HP18 . 41 F8
Oak Gn HP21 . . . . 115 C3
Oak Green Sch
HP21 . . . . 115 C3
OAKGROVE 35 D2
Oakgrove L Ctr MK10 35 F2
Oakgrove Prim & Nur
Sch MK10 . . . . . . 35 D2
Oakgrove Rdbt MK10 35 F2
Oakgrove Sch MK10 . 35 D2
Oakhall Ct HP18 . . 109 F1
Oakham Rise MK4 . . 45 E1
OAKHILL 66 B5
Oakhill Cl
Maple Cross WD3 . . 178 E6
Milton Keynes MK5 . . 45 E6
Oakhill La
Calverton MK12 . . . . 33 A1
Whitehouse MK19 . . . 45 B8
Oakhill Rd
Maple Cross WD3 . . 178 D6
Milton Keynes, Hazeley
MK5 . . . . 45 D5
Milton Keynes, Shenley
Church End MK5 . . . 45 F6
Oakhill Rdbt MK5 . . . 45 D5
Oakhurst SL6 . . . . 196 B4
Oakington Ave HP6 166 E8
Oak La
Buckland Common
HP23 . . . . 133 A2
Windsor SL4 . . . . . 210 A6
Oaklands HP4 . . . . 135 A4
Oaklands Ct HP6 . . 154 C1
Oaklands Gr SL6 . . 203 A3
Oakland Way HP10 174 A1
Oak Lawn HP23 . . . 119 A3
OAKLEY
Brill 109 D5
Chinnor 147 B5
Oakley Ho 185 F7
Oakley CE Comb Sch
HP18 . . . . 109 D4
Oakley Cres SL1 . . 205 E6
Oakley Gdns MK15 . . 35 E3
Oakley Gn Rd SL4 . 209 C2
OAKLEY GREEN . . 209 B5
Oakley Green Rd
SL4 . . . . 209 B5
Oakley Hill Wildlife
Reserve OX39 . . . 147 D4
Oakley La OX39 . . . 147 B6
Oakley Rd
Brill HP18 . . . . . . 109 F7
Brill HP18 . . . . . . 110 A8
Chinnor OX39 . . . . 147 C6
Horton-cum-S OX33 138 C5
Worminghall HP18 . . 123 C6
Oak Leys MK18 . . . . 63 E3
Oak Pl HP22 . . . . . 116 B4
Oak Rd HP27 . . . . 139 C3
Oakridge MK4 . . . . . 46 C4
Oakridge Ct HP12 . 172 C6
Oakridge Pl SL2 . . 198 C8
Oakridge Rd HP11 . 172 C7
Oakridge Sch HP11 172 C7
Oakside UB9 . . . . . 201 B6

Oaks Rd TW19 . . . . 213 D2
Oaks The HP4 . . . . 135 A4
Oak Stubbs La SL6 . 203 F4
Oak Tree Ave SL7 . . 183 D3
Oaktree Cl HP10 . . 163 B2
Oak Tree Cl SL7 . . . 183 D3
Oak Tree Cotts HP18 83 B5
Oaktree Ct MK15 . . . 35 C7
Oak Tree Dr
Lane End HP14 . . . 171 C5
Slough SL3 . . . . . . 207 B1
Oak Tree Rd SL7 . . 183 D4
Oakview HP6 . . . . . 153 D4
Oak View
Great Kingshill
HP15 . . . . 162 D8
Towcester NN12 . . . 18 D3
Oakview Gdns SL3 . 206 F2
Oakway
Amersham HP6 . . . 154 B4
Winslow MK18 . . . . 66 A4
Oakwell Cl LU6 . . . . 93 F7
Oakwood HP10 . . . 174 A2
Oak wood HP4 . . . . 134 F3
Oakwood Cl HP22 . . 131 E6
Oakwood Dr
Bletchley MK2 . . . . 58 E7
Milton Keynes MK2 . . 58 E7
Oakwood Pl HP14 . . 171 B4
Oak Wood Pl SL9 . . 188 F2
Oakworth Ave MK10 . 36 A4
Oat Cl HP21 . . . . . 115 C3
Oatlands Dr SL1 . . . 205 C8
Oatleys Rd NN13 . . . 38 C8
Oban Ct SL1 . . . . . 205 D5
Oberon Way MK4 . . . 45 D2
Observatory Sh Ctr 4
SL1 . . . . 205 E5
Oceans Cl MK10 . . . 36 D3
Ockfields Nature Reserve
SL6 . . . . 202 E2
Ockwells Nature Reserve
SL6 . . . . 202 C2
Octagon Arc 10
HP11 . . . . 173 A7
Octagon Par 6
HP11 . . . . 173 A7
Octavian Dr MK13 . . 33 F5
Octavian Way NN13 . 38 A7
Oddley La HP27 . . . 148 D8
Odds Farm Est
HP10 . . . . 186 B4
Odds Farm Park★
HP10 . . . . 186 B4
Oddy Hill
Tring HP23 . . . . . . 119 C3
Wigginton HP23 . . . 119 C2
Odell Cl MK6 . . . . . 47 C8
Odencroft Rd SL2 . . 198 B4
Odney La SL6 . . . . 196 B7
Offa Pl HP23 . . . . . 125 D1
Offas La MK18 . . . . 66 B5
Ogilvie Cl 1 HP22 . . 131 E6
Ogilvie Rd HP12 . . . 172 B2
O'Grady Way HP19 . 101 A3
Okeford Cl HP23 . . . 118 F4
Okeford Dr HP23 . . . 118 F4
Okeford End LU7 . . . 118 F4
Okeley La HP23 . . . 118 E3
Oldacres SL6 . . . . 203 B7
Old Airfield Ind Est
HP23 . . . . 104 D6
Old Amersham Rd
SL9 . . . . 189 B3
Old Bakery Ct SL0 . 207 F7
Old Bakery The
Aston Abbotts HP22 . 88 D5
Lane End HP14 . . . 171 B4
Old Barn Cl MK18 . . 52 A4
Old Bells Ct 2 HP5 154 B7
Old Bix Rd RG9 . . . 191 A6
Old Brewery Cl
HP21 . . . . 115 E7
Old Brewery La
RG9 . . . . 191 E2
Old Brickyard Cl MK46 7 E8
Old Brickyard The
HP22 . . . . 87 B5
OLDBROOK 46 E8
Oldbrook Bvd MK6 . . 46 E8
Oldbrook Fst Sch
MK6 . . . . 46 E8
Old Bryers Cl HP18 124 C2
Old Burrs HP21 . . . 115 D3
Oldbury Gr HP9 . . . 175 D5
Oldcastle Croft MK4 . 46 A1
Old Chapel Ct HP17 129 E3
Old Coach Dr HP11 174 A4
Old Coal Yd LU7 . . . 78 E7
Old College Gdns
SL6 . . . . 202 D7
Old Common Rd
WD3 . . . . 167 D5
Old Court Cl SL6 . . 202 B3
Old Dashwood Hill
HP14 . . . . 159 F2
Old Dean HP3 . . . . 146 A4
Old Drovers View
MK17 . . . . 67 B3
Olde Bell Cl MK17 . . 69 E7
Olde Bell La MK5 . . . 46 A7
Old End MK18 . . . . 53 B2
Old English Cl MK17 44 C1
Oldershaw Mews
SL6 . . . . 202 B8
Old Farm LU7 . . . . 105 D4

Old Farm Cl
Beaconsfield HP9 . . . 175 C5
Slapton LU7. . . . . 91 A3
Worminghall HP18 . . 123 E5
Old Farm La
Amersham HP7. . . . . 165 E6
Ashton NN12. . . . . 9 F8
OLD FARM PARK . . 48 E5
Old Farm Rd
High Wycombe
HP13. . . . . 161 E2
West Drayton UB7. . . 208 D4
Old Ferry Dr TW19 . . 211 D1
Old Field Cl HP6 . . 166 E8
Oldfield Prim Sch
SL6. . . . . 203 B6
Oldfield Rd SL6 . . . . 203 B7
Oldfield St HP10 . . . 100 F4
Old Fishery La HP1. 146 E5
Old Fives Ct SL1. . . . 197 C2
Old Forge Cl
Maidenhead SL6 . . . . 203 A3
Tingewick MK18 . . . . 51 B6
Old Forge Gdns
HP22. . . . . 102 B4
Old Forge Rd HP10. 174 C2
Old Forge The
HP23. . . . . 104 B4
Old Furlong The
MK43 . . . . 25 B2
MK18. . . . . 41 D1
Old Gaol Mus★
Old Garden Ctr The
HP27. . . . . 139 B3
Old Gated Rd The
HP16. . . . . 140 E2
Old Greys La RG9. . 191 D1
Old Groveway MK6. . 47 D5
Oldham Rise MK5 . . . 45 E5
Oldhams Mdw 8
HP20. . . . . 101 F2
Old Hardenwaye
HP13. . . . . 162 E1
Old Heatherdene Cotts
HP15. . . . . 162 D8
Old High St NN7. . . . . 1 B6
Old Horns La SL7. . . 172 A3
Oldhouse Cl HP11. . 172 E3
Old House Ct SL3. . . 206 D7
Old Kiln Rd
Flackwell Heath
HP10. . . . . 185 A8
Tylers Green HP10 . . 163 C2
OLD LINSLADE 70 D2
Old Linslade Rd LU7. 70 E3
Old Lodge Dr HP9 . . 175 E1
Old Long Gr HP9 . . . 176 C4
Old Maltings The
Buckingham MK18 . . . 52 C7
Thame OX9 . . . . 125 E1
Old Manor Cl
Askett HP27. . . . . 139 C7
Whaddon MK17. . . . . 45 B1
Old Manor La 78 E8
Old Marsh La SL6 . . 203 F4
Old Mead SL9. . . . . . 177 E4
Old Meadow Cl
HP4. . . . . 135 A2
Old Mews The MK46. . 6 F4
Old Mill Cl
Haddenham HP17 . . . 127 A6
Yiewsley UB8 . . . . . . 208 C8
Old Mill Furlong
MK18. . . . . 66 A5
Old Mill Gdns 12
HP4. . . . . 135 D4
Old Mill La
Maidenhead SL6 . . . . 203 D4
Uxbridge UB8 . . . . . . 208 B8
Old Mill Pl
Aston Clinton HP22 . . 117 D4
Wraysbury TW19 . . . 212 B1
Old Mill Rd UB9. . . . 190 A1
Old Moor La HP10 . . 185 E8
Old Northampton Rd
NN12. . . . . 9 B5
Old Nursery Ct SL2. 187 C4
Old Oak Gdns HP4. . 134 E7
Old Orch
Henton OX39. . . . . . . 137 E2
Iver SL0. . . . . 207 F7
Old Orchard Mews 1
HP4. . . . . 135 C4
Old Orchards HP22. 102 A3
Old Orchard The
HP15. . . . . 151 D1
Old Oxford Rd HP14 160 C1
Old Palace Ct SL3 . . 212 D6
Old Papermill Cl
HP10. . . . . 185 E8
Old Post Office La 11
SL6. . . . . 202 F7
Old Rd LU7. . . . . 80 E7
Old Rd The RG9 . . . . 179 C8
Old Rectory Cl MK18. .65 F4
Old Rectory La
UB9. . . . . 189 E4
Old Rickyard Piece
HP22. . . . . 116 E6
Old Risborough Rd
HP22. . . . . 130 A8
Old Saw Mill La
HP27. . . . . 150 B8
Old Sawmill Pl
OX39. . . . . 147 D6

Old Saw Mill Pl
Little Chalfont HP6 . . 155 B1
1 Little Chalfont
HP6. . . . . 166 B8
Old Sax La HP5. . . . . 143 D4
Old School Cl HP22. 117 C1
Old School Cotts
HP5. . . . . 145 D5
Old School Ct
1 Buckingham
MK18 . . . . 52 C8
Eaton Bray LU6. . . . . 92 E6
Old School Hill HP5 155 C8
Old School La MK17. 69 E8
Old School La The
MK18 . . . . 63 D3
Old School Rd UB8. 201 F1
Old School The
HP10. . . . . 185 D4
Old Shire La
Chalfont St Peter
SL9. . . . . 178 A1
Chorleywood WD3. . . 167 B3
Old Slade La SL0 . . . 207 F2
Old Springfields
MK18 . . . . 53 C2
Old Stable Yd MK19 . 32 C7
Old Stable Yd The
MK18 . . . . .65 F4
Old Station Cl MK18. 66 A5
Old Station La
TW19 . . . . 212 A1
Old Station Way
HP10. . . . . 185 E5
Old Station Yard
NN12. . . . . .19 F5
Old Stoke Rd HP21. 115 D6
Old Stoneyard Cl
MK46. . . . . .8 A7
OLD STRATFORD . . 32 B7
Old Stratford Prim Sch
MK19 . . . . 32 B6
Old Sun Cl HP14. . . . 171 C4
OLD TOWN 38 A7
Old Town NN13 . . . . 38 A7
Old Town Cl HP9 . . . 175 E1
Old Town Farm
HP16. . . . . 152 A4
Old Union Way OX9 125 E1
Old Uxbridge Rd
Maple Cross WD3 . . . 178 E3
Maple Cross WD3 . . . 178 E3
Old Vicarage Way
HP10. . . . . 185 D4
Old Watery La HP10 185 E5
Oldway La SL1. . . . . . 204 D5
Old Weavers Pl
HP23. . . . . 119 A3
Old Windmill Way
HP18. . . . . 125 C7
OLD WINDSOR 211 A1
OLD WOLVERTON . . 33 D8
Old Wolverton Rd
MK12 . . . . 33 C8
Oliffe Cl HP20. . . . . . 101 D3
Oliffe Way HP20. . . . 101 D3
Oliver Rd MK2 . . . . . . 58 C8
Oliver Row 4 MK4 . . 45 E3
Oliver's Paddock
SL7. . . . . 183 D5
Olivia Dr SL3. . . . . . . 206 F1
Olivier Way HP20. . . 116 A8
Olleberrie La WD4 . 156 D7
OLNEY. 6 E4
Olney Ind EstMK46. . . 6 F6
Olney Infant Acad
MK46. . . . . .6 F3
Olney Mid SchMK46. . 6 F5
Olney Rd
Emberton MK46 . . . . .13 F8
Lavendon MK46 . . . . . 7 E7
Weston Underwood
MK46. . . . . .6 C2
Yardley Hastings NN7. . 1 C4
Olson Cotts HP14 . . . 158 F4
Olympia Way HP18 . 100 C5
Olympic Cres MK10. . 36 D4
Olympic Ho UB8 . . . . 201 F1
Olympic Way HP13. . 174 A6
O'Neill Rd MK8. . . . . . 45 D6
One Pin La SL2. . . . . 187 D1
One Pin Pl SL2. . . . . 187 D1
One Tree La HP9 . . . 175 E3
Onslow Ct MK7. . . . . . 48 A4
Onslow Dr OX9. . . . . 126 E1
Onslow Gdns HP13 . 173 E7
Onslow MillsUB7 . . . 208 D6
Opal Cl SL3. . . . . 199 C1
Opal Dr MK15 . . . . . . .35 F4
Opal Mews HP18. . . . 100 E3
Opecks Cl SL3 . . . . . 199 B1
Opendale Rd SL1. . . 204 B8
Open University (Walton
Hall) TheMK7. . . . . . .47 D7
Oram Ct 3 SL7. . . . . 183 D2
Orbell Ct SL7. . . . . . . 139 B3
Orbison Ct MK8. . . . . 45 D7
Orchard AcadMK6 . . 35 B2
Orchard Ave
Berkhamsted HP4. . . 134 F6
Berkhamsted HP4. . . 135 A4
Slough SL1 . . . . 204 D8
Windsor SL4. . . . . . . 210 A6
Orchard Bglws SL2. 197 F5
Orchard Cl
15 Aylesbury HP20 . . 101 F3
Beaconsfield HP9 . . . 175 D3
Chorleywood WD3. . . 167 D5

Orchard Cl *continued*
Cosgrove MK19. . . . . 19 E2
Cranfield MK43. . . . . 25 A1
Hughenden Valley
HP14. . . . . 162 A7
Longwick HP27 . . . . 138 D7
Maidenhead SL6 . . . 203 A3
Milton Keynes MK3 . . .57 F7
New Denham UB9 . . 201 B6
Newton Longville
MK17. . . . . 57 C3
Oakley HP18 . . . . 109 D4
Slough SL1 . . . . 197 B1
Stoke Mandeville
HP22. . . . . 116 B1
Thornborough MK18. 54 B7
Upper Arncott OX25. 94 D6
Waddesdon HP18 . . . 99 A7
Wendover HP22 . . . . 131 A5
Wingrave HP22. . . . . 89 B3
Yardley Gobion NN12. .18 F6
Orchard Ct
Aylesbury HP21. . . . . 115 F6
Bovingdon HP3 . . . . 146 A4
Seer Green HP9 . . . . 176 C5
Orchard Dene MK18. 41 D1
Orchard Dr
Aston Clinton HP22 . . 117 E5
Chorleywood WD3. . . 167 D5
Hazelmere HP15. . . . 163 A3
Leighton Buzzard LU7. 80 D6
Uxbridge UB8 . . . . . . 201 D1
Wooburn HP10 . . . . . 185 D4
Orchard End
Edlesborough LU6. . . 92 E4
Hazelmere HP15. . . . 163 B6
Orchard End Ave
HP7. . . . . 165 F8
Orchard Gate SL2 . . 198 C7
Orchard Gdns HP23 119 C5
Orchard Gn HP9 . . . 186 E8
Orchard Gr
Chalfont St Peter
SL9. . . . . 177 C2
Flackwell Heath
HP10. . . . . 185 B7
Maidenhead SL6 . . . 202 C7
7 Wolverton MK12 . . 33 A6
Orchard Ho
8 Bourne End SL8 . . 185 A4
Milton Keynes MK12 . 33 D6
Orchard La
Amersham HP6. . . . . 154 D1
Harrold MK43 . . . . . . .3 F7
Prestwood HP16. . . . 151 C6
Stewkley LU7 . . . . . . 78 E7
ORCHARD LEIGH . . 145 B3
Orchard Leigh Villas
HP5. . . . . 145 A4
Orchard Lodge SL1. 204 E5
Orchard Mews HP9. 176 C5
Orchard Mill SL8. . . 185 B1
Orchard Mill La
Great Brickhill MK17. .58 F2
Great Brickhill MK17. 59 A2
Orchard Pk HP15. . . 163 C6
Orchard Pl
Monks Risborough
HP27. . . . . 139 C5
Stokenchurch HP14. . 158 E5
Uxbridge UB8 . . . . . . 201 D5
Westbury NN13. . . . . 39 A4
Orchard Rd
Beaconsfield HP9 . . . 175 F1
Chalfont St Giles HP8 177 C8
Loudwater HP13. . . . 174 A4
Old Windsor SL4 . . . 211 B1
Seer Green HP9 . . . . 176 C5
Orchard Rise MK46. . 6 F3
Orchard Row HP14 . 171 A4
Orchards The
Eaton Bray LU6. . . . . 92 E7
Little Kingshill HP16 . 152 A2
Slough SL3 . . . . 206 F5
Tring HP23 . . . . 118 F3
Orchard The
Aston Clinton HP22. . 117 E5
Flackwell Heath
HP10. . . . . 185 B7
Halton HP22 . . . . 131 C8
Hazelmere HP15 . . . 163 A6
Hillesden MK18. . . . . 63 A7
Marlow SL7. . . . . 183 E3
Potterspury NN12. . . 18 C3
Walter's Ash HP14 . . 161 E6
Orchard View
Hillesden MK18. . . . . 63 B7
Uxbridge UB8 . . . . . . 201 D1
ORCHARDVILLE . . . 197 B1
Orchardville SL1. . . . 197 B1
Orchard Way
Aylesbury HP20. . . . . 101 F2
Bovingdon HP3 . . . . 146 A3
Chinnor OX39. . . . . . 147 C5
Cranfield MK43. . . . . 25 A1
East Claydon MK18. . 74 E6
Eaton Bray LU6. . . . . 92 F5
Holmer Green HP15 . 163 C6
North Crawley MK16. . 24 A6
Pitstone LU7 . . . . 105 E4
Slough SL3 . . . . 206 F5
Stoke Goldington
MK16. . . . . 12 B7
Wing LU7. . . . . 79 E2
Orchard Waye UB8 201 D3
Orchard Wlk MK46. . .7 F7
Orchehill Ave SL9 . . 188 D7
Orchehill Ct SL9 . . . 188 E6

Orchehill Rise SL9 . 188 D6
Oregano Cl UB7. . . . 208 F6
Orford Ct MK5 . . . . . . 46 B6
Oriel Cl MK12 . . . . . . 33 B6
Oriel Cotts MK18 . . . 63 D2
Orient Chase 1
MK10 . . . . 36 B5
Orkney Cl
Milton Keynes MK3 . . 46 F2
Stewkley LU7 . . . . . . .78 E8
Orkney Ct SL6 . . . . . 196 E5
Orkney Way MK8. . . . 45 C7
Ormesby Cl HP21. . . 116 A5
Ormonde MK14 . . . . . 34 D7
Ormond Rd OX9. . . . 126 A1
Ormsgill Ct MK13 . . . 34 B5
Orne Gdns MK5. . . . . 35 A7
Orpington Gr MK5. . . 46 B4
Orrell Pl MK18 . . . . . . 65 E5
Ortensia Dr MK7 . . . . 48 C7
Ortman Cl SL9 . . . . . 188 E4
Orwell Cl
Aylesbury HP21. . . . . 115 D4
Newport Pagnell MK16 21 F5
Windsor SL4 . . . . 210 D4
Orwell Dr HP21. . . . . 115 D4
Osborne Ct SL4 . . . . 210 C5
Osborne Mews SL4. 210 C5
Osborne Rd SL4. . . . 210 D4
Osborne St
Milton Keynes MK2 . . 58 C7
Slough SL1 . . . . 205 F4
Osborne Way HP23 119 D1
Osborn Rd UB8 . . . . 201 C5
Osborns Ct MK46. . . . 6 F3
Osborn's Ct 5 MK46. . 6 F3
Osbourne Cnr MK43. 25 B3
Osbourne St MK12 . . 33 D6
Osea Gr MK3. . . . . 58 B4
Osier La MK5 . . . . 46 B4
Osier Way
Aylesbury HP20. . . . . 102 A1
Aylesbury HP20. . . . . 115 F8
Buckingham MK18 . . 52 C6
Olney MK46. . . . . 6 F6
Osiris Gr MK17 . . . . . 36 E3
Osmington Pl HP23. 118 F4
Osney Rd SL6 . . . . . . 195 E2
Osprey Cl
Milton Keynes MK6 . . 47 B8
West Drayton UB7. . . 208 E4
Osprey The HP19 . . . 101 E4
Osprey Wlk
Aylesbury HP19. . . . . 101 E4
Buckingham MK18 . . 52 F7
Ossulbury La HP19. 101 C4
Osterley Cl MK16. . . . 22 C3
Ostler Gate SL6 . . . . 195 C1
Ostlers Ct HP11 . . . . 174 A4
Ostlers La MK11. . . . 32 D6
Oswald Way MK18. . . 52 B8
Otterburn Cres MK5. 45 D5
Otter Cl
Brackley NN13 . . . . . 26 A2
Milton Keynes MK3 . . 46 D1
Otterfield Rd UB7 . . 208 E6
Otters Brook MK18 . . 52 E7
Otter Wy UB7. . . . . . 208 E5
Otway Cl
Aylesbury HP21. . . . . 115 E3
17 Broughton MK10. . 36 C4
Oulton Cl HP21. . . . . 116 A5
Our Lady of Peace RC
Prim and Inf Sch
SL1. . . . . 197 C8
Our Lady's RC Prim Sch
HP6. . . . . 154 B4
Ousebank St MK16 . . 22 C5
Ousebank Way MK11 32 D5
Ousedale Sch
Newport Pagnell
MK16. . . . . 22 B3
Olney MK46. . . . . 6 E4
Ouseley Rd TW19 . . 211 D1
Ouseley Way LU6. . . 107 E8
Outfield Rd SL9 . . . . 177 D3
Outlook Dr HP8 . . . . 177 D7
Ouzel Cl MK3 . . . . . . 46 E1
Oval The MK6. . . . . . . 46 F2
Oval Way SL9 . . . . . . 188 E2
Overdale Rd MK8. . . 44 B3
Overdales HP15 . . . . 162 F3
Overend Cl MK13. . . 34 A3
Overgate MK6, MK9,
MK14. . . . . 35 B4
Over Hampden
HP16. . . . . 151 C7
Overhills MK6. . . . . . . 6 E4
Overlord Cl UB8. . . . 201 E5
Overn Ave MK18. . . . 41 C1
Overn Cl MK18 . . . . . 41 D1
Overn Cres MK18. . . 41 C1
Overshot Ho HP10. . 174 C2
Oversley Rd MK14 . . 22 A1
Overstone Cl
Wing LU7 . . . . 79 E2
Wing LU7 . . . . 79 E2
Overstone Comb Sch
LU7. . . . . 79 E2
Overstrand MK12 . . . 117 E5
Overstreet MK15 . . . 35 A4
Over the Misbourne
UB9. . . . . 189 B5
Over the Misbourne Rd
UB9. . . . . 189 C5
Overton Dr OX9. . . . 126 B1
Oville Ct MK5 . . . . . . 46 B5
OVING 86 D8

Oving Rd
Quainton HP22 . . . . . .85 F3
Whitchurch HP22 . . . 86 E7
Ovitts Cl MK18 . . . . . 66 A5
Owl Cl 5 HP19. . . . . . 101 F3
Owlsears Cl HP9 . . . 175 D4
OWLSWICK. 128 C1
Owlswick HP27 . . . . . 128 E2
Owlswick La
Longwick HP17 . . . . . 139 A7
Longwick HP27 . . . . . 138 E8
Owlswick Rd HP17 . 128 C4
Oxendon Ct LU7. . . . .70 F2
Oxenhope Way MK10 36 A4
Oxfield Cl HP4 . . . . . 135 A3
Oxfield Park Dr
MK19 . . . . 32 C7
Oxford Ave
Burnham SL1. . . . . . . 197 B3
Slough SL1 . . . . 204 F8
Oxford Brookes Univ
(Wheatley Campus)
OX33. . . . . 122 C1
Oxford Down OX39 147 C7
Oxford Gdns UB9. . . 190 A1
Oxford La HP18 . . . . . 83 D3
Oxford Rd
Aylesbury HP17,
HP21. . . . . 115 D4
Denham UB9 . . . . . . 189 D2
Denham UB9 . . . . . . 201 A8
Dinton HP17 . . . . 113 E2
Gerrards Cross SL9. 188 D5
High Wycombe HP11. 173 A4
Marlow SL7. . . . . 183 D2
Oakley HP18 . . . . 109 D5
Piddington HP14. . . . 160 D1
Stokenchurch HP14. . 158 D5
Stone HP17 . . . . 114 C5
Thame HP23 . . . . 125 A1
Thame OX9 . . . . 125 E1
Tiddington OX9 . . . . . 136 D7
Uxbridge UB8. UB9. . 201 B6
Windsor SL4 . . . . 210 C6
Oxford Road E SL4 . 210 C6
Oxford St
5 High Wycombe
HP11. . . . . 173 A7
Lee Common HP16 . . 142 D5
Ox Gd HP18 . . . . 100 D4
Ox Ground HP18 . . . 100 D4
Oxhouse Ct MK5 . . . . 46 A3
Oxlade Dr SL1 . . . . . 206 C2
OXLEY PARK 45 E3
Oxley Park Acad
MK4 . . . . 45 E2
Oxley Park Rdbt MK5 45 E3
Oxleys MK46. . . . . . . .6 E4
Oxman La MK12. . . . . 33 A5
Oxpen HP18 . . . . 100 D4
Oxwich Gr MK4 . . . . . 57 B8
Oxyard HP18 . . . . . . 100 D4

P

Pablo Ct HP5 . . . . . . 144 A3
Pace Ctr The HP19. . 101 B2
Pacific Ave MK10. . . . 36 C4
Packet Boat La UB8 208 C7
Packhorse Rd SL9. . 188 E6
Pack & Prime La
RG9. . . . . 191 C2
PADBURY 53 B2
Padbury CE Sch
MK18 . . . . 53 C2
Padbury Oaks UB7 . 213 B6
Padbury Rd MK18. . . 53 F6
Padcroft Rd UB7. . . 208 D5
Padda Mws MK18 . . . 52 B8
Paddington La
HP22. . . . . 102 D2
Paddock Cl
8 Aylesbury HP19. . 100 F1
Castlethorpe MK19. . 20 A5
Maidenhead SL6 . . . 202 A2
Milton Keynes MK14 . 34 E8
Windsor SL4 . . . . 209 F6
Paddock Cotts SL6. 202 A2
Paddocks Clinic The
(BMI)HP27 . . . . 139 C4
Paddocks End HP9. 176 C4
Paddocks La MK17. . 48 F4
Paddocks The
Amersham HP6. . . . . 154 E2
Chinnor OX39. . . . . . 147 D8
Chorleywood WD3. . . 167 F5
Flackwell Heath
HP10. . . . . 185 B8
Haddenham HP17. . . 127 A5
High Wycombe HP12. 172 B3
Leighton Buzzard LU7. 80 F8
Prestwood HP16. . . . 151 C5
Steeple Claydon MK18 63 E3
Wendover HP22 . . . . 131 B5
Widmer End HP15. . . 162 E5
Paddock The
Aylesbury HP21. . . . . 116 C7
Chalfont St Peter SL9 177 E5

Paddock The *continued*
Datchet SL3. . . . . 211 B6
Emberton MK46 . . . . .13 E8
Maidenhead SL6 . . . 195 C2
Maids Moreton MK18. 41 E7
Paddock View MK19. 32 B6
Paddock Way
Ashley Green HP5 . . 144 F7
Milton Keynes MK2 . . 47 D1
Padstow Ave MK6 . . . 34 F1
Padstow Cl
Aylesbury HP20. . . . . 101 F1
Slough SL3 . . . . 206 E3
PAGE HILL. 41 F2
Page Hill Ave MK18. . 41 E1
Pages Croft HP4 . . . 135 A6
Pages La UB8 . . . . . . 201 C6
Pages Wharf SL6. . . 203 C8
Paget Cl SL7. . . . . . . 183 F4
Paget Ct UB7 . . . . . . 208 E4
Paget Dr SL6 . . . . . . 202 A4
Paget Rd SL3 . . . . . . 206 F2
Pagg's Ct MK16. . . . . 22 D4
Pagoda Rdbt MK5 . . 35 C5
Pagoda The SL6. . . . 196 B1
Paignton Way 2
MK10 . . . . 36 A3
Paines Orch LU7 . . . 105 A8
Painsend Rd
Hastoe HP23. . . . . . . 132 D8
Tring LU7. . . . . 118 E1
Pakenham Cl HP19. 114 F8
Palace Cl SL1. . . . . . 204 F5
Palace Sq MK6. . . . . .46 F7
Palfreyman St
HP19. . . . . 101 D4
Pallatia Ct 2 HP13. . 162 A1
Palliser Rd HP8 . . . . 177 B6
Palmer Ave
Aylesbury HP19. . . . . 115 C8
Upper Arncott OX25 . .94 F3
Palmers Rise SL6. . . 202 A3
PALMERS MOOR . . . 201 A1
Palmers Moor MK18. 54 A8
Palmer's Moor La
SL0. . . . . 201 A1
Palmers Path MK18 . 65 F5
Palmers Rd MK46 . . . 7 A3
Palmerston Ave
SL3. . . . . 206 B3
Panama La MK10. . . . 36 D4
Pankridge Dr HP16. 151 C2
Panleigh Cotts
HP14. . . . . 171 B3
Pannier Pl MK14 . . . . 35 A5
Pann Mill HP13 . . . . . 173 C6
Panshill OX5. . . . . 94 D2
Panters Cl MK17. . . . 44 C1
Pantile Row SL3 . . . 207 A2
Pantile Wlk UB8 . . . 201 C5
Papermill La MK17. . 69 F7
Paprika Ct MK7. . . . . 48 B5
Papworth Pl MK16. . . 22 F3
Parade Ct 7 SL8. . . 185 A4
Parade The
Bourne End SL8. . . . 185 A3
Farnham Common
SL2 . . . . 198 C6
High Wycombe HP11. 172 F6
Uxbridge UB8 . . . . . . 208 C8
Windsor SL4 . . . . 209 D6
Paradine St MK18 . . . 63 E3
Paradise MK11. . . . . . 57 D4
Paradise Mews
RG9. . . . . 191 E2
Paradise Orchard
Aylesbury HP18. . . . . 100 D4
Berryfields HP18. . . . 100 E4
Paradise Rd RG9 . . . 191 C1
Parchment Cl HP6. . 154 E2
Parish La SL2. . . . . . 187 C1
Parish Piece HP15 . 163 C7
Park Ave
Newport Pagnell
MK16. . . . . 22 B4
Totternhoe LU6. . . . . 93 B8
Wraysbury TW19 . . . 211 D3
Park Cl
Cosgrove MK19. . . . . .19 E2
Dunton MK18 . . . . . . 77 E5
Lane End HP14 . . . . . 171 C5
Windsor SL4 . . . . 210 D5
Park Cnr SL4. . . . . . . 209 E4
Park Ct UB8 . . . . 201 D4
Parker Cl MK13 . . . . . 34 A6
Parker Gdns SL4 . . . 211 B1
Parker Knoll Way
HP13. . . . . 173 A7
Parker Wlk HP19. . . 101 D3
Park Farm Rd HP12. 161 B1
Park Farm Way
HP14. . . . . 171 C5
Parkfield WD3 . . . . . . 167 E5
Parkfield Ave HP6. . 154 D2
Parkfield Rise HP27 139 B2
Parkgate SL1. . . . . . . 197 C1
Park Gate LU7 . . . . . . 79 E1
Park Gdns MK3 . . . . . 47 A1
Park Gr
Beaconsfield HP9 . . . 175 C7
Little Chalfont HP8 . . 166 D6
Park Hill OX33 . . . . . 122 B1
Park Ho
Berkhamsted HP4. . . 135 D4
Gerrards Cross SL9. 188 E4
Maidenhead SL6 . . . 202 E6
Park House Bsns Ctr
HP12. . . . . 172 E8

Park House Dr MK5 . .45 F6
Park La
  Beaconsfield HP9 . . . . . 175 F1
  Burnham SL1 . . . . 197 E7
  Eaton Bray LU6 . . . . 92 D6
  Hazelmere HP15 . . . . . 163 A4
  Horton SL3 . . . . 212 A4
  Lane End HP14 . . . . . . 171 D5
  Maidensgrove RG9 . . . 179 D6
  Paulerspury NN12. . . . . 17 B7
  Slough SL3 . . . . 206 B3
  Stokenchurch HP14. . . 158 E6
Parkland Ave SL3 . . . . 206 D2
Parklands MK14. . . . . 21 D1
Park Lane Ct HP14 . . 158 E5
Park Lawn SL2. . . . . . 198 C2
Park Lodge Ave
  UB7. . . . . 208 F7
Park Manor Industries
  MK18 . . . . 41 D3
Park Mdw HP27 . . . . . 139 A3
Parkminster MK10 . . . 36 A1
Park Parade SL2 . . . . 198 C3
Park Parade Ctr The
  HP15 . . . . 163 A5
Park Pl
  Amersham HP6 . . . . . 154 F1
  Seer Green HP9 . . . . 176 D5
Park Rd
  Amersham HP6 . . . . . 154 F2
  Chesham HP5 . . . . . . 154 B8
  Farnham Royal SL2 . . 198 E3
  Granborough HP18. . . . .75 F6
  Grendon Underwood
    HP18. . . . . .82 F8
  Hanslope MK19. . . . . . 11 B1
  Hartwell NN7 . . . . 10 C8
  Henley-on-Thames
    RG9. . . . . 191 A1
  Milton Keynes MK11 . . 32 D5
  Sherington MK16 . . . . 14 A2
  Stanwell TW19. . . . . . 213 C1
  Tring HP23 . . . . 118 F2
  Uxbridge UB8 . . . . . . 201 E6
  Winslow MK18 . . . . . . .65 F5
Park Rise HP4 . . . . . . 134 E6
Park Road E UB10 . . 201 D3
Park Road S MK18. . . .65 F5
Parkside
  Gerrards Cross SL9. . . 188 F7
  Henley-on-Thames
    RG9. . . . . 191 C2
  Maidenhead SL6 . . . . 195 D1
  Milton Keynes MK4 . . . 46 E3
  Naphill HP14. . . . . . . 150 B1
Parkside Wlk SL1 . . . 206 A3
Park Sports Ctr
  OX33. . . . . 222 B1
Park St
  Aylesbury HP20. . . . . 115 F8
  Berkhamsted HP4. . . . 135 B5
  High Wycombe HP11 . . 173 D6
  Maidenhead SL6 . . . . 202 F7
  Poyle SL3 . . . . 212 D6
  Princes Risborough
    HP27. . . . . 139 B3
  Slough SL1 . . . . 205 F4
  Tring HP23 . . . . 119 A3
  Windsor SL4 . . . . 210 D6
  Woburn MK17. . . . . . . .60 F7
Parkstone Lodge
  SL3 . . . . 206 A3
Park Street Ind Est
  HP20. . . . . 115 F8
Parkview
  Flackwell Heath
    HP10. . . . . 185 B7
  Maidenhead SL6 . . . . 202 F7
Park View
  Newport Pagnell
    MK16 . . . . 22 D4
  West Drayton UB7. . . 208 E6
Parkview Chase
  SL1 . . . . 204 E7
Park View Ct
  Berkhamsted HP4. . . . 135 B4
  High Wycombe HP12 172 E8
  4 Leighton Buzzard
    LU7. . . . . 80 E7
Park View Rd
  Berkhamsted HP4. . . . 135 B4
  Uxbridge UB8 . . . . . . 208 F7
Parkway
  Bow Brickhill MK17. . . 48 D2
  Marlow SL7. . . . . 184 A3
  Woburn Sands MK17. . 49 A6
Parkway The SL0. . . . 200 C4
Parkwood HP14. . . . . 150 A2
Park Wood, Gouldings
  Wood Nature Reserve
  SL6. . . . . 194 E4
Parlaunt Rd SL3. . . . 207 B2
Parliament Cl HP16 151 B7
Parliament La SL6,
  SL1. . . . . 196 F5
Parliament Rd OX9. . 125 C1
Parmiter Cl HP19. . . 115 B8
PARMOOR. 181 F7
Parmoor Croft La
  Hambleden SL7. . . . . 182 A7
  Parmoor RG9 . . . . . . 181 F7
Parmoor La
  Frieth RG9. . . . . 170 E1
  Parmoor RG9 . . . . . . 181 F8
Parneleys MK10. . . . . .35 F2
Parrin Dr HP22. . . . . 131 E6
Parrishs Piece HP22. 87 B3
Parrock La MK10. . . . . 36 A2

Parrot Cl HP21. . . . . 115 B6
Parrott Ct MK17. . . . . 58 C2
Parrott's La HP23 . . . 133 A4
Parrs Rd HP14 . . . . . 158 E4
Parry Cotts SL9 . . . . 177 E6
Parry Green N SL3 . . 206 F2
Parry Green S SL3. . . 207 A2
Parsley Cl
  Aston Clinton HP22. . 117 C5
  Walton MK7 . . . . 48 B5
Parslow Cl HP21 . . . . 115 D3
Parslow Ct HP21. . . . 115 D3
Parsonage Cl
  High Wycombe
    HP13. . . . . 173 C6
  Tring HP23 . . . . 119 A4
Parsonage Ct **1**
  HP23. . . . . 119 A3
Parsonage Farm
  HP22. . . . . .89 B3
Parsonage Gdns
  SL7 . . . . 183 E1
Parsonage La
  Chesham HP5 . . . . . . 154 B8
  Farnham Common
    SL2. . . . . 198 D5
  Windsor SL4 . . . . 210 A6
Parsonage Pl HP7. . . 165 C8
Parsonage Rd HP8 . . 177 B7
Parson Cl MK18. . . . . .65 F4
Parsons Cl HP5 . . . . 154 B8
Parsons Cres MK5. . . .46 C5
Parson's Fee HP20 . . 115 D8
Parsons La HP22. . . . 102 B3
Parsons Rd SL3 . . . . 206 F1
Parsons Wlk HP15. . . 163 C6
Parson's Wood La
  SL2 . . . . 198 D5
Parton Cl HP22. . . . . 131 A5
Parton Rd HP20 . . . . 116 B8
Partridge Cl
  Buckingham MK18 . . .52 F7
  Chesham HP5 . . . . . . 144 E3
  Leighton Buzzard LU7 104 F7
  4 Uxbridge UB10 . . . . 201 F4
Partridge Hill MK17 . 70 B6
Partridge Mead
  SL6 . . . . 195 F2
Partridge Piece
  MK43 . . . . 25 C3
Partridge Way
  7 Aylesbury HP19 . . . 101 F3
  High Wycombe HP13 . . 161 C2
Pascal Dr MK5 . . . . . 45 E5
Pascal Mws MK10. . . . 35 E2
Pascomb Rd LU6. . . . .93 F8
Passalewe La MK7 . . 48 D7
PASSENHAM. 32 C4
Passenham Rd
  Deanshanger MK19. . . 32 A4
  Old Stratford MK19. . . 32 B4
Passmore MK6. . . . . . 47 D6
Pastern Pl MK14 . . . . 35 A5
Pastures The
  Aylesbury HP20. . . . . 102 B2
  Edlesborough LU6. . . .92 F3
  High Wycombe HP13 . . 161 E1
Patch Cl UB10. . . . . 201 F4
Patches Field SL7 . . 183 E5
Pateman Rd MK18 . . . 41 C1
Patemore La RG9 . . . 168 A1
Paterson Rd HP21. . . 115 C6
Pathia Cl HP17 **1** . . 10 C4
Patricia Cl SL1. . . . . 204 E6
Patrick Haugh Rd
  OX25. . . . . .94 F7
Patricks La MK19. . . . 31 F4
Patrick Way HP21. . . 116 A4
Patrington Cl UB8. . . 201 C2
Patriot Dr MK13. . . . . 34 B2
Patrons Way E UB9. 189 F5
Patrons Way W UB9 189 F5
Patterson Rd HP10. . 185 E7
Patterson Rd HP5 . . 144 B3
Pattison La MK15. . . . 35 C3
Paulerspury CE Prim
  Sch NN12. . . . . 17 B8
Paulerspury Rd
  MK18 . . . . 17 B2
Pauling Cl HP22. . . . 117 C5
Pauls Hill HP10 . . . . 174 F6
Paul's Row HP11. . . . 173 B6
Pavers Ct HP21 . . . . 115 D3
Pavilion Cl
  Aylesbury HP20. . . . . 116 A8
  Padbury MK18. . . . . . 53 D2
Pavilion End HP9. . . 175 C5
Pavilion Gdns HP22 117 E4
Pavilions The (Sh Ctr)
  UB8. . . . . 201 C5
Pavilion Way HP6 . . 166 C8
Pavis Cl LU7 . . . . . . 118 E3
Paxton Ave SL1 . . . . 205 C3
Paxton Cl MK46 . . . . .6 F3
Paxton Cres MK5. . . . 46 B5
Paxton Rd HP4. . . . . 135 D4
Payne Rd MK17 . . . . .36 F1
Paynes Dr MK18. . . . . 41 D1
Paynes Dr MK5. . . . . 46 A8
Paynes Field Cl
  HP4. . . . . 134 D7
Payton Gdns SL6. . . 195 D6
Payton Hos SL6. . . . 195 E6
Peace La SL6 . . . . . 195 F6
Peace Rd SL0, SL3 . . 200 A3
Peachey Cl UB8. . . . 208 D7
Peachey La UB8. . . . 208 D8

Peach Tree Ave
  UB7. . . . . 208 F7
Peacock Hay MK4 . . . 46 C2
Peacock La HP19. . . . 101 B4
Peacock Rd SL7. . . . 184 A3
Peacocks Cl HP4. . . . 134 F6
Pea La HP4 . . . . 134 D7
Pearce Cl
  Aylesbury HP21. . . . . 115 E4
  Maidenhead SL6. . . . 195 F1
Pearce Ctyd HP18 . . 109 E5
Pearce Dr SL6 . . . . . 195 F1
Pearce Rd
  Chesham HP5 . . . . . . 144 B2
  Maidenhead SL6. . . . 195 F1
Pearce's Orch RG9 191 D3
Peard Ct HP22 . . . . . 102 B1
Pearl Cl MK18. . . . . . .52 F6
Pearl Gdns SL1 . . . . 205 B5
Pearmain CI MK16 . . 22 B4
Pearse Gr MK7. . . . . 48 A8
Pearson Cl HP19 . . . 115 B6
Pear Tree Ave UB7 . . 208 F7
Peartree Cl SL1 . . . . 204 F5
Pear Tree Cl
  Amersham HP7 . . . . . 165 F8
  Amersham HP7. . . . . 165 F8
  Seer Green HP9 . . . . 176 C4
Pear Tree Ct HP15. . . 163 C6
Pear Tree Farm Ind
  Units OX27 . . . . 71 E2
Pear Tree La
  Loughton MK5. . . . . . 46 E5
  Milton Keynes MK6 . . .46 F5
Peartrees UB7 . . . . 208 E6
Peascod Pl **12** SL4. . 210 D6
Peascod St SL4 . . . . 210 D6
Peascroft HP18 . . . . 125 D6
Peatey Ct HP21 . . . . 173 D6
Pebble Brook Sch
  HP21. . . . . 115 C7
Pebble La
  20 Aylesbury HP20 . . 115 D8
  Brackley NN13 . . . . . 38 A7
Pebblemoor LU6. . . .92 F3
Pebody Pl **10** MK46 . . .6 F3
Peck Ct MK4 . . . . 45 E4
Peckover Ct **7** MK8 . .33 F1
Pecks Farm Cl
  HP22. . . . . 102 C4
Peddle Cl HP11 . . . . 172 F7
Pednor Bottom HP5 143 B3
PEDNORMEAD
  END 154 A7
Pednormead End
  HP5. . . . . 154 B7
Pednor Rd HP5 . . . . 143 E2
Peebles Rd MK3 . . . .46 F3
Peel Cl
  Tatling End SL9 . . . . 189 B3
  Windsor SL4 . . . . 210 B4
Peel Ct
  Monks Risborough
    HP27. . . . . 139 B4
  Slough SL1 . . . . 205 B8
Peel Rd MK12 . . . . . 33 C6
Peel Way UB8. . . . . . 208 E8
Peerless Dr UB9 . . . 190 C7
Peers Dr MK17 . . . . . 49 E3
Peers La MK5. . . . . . .46 B6
Pegasus Way HP17. . 126 F7
Pegasus Wy HP17 . . 126 D6
Peggs La HP22 . . . . 117 F5
Pelham Ct SL6 . . . . . 202 E7
Pelham Pl MK14 . . . . .34 F5
Pelham Rd OX9 . . . . 126 B1
Pelton Ct MK5 . . . . . 46 C5
Pemberley Lodge
  SL4 . . . . 210 A4
Pemberton Cl HP21 115 F5
Pemberton Dr MK17. .60 F7
Pemberton Rd SL2. . 197 E1
Pembridge Cl **3**
  HP3. . . . . 146 A3
Pembridge Gr MK4. . 45 E1
Pembridge Rd HP3. . 146 A3
Pembroke Ho
  2 Milton Keynes
    MK3. . . . . .46 F1
  7 Olney MK46. . . . . . .6 F3
Pembroke La MK19. . 45 D8
Pembroke Rd HP20. . 101 F1
Penard Cres **18** MK4. 56 E8
Pencarrow Pl MK6 . . 35 A1
Penda Rd MK18 . . . . 52 B8
Pendeen Cres MK4. . 57 B7
Pendeen Ct SL1. . . . 205 A5
Pendennis Cl MK4 . . 57 A8
Pendles Paddocks
  HP14. . . . . 158 F2
Pendrill Ho **2** HP12 172 E7
Penfold HP22. . . . . . 116 C7
Penfold Cotts HP15 163 D7
Penfold La
  Holmer Green
    HP15. . . . . 163 E8
  Hyde Heath HP7,
    HP15. . . . . 152 F1
  Little Missenden HP7 152 F1
Pengelly Ct **2** MK6. . 35 A1
Penhale Cl MK4 . . . . 57 B8
Penhow Rise MK4. . . 45 E1
Penina Cl MK3 . . . . . 46 D1
Penington Rd HP9 . . 186 B8
Peninsular Ct **4**
  MK10 . . . . 36 D4
Penlee Rise MK4 . . . 57 B8

Penley Cl OX39. . . . . 147 B6
Penling Cl SL6 . . . . . 195 E6
Penmans Hill WD4 . 156 F6
Penmon Cl MK10. . . . .35 F1
Penmoor Cl HP12 . . . 172 C8
PENN 174 E7
Penn Ave HP5. . . . . . 144 A1
Penn Bottom
  Hazelmere HP10. . . . 163 D4
  High Wycombe HP10. . 163 F2
Penn Cl
  Chorleywood WD3. . . 167 D3
  Uxbridge UB8 . . . . . . 201 D1
Penn Ct
  14 Marlow SL7. . . . . . 183 E2
  Tylers Green HP10 . . 174 B8
Penn Dr UB9 . . . . . . 189 F5
Penn Gaskell La
  SL9 . . . . 177 F5
Penn Gn HP9 . . . . . . 175 D4
Penn Haven SL9 . . . . 188 F6
Pennine Rd SL2 . . . . 205 A8
Penning Cl MK14. . . . 21 C1
Pennings The HP22 131 B5
Pennington Pl OX9. 126 B1
Pennington Rd
  Chalfont St Peter
    SL9 . . . . 177 D3
  High Wycombe HP13. . 173 F6
Pennings The
  HP6. . . . . 154 E2
Penn Mdw SL2. . . . . 198 F4
Penn Mead HP10. . . . 174 F7
Penn Rd
  Aylesbury HP21. . . . . 115 F6
  Beaconsfield HP9 . . . 175 C5
  Chalfont St Peter SL9 177 D2
  Chorleywood WD3. . . 167 F1
  Datchet SL3. . . . . . . 211 D6
  Hazelmere HP15. . . . 163 B3
  Milton Keynes MK2 . . 58 E8
  Slough SL2 . . . . 198 D1
Penn Rd Service Rd
  HP15. . . . . 163 A4
PENN STREET. 164 B5
Penn Street Works Ind
  Est HP7 . . . . 164 A4
Penn Way WD3 . . . . 167 D3
Penn Wood Prim Sch
  SL2 . . . . 198 D1
Penn Wood View
  HP7. . . . . 164 A4
Pennycress Way
  MK16 . . . . .21 F4
Pennycuik MK17 . . . . 59 C1
PENNYLAND 35 A6
Pennylets Gn SL2 . . 199 A5
Pennyroyal MK7 . . . . 48 B7
Pennyroyal Dr UB7. 208 F4
Pennyroyal
  HP22. . . . . 102 D3
Pennyworth Pl HP9 186 D8
Penrith Cl UB8. . . . . 201 D5
Penrith Way HP21. . . 116 B7
Penryn Ave MK6 . . . . 35 A2
Penshurst Cl SL9. . . 177 D1
Penshurst Cres MK6. 47 D4
Penshurst Rd SL6. . 202 D5
Pentewan Gate MK6. .34 F2
Pentland Rd
  Aylesbury HP21. . . . . 115 F6
  Slough SL2 . . . . 205 A8
Pentlands MK11. . . . . 32 F4
Pentlands Ct
  High Wycombe
    HP11. . . . . 174 B4
  Loudwater HP13. . . . 174 B4
Pentlands The
  HP13. . . . . 174 B4
Penwood Ct SL6 . . . . 202 B7
Penwood La SL7 . . . 183 C1
Penwynne Gdns
  SL9 . . . . 177 B5
Penyston Rd SL6 . . . 202 C7
Penzance Spur SL2. 198 B1
Peplar Way SL1 . . . . 197 B2
Peplow Cl UB7 . . . . . 208 D5
Peppard Mdw HP16 151 D5
Pepper Hill Sch
  MK13 . . . . 34 A7
Peppeards Gn HP5. . 143 D8
Peppiatts The LU6 . . 92 B5
Pepys Cl SL3 . . . . . . 212 B8
Pepys Dr HP16 . . . . 151 C6
Perch Cl
  Marlow SL7. . . . . 183 C1
  Marlow SL7. . . . . 194 C8
Percheron Pl MK14. .34 F7
Perch Mdws HP22. . . 131 B8
Percy Bush Rd UB7. 208 F3
Percy Pl SL3. . . . . . . 211 B6
Percy Terr HP8 . . . . 177 A7
Peregrine HP19. . . . . 101 E3
Peregrine Bsns Pk
  HP13. . . . . 174 A5
Peregrine Cl MK6. . . 47 B8
Perivale MK10 . . . . . 36 E3
Perks La HP16 . . . . . 151 C3
Permayne MK13 . . . . 34 A7
Perracombe MK4 . . . 46 E3
Perran Ave
  4 Central Milton Keynes
    MK6 . . . . .34 F1
  Milton Keynes MK6 . . .34 F1
Perrine Cl HP18. . . . 100 E5
Perrin Springs La
  RG9. . . . . 170 F1

Perry Cl MK17. . . . . . 58 C2
Perrycroft SL4 . . . . . 209 D6
Perryfield Ct HP27 . . 138 C1
Perryfields Way
  SL1. . . . . 197 B1
Perry Hill HP18 . . . . . 73 C3
Perry Ho SL1 . . . . . . 197 B2
Perry La
  Bledlow HP27. . . . . . 138 C1
  Bledlow HP27. . . . . . 138 C2
  Sherington MK16 . . . 14 B2
Perryman Way SL2 . . 197 F2
Perry Mead LU6. . . . . 92 C6
Perry St HP22. . . . . . 131 A5
Perrys The HP22 . . . . 131 B5
Pershore Croft **1**
  MK10 . . . . 36 A1
Pershore Wy HP18 . . 100 E3
Perth Ave SL1. . . . . . 205 B7
Perth Cl MK3 . . . . . . .46 F2
Perth Rd HP13 . . . . . 173 D8
Perth Trad Est SL1. . 205 B8
Peterborough Ave **2**
  HP13. . . . . 173 C7
Peterborough Gate
  MK15 . . . . 35 C6
Peter Dwight Dr
  HP6. . . . . 154 E1
Peterhead Mews
  SL3 . . . . 207 A1
Peterhill Cl SL9 . . . . 177 E5
Peterley Ave HP15,
  HP16. . . . . 151 E3
Peterley La HP16. . . 151 E3
Peter's Cl HP16 . . . . 151 C6
Petersfield HP22 . . . 116 C3
Petersfield Ave SL2 206 A5
Petersfield Gn **5**
  MK9 . . . . 34 E1
Petersham Cl MK16. 22 C2
Peters La
  Great Hampden
    HP27. . . . . 150 B8
  Little Hampden HP27 140 A1
  Princes Risborough
    HP27. . . . . 139 E4
Peter's Pl HP4 . . . . . 134 E6
Petronel Rd HP19 . . 101 D4
PETSOE END 14 A7
Petsoe End MK46 . . . 14 C7
Pettifer Way HP12. . 172 D6
Pettingrew Cl MK7 . . 48 B6
Petty Cross SL1 . . . . 204 E7
Petworth MK8 . . . . . . 33 E1
Petworth Ct SL4 . . . 210 B6
Petworth Ho **2** MK8. .33 F1
Pevensey Cl
  Aylesbury HP21. . . . . 116 B5
  Milton Keynes MK3 . . 57 E2
Pevensey Rd
  Slough SL1 . . . . 204 F8
  Slough SL2 . . . . 205 A8
Peverel Dr MK1 . . . . 47 B3
Pever Green MK17 . . 37 A1
Peveril Cl HP21 . . . . 116 B5
Pevers La MK46 . . . . .6 A1
Pfullmann St HP22. . 117 C5
Pheasant Cl
  Amersham HP6. . . . . 154 E2
  Berkhamsted HP4. . . 135 C3
  Tring HP23 . . . . 119 B6
Pheasant Dr HP13. . . 161 C2
Pheasant Hill HP8 . . 177 C8
Pheasant Rise HP5 . 154 D6
PHEASANTS 181 E6
Pheasants Croft
  SL6. . . . . 202 A4
Pheasants Dr HP15. . 163 B5
Pheasants Hill RG9. 181 C3
PHEASANT'S HILL . . 181 D3
Pheasants Ridge
  SL7 . . . . 183 C7
Pheasant Wlk SL9. . 177 E6
Phelps Rd MK2. . . . . 58 E6
Philbe Mews SL1. . . 204 F4
Philip Cotts SL8. . . . 185 C3
Philip Dr HP10 . . . . . 185 C7
Philip Rd HP13. . . . . 173 D7
Philipshill Wood
  Reserve* WD3 . . . . 167 A2
Philips Rd HP19. . . . 115 A3
Phillimore Cl MK15. . 35 B7
Phillip Ct MK5 . . . . . 46 B6
Phillips Way **4**
  HP6. . . . . 154 E1
Philpots Cl UB7 . . . . 208 D6
Philps Cl HP14 . . . . 171 C4
Phipps Cl
  Aylesbury HP20. . . . . 102 A2
  Maidenhead SL6. . . . 202 A2
Phipps Rd SL1 . . . . 204 E8
Phoebe La MK17 . . . 48 E6
Phoebes Orch MK7 . 69 E7
Phoenix Bsns Ctr **3**
  HP5. . . . . 144 B1
Phoenix Cl SL9. . . . . 189 A3
Phoenix Ct SL6. . . . . 202 D4
Phoenix Dr MK6. . . . . 46 E6
Phoenix Ho **7**
  HP19. . . . . 115 A4
Phoenix House Bsns Ctr
  HP12. . . . . 172 E8
Phoenix Inf Acad
  SL1. . . . . 205 C8
Phygtle The SL9. . . . 177 E4
Phyllis Court Dr
  RG9. . . . . 191 E3
Picasso Pl HP19. . . . 100 F2

Piccadilly Mews
  MK18 . . . . 66 A5
Pickering Dr MK4. . . 46 B2
Pickford Dr SL3. . . . 207 A5
Pickfords Gdns SL1 205 E5
Pickins Piece SL3. . . 212 A5
Pickwick Terr SL2. . . 206 B6
Picton St MK4 . . . . . 45 E1
Picts La HP27 . . . . . 139 C4
PIDDINGTON
  Blackthorn. 95 E7
  High Wycombe 160 B1
  Northamptonshire. 4 B8
Piddington La HP14 171 B8
Piddington Rd
  Ludgershall HP18 . . . 96 A8
  Ludgershall OX25 . . . 95 A8
  Marsh Gibbon OX27 . .71 F1
  Marsh Gibbon OX27 . .81 F8
Piece Cl OX27. . . . . . .71 F3
Pield Heath House Sch
  UB8. . . . . 201 F1
Pield Heath Rd UB8 201 F1
Pierrepoint Way
  Hanslope MK19. . . . . 11 A2
  Hanslope MK19. . . . . 11 A2
  Hanslope MK19. . . . . 11 A2
Pierson St SL4 . . . . . 209 D6
Pigeon Farm Rd
  HP14. . . . . 158 E5
Piggotts End **6**
  HP7. . . . . 165 B7
Piggott's Hill HP14 . 150 E1
Piggotts Orch HP7 . 165 B7
Piggy La WD3. . . . . . 167 B3
Pightle Cres MK18 . . 41 D2
Pightle The
  Buckingham MK18 . . . 41 D1
  Maids Moreton MK18 . .41 F4
  Oving HP22. . . . . 86 D7
  Pitstone LU7 . . . . . . 105 D3
Pigott Dr MK5. . . . . . 46 A5
Pigott Orch HP22 . . 85 A5
Pike Cl
  Marlow SL7. . . . . 194 C8
  Uxbridge UB10 . . . . . 201 F4
Pike Cnr HP21 . . . . . 116 C5
Pilch Field Wildlife
  Reserve MK17 . . . . . 54 B5
Pilch La MK17. . . . . . 54 D4
Pilgrims Cl HP27 . . . 139 B5
Pilgrim St MK15. . . . 35 A4
Pillow Wy MK18. . . . .52 F6
Pilmore Mdw OX39. 147 B3
Pilots Pl HP17. . . . . 126 E6
Pilot Trad Est HP12 172 E8
PIMLICO. 26 F6
Pimlico Ct **4** MK10. . .35 F1
Pimms Cl HP13 . . . . 174 A6
Pimms Gr HP13 . . . . 174 A5
Pimpernel Gr MK7 . . 48 B6
Pinafore Gdns MK17. 36 E3
Pinchfield WD3 . . . . 178 D5
Pincords La MK43 . . 25 D5
Pinders Croft MK12. . 33 B5
PINDON END
  10 C4
  Castlethorpe MK19. . . 10 B3
Pindon End NN7 . . . . .9 F5
Pineapple Rd HP7. . 165 F8
Pine Chase HP12. . . 172 B3
Pine Cl
  Berkhamsted HP4. . . 135 B4
  Buckingham MK18 . . . 41 E3
  Hazelmere HP15. . . . 163 B3
  Maidenhead SL6. . . . 202 B7
Pine Crest Mews
  LU7. . . . . 80 E6
Pinecroft SL7. . . . . . 183 D4
Pine Ct HP5. . . . . . . 154 C8
Pine Gr MK17 . . . . . . 49 A4
PINEHAM. 35 E7
Pineham Rdbt MK15. 35 E7
Pine Hill HP15 . . . . . 162 F3
Pinels Way HP11. . . . 172 E3
Piner Cotts SL4 . . . . 209 E4
Pine Rd LU6 . . . . . . 106 F8
Pines Cl
  Amersham HP6. . . . . 154 B2
  Little Kingshill HP16 . 152 B4
Pine St HP19. . . . . . 115 A8
Pines The
  Felden HP3 . . . . 146 F7
  Slough SL3 . . . . 206 F5
  Slough SL3 . . . . 206 F5
  Tylers Green HP10 . . 163 B1
Pinetree Cl SL9 . . . . 177 C3
Pine Trees Dr UB10. 201 E8
Pine Wlk
  Berkhamsted HP4. . . 134 D7
  Hazelmere HP15. . . . 163 B3
Pinewood Ave UB8. 208 F7
Pinewood Cl
  Gerrards Cross SL9. . 188 E4
  Iver Heath SL0 . . . . . 200 C5
Pinewood Dr MK2. . . 58 E7
Pinewood Film Studios
  SL0. . . . . 200 B5
Pinewood Gn SL0 . . 200 C5
Pinewood Mews
  TW19 . . . . 213 D1
Pinewood Rd
  High Wycombe
    HP12. . . . . 172 C7
  Iver Heath SL0 . . . . . 200 B4

Pineywoods La MK8. 45 C7
Pinfold MK7 . . . . 48 B6
PINFOLDPOND 60 E6
Pinfold Yd MK18 . . 51 B6
Pinglestone Cl UB7. 213 E7
Pinions Rd HP13 . . 173 E5
Pinkard Ct MK6 . . . 47 C8
Pink Hill HP27 . . . 149 E8
Pink La SL1 . . . . 197 B3
Pinkneys Dr
  Maidenhead SL6 . . 195 A1
  Maidenhead SL6 . . 202 A8
PINKNEYS GREEN . . 195 A1
Pinkneys Rd SL6 . . 202 A8
Pink Rd
  Great Hampden
  HP27 . . . . 150 B8
  Lacey Green HP27. 149 E7
Pinks Cl MK5 . . . . 46 C8
Pinkworthy MK4 . . 46 D4
Pinn Cl UB8. . . . 208 D7
Pinners Way HP23. 125 D7
Pinstone Way SL9 . 189 B2
Pintail Cl HP19. . . 101 E4
Pintail Wy SL6 . . . 203 B8
Pipard MK14. . . . 34 E7
Pipers Cl SL1 . . . . 197 C2
Pipers Corner Sch
  HP15. . . . 162 B7
Pipers Croft LU6 . . 93 F7
Pipers Ct SL1 . . . . 197 C2
Pipers La HP15. . . 162 C8
Pipers Wood Cotts
  HP7. . . . 153 C2
Pipit Gdns 7 HP19. 101 E4
Pipit Wlk 6 HP19 . 101 E4
Pippin Cl
  Newport Pagnell
  MK16 . . . . 22 B3
  Slough SL1 . . . . 205 C8
Pippin Rd HP18 . . 100 E5
Pippins Cl UB7. . . 208 D3
Pippins Sch SL3. . . 212 F6
Pippins The SL3. . . 206 F5
Pipston Gn
  Milton Keynes MK7. 48 B7
  Walton MK7 . . . . 48 B7
PISHILL 179 D8
PISHILL BANK. . . 168 B1
Pishill Bank RG9 . . 168 B1
PISHILL BOTTOM . . 168 A1
Pistone Green Bsns Pk
  LU7 . . . . 105 D2
PITCHCOTT 86 B5
Pitchcott Hill HP22. .85 F4
Pitchcott Rd HP22. . 86 B6
Pitcher La MK5 . . . 46 B8
Pitcher Wlk HP19 . 115 A7
Pitchford Ave MK18 . 41 E2
Pitchford Wlk MK18 . 41 F1
PITCH GREEN . . . 138 B3
Pitch Pond Cl HP9. 175 C5
Pitch The HP14 . . . 159 D3
Pitfield MK11. . . . 33 B3
PITSTONE 105 C4
Pitstone Green Farm
  Mus* LU7. . . . 105 D4
Pitstone Rd LU7. . . 105 B5
Pitstone Windmill*
  LU7. . . . 105 F4
Pitters Piece HP18 . 125 F7
Pitt Gn MK18. . . . .41 F1
Pitts Rd SL1 . . . . 205 C5
Pixel Wy MK10 . . . 35 E2
Pixie Rd HP18. . . . 100 E5
Pk La Ct HP14. . . . 158 E5
Pk Mill HP27 . . . . 138 F3
Pk St
  Central Milton Keynes
  MK9 . . . . 35 B4
  17 Slough SL1. . . 205 F4
Pk View HP22. . . . 117 E4
Place Farm Ho
  HP27 . . . . 139 B6
Place Farm Way
  HP27 . . . . 139 B5
Plackett Way SL1 . 204 D5
Plaines Cl SL1 . . . 204 F5
Plaistow Cres MK10 . 35 F1
Plaiters Cl HP23. . . 119 B4
Plantain Ct MK7. . . 48 B6
Plantation Pl MK5. . 46 A4
Plantation Rd
  Amersham HP6. . . 154 E2
  High Wycombe HP13. 174 A7
  Leighton Buzzard LU7 . .70 F3
Plantation Way HP6 154 E2
Platers Rd HP17. . . 126 F7
Platform St HP22. . 102 C2
Platt The HP7. . . . 165 B7
Playing Field Rd
  NN13. . . . 39 A4
Pleasant Cotts SL0 . 200 B2
Pleasant Pl WD3 . . 178 E3
Pleasaunce The
  HP22. . . . 117 E5
Pleshey Cl MK5 . . . 46 B6
Plested Ct HP22. . . 116 C2
Pliny La MK11. . . . .32 F3
Plomer Green Ave
  HP13. . . . 161 D2
Plomer Green La
  HP13. . . . 161 D3
Plomer Hill HP13. . 161 D1
Plough HP21 . . . 115 E3

Plough End HP22 . . 102 B4
Plough La
  Sarratt WD4 . . . . 156 F6
  Wexham Street SL2. . 199 B4
Ploughlees La SL1 . 205 E6
Ploughley Rd OX25. . 94 E8
Plough Orch HP22. . 116 F3
Plover Cl
  1 Berkhamsted
  HP4. . . . 135 C3
  Buckingham MK18 . . 52 E7
  Newport Pagnell MK16 22 F3
Plover The 4 HP19. 101 E4
Plover Wlk 3 HP19. 101 E4
Plowman Cl MK12. . 33 B5
Plumer Rd HP11 . . 172 E7
Plum Park La NN12. . 17 D8
PLUMPTON END. . . 17 C7
Plumpton End NN12. 17 C8
Plumstead Ave MK13 34 D3
Plumton End NN12. . 17 C4
Pluto Cl SL1 . . . . 204 E4
Pluto Way HP19. . . 101 D4
Plym Cl HP21 . . . . 115 C5
Plymouth Gr MK4 . . 46 B1
Plymouth Rd SL1. . 204 E8
Plysu Wy 1 MK17. . 49 A5
Pockersdell La HP3 145 E2
Pocketts Yd SL6 . . 196 B7
Pocock Ave UB7 . . 208 F3
Pococks La SL4 . . . 205 E1
Poets Chase HP21. 115 F6
Points The SL6. . . . 202 B3
Polar Pk UB7 . . . . 213 F7
Polecat End La
  OX33. . . . 122 A5
Poles Hill
  Chesham HP5 . . . 144 A2
  Sarratt WD4 . . . . 156 E6
Police Hos SL9. . . 189 B3
Polidoris La HP15 . 163 C7
Polish Ave HP22 . . 131 E8
Pollard Ave UB9 . . 189 F5
Pollard Cl SL4 . . . 211 B2
Pollards WD3. . . . 178 D5
Pollys Yd MK14 . . . 22 D5
Pollywick Rd HP23 . 119 D1
Polmartin Ct 1 MK6 35 A1
Polruan Pl
  Fishermead MK6. . . 47 A8
  Milton Keynes MK6 . . 35 A1
Polygon Bsns Ctr
  SL3. . . . 212 F5
Pomander Cres MK7 48 B7
Pomeroy Cl HP7 . . 165 D7
Pomeroy Ct HP18. . 100 E5
Pompeii Gr MK11 . . .32 F2
Pond App HP15 . . . 163 C7
Pond Cl
  Newton Longville
  MK17. . . . 57 C2
  Tring HP23 . . . . 119 A4
  Winchmore Hill HP7. 164 C3
Pond Cotts HP14 . . 171 B4
Pondecroft HP18. . 100 D4
Pondgate MK7. . . . 48 B8
Pond Gate MK14 . . .21 F3
Pond La
  Chalfont St Peter
  SL9 . . . . 177 C2
  Little Gaddesden HP4 121 E7
POND PARK 144 A2
Pond Park Rd HP5. . 144 B2
Pondwicks HP7 . . . 165 B8
Ponies Cl HP23 . . . 104 F7
Pontefract Ave 11
  MK4 . . . . 56 E8
Pony Field The
  HP22. . . . 116 D1
Poole Cl 8 HP21 . . 115 E4
Pool La SL1. . . . 205 E6
Poolmans Rd SL4 . 209 D4
Pope Ct HP23 . . . . 118 F3
Popes Acre HP17. . 126 F5
Popes Cl
  Amersham HP6 . . . 154 F2
  Colnbrook SL3. . . 212 C7
Popes La SL6 . . . . 195 C2
Pope Way 3 HP21 . 115 E4
Poplar Ave UB7 . . . 208 F6
Poplar Cl
  Aylesbury HP20. . . 102 A2
  Chesham HP5 . . . 144 C3
  Milton Keynes MK6 . . 47 E5
  Poyle SL3 . . . . 212 E6
Poplar Farm Caravan Pk
  LU6. . . . 93 A8
Poplar Ho SL3 . . . 206 F1
Poplars Cl HP17. . . 114 C5
Poplars Gr SL6 . . . 196 B2
Poplars Rd MK18. . 52 D8
Poplars The HP22 . 131 D5
Poplar Wy
  Ickford HP18. . . . 123 F4
  Ickford HP18. . . . 124 A4
Poppy Ave MK10 . . 36 B4
Poppy Cl
  Slough SL1 . . . . 206 C2
  West Drayton UB7. . 208 E3
Poppyfield Wy NN13. 26 A2
Poppy La 2 LU7 . . . 69 E2
Poppy Rd HP27 . . . 139 A2
Porchester Cl MK3 . .57 F8

Porlock La MK4 . . . 46 C4
Portage Pl UB7 . . . 208 E5
Portal Cl UB10 . . . 201 F5
Portal Rd HP22. . . 131 D6
Portchester Ct 1
  MK8 . . . . .33 F1
Porter La HP22. . . . 102 C2
Porter's Cl MK19 . . 31 E4
Porters Way UB7. . 208 F4
Portfield Cl MK18 . . 52 E8
Port Field Farm
  MK16 . . . . .21 F5
Portfields Prim Sch
  MK16 . . . . 22 A5
Portfields Rd MK16. . 22 B4
Portfield Way MK18. 52 E8
Porthcawl Gn MK3 . 57 C8
Porthleven Pl MK6 . 35 A2
Porthmellin Ct MK4 . 57 B8
Portishead Dr
  Milton Keynes MK4 . . 56 F8
  Shenley Brook End
  MK4 . . . . 57 A8
Portland Ave
  Whitehouse MK19. . 33 C1
  3 Whitehouse MK19 . 45 D8
Portland Bsns Ctr
  SL3. . . . 211 B6
Portland Cl
  Broughton HP22. . 102 E3
  Slough SL2. . . . 197 D1
Portland Cres SL7. . 183 D1
Portland Ct MK14 . . 21 C1
Portland Dr MK15. . 35 C7
Portland Gdns SL7 . 183 D1
Portland Ho HP13 . 173 D8
Portland Pk SL9. . . 188 D5
Portland Rd HP11 . . 173 E4
Portlands Alley SL7 183 D1
Portlands Mews 1
  SL7. . . . 183 D1
Port Line Rd
  Atterbury MK10 . . . 36 C4
  Broughton MK10. . . 36 D4
Portlock Rd SL6 . . . 202 C7
Portman Mews
  HP19. . . . 114 F8
Portmarnock Cl MK3 57 D7
Portnall Pl MK43 . . 25 B2
Portobello Cl HP5. . 144 A2
Portobello Cotts
  Lacey Green HP27. . 149 E5
  Lewknor OX49. . . . 157 C2
Portrush Cl MK3 . . 57 D8
Portsmouth Ct SL1 . 205 E6
Portway
  Milton Keynes, Bradwell
  Common MK5, MK9, MK13,
  MK14, MK15 . . . . 34 D2
  Milton Keynes, Shenley
  Church End MK8,
  MK5 . . . . 45 F6
  North Marston HP22. 86 B8
  North Marston MK18. 76 B1
  Stone HP17 . . . . 114 E4
Portway Dr HP12. . 161 B1
Portway Rd
  Stone HP17 . . . . 114 E4
  Twyford MK18. . . . 62 D1
Portway Rdbt MK5 . 34 B1
PORTWAYS 168 B8
Posting Ho HP23 . . 120 A5
Post Mdw SL0 . . . 200 D2
Post Office Cotts
  SL2. . . . 199 A5
Post Office La
  Beaconsfield HP9 . 175 D3
  Hoggeston MK18 . . 77 B7
  Hoggeston MK18 . . 77 B7
  Slough SL3 . . . . 206 D7
  Whitchurch HP22 . . 87 A6
Potash Cl HP17 . . . 126 F5
Potash La HP23. . . 104 A5
Potkiln La HP9. . . . 176 D1
Potter Row HP16. . 142 C1
Potters Cl HP16. . . 151 B7
Potters Cross SL2 . 200 E2
Potters Cross Cres
  HP15. . . . 162 E2
Potters Glen MK18 . 53 B1
Potters La MK11 . . 33 B4
POTTERSPURY . . . 18 D2
Potterspury Lodge Sch
  NN12. . . . 18 B6
Potterspury Rd
  Deanshanger NN12. . 18 B1
  Deanshanger NN12. . 31 A7
Pottery Cl HP19. . . 115 A7
Pottery Ct HP19. . . 115 A7
Potts Pl 8 SL7. . . . 183 D2
Poulcott TW19 . . . 211 E1
Poulter Cft MK10. . 35 E3
Poultons Mdw 5
  LU7. . . . 105 C4
Pound Cl
  Steeple Claydon
  MK18. . . . 63 D3
  Wicken MK19 . . . 31 A4
Pound Cres SL7. . . 183 C1
Poundfield La SL6. . 195 F7
Poundfield Rd NN12. 18 E2
Pound Hill
  Great Brickhill MK17. 59 C1
  Poundon OX27 . . . 71 D7
Pound La
  Heath End HP5 . . . 134 A1
  Little Marlow SL7 . . 184 C4
  Marlow SL7. . . . 183 D1

Pound La continued
  North Crawley MK16. . 24 B7
  Princes Risborough HP18. 51 C1
POUNDON. . . . 71 E7
Poundon Rd OX26. . 71 C6
Pound Riding NN7 . . .1 B1
Pounds Cl MK43. . . 25 B1
Pound St MK16 . . . 131 B4
Pound The
  Cookham SL6 . . . 196 A7
  Cookham Rise SL6. . 195 F7
  Slough SL1 . . . . 197 D1
  Syresham NN13 . . . 27 B7
Powell Haven MK10. 35 E3
Powis Cl SL6. . . . 202 B4
Powis La MK4 . . . . .45 F2
Powney Rd SL6 . . . 202 C7
POYLE 212 E6
Poyle 14 Trad Est
  SL3 . . . . 212 E4
Poyle La SL1 . . . . 197 B3
Poyle New Cotts
  SL3 . . . . 212 E5
Poyle Pk SL3. . . . 212 E4
Poyle Rd SL3 . . . . 212 E5
Poyle Tech Ctr The
  SL3 . . . . 212 E5
Poyning La MK10. . 35 E3
Poynings The SL0 . . 207 F2
Pratt Ho HP6 . . . . 154 F1
Prebendal Ave
  HP21. . . . 115 D7
Prebendal Ct
  1 Aylesbury HP20. 115 D8
  11 Aylesbury HP20. 115 D8
PREBENDAL FARM. 115 D8
Precedent Dr MK13. 34 B7
Precincts The SL1. . 197 C1
Premier Acad The
  MK2 . . . . 58 D6
Premier Way 12
  HP13. . . . 173 A7
Prentice Gr MK5 . . 46 B3
Prescott Rd SL3. . . 212 E5
Prescotts The UB9 . 189 F3
President Rd HP19 . 100 D5
Presley Way MK8. . 45 E7
Press Rd UB8. . . . 201 D6
PRESTON BISSETT. . 62 B8
Preston Bissett Rd
  Chetwode MK18 . . 61 E7
  Preston Bissett MK18. 62 A6
  Preston MK15 . . . 35 B7
Preston Hill HP5 . . 144 D2
Preston Rd
  Slough SL2 . . . . 206 C6
  Tingewick MK18 . . . 51 D4
Prestwick Cl MK3 . . 57 D7
Prestwold Ho HP19. 115 A7
Prestwold Way
  HP19. . . . 115 A7
PRESTWOOD 151 D6
Prestwood SL2 . . . 206 B7
Prestwood Cl HP12 172 D8
Prestwood Inf Sch
  HP16. . . . 151 C7
Prestwood Jun Sch
  HP16. . . . 151 C6
Prestwood Nature
  Reserve HP16. . . 151 B3
Prestwood Pl HP16. 151 C6
Pretoria Rd HP13. . 173 C8
Priest End OX9. . . . 125 E1
Priestland Gdns
  HP4. . . . 135 C6
Priestley Ct HP13 . 173 D6
Priestley Dr MK4 . . 56 E7
Priests Paddock
  HP9. . . . 175 B5
Prima Rd HP18 . . . 100 E5
Primary Rd SL1 . . 205 D3
Primatt Cres MK5 . 46 B6
Primrose Cotts
  HP14. . . . 150 A1
Primrose Ct HP21. 115 B6
Primrose Dr
  Aylesbury HP21. . . 115 B5
  West Drayton UB7. . 208 D2
Primrose Gdns LU7. 80 C7
Primrose Gn HP15. 162 F6
Primrose Hill HP15. 162 F7
Primrose La MK10. . 36 C3
Primrose Lea SL7. . 183 D2
Primrose Rd MK13 . 34 A4
Primrose Terr HP18 110 A8
Primrose Way MK18. 52 C7
Prince Albert's Wlk SL3,
  SL4 . . . . 211 B5
Prince Andrew Cl 1
  SL6. . . . 203 B8
Prince Andrew Rd
  SL6 . . . . 196 B1
Prince Consort Cotts
  SL4 . . . . 210 D5
Prince Consort's Dr
  SL4 . . . . 210 A2
Prince Edward St
  HP4. . . . 135 C4
Prince Philip Ave
  MK43 . . . . 24 D2
Prince Rupert Dr
  HP19. . . . 101 C4
Princes Cl
  Berkhamsted HP4. 135 A6
  Chilton HP18. . . . 111 B3
  Eton Wick SL4 . . . 204 F1
Princes Ct LU7. . . . .80 F8
Princes Gate HP13 . 173 D1

Princes Gdns HP27. 139 B3
Princes La HP16 . . 142 D5
Princes Pl HP27. . . 139 B1
Princes Rd SL8. . . 185 C3
Prince's Rd HP21. . 115 E8
PRINCES
  RISBOROUGH . . . 139 D4
Princes Risborough Sch
  Monks Risborough
  HP27. . . . 139 B5
  Princes Risborough
  HP27. . . . 139 C2
Princes Risborough Sta
  HP27. . . . 138 F2
Princess Cl SL4. . . 210 B4
Princess Gr HP9 . . 176 D6
Princess Margaret Hospl
  The (private) SL4 . 210 D1
Princess Mary Dr 5
  HP22. . . . 131 D6
Princess St SL6 . . 202 F6
Princes St
  Piddington HP14. . . 160 B1
  2 Slough SL1. . . . 206 B4
Princes Terr SL8. . . 185 C3
Princes Way MK2 . . 58 C8
Princes Way Rdbt
  MK2 . . . . 58 B8
Printers End
  Aylesbury HP19. . . 101 B1
  Aylesbury HP19. . . 115 B8
Printers Piece 5
  HP17. . . . 127 A6
Prior Gr HP5 . . . . 144 C1
Priors Cl
  Maidenhead SL6 . . 203 B2
  4 Slough SL1. . . . 206 A3
Priors Pk MK4 . . . 46 D2
Priors Rd SL4 . . . . 209 D4
Priors Way SL6 . . . 203 B2
Priors Way Ind Est
  SL6 . . . . 203 B2
Priory Ave
  High Wycombe
  HP13. . . . 173 B7
  South Harefield UB9. 190 C7
Priory Cl
  Aylesbury HP19. . . 101 C1
  Denham UB9 . . . 190 A1
  Horton-cum-S OX33. 108 B5
  Newport Pagnell MK16 22 E4
  South Harefield UB9. 190 C7
Priory Common Sch
  MK13 . . . . 34 B4
Priory Cotts UB9 . . 190 C7
Priory Cres HP19. . 101 C2
Priory Farm Cotts
  OX27 . . . . 71 E2
Priory Gdns
  Berkhamsted HP4. . 135 C4
  South Harefield UB9. 190 C7
Priory Rd
  Gerrards Cross SL9. 188 D8
  High Wycombe HP13. 173 B7
  Slough SL1 . . . . 204 C8
Priory Rise Sch MK4. 56 D7
Priory Sch SL1. . . . 204 B8
Priory St MK16 . . . 22 E4
Priory Way
  Datchet SL3. . . . 211 B7
  Gerrards Cross SL9. 188 D8
  Harmondsworth UB7. 213 E8
Pritchard Ct MK14. . 34 E8
Proctor Mews MK17. 58 B2
Proctor Rise MK8 . . 45 C6
Progress Bsns Ctr
  SL1 . . . . 204 D7
Progress Rd HP12. . 172 B7
Promenade SL4. . . 210 C7
Prospect Cl MK17 . 68 D6
Prospect Cotts
  HP14. . . . 150 A1
Prospect Ct NN12 . . 18 F6
Prospect Pl
  Castlethorpe MK19. . 19 F5
  Hurley SL6. . . . 193 C3
  3 Windsor SL4. . . 210 D4
  Wing LU7 . . . . 79 E2
Prospect Rd
  Marlow SL7 . . . . 183 D2
  Milton Keynes MK11. 32 C5
Prothero Cl 6
  HP21. . . . 115 E4
Protheroe Rd MK7 48 D4
Providence Pl
  9 Maidenhead SL6. 202 F7
  2 Milton Keynes
  MK13 . . . . 34 A4
Providence Rd UB7. 208 F5
Provis Wharf HP20. 102 B1
Prudential Bldgs 1
  SL1 . . . . 205 F4
Puddle End HP22. . 102 C2
PUDDS CROSS . . . 145 E2
Pudds Cross HP3. . 145 E2
Pudseys Cl SL6. . . 195 B6
Puers Field HP9. . . 176 E4
Puers La HP9. . . . 176 E4
Puffin Way HP19. . 101 F3
Pulborough Cl MK3. 46 D1
Pulford Rd LU7 . . . 80 F6
Pulfields HP5 . . . . 144 A1
Pulpit Cl HP19. . . . 101 C4
Pulpit La HP22. . . . .76 D1
Pulver Rd HP22 . . . 117 E5
Pumpkin Hill SL1. . 197 E6
Pump La HP5. . . . 154 C1
Pump Lane N SL7 . 183 F6

Pump Lane S SL7 . 184 A4
Pump Mdw HP16. . 152 A8
Pump Pl MK19 . . . .32 B7
Pumpus Gn MK18. . 66 A4
Punch Bowl La HP5 154 C7
Purbeck MK13 . . . 34 C6
Purbeck Cl HP21 . . 116 B5
Purcel Dr MK16 . . . 22 C3
Purcell Way MK17 . 59 A7
Purse La
  Stoke Goldington
  MK16 . . . . .4 E1
Pursers SL1. . . . 205 E7
Purssell Cl SL6. . . 202 A3
Purssell Pl HP27 . . 139 B5
Purssell Rd HP22 . . 116 C2
Purssells Mdw
  HP14. . . . 161 C7
Purton Ct SL2. . . . 198 C5
Purton La SL2. . . . 198 C5
PURY END 17 A7
Pury Rd
  Alderton NN12 . . . .9 A2
  Alderton NN12 . . . .9 C4
Pusey Way HP14 . . 171 C5
Putlowes Dr HP18. . 100 C3
Putman Ho MK4. . . 46 C5
Putman St HP19. . . 101 C1
Putnams Dr HP22 . 117 D5
PUTTENHAM . . . 103 F2
Puttenham Ct
  HP23. . . . 103 F2
Puttenham Rd
  Buckland HP23. . . 117 F8
  Drayton Beauchamp
  LU7. . . . 118 A7
  Puttenham HP23. . 103 F1
PUXLEY 31 D7
Puxley Rd
  Deanshanger MK19 . 31 D5
  Deanshanger NN12. . 31 D7
  Milton Keynes MK19. 32 A5
  Pottspury NN12. . 18 D1
Pyatts Farm La
  HP14. . . . 171 D5
Pye Bridge End
  MK10 . . . . 36 A4
Pyebush La HP9. . . 187 A8
Pyghtles The HP22. 85 B5
Pyghtle The
  Denham UB9 . . . 190 A3
  Olney MK46. . . . . .6 F3
  Turvey MK43. . . . .8 E6
Pyke Hayes MK8 . . 33 D3
Pymcombe Cl HP27 139 B5
Pyms Stables MK16 . 22 F2
Pym Wlk OX9 . . . 125 F1
Pynefield Ho WD3. . 167 F2
Pyxe Ct MK7 . . . . 48 A4

Q

Quadrangle The
  HP13. . . . 173 E7
Quadrans Cl MK15. . 35 A7
Quadrant The
  High Wycombe
  HP13. . . . 162 E1
  Maidenhead SL6. . 203 A6
  Maidenhead SL6. . 203 A6
QUAINTON 85 B5
Quainton CE Comb Sch
  HP22. . . . 85 A5
QUAINTON HILL . . 75 B1
Quainton Rd
  East Claydon MK18. . 74 F4
  North Marston MK18. 76 A2
  Quainton, Waddesdon
  HP18. . . . .84 F1
  Waddesdon HP18 . .99 A7
Quainton Road Sta* . 84 F2
Quainton Windmill*
  HP22. . . . 85 B5
Quaker's Mead
  HP22. . . . 116 F3
Quakers Mede
  HP17. . . . 127 A6
Quantock Cl SL3 . . 207 A1
Quantock Cres MK4 . 46 D2
QUARRENDON . . . 101 B3
Quarrendon Ave
  HP19. . . . 101 B2
Quarrendon Rd
  HP7. . . . 165 E7
Quarry Cl HP18 . . . 125 C7
Quarry Ct LU7. . . . 105 D2
Quarrydale Dr SL7 . 183 F2
Quarry Green Cl
  MK19 . . . . 31 B3
Quarry Hall Spinney
  MK16 . . . . 21 E8
Quarry Rd LU7 . . . 105 D2
Quarry Wood Rd SL6,
  SL7. . . . 195 A8
Quaves Rd SL3 . . . 206 C3
Quebec Rd HP13 . . 173 E6
Queen Alexandra Rd
  HP11. . . . 173 A6
Queen Anne Royal Free
  CE Fst Sch The
  SL4 . . . . 210 D4
Queen Anne's Ct 10
  SL4 . . . . 210 C6

Queen Anne's Rd
SL4. . . . . .210 C3
Queen Anne St MK13 .33 F7
Queen Catherine Rd
Steeple Claydon
MK18. . . . . 63 E2
Steeple Claydon MK18 74 B8
Queen Charlotte St
10 SL4. . . . . 210 D6
Queen Cl RG9. . . . . . . 191 E1
Queen Eleanor Prim Sch
MK11. . . . . .32 F4
Queen Eleanor St
MK11. . . . . 32 E6
Queen Elizabeth's Wlk
SL4. . . . . 210 F5
Queen Mother's Dr
UB9. . . . . 189 F5
Queens Acre
High Wycombe
HP13. . . . . 173 D6
Windsor SL4. . . . . . . 210 D3
Queen's Acre SL4. . . 210 D3
Queen's Acre Ho **6**
SL4. . . . . 210 D4
Queen St Mews
RG9. . . . . 191 E1
Queens Ave MK16. . . 22 C4
Queensbury La
MK10. . . . . 35 E1
Queens Cl OX9. . . . . 125 F2
Queen's Cl SL4. . . . . 211 A2
Queens Ct HP13. . . . 173 C6
Queen's Ct SL1 . . . . 205 F6
Queen's Dr SL3 . . . . 199 F4
Queen's Dr The
WD3. . . . . 167 F2
Queensgate HP19 . . 115 A8
Queen's Gate SL4. . . 210 D3
Queen's La **12** SL6. . . 202 F7
Queensmead SL3 . . . 211 B6
Queens Mead HP21 116 C7
Queensmead Ho
HP10. . . . . 174 C2
Queensmead Rd
HP10. . . . . 174 C2
Queensmere Rd
SL1 . . . . 205 F4
Queensmere (Sh Ctr)
SL1 . . . . 205 F4
Queens Park Arts Ctr
HP21. . . . . 115 F8
Queen's Pk HP21. . . 115 F8
Queen Sq **8** HP11. . 173 A7
Queens Rd
Berkhamsted HP4. . . 135 A5
1 Chesham HP5. . . 144 C1
Eton Wick SL4. . . . . 204 F1
High Wycombe
HP13. . . . . 173 C6
Princes Risborough
HP27. . . . . 139 C4
Slough SL1 . . . . 205 F6
West Drayton UB7. . . 208 F4
Queen's Rd
Datchet SL3. . . . . . . 211 B7
Marlow SL7. . . . . 183 D2
Uxbridge UB8 . . . . . 201 C2
Windsor SL4 . . . . . . 210 C5
Queen St
Aylesbury HP20. . . . . 116 A8
Henley-on-Thames
RG9. . . . . 191 E1
High Wycombe HP13. . 173 C7
Leighton Buzzard LU7. .80 F8
Maidenhead SL6. . . . 202 F7
Milton Keynes MK11 . . 32 E6
Piddington HP14. . . . 160 B1
Pitstone LU7. . . . . . . 105 C4
Tring HP23 . . . . 119 A3
Waddesdon HP18. . . . .98 F6
Queen's Terr **5**
SL4. . . . . 210 D4
Queensway
Bletchley MK2. . . . . . 58 C8
Hazelmere HP15. . . . 163 A4
Maidenhead SL6. . . . 195 E2
Milton Keynes MK2. . 58 D8
Queensway The
SL9. . . . . 188 D7
Queen Victoria Rd
HP11. . . . . 173 B6
Queen Victoria's Wlk
SL4. . . . . 210 D4
Quercetum Cl **3**
HP19. . . . . 101 C1
Quickberry Pl HP7 . 165 C8
Quickley La WD3. . . 167 C3
Quickley Rise WD3. 167 B3
Quickly Brow WD3. 167 B3
Quill Hall La
Amersham HP5. . . . . 154 F2
Amersham HP6. . . . . 154 F2
Quilter Mdw MK7. . . 48 D5
Quilters Way HP7 . . . 48 D5
Quimby Rise MK17. . 59 A7
Quinbrookes SL2. . . 206 C7
Quince Cl MK7. . . . . 48 B5
Quindell Cl HP18. . . 100 E4
Quinn Mdws MK4. . . 45 E3
Quintin Cl SL6. . . . . 203 A5
Quinton Cl MK13. . . 203 A6
Quinton Dr MK13. . . 34 B3
Quintus Cl MK11. . . 33 A3
Quoitings Dr SL7 . . 183 C2
Quoitings Gdns
SL7. . . . . 183 C2
Quoiting Sq SL7. . . 183 D2

R

Raans Rd HP6. . . . . . 154 F1
Rabans Cl
Aylesbury HP19. . . . . 100 E1
Olney MK46. . . . . .6 E5
Rabans La HP19. . . . 100 E1
Rabans Lane Ind Est
UB7. . . . . 100 F1
Rabbits La
Ley Hill HP5. . . . . . . 145 D1
Ley Hill HP5. . . . . . . 155 C8
Rabbsfarm Prim Sch
MK12. . . . . 33 B6
Rabbs Mill Ho UB8. . 201 D3
Rachels Way HP5 . . 154 D5
Rackstraw Gr MK7. . 48 D5
Radcliffe Sch The
MK12. . . . . 33 B6
Radcliffe St MK12. . . 33 D6
RADCLIVE 51 E8
Radclive Rd
Gawcott MK18. . . . . . .51 F7
Gawcott MK18. . . . . . .51 F7
Radcot Ave SL3 . . . 207 B3
Radcot Cl SL6. . . . . 195 E3
Radcote Lodge MK8. 33 E1
Radian Ct MK5. . . . . 46 C7
Radman Gr MK12. . . 33 B5
RADNAGE 159 C7
Radnage CE (VA) Prim
Sch HP14. . . . . 159 D6
Radnage Common Rd
HP14. . . . . 159 D5
Radnage La HP14 . . 148 C2
Radnor Cl RG9. . . . . 191 E2
Radnor End HP20 . . 101 E2
Radnor Way SL3 . . . 206 C2
Radstock Cres MK10. 36 A4
RADSTONE 26 A6
Radstone Rd NN13 . . 26 B4
Radworthy MK4. . . . 46 C3
Raeside Cl HP9 . . . . 176 C5
RAF High Wycombe
Hughenden HP14 . . . 161 C8
Walter's Ash HP27 . . 150 B1
Raft Way MK4. . . . . . 45 D2
Ragmans Cl SL7. . . . 183 C8
Ragmans La
Marlow Bottom HP10,
SL7. . . . . 172 D1
Marlow Bottom SL7. . 183 D1
Ragnall's La OX33 . . 108 A8
Ragstone Rd SL1. . . 205 E3
Ragstones HP10 . . . 174 A1
Railway Cotts
Steeple Claydon
MK18. . . . . 64 A1
Wigginton HP23. . . . 119 F5
Railway Pl **1** HP11 . 173 C6
Railway St **2** HP20. 115 E8
Railway Terr SL2. . . 205 F5
Rainborough Gdns
HP20. . . . . 101 E2
Rainbow Dr MK6. . . .46 F7
Rainbow Ind Est
UB7. . . . . 208 D6
Rainier Cl MK16. . . . .22 F3
Rainsborough
MK14. 35 A8
Rainsborough Chase
SL6. . . . . 202 B3
Rains Rd MK4. . . . . . 45 E3
Rake Way HP21 . . . . 115 D3
Raleigh Cl SL1 . . . . 205 A5
Ralphs Retreat
HP15. . . . . 162 F4
Ralston Ct **20** SL4 . . 210 D6
RAM ALLEY 12 B5
Ram Alley MK16. . . . 12 B6
Rambler Cl SL6. . . . 204 B7
Rambler La SL3 . . . . 206 E2
Rambouillet Dr MK8. 33 C1
Ramsay Cl MK13 . . . 34 B3
Ramsay View HP15 163 A3
Ramscote La
Bellingdon HP5. . . . . 143 F7
Chesham HP5. . . . . . 144 B5
Ramsey Cres MK17. . 58 C2
Ramsey Ct SL2. . . . . 197 D1
Ramsgill Ct MK13 . . 34 C5
Ramsons Ave MK14. . 34 E4
Ramsthorn Gr MK7. . 48 B6
Ramworth Way
HP21. . . . . 116 A6
Randall Ave MK19 . . 45 D8
Randall Cl SL3. . . . . 206 F1
Randall Ct SL4. . . . . 211 A1
Randall Dr MK4. . . . . 45 D2
Randallpl UB8 . . . . . 201 C5
Randall Way HP5. . . 154 D6
Randolph Cl MK13. . 34 A6
Randolph Rd SL3. . . 206 D6
Ranelagh Gdns MK16 22 C2
Rangers Cl MK8. . . . 33 F1
Rannal Dr OX39 . . . 147 C6
Rannoch Cl MK2. . . . 58 D5
Rannock Gdns LU7. . 80 D7
Ranston Cl UB9 . . . . 189 F5
Rashleigh Pl MK6 . . 46 E5
Ratcliff MK46. . . . . . . .6 E5
Ratcliffe Cl
Old Stratford MK19. . .32 B7
Uxbridge UB8. . . . . . 201 D2
Rathbone Cl MK4. . . 45 E7
Ravel Cl MK7. . . . . . 48 D6
Ravel La HP21. . . . . 115 E3
Raven Cl **3** HP19. . . 101 F3

Raven Cres HP18. . . 98 C6
Raven Dr SL6. . . . . . 203 A8
Raven Forge HP17. . 114 D5
Raven Rd HP14. . . . . 158 F4
Ravensbourne Pl
MK6. . . . . 35 B2
Ravensbourne Rd
HP21. . . . . 115 D4
Ravenscar Ct MK4. . 46 C2
Ravenscourt SL7. . . 184 A3
Ravenscroft Rd
RG9. . . . . 191 D2
Ravens Ct
Berkhamsted HP4. . . 135 E6
High Wycombe HP13. 161 E3
Long Marston HP23. . 104 B4
Ravens Field SL3. . . 206 D4
Ravensgill MK13. . . . 34 C5
Ravensglass Croft **6**
MK10. . . . . 36 B3
Ravenshoe Cl SL8. . 185 A3
Ravens La HP4. . . . . 135 D4
Ravensmead
Chalfont St Peter
SL9. . . . . 177 F5
Chinnor OX39 . . . . . 147 C6
RAVENSTONE 5 D2
Ravenstone La NN7 . . 5 A8
Ravenstone Mill Rd
MK46. . . . . 12 E7
Ravens Wharf HP4. . 135 D4
Ravensworth Rd
SL2. . . . . 198 A2
Ravigill Pl MK12. . . . 33 D4
Ravi Way MK17. . . . . 48 E8
Rawcliffe Ho SL6. . . 203 A6
Rawlings Ct ML17 . . .60 F7
Rawlings La HP9 . . . 176 D7
Rawlins Rd MK13. . . 34 A4
Ray Dr SL6. . . . . 203 B7
Rayfield SL6. . . . . . . 203 B8
Ray Ho **5** SL6. . . . . 185 A4
Raylands Mead SL9 188 C6
Ray Lea Cl SL6. . . . . 203 B8
Ray Lea Rd SL6. . . . 203 B8
Rayleigh Cl MK5 . . . . 46 B6
Raylens HP12 . . . . . 172 B5
Ray Lodge SL6. . . . . 203 B7
Ray Lodge Mews
SL6. . . . . 203 B7
Ray Mdw SL6 . . . . . 196 A1
Ray Mead Cl SL6 . . 196 C1
Ray Mead Rd SL6. . . 203 C8
Ray Mill Road E SL6 196 B1
Ray Mill Road W
SL6. . . . . 203 A8
Raymond Cl SL3 . . . 212 E6
Raymond Munday Rd
HP22. . . . . 116 A2
Raymond Rd
Maidenhead SL6. . . . 202 D7
Slough SL3 . . . . 207 A3
Rayners Ave HP10. . 174 B3
Rayners Cl
Colnbrook SL3. . . . . 212 C7
Loudwater HP10. . . . 174 C3
Rayners La MK5 . . . . 46 A5
Ray Park Ave SL6. . . 203 B8
Ray Park La SL6. . . . 203 B8
Ray Park Rd SL6 . . . 203 B8
Rays Ave SL4 . . . . . 209 F7
Rays Cl MK2. . . . . . . 58 E6
Ray's Hill HP5. . . . . 133 C2
Rays La HP10 . . . . . 163 C1
Ray St SL6. . . . . 203 B7
Razzaq Pl HP12 . . . 172 E7
Reach Free Sch The
WD3 . . . . 178 F8
Read Dr HP22. . . . . 102 C4
Reade Ct SL2 . . . . . 198 C6
Read Ho HP19 . . . . 101 A3
Reading Rd
Aylesbury HP19. . . . . 100 F3
Henley-on-Thames
RG9. . . . . 191 E1
Readings The WD3. 167 F6
Read Loke MK2 . . . . .58 F7
Reads La LU7 . . . . . . 78 D1
Recreation Rd SL8. 185 B3
Rectory Ave HP13 . . 173 C7
Rectory Cl
Farnham Royal SL2. . 198 C2
High Wycombe HP13. 173 C7
Marsh Gibbon OX27 . .71 F3
Slapton LU7. . . . . 91 D6
Windsor SL4 . . . . . . 210 A6
Rectory Ct
2 Amersham HP7 . . 165 B7
3 High Wycombe
HP13. . . . . 173 F5
Lewknor OX49. . . . . 157 B8
Princes Risborough
HP27. . . . . 139 B3
West Drayton UB7. . . 208 E4
Rectory Dr HP18. . . . 99 A6
Rectory Fields
MK15. . . . . 35 D3
Rectory Gdns HP8. . 177 B7
Rectory Hill
Amersham HP7. . . . . 165 B8
Hambleden RG9 . . . . 181 C4
Rectory La
Amersham HP7. . . . . 165 B7
Berkhamsted HP4. . . 135 C4
Bix RG9. . . . . 179 D1
Bradenham HP14 . . . 160 F6

Rectory La continued
Great Hampden
HP16. . . . . 150 E6
Yardley Hastings NN7 . .1 A7
Rectory Mdw OX39 147 D6
Rectory Orch MK46. . .7 F8
Rectory Rd SL6 . . . . 196 E1
Rectory Terr SL2. . . 198 C3
Red Admiral St
HP19. . . . . 101 C4
Redbourne Ct MK11. .32 F5
Redbridge MK4. . . . . 34 D7
Redcliffe Wlk HP19. 101 B2
Redcote Manor MK7. 48 A4
Red Cottage HP23. . 119 C1
Red Cottage Mews **6**
SL3 . . . . 206 C3
Red Ct SL1. . . . . 205 E5
Redcurrant Ave
HP18. . . . . 100 D5
Redding Ct HP17. . . 129 E2
Redding Dr HP6. . . . 154 A2
Redding Gr MK8. . . . 45 E6
Reddings Cl HP22 . . 131 B6
Reddington Dr SL3. 206 E2
Rede Cl HP19 . . . . . 101 B4
Redfern Cl UB8 . . . . 201 C4
Redfield Ct LU6 . . . . 93 E8
Redford Rd SL4 . . . . 209 D6
Redford Way UB8. . . 201 D5
Red Friars Square Sh Ctr
21 HP20. . . . . 115 D8
Redgrave Dr **2** MK4. 45 E2
Redgrave Pl SL7 . . . 183 F3
Redhill UB9. . . . . . . 189 D2
Redhouse Cl HP11. . 172 E3
Red House Cl
Beaconsfield HP9 . . . 175 B4
Newton Longville
MK17 . . . . 57 D4
Redhuish Cl MK4. . . 46 D3
Red Kite Cl HP13 . . . 161 D1
Red Kite View MK18. 73 B5
Red Kite Wy HP13 . . 172 F8
Red La
Chinnor OX39 . . . . . 147 F3
Chinnor OX39 . . . . . 148 A3
Redland Cl MK18. . . 63 D2
Redland Dr MK5. . . . 46 C7
Redland End HP27. . 150 A8
Redlands Bank MK43 25 B2
Redland Way HP21. . 116 A5
Red Leaf Cl SL3 . . . 206 F5
Red Leys UB10 . . . . 201 E5
Redling Dr
Bovingdon HP3 . . . . 145 F1
Bovingdon HP3. . . . 146 A1
Red Lion Cl MK43 . . 25 B1
Red Lion Cotts SL2 . 199 B1
Red Lion Dr HP14 . . 158 D5
Red Lion St HP5. . . . 154 B7
Red Lion Way HP10. 185 E6
Red Lodge Gdns
HP4. . . . . 135 A3
Redman Rd HP12. . . 172 B3
REDMOOR 47 A4
Redmoor Ind Est
MK6 . . . . 47 A4
Red Oak La NN13. . . 38 F4
Redpitch Pk HP10 . . 185 F6
Red Poll Wy MK19. . 45 C8
Redriff Cl SL6. . . . . . 202 D6
Red Roofs SL6. . . . . 203 C7
Redruth Gate MK10. 36 D3
Redshaw Cl HP14. . . 41 E1
Redshots Cl SL7. . . . 183 E4
Redvers Gate MK15. 35 B7
Redway
MK14. . . . . .34 F7
Redway Sch The
MK6. . . . . 47 C6
Red Wing HP20. . . . 101 E3
Redwood SL1. . . . . . 197 B3
Redwood Cl
Hazelmere HP15. . . . 163 B3
Wing LU7 . . . . 79 E2
Redwood Dr
Aylesbury HP21. . . . . 115 E7
Wing LU7 . . . . 79 E2
Redwood Gate MK5. 46 C4
Redwood Gdns SL1 205 D6
Redwood Glade LU7. .70 F3
Redwood Pl HP9 . . . 175 D1
Redwoods The SL4 210 D4
Reed Cl SL0. . . . . . . 207 E7
Reedham Rd SL1. . . 197 C2
Reed Way
Slough SL1 . . . . 204 F6
Windsor SL4 . . . . . . 209 D6
Reeves Cl HP22. . . . 117 D6
Reeves Croft MK12. . 33 C4
Reform Rd SL6. . . . . 203 B7
Reform Road Ind Est
SL6. . . . . 203 B7
Regal Ct
Maidenhead SL6. . . . 203 B2
14 Tring HP23 . . . . . 119 A3
Regency Ct HP21. . . 116 B7
Regency Mews **2**
MK17 . . . . 49 A5
Regent Ct
3 Maidenhead SL6. 202 F7
Slough SL1. . . . . 205 E7
Windsor SL4. . . . . . . 210 A5
Regent Pk HP22. . . . 138 F3
Regent Rd HP21. . . . 116 B7
Regents Hall MK11. . 32 E5

Regents Pl SL6. . . . . 202 D6
Regent St MK2. . . . . . 58 C8
Regius Ct SL0. . . . . . 174 D8
Regory Rd SL2. . . . . 187 D2
Reid Ave SL6. . . . . . 202 E5
Reliance La MK9 . . . . 35 B3
Rembrandt End
HP19. . . . . 100 F2
REMENHAM 192 C3
Remenham Church La
RG9. . . . . 192 A4
REMENHAM HILL . . . 192 C2
Remenham La
Remenham RG9 . . . . 192 B5
Remenham Hill RG9 191 F3
Remenham Row
RG9. . . . . 191 F2
Remenham Terr
RG9. . . . . 192 C2
Remus Cl MK11 . . . . .32 F3
Remus Gate NN13. . 38 A6
Rendlesham MK15. . 35 C3
Rendlesham Way
WD3 . . . . 167 C3
Renfrew Way MK3. . .46 F3
Rennie Cl HP13 . . . . 161 F1
Renny Pk Rd MK16 . . 22 F3
Repton Cl SL6. . . . . 202 C3
Repton Dr
Hanslope MK19. . . . . .10 F2
Hanslope MK19. . . . . 11 A2
Hanslope MK19. . . . . 11 A2
Repton Pl HP7 . . . . 166 A8
Restharrow Way
HP22. . . . . 102 D3
Retreat La HP14. . . . 148 D2
Retreat The
Little Chalfont HP6 . . 166 E8
Milton Keynes MK11. . 32 C5
Princes Risborough
HP27. . . . . 139 B4
Revel Rd HP10 . . . . 185 D8
Revesby Cl SL6. . . . 202 D3
Reyners Gn HP16. . . 152 B4
Reynold Dr HP20. . . 102 A2
Reynolds Cl
Cranfield MK43. . . . . 24 E2
High Wycombe HP13. 173 E8
Reynolds Mead
HP23. . . . . 104 F8
Reynolds Pl MK8. . . 45 D6
Reynolds Rd HP9. . . 175 D3
Reynolds Wlk HP5. . 144 A4
Reynolds Yard HP5. 154 B7
Rhodes Pl MK6. . . . . 46 E7
Rhondda Cl MK1 . . . 47 E1
Rhoscolyn Dr MK3 . 57 C8
Rhuddlan Cl MK5. . . .45 F7
Rhymer Cl MK19 . . . .10 F4
Ribble Cl MK16. . . . . 22 C4
Ribble Cres MK3. . . . 57 D8
Ribstone Rd SL6. . . 202 B3
Richard Gdns HP13. 173 E8
Richardson Cl **3**
HP19. . . . . 101 B1
Richardson Pl **2**
MK6. . . . . 34 E1
Richards Way SL1. . 204 F5
Richborough MK13. 34 A6
RICHINGS PARK . . . 207 E3
Richings Pl SL0. . . . 207 E3
Richings Way SL0. . 207 F3
Richmond Cl
1 Amersham HP6 . . 154 F1
Milton Keynes MK3. . 46 D7
Richmond Cres SL1 206 A5
Richmond Ct
Dunstable LU6. . . . . . 92 E6
High Wycombe HP13. 173 C7
Richmond Pl SL9. . . 188 C2
Richmond Rd SL6. . 202 F7
Richmond Way MK16 22 D3
Rickard Cl
Aylesbury HP21. . . . . 115 D3
West Drayton UB7. . . 208 D1
Ricketts Cl **3** HP17. 127 A6
Rickford's Hill HP20 115 D8
Rickley La MK3. . . . . 58 A8
Rickley Park Prim Sch
MK3. . . . . .57 F8
Rickman's La SL2 . . 198 E6
RICKMANSWORTH . . 167 F1
Rickmansworth La
SL9. . . . . 177 F5
Rickmansworth Rd
Amersham HP6. . . . . 154 C2
Chorleywood WD3. . 167 F6
Rickman Wlk HP19. 115 A7
Rickyard Cl
1 Milton Keynes
MK13 . . . . 34 A4
Whitchurch HP22. . . . 87 A7
Rickyard Gr HP18. . . 83 B5
Rickyard The
Clifton Reynes MK46. . . .7 C2
Ride The LU6 . . . . . . 93 B6
Ridgebank SL1. . . . . 204 F6
Ridgebarn Farm La
HP17. . . . . 113 C4
Ridge Cl
Aylesbury HP21. . . . . 115 D3
Lane End HP14 . . . . 171 C4
Ridge Ct SL4. . . . . . 210 C4

Ridgemount End
SL9. . . . . 177 E5
Ridge Side HP14 . . . 160 A8
Ridge View HP23. . . 119 C5
Ridgeway
Berkhamsted HP4. . . 134 F4
4 High Wycombe
HP11. . . . . 173 A6
Milton Keynes, Stony
Stratford MK11. . . . . .32 F4
Milton Keynes, Wolverton
Mill MK12 . . . . 33 A5
Wing LU7 . . . . 79 E3
Ridge Way
High Wycombe
HP13. . . . . 162 C1
Long Crendon HP18. 125 F4
Ridgeway Cl
Chesham HP5 . . . . . 144 B3
Marlow SL7. . . . . 183 E4
Ridgeway Cotts
MK17 . . . . 67 B3
Ridgeway Ct **3**
HP20. . . . . 101 E1
Ridgeway Gdns
HP23. . . . . 119 B6
Ridgeway Meads
HP27 . . . . 138 B2
Ridgeway Rd HP5. . 144 B3
Ridgeway The
Amersham HP7. . . . . 165 E7
Gerrards Cross SL9. 188 D8
Iver SL0 . . . . 207 F6
Marlow SL7. . . . . 183 E4
Ridgeway Trad Est The
SL0. . . . . 207 E6
Ridge Wlk HP27. . . . 138 D6
Ridgewood RG9. . . . 181 C1
Ridgmont MK19. . . . 31 E5
Ridgmont MK19 . . . . 31 E5
Ridgway MK17. . . . . 49 B6
Riding Court Rd
SL3. . . . . 211 D7
Riding Ct SL3 . . . . . 211 C8
Riding La HP9, HP10 174 F3
Ridings Cotts HP15 163 D6
Ridings The
Amersham HP6. . . . . 154 D4
Iver SL0 . . . . 207 F2
Latimer HP5. . . . . . . 155 D3
Maidenhead SL6. . . . 202 A7
Ridings Way LU7. . . 78 B1
Riding The MK19 . . . 31 E5
Rifle Range La
HP17. . . . . 139 E7
Rigby Lodge SL1 . . 205 E7
Rigeway View LU7 . 105 D4
Rignall Rd
Great Missenden
HP16. . . . . 151 E8
Hampden Bottom
HP16. . . . . 141 B1
Little Hampden HP16 140 F2
Riley Cl
Aylesbury HP20. . . . . 115 C8
Brackley NN13 . . . . . 26 A1
Riley Rd SL7 . . . . . . 183 D2
Rillington Gdns MK4 46 B3
Rimmington Way
HP19. . . . . 101 B1
Rimsdale Ct MK2. . . 58 D3
Ringlet Way HP19 . . 101 C4
Ring Rd HP10. . . . . . 173 F2
Ring Road E MK7. . . .47 F7
Ring Road N MK7. . . .47 F7
Ring Road W MK7. . .47 F7
RINGSHALL 107 B1
Ringshall Dr HP4. . . 121 C8
Ringshall Rd
Dagnall HP4. . . . . . . 107 B3
Little Gaddesden
HP4. . . . . 121 A8
Ringshall HP4 . . . . . 107 A1
Ringstead Way
HP21. . . . . 116 A5
Ripley Cl
High Wycombe
HP13. . . . . 173 A8
Milton Keynes MK4 . . 45 E1
Slough SL3 . . . . 206 E2
Ripley Rd **12** MK10. . 36 C3
Ripon Ho HP21. . . . . 115 F6
Ripon St **7** HP20. . . 101 D1
Risborough Rd
Aston Sandford
HP17. . . . . 127 E3
Great Kimble HP17,
HP27. . . . . 139 E8
Kingsey HP17 . . . . . 127 D2
Maidenhead SL6. . . . 202 E8
Owlswick HP27. . . . . 128 A1
Stoke Mandeville
HP17. . . . . 130 B7
Risborough Springs
Swim & Fitness Ctr
HP27. . . . . 139 A4
Rise Hag Hill SL6. . . 204 A7
Riseley Rd SL6. . . . . 202 D2
Rise The
Amersham HP7. . . . . 165 C8
Gawcott MK18. . . . . . .51 F4
Hazelmere HP15. . . . 163 A5
Loudwater HP13. . . . 174 B4
Uxbridge UB10 . . . . 201 F3
Risings The HP13 . . 162 B1

Ritson La HP18. . . . . . 100 E4
Riverbank Point
UB8. . . . . 201 C6
Riverbank The SL4 . 210 B7
River Cl MK16. . . . . . 22 D4
Rivercrest Rd MK19 . 32 B6
River Ct SL6. . . . . . . 203 C7
River Gdns SL6. . . . . 203 D4
Rivermead Ct SL7. . 194 E8
Riverpark Dr SL7. . . 183 F1
River Park Ind Est
HP4. . . . . 135 A5
River Rd SL6. . . . . . 203 D4
River & Rowing Mus★
RG9. . . . . 191 F1
Riversdale SL8. . . . . 185 B1
Riversdale Cotts
SL8. . . . . 185 B1
Riversdale Ct SL8 . . 185 A1
Rivers Edge
Loudwater HP11. . . 174 A3
Wooburn Green
HP10. . . . . 185 F5
Riverside
Cookham SL8 . . . . . 184 E3
Marlow SL7. . . . . . 183 D1
River Side MK16 . . . . 22 D4
Riverside Cotts
West Drayton UB7. . 208 C1
Wooburn Green
HP10. . . . . 185 E8
Riverside Cvn Pk
UB7. . . . . 208 C3
Riverside Gdns HP4 135 A5
Riverside Mews
MK18. . . . . 52 D8
Riverside Pk SL3. . . 212 E5
Riverside Pl TW19. . 213 E1
Riverside Rd TW19. . 213 E1
Riverside Way UB8. 201 B4
Riverside West
HP10. . . . . 185 D8
Riverside Wlk SL4. . 210 D7
River St SL4. . . . . . . 210 D7
Riverswood Gdns
HP11. . . . . 174 B3
River View
Flackwell Heath
HP10. . . . . 185 B7
Old Stratford MK19. . 32 B6
Riverway SL4 . . . . . . 210 C7
River Wlk UB9 . . . . . 201 C7
Riverwood Ave SL7. 184 A1
Riverwoods Dr SL7. 184 A1
Rivets Cl HP21. . . . . 115 E6
Rivetts Cl MK46. . . . . .6 E4
Rivington Gdns
HP4. . . . . 134 D7
Rixband Cl MK7. . . . . 48 B4
Rixman Cl SL6. . . . . 202 D5
Rixon Cl SL3. . . . . . . 206 E2
Rixons Mdw HP19. . 115 B7
Roade Hill NN7 . . . . . . .9 F8
Roald Dahl Mus & Story
Ctr HP16 . . . . 152 A7
Robert Rd SL2 . . . . . 187 D2
Roberts Cl
Deanshanger MK19 . . 31 E4
Stanwell TW19 . . . . 213 E1
West Drayton UB7. . 208 E5
Robert's Dr HP19. . . 101 D2
Roberts La SL9. . . . . 178 B5
Robertson Cl MK5. . .45 F7
Robertson Pl HP11 . 173 B4
Robertson Rd 6
HP4. . . . . 135 D4
Roberts Rd
Haddenham HP17. . 127 B6
High Wycombe HP13. 173 B8
Roberts Ride HP15 . 163 A5
Roberts Way HP21 . 115 B6
Roberts Wood Dr
SL9 . . . . 177 F5
Robertswood Sch
SL9 . . . . 177 F3
Robeson Pl MK8 . . . . 45 E8
Robin Cl
Aylesbury HP19. . . . 101 F3
Buckingham MK18. . .52 F7
Great Kingshill HP15 151 D1
Robin Hill
Berkhamsted HP4. . 135 C3
Maidenhead SL6. . . 202 E4
Robin Ho HP11. . . . . 174 A4
Robin Hood Cl SL1. 204 F5
Robin Par 2 SL2. . . 198 C7
Robins Cl
High Wycombe
HP12. . . . . 172 D5
Uxbridge UB8 . . . . 208 C8
Robins Dr HP12. . . . 172 B3
Robins Hill MK6. . . . . 47 A6
Robinson Cl
Aylesbury HP19. . . . 100 F3
Princes Risborough
HP27. . . . . 139 B4
Robinson Cres MK17 37 A1
Robinson Ct SL6. . . 202 E4
Robinson Rd 8 . . . . 174 B4
Robinson Row 5
MK10. . . . . 35 E2
Robinson St 2 MK3. 58 B8
Robins Orch SL9. . . 159 E5
Robins Platt OX39. . 147 B6

Robins St HP22 . . . . 102 C2
Robinswood Cl
Beaconsfield HP9 . . 175 C5
Leighton Buzzard LU7 . .70 F2
Robin Willis Way
SL4 . . . . 211 A1
Robinwood Gr UB8. 201 F1
Roblin Cl HP21. . . . . 115 E4
Robson Cl SL9 . . . . . 177 E5
Robson Ct 4 HP16 . 152 A8
Roche Gdns MK3. . . . 58 A8
Rochester Ct MK5. . . 46 A5
Rochester Mews LU7 80 E6
Rochester Pl HP19 . 115 B8
Rochfords MK6. . . . . .46 F6
Rochfords Gdns
SL2. . . . . 206 C5
Rochford Way SL6 . 204 A7
Rockall Ct SL3 . . . . . 207 B3
Rock Cl LU7 . . . . 80 D6
Rockingham Cl
Pitstone LU7 . . . . . 105 D3
Uxbridge UB8 . . . . 201 C4
Rockingham Dr
MK14. . . . . 34 E6
Rockingham Par
UB8. . . . . 201 C5
Rockingham Pl HP9 175 F1
Rockingham Rd
UB8. . . . . 201 C4
Rockingham Wharf
UB8. . . . . 201 B4
Rock La LU7 . . . . 80 D7
Rockleigh Ct 3 LU7. 80 E7
Rockspray Gr MK7 . . 48 B5
ROCKWELL END 181 F5
Rockwell End Hill
RG9. . . . . 181 D4
Rockwell End La
RG9. . . . . 181 F5
Rocky La
Kingsash HP16 . . . . 141 F8
Wendover HP22,
HP16. . . . . 141 E8
Rodney Way SL3 . . . 212 E6
Rodwell Gdns MK7 . 48 D4
Rodwell Yd 3
HP23. . . . . 119 A3
Roebuck Ave HP13 . 173 F6
Roebuck Gn SL1 . . . 204 E5
Roebuck Mews LU6 . 92 E6
Roeburn Way MK5 . . 46 C6
Roeburn Cres MK4 . . 46 C1
Roes The MK43 . . . . . 25 B3
Rogers Croft MK6 . . . 47 D7
Rogers La
7 Buckingham
MK18. . . . . 41 E3
Stoke Poges SL2 . . . 198 F4
Rogers Wy MK18. . . . 65 E4
Roker Park Ave
UB10. . . . . 201 E8
Rokesby Rd SL2. . . . 197 F2
Rolfe Cl
Beaconsfield HP9 . . 175 E1
Winslow MK18 . . . . .65 F4
Rolls La HP16 . . . . . . 150 F5
Rolvenden Gr MK7 . . 48 F3
Roman Fields Acad
HP3. . . . . 146 F8
Roman Lea SL6 . . . . 195 F7
Roman Pl SL6. . . . . . 202 C6
Roman Rdbts MK1 . . 47 C2
Romans Field Sch
MK3 . . . . 46 E1
Roman Way
Aylesbury HP19. . . . 115 B8
Bourne End SL8. . . . 185 B4
Brackley NN13 . . . . . 38 A7
Thame HP23 . . . . . . 125 D1
Romar Ct MK1 . . . . . . 47 C2
Romarin Ct MK17 . . . 48 E8
Rome Ave HP21 . . . . 115 F3
Romney Ct 11 SL7. . 183 F3
Romney La
Quainton HP22. . . . .84 F3
Quainton HP22. . . . . 85 A3
Romney Lock Rd
SL4 . . . . 210 D7
Romney Rd HP21. . . 115 E4
Romney Wy
1 Abbey Hill MK19. . 33 D1
Two Mile Ash MK8. . . 33 D1
Romsey Cl SL3. . . . . 206 F3
Romsey Dr SL2. . . . . 187 D1
Romsey Way HP11 . 173 B4
Romulus Way
Brackley NN13 . . . . . 38 A6
Fairfields MK11. . . . . 33 A2
Ronald Allen Dr
HP22. . . . . 116 A2
Ronald Rd HP9. . . . . 175 F2
Ronaldsay 1 MK18. . 41 E3
Ronaldsay Gr 3
MK19 . . . . 33 D1
Ronaldsay Spur SL1 205 E8
Ronan Way UB9. . . . 189 F2
Ronnie Mdws MK17 . 48 E8
Rookery Ct SL7 . . . . 183 D2
Rookery Gdns 11
SL3 . . . . 183 D2
Rookery Mdw HP15 163 C7
Rookery Piece
HP17. . . . . 127 B6
Rookery Wlk MK18. . .63 F3
Rook Rd HP10. . . . . . 185 D4
ROOKSLEY 34 B2
Rooksley Rdbt MK13. 34 B3

Rooks Terr UB7 . . . . 208 E4
RookTree Farm Ind Est
MK17. . . . . .37 F3
Rook Tree Farm Rd
MK17. . . . . .37 F1
Rook Wood Way
HP16. . . . . 152 B5
Ropa Ct 6 LU7 . . . . . 80 F7
Roperies The HP11. 173 E6
Ropley Way 3 MK10 36 B3
Rosamonds Cotts
HP18. . . . . 83 B2
Rosary The HP15. . . 163 C7
Roseary Cl UB7 . . . . 208 D2
Rose Ave
Aylesbury HP19. . . . 101 C4
Hazelmere HP15. . . 163 B2
Rosebank Cl SL6. . . 195 E7
Rosebank Cotts
HP10. . . . . 174 B3
Rosebarn La HP23. . 104 D1
Rosebay Ave SL2. . . 206 B8
Rosebay Cl MK7. . . . 48 B5
Rosebery Ave
High Wycombe
HP13. . . . . 173 C5
Leighton Buzzard LU7 . 80 E7
Rosebery Ct 4 LU7. . .80 F7
Rosebery Mews LU7 . 90 D4
Rosebery Mws 8
HP11. . . . . 173 C5
Rosebery Rd HP22 . 117 C5
Rosebery Way HP23 119 B5
Rose Cnr HP14. . . . . 158 E5
Rosecomb Pl MK5. . . 46 A4
Rose Cotts SL6. . . . . 202 C3
Rose Ct
Amersham HP6. . . . 154 E2
Chesham HP5 . . . . . 154 D6
Eaton Bray LU6. . . . . 92 D6
3 Olney MK46 . . . . . .6 F3
Wolverton MK12. . . . 33 E6
Rosedale MK10 . . . . . 35 F1
Rosedene Mws UB8 201 C2
Rose Dr HP5. . . . . . . 154 D7
Rosehall Green
WD3 . . . . 156 E5
Rosehill HP4. . . . . . . 135 B4
Rose Hill SL1 . . . . . . 197 A5
Rosehill Cres MK18. . 62 D1
Rosehill Ct SL1. . . . . 206 A3
Rose Ind Est SL7 . . . 183 D5
Rose La RG9 . . . . 193 A1
Roseleigh Cl SL6. . . 202 A7
Rosemary Cl
Buckingham MK18 . . .52 F6
High Wycombe HP12. 161 B1
Rosemary Ct
High Wycombe
HP12. . . . . 161 B1
3 Walton MK7 . . . . 48 A5
Rosemary La HP17 . 127 A7
Rose Mdw HP17. . . . 127 B5
Rosemead HP22 . . . 117 E1
Rosemoor Ct MK4 . . 45 E2
Rosemoor Mews
HP19. . . . . 114 F8
Rosemullion Ave
Milton Keynes MK4 . . 57 B8
Shenley Brook End
MK4. . . . . 57 B8
Rosery The 5 SL8. . 185 A3
Roses Cl LU7. . . . . . . 78 B1
Roses La SL4 . . . . . . 209 D5
Rosetree Cl HP16 . . 151 C6
Rosevear Pl MK3. . . . 58 B4
Rose Wlk SL2 . . . . . . 205 B8
Rosewood Gdns
HP12. . . . . 172 C4
Rosewood Way SL2 198 C7
Rosken Gr SL2. . . . . 198 B3
Roslyn Ct MK15. . . . . 35 D7
Rossal Pl MK12 . . . . . 33 D4
Rossendale MK14 . . . 34 D7
Rossetti Pl HP15 . . . 163 C7
Rossini Pl MK7. . . . . 48 D5
Rossiter Cl SL3. . . . . 206 E2
Ross Rd
Aston Abbotts HP22 . . 88 D5
Maidenhead SL6. . . 202 E4
Rossway HP4 . . . . . . 134 B3
Ross Way SL3. . . . . . .46 F2
Rossway La HP4 . . . 134 A7
Rostrevor Gdns SL0 200 D3
Rothersthorpe MK14 35 A8
Rothesay Cl HP20. . 101 E1
Rothesay Ct HP4. . . 135 A4
Rothley Rd MK10. . . . 36 C2
Rothschild Ave
HP22. . . . . 117 C5
Rothschild Pl 19
HP23. . . . . 119 A3
Rothschild Rd
Leighton Buzzard LU7 . 80 F8
Wing LU7 . . . . 79 E2
ROTTEN ROW 181 F2
Rotten Row MK17 . . 59 C2
Roughwood La HP8 166 E3
Roundhead Dr OX9 125 F1
Roundheads End
HP9. . . . . 175 D4
Round Hill HP17 . . . 114 D5
Roundhill Ct HP17. . 126 E8
Roundhill View
HP17. . . . . 127 A7
Roundhouse Cl
HP22. . . . . 117 F4

Roundhouse La
RG9. . . . . 180 D5
Roundlands HP27 . . 149 E5
Roundwood Prim Sch
(Inf) MK18. . . . . 51 B6
Roundwood Prim Sch
(Jun) MK18. . . . . . . .51 F4
Roundwood Rd
HP12. . . . . 172 C7
Round Wood Rd
HP6. . . . . 154 F2
Rouse Ct SL9 . . . . . . 188 F6
Routs Gn HP14. . . . . 148 D2
Roseary Cl UB7 . . . . 208 D2
ROUT'S GREEN. . . . 148 D2
Roveley Ct MK11 . . . .32 F5
Rowan Ave HP13. . . 173 D8
Rowan Cl
Aylesbury HP21. . . . 115 E4
Beaconsfield HP9 . . 175 B1
Hazelmere HP15. . . 163 A3
Rowan Dr MK19 . . . . 20 D2
Rowan Gdns SL0 . . . 200 C3
Rowan Ho 1 SL8. . . 185 A4
Rowanhurst Dr SL2. 198 C7
Rowan Pl HP6 . . . . . 154 F1
Rowan Rd HP18. . . . 208 E2
Rowans The SL9 . . . 188 E8
Rowan Way SL2. . . . 205 B8
Rowan Wlk HP5. . . . 144 A1
Rowborough Rd
HP22. . . . . 131 D7
Rowden Farm La
LU7 . . . . 90 E6
Rowditch Furlong
MK14. . . . . 21 F3
Rowland Cl
Pitstone LU7 . . . . . 105 D3
Windsor SL4 . . . . . 209 D4
Rowland Ho HP9 . . . 175 F1
Rowlands Cl MK2 . . . 58 E8
Rowlandson Way
MK13. . . . . 34 A8
Rowland Way HP19. 115 B7
Rowle Cl MK14. . . . . . 34 E7
Rowley Furrows LU7 80 D8
Rowley La SL3 . . . . . 199 D4
Rowlheys Pl HP7. . . 208 E3
Rowliff Rd HP12. . . . 172 C6
ROWSHAM 102 D8
Rowsham Dell HP22 102 C5
Row The
Cholesbury HP5 . . . 133 D2
Cold Brayfield MK46 . .8 B6
Lane End HP14 . . . . 171 B4
Newton Blossomville
MK43 . . . . .8 B3
Winchmore Hill HP7 . 164 C3
Rowton Heath MK5 . 45 C5
Roxburgh Way MK3 . 46 F3
Roxhill Rd MK43. . . . . 25 F3
Roxwell Cl SL1. . . . . 204 E5
Roxwell Path 5
HP20. . . . . 101 F2
Royal Buckinghamshire
Hospl HP21. . . . . . 101 D1
Royal Cl UB7, UB8. . 208 E7
Royal Cotts SL6 . . . 195 C7
Royal Cotts HP7. . . 164 C2
Royal Ct HP23. . . . . 120 A5
Royal Free Ct 13
SL4 . . . . 210 D4
Royal Gram Sch The
HP13. . . . . 162 C1
Royal La UB8 . . . . . . 201 F1
Royal Latin Sch The
MK18. . . . . 52 D7
Royal Mansions
RG9. . . . . 191 E1
Royal Mead HP17 . . 130 C5
Royal Oak Mws
HP15. . . . . 162 D8
Royal Windsor
Racecourse SL4 . . 209 E7
Royal Windsor Way
Eton SL4 . . . . 205 B1
Eton SL4 . . . . 210 B7
Royce Cl LU6 . . . . . . .93 F7
Royce Rd MK43. . . . . 24 D3
Roylands
Stoke Mandeville
HP22. . . . . 116 A1
Stoke Mandeville
HP22. . . . . 130 A8
Royle Cl SL9 . . . . . . 177 E3
Royston Way SL1. . . 204 D8
Rubbra Cl MK7. . . . . 48 C5
Rubens Cl HP19 . . . 100 F2
Rubus Cl LU7 . . . . . . .79 F3
Ruby Cl SL1. . . . . . . 205 A4
Ruby Cres HP19. . . . 100 E6
Ruckles Way HP7. . . 165 C5
Ruddington Ave
1 Milton Keynes
MK10. . . . . 35 F4
6 Milton Keynes
MK10. . . . . 36 A4
Ruddlesway SL4 . . . 209 D6
Rudds Cl MK18. . . . . 66 A5
Rudd's La HP17 . . . . . 99 F5
Rudsworth Cl SL3. . 212 D7
Ruffle Cl UB7 . . . . . . 208 E4
Rugby Rise HP11. . . 173 A2
Rugwood Rd HP10 . 173 F2
Rumpenny OX9 . . . . 147 D8
Rumptons Paddock
HP18. . . . . .82 F6
Runford Ct MK5. . . . 46 C5

Run Furrow HP17 . . 127 A7
Runnymede MK14. . . .21 F2
Runrig Hill HP6 . . . . 154 F4
Rupert Ave HP12. . . 172 E4
Rupert Cl RG9 . . . . . 191 E3
Rupert House Sch
RG9. . . . . 191 E2
Rupert's La 191 E3
Rupert Way OX9 . . . 126 A1
Ruscombe Gdns
SL3 . . . . 211 A7
Ruscote MK4. . . . . . 135 A3
Rushall Rd OX9 . . . . 126 A1
Rushbeds Wood Wildlife
Reserve★ HP18. . . .96 D4
Rushbrooke Cl
HP13. . . . . 162 F2
Rushburn` HP10 . . . 185 F6
Rushendon Furlong
LU7 . . . . 105 E5
Rushes Mead UB8. . 201 C4
Rushes The
Maidenhead SL6. . . 203 C6
Marlow SL7. . . . . . 183 C1
Marlow SL7. . . . . . 194 C8
Rushfields 12 MK4 .45 F1
RUSH GREEN. 200 E8
Rushington Ave SL6 202 F5
Rushington Cl HP17 115 A2
Rushington Mdw
HP22. . . . . 116 E1
Rushland Field
OX39. . . . . 147 E8
Rushleys Cl MK5. . . . 46 A8
RUSHMERE 70 E4
Rushmere Ct MK17. . 48 D2
Rushmere La
Ashley Green HP5. . 145 B3
Lye Green HP5. . . . . 144 F3
Rushmere Ret Pk
MK1 . . . . 47 D2
Rushmoor Ave
HP15. . . . . 163 B3
Ruskin Ct MK16 . . . . 22 C2
Rusland Cir MK4 . . . . 46 C2
Russel Ct HP14. . . . . 161 C8
Russell Ave HP21. . . 115 C6
Russell Cl
Little Chalfont HP6 . 166 D8
Tylers Green HP10 . 163 B1
Russell Ct
Aylesbury HP21. . . . 115 E6
Chesham HP5 . . . . . 144 D2
Maidenhead SL6. . . 202 F7
Wendover HP22 . . . 131 B5
Russell Dr TW19 . . . 213 D1
Russell Ho 4 SL8 . . 185 A4
Russell Sch The
WD3 . . . . 167 B5
Russell St
Milton Keynes MK11 . 32 D5
Windsor SL4 . . . . . 210 D6
Woburn Sands MK17. 49 B4
Russell Street Sch
MK11. . . . . 32 D5
Russet Cl TW19 . . . . 212 F1
Russet Rd SL6 . . . . . 202 C3
Russet St HP19. . . . 100 D5
Russets The SL9 . . . 177 E2
Russett Hill SL9. . . . 188 E8
Russwell La MK17 . . 59 C6
Rustics Cl MK18. . . . 73 B5
Rustic St HP22 . . . . 102 E2
Rustlings Gate
HP14. . . . . 171 C5
Rutherford Cl
Uxbridge UB8 . . . . 201 F1
Windsor SL4 . . . . . 209 F6
Rutherford Gate
MK5 . . . . 46 C5
Rutherford Rd HP21 115 E4
Ruthven Cl MK2. . . . . 58 C4
Rutland Ave
High Wycombe
HP12. . . . . 172 D6
Slough SL1 . . . . . . 205 C8
Rutland Ct SL6 . . . . 203 C8
Rutland Ct 2 HP11. 173 A6
Rutland Gate SL6. . 202 C6
Rutland Ho 3 MK3. .46 F1
Rutland Pl SL6. . . . . 202 C6
Rutland Rd SL6. . . . 202 C6
Rutland St HP11. . . 173 A6
Ryans Mount SL7. . . 183 A2
Rycote Farm OX9 . . 136 C7
Rycote La SL6 . . . . . 203 C8
Rycote Lane Ind Est
OX9. . . . . 136 C4
Rycroft
Milton Keynes MK4 . . 46 E3
Windsor SL4 . . . . . 209 F4
Rydal Way
High Wycombe
HP12. . . . . 172 B5
Milton Keynes MK2 . . 58 D5
Ryder Cl HP3 . . . . . . 146 A4
Rydings SL4. . . . . . . 209 F4
Ryding The MK5 . . . . 46 A4
Rye Cl
Aylesbury HP21. . . . 115 D4
Maidenhead SL6. . . 202 A4
Ryecote Chapel★
OX9. . . . . 136 D6
Ryecroft Rd HP5 . . . 154 A7
Rye Ct 3 SL3 . . . . . . 206 E3
Ryefield Terr SL3 . . 212 D7
Ryeland MK11 . . . . . . 32 E6
Ryeland Ct UB7 . . . . 208 E7

Ryeland Croft MK14 . 21 C4
Ryeland Dr MK19. . . . 33 B1
Ryemead Way HP11 173 F4
Rye The LU6, LU7. . . . 92 B8
Rye View HP13. . . . . 173 C7
Rylstone Cl
Maidenhead SL6 . . . 202 C3
Milton Keynes MK13 . 34 B3
Ryman Ct WD3. . . . . 167 C3
Rymill Cl HP3. . . . . . 146 A3
Rynn Cl 1 HP13. . . . 162 A1
Ryton Pl MK4 . . . . . . 46 C3
Ryvers End SL3 . . . . 206 F3
Ryvers Prim Sch
SL3 . . . . 206 D3
Ryvers Rd SL3 . . . . . 206 D3

S

Sabina Cl
Fairfields MK11. . . . . 32 F3
High Wycombe HP12. 172 E6
Sacred Heart RC Prim
Sch RG9. . . . . 191 D1
Saddington MK6 . . . . 47 D6
Saddlers Pl MK14 . . . 35 A5
Sadleirs Gn MK17 . . . 49 B5
Sadlers Mews SL6. . 203 B7
Saffrey Mws HP17. . 126 E6
Saffron Cl SL3 . . . . . 211 B6
Saffron Ct HP13. . . . 173 C6
Saffron Rise LU6. . . . 92 E6
Saffron St MK2. . . . . 58 D7
Saham Croft Cl MK18 65 E4
Sailing Club Rd SL8 185 A3
St Abbs Ct MK4 . . . . .56 F8
St Adrian's Cl SL6 . . 202 B4
St Agnes Gate HP22 131 C5
St Agnes Way MK4 . . 57 A8
St Aidan's Cl MK3 . . . 57 E6
St Albans Cl 7 SL4 . 210 D6
St Alban's Rd MK18. .65 F4
St Alban's St SL4. . . 210 D6
St Andrew's Ave
SL4 . . . . 209 F5
St Andrew's CE Inf Sch
MK14 . . . . 34 E8
St Andrew's CE Prim Sch
Chinnor OX39 . . . . 147 C7
Uxbridge UB8 . . . . 201 D4
St Andrew's Cl
High Wycombe
HP13. . . . . 162 F1
Old Windsor SL4 . . . 211 A1
Wraysbury TW19. . . 211 E1
St Andrews Cotts 1
SL4 . . . . 210 A5
St Andrew's Cres
SL4 . . . . 209 F5
St Andrews Ct
Colnbrook SL3. . . . . 212 D7
2 Slough SL1. . . . . 205 E3
St Andrews Ho
OX39. . . . . 147 C6
St Andrew's Rd
Chinnor OX39 . . . . 147 C5
Milton Keynes MK3 . . 57 E7
Uxbridge UB10 . . . 201 E5
1 Uxbridge UB10. . 201 F4
St Andrews Way
SL1 . . . . 204 D6
St Andrews Way Ind Est
6 HP19 . . . . 101 C1
St Anne's Cl
Henley-on-Thames
RG9. . . . . 191 D1
Wendover HP22 . . . 131 B5
St Annes Mws 7
SL4 . . . . 210 A5
St Anne's Rd
Aylesbury HP19. . . . 115 B8
South Harefield UB9 190 C8
St Ann's HP10. . . . . 174 C2
St Ann's Ct HP10. . . 174 C2
St Anthony's Cath Prim
Sch SL2 . . . . 198 C2
St Anthony's Cl
HP19. . . . . 115 B8
St Anthony's Ct
HP9. . . . . 186 C8
St Anthony's Pl MK4. 57 B8
St Augustus Cl MK3 . 57 E7
St Bartholomews
MK10 . . . . 36 A1
St Bartholomew's CE
Sch HP23. . . . . 119 D3
St Bees MK10. . . . . . 36 B1
St Bernadette's RC Prim
Sch MK10. . . . . .47 F8
St Bernard's Cath Gram
Sch SL3 . . . . 206 C4
St Bernards Ct
HP13. . . . . 173 C6
St Bernard's Prep Sch
SL1 . . . . 206 B4
St Bernards Rd SL3. 206 C3
St Birinus Rd HP11 . 174 A2
St Brides Cl MK6 . . . 35 C2
St Catherine RC Prim
Sch UB7. . . . . 208 D4
St Catherine's Ave
MK3 . . . . 57 D6
St Catherines Ct 3
SL4 . . . . 210 A5
St Catherine's Ct
HP19. . . . . 115 B8
St Chad's Rd SL6. . . 202 B4

St Christopher Rd
UB8 . . . . 208 D8
St Christopher's Cl
HP16 . . . . 152 B3
St Christophers Ct
WD3 . . . . 167 D5
St Clement Cl UB8. . 208 D7
St Clement Danes Sch
WD3 . . . . 167 D7
St Clement's Dr MK3 57 D6
Saint-Cloud Way
SL6 . . . . 203 A7
St Columba's Cl SL6 202 B4
St Cuthburt La UB8 208 D7
St David Cl UB8 . . . . 208 D8
St Davids Cl SL0. . . 200 D4
St David's Cl
Iver Heath SL0 . . . . 200 D4
Maidenhead SL6 . . . 202 A4
St David's Ct NN13 . . 38 A8
St David's Par SL0. . 200 D4
St David's Rd MK3. . . 57 E6
St Denis Cl SL1. . . . 204 C7
St Dunstans MK6. . . . 47 A6
St Dunstans Cl
HP27. . . . . 139 C6
St Edmund Campion RC
Prim Sch SL6 . . . . 202 B5
St Edmunds HP4 . . . 135 C3
St Edmund's Cl
HP19. . . . . 115 B8
St Edwards Ct [1]
MK14 . . . . 34 F7
St Edward's RC Fst Sch
SL4 . . . . 210 A6
St Edward's RC Jun Sch
HP21. . . . . 116 A7
St Edward's Royal Free
Middle Sch SL4 . . 210 A6
St Elmo Cl SL2 . . . . 198 D1
St Elmo Cres SL2. . . 198 D1
St Ethelbert's RC Prim
Sch SL2 . . . . 206 A7
St Faith's Cl MK17. . . 57 D3
St Francis Cl
Berkhamsted HP4. . . 135 A5
Tring LU7. . . . . 118 E3
St Francis Rd
Beacon's Bottom
HP14. . . . . 159 D3
Denham Green UB9. . 189 F5
Highway SL6 . . . . . . 202 B7
St George's CE Inf Sch
[4] HP7 . . . . 165 E8
St George's Cl
High Wycombe
HP13. . . . . 173 D7
Windsor SL4 . . . . . . 209 E6
St Georges Cres
SL1 . . . . 204 D6
St Georges Ct [2]
HP12. . . . . 172 D8
St George's Dr
UB10. . . . . 190 F1
St Georges Ind Est
HP7. . . . . 165 F8
St Georges Lodge
SL6 . . . . 196 B7
St George's Rd MK3. . 57 E6
St George's Sch
SL4 . . . . 210 D7
St Georges Way 33 D7
St Giles Mews MK1. . 32 D6
St Giles St MK13 . . . . 33 F7
St Govans Cl MK4 . . . 57 B8
St Helena Ave MK3. . 58 C3
St Helen Cl UB8 . . . . 208 D8
St Helens Gr MK47 . . 47 F8
St Hilda's Ct HP19. . 115 B8
St Hilda's Way
HP10. . . . . 174 A2
St Huberts Cl SL9 . . 188 E2
St Huberts Cotts
SL9 . . . . 188 E4
St Huberts La SL9 . . 188 F2
St Hugh's HP14. . . . 158 F4
St Hugh's Ave HP13 173 F6
St Hughs Pl HP14. . . 158 F4
St Ives Cres MK4 . . . 57 B8
St Ives Rd SL6. . . . . 203 A7
St James Cl MK19 . . . 11 A2
St James Ctyd [8]
SL7 . . . . 183 E2
St James Pl SL1. . . . 204 C7
St James & St John CE
Prim Sch Infant Site
MK18 . . . . 41 E4
St James & St John CE
Prim Sch Junior Site
MK18 . . . . 41 B4
St James St MK13 . . . 33 F7
St James Way HP22 102 B3
St James Wlk SL0 . . 207 B8
St John's Ave HP10. 174 B8
St John's CE Comb Sch
HP27. . . . . 149 F4
St John's CE Comb Sch
HP27. . . . . 149 F4
St Johns Cl HP10 . . 163 B1
St John's Cl UB8 . . . 201 B4
St Johns Cres MK12 . 33 D5
St Johns Dr
Stone HP17. . . . . . . 114 B5
Windsor SL4 . . . . . . 210 A5
St Johns La MK18 . . . 75 F2
St John's La MK19. . . 31 B4
St John's Manor Ho
HP15. . . . . 162 E2

St Johns Rd
Slough SL2 . . . . 206 A6
Tylers Green HP10 . . 163 B1
Windsor SL4 . . . . . . 210 A5
St John's Rd
[4] Aylesbury HP20 . 101 E1
Hazlemere HP15. . . . 162 F2
Milton Keynes MK3. . 57 E6
Uxbridge UB8 . . . . . 201 B4
St Johns Sq SL4 . . . 210 C8
St John's St HP20 . . 101 E1
St John St MK16. . . . 22 D4
St John's Terr MK16. 22 D4
St John's Well Ct
HP4. . . . . 135 B5
St John's Well La
HP4. . . . . 135 B5
St Joseph's Cath Prim
Sch [1] HP23 . . . . 118 C8
St Josephs Cl MK46. . 6 F4
St Josephs Mews
HP9. . . . . 175 F2
St Joseph's RC High Sch
SL2 . . . . 206 A7
St Joseph's RC Inf Sch
HP21. . . . . 116 A7
St Joseph's RC Prim Sch
SL9 . . . . 188 C8
St Katherine's Way
HP4. . . . . 134 F7
St Laurence Cl UB8. 208 C8
St Laurence Rd MK18 65 F4
St Laurence Way
SL1 . . . . 206 A3
St Lawrence View
MK13 . . . . 34 A4
St Leger Ct MK14. . . 34 E8
St Leger Dr MK14 . . . 34 E7
ST LEONARDS. 132 E3
St Leonard's Ave [2]
SL4 . . . . 210 C5
St Leonard's Hill
SL4 . . . . 209 E4
St Leonards Rd
Amersham HP6. . . . . 154 E4
Hastoe HP23. . . . . . 132 C7
St Leonard's Rd
Oakley Green SL4 . . 209 D1
Windsor SL4 . . . . . . 210 C4
St Leonard's Way
LU6 . . . . 92 E1
St Leonards Wlk
SL0 . . . . 207 F3
St Louis RC Prim Sch [13]
HP20. . . . . 101 F2
St Lucia Cres MK17. . 58 B3
St Luke Cl UB8 . . . . 208 D7
St Luke's CE Prim Sch [2]
SL6 . . . . 202 F8
St Luke's Rd
Maidenhead SL6 . . . 202 F8
Old Windsor SL4 . . . 211 A1
Uxbridge UB8 . . . . . 201 E5
St Margaret Ct MK2 . 58 E8
St Margarets Cl
Iver Heath SL0 . . . . 200 D3
Newport Pagnell MK16 22 E4
St Margaret's Cl
Berkhamsted HP4. . . 135 D3
Iver Heath SL0 . . . . 200 D3
Tylers Green HP10 . . 174 C8
St Margaret's Ct
SL0 . . . . 200 D3
St Margaret's Gate
SL0 . . . . 200 D3
St Margarets Gr
HP15. . . . . 151 E1
St Margaret's Rd
SL6 . . . . 202 A7
St Margaret Way
SL1 . . . . 204 F4
St Margaret Wy [7]
SL1 . . . . 204 F4
St Marks Rd HP13. . 173 D7
St Mark's Cres SL6. 202 B7
St Mark's Hosp
SL6 . . . . 202 C7
St Mark's Pl SL4 . . . 210 C5
St Mark's Rd
Aylesbury HP21. . . . 115 C7
Henley-on-Thames
RG9. . . . . 191 E1
Maidenhead SL6 . . . 202 D7
Windsor SL4 . . . . . . 210 C5
St Martin Cl UB8 . . 208 D7
St Martin's Prim Sch
UB7. . . . . 208 D3
St Martin's Rd UB7. 208 D3
St Martin's Sch MK2 . 58 C8
St Mary & All Saints CE
Prim Sch HP9. . . . 175 E3
St Mary Magdalene RC
Prim Sch MK12 . . . 33 A5
St Mary & St Giles CE
Jun Sch MK11. . . . . 32 E6
St Mary's Ave
Berkhamsted HP4. . . 134 D6
Milton Keynes MK3. . 57 E7
Milton Keynes, Stony
Stratford MK11. . . . 32 E6
St Marys CE Prim Sch
MK17 . . . . 37 B1
St Mary's CE Prim Sch
Amersham HP7. . . . 165 A8
Berkhamsted HP4. . . 134 E6
Slough SL1 . . . . 206 A3

St Mary's CE Sch
HP19. . . . . 115 A8
St Marys Cl
East Claydon MK18 . . 74 F8
Farnham Royal SL2 . 198 C2
Lee Common HP16 . . 142 D5
Mursley MK17. . . . . . 67 D6
St Mary's Cl
Maidenhead SL6 . . . 203 A4
South Harefield UB9 190 B8
Wavendon MK17. . . . 48 E7
St Marys Ct MK4. . . . 51 B7
St Mary's Farnham Royal
CE Prim Sch SL2 . . 198 C2
St Mary's Glebe LU6. 92 E4
St Mary's RC Prim Sch
Maidenhead SL6 . . . 195 F2
Uxbridge UB8 . . . . . 201 C4
St Marys Rd MK18 . . 74 F7
St Mary's Rd
Denham Green UB9. . 189 F5
Slough SL3 . . . . 206 A4
South Harefield UB9 190 B8
St Mary's Row [7]
HP20. . . . . 115 D8
St Mary's Sch SL9 . . 188 E7
St Mary's Sq [3]
HP20. . . . . 115 D8
St Mary St
High Wycombe
HP11. . . . . 173 B6
Milton Keynes MK13. . 33 F7
St Mary's Wavendon CE
Prim Sch MK17 . . . 48 E7
St Mary's Way
Chalfont St Peter
SL9 . . . . 177 D1
Chesham HP5 . . . . . 154 B8
Leighton Buzzard LU7 . 80 D7
St Mary's Wlk [10]
SL6 . . . . 202 F7
St Matthew Cl UB8 . 208 D7
St Matthew's CE Prim
Sch UB7. . . . . 208 C5
St Matthews Ct
[3] Maidenhead SL6 . 202 B8
Milton Keynes MK3. . 57 E6
St Michael's Catholic
Sch HP11. . . . . . . 173 A4
St Michael's Cath Sch
HP19. . . . . 101 C1
St Michael's CE Comb
Sch LU7 . . . . 68 C1
St Michaels Cl
Edgcott HP18. . . . . . 72 F7
Halton HP22 . . . . . . 131 C8
Stewkley LU7. . . . . . 68 E1
St Michael's Cl
HP22. . . . . 117 C1
St Michaels Croft
HP5. . . . . 145 D5
St Michael's Ct
Ashton NN7. . . . . 9 F8
Slough SL3 . . . . 197 D1
St Michaels Dr
Milton Keynes MK7. . 47 F6
Walton MK7 . . . . 47 E7
St Michael's Gn
HP9. . . . . 175 E3
St Michaels Way
MK18 . . . . 63 E3
St Monica's RC Prim Sch
MK14 . . . . 34 F6
St Nicholas CE Comb
Sch SL6 . . . . 196 E1
St Nicholas Cl
Cublington LU7 . . . . 78 B1
Little Chalfont HP7 . . 166 B8
Uxbridge UB8 . . . . . 208 D7
St Patrick's Cl SL6 . 202 D7
St Patrick's Way MK3 57 E6
St Paul Cl UB8 . . . . 208 D8
St Pauls Ave SL2 . . 206 A5
St Paul's CE Comb Sch
HP10. . . . . 185 D4
St Pauls Ct MK11 . . . 32 D6
St Paul's Ct SL6 . . . 202 F6
St Pauls Gdns SL6. . 202 B8
St Pauls RC Sch MK6 . 46 F7
St Paul's Rd MK3 . . . 57 E6
St Pauls Yd MK16 . . . 22 D4
St Peter's Ave HP19 101 C3
St Peter's CE Mid Sch
SL4 . . . . 210 F1
St Peter's CE Prim Sch
SL1 . . . . 197 B2
St Peters Cl
Loudwater HP11. . . . 174 B1
Speen HP27. . . . . . . 150 C4
St Peter's Cl
Burnham SL1. . . . . . 197 B1
Old Windsor SL4 . . . 211 A4
St Peter's Ct SL9 . . . 177 E2
St Peters Gate NN13 38 A7
St Peters Hill HP23 . 119 A4
St Peter's RC Prim Sch
SL7 . . . . 183 D3
St Peters Rd NN13. . 38 A8
St Peter's Rd
Maidenhead SL6 . . . 195 D2
Uxbridge UB8 . . . . . 208 D8
St Peter St SL7. . . . 183 E1
St Peters Way
Chorleywood WD3. . . 167 B5
Milton Keynes MK13. 34 A8
St Pirans Sch SL6 . . 195 C1
St Rumbold's La [3]
MK18 . . . . 52 C8

St Stephens Dr MK15 35 B7
St Stephen's Rd
MK7. . . . . 208 D5
St Teresa's Cl HP27 139 B4
St Teresa's Sch
HP27. . . . . 139 B4
StThomas Aquinas
Catholic Prim Sch
MK3 . . . . 57 E7
St Thomas Ct MK4. . 45 F1
StThomas More RC
Prim Sch HP4. . . . 135 A4
St Thomas Wlk SL3 212 D7
Saint Vincent Ave
MK17 . . . . 58 B3
St Vincents MK17 . . . 49 C4
Sakura Wlk MK15 . . 35 C6
Salcey Forest Trail ★
MK16 . . . . 4 C2
SALCEY GREEN 11 B7
SALDEN. 67 F8
Salden Cl
Drayton Parslow
MK17. . . . . 68 C6
Milton Keynes MK5 . . 46 B6
Salden La MK17 . . . . 56 E2
SALFORD. 37 C3
Salford Rd
Aspley Guise MK17 . . 49 D7
Broughton MK17. . . . 36 F3
Hulcote MK17 . . . . . . 37 F1
Milton Keynes MK17 . 49 D4
Salisbury Ave SL2 . 205 C8
Salisbury Cl
Amersham HP7 . . . . 165 E8
Princes Risborough
HP27. . . . . 139 C3
Salisbury Ct SL6 . . 202 E5
Salisbury Gr MK14. . 21 F7
Salisbury Mews
SL2 . . . . 198 C1
Salisbury Rd
High Wycombe
HP13. . . . . 162 D1
Uxbridge UB8 . . . . . 201 B3
Sallowsprings LU6 . 93 F2
Salmons La HP16. . . 151 D6
Salop Ho MK3. . . . . . 46 F7
Salorn Way [10] MK8. 45 D8
Saltash Cl MK13 . . . 174 B4
Salt Box The MK46 . . 7 F7
Salters Cl SL6. . . . . 203 A7
Salter's Cl HP4. . . . 134 F6
Salters La HP18 . . . . 96 C8
Salters Mews MK14 . 34 F6
Salters Rd SL6. . . . 203 B7
Salters Row HP10 . . 186 A4
SALT HILL 205 D5
Salt Hill Ave SL1 . . 205 C5
Salt Hill Cl SL1. . . . 201 E7
Salt Hill Dr SL1. . . . 205 C5
Salt Hill Mans SL1. . 205 C5
Salt Hill Way SL1. . . 205 D5
Salton Link MK4 . . . 46 B2
Saltwood Ave
[3] Church Hill MK4. . 56 E8
Milton Keynes MK4. . 45 E1
Samian Wy HP22 . . . 117 D8
Samphire Ct
Walton MK7 . . . . 48 A6
Walton MK7 . . . . 48 A6
Sampsons Gn SL2 . . 197 F2
Sampsons Hill HP7. 164 E2
Samuel Cl MK16. . . . 22 E3
San Andres Dr MK3. 58 B4
Sanctuary Rd HP15 363 B5
Sandage Rd HP14 . . 171 B5
Sandal Ct MK5 . . . . . 46 A5
Sandbrier Cl MK7 . . . 48 B6
Sandbrook La HP23 104 C1
Sandels Way HP9 . . 175 D4
Sandles The SL4 . . . 205 B1
Sandleswood Cl
HP9. . . . . 175 D5
Sandleswood End
HP9. . . . . 175 D5
Sandmartin Cl MK18. 41 E1
Sandon Cl HP23. . . . 118 F4
Sandown Ct
[8] High Wycombe
HP12. . . . . 172 D8
Milton Keynes MK3. . 57 D6
Sandown Rd SL2. . . 204 F8
Sandpiper [1] HP19. 101 E4
Sandpipers Pl SL6. . 195 E6
Sandpit Hill MK18 . . 50 F6
Sandpit Hill Cotts
HP23. . . . . 133 B3
Sandpits La HP27 . . 138 B4
Sandpits La HP10 . . 174 D1
Sandringham Ct
[8] High Wycombe
HP13. . . . . 173 B7

Sandringham Pl
MK2 . . . . 58 C8
Sandringham Rd
Maidenhead SL6 . . . 195 E2
Stanwell TW6 . . . . . 213 E2
SANDS. 172 B7
Sands Bank Nature
Reserve ★ HP12. . . 172 A7
Sandsdown Cl
HP12. . . . . 172 C8
Sands Farm Dr SL1. 197 C1
Sands Ind Est HP12 172 C8
Sandstone Cl MK18. . 73 B5
Sandwell Ct MK8 . . . 33 C2
Sandy Cl
Buckingham MK18 . . 52 F8
Milton Keynes MK14 . 34 D8
Woburn Sands MK17. 49 B4
Sandycroft Rd HP6. 155 C1
Sandygate Cl SL7 . . 183 D3
Sandygate Rd SL7. . 183 D3
Sandy La
Aspley Heath MK17 . . 49 B2
Leighton Buzzard LU7 . 70 F3
Long Crendon HP18. 125 B6
Sandy Mead SL6 . . . 203 C1
Sandy Rd MK18 . . . . 73 B5
Sandy Rise SL9 . . . . 177 E2
Sandywell Dr MK15. . 35 A6
Santa Cruz Ave
MK17. . . . . 58 A3
Santa Maria La MK17 58 B2
Santen Gr MK2. . . . . 58 D4
Santesdune Way
HP27. . . . . 149 C1
Santoon St John Rd
HP18. . . . . 109 A6
Sargeant Cl UB8 . . 201 D2
Sark Dr MK2 . . . . . . 58 C4
Saro Mws HP20. . . . 116 D7
SARRATT 156 F4
Sarum Complex
UB8. . . . . 201 B3
Satis Ho SL3 . . . . . . 211 C7
Saturn Ave MK11. . . . 32 F3
Saunders Cl MK7. . . 48 D6
Saunders Ct [1]
HP13. . . . . 173 F6
Saunders End HP6 . 153 C5
Saunders Pl HP19 . . 115 A7
Saunders Rd UB8 . . 201 F4
Saunders Wood Copse
HP14. . . . . 158 F4
SAUNDERTON
Bledlow Ridge. 149 C1
Princes Risborough. 138 E1
SAUNDERTON LEE. . 149 A4
Saunderton Sta
HP14. . . . . 149 C1
Saunderton Vale
HP14. . . . . 149 C1
Savage Croft MK10 . 35 E3
Savay Cl UB9 . . . . . 190 A4
Savay La UB9 . . . . . 190 A5
Savernake Rd HP19 101 D3
Savill La
Milton Keynes MK4,
MK5 . . . . 45 F2
[2] Shenley Brook End
MK5 . . . . 46 A3
Savill Way SL7 . . . . 183 E2
Savoy Cres MK9. . . . 34 F3
Savoy Ct SL6 . . . . . 195 F1
Sawdy Dr MK27 . . . 117 B4
Sawley Ho [5] MK3. . 46 F1
Sawmill Cotts SL3 . 199 F2
Sawmill Rd HP27. . . 138 D7
Sawpit Hill HP15 . . . 163 B5
Sawyers Cl SL6 . . . 202 A2
Sawyer's Cl SL4 . . . 209 E7
Sawyers Cres SL6 . . 202 A2
Saxeway Dr HP5 . . . 143 E3
Saxaxeys Bsns Ctr
HP5. . . . . 143 E3
Saxhorn Rd HP14. . . 171 C4
Saxon Cl
Amersham HP6. . . . . 154 D1
Dunstable LU6. . . . . 93 E8
Milton Keynes MK19 . 11 B2
Slough SL3 . . . . 206 F4
Uxbridge UB8 . . . . . 208 E8
Saxon Ct
High Wycombe
HP12. . . . . 172 D8
Stanwell TW19 . . . . 213 A2
Saxon Gate MK9 . . . 34 E2
Saxon Gate East MK9 34 E2
Saxon Gdns SL6. . . . 196 D1
Saxonia Bvd MK16. . 36 B5
Saxon Lodge SL1. . . 204 F5
Saxon Park Ind Est
MK1 . . . . 47 D2
Saxon Sq HP23. . . . 125 D1
Saxon St
Great Linford MK13. . 34 D4
Milton Keynes MK2 . . 58 C8
Milton Keynes, Ashland
MK1, MK6 . . . . 47 C4
Milton Keynes, Heelands
MK6, MK13, MK14. . 34 C5
Stantonbury MK13. . 34 B4
Woughton on the Green
MK3 . . . . 47 A7
Saxon Way
Harmondsworth
UB7. . . . . 213 D8
Newport Pagnell MK16 22 B3
Slough SL1 . . . . 211 B1

St C–Sco 247

Saxon Way Trad Ctr
UB7. . . . . 213 C8
Sayers Ct MK4 . . . . . 56 F8
Sayers Gdns HP4 . . 135 A6
Saye & Sele Cl HP18 . 92 F4
Scafell Rd SL2 . . . . 204 F8
Scaldwell Pl [4]
HP21. . . . . 115 F4
Scarborough Gdns
MK4 . . . . 45 E1
Scarborough Way
SL1 . . . . 205 B4
Scardale MK13. . . . . 34 C5
Scarlett Ave
Wendover HP22 . . . 131 E6
Wendover HP22 . . . 131 E6
Scatterdells La
WD4 . . . . 146 F1
Scatterill Cl MK13. . . 34 A4
Scholars Rise HP14 158 E4
Scholars Way HP6. . 154 F1
Scholars Wlk
Chalfont St Peter
SL9 . . . . 177 E4
Chalfont St Peter SL9 188 E7
Slough SL3 . . . . 207 A4
School Cl
Asheridge HP5 . . . . 143 E5
Brackley NN13 . . . . . 39 A4
Cryers Hill HP15 . . . 162 C6
High Wycombe HP11. 173 A4
High Wycombe, Downley
HP13. . . . . 161 D2
Holmer Green HP15 . 163 C7
Ickford HP18. . . . . . 124 A3
School Dr MK17. . . . . 57 C3
School End
Chetwode MK18 . . . . 61 D8
Great Horwood MK7 . 55 A3
School Hill
Charndon OX27. . . . . 73 A6
North Marston MK18. 76 B2
School Ho TW19 . . . 213 E1
Schoolla HP16. . . . . 150 E7
School La
Amersham HP7. . . . . 165 A8
Buckingham MK18 . . 52 C8
Castlethorpe MK19. . 19 F5
Chalfont St Giles HP8 177 B7
Chalfont St Peter
SL9 . . . . 177 D1
Cookham SL6 . . . . . 196 B7
Cookham Dean SL6. . 195 B7
Dinton HP17. . . . . . 113 F2
Eaton Bray LU6 . . . . 92 F6
Harrold MK43 . . . . . . 3 F6
Henley-on-Thames
RG9. . . . . 191 D1
Leighton Buzzard LU7 . 68 C1
Little Marlow SL7 . . 184 C5
Maidenhead SL6 . . . 195 D1
Medmenham SL7. . . 193 B6
Milton Keynes MK5. . 46 B8
Oakley HP18 . . . . . . 109 C5
Penn Street HP7 . . . 164 B5
Preston Bissett MK18. 62 B8
Seer Green HP9 . . . 176 D4
Shabbington HP18. . 124 D3
Sherington MK16 . . . 14 A2
Slough SL2 . . . . 205 F6
Thornborough MK18. 54 A8
Tiddington OX9 . . . . 136 A6
Turville RG9. . . . . . . 169 F3
Twyford MK18. . . . . . 62 D2
Upper Winchendon
HP18. . . . . 99 A1
Waddesdon HP18. . . 99 A6
Weston Turville HP22 116 F1
Wexham Street SL2. 199 B5
Yardley Gobion NN12 . 18 E6
School Rd
Harmondsworth
UB7. . . . . 213 D8
Tylers Green HP10 . . 174 D8
Wooburn Green
HP10. . . . . 185 E6
School St MK13 . . . . 33 F7
School The HP23 . . . 118 C8
School Way HP11 . . 174 B2
Schorne La MK18 . . . 76 B2
Schumann Cl MK7. . 48 C4
Scotch Firs MK7 . . . . 48 C6
Scotchy La RG9 . . . . 170 B1
Scotlands Dr SL2. . . 198 B6
Scotney Gdns MK3 . . 57 E8
Scotsgrove Cotts
OX9. . . . . 126 A4
Scotsgrove Hill
Thame HP23 . . . . . . 125 F3
Thame OX9 . . . . 126 A3
Scotswood Cl HP9 . 175 D5
Scott Cl
Farnham Common
SL2 . . . . 198 C7
West Drayton UB7. . 208 F2
Scott Ct MK17. . . . . . 48 D8
Scott Dr MK16 . . . . . 22 A5
Scott End HP19 . . . . 100 F2
Scott Evans Ct MK18. 66 A5
Scotts Cl
Marsh Gibbon OX27 . 72 A3
Stoke Hammond MK17 69 E8
Scotts Cnr NN13 . . . . 39 A4
Scotts Farm Cl MK18 41 E4

Scotts La
Adstock MK18 . . . . .53 F1
Buckingham MK18 . . . . 41 E3
Marsh Gibbon OX27 . . 71 E2
Scribe Pl UB7. . . . . . 208 F2
Scriven Ct MK15 . . . . 35 E7
Scriveners La NN12 . 17 A8
Scrubb's La HP14 . . 160 B7
Seabright Way
HP18 . . . . 100 E4
Seabrooke Ct MK8 . . 45 D6
Seabrook Farm La
LU7 . . . . 105 B6
Seacourt Rd SL3. . . 207 B2
Seaford Rd TW6 . . . 213 D2
Seagrave Ct MK7. . . . 48 A4
Seagrave Rd HP9 . . 175 C4
Sears Dr LU7. . . . . 118 E3
Sears The LU6 . . . . . 92 B5
Seaton Dr HP21. . . . 115 D4
Seaton Gr MK10 . . . . 36 A4
Sebright Cl MK5 . . . . 46 A4
Secklow Gate MK9 . .34 F3
Second Ave MK1. . . . 47 C2
Second Cres SL1. . . 205 C8
Sedgemere MK8 . . . . 33 D2
Sedgemoor Dr OX9. 126 A1
Sedgmoor Cl HP10. 185 A7
Sedgmoor Gdns
HP10. . . . . 185 A8
Sedgmoor La HP10. 185 B7
Sedgmoor Rd HP10. 185 A8
Sedgwick St HP17. . 126 E7
Sedley Gr UB9 . . . . 190 C7
SEDRUP. 114 F3
Sedrup La HP17. . . . 114 F4
Seebeck Cl MK5. . . . 46 C7
Seechfield HP22. . . . 85 A3
Seeleys Cl HP9. . . . . 175 C4
Seeleys Cl HP9. . . . . 175 D3
Seeleys La HP9 . . . 175 D3
Seeleys Rd
Beaconsfield HP9 . . 175 C4
Beaconsfield HP9 . . 175 C5
SEER GREEN 176 D4
Seer Green CE Comb
Sch HP9. . . . . 176 C4
Seer Green & Jordans
Sta HP9. . . . . 176 C3
Seer Green La HP9. 176 E3
Seer Mead HP9 . . . . 176 D4
Sefton Cl SL2 . . . . . . 198 F4
Sefton Paddock
SL2 . . . . 199 A5
Sefton Park Cotts
SL2 . . . . 199 A4
Sefton Way UB8. . . 208 C7
Selbourne Ave MK3 .57 F7
Selbourne Ho [10]
SL8 . . . . 185 A4
Selby Gdns
Wavendon MK17. . . 37 A1
Wavendon MK17. . . 49 A8
Selby Gr MK5 . . . . . 46 B5
Selim Ct [4] SL1 . . 206 B4
Selkirk Dr
Stantonbury MK13. . 34 B8
Stantonbury MK14 . . 21 C1
Selkirk Gr MK3. . . . .46 F2
Selwood Cl TW19 . . 213 C1
Selwood Gdns
TW19 . . . . 213 C1
Selwood Way HP13. 161 E2
Selworthy MK4 . . . . 46 D3
Selwyn Cl SL4. . . . . 209 E5
Selwyn Ct HP21. . . . 116 B6
Selwyn Gr MK3. . . . . 58 B8
Selwyn Pl SL1. . . . . 204 F6
Seneca Cl [5] HP18 . 100 C5
September Ct
UB10. . . . . 201 D3
Seren Pl SL2. . . . . . 198 B5
Sergius Cl MK11. . . .32 F3
Serjeants Gn MK14 . .34 F6
Serles Ct MK6. . . . . 47 A6
Sermed Ct SL2. . . . 206 C5
Serpentine Ct MK2. . 58 D5
Serpentine The
HP19. . . . . 115 C8
Servite Ho SL6. . . . 203 B8
Seven Acre Ho
HP10. . . . . 174 C2
Seven Acres HP18. . 125 B7
Seven Gables MK18. 65 D6
Sevenhills Rd SL0. . 200 C6
Sevens Cl [6] HP4. . 135 D4
Severalls Ave HP5. . 144 C2
Severn Cres SL3. . . 207 B1
Severn Dr MK16. . . . 22 E4
Severn Ho HP13. . . . 173 F7
Severn Way MK3. . . 57 D8
Sewell Cl HP19. . . . 100 F2
Seymour Cl
Flackwell Heath
HP10. . . . . 173 F2
Maidenhead SL6. . . 202 B3
Seymour Court La
SL7 . . . . 183 B5
Seymour Court Rd
SL7 . . . . 183 C4
Seymour Ct
Berkhamsted HP4. . . 134 E6
Tring HP23 . . . . 119 A4

Seymour Ho
High Wycombe
HP12. . . . . 172 E4
Slough SL3 . . . . 206 E4
Seymour Park Rd
SL7 . . . . 183 D3
Seymour Pk Rd
OX39. . . . . 147 D6
Seymour Plain SL7. 183 C5
Seymour Rd
Berkhamsted HP4. . . 134 E6
Chalfont St Giles HP8 177 C6
Slough SL1 . . . . 205 D4
Seymour St HP22. . . 102 D3
SHABBINGTON. . . . 124 D3
Shabbington Rd
Ickford OX9. . . . . . . 124 A4
Long Crendon HP18. 125 A5
Shabbington HP18. . 124 E4
Worminghall HP18. . 123 E5
Shackerstone Cl
MK10. . . . . 36 B4
Shackleton Ct [6]
TW19. . . . . 213 E1
Shackleton Pl MK6. 34 E1
Shackleton Rd
High Wycombe
HP12. . . . . 172 E5
Slough SL1 . . . . 205 F6
Shaftesbury Cres
MK3. . . . . 47 A1
Shaftesbury Ct
Maidenhead SL6. . . 202 E5
[6] Slough SL1. . . . 205 E4
Winslow MK18 . . . . .65 F5
Shaftesbury Ho
HP21. . . . . 116 C7
Shaftesbury St
HP11. . . . . 172 F8
Shaggy Calf La SL2. 206 A6
Shakespeare Cl
MK16. . . . . 22 A5
Shakespeare Lodge
SL1. . . . . 204 F5
Shakespeare Orch
HP18. . . . . .82 F6
Shakespeare Way
HP20. . . . . 116 A8
Shallowford Gr MK4. 46 D4
SHALSTONE. 39 E6
Shamaa Ho [18] SL1. 205 E4
Shamrock Ct MK7. . 48 B6
Shannon Ct
Chesham HP5. . . . . 144 C1
Milton Keynes MK14. 35 A6
Shantock Hall La
HP3. . . . . 145 E1
Shantock La HP3. . . 145 E1
Shantung Ho HP5. . 154 C6
Shardeloes HP7. . . . 164 D8
Sharkham Ct MK4. . 46 B1
Sharman Row [8]
SL3. . . . . 206 F1
Sharman Wlk MK13. 34 A3
Sharney Ave SL3. . . 207 B3
Sharp Cl HP21. . . . . 115 E5
Sharps Cl HP18. . . . 99 B6
Sharrow Vale HP12. 172 E4
Shaw Cl
Aylesbury HP20. . . . 116 A8
Newport Pagnell MK16 22 A5
Shaw Ct
Aylesbury HP21. . . . 115 E3
Old Windsor SL4. . . 211 A2
Shawfield Cl SL4. . 208 E3
Shaw Gdns [11] SL3. 206 F1
Shaw Savill Wy
MK10. . . . . 36 C4
Shaws Cl HP16. . . . 151 D5
Shaw The SL6. . . . . 195 E6
Shearmans MK11. . . 33 A4
Sheehy Way SL2. . . 206 B6
Sheelin Gr MK2. . . . 58 D4
Sheepcoat Cl MK5. . 46 A5
Sheepcote Cl HP9. . 175 C4
Sheepcote Dell Rd
HP15. . . . . 163 E7
Sheepcote Gdns
UB9. . . . . 190 A5
Sheepcote La HP10,
SL1. . . . . 186 A2
Sheepcote Rd
Eton Wick SL4. . . . . 205 A1
Windsor SL4. . . . . . 209 E5
Sheepfold La HP7. . 165 D7
Sheephouse Rd SL6 196 B2
Sheep La MK17. . . . 60 D4
Sheeplane MK17. . . 60 C2
SHEEPRIDGE. 184 E7
Sheepridge La SL7,
SL8. . . . . 184 E7
Sheep St MK18. . . . 66 A4
Sheep Wy MK14. . . . .21 F3
Sheer Croft HP5. . . 143 F2
Sheering Gr MK13. . 34 B8
Sheerness Ct MK4. . 57 A8
Sheerstock HP17. . . 126 E5
Sheerwater HP19. . 101 E4
Sheet St SL4. . . . . . 210 D6
Sheet Street Rd
SL4. . . . . 210 C2
Sheffield Dr HP21. 115 E6
Sheffield Rd SL1. . 205 C7
Shelburne Ct HP12. 172 E4
Shelburne Rd HP12. 172 E4
Sheldon Ct MK8. . . .33 F1
Sheldon Rd HP18. . 124 A3
Sheldon Way HP4. . 135 A5

Shelduck Cl [3]
HP19. . . . . 101 E3
Shelley Cl
Langley SL3. . . . . . 207 A1
Medmenham SL7. . . 193 D7
Newport Pagnell MK16 22 B4
Slough SL3 . . . . 206 F1
Wooburn Green
HP10. . . . . 185 E8
Shelley Dr MK3. . . . .57 F7
Shelley Rd
Chesham HP5. . . . . 144 B2
High Wycombe HP11. 172 F5
[12] Marlow SL7 . . . 183 F3
Shellfield Cl TW19. 213 A2
Shelsley Ave MK6. . 47 C5
Shelsmore MK14. . . 35 A8
Shelton Ct
Slough SL3 . . . . 206 C3
Woburn Sands MK17. 49 B4
SHENLEY BROOK
END. 46 A2
Shenley Brook End Sch
Milton Keynes MK5. . 46 A2
Milton Keynes MK5. . 46 B4
SHENLEY CHURCH
END. 45 E6
Shenley L Ctr MK5. . 46 A7
SHENLEY LODGE. . . 46 C5
Shenley Rd
Milton Keynes, Bletchley
MK3. . . . . 46 E1
Milton Keynes, Loughton
MK5. . . . . 46 A7
Whaddon MK17. . . . 56 C8
Shenley Rdbt MK5. . 46 A6
SHENLEY WOOD. . . .45 F4
Shenston Ct [13] SL4. 210 C6
Shenstone Dr SL1. . 197 D1
Shenstone Hill HP4. 135 E5
Shenton MK16. . . . . 36 C3
Shepherd Rd HP20. 102 A2
Shepherds MK11. . . 33 A4
Shepherds Cft LU6. . 93 E8
Shepherds Cl
Beaconsfield HP9. . 175 F1
Hurley SL6. . . . . . . 193 F3
Uxbridge UB8. . . . . 201 C1
Shepherds Ct SL4. . 209 E5
Shepherds Fold
HP15. . . . . 163 D8
Shepherds Gate
HP16. . . . . 152 A2
Shepherds Hey MK14 21 C1
Shepherds La
Beaconsfield HP9. . 175 F1
Hazlemere HP15. . . 162 F5
Hurley SL6. . . . . . . 193 E4
Rickmansworth WD3. 167 E2
Shepherds Row
MK18. . . . . 66 A4
Shepherds Way
HP5. . . . . 154 D6
Shepherdswell Acad
MK6. . . . . 35 B2
Sheppard Gr MK17. . 37 B1
Sheppards Cl MK16. 22 C4
Sheppards Cl MK18. 76 A2
Shepperds Gn MK5. .45 F6
Shepperton Ct MK19 .19 F5
Shepton Rd [4] MK10. 36 B4
Sheraton Dr HP13. . 162 D1
Sheraton Ho WD3. . 167 C5
Sherborne Cl SL3. . 212 E6
Sherborne Ct SL6. . 202 E5
Sherbourne Dr
Dow Brickhill MK7. . 48 B4
Maidenhead SL6. . . 202 C2
Windsor SL4. . . . . . 209 F3
Sherbourne Wlk
SL2. . . . . 198 C8
Shereway HP19. . . . 115 B8
Shergold Way SL6. . 195 F6
Sheridan Cl HP21. . 115 D3
Sheridan Ct
High Wycombe
HP12. . . . . 172 C3
Maidenhead SL6. . . 203 B8
Slough SL1 . . . . 204 E6
Sheridan Gr MK4. . . 45 D2
Sheriff Cl HP19. . . . 115 B8
Sheringham Ct SL6. 202 E7
SHERINGTON. 14 A2
Sherington Ce Prim Sch
MK16. . . . . 14 A2
Sherington Rd
Emberton MK46. . . .13 F6
Lathbury MK16. . . . 22 E7
Sherman Rd SL1. . . 205 E8
Shernfold MK7. . . . . 48 B7
Sherriff Cotts HP18. 99 A7
Sherwood Ct SL3. . 206 E3
Sherwood Ct
Colnbrook SL3. . . . 212 D7
[10] Slough SL3. . . 206 F1
Sherwood Dr
Maidenhead SL6. . . 202 A6
Milton Keynes MK1, MK2,
MK3. . . . . 47 B1
Shetland [1] MK18. . 41 D3
Shetland Dr
Whitehouse MK19. . 33 B1
Whitehouse MK19. . 45 C8
Shetland Mdws
MK17. . . . . 58 A3
Shields Ct HP10. . . 163 B1
Shifford Cres SL6. . 195 E3
Shilling Cl MK15. . . 35 A7

Shillingridge Pk
SL7 . . . . 182 E5
Shinfield Cl MK18. . 63 D2
Ship Hill SL1. . . . . . 186 E4
Ship La
Marsworth HP23. . . 104 F2
Marsworth HP23. . . 105 A3
Pitstone LU7. . . . . 105 D3
Shiplake Ho SL8. . . 185 B4
Shipley Rd MK16. . . 22 B4
Shipman Ct MK15. . 35 B7
Ship Rd LU7. . . . . . 80 E6
Ship St HP11. . . . . . 173 A7
Shipton MK18. . . . . 66 B3
Shipton Hill MK13. . 34 B6
Shiptonlee HP22. . . .83 E7
SHIPTON LEE. 84 D7
Shipton Lee MK18. . 84 C6
Shipton Lee Rd
Edgcott HP18. . . . . 73 D1
Grendon Underwood
HP18. . . . . 83 D8
Shipton Rd UB10. . 201 E8
Shirburn Rd OX49. . 157 A7
Shire Ct MK14. . . . . 35 A5
Shire La
Chalfont St Peter HP8,
SL9. . . . . 178 B6
Chalfont St Peter SL9 178 B4
Cholesbury HP23. . 133 B4
Chorleywood WD3. . 167 C4
North Crawley MK16. 24 C4
Shires Bsns Pk The
NN13. . . . . 38 A6
Shires Rd NN13. . . . 38 A6
Shirley Ave SL4. . . 209 F6
Shirley Cl HP20. . . . 101 D2
Shirley Moor MK7. . 48 B8
Shirley Rd SL6. . . . 202 C5
Shirwell Cres MK4. . 46 D5
Shogmoor La RG9. . 170 C1
Shootacre Cnr
HP27. . . . . 149 A8
Shootacre La HP27. 149 A8
SHOOTERSWAY. . . . 134 E4
Shootersway HP4. . 134 E4
Shootersway La
HP4. . . . . 134 F4
Shootersway Pk
HP4. . . . . 134 F3
Shop La NN7. . . . . . .1 B6
Shoppenhanger's Rd
SL6. . . . . 202 E4
Shorediche Cl UB10 190 F1
Shoreham Rise SL2 197 D1
Shoreham Road (E)
TW6. . . . . 213 E2
Shoreham Road (W)
TW6. . . . . 213 E2
Shorham Rise MK8. . 33 E2
Shortborough Ave
HP27. . . . . 139 D5
Short Ditch HP17. . 127 A7
Shortfern SL2. . . . . 206 C7
Short Hale LU7. . . . 105 D3
Shorthorn Dr MK8. . 45 D7
Short La SL7. . . . . . 193 F8
Short Massey MK46. 26 E5
Short Rd TW6. . . . . 213 E1
Short St HP11. . . . . 172 F7
Shortway
Amersham HP6. . . . 154 D2
Chesham HP5. . . . . 144 B2
Shotfield Rd HP14. 171 C4
Shothanger Way
HP3. . . . . 146 B4
Shouler Cl MK5. . . . 46 A5
SHREDING GREEN. . 207 C7
Shrewsbury Cl MK10 36 A2
Shrimpton Cl
Beaconsfield HP9. . 175 D6
Long Crendon HP18. 125 B6
Shrimpton Rd
Beaconsfield HP9. . 175 D6
High Wycombe HP12. 172 B3
Shropshire Ct MK3. 46 E1
Shrubbery Cl HP13. 173 B8
Shrubbery Rd HP13 173 B8
Shrublands Ave
HP4. . . . . 135 A4
Shrublands Rd HP4 135 A5
Shucklow Hill MK17. 55 E3
Shugars Gn HP23. . 119 B5
Shupps La HP18. . . 112 B1
Shutlanger Rd NN12 .9 A8
Shuttleworth Gr
MK7. . . . . 48 D6
Siareys Cl OX39. . . 147 C6
Sibleys Rise HP16. . 152 D8
Siddington Dr HP18 100 E5
Side Rd UB9. . . . . . 189 D4
Siding Rd HP22. . . . 102 C2
Sidings Ind Est The
NN13. . . . . 38 A8
Sidings The
Loudwater HP11. . . 174 B3
Milton Keynes MK2. . 47 E1
Sidlow Ct MK11. . . . .32 F4
Sidney Cl
Lane End HP14. . . . 171 C5
Milton Keynes MK10. 35 E3
Sidney Rd SL4. . . . . 209 C4
Sidney Terr HP22. . 131 B5
Sierra Dr HP19. . . . 100 F4
Sierra Rd
High Wycombe
HP11. . . . . 173 E4

Sierra Rd continued
Wycombe Marsh
HP11. . . . . 173 E5
Silbury Arc MK9. . . . 34 E3
Silbury Boulevard
MK9. . . . . 34 C1
Silbury Bvd MK9 . . . 34 D2
Silbury Rdbt MK9. . 34 C1
Silchester Ho SL6. . 203 B8
Silco Dr SL6. . . . . . 202 E6
Silicon Ct MK5. . . . 46 C5
Silk Cl MK18. . . . . . .52 F5
Silk Mill Way HP23 . 119 A5
Silk St
Waddesdon HP18. . .98 F4
Waddesdon HP18. . 99 A3
Waddesdon HP18. . 99 A6
Silkwood Ct SL1. . . 205 F6
Sillswood MK46. . . . . 6 E4
Silsden Cres HP8. . 177 D7
Silverbeck Way
TW19. . . . . 213 A2
Silver Birch Cl
UB10. . . . . 201 E8
Silver Birch Dr
HP27. . . . . 149 E5
Silverbirches La
MK17. . . . . 49 C2
Silver Birch Way
HP22. . . . . 116 B4
Silver Cl SL6. . . . . . 202 A5
Silverdale Cl
[4] Aylesbury HP20. 101 C1
Tylers Green HP10. 163 A1
Silver End MK46. . . .7 A3
Silver Hill HP8. . . . 177 B8
Silverhill Ct SL1. . 205 C8
Silvermead HP18. . 123 D5
Silver St
Cublington LU7. . . . 78 B1
Milton Keynes MK11. 32 D5
Newport Pagnell
MK16. . . . . 22 D4
Silverstone Mews
Forty Green OX39. . 137 F3
Skittle Green HP27. 138 A2
*Silverstone Motor
Racing Circuit★*
MK18. . . . . 28 F8
Silverstone Rd
Dadford MK18. . . . 28 D3
Lillingstone Dayrell
MK18. . . . . 28 D8
Silvertrees Dr SL6. 202 A5
Silverweed Ct MK7. 48 B5
Simatt Ho HP10. . . 174 C2
Simdims MK43. . . . 25 A1
Simford Way [2]
MK19. . . . . 45 D8
Simmental Way
MK19. . . . . 33 B1
Simmons Cl SL3. . . 207 A2
Simmons Ct
Aylesbury HP21. . . 115 E4
High Wycombe HP12. 172 E7
Simmons Rd RG9. . 191 D3
Simmons Way
Lane End HP14. . . . 171 C4
Thame OX9. . . . . . . 125 F1
Simms Croft MK10. 36 A3
Simnel MK6. . . . . . . 47 B6
Simon Dean HP3. . . 146 A4
Simonsbath MK4. . . 46 D2
Simons Lea MK13. . 34 B4
Simons Paddock
MK17. . . . . 49 E7
Simon's Way MK18. 39 E7
Simpson Cl SL6. . . 203 B8
Simpson Dr MK6. . . 47 E5
Simpson Pl HP21. . 115 E5
Simpson Rd
Milton Keynes MK1, MK2,
MK6. . . . . 47 E3
Walton MK7. . . . . . .47 F5
Simpson Rdbt MK6. 47 D5
Simpsons Way SL1. 205 E5
Sinatra Dr MK4. . . . 45 E3
Sinclair Ct MK1. . . . 47 B3
Sinclair Rd SL4. . . 210 C4
Singers La RG9. . . . 191 E1
SINGLEBOROUGH. . .54 F5
Singleborough La
Great Horwood
MK17. . . . . 54 F7
Great Horwood MK17. 54 F4
Singleborough Rd
Nash MK17. . . . . . . .54 F7
Thornborough MK17. 43 E1
Singleton Dr MK8. . 45 D6
Singleton Way [8]
HP19. . . . . 115 A8
Singret Pl UB8. . . . 201 C1
Sion Hill
East Claydon MK18. .74 F8
East Claydon MK18. 75 A8
Sion Terr MK18. . . . 51 B6
Sipson Rd UB7. . . . 208 F3
Sipthorp Cl MK7. . . 48 C6
Sirett Cl LU7. . . . . . .79 F3
Sir Henry Floyd Gram
Sch HP21. . . . . 115 C7
Sir Henry Lee Cres
Aylesbury HP18. . . 100 D3
Aylesbury HP18. . . 100 E3
Sir Henry Peakes Dr
SL2. . . . . 198 A6
Sir Herbert Leon Acad
MK2. . . . . 58 C5
Sir Peter's Way HP4 107 E6

Sir Robert Mews
SL3 . . . . 207 A1
Sir Sydney Camm Ho
SL4 . . . . 210 B6
Sir Thomas Fremantle
Sch MK18. . . . . .65 F5
Sir William Borlase's
Gram Sch SL7. . . . 183 C1
Sir William Ramsay Sch
HP15. . . . . 163 A3
Sissinghurst Dr MK4 45 E2
Sitwell Cl MK16. . . . .21 F5
Six Cotts MK18. . . . 29 E5
Sixty Acres Rd
HP16. . . . . 151 C6
Skeats Wharf MK15. 35 A7
Skeldon Gate MK14. 35 A4
Skeldon Rdbt MK9. . 35 A4
Skeleton Rd [6]
MK18. . . . . 41 E3
Skelton Cl HP9. . . . 186 A8
Skelton Rd [7] MK18. 41 E3
Skene Cl MK2. . . . . 58 C4
Skerries Ct SL3. . . 207 A2
Skimmers Cl HP15. 163 C6
Skimmers End
HP15. . . . . 163 C6
Skimmers Field
HP15. . . . . 163 C6
Skinner Rd HP19. . 101 B4
Skinners Cl MK14. . 21 F3
Skip La UB9. . . . . . 190 E3
Skipper Cl
Aylesbury HP19. . . 101 C4
Chinnor OX39. . . . 147 C5
Skippon Way OX9. . 125 F2
Skipton Cl MK15. . . 35 C6
SKIRMETT. 170 A1
Skirmett Rd
Colstrope RG9. . . . 181 B5
Hambleden RG9. . . 181 C1
Mill End RG10. . . . 192 D8
Skirmett RG9. . . . . 170 A2
Skittle Gn
Forty Green OX39. . 137 F3
Skittle Green HP27. 138 A2
SKITTLE GREEN. . . 138 A3
Skydmore Path SL2 197 F1
Skye Cres MK17. . . 58 C3
Skye Lodge SL1. . . 205 E5
Skylark Cl HP17. . . 127 B6
Skylark Rd UB9. . . 189 C3
Skyline Mews HP12 172 C4
Skyport Dr UB7. . . 213 D2
Skyway 14 Trad Est
SL3. . . . . 212 D1
Slade Hill
Aylesbury HP19. . . 115 A7
Mixbury NN13. . . . 38 D1
Mixbury NN13. . . . 38 D1
Slade La MK11. . . . 33 A4
Slade Oak La
Denham UB9. . . . . 189 C6
Denham Green UB9. 189 C5
Slade Rd HP14. . . . 158 E4
Slade The MK17. . . 57 D3
Slad La HP27. . . . . 149 F3
SLAPTON. 91 C5
Slapton Bridge La
LU7. . . . . .91 F5
Slapton La LU6. . . . .91 F6
Slapton Rd
Slapton LU6. . . . . . 91 C8
Slapton LU7. . . . . . 91 E3
Slated Row MK12. . 33 B7
Slated Row Sch
MK12. . . . . 33 A4
Slatepits Croft
Olney MK46. . . . . . .6 E4
Olney MK46. . . . . . .6 F4
Slater St HP13. . . . 173 C6
Slattenham Cl HP19 115 B7
Slave Hill HP17. . . 126 F5
Slayter Rd HP14. . . 171 C4
Slicketts La LU6. . . 93 A3
Slickett's La LU6. . .92 F3
Slipe The LU7. . . . . 105 A7
SLOUGH. 205 D5
Slough & Eton CE Bsns
& Enterprise Coll
SL1. . . . . 205 D3
Slough Gram Sch
SL3. . . . . 206 B3
Slough Ice Arena
SL1. . . . . 205 D4
Slough Interchange
Ind Est SL2. . . . . . 206 A5
Slough La HP14. . . 160 C6
Slough Rd
Beaconsfield HP9. . 187 A8
Datchet SL3. . . . . . 211 B8
Eton SL4. . . . . 205 F1
Iver Heath SL0. . . 200 D3
Iver Heath SL0. . . 200 E3
Slough SL4. . . . . . 205 E3
Slough Sta SL1. . . . 205 F5
Slough Trad Est
SL1. . . . . 205 B7
Sly Corner HP16. . . 142 E4
Smabridge Wlk
MK15. . . . . 35 D7
SMAE Inst The SL6. 202 B6
Smallbrook MK43. . 25 B2
Smallbrook La HP27. 149 E2
Small Cres MK18. . .52 F7
Smalldean La HP27. 149 E2
Small Dean La
HP22. . . . . 141 B8
Smarden Bell MK7. . 48 B8

Smeaton Cl
Aylesbury HP19.....101 A1
Blakelands MK14.....22 A2
Smewin Ct HP11....172 E7
Smith Cl HP20.....116 B7
Smith Ctr The RG9..191 B5
Smithergill Ct MK13..34 C5
Smithfield End MK4..161 C8
Smithfield Rd SL6...202 A3
Smith's La
  Waterperry Common
  OX33.............122 F7
  Windsor SL4.......209 E6
Smithsons Pl MK9...35 B3
Smiths Rd HP14.....161 C8
Smithy The MK19....31 E4
Smoothing Iron
  Flaunden HP3.....156 A5
  Heath End HP5....134 A3
Smyth End HP22....117 D5
Snaith Cres MK5....46 B7
Snakeley Ct HP10..174 C1
Snakemoor Nature
  Reserve HP17...126 D6
Snape Spur SL1...205 E7
Snells La HP7......166 C7
Snells Wood Ct
  HP7..............166 C7
SNELSHALL EAST....57 B7
Snelshall St
  Milton Keynes MK4..56 F8
  5 Shenley Brook End
  MK4..............56 F8
SNELSHALL WEST....57 A7
Snowball Hill SL6..202 A1
Snowberry Cl MK12..33 D5
Snowden Cl SL4....209 D3
Snowdon Dr MK6....46 D7
Snowdrop Way
  HP15.............162 F7
Snowhill Cotts HP5.144 F7
Snowshill MK14....21 F2
Soames Cl MK46.....7 F7
Soane Wlk HP13...173 A8
Soay Way MK8.....33 C1
Soho Cres HP10...185 D4
Soho Mills Ind Est
  HP10.............185 D4
Sokeman Cl MK12...33 A5
Solar Ct MK14.....21 E1
Solesbridge Cl WD3.167 F6
Solesbridge La
  WD3.............167 F6
Solters Ct HP18...196 C8
Somerford Cl SL6..203 B8
Somerford Rd HP9..175 D3
Somerlea SL6.....196 C3
Somersby Cres SL6.202 E3
Somerset Cl MK3...46 F1
Somerset Lodge **3**
  SL6..............202 E3
Somerset Way SL0.207 F4
Somerset Wlk MK10.36 D3
Somers Lees **13**
  HP19............115 A8
Somerville Rd SL4.205 C1
Somerville Way
  HP19............115 D8
Sophie Gdns SL3..206 D4
Sorensen Ct MK5...45 E4
Sorrell Dr MK16....21 F4
Sorrel Way HP22...102 E2
Soskin Dr MK14....34 D6
Sospel Ct SL2.....198 C3
SOULBURY........69 E3
Soulbury Ct LU7...69 E2
Soulbury Rd
  Burcott LU7.......79 D4
  Leighton Buzzard LU7..80 D7
  Stewkley LU7......68 F1
  Wing LU7.........79 E5
Sounding Arch Wy
  SL6..............202 D5
Southampton Road E
  TW6.............213 F1
Southampton Road W
  TW6.............213 F1
South Bank
  Turweston NN13...38 C7
  Turweston NN13...38 C7
South Bank Rd HP4.134 F6
Southbourne **1**
  HP13............173 C7
Southbourne Dr
  SL8..............185 A3
Southbridge Gr MK7.48 A7
South Cl
  Medmenham SL7..193 D7
  Slough SL1.......204 D6
  West Drayton UB7.208 F3
Southcliffe Dr SL9.177 E5
South Common Rd
  UB8.............201 E6
Southcote Way
  HP10............163 B1
South Cottage Dr
  WD3.............167 F4
South Cottage Gdns
  WD3.............167 F4
Southcott Lower Sch
  LU7.............80 D8
Southcott Village
  LU7.............80 D6
Southcott Way MK6..47 D5
SOUTHCOURT......115 D6
Southcourt Ave LU7.80 D6
Southcourt Ho LU7..80 D7
Southcourt Rd LU7..80 D7

Southcroft SL2.....198 B1
Southdown Gr **2**
  MK19............33 D1
South Dr
  Beaconsfield HP9..186 B8
  High Wycombe HP13.173 D8
South Eighth St MK9.34 E2
SOUTHEND........180 C8
  Leckhampstead......42 E7
  Stewkley.........78 E8
South End HP17....126 F5
South End MK18....42 E6
Southend Common
  RG9.............180 C8
South End La LU6...92 B4
South Enmore Rdbt
  MK6.............35 B3
Southern Cotts
  TW19............213 A2
Southern Perimeter Rd
  TW6, TW19.......213 D2
Southern Rd
  Aylesbury HP19...101 C1
  Thame OX9.......125 E1
Southern Way MK12.33 D5
Southfield Cl MK15..35 E7
South Field Cl SL4..204 C3
Southfield Cotts
  HP17............130 C3
Southfield Dr HP15.163 A6
Southfield Gdns
  SL1.............204 B8
Southfield Rd
  Aylesbury HP20..116 B8
  Flackwell Heath
  HP10............174 A1
  High Wycombe HP13.161 D1
  Princes Risborough
  HP27............139 C3
South Fifth St MK9..34 E2
South Fourth St MK9.34 D5
Southgate Ho SL2..202 F8
Southlands Rd
  Denham UB9......189 F1
  Iver Heath SL0....200 E5
South Lawne MK3...57 F8
Southlea Rd SL3,
  SL4.............211 B5
South Loop Rd UB8.201 E1
South Maundin
  HP14............162 A7
South Meadow La
  SL4.............210 C8
South Ninth St MK9..34 F2
South Overgate Rdbt
  MK6.............35 B3
South Park Ave
  WD3.............167 F4
South Park Cres
  SL9.............188 F7
South Park Ct SL9..188 E6
South Park Dr SL9..188 E7
South Park Gdns
  HP4.............135 B5
South Park View
  SL9.............188 F7
South Path SL4....210 C5
South Pk SL9......188 F6
South Pl SL7.......183 E1
South Rd
  Amersham HP6...154 C3
  Chorleywood WD3.167 C4
  Maidenhead SL6..202 E6
  West Drayton UB7.208 F3
South Row
  Fulmer SL3.......199 E8
  Milton Keynes MK9..34 E1
  Milton Keynes MK9..46 D8
South Saxon Rdbt
  MK9.............34 F1
South Second St
  MK9.............34 D1
South Seventh St
  MK9.............34 E1
South Side Cl UB8.188 D8
Southside Cl UB8..201 E5
South Sixth St MK9..34 E1
South St
  Castlethorpe MK19..19 F5
  Wendover HP22...131 B4
South Tenth St MK9..34 F2
South Terr
  Milton Keynes MK2..58 C8
  Windsor SL4......210 E6
South Vale NN7.....1 A5
South View
  Cookham Rise SL6..195 F7
  Eton SL4.........205 B1
  High Wycombe HP13.161 D2
  High Wycombe HP13.173 D2
  Wooburn Green
  HP10............185 D8
Southview Rd SL7..183 E4
South View Rd SL9..188 D7
South Way HP9....186 A8

Southwick Ct MK8...45 F8
South Witan Rdbt
  MK6.............34 E1
Southwold Cl HP21.116 A6
Southwold Cres
  MK10............36 C3
Southwold Spur
  SL3.............207 C4
Southwood Gdns
  SL6.............195 E5
Southwood Rd SL6..195 E5
Southwood Sch
  MK14............34 E5
Sovereign Beeches
  SL2.............198 B6
Sovereign Cl
  Granborough MK18...75 F7
  5 Linslade LU7....80 F8
Sovereign Ct
  Aylesbury HP19...101 D1
  High Wycombe HP13.173 D6
Sovereign Dr MK15..35 A7
Sovereign Hts SL3..212 A8
Sovereign Lodge
  MK15............35 A7
Sovereigns Way MK6.47 D1
Spackmans Way
  SL1.............205 D3
Spa Cl HP18.......110 B8
Spade Oak Farm
  SL8.............184 E3
Spade Oak Mdw
  SL8.............184 E4
Spade Oak Reach
  SL6.............184 D2
Span Geen La HP18..95 E1
Span Green La
  HP18............109 D8
Spans The HP18....95 E1
Spark Way MK16....21 F5
Sparrow Cl HP19...101 F3
Sparrow Hall Bsns Pk
  LU6.............92 D3
Sparrow Hall Farm
  LU6.............92 D3
Sparrows Herne
  HP4.............134 E4
Sparsholt Cl **5** MK4.46 C2
Spartlet Mews
  HP18............100 E4
Spearing Rd HP12..172 C7
Spearmast Ind Est
  HP12............172 B6
Spearmint Cl MK7...48 B5
Specklands MK5....46 A8
Speedbird Way UB7.213 B7
Speedwell Pl MK4...34 E4
SPEEN..........150 C4
Speen CE Sch HP27.150 B4
Speen Rd
  Hughenden Valley
  HP14............162 A8
  Naphill HP14, HP16,
  HP27............150 D2
Speldhurst Ct MK7...48 B7
Spencer MK14.....34 C8
Spencer Cl UB8....201 C2
Spencer Gdns OX27.72 E5
Spencers Cl SL6...202 D8
Spencers Rd SL3...206 F3
Spencer St MK13....33 F7
Spencer Villas SL1.204 F5
SPENCERSGREEN...132 C7
Spencers La SL6...195 E6
Spenlows Rd MK3...47 A3
Spens SL6........202 F8
Spenser Ho HP21...115 F6
Spenser Rd HP21...115 F6
Sperling Rd SL6....195 F1
Spicers Yard **4**
  HP17............127 A6
Spicers Yd HP17...127 A6
Spickett's La HP18.113 A3
Spiers La OX27.....71 F2
Spiert The HP17....114 D5
Spindle Cl HP15....163 A3
Spindle Ct HP12...172 E7
Spindle Gn HP22...116 D6
Spindle Mews MK18.52 F6
Spinfield La SL7...183 B2
Spinfield Lane W
  SL7.............183 B1
Spinfield Mount
  SL7.............183 B1
Spinfield Pk SL7...183 C1
Spinfield Sch SL7..183 B2
Spinnaker Cft MK17.48 D7
Spinners Wlk
  Marlow SL7.......183 C1
  Stantonbury MK14..21 C1
  Windsor SL4......210 C6
Spinney SL1......205 B5
Spinney Bank LU7...79 E3
Spinney Bglws LU7..91 C6
Spinney Cl
  Steeple Claydon
  MK18............63 E2
  West Drayton UB7..208 E6
Spinney Cotts OX33.123 B1
Spinney Cres LU6...93 F8
Spinney Hill Rd MK46..6 B3
Spinney La MK17....49 F4
Spinneys The HP10.174 B1
Spinney The
  Aston Clinton HP22.117 D5
  Beaconsfield HP9..175 E1
  Berkhamsted HP4..134 F3

Spinney The *continued*
  Chesham HP5.....144 D2
  Gerrards Cross SL9..188 D3
  High Wycombe HP11.173 A4
  Holmer Green HP15.163 D7
  Milton Keynes MK13..34 A4
  Winslow MK18....66 A6
Spinney View MK19..31 F5
Spire Thames Valley
  Hosp SL3.......199 C4
Spire View TW19...213 D1
SPITAL..........210 B3
Spitfire Cl SL3....207 A2
Spittal St SL7.....183 D2
Spoondell LU6.....93 F7
Spoonley Wood
  MK13............33 E5
Sportsman Cl MK18..63 D3
Sportsmans Way
  HP27............138 E5
Spout La TW19.....213 A3
Spout Lane N TW19.213 B3
SPRIG'S ALLEY....147 F1
Sprigs Holly OX39..147 E1
Sprigs Holly La
  HP14............159 B8
Springate Field SL3.206 E4
Springbank Ct MK16.12 B7
Springbank Rd **5**
  HP14............171 C4
Spring Cl
  High Wycombe
  HP13............173 F7
  Latimer HP5......155 D3
  Maidenhead SL6..195 F2
  Milton Keynes MK17..55 A2
Spring Coppice
  HP27............171 F5
Spring Coppice La
  HP27............171 F5
Springdale Cotts
  SL8.............185 B2
Spring Dr HP27....138 C6
Springett Pl HP6...154 F2
SPRINGFIELD.....35 B2
Springfield SL1....206 A3
Springfield Bvd MK6.35 B2
Springfield Cl
  Aylesbury HP21...115 C8
  Chesham HP5.....154 C7
  Windsor SL4......210 B5
Springfield Ct
  1 Leighton Buzzard
  LU7.............80 E7
  1 Maidenhead SL6.203 B7
  Milton Keynes MK6..35 B2
Springfield Gdns
  Chinnor OX39....147 C7
  Deanshanger MK19..31 E4
Springfield Hollow
  HP14............158 E5
Springfield Pk SL6.203 C1
Springfield Rd
  Chesham HP5.....154 C7
  Chesham HP5.....154 C7
  Dunstable LU6....93 D5
  Leighton Buzzard LU7..80 E7
  Olney MK46........6 F4
  Slough SL3.......212 B7
  Stokenchurch HP14..158 F4
  Windsor SL4......210 B5
Spring Field Rd
  Berkhamsted HP4..134 F6
  Berkhamsted HP4..135 A6
Springfield Rdbt
  MK6.............35 A2
Springfields
  Amersham HP6...154 C2
  Padbury MK18....53 C1
  Tylers Green HP10..163 A8
Springfields Cl MK18.53 C2
Springfields Ct MK18.53 C1
Springfield Way
  MK43............25 C2
Spring Gardens Rd
  HP13............173 E5
Spring Gdn La HP4.134 D5
Spring Gdns
  Bourne End SL8...185 A4
  Marlow SL7.......183 E3
  Newport Pagnell MK16.22 C4
  Wooburn Green
  HP10............185 E8
Spring Gr HP17....49 B5
Springhall Hill
  HP23............132 F2
Spring Hill SL6....202 E3
Springhill Rd
  Edgcott HP18.....82 F8
  Edgcott HP18.....83 A8
Spring Ho SL7.....183 E3
Spring La
  Alderton NN12.....9 A2
  Clifton Reynes MK46..7 C3
  Cookham Dean SL6.195 C5
  Farnham Common
  SL2.............198 C5
  Flackwell Heath
  HP10............173 F3
  Great Horwood MK17.55 A2
  Olney MK46........6 F3
  Slough SL1.......204 F5
Spring Mdw HP18...97 A1
Spring Promenade **4**
  HP7.............208 F4
Spring Rose Way
  MK5.............46 F6
Springs Cl HP17...130 B2

Springside **2** LU7...80 E7
Springs La HP17...130 B3
Spring Valley Dr
  HP14............162 A7
Springwater Mill
  HP11............173 E4
Springwood HP27..150 C4
Sproggit Ind Est
  HP16............151 A7
Spruce Ct **5** SL1...205 F3
Spruce Dene HP15.162 F2
Spruce Rd **1** HP19..100 F1
SPURGROVE......170 E2
Spurgrove La RG9..170 E2
SPURLANDS END...163 A8
Spurlands End Rd
  HP15............163 A8
Spur The SL1......204 D8
Spurt St HP18......112 F3
Square Close Cotts
  RG9.............169 F3
Square The
  Akeley MK18......41 F8
  Aspley Guise MK17...49 E4
  Brill HP18........110 A8
  Great Missenden
  HP16............152 B7
  Harmondsworth UB7.213 B6
  Long Crendon HP18.125 C6
  Milton Keynes MK12..33 D6
  Preston Bissett MK18.62 B8
  Waddesdon HP18...99 A6
  Yardley Hastings NN7..1 A6
Squires Cl MK6....47 A6
Squirrel Cl MN13...26 A2
Squirrel La HP12...172 C5
Squirrel Rise SL2..183 D6
Squirrels Way MK18.52 E7
Sta App **19** HP13...173 B7
Stableford Rd
  HP22............117 F3
Stable Cotts SL7...194 C5
Stable La HP9.....176 C4
Stable Rd HP22....131 E7
Stables Cl SL7.....183 B1
Stables The MK19...20 F3
Stacey Ave MK12...33 D6
Stacey Ho HP12....172 E4
Stacey's Ct HP8...177 C8
Stacey Bushes Trad Ctr
  MK12............33 E4
Staddle Stones
  HP27............139 B4
Stadium App **7**
  HP21............115 E4
Stadium MK (MK Dons
  FC) MK1........47 C3
Stadium Way East
  MK1.............47 C3
Stadium Way West
  MK1.............47 B3
Stafferton Link SL6.203 A6
Stafferton Way
  17 Maidenhead SL6..202 A6
  Maidenhead SL6..203 A6
Stafford Ave SL2..198 C1
Stafford Cl SL6....204 B7
Stafford Gr MK5....46 B6
Stafford Keep HP19.115 A8
Stag Ct WD3......167 C5
Stag La
  Berkhamsted HP4..135 B5
  Chorleywood WD3..167 C3
  Great Kingshill HP15.151 D1
Stag Row OX9.....124 C2
Stagsden By Pass
  MK43............16 F1
STAGSDEN WEST
  END............16 D3
Stagshaw Gr **5** MK4.46 B7
Stainby Cl UB7....208 E3
Stainton Dr MK13...34 C4
Stairs La MK18.....63 E3
Stamford Ave MK6..35 B2
Stamford Rd SL6...202 C6
Stanbridge Ct HP27.122 A7
Stanbridge Ct MK11..32 F5
Stanbridge Rd
  Haddenham HP17..127 A8
  Haddenham HP17..127 B6
Stanbrook Pl MK10..36 A1
Standfield Cl HP19.115 A8
Standing Way
  Milton Keynes,
  Coldharbour Spinney MK3,
  MK4.............46 B3
  Milton Keynes, Kingston
  MK10............36 C1
  Milton Keynes, Peartree
  Bridge MK10, MK4,
  MK6.............47 C7
  Milton Keynes, Snelshall
  East MK4.........57 B7
Standring Pl HP20..101 F2
Stanhope Cl HP22..131 B7
Stanhope Heath
  TW19............213 C1
Stanhope Rd
  Aylesbury HP20..116 A8
  Slough SL1.......204 D7
Stanhope Way
  TW19............213 C1
Stanier Rise HP4...134 F7

Stanier Sq **5** MK2...58 C8
Stanley Ave HP5...154 B8
Stanley Cl
  Marlow SL7.......183 F3
  Uxbridge UB8....201 C3
Stanley Cotts SL2..205 F5
Stanley Ct MK46.....6 F3
Stanley Gdns HP23.118 F3
Stanley Green E
  SL3.............206 F2
Stanley Green W
  SL3.............206 F2
Stanley Hill HP7...165 E7
Stanley Hill Ave
  HP7.............165 E8
Stanley Ho SL4....211 A2
Stanley Kubrick Rd
  UB9.............190 A6
Stanley Rd HP12...172 C7
Stanley Spencer Gall *
  SL6.............196 F7
Stanmore Gdns
  MK16............22 B2
Stanmore La HP14.160 C3
Stanstead Pl HP7..165 E8
Stansted Rd TW19.213 F1
Stanton Ave MK13...34 A6
STANTONBURY
  MK14............34 C7
Stantonbury Campus
  MK14............34 C7
Stantonbury Campus L
  Ctr MK14.......34 C7
Stantonbury Cl MK13.34 A8
Stanton Gate MK14.34 D8
Stanton St John Rd
  HP18............108 E5
Stanton Sch MK13...34 B7
Stanton Way SL3...206 E2
Stanton Wood Rdbt
  MK14............34 D4
Stanway Cl MK15...35 B6
STANWELL.......213 C1
Stanwell Cl TW19..213 D1
Stanwell Fields CE Prim
  Sch TW19.......213 C1
Stanwell Gdns
  TW19............213 D1
STANWELL MOOR..212 E1
Stanwell Moor Rd
  Harmondsworth TW6,
  TW19, UB7.......213 B4
  Stanwell TW19...213 B1
Stanwell St SL3....212 C4
Stanwyck La **4**
  MK4.............45 D2
Stapeley Ct **1** MK4..45 F1
Stapleford Mill LU7..70 B5
Stapleford Mill Rd
  MK17............70 B5
Staple Hall Rd MK1..47 E1
Staple Oak MK4....46 C3
Stapleton Cl SL7...183 F4
Starling Cres SL1..206 C2
Starling Mews
  HP19............114 E8
Starlings The SL0..200 D1
Stars La HP17.....113 E2
Startins La SL6....195 C8
STARTOP'S END....104 F1
Starveall Cl UB7...208 F3
Starwood Ct **1** SL3.206 C3
Staters Pound MK15..35 A7
Statham Pl MK6.....46 F8
Station App
  Amersham HP6...154 C1
  Chorleywood WD3..167 D5
  Denham UB9......189 D4
  Gerrards Cross SL9..188 E6
  Great Missenden
  HP16............152 A7
  Langley SL3......207 A4
  Little Chalfont HP7..166 D8
  Maidenhead SL6..202 F6
  Marlow SL7.......183 E2
  Wendover HP22...131 B4
  West Drayton UB7..208 E5
Station Approach
  HP27............138 F2
Station Bvd HP20..115 D8
Station Cl HP13....173 B7
Station Cotts
  Denham UB9......190 A4
  Winslow MK18....66 A5
Station Hill SL6...195 F7
Station Par
  Beaconsfield HP9..175 D3
  Cookham Rise SL8..155 F6
  Denham Green UB9.190 A4
Station Rd
  Aldbury HP23....120 B5
  Amersham HP7...165 C8
  Beaconsfield HP9..175 E2
  Berkhamsted HP4..135 D4
  Blackthorn OX25...81 A4
  Bourne End SL8...185 A3
  Bow Brickhill MK17..48 C2
  Buckingham MK18..52 C7
  Castlethorpe MK19..19 F5
  Cheddington LU7...90 F1
  Cheddington LU7...91 A1
  Chesham HP5.....154 C8
  Chinnor OX39....147 C6
  Cookham Rise SL6..195 F7
  Gerrards Cross SL9..188 E6
  Haddenham HP17..126 E5

Station Rd continued
Henley-on-Thames
RG9. . . . . **191** E1
High Wycombe HP13. **173** C6
Ivinghoe LU7. . . . . . **105** E5
Leighton Buzzard LU7 **80** E7
Little Kimble HP17. . . **129** E2
Long Marston HP23. . **103** E6
Long Marston HP23. . **104** B4
Loudwater HP10. . . . **174** C2
Marlow SL7. . . . . . . **183** E1
Marsh Gibbon OX27 . . **71** F3
Mursley MK17. . . . . . **67** B7
Newport Pagnell MK16 **22** C4
Padbury MK18. . . . . . **53** B1
Poundon OX26 . . . . . **71** A5
Princes Risborough
HP27. . . . . **139** A2
Quainton HP22 . . . . . **85** A4
Quainton HP22 . . . . . **85** A4
Slough SL1 . . . . **204** E7
Slough, Langley SL3 . **207** A4
Stoke Mandeville
HP22. . . . . **116** B2
Swanbourne MK17 . . . **66** F5
Swanbourne MK17 . . . **67** A4
Taplow SL6. . . . . . . **203** F7
Tring HP23 . . . . **119** D4
Uxbridge UB8 . . . . . **201** D1
West Drayton UB7. . . **208** E4
West Drayton UB7. . . **208** E4
Winslow MK18 . . . . . . **66** A5
Woburn Sands MK17. . **49** B5
Wraysbury TW19 . . . . **212** A1
Station Rd Ind Est
MK18 . . . . **66** A5
Station Rd South
Quainton, Waddesdon
HP18. . . . . **84** E1
Westcott HP18 . . . . . . **98** D8
Station Rise SL7 . . **183** E2
Station Sq
Loughton MK5. . . . . . **46** C8
Milton Keynes MK9 . . **34** C1
Station Terr
Buckingham MK18 . . . **52** C7
Milton Keynes MK14 . **21** E2
Station Way E HP20 **115** D7
Station Way W E
HP20. . . . . **115** D8
Staunton Ho MK17 . . **60** D7
Staunton Rd SL2 . . . **205** D8
Staveley Cl HP21 . . **116** C6
Staverton Gr MK10 . . **36** B2
Stavordale 2 MK10 . . **36** A1
Stayning La MK14 . . . **34** F6
Stebbe's La MK18 . . . **52** B8
Steeple Cl MK4 . . . . . **57** A8
STEEPLE CLAYDON . . **63** C3
Steepleclaydon Rd
MK18 . . . . **53** A1
Steeple Claydon Rd
Middle Claydon
MK18 . . . . **64** A1
Padbury MK18. . . . . . **64** A8
Twyford MK18. . . . . . **72** E8
Steeple Claydon Sch
MK18 . . . . **63** E3
Steinbeck Cres MK4. **56** F7
Stephenson Acad
MK14 . . . . **34** D7
Stephenson Cl
Aylesbury HP19. . . . **115** B7
High Wycombe HP13 . **161** F1
Leighton Buzzard LU7 **80** E6
Stephenson Ct 12
SL1 . . . . **205** F4
Stephenson Dr SL4. . **210** B7
Stepnells HP23 . . . . **105** A1
Steppingstones LU6. **93** F8
Sterling Bus Pk
MK18 . . . . **52** D6
Sterling Cl MK15 . . . **35** A6
Stert Way MK3. . . . . . **58** A4
Stevens Cl
Holmer Green
HP15. . . . . **163** B7
Prestwood HP16. . . . **151** D5
Stevens Field MK7 . . **48** D6
Stevens Ho 8 HP7. . **165** B7
Stevenson Rd SL2. . **187** D2
Stevens Wy HP7. . . . **165** B7
Stewart Ave SL1 . . . **205** F8
Stewart Ct UB9 . . . . **189** F6
Stewarts Dr SL2. . . **198** B7
Stewarts La MK46. . . . **6** B2
Stewarts Way SL7 . . **183** D7
STEWKLEY **68** E2
STEWKLEY DEAN **68** B1
Stewkley La MK17. . . . **67** E4
Stewkley Rd
Cublington LU7 . . . . . **78** C3
Cublington LU7 . . . . . **78** C3
Drayton Parslow
MK17 . . . . **68** E6
Hollington LU7 . . . . . **69** C2
Wing LU7 . . . . **79** B3
Stilebrook Rd MK46. . . **6** F6
Stile Mdw HP9 . . . . . **175** E3
Stile Rd SL3 . . . . . . **206** D3
Stilliters Farm Rd
MK43 . . . . **37** E8
Stilton Cl 4 HP19. . **101** C1
Stilwell Dr UB8 . . . **201** F1
Stirling Ave HP20 . . **101** E1

Stirling Cl
Uxbridge UB8 . . . . . **201** C2
Windsor SL4 . . . . . . **209** D5
Stirling Gr SL6 . . . . **202** A8
Stirling Ho
2 High Wycombe
HP13. . . . . **173** F7
Milton Keynes MK3. . . **57** D7
Stirling Mews 2
MK10 . . . . **36** C3
Stirling Rd
High Wycombe
HP12. . . . . **172** D5
Slough SL1 . . . . **205** A8
Stanwell TW6 . . . . . **213** F1
Stoches Cl
Stoke Mandeville
HP22. . . . . **116** A1
Stoke Mandeville
HP22. . . . . **130** A8
Stockaway HP22 . . . . **87** C1
Stockdale MK13. . . . . **34** C5
Stockdales Rd SL4 . **204** F2
Stocken Cl MK46. . . . . **6** E4
Stock Field Cl HP15 **163** B3
Stockfields Pl HP14 **158** D5
Stockgrove Ctry Pk★
LU7 . . . . **70** F7
Stockgrove Park Ho
LU7 . . . . **70** F8
Stockhall Cres LU7. . **68** D2
Stockholm Chase
MK10 . . . . **36** C2
Stocking Green Cl
MK19 . . . . **11** A3
Stocking La HP14 . . **161** E7
Stock La MK17 . . . . . **45** B1
Stocklake
Aylesbury HP20. . . . **101** F1
Aylesbury HP21. . . . **102** B1
Stocklake Ind Est
HP20. . . . . **101** F1
Stocklake Park Sch
HP20. . . . . **101** F1
Stocklands Way
HP16. . . . . **151** D5
Stockley Academy
UB8. . . . . **208** F7
Stockleys La MK18 . . **51** B6
Stockport Rd WD3 . . **167** C2
Stocks Cl MK18 . . . . . **65** F4
Stocks La MK18 . . . . . **65** F4
Stocks Rd
Aldbury HP23 . . . . . **120** C7
Ivinghoe HP23 . . . . . **106** B2
Stocks The MK19. . . . **19** C1
Stockwell HP17 . . . . **127** A6
Stockwell Furlong
HP17. . . . . **127** A6
Stockwell La
Longwick HP17 . . . . **139** A8
Waterperry OX33 . . . **123** D1
Wavendon MK17. . . . **48** D7
Stockwells SL6 . . . . **196** C1
STOKE BRUERNE. **9** B8
Stoke Bruerne CE Prim
Sch NN12. . . . . **9** A8
Stoke Common Rd SL2,
SL3 . . . . **199** B8
Stoke Court Dr SL2. **198** F4
Stoke Farm La 1
HP21. . . . . **115** C3
Stoke Gdns SL1 . . . **205** F5
Stoke Gn SL2 . . . . . **199** A1
**STOKE
GOLDINGTON** **12** A6
Stoke Goldington Ce Sch
MK16 . . . . **12** B6
Stoke Goldington Rd
Hartwell MK16 . . . . . . **4** C2
Ravenstone MK16. . . . **12** C8
Ravenstone MK46. . . . **5** D1
STOKE GREEN. **199** B3
STOKE HAMMOND. . . . **69** E6
**Stoke Hammond and
Linslade Bypass**
LU7 . . . . **80** B5
Stoke Hammond Bypass
Soulbury MK17 . . . . . **70** A4
Stoke Hammond MK17 **58** C2
Stoke Hammond MK17 **69** E6
Stoke Ho 2 SL1. . . . **205** F3
Stoke La MK17 . . . . . **59** C1
Stoke Leys Cl HP21. **115** E3
**STOKE
MANDEVILLE** **116** A2
Stoke Mandeville Comb
Sch HP22. . . . . **116** A2
Stoke Mandeville Hospl
HP21. . . . . **115** F4
Stoke Mandeville Sta
HP22. . . . . **116** B2
STOKENCHURCH. . . . **158** E5
Stokenchurch Pl
MK13 . . . . **34** C3
Stokenchurch Prim Sch
HP14. . . . . **158** E5
Stokenchurch Rd
HP14. . . . . **170** E5
Stoke Park Ave SL2 **198** C2
Stoke Pk Ave SL2 . . **198** C2
Stoke Pk Pavilions
NN12. . . . . **9** A6
STOKE POGES. **198** F4
Stoke Poges La
SL1 . . . . **205** E7
Stoke Poges Sch The
SL2 . . . . **198** F5

Stoke Rd
Ashton NN7. . . . . **9** E8
Aylesbury HP21. . . . **115** E6
Leighton Buzzard LU7 **70** D1
Milton Keynes MK2 . . **58** E5
Newton Longville
MK17 . . . . **57** F3
Newton Longville
MK17 . . . . **58** A2
Slough SL2 . . . . **205** F7
Slough SL2 . . . . **206** A8
Stoke Hammond MK17 **58** E3
Stoke Poges SL2 . . . **198** F1
Stokesay
Slough SL2 . . . . **205** F6
Slough SL2 . . . . **206** A6
Stokesay St MK4 . . . . **45** E2
Stokes Croft HP17. . **127** A6
Stokes End HP17 . . . **127** A7
Stokes Grove MK19. . **.10** C7
Stokes La HP17 . . . . **127** A7
Stokesley Rise
HP10. . . . . **185** E8
Stoke View SL1 . . . . **205** F5
Stoke Wood SL2 . . . **198** B8
Stolford Rise MK4. . . **46** B1
Stompits Rd SL6 . . . **203** C1
Stomp Rd SL1. . . . . . **204** B8
STONE **114** C5
STONEBRIDGE. **33** F7
Stonebridge Field
SL4. . . . . **205** B1
Stonebridge Gr
MK10 . . . . **35** E1
Stonebridge Rd
HP19. . . . . **101** B3
Stonebridge Rdbt
MK13 . . . . **33** E8
Stone CE Comb Sch
HP17. . . . . **114** C5
Stonechat HP19. . . . **101** E3
Stone Cl HP17 . . . . . **208** F5
Stonecroft HP6 . . . . **153** C4
Stone Croft HP17. . . **114** D5
Stonecroft Way SL0. **207** E2
Stonecrop Pl MK14. . **34** E4
Stone Ct MK46 . . . . . **13** E8
Stonefield Pk SL6. . **202** C7
Stonefield Rd HP14 **161** C8
Stonegate MK13 . . . . **34** A5
Stonehaven Rd
HP19. . . . . **101** B2
Stone Hill MK8. . . . . **33** D1
Stone House La
SL6. . . . . **184** C1
Stoneleigh St MK4. . **45** E1
Stonemasons Cl 11
MK46 . . . . **6** F3
Stone Pit Cl MK46. . . . **6** E3
Stonepitts Pk HP18. **111** B3
Stone Rd HP18 . . . . . **72** E1
Stones Courtyard
HP5. . . . . **154** C4
Stones Row HP11 . . . **173** F4
Stones Way MK17 . . . . **68** C6
Stone View HP22. . . . **86** D7
Stoney Cl HP4 . . . . . **134** F6
Stoneycroft HP23 . . **120** C5
Stoneyfield SL9. . . . **188** C3
Stoney Furlong
HP18. . . . . **112** B2
Stoney Gr HP5 . . . . . **144** D1
Stoney Grove HP5. . . **144** C1
Stoney La
Berkhamsted HP1. . . **146** B8
Bovingdon HP3 . . . . **146** C5
Chipperfield WD4 . . . **146** F1
Cholesbury HP5 . . . . **133** F1
East Burnham SL2. . . **198** A4
Stoney Meade SL1 . **205** B5
Stoney Ware SL7. . . **194** B8
Stoney Ware Cl SL7 **194** D8
STONOR. **179** F6
Stonor Ho & Gdns★
RG9. . . . . **180** A7
Stony Dean Sch
HP6. . . . . **165** F8
STONY GREEN **151** A4
Stony Hill NN12 . . . . **17** C8
Stony La
Little Chalfont HP6 . . **155** F1
Little Kingshill HP16 . **152** C3
Stopps Orch HP27. . **139** C5
Stork Cl 2 HP19 . . . **101** F3
Stornaway Rd SL3. . **207** C2
Stotfold Ct MK11 . . . **32** E4
Stour Cl
Aylesbury HP21. . . . **115** C4
Milton Keynes MK3 . . **57** E8
Newport Pagnell MK16 **22** E1
Slough SL1 . . . . **205** B3
Stourhead Gate MK4 **45** E2
Stovell Rd SL4 . . . . **210** B7
Stowe Ave MK18 . . . . **41** B3
Stowe Castle Bsns Pk
MK18 . . . . **41** B7
Stowe Castle Rd
Lillingstone Dayrell
MK18 . . . . **29** B2
Stowe MK18. . . . . . . **41** B8
Stowe Cl MK18. . . . . . **41** C1
Stowe Ct MK4. . . . . . **45** E1
Stowe Landscape Gdns★
MK18 . . . . **40** F7
STOWE PARK. **40** F7
Stowe Rd
Slough SL1 . . . . **204** E6
Water Stratford MK18. **40** A2

Stowe Rise MK18. . . . **41** C1
Stowe Sch MK18 . . . . **40** F7
Stowe View MK18 . . . **51** A7
Straight Bit HP10. . . **185** B8
Straight Mile The
OX33. . . . . **108** A5
Straight Rd SL4 . . . . **211** B1
Strande Pk SL6 . . . . **195** F5
Strande View Wlk
SL6. . . . . **195** F5
Strand La SL6. . . . . **195** F5
Strand The HP22. . . . **85** B5
Strangers La MK18. . **51** A6
Strangford Dr MK2 . . **58** C8
Stranraer Gdns SL1 **205** C6
Stranraer Rd TW19 . **213** E1
Stranraer Way 1
TW6 . . . . **213** E1
Strarron Audley Rd
MK18 . . . . **61** C7
Stratfield Ct
Maidenhead SL6 . . . **203** B8
Milton Keynes MK8 . . **33** F1
Stratfield Rd SL4 . . **206** A4
Stratford Ave UB10 **201** F3
Stratford Cl
Aylesbury HP22. . . . **117** C5
Slough SL2 . . . . **197** D1
Stratford Dr
Aylesbury HP21. . . . **115** B6
Wooburn HP10. . . . . **185** D4
Stratford Gdns SL6. **202** C4
Stratford Rd
Beachampton MK19. . **44** B7
Buckingham MK18 . . . **41** E1
Calverton MK19 . . . . **32** C2
Calverton MK19 . . . . **32** C2
Cosgrove MK19. . . . . **19** D1
Deanshanger MK19. . **31** F4
Deanshanger MK19. . **32** A4
Leckhampstead MK19. **43** B6
Maids Moreton MK18. **42** C2
Milton Keynes MK12 . **33** C7
Nash MK17. . . . . **44** B2
Nash MK17. . . . . **44** C1
Old Stratford MK19. . . **32** B5
Whaddon MK17. . . . . **45** A4
Wicken MK19 . . . . . . **31** D1
Wicken MK19 . . . . . . **43** C8
Wolverton MK12. . . . **33** E7
Yardley Gobion NN12 . **18** F6
Yardley Gobion NN12 . **19** A5
Stratfords Way 1
HP17. . . . . **127** A6
Strathcona Cl HP10 **185** C7
Strathcona Way
HP10. . . . . **185** C7
Strathnaver Pl MK12 **33** D4
Strathspey Gate
MK10 . . . . **36** C3
Stratton Audley Rd
Godington MK17. . . . **61** C1
Poundon OX27 . . . . . **71** F8
Stratton Chase Dr
Chalfont St Giles
HP8. . . . . **177** B8
Chalfont St Peter
HP8. . . . . **177** A8
Stratton Gn HP21 . . **116** B6
Stratton Rd
Beaconsfield HP9 . . . **175** B2
Princes Risborough
HP27. . . . . **139** A3
Stratus Pk MK10 . . . . **48** C7
Strauss Gr MK7 . . . . . **48** C4
Strawberry Cl HP16 **151** D5
Strawberry Fields
MK17 . . . . **70** B6
Strawberry Hill SL9 **188** E2
Straws Hadley Ct
HP22. . . . . **89** B2
Streamside SL1. . . . **204** F5
Streamside Wlk
HP21. . . . . **115** C6
Streatham Pl MK13. . **34** C2
Stretton Cl HP10 . . . **174** C8
Stretton Pl 3 HP6 . **154** F1
Stringers Cotts 1
SL9. . . . . **177** D2
Stringfellow Cl MK43 **24** E2
Stroma Ct SL1 . . . . **204** D6
Stroud Cl SL4 . . . . . **209** D4
Strudwick Dr MK6. . . **46** F8
Stuart Cl
Milton Keynes MK2 . . **47** D1
Windsor SL4 . . . . . . **209** F5
Stuart Ct 6 HP6 . . . **154** D1
Stuart Rd HP13 . . . . **173** C6
Stuart's La RG9 . . . . **191** D1
Stuart Way
Thame OX9 . . . . **126** A1
Windsor SL4 . . . . . . **209** F5
Stubbings Cl LU7. . . **118** E3
Stubble Hill HP19 . . **115** A8
Stubbles La SL6. . . . **195** B6
Stubbs End Cl HP6 . **154** E2
Stubbs Field MK5 . . . **46** A3
Stubbs Wood HP6. . . **154** E3
Stuchbury Cl HP19 . **115** A8
Studdridge Ct HP14 **158** C4
Studham La
Dagnall HP4 . . . . . . **107** D4
Whipsnade LU6. . . . **107** F8
Studland Pl MK18. . . **116** B5
STUDLEY GREEN . . . **159** E3
Studley Knapp
Milton Keynes MK7 . . **48** B5

Studley Knapp continued
Walnut Tree MK7. . . . **48** B7
Studley Rd
Boarstall HP18 . . . . . **94** F1
Boarstall HP18 . . . . **109** A8
Sturdy La MK17 . . . . . **49** A5
Sturges Cl MK7 . . . . . **48** A5
Sturgess Ave MK17. . **37** B1
Sturgess Rd HP15 . . **163** A6
Sturgess Rd MK17. . **163** A6
Sturman Ho HP6 . . . **154** C2
Stylecroft Rd HP8. . **177** D8
Styles Cl OX27 . . . . . **71** C2
Styles Ct HP18 . . . . . **99** A7
Sudbury Chase MK10 **35** C1
Sudeley Pl 10 MK4. . **56** E8
Sudgrove Ho MK15 . . **35** A6
Suffield Hill 6
HP11. . . . . **173** A6
Suffield Rd HP11. . . **172** F6
Suffolk Cl
Maidenhead SL6 . . . **202** F8
Marsh Gibbon OX27 . . **71** F3
Suffolk Ho HP10 . . . **185** A6
Suffolk Punch Cl
MK13 . . . . **34** C5
Suffolk Rd SL6 . . . . **202** D4
Sugar La HP4 . . . . . **135** D2
Sulby Cl HP21. . . . . **115** C5
Sulgrave Cres HP23 **119** C5
Sullivan Cres MK7. . **48** C5
Sulman Gr MK10 . . . . **48** D8
Sultan Croft MK5. . . **46** A4
Sumatra Cres
7 Bletchley MK17. . **58** B3
Milton Keynes MK3 . . **58** B3
Sumburgh Way SL1 **205** B8
Summer Dr UB7. . . . **208** F4
Summerfield Sch
MK13 . . . . **34** C3
Summergill Ct MK13 **34** C5
Summerhayes MK14. **34** F7
Summer House Hill 9
MK18 . . . . **41** D1
Summerhouse La
UB7. . . . . **213** D8
Summerlea SL1. . . . **205** B5
Summerleaze Rd
SL6. . . . . **196** B1
Summerleys LU6. . . . **92** E4
Summerleys Farm Rd
HP27. . . . . **138** F4
Summerleys Rd
Princes Risborough
HP27. . . . . **138** F3
Princes Risborough
HP27. . . . . **138** F4
Summerlin Dr
Milton Keynes MK17. . **49** B5
Woburn Sands MK17. . **49** B5
Summersby Ct SL1 . **206** C1
Summerson Ct MK6. **46** F5
Summerson Rd
Bleak Hall MK6 . . . . **47** A5
Milton Keynes MK6. . **46** F5
Summers Rd SL1. . . **197** C2
Summit Ctr UB7. . . . **213** D7
Sumner Ct MK5 . . . . . **46** A8
Sunbury Cl MK13. . . . **34** A6
Sunbury Ct SL4 . . . **210** D8
Sunbury Rd SL4. . . **210** D8
Sun Cl SL4 . . . . **210** D8
Sun Cres HP18 . . . . **109** D5
Sunderland Ct
Milton Keynes MK4 . . **45** F1
11 Stanwell TW19. . **213** E1
Sunderland Rd SL6. **202** B8
Sun La SL6 . . . . **202** F7
Sunningdale Cl
HP21. . . . . **172** B5
Sunningdale Way
MK3 . . . . **57** D8
Sunnybank SL7 . . . . **183** D4
Sunny Bank
Cheddington LU7. . . **104** F7
Hazlemere HP15. . . . **162** F6
Widmer End HP15. . . **163** A6
Sunny Brook Cl
HP22. . . . . **117** D6
Sunny Croft HP13 . . **161** C2
Sunnyhill Rd WD3. . **178** D4
SUNNYMEADS **211** E4
Sunnymeads Sta
TW19 . . . . **211** E4
Sunnymede Ave
HP5. . . . . **144** E3
Sunnymede Cotts
SL6. . . . . **196** B5
Sunnyside Cotts
HP5. . . . . **145** A5
Sunnyside Rd HP5. . **144** C1
Sunny View NN7 . . . . **1** B6
Sunray Ave UB7. . . . **208** D4
Sunridge Cl MK16. . . **22** C3
Sunrise Parkway
MK14 . . . . **34** E6
Sunset Cl MK2 . . . . . **58** C7
Sunset Wlk MK9 . . . . **34** E2
Sunters End HP12. . **172** A7
Sunters Wood Cl
HP12. . . . . **172** B5
Surly Hall Wlk SL4 . **209** F6
Surrey Ave SL2. . . . **198** C1

Surrey Pl
Milton Keynes MK3 . . **46** F2
Tring HP23 . . . . **119** A3
Surrey Rd MK3. . . . . . **46** F2
Sussex Cl
Aylesbury HP19. . . . **101** A3
Chalfont St Giles HP8 **177** B8
High Wycombe HP13 . **162** D1
Slough SL1 . . . . **206** B4
Sussex Ho 7 SL1 . . **206** B4
Sussex Keep 7 SL1 **206** B4
Sussex Lodge 7
SL6. . . . . **202** F6
Sussex Pl SL1. . . . . **206** B4
Sussex Rd MK3. . . . . . **46** F1
Sutcliffe Ave MK6. . **34** E1
Sutherland Gr MK3. . **46** F3
Sutherland Grange
SL4 . . . . **209** D7
**Sutherland Grange
Nature Reserve**
SL4 . . . . **209** D7
Sutherland Wlk
HP21. . . . . **115** F5
Sutleye Ct MK5 . . . . **46** A5
SUTTON **207** C1
Sutton Ave SL3 . . . **206** C4
Sutton Cl
Cookham SL6 . . . . . **196** B7
Maidenhead SL6 . . . **202** C5
Tring HP23 . . . . **119** B6
Sutton Ct MK4 . . . . . **46** C1
Sutton La SL3 . . . . . **207** B1
Sutton Pl SL3 . . . . . **212** B8
Sutton Rd SL6 . . . . **196** B6
Swabey Rd SL3 . . . **207** A2
Swains Cl UB7 . . . . **208** E4
Swains La
Flackwell Heath
HP10. . . . . **174** B1
4 Flackwell Heath
HP10. . . . . **185** A8
Swains Mkt HP10. . . **174** A1
Swakeleys Dr UB10. **201** F8
Swakeleys Rd UB10 **201** E8
Swaledale End
MK14 . . . . **21** C1
Swale Rd HP21. . . . . **115** C5
Swallow Cl
Buckingham MK18 . . . **52** E7
Olney MK46. . . . . **6** E6
Swallowdale SL0. . . **200** D2
Swallow Dr HP15. . . **163** B5
Swallowfield MK8. . . **33** E1
Swallowfield Lower Sch
MK17 . . . . **49** B5
Swallow Fields SL0 **200** D1
Swallow Ho SL7. . . **184** A2
Swallow La
Aylesbury HP19. . . . **114** F8
Stoke Mandeville
HP22. . . . . **116** A1
Swallow St
Iver SL0 . . . . **207** D8
Iver Heath SL0 . . . . **200** D1
Swallowtail Wlk
HP4. . . . . **134** F7
Swan Bottom Rd
HP16. . . . . **142** B6
SWANBOURNE **67** B3
Swanbourne CE Sch
MK17 . . . . **67** A3
Swanbourne House Sch
MK17 . . . . **66** F3
Swanbourne Rd
MK17 . . . . **67** D4
Swanbrook Ct SL6 . **203** A7
Swan Bsns Pk MK18 . **52** C6
Swan Cl
Aylesbury HP19. . . . **101** F3
Blackthorn OX25. . . . **81** A3
Buckingham MK18 . . . **52** E7
Chesham HP5 . . . . . **144** B4
Ivinghoe Aston LU7. . **92** A1
Whitchurch HP22 . . . . **87** B5
Swan Cotts HP17. . . **129** D1
Swan Ct
Buckingham MK18 . . . **65** F5
Chorleywood WD3. . . **167** C5
Datchet SL3. . . . . . . **211** B6
Leighton Buzzard LU7 . **80** E6
Olney MK46. . . . . **7** A4
Westcott HP18 . . . . . **98** B7
West Drayton UB7. . . **208** D4
Swan Hill HP18 . . . . **112** F3
Swan Hill Cotts
HP18. . . . . **112** F3
Swan Hunter Cl 8
MK10 . . . . **36** C4
Swan La
Lee Gate HP16 . . . . **142** C8
Marsh Gibbon OX6 . . **72** A3
St Leonards HP23 . . . **132** C2
The Lee HP16 . . . . . **142** C8
Swan Mews HP22 . . **131** B5
Swannells Wk WD3. **167** F2
Swann Rd HP22 . . . . **131** D8
Swan Rd MK19. . . . . . **32** B7
Swan Pool & L Ctr
MK18 . . . . **52** D7
Swan Rd
Iver SL0 . . . . **207** F7
West Drayton UB7. . . **208** D4
Swanson Dr MK4. . . . **45** D3
Swansons LU6 . . . . . **92** F3
Swan Terr
Milton Keynes MK11. . **32** D5
Windsor SL4 . . . . . . **210** A7

Swan Wharf Bsns Ctr
UB8 . . . . 201 C3
Swanwick La MK10 . . . 36 B3
Swan Yard HP14 . . . 160 F2
Swayne Rise MK10 . . 36 A2
Sweet Briar HP22 . . 116 D6
Sweetcroft UB10 . . 201 F6
Sweetlands Cnr MK7 48 B8
Swift Cl
Aylesbury HP19 . . . . . 101 F3
Newport Pagnell MK16 22 A5
Slough SL1 . . . . 204 F6
Swift Ho SL7 . . . . . . 184 A2
Swiftsure Dr MK17 . . 36 E3
SWILLET THE 167 B3
Swimbridge La MK4 . 46 D4
Swinden Ct MK13 . . . 34 B4
Swing Gate Fst Sch
HP4 . . . . 135 D3
Swing Gate La HP4 135 D2
Swinnerton Ho RG9 191 E3
Switchback Cl SL6 . 195 D2
Switchback Office Pk
SL6 . . . . 195 D2
Switchback Road N
SL6 . . . . 195 D3
Switchback Road S
SL6 . . . . 195 D2
Switchback The
SL6 . . . . 195 D2
Swithin La MK18 . . . 52 B8
Swithland 8 MK10 . . 36 C3
Sycamore Ave
Bletchley MK2 . . . . . . 58 E8
Milton Keynes MK2 . . . 58 E8
Sycamore Cl
Amersham HP6 . . . . . 154 D2
3 Bourne End SL8 . 185 B3
Buckingham MK18 . . . 52 F7
Chalfont St Giles HP8 177 A7
Long Crendon HP18 . . 125 C6
Maidenhead SL6 . . . . 202 C3
Stewkley LU7 . . . . 68 D2
West Drayton UB7 . . 208 F6
Sycamore Cnr HP6 154 D2
Sycamore Ct
Aylesbury HP19 . . . . . 101 D1
High Wycombe HP12 . 172 C4
Windsor SL4 . . . . . . 210 C4
Sycamore Dene
HP5 . . . . 144 D3
Sycamore Dr
Marlow Bottom SL7 . 183 D5
Tring HP23 . . . . 119 B4
Sycamore Gr HP22 . 116 B4
Sycamore Ho
Amersham HP6 . . . . . 154 D2
Princes Risborough
HP27 . . . . 139 B3
Sycamore Leys MK18 63 E3
Sycamore Pl HP6 . . 154 C1
Sycamore Rd
Amersham HP6 . . . . . 154 D2
Chalfont St Giles HP8 177 A7
High Wycombe HP12 . 172 C4
Sycamore Rise
Berkhamsted HP4 . . 135 D3
Chalfont St Giles HP8 177 A7
Sycamore Way
HP15 . . . . 163 A3
Sycamore Wlk SL3 . 206 E7
Sydney Gr SL1 . . . . 205 C7
Sydney St HP21 . . . 115 F4
Sygnus Ct 8 SL6 . . 202 F7
Syke Cluan SL0 . . . 207 E4
Syke Ings SL0 . . . . 207 E4
Sykes Croft MK4 . . . 46 C1
Sykes Rd SL1 . . . . . 205 B8
Sylvana Cl UB10 . . . 201 F4
Sylvania Gdns 1
MK16 . . . . 36 C4
Sylvester Rd SL6 . . 195 E2
Sylvia Cl HP16 . . . . 152 B4
Symington Ct MK5 . . 46 B5
Symonds Cl 7
HP22 . . . . 117 D5
Syon Gdns MK16 . . . 22 C2
SYRESHAM 27 B8
Syresham St James CE
Prim Sch NN13 . . . . . 27 C8
Syward Row MK12 . . 33 B6

T

Tabard Gdns MK16 . . 22 C2
Tachbrook Rd UB8 . 201 D1
Tacknell Dr MK5 . . . 46 A4
Tacks La HP17 . . . . 126 F6
Tadmere MK8 . . . . . . 33 D1
Tadros Ct HP13 . . . 173 D6
Tahiti Row MK17 . . . 58 A3
Talbot Ave
High Wycombe
HP13 . . . . 161 D2
Slough SL3 . . . . 206 F4
Talbot Cl HP3 . . . . . 146 B4
Talbot Ct
Milton Keynes MK15 . 35 C1
Windsor SL4 . . . . . . 210 B4
Talbot Pl SL3 . . . . . 211 C6
Talbot Rd HP22 . . . 117 E5
Talbots Dr SL6 . . . . 202 B6
Talbots Hyde MK46 . . 6 F4
Talland Ave MK6 . . . 34 F1
Tallis La MK7 . . . . . . 48 C5
Tall Oaks HP6 . . . . . 154 D2

Tall Pines LU7 . . . . . . 70 F2
Tall Trees SL3 . . . . 212 E6
Tamar Cl
Aylesbury HP21 . . . . . 115 C3
Loudwater HP13 . . . . 174 B4
Tamar Ho
High Wycombe
HP13 . . . . 173 F7
Milton Keynes MK3 . . 46 E1
Tamarisk Cl MK14 . . 22 B1
Tamarisk Way
Aylesbury HP22 . . . . . 116 C4
Slough SL1 . . . . 205 B5
Tamar Way SL3 . . . 207 B2
Tamworth Stubb
MK7 . . . . 48 A5
Tancred Rd MK18 . . 162 A1
Tanders Gr MK46 . . . . 7 F7
Tandra MK6 . . . . 47 B5
Tandy Rise MK8 . . . 45 D6
Tandys Cl MK43 . . . . . 8 E5
Tanfield La MK16 . . . 36 A3
Tangier Ct SL4 . . . . 210 D8
Tangier La SL4 . . . . 210 D8
Tangmere Cres
UB10 . . . . 201 E4
Tankard Cl MK16 . . . 22 C4
Tank House Rd MK18 66 B6
Tanners Dr MK14 . . . 22 A2
Tannery Rd HP13 . . 174 A4
Tannery Road Ind Est
HP13 . . . . 174 A4
Tannery The MK18 . . 65 F4
Tansley La MK17 . . . 49 B5
Tansley Rd
Wavendon MK17 . . . . 36 F1
Wavendon MK17 . . . . 48 F8
Tansman La MK5 . . . 48 D5
Tanton Ho MK16 . . . 151 F8
Tapestries Hall SL4 211 A2
Tapestries The SL4 . 211 A2
Taplin Way HP10 . . 163 C1
TAPLOW 196 E1
Taplow Common Rd
SL1 . . . . 197 A3
Taplow Rd SL6 . . . . 204 A7
Taplow Sta SL6 . . . 203 F7
Tapping Rd HP14 . . 171 C5
Taranis Cl MK7 . . . . 48 C7
Tarbay La SL4 . . . . 209 B5
Tarbert Cl MK2 . . . . 58 C5
Tarka Mws MK10 . . . 36 C3
Tarmac Way UB7 . . 213 B4
Tarnbrook Cl 6 MK4 46 B2
Tarry Ct MK13 . . . . . 34 B6
Taskers Row LU6 . . . 92 F4
Taskers Row Cotts
LU6 . . . . 92 F4
Task The MK46 . . . . . . 7 A4
Tasmania Gr MK3 . . 58 C4
Tatchbrook Cl SL6 . 203 A8
Tate Rd SL9 . . . . . . 177 F5
TATHALL END 11 E2
TATLING END 189 B3
Tatling Gr MK7 . . . . 48 A6
Tattam Cl MK15 . . . . 35 C2
Tattams La MK17 . . . 67 B3
TATTENHOE 57 A8
Tattenhoe La MK3 . . 57 D8
Tattenhoe Pavilion
MK4 . . . . 57 A8
Tattenhoe St
Milton Keynes MK5 . . 45 E4
Woodhill MK4 . . . . . . 45 F3
Tattershall Cl MK5 . . 46 A6
Tattlers Hill HP22 . . 89 B3
Taunton Deane MK4 . 46 D2
Taurus Cl MK18 . . . . 63 D2
Tavelhurst MK8 . . . . 33 E1
Taverner Cl MK7 . . . 48 D5
Tavistock Cl
Maidenhead SL6 . . . . 202 A8
Woburn Sands MK17 . 49 B6
Tavistock Mews
HP12 . . . . 172 E7
Tavistock Rd UB7 . . 208 D5
Tavistock St MK2 . . . 47 D1
Tavistock Wlk HP20 101 E2
Taylor Cl
Bletchley MK17 . . . . . 58 F7
Fenny Stratford MK17 . 59 A7
Steeple Claydon MK18 63 C2
Taylor Mdws MK4 . . . 45 E3
Taylor Rd HP21 . . . 115 D5
Taylors Cl SL7 . . . . 183 F2
Taylors Cnr HP18 . . . 99 A7
Taylors Corner MK17 67 C6
Taylors Cl SL6 . . . . 202 B8
Taylors La
Little Missenden
HP7 . . . . 153 A3
St Leonards HP23 . . . 132 C3
Stewkley LU7 . . . . 78 E7
Taylors Mews MK14 34 F6
Taylors Rd HP5 . . . . 144 D2
Taylor's Ride LU7 . . . 70 F2
Taylors Turn HP13 . 161 D3
Taymouth Pl MK9 . . 35 B3
Tay Rd MK3 . . . . 46 E1
Teale Cl OX25 . . . . . 94 E7
Teal Ho HP11 . . . . . 173 C6
Teasel Ave MK14 . . . 34 E5
Teasel St HP22 . . . . 102 C2
Tedder Cl UB10 . . . 201 F5
Tedder Rd MK22 . . 131 D5
Tees Rd HP21 . . . . . 115 C5
Teesdale Rd SL2 . . 204 F8
Teeswater 3 MK18 . 41 D2

Teeswater Wy MK8 . 33 D1
Tees Way MK3 . . . . . 46 D1
Teign Cl MK16 . . . . . 22 D4
Teikyo Sch UK SL2 . 199 D5
Telford Cl HP19 . . . 100 F1
Telford Dr SL1 . . . . 205 A4
Telford Way
High Wycombe
HP13 . . . . 162 A1
Milton Keynes MK14 . 22 B1
Telston Cl SL8 . . . . 185 A5
Temperance Terr
MK11 . . . . 32 C6
Templars Pl 2 SL7 . 183 F2
TEMPLE 194 C5
Temple MK14 . . . . . . 34 C7
Temple Cl
Buckingham MK18 . . . 41 E2
Milton Keynes MK3 . . 57 D7
Temple Cres MK4 . . 45 D3
Templecroft Terr
HP17 . . . . 114 A4
Temple End HP13 . . 173 A8
Temple Gate HP13 . 173 A7
Temple Ho RG9 . . . 191 E3
Temple La SL7 . . . . 194 D6
Temple Mill Cotts
SL7 . . . . 194 C5
Temple Mill Island
SL7 . . . . 194 C5
Temple Orch HP13 . 173 B7
Temple Pk SL6 . . . . 193 F3
Temple Rd SL4 . . . . 210 D5
Templeside Gdns
HP12 . . . . 172 E8
Temple Sq 17 HP20 115 D8
Temple St
19 Aylesbury HP20 . 115 D8
Brill HP18 . . . . 96 B1
Temple Way SL2 . . 198 C7
Templewood HP14 . 150 B1
Templewood Gate
SL2 . . . . 198 C7
Templewood La
SL2 . . . . 198 E8
Tenby Gr
1 Church Hill MK4 . . 56 E8
Milton Keynes MK4 . . 45 D1
Tene Acres MK5 . . . . 45 F6
Tennis La MK18 . . . . 66 A3
Tennyson Dr MK16 . . 22 A4
Tennyson Gr 1
MK3 . . . . 57 F7
Tennyson Rd
Aylesbury HP21 . . . . . 115 F6
High Wycombe HP13 . 173 A5
Tennyson Way SL2 . 197 E1
Tenor Cl MK18 . . . . . 52 C8
Tenterden Cres MK7 48 B7
Tenzing Dr HP13 . . 173 E6
Terrace The
Aspley Guise MK17 . . 49 E5
Bray SL6 . . . . 203 C3
7 Tring HP23 . . . . . 119 A3
Terrent Ct SL4 . . . . 210 A5
TERRICK 130 C5
Terrick Row HP17 . . 130 B5
TERRIERS 162 D2
Terriers Dr HP13 . . . 162 D2
Terriers End HP13 . . 162 D2
Terry Dr HP19 . . . . . 101 C3
Terryfield Rd HP13 . 173 E6
Terry Orch HP13 . . . 173 C8
Terry Pl UB8 . . . . . . 208 C8
Terry Rd HP13 . . . . 173 C8
Terry's La
Cookham Rise SL6 . . 184 E1
Cookham Rise SL6 . . 195 F8
Testwood Rd SL4 . . 209 D6
TETCHWICK 82 F7
Tetchwick Farm Rd
Kingswood HP18 . . . . 83 A3
Ludgershall HP18 . . . 82 F7
Tetley Rise MK17 . . . 37 A1
Tewkesbury La 1
MK10 . . . . 35 F1
TEW'S END 17 C8
Tews End La NN12 . . 17 B8
Texel Cl MK13 . . . . . 34 B8
Thackeray End
HP19 . . . . 100 F2
THAME 125 E2
Thame Ho 5 HP13 . 173 B7
Thame Rd
Aylesbury HP17 . . . . . 127 C2
Aylesbury HP21 . . . . . 115 C7
Aylesbury HP21 . . . . . 115 D7
Blackthorn OX25 . . . . 81 A3
Brill HP18 . . . . 110 B7
Chilton HP18 . . . . . . 111 B3
Chinnor OX39 . . . . . 147 B8
Haddenham HP17 . . . 126 D5
Kingsey HP17 . . . . . 126 F2
Long Crendon HP18,
OX9 . . . . 125 D4
Longwick HP27 . . . . 138 E6
Oakley HP18 . . . . . . 110 C3
Piddington OX25 . . . . 95 D6
Thame OX9 . . . . 136 C7
Thame Road S
HP21 . . . . 115 B6
Thames Ave SL4 . . 210 D7
Thames Bank SL6 . 203 C7
Thamesbourne Mews 3
SL8 . . . . 185 A3

Thames Cl
Bourne End SL8 . . . . 185 A4
Milton Keynes MK3 . . 57 E8
Thames Cres SL6 . . 196 B5
Thames Dr MK16 . . . 22 E3
Thamesfield Gdns
SL7 . . . . 183 E1
Thames Ho
Datchet SL3 . . . . 211 B6
Henley-on-Thames
RG9 . . . . 191 E3
Thames Ind Est SL7 183 F2
Thames Mead SL4 . 209 E6
Thames Rd SL3 . . . 207 B3
Thames Reach SL7 193 D6
Thames Side
Henley-on-Thames
RG9 . . . . 191 E2
Windsor SL4 . . . . . . 210 D7
Thames St SL4 . . . . 210 D7
Thames Valley Athletics
Ctr SL4 . . . . 205 E1
Thane Ct MK14 . . . . 34 C7
Thanestead Copse
HP10 . . . . 174 C2
Thanestead Ct
HP10 . . . . 174 C2
Thatcher Cl UB7 . . . 208 E4
Thatchers Dr SL6 . . 202 A5
Theatre Wlk MK9 . . . 34 F3
Thellusson Way
WD3 . . . . 167 F2
Theseus Terr 4
MK16 . . . . 36 B5
Theydon Ave MK17 . 49 B4
Thicket The
Tylers Green HP10 . . 163 A1
West Drayton UB7 . . 208 E7
Thimble Cl MK18 . . . 52 F6
Third Ave
Marlow SL7 . . . . 183 F2
Milton Keynes MK1 . . 47 B2
Third Cres SL1 . . . . 205 C8
Thirkleby Cl SL1 . . . 205 C5
Thirlby La MK5 . . . . 46 A6
Thirlmere Ave
Milton Keynes MK2 . . 58 D6
Slough SL1 . . . . 204 C8
Thirsk Gdns MK3 . . . 57 C6
Thistle Ct HP21 . . . 115 C5
Thomas Bourne Ho 1
HP4 . . . . 135 D4
Thomas Coram CE Sch
The HP4 . . . . 135 D2
Thomas Ct
Berkhamsted HP4 . . 134 E6
Maidenhead SL6 . . . . 202 A2
Thomas Dr
Newport Pagnell
MK16 . . . . 22 A6
Uxbridge UB10 . . . . 201 E6
Thomas Gdns HP23 119 B4
Thomas Harding Jun
Sch HP5 . . . . 154 B7
Thomas Hickman Sch
HP19 . . . . 101 A3
Thomas Rd HP10 . . 185 D4
Thomas Valentine Ho
HP8 . . . . 177 B7
Thompkins La SL2 . 198 A5
Thompson Ave
Wavendon MK17 . . . . 37 A1
Wavendon MK17 . . . . 49 A8
Thompson Cl SL3 . . 207 A2
Thompson Mws
HP17 . . . . 127 B5
Thompson Rd UB10 201 E5
Thompson St MK13 . 34 A7
Thornaby Pl HP10 . . 185 E8
Thornbank Cl TW19 213 A2
Thornberry Gdns
HP10 . . . . 173 D3
THORNBOROUGH . . . 54 A8
Thornborough Inf Sch
MK18 . . . . 54 A8
Thornborough Rd
Adstock MK18 . . . . . . 53 F2
Nash MK17 . . . . 55 B8
Padbury MK18 . . . . . 53 D4
Thornborough MK18 . 42 F1
Thornton MK17 . . . . 43 A3
Thornbridge Rd
SL0 . . . . 200 C4
Thornbury MK6 . . . . 47 B4
Thornbury Pl HP11 . 173 A4
Thorncliffe MK8 . . . . 33 D1
Thorndike SL2 . . . . 205 B8
Thorn Dr SL3 . . . . . 206 E7
Thorne Rd
Lane End HP14 . . . . 171 C4
Slough SL1 . . . . 206 C1
Thorne Way
Aston Clinton HP22 . . 118 A4
Aylesbury HP20 . . . . . 101 F2
THORNEY 208 B3
Thorneycroft La
MK15 . . . . 35 B5
Thorney Cntry Pk
UB7 . . . . 208 B3
Thorney Lane N SL0 207 F6
Thorney Lane S SL0 207 D7
Thorney Mill Rd
Richings Park SL0,
UB7 . . . . 208 B3
West Drayton UB7 . . 208 C3
Thornhill MK18 . . . . 54 B8

Thornhill HP7 . . . . . 165 B7
Thornhill Rd UB10 . 201 F8
Thornlea Croft MK15 . 35 A6
Thornley Cl HP18 . . 100 E4
Thornley Croft MK4 . 46 C2
Thorns HP27 . . . . . 139 D5
Thorns La HP27 . . . 139 E5
THORNTON 43 C4
Thornton Ave UB7 . 208 F3
Thornton Chase
MK14 . . . . 34 E6
Thornton Cl UB7 . . 208 F3
Thornton Coll HP17 . 43 C5
Thornton Cres
HP22 . . . . 131 A5
Thornton Rd
Beachampton MK19 . . 43 F6
Beachampton MK19 . . 44 A7
Nash MK17 . . . . 44 A1
Thorntree Dr HP23 . 118 F4
Thorpe Cl HP21 . . . 116 A4
Thorpe House Pre-Prep
Sch SL9 . . . . 188 E8
Thorpe House Senior
Sch SL9 . . . . 188 E7
Thorpeness Cft MK4 . 57 A8
Thorpeness Croft 2
MK4 . . . . 56 F8
Thorwold Pl MK5 . . . 46 B6
Thrasher Rd HP21 . 115 D5
Threads La MK18 . . . 52 F6
Three Close La HP4 135 C4
Three Gables HP9 . 175 E2
THREE
HOUSEHOLDS 176 F7
Three Households
HP8 . . . . 176 F6
Three Oaks Cl UB10 190 F1
Three Points La
East Claydon MK18 . . 74 D4
Steeple Claydon MK18 74 A6
Threeways LU6 . . . . 92 C4
Threlkeld Cl HP11 . . 173 B4
Thresher Gr MK12 . . 33 A5
Thresher Rd HP27 . 138 D6
Thrift La SL6 . . . . . 202 D1
Thrift View MK43 . . . 25 C2
Thrupp Cl MK19 . . . 20 A6
Thrupp Wharf NN12 . 19 D3
Thrush Cl
6 Aylesbury HP19 . . 101 F3
High Wycombe HP12 172 C4
Thurlby Way SL6 . . 202 D3
Thurley Cotts SL2 . 199 B3
Thurne Ct MK16 . . . 22 E3
Thursby Cl MK15 . . . 35 D7
Thurston Rd SL1 . . 205 E7
Thyme Cl MK16 . . . . 21 F5
Tibbs Rd HP17 . . . . 126 E6
Tibbys La HP18 . . . 112 F3
Tiberius Dr MK11 . . . 33 A3
Ticehirst Cl MK17 . . 48 B7
Ticehurst Cl MK7 . . . 48 B7
Tichborne WD3 . . . 178 D5
Tickford Arc MK16 . . 22 D4
TICKFORD END 22 F4
Tickford Park Prim Sch
MK16 . . . . 22 D3
Tickford St MK16 . . . 22 E4
Tidbury Cl MK17 . . . 49 A4
Tiddenfoot Waterside
Pk * LU7 . . . . 80 E4
TIDDINGTON 136 A7
Tierney 5 MK4 . . . . 45 D2
Tierney Ct 3 SL7 . . 183 E1
Tiffany Cl MK17 . . . . 58 D6
Tiggywinkles Wildlife
Hospl * HP17 . . . . . 127 C4
TILBROOK 48 C3
Tilbrook Ind Est MK7 48 B3
Tilbrook Rdbt MK7 . . 48 B2
Tilbury Wlk SL3 . . . 207 B3
Tilburywood Cl
HP13 . . . . 161 C2
Tilcolumn Cl SL7 . . 183 C2
Tilehouse Comb Sch
UB9 . . . . 189 F5
Tilehouse La UB9 . . 189 E6
Tile House Rd MK18 . 29 C3
Tilehouse Way UB9 189 F4
Tilers Rd MK11 . . . . 33 B2
Tilia Cl SL4 . . . . 209 D5
Tilling Cres HP13 . . 174 A7
Tillman Cl MK12 . . . 33 C5
Tillson Square 5
HP21 . . . . 115 F4
Tilstone Ave SL4 . . 204 E2
Tilstone Cl SL4 . . . . 204 E1
Tilsworth Rd HP9 . . 175 C1
Tiltman La MK3 . . . . 58 B8
Timber La MK17 . . . . 60 F7
Timberley La
Lee Gate HP16 . . . . 142 A8
The Lee HP23 . . . . . 132 B8
Timberscombe MK4 . 46 D3
Timbers Wlk SL6 . . 202 B5
Timber Way OX39 . 147 C6
Timberwood SL2 . . 187 D1
Timbold Dr
Milton Keynes MK7 . . 48 A7
Walton MK7 . . . . 47 F7
Timms Ct HP20 . . . 101 F2
Timor Cl MK11 . . . . . 32 D6
Timothy's Cl MK12 . 33 C7
Timpson Ct HP15 . . 162 D8
Timpson La MK46 . . . 7 C3
Timpsons Row MK46 . 7 A3

Tindal Rd HP20 . . . 101 E2
TINGEWICK 51 B7
Tingewick Bypass
Tingewick MK18 . . . . 50 F5
Tingewick MK18 . . . . 51 B6
Tingewick Rd
Buckingham MK18 . . . 52 B8
Gawcott MK18 . . . . . 51 E5
Radclive MK18 . . . . . 51 E5
Tingewick Road Ind Est
MK18 . . . . 52 B8
Tinick Cres MK46 . . . 7 F7
TINKERS BRIDGE . . . 47 D6
Tinkers Dr MK18 . . . 65 F3
TINKERS END 65 F3
Tinkers La
Berkhamsted HP23 . . 134 A6
Windsor SL4 . . . . . . 209 D5
Tinkers Wood Rd
HP13 . . . . 161 E1
Tintagel Ct MK6 . . . . 47 A8
Tintagel Ho SL1 . . . 205 C5
Tintern Cl SL1 . . . . 205 C3
Tinterne Cl HP21 . . 116 C6
Tippet Cl MK7 . . . . . 48 D4
Tipton Cres HP22 . . 102 C1
Tiree Cl MK3 . . . . . . 58 C3
Tiree Ho SL2 . . . . . 205 B8
Titan Terr 4 MK10 . 35 E2
Titchmarsh Ct MK6 . 46 E8
Tithe Barn Dr SL6 . 203 E1
Tithe Cl SL6 . . . . . . 203 C1
Tithe Ct SL3 . . . . . . 207 A2
Tithe La
Wraysbury TW19 . . . 211 F1
Wraysbury TW19 . . . 212 A1
Tithe Mdw MK18 . . . 51 A6
Titmus Rd HP22 . . . 131 E2
Titus Cl MK11 . . . . . 32 F3
Tiverton Cres
Aylesbury HP19 . . . . . 101 C3
Milton Keynes MK4 . . 45 E1
Tobago Dr MK3 . . . . 58 B3
Tobermory Cl SL3 . 206 E2
Tockley Rd SL1 . . . 197 B2
Todd Cl
Aylesbury HP21 . . . . . 115 B6
Holmer Green HP15 . 163 B6
Tofield Cl HP19 . . . 101 D3
Toki Rd MK18 . . . . . 52 A8
Tolcarne Ave MK6 . . 35 A1
Tolkien Mdws MK4 . . 56 F8
Toll Bar Cnr HP27 . 138 D7
Tollgate SL6 . . . . . 202 A6
Tollgate Cl WD3 . . 167 F5
Tollgate St MK18 . . . 51 B6
Tolman Ct HP21 . . . 115 B6
Tomlin Rd SL2 . . . . 197 E1
Tomo Ind Est UB8 . 208 C7
Tompion Rd HP19 . 100 F1
Tompkins Cl
Aston Clinton HP27 . . 117 F4
Milton Keynes MK5 . . 46 B3
Tom Scott Ho HP5 . 144 B2
Toms Hill Cl HP23 . 120 D5
Toms Hill Rd HP23 . 120 D5
Toms Turn HP15 . . 162 F5
TONGWELL 35 C8
Tongwell Ind Est
MK15 . . . . 35 C8
Tongwell La MK15,
MK16 . . . . 22 C2
Tongwell Rdbt MK15 35 D8
Tongwell St
Milton Keynes, Broughton
MK10 . . . . 36 A3
Milton Keynes, Northfield
MK15 . . . . 35 F5
Milton Keynes, Pineham
MK15 . . . . 35 E7
Walnut Tree MK7 . . . 48 C6
Toot Hill Cl MK5 . . . 46 A5
Top Angel MK18 . . . 52 D5
Topaz Cl SL1 . . . . . 205 B5
Topaz La HP19 . . . 100 E6
Top Fair Furlong
MK14 . . . . 21 F3
Top Farm Cl HP9 . . 175 A1
Top Fox Wy MK14 . . 21 F3
Topland Rd SL9 . . . 177 D3
Top Mdw
Bow Brickhill MK7 . . . 48 B3
Milton Keynes MK3 . . 47 A3
Topping La UB8 . . . 201 D2
Top Pk SL9 . . . . . . 188 C5
Top Station Rd
NN13 . . . . 38 A8
Top Station Road
Ind Est NN13 . . . . . 38 A8
Torbay HP22 . . . . . . 85 B4
Tornay Ct LU7 . . . . . 91 D6
Torquay Spur SL2 . 198 B2
Torre Cl MK3 . . . . . . 47 A2
Torridge Rd
Aylesbury HP21 . . . . . 115 D4
Slough SL3 . . . . 212 B8
Torridon Ct MK2 . . . 58 D4
Torrington Rd HP4 . 135 B4
Tortoiseshell Rd
HP19 . . . . 101 C4
Tortoiseshell Way
HP4 . . . . 134 F6
Torwood Cl HP4 . . 134 F4
TOTTERIDGE 173 F8

Totteridge Ave
HP13. . . . .**173** D6
Totteridge Common
Cotts HP13. . . . . . **173** F8
Totteridge Dr HP13. **162** E1
Totteridge Ho HP13 **173** E8
Totteridge La HP13. **162** E1
Totteridge Par
HP13. . . . .**173** E8
Totteridge Rd HP13 **173** D7
TOTTERNHOE. **93** B7
Totternhoe Knolls &
Quarry★ LU6 . . . . . **93** B8
Totternhoe Lower Sch
. . . .**93** B7
Totternhoe Rd
Dunstable LU6. . . . . **93** C7
Eaton Bray LU6 . . . . **92** D7
TOUCHBRIDGE. . . . **95** E1
Towan Ave
Fishermead MK6. . . . **47** A8
Milton Keynes MK6. . **35** A1
Towcester Dr NN12 . **18** B3
Towcester Rd
Buckingham MK18 . . **41** E4
Lillingstone Dayrell
MK18 . . . . **29** E3
Old Stratford MK19. . **32** B7
TOWERAGE. **171** F8
Tower Cl
Berkhamsted HP4. . .**135** A3
Emberton MK16 . . . **13** C5
Flackwell Heath
HP10. . . . .**185** C7
Tower Cres MK14. . . **34** F6
Tower Ct HP27. . . . . **139** B3
Tower Dr MK14 . . . . . **34** F7
Towergate Cl UB8. . . **201** E5
TOWER HILL. **146** F2
Tower Hill WD4 . . . . **146** F1
Tower Hill Bsns Pk
OX27. . . . .**71** D7
Tower Ho
Iver SL0. . . . . **207** E7
4 Slough SL1 . . . . **205** E4
Toweridge La
High Wycombe
HP12. . . . .**172** C8
West Wycombe HP14 **160** F1
Tower Rd HP7 . . . . . **165** A4
Towersey Way
HP21. . . . .**115** B7
Towers Lea HP13. . . **173** C7
Tower St HP13. . . . . **162** D2
Town Bridge Ct
HP5. . . . .**154** B7
Town Bridge Mill
LU7. . . . .**80** F6
Town Cl MK18 . . . . . **50** D6
TOWN END. **130** D8
Town End Cres MK16 **12** B5
Town End Rd HP14 . **159** C8
Town Farm LU7 . . . . **105** A7
Town Farm Barns
HP27. . . . .**139** B3
Town Farm Cl OX49 **157** B8
Townfield HP5. . . . . **154** C7
Town Field La HP8 . **177** C7
Townfield Rd **5**
HP13. . . . .**173** C7
Town La
Marlow SL7. . . . . . . **183** D2
Stanwell TW19 . . . . **213** D1
Wooburn HP10 . . . . **185** D4
Townlands Cres **9**
MK12 . . . .**33** A6
Townlands Meml Hospl
RG9. . . . .**191** D2
TOWNSEND
Haddenham **127** A7
North Marston **76** B2
Townsend
Haddenham HP17. . . **127** A7
Marsh Gibbon OX27. . **71** E2
Quainton HP22 . . . . . **85** A5
TOWN'S END. **71** D2
TOWN'S END Cotts
Great Horwood
MK17. . . . . **55** B3
Middle Claydon MK18 **74** C8
Townsend Gate
HP4. . . . .**135** E3
Townsend Gr MK13. . **34** B8
Townsend La OX27. . **71** E2
Townsend Piece
HP19. . . . .**101** C1
Townsend Rd HP5. . **144** C1
Townside
Edlesborough LU6. . . .**92** F3
Haddenham HP17. . . **126** F5
Haddenham HP17. . . **126** F6
Town Sq **8** SL1 . . . . **205** F4
Tozer Wlk SL4 . . . . . **209** D4
Tracy Cl SL3. . . . . . . **206** F1
Tracy Way **3** MK4. . . **45** E3
Trafalgar Ave MK3 . . **46** E2
Trafalgar Pl MK21 . . **115** F6
Trafalgar Dr MK16 . . **36** B5
Trafford Cl HP16 . . . **152** A6
Trafford Rd HP16 . . **152** A7
Tram Hill HP18. . . . . **96** B2
Tranlands Brigg
MK13 . . . .**34** B4
Transcend **10** SL4 . **210** C5
Trapp's Ct HP5. . . . . **154** C6

Trapp's La HP5 . . . . **154** C6
Travell Ct MK13 . . . . **34** B3
Travic Rd SL2. . . . . . **197** F2
Travis Ct SL2 . . . . . . **198** B2
Travis Gr MK3. . . . . . **58** A8
Treachers Cl LU7. . . **105** D5
Treacher's Cl HP5. . **154** B8
Treadaway Bsns Ctr
HP10. . . . .**174** C1
Treadaway Hill
HP10. . . . .**174** B1
Treadaway Rd HP10 **174** B1
Trebah Sq HP19. . . . **114** F8
Treble Cl **9** MK18 . . **52** C8
Treborough MK4. . . . **46** D2
Tredington Gr MK7. . **48** B4
Treefields MK18 . . . . **52** C8
Treehanger Cl
HP23. . . . .**119** B4
Tree Riding
Yardley Hastings NN7 . . **1** B1
Yardley Hastings NN7. . .**6** A8
Trees Ave HP14. . . . **162** A6
Treeside Cl UB7. . . . **208** D2
Treesmill Dr SL6. . . . **202** C3
Trees Rd
Bourne End SL8. . . . **185** B3
Hughenden Valley
HP14. . . . . **162** A6
Trelawney Ave SL3. . **206** E3
Trelissick Way MK4 . **45** E2
Tremayne Ct MK6 . . . **47** A8
Trenchard Ave
HP22. . . . .**131** D6
Trenchard St HP19. . **115** A8
Trenches La SL3 . . . **207** A6
Trengothal Ct NN13 . **26** D4
Trent Dr MK16 . . . . . . **22** D4
Trentishoe Cres MK4 **46** D3
Trent Rd
Milton Keynes MK3 . . **46** E1
Slough SL3. . . . . **206** F3
Trent Villas Est SL3. **211** B6
Tresco Gr MK3. . . . . **58** B4
Tresco Rd HP4. . . . . **134** F5
Tresham Ct MK5 . . . . **46** A7
Tressell The SL6. . . . **202** D6
Trevelyan Ct SL4. . . **210** A5
Trevelyan Mid Sch
SL4 . . . .**210** C3
Trevelyan Way
Berkhamsted HP4. . . **135** B6
Wolverton MK12 . . . . **33** B7
Treverne Courtyard
OX39. . . . .**147** D7
Treves Gr HP21. . . . . **115** E5
Trevithick La MK5. . . **46** B5
Trevone Ct MK6. . . . . **47** A8
Trevor Ct TW19 . . . . **213** A2
Trewarden Ave SL0 **200** D3
Triangle Bsns Pk
HP22. . . . .**130** D8
Triangle Mws UB7. . **208** F5
Trident Ind Est SL3. **212** E4
TRING **119** C3
Tring Bsns Ctr
HP23. . . . .**118** E4
TRINGFORD. **118** F8
Tringford La HP22. . **102** D2
Tringford Rd HP23. . **119** A7
Tring Ford Rd HP23 **119** A7
Tring Hill HP23. . . . **118** C3
Tring Park Sch for the
Performing Arts
HP23. . . . .**119** B3
Tring Rd
Aylesbury HP21. . . . . **116** B7
Berkhamsted HP4. . . **134** D7
Dunstable LU6. . . . . . **93** E7
Edlesborough LU6. . . **106** E8
Ivinghoe LU7. . . . . . . **105** F4
Ivinghoe LU7. . . . . . . **106** A3
Long Marston HP23. . **104** C3
Tring HP23 . . . . **119** C3
Tring HP23 . . . . **119** C3
Wendover HP22 . . . . **131** C5
Wilstone HP23 . . . . . **104** C1
Wingrave HP22 . . . . . **89** C1
Tring Reservoirs
(Wildlife Trust
Reserves) HP23. . . **118** E7
Tring Sch HP23 . . . . **119** B4
Tring Sta HP23. . . . . **120** A5
Trinidad Gr MK17 . . . **58** A3
Trinity Ave SL7. . . . . **183** D3
Trinity CE Prim Sch
RG9. . . . .**191** D1
Trinity Circle HP11. **173** B4
Trinity Cl
Old Stratford MK19. . . **32** B7
Stanwell TW19 . . . . . **213** C1
Trinity Ct
Aylesbury HP19. . . . . **101** C1
Chesham HP5 . . . . . **154** C7
Marlow SL7. . . . . **183** D3
Trinity Ho SL8 . . . . . **195** F6
Trinity Pl SL4 . . . . . . **210** C5
Trinity Rd
Hazlemere HP15. . . . **162** F3
Marlow SL7. . . . . **183** D2
Milton Keynes MK12. . . **33** B7
Trinity St Stephen CE
(VA) Fst Sch SL4 . . **210** B6
Tripps Hill Cl HP8 . . **177** A7
Trispen Ct MK6 . . . . **47** A8
Trooper Rd HP23 . . . **120** C5
Troutbeck MK6. . . . . **47** C8

Troutbeck Cl SL2. . . **206** A6
Trout Cl SL7 . . . . **194** C8
Trout Hollow HP27. . **148** F8
Trout La UB7 . . . . . . **208** C5
Trout Rd
West Drayton UB7. . . **208** D6
Yiewsley UB8 . . . . . . **208** C6
Trubys Gdn MK6. . . . **47** A7
Trueman Pl MK6 . . . . **46** F8
Truesdale Dr UB9 . . **190** C7
Trumper Way
Slough SL1 . . . . **204** F5
Uxbridge UB8. . . . . . **201** C4
Trumpton La MK7. . . **48** C7
Trunk Furlong MK12. **49** D6
Truro Cl SL6. . . . . . . **202** A7
Trust Cotts HP4 . . . . **107** A1
Trustees Cl UB9. . . . **189** F5
Trywright Ct **3**
MK10 . . . .**36** D4
Tubwell Rd SL2 . . . . **199** B4
Tucker Cl HP13 . . . . **173** C8
Tuckers Dr HP15 . . . **163** C7
Tudanca Chase MK8 **45** D6
Tudeley Hale MK7. . . **48** B8
Tudor Ct
4 Amersham HP6 . . **154** D1
5 Leighton Buzzard
LU7. . . . .**80** F7
Maidenhead SL6 . . . **196** C2
Piddington HP14 . . . **160** C1
3 Stanwell TW19 . . **213** E1
Tudor Gdns
Milton Keynes MK11 . . **32** E4
Slough SL1 . . . . **204** C8
Steeple Claydon MK18 **63** D3
Tudor Mill HP10. . . . **185** E6
Tudor Orch HP4. . . . **134** E6
Tudor Pk HP6. . . . . . **154** D2
Tudor Rd HP15. . . . . **163** C3
Tudors Cl MK18 . . . . **73** B4
Tudor Way SL4. . . . . **209** E6
Tuffnell Cl MK15 . . . . **35** E7
Tuffnell Gn MK10. . . . **35** E1
Tulip Way UB7. . . . . **208** D2
Tulkers Cl HP16. . . . **151** D5
Tulla Ct MK2. . . . . . . **58** C4
Tummell Way MK2. . . **58** C6
Tunbridge Gr MK7. . . **48** B8
Tunfurlong LU7. . . . . **105** E3
Tunmers Ct SL9. . . . **177** C2
Tunmers End SL9 . . **177** C2
Tunmers Ho SL9 . . . **177** C2
Tunnel Way LU7. . . . **105** C2
Tunny End MK3 . . . . . **47** A1
Tuns La
Henley-on-Thames
RG9. . . . .**191** E2
Slough SL1 . . . . **205** C4
Turing Gate MK3. . . . **47** B1
Turks Head Ct SL4 . **210** C7
Turnberry Cl MK3. . . . **57** D7
Turner Cl HP20 . . . . . **101** F3
Turner Ct HP4 . . . . . **135** A5
Turner Rd SL3. . . . . **206** C4
Turners Dr HP13. . . . **173** E8
Turners Field HP13. . **161** E3
Turner's Mdw MK14. . **34** F6
Turners Mews MK14. . **34** F6
Turners Pl HP15. . . . **163** C6
Turners Wlk **4**
HP5. . . . .**144** C1
Turners Wood Dr
HP8. . . . .**177** D7
Turner Wlk **12** HP20 **101** F3
Turneys Dr MK12. . . . **33** A6
Turney St HP22 . . . . **102** B1
Turnfields HP18. . . . **124** A3
Turnfurlong HP21 . . **115** F7
Turnfurlong Inf Sch
HP21. . . . .**116** A6
Turnfurlong Jun Sch
HP21. . . . .**116** A6
Turnfurlong La
HP21. . . . .**116** A6
Turnfurlong Row
HP21. . . . .**116** A6
Turnham Cl MK18 . . . **65** E5
Turnham Way HP19 **116** B7
Turnmill Ave MK6. . . . **35** B2
Turnmill St MK6. . . . . **35** B2
Turnoak Pk SL4. . . . **209** E3
Turnpike Ct MK17. . . . **49** A5
Turnpike La UB10 . . **201** E3
Turnpike Rd HP12. . . **172** A4
Turnpike The HP18 **109** D5
Turnpike Way HP12 **172** C4
Turnpin Cl MK18 . . . . .**52** F6
Turnside St MK18. . . .**52** F6
Turnstone Way
HP19. . . . .**101** E3
Turpins Gn SL6 . . . . **202** A5
Turpyn Ct MK6. . . . . . **47** D8
Turton Way SL1. . . . **205** D3
TURVEY. **8** F6
Turvey Cl HP22. . . . . **117** C5
Turvey Loop MK46 . . . .**8** E5
Turvey Mill MK43. . . . . .**8** E6
Turvey Prim Sch MK43 **8** E6
Turvey Rd
Astwood MK16. . . . . . **15** C5
Stagsden MK43 . . . . . **16** F8
Turvey MK43 . . . . **3** E2
TURVILLE. **169** F3
TURVILLE HEATH. . **169** A3

Turville Heath RG9. **169** A2
Turvill End MK5. . . . . **46** B8
Turville Rd HP11. . . . **116** C6
Turville Valley Rd
Fingest RG9 . . . . **170** A2
Turville RG9. . . . . . . **169** E3
TURWESTON. **38** C8
Turweston Rd
Brackley NN13 . . . . . . **26** A1
Evenley NN13 . . . . . . **38** B3
Tuscans MK18 . . . . . **73** B5
Tutbury La **14** MK4 . . **56** E8
Twain Wy MK4. . . . . . **56** F7
Tweedale Cl MK17. . . **67** C7
Tweed Cl HP4. . . . . . **135** B5
Tweed Dr MK3. . . . . . **46** D1
Tweed Rd SL3. . . . . **212** B8
Tweenways HP5 . . . **144** E1
Twelve Leys HP22. . . **89** B3
Twickenham Rd **2**
MK18 . . . .**41** E3
Twinches La SL1. . . . **205** B5
Twinflower MK7. . . . . **48** B6
Twiselton Heath
MK12 . . . .**33** A6
Twist The HP23 . . . . **119** D2
Twist Way
Slough SL2 . . . . **197** F1
Slough SL2 . . . . **198** A1
Twitchell La HP22. . . **117** E5
Twitchell Rd HP16. . **152** E3
Twitchell's La
Chalfont St Giles
HP9. . . . .**176** F5
Seer Green HP9 . . . . **176** F5
Twitchen La MK4. . . . **46** D3
Twizel Cl MK13. . . . . . **33** E6
Two Dells La
Ashley Green HP5. . . **145** A4
Chesham HP5 . . . . . **155** B8
Two Gates La HP5 . . **143** D7
TWO MILE ASH. **33** D2
Two Mile Ash Sch
MK8 . . . .**33** E1
Two Mile Dr SL1 . . . **204** E4
Two Ponds La HP4 . **134** C7
TWYFORD. **62** C1
Twyford CE Sch
MK18 . . . .**62** C2
Twyford La MK7. . . . . **48** C5
Twyford Mill Rd
OX27. . . . .**62** A2
Twyford Rd
Poundon OX27 . . . . . .**71** F7
Twyford MK18 . . . . . . **62** A4
Twyford OX27 . . . . **62** A1
Twyford OX27 . . . . **72** A8
Twynham Rd SL6. . . **202** B7
Tyburn Ave MK6 . . . . **35** B2
Tydemans Ct HP19 . **100** E5
Tyhurst
Milton Keynes MK10 . . .**35** F2
Milton Keynes MK10 . . **36** F2
Tyle Pl SL4 . . . . **211** A2
Tylers Cres HP15 . . **163** B2
Tylers Gn MK13. . . . . **34** D3
Tylers Green Fst Sch
HP10. . . . .**174** D8
Tylers Green Mid Sch
HP10. . . . .**174** B8
Tylers Hill Rd HP5 . **154** F8
Tylers Rd HP15. . . . **163** B5
Tyler Wlk **3** SL3 . . . **206** F1
Tylsworth Cl **3**
HP6. . . . .**154** C1
Tyndale Mews SL1 . **205** B4
Tyneham Cl HP21 . . **116** B4
Tynemouth Rise **3**
MK10 . . . .**36** A1
Tyne Rd HP21 . . . . . **115** D4
Tyne Sq MK3. . . . . . . **46** D1
Tyrell Cl
Buckingham MK18 . . . **52** C7
Milton Keynes MK19 . . **20** A5
Tyrell Gdns SL4 . . . **209** F4
Tyrells Gdns MK17 . . **69** E8
Tyrells Rd MK17. . . . . **69** E8
Tyrill MK14. . . . . **34** C7
Tyson Pl MK6. . . . . . . **46** E8
Tyson Rd HP18. . . . . **100** E4
Tythe Cl LU7 . . . . **78** E8
Tythe Gdns LU7. . . . . **78** E8
Tythe Mews LU6 . . . . **92** E3
Tythrop Way HP23 . . **125** F2
Tyzack Rd HP13. . . . **162** E1

U

Ufton Court Yd SL8. **185** B4
Ufton Ct SL8. . . . . . . **185** B4
Ullswater Cl SL1 . . . **204** C8
Ullswater Dr LU7. . . . **80** C7
Ultra Ave MK3 . . . . . . **47** A1
Ulverscroft MK10 . . . **36** B2
Ulverston Cres MK10 **36** B2
Ulyett Pl MK6 . . . . **46** E8
Umberville Way SL2 **197** F2
Underhill Cl SL6. . . . **202** B6
Underwood Cotts
HP7. . . . .**164** C2
Underwood Pl MK6. . **46** E8
Underwood Rd
HP13. . . . .**173** D8
Union Bldgs UB8 . . **201** B2

Union Bsns Pk UB8. **201** B5
Union Castle Row **9**
MK10 . . . .**36** C4
Union Cl **11** HP4. . . **135** D4
Union Ind Est HP22 **172** A7
Union St MK16 . . . . . **22** D5
Univ Campus Aylesbury
Vale **6** HP21. . . . . **115** E7
University Way MK43 **24** D1
Univ of Buckingham
(Hunter St) The
MK18. . . . .**52** C8
Univ of Buckingham The
(Chandos Rd)
MK18. . . . .**52** C7
Univ of Buckingham The
(Verney Pk) MK18 . . **52** E7
Up Corner HP8. . . . . **177** C8
Up Corner Cl HP8 . . **177** B8
Upcroft SL4. . . . . **210** B4
UP END. **24** A8
Upende HP18. . . . . . **100** D4
Up End Rd MK43 . . . . **16** E6
Upland Ave HP5. . . . **144** B3
Uplands SL7 . . . . . . **183** D6
Uplands Cl
Gerrards Cross SL9. . **188** C3
High Wycombe HP13. **173** E8
Uplands Cl HP5. . . . **144** C1
Uplands The SL9 . . **188** E2
Upminster MK10. . . . **35** E1
Upper Abbotts Hill
HP19. . . . .**115** A7
UPPER ARNCOTT. . . **94** E7
Upper Ashlyns Rd
HP4. . . . .**135** B3
Upper Barn Farm
HP18. . . . .**84** B1
Upper Belmont Rd
HP5. . . . .**144** B3
Upper Bourne End La
Berkhamsted HP1. . . **146** B7
Bovingdon HP3 . . . . **146** B8
Upper Bray Rd SL6 . **203** C3
Upper Church St
MK18. . . . .**112** F3
Upper Coombe Cl . . **80** E8
Upper Culham La
RG10. . . . .**192** D1
Upper Dr HP9. . . . . . **175** D5
UPPER DUNSLEY . . **119** C4
Upper Field OX39 . . **147** C5
Upper Fifth St MK9 . . **34** D2
Upper Fourth St
MK9 . . . .**34** D2
Upper George St
HP5. . . . .**144** C1
Upper Gladstone Rd **2**
HP5. . . . .**144** C1
Upper Green St
HP11. . . . .**172** E7
Upper Hall Pk HP4 . **135** E2
Upper Hartwell
HP17. . . . .**114** E5
Upper Hollis HP16. . **151** F7
Upper Hundreds Way
HP20. . . . .**115** E8
Upper Icknield Way
Askett HP27 . . . . **139** E7
Bledlow OX39. . . . . . **148** B7
Chinnor OX39 . . . . . **147** E6
Halton HP22 . . . . **117** F2
Ivinghoe LU7. . . . . . . **106** A3
Monks Risborough
HP27. . . . . **139** D6
Pitstone IIP23, LU7. . **105** E1
Princes Risborough
HP27. . . . . **139** B2
Saunderton HP27 . . . **148** F7
Upper Lees Rd SL2 . **198** B2
Upper Lodge La
Hazlemere HP15. . . . **162** F6
Hazlemere HP15. . . . **163** A6
UPPER
MAIDENSGROVE. . **179** A7
Upper Mdw **2** HP5. **144** B1
UPPER NORTH
DEAN. **150** E2
UPPER POLLICOTT . **111** E8
Upper Pollicott
HP18. . . . .**111** E8
Upper Ray Mdws
Wildlife Reserve
OX25. . . . .**81** D4
Upper Rd UB9. . . . . **189** D4
Upper Riding HP5. . **175** B2
Upper Second St
MK9 . . . .**34** D1
Upper Seventh St
MK9 . . . .**34** E2
Upper St
Quainton HP22 . . . . . .**85** A5
Tingewick MK18 . . . . . **51** B6
Upper Stonehayes
MK14 . . . .**34** F8
Upper Thames Way
SL8. . . . .**184** F3
Upper Third St MK9 . . **34** D1
Upper Tring Pk
HP23. . . . .**119** D1
Upper Ventnor Cotts
SL6. . . . .**195** C8
Upper Way MK17. . . . **59** C2
UPPER WEALD MK19 . **32** F1
Upper Weald
Calverton MK19 . . . . . **44** F8
Calverton MK19 . . . . . **45** A8
Whitehouse MK5. . . . . **45** A8

UPPER
WINCHENDON. . . . **99** B1
Upperwood Cl **1**
MK5 . . . .**46** A3
Upper Wood Cl **4**
. . . .**45** F3
UPTON
Slough. **206** D3
Stone **114** A4
Upton Cl
Henley-on-Thames
RG9. . . . .**191** E1
5 Slough SL1 . . . . **205** F3
Upton Court Rd SL3 **206** B2
Upton Gr
Milton Keynes MK5 . . . **46** C4
Shenley Brook End
MK5 . . . . **46** C4
Upton Hospl SL1 . . . **205** F4
Upton House Sch
SL4. . . . .**210** C5
UPTON LEA. **206** A7
Upton Lea Par SL2. . **206** B6
UPTON PARK. **205** F3
Upton Pk SL1 . . . . . . **205** F3
Upton Rd
Dinton HP17. . . . . . . **114** A3
Slough SL1 . . . . **206** A3
Upton Terr HP17 . . . **114** A3
Upway SL9 . . . . **177** F2
Ushercombe View
MK18 . . . .**50** D6
Utah Way HP11 . . . . **173** B3
UXBRIDGE. **201** E5
Uxbridge Coll UB8 . **201** E5
Uxbridge High Sch
UB8. . . . .**201** D3
Uxbridge Ind Est
UB8. . . . .**201** B4
UXBRIDGE MOOR. . **201** B4
Uxbridge Rd
Iver Heath SL0,
SL3. . . . .**200** D3
Rickmansworth WD3. **178** F5
Slough SL1, SL3. . . . **206** C7
Uxbridge UB10 . . . . **201** F2
5 Wendover HP22. . **131** E6
Uxbridge U Sta
UB8. . . . .**201** D5

V

Vache La
Chalfont St Giles
HP8. . . . .**177** C8
Milton Keynes MK5 . . . **45** F6
Vaisey Cl LU7 . . . . . . **118** E3
Vale Cl SL9 . . . . **177** D2
Vale Ct MK43 . . . . **25** D2
Vale Gr SL1. . . . . **205** E3
Vale House HP19. . . **115** C8
Vale Ind Ctr The
HP19. . . . .**101** C1
Valens Cl MK8 . . . . . . **45** E7
Valentina Ct MK11 . . . **32** F3
Valentine Ct MK8 . . . . **45** E7
Valentine Way HP8 **177** D7
Vale Park Dr HP20. . **115** C8
Vale Rd
Aylesbury HP20. . . . . **101** C4
Chesham HP5 . . . . . **144** C4
Windsor SL4 . . . . . . **209** F6
Vale Ret Pk HP20. . . **115** C8
Valerian Pl MK16 . . . . **21** F4
Valerian St HP22 . . . **102** D3
Valerie Way **2**
HP18. . . . .**100** C5
Vale Rise HP5. . . . . . **144** C3
Valeside Ave HP10 . **173** D3
Vale The
Ashley Green HP5. . . **144** C6
Chalfont St Peter SL9 **177** D2
Valiant Cl MK17 . . . . . **36** E3
Valley Cl
Brackley NN13 . . . . . . **38** A8
Whipsnade HP4 . . . . **107** E7
Valley Cres NN13. . . . **38** A8
Valley Ctr The HP13. **173** C6
Valley End SL3 . . . . **199** C1
Valley Rd
Berkhamsted HP4. . . **134** F6
Brackley NN13 . . . . . . **38** A8
Buckingham MK18 . . . **41** F1
Buckingham MK18 . . . **52** F8
Finmere MK18 . . . . . . **50** D6
Henley-on-Thames
RG9. . . . .**191** C1
Hughenden Valley
HP14. . . . . **162** A5
Hughenden Valley
HP14. . . . . **162** A7
Uxbridge UB10 . . . . **201** E3
Valley Rise NN13 . . . . **38** A8
Valley View HP5 . . . **144** B2
Valley Way SL9 . . . . **188** D5
Valor Dr HP18. . . . . . **100** E3
Valpy Cl HP23. . . . . . **119** D1
Van Der Bilt Ct MK13 **33** F6
Van Diemens Cl
OX39. . . . .**147** C7
Vandyke Cl MK17. . . . **49** B6
Vane Rd OX9. . . . . . . **126** B1
Vanguard Circle
MK10 . . . .**36** D3
Vanguard Cl HP12. . **172** D7
Vanguard Ho **5**
TW19 . . . .**213** E1

Van–Wav 253

Vansittart Rd
Bisham SL7 194 E7
Windsor SL4 210 B6
Vantage Ct MK16 22 F3
Vantage Rd SL1 205 B5
Vantage St HP22 117 F4
Vanwall Bsns Pk
SL6 202 C5
Vanwall Rd SL6 202 C4
Varnell Terr RG9 181 C2
Vatches Farm Rd
HP22 117 B6
Vaughan Copse
SL4 205 D2
Vaughan Gdns SL4 204 F2
Vaughan Way SL2 197 E1
Vauxhall MK13 34 B6
Vaynol Cl MK19 45 C8
Vector Wlk MK10 35 E2
Vellan Ave MK6 35 B1
Venables La MK15 35 B7
Vendeen MK14 21 C1
Venetian Ct MK7 48 C7
Venics Way [5]
HP11 173 E5
Ventfield Cl OX33 108 A5
Venturer Gate MK10 35 F2
Venus Cl
Fairfields MK11 32 F3
Slough SL2 197 F1
VENUS HILL 156 B8
Venus Hill
Bovingdon HP3 156 A8
Bovingdon HP5 155 F8
Verbena Cl UB7 208 D1
Verdi Cl MK7 48 D5
Verdon Ct SL2 198 B2
Verdon Dr MK15 35 B7
Verity Pl MK6 34 F1
Verley Cl MK6 47 C8
Vermont Pl MK15 22 C1
Vermont Rd SL2 197 F1
Verney Ave HP12 172 D4
Verney Cl
Berkhamsted HP4 134 F5
[6] Buckingham MK18 41 D1
Marlow SL7 183 D2
Tring HP23 119 C5
Verney Farm Cl
MK18 74 F8
Verney Junc Bsns Pk
MK18 64 E3
VERNEY JUNCTION 64 F4
Verney Rd
Addington MK18 64 F4
Middle Claydon MK18 64 E4
Slough SL3 207 A2
Winslow MK18 65 E4
Verney Wlk HP21 115 D6
Vernier Cres MK5 45 E5
Vernon Bldg [7]
HP11 172 F7
Verona Cl UB8 208 C7
Verwood Rd HP20 101 E2
Veryan Pl MK6 35 B1
Vespasian Rd
Milton Keynes MK11 33 A3
Milton Keynes MK13 33 E7
Vesta Cl MK11 33 A2
Vianesa Gr MK8 45 C7
Vicarage Cl
Cookham SL6 196 B7
Seer Green HP9 176 D3
Steeple Claydon MK18 63 D2
Wendover HP22 131 B5
Vicarage Ct
Hanslope MK19 11 B2
Steeple Claydon MK18 63 D3
Vicarage Dr SL6 203 C4
Vicarage Flats SL4 210 D8
Vicarage Gdns
Leighton Buzzard LU7 80 E6
Marsworth HP23 105 A2
[3] Milton Keynes
MK13 34 A4
Vicarage La
Bovingdon HP3 146 B4
Ivinghoe LU7 105 F5
Piddington OX25 95 E6
Steeple Claydon MK18 63 D2
Wing LU7 79 E2
Vicarage Mews [2]
SL6 202 D6
Vicarage Rd
Aylesbury HP21 115 D5
Henley-on-Thames
RG9 191 E1
Leighton Buzzard LU7 80 E6
Maidenhead SL6 202 F8
Milton Keynes, Bradwell
MK13 34 A4
Milton Keynes, Fenny
Stratford MK2 58 E8
Milton Keynes, Stony
Stratford MK13 32 D6
Pitstone LU7 105 D2
Whaddon MK17 56 B8
Wigginton HP23 119 D1
Winslow MK17 66 A4
Winslow MK18 65 F4
Yardley Gobion NN12 18 D6
Vicarage St MK17 49 C4
Vicarage Way
Colnbrook SL3 212 D7
Gerrards Cross SL9 188 F5
Vicarage Wlk MK11 32 D6
Vickers Ct [9] TW19 213 E1
Vickery Cl HP21 115 E5
Vickery Way HP21 115 E5
Victor Cl
Berryfields HP18 100 E4
Maidenhead SL6 202 B8
Victoria CE Fst Sch
Berkhamsted HP4 135 C4
Victoria Cotts SL6 195 C8
Victoria Cres SL0 208 A6
Victoria Ct
Henley-on-Thames
RG9 191 E1
High Wycombe HP11 172 F8
[4] Marlow SL7 183 E2
Slough SL1 205 E5
[21] Windsor SL4 210 D6
Victoria Dr
Burnham SL1, SL2 197 F6
Wavendon MK17 48 E8
Victoria Gdns
High Wycombe
HP11 172 F4
Marlow SL7 183 E2
Victoria Ho SL4 211 A2
VICTORIA PARK 116 B8
Victoria Rd
Berkhamsted HP4 135 C4
Chesham HP5 144 C1
Eton Wick SL4 204 F1
Farnham Common
SL2 198 C6
Leighton Buzzard LU7 80 E6
Marlow SL7 183 E2
Milton Keynes MK2 47 E1
Slough SL2 206 B5
Uxbridge UB8 201 C5
Victoria Row MK18 52 D8
Victoria St
Aylesbury HP20 115 F8
High Wycombe HP11 172 F7
Milton Keynes MK12 33 D6
[9] Slough SL1 205 F4
Windsor SL4 210 D6
Victor Lay Place
HP11 173 F4
Victor Rd SL4 210 C4
Victory Ave MK16 36 B5
Victory Ct MK1 47 B2
Victory Dr MK10 36 D4
Victory Rd
Berkhamsted HP4 135 A5
Steeple Claydon MK18 63 D2
Wendover HP22 131 B5
Vicus Way SL6 203 A5
Vienna Gr MK13 33 E6
Village Cl MK16 13 F2
Village Cl The OX25 94 D7
Village Ct LU7 80 D6
Village La SL2 187 D4
Village Mews [2]
HP3 146 A4
Village Rd
Coleshill HP7 164 F3
Denham UB9 190 A2
Dorney SL4 204 B3
Village The HP5 155 E2
Village Way HP7 166 D7
Villa Park (Mobile Home
Pk) MK43 37 F7
Villa Pk MK17 37 F7
Villiers Bldgs [8]
HP20 115 D8
Villiers Cl MK18 41 E2
Villiers Ct SL4 210 A7
Villiers Rd
[4] Slough SL2 198 D1
Slough SL2 205 D8
Villier St UB8 201 D3
Vimy Ct LU7 80 F7
Vimy Rd LU7 80 F7
Vincent Ave MK8 45 F8
Vincent Dr UB10 201 F4
Vincent Rd HP19 101 A3
Vincents Way HP14 161 D6
Vine Cl
Hazlemere HP15 163 A3
Stanwell TW19 213 A2
Vine Ct SL2 199 A6
Vine End NN12 17 B8
Vine Gr UB10 201 F5
Vine La UB10 201 F4
Vine Rd SL2 198 F6
Vine Row MK43 8 E6
Vine St UB8 201 C4
Vine The HP18 124 D3
Vinetrees HP22 131 B4
Vineyard Dr SL8 185 A5
Vineyards The
HP27 138 A2
Viney La HP19 114 F8
Vinlake Ave UB10 190 F1
Vintners Mews MK14 34 F6
Violet Ave UB8 208 F8
Violet Cl HP27 149 D6
Violets Cl MK16 24 B6
Vipont Ct HP12 172 E7
Virage HP22 117 F4
Virginia MK6 47 A7
Virginia Gdns HP14 159 F8
Viridian Sq HP21 115 E7
Viscount Ct [12] SL4 210 C6
Viscount Ind Est
SL3 212 E4
Viscount Way MK2 47 C1
Vitalograph Bsns Pk
MK18 41 F4
Vivaldi Ct MK7 48 D5
Vivien Cl SL6 195 F6
Volta Rise MK5 46 C4
Vulcan Croft MK11 33 A2
Vyne Cres MK8 33 F1
Vyners Sch UB10 201 F8

W

Waborne Rd SL8 185 B4
WADDESDON 99 B7
Waddesdon CE Sch
HP18 99 A6
Waddesdon Cl [6]
MK8 45 F8
Waddesdon Green [5]
HP21 115 E4
Waddesdon Hill
HP18 99 C3
Waddesdon Manor*
HP18 98 E5
Waddesdon Manor Est
Waddesdon HP18 98 F5
Waddesdon HP18 98 F6
Waddesdon HP18 99 B5
Waddesdon Manor Flats
HP18 98 E6
Waddesdon Village Prim
Sch HP18 99 A6
Wade Dr SL1 205 A5
Wadesmill La MK7 48 A4
Wadhurst La MK10 36 B1
Wadworth Holme
MK10 35 E3
Wafandun La MK17 37 B1
Waffas Hill MK17 49 A8
Waggoners Ct [5]
HP17 126 F6
Waglands Gdn MK18 52 D7
Wagner Cl MK7 48 C4
Wagstaff Way [12]
MK46 6 F3
Wagtail Rd TW6 213 B5
Waine Cl MK18 52 D7
Wainers Croft MK12 33 B4
Wainhill OX39 147 F7
Wainscot Gn HP22 102 D3
Wainwrights HP18 125 D6
Waivers Way HP21 116 A5
Wakefield Cl MK14 34 F7
Wakefield Cres SL2 198 F6
Wakefield Lodge Estate
NN12 18 A2
Wakelins End SL6 195 E7
Wakeman Rd SL8 185 A3
Walbank Gr [5] MK5 46 A3
Walbrook Ave MK6 35 B3
Waldeck Ho SL6 203 A7
Waldeck Rd SL6 203 A7
Waldenbury Pl HP9 186 A8
Walden Croft MK6 47 E4
Waldens Cl [4] SL8 185 A3
Walducks Cl LU7 78 E8
Walford Rd UB8 201 D3
Walgrave Dr MK13 34 B4
Walker Ave MK12 33 A6
Walker Cres SL3 206 F1
Walker Ct SL6 202 D7
Walker Pl [4] HP21 115 E5
Walker Rd SL6 203 A4
Walkers Rd HP27 138 D7
Walkham Cl HP13 174 B4
Walkhampton Ave
MK13 34 C3
Walk House Cl MK43 25 B1
Walk The
Eton Wick SL4 205 A1
Winslow MK18 65 F4
Walkwood End HP9 175 C1
Walkwood Rise
HP9 186 C8
Wallace Cl
Marlow SL7 183 F4
Uxbridge UB10 201 E3
Wallace Dr LU6 92 E6
Wallace End HP21 116 A6
Wallace Mews LU6 92 E6
Wallace St MK13 33 E7
Wallace Wlk SL4 205 F1
Wallasea Ave MK3 58 B4
Wallbridge Cl HP19 115 B7
Wall Brown Way
HP19 101 C4
Wallen Cl HP11 173 F5
Waller Rd HP9 175 F2
Waller Wy HP5 144 D3
Wallinger Dr MK5 46 A3
Wallingford MK13 34 B5
Wallingford Gdns
HP11 173 B4
Wallingford Rd UB8 201 B2
Wallingford Way
SL6 203 A6
Wallington Rd HP5 144 B1
Wallis Ct SL1 206 A3
Wallis Rd TW6 213 B4
Wallmead Gdns MK5 46 B7
Walmer Wy MK4 56 E8
Walney Pl MK4 45 F1
Walnut Cl
Great Missenden
HP16 152 A7
Long Crendon HP18 125 C7
Newport Pagnell MK16 22 A3
Stoke Mandeville
HP22 116 C2
Walnut Cres HP27 138 D7
Walnut Dr
Maids Moreton MK18 41 F4
Milton Keynes MK2 58 E8
Walnut Dr *continued*
Wendover HP22 131 B6
Walnut Gr HP10 185 E6
Walnut Lodge SL1 205 D4
Walnut Mws HP7 165 C7
Walnuts Sch The
Milton Keynes MK3 46 E1
Milton Keynes MK8 45 D5
WALNUT TREE 48 C6
Walnut Tree Cl
Bourne End SL8 185 B2
Chinnor OX39 147 D8
High Wycombe HP12 172 C8
Uxbridge UB10 201 E8
Winslow MK18 65 F4
Walnut Tree Ct
HP22 116 C3
Walnut Tree Ho
HP11 174 B3
Walnut Tree La
HP27 138 D6
Walnut Tree Rdbt
MK7 48 C7
Walnut Way
Bourne End SL8 185 B2
Hyde Heath HP6 153 C4
Walpole Rd SL1 204 D7
Walsh's Manor MK14 34 D7
Walsingham Gate
HP11 173 A4
WALTER'S ASH 150 C1
Waltham Chase
SL6 202 A2
Waltham Dr MK10 36 A1
Waltham Ho [4] MK3 46 F1
WALTON
Aylesbury 115 F7
Milton Keynes 47 F5
Walton Cl HP13 162 E1
WALTON COURT 115 C5
Walton Court Ctr
HP21 115 C5
Walton Dene HP21 115 F7
Walton Dr
High Wycombe
HP13 162 E1
Walton MK7 47 E4
Walton End MK7 48 C6
Walton Gn HP21 115 E7
Walton Gr HP21 115 E7
Walton Heath MK3 57 D7
Walton High Brooklands
Campus MK10 36 D4
Walton High Sch
MK7 48 C6
Walton La SL2 197 F3
WALTON MANOR 48 A6
WALTON PARK 48 A4
Walton Park Rdbt
MK7 48 B4
Walton Pl HP22 116 F3
Walton Rd
Aylesbury HP21 115 F7
Caldecotte MK7 48 B3
Milton Keynes MK10 36 A2
Simpson MK6 47 E5
Walton MK7 48 B6
Wavendon MK10,
MK17 48 D7
Walton St
Aylesbury HP21 115 E7
[3] Aylesbury HP21 115 E7
Walton Terr HP21 115 E7
Walton Way HP21 116 A7
Wandlebury MK14 35 A8
Wandsworth Pl
MK13 34 D3
Wannamaker Gdns
MK4 45 E3
Wannions Cl HP5 145 A1
Wansford Ave [5]
MK10 35 F4
Wantage Cl LU7 79 E3
Wantage Cres LU7 79 E3
Wappenham Rd
NN13 27 B8
Wapping HP18 125 D6
Wapseys La SL2 187 F4
Warbler Cl HP19 114 F8
Warburg Nature
Reserve* RG9 179 B5
Ward Cl SL0 207 F7
Wardes Cl HP16 151 C5
Ward Gdns SL1 204 E5
Wardle Pl MK6 46 E8
Ward Pl HP7 165 B7
Ward Rd
Brackley NN13 38 A5
Milton Keynes MK1 47 E3
Wardrobes La HP27 149 D8
Ward Royal [6] SL4 210 C6
Ward Royal Parade [3]
SL4 210 C6
Wards Dr WD3 156 F3
Ward St HP22 116 D7
Wardstone End MK4 46 B2
Ware Leys Cl OX27 71 E3
Wargrave Rd RG9 191 F1
Waring Cres HP22 117 D6
Warmington Gdns
MK15 35 B5
Warmstone Cl HP18 99 B6
Warmstone La HP18 99 B6
Warmstone Layby
HP18 99 B6
Warneford Ave
HP22 131 D5
Warneford Rd TW6 213 B5
Warner Cl SL1 204 E5
Warners Cl MK17 59 D1
Warners Hill SL6 195 D8
Warners Rd MK17 57 D3
Warren Bank MK6 47 E5
Warren Cl
Buckingham MK18 52 E7
Slough SL3 206 E3
Stone HP17 114 B5
Warren Ct
Farnham Common
SL2 198 C7
Little Horwood MK17 55 E5
Warrendene Rd
HP14 162 A8
Warrender Rd HP5 144 E2
Warren Farm Cotts
MK18 50 A7
Warren Field SL0 200 C3
Warren Ho HP19 101 B1
Warren Nature Reserve
HP10 185 E5
Warren Parade SL2 206 C5
Warren Rd
Ickenham UB10 201 F8
Little Horwood MK17 55 F5
Yardley Gobion NN12 18 F6
Warren The
Aylesbury HP18 100 D4
Chalfont St Peter SL9 177 F3
Chartridge HP5 143 E3
Hazelmere HP15 163 A5
Warren Way MK17 36 F1
Warren Wood Dr
HP11 173 C5
Warren Yd MK12 33 A6
WARRINGTON 2 B1
Warrington Ave
SL1 205 C7
Warrington Rd MK46 7 B7
Warwick Ave
High Wycombe
HP12 172 B6
Milton Keynes MK10 36 C3
Slough SL2 198 C1
Warwick Cl
Aston Clinton HP22 117 E5
Maidenhead SL6 202 B4
Warwick Ct
Beaconsfield HP9 175 D3
Chorleywood WD3 167 F6
[7] Windsor SL4 210 C5
Warwick Dr LU7 79 E2
Warwick Ho [7]
HP13 173 F7
Warwick Pl
Long Crendon
HP23 125 D7
Milton Keynes MK3 57 E7
Uxbridge UB8 201 C5
Warwick Rd
Beaconsfield HP9 175 D3
Hanslope MK19 11 A3
Milton Keynes MK3 57 F7
Pitstone LU7 105 D2
West Drayton UB7 208 E5
Warwick Row
HP20 102 A1
Washfield MK4 46 D3
Wash Hill HP10 185 E3
Wash Hill Lea HP10 185 E4
Wash Hill Mobile Home
Pk HP10 185 E3
Washingleys MK43 25 C2
Washington Ct SL7 184 A3
Washington Dr
Slough SL1 204 D6
Windsor SL4 209 E4
Washington Row
HP7 165 C7
Wastel MK6 47 B5
Watchcroft Dr MK18 41 E2
Watchet Ct MK4 46 D3
Watchet La
Holmer Green
HP15 163 B7
Little Kingshill HP16 152 C1
Waterbeach Cl SL1 205 D7
Waterbeach Rd SL1 205 D7
Waterborne Wlk LU7 80 F7
Water Cl MK19 32 B7
Watercress Way
[9] Broughton MK10 36 B3
Milton Keynes MK10 36 B3
Watercroft La HP14 170 E6
WATER EATON 58 D5
Water Eaton Ind Est
MK2 58 C6
Water Eaton Rd MK2,
MK3 58 C7
WATEREND 159 C5
Water End Rd
Beacon's Bottom
HP14 159 D3
Beacon's Bottom,
Waterend HP14 159 C5
Waterfield WD3 167 C2
Waterford Cl MK3 46 E1
Waterford Ho UB7 208 C3
Watergate Farm La
MK18 61 B8
Water Gdns The
HP15 162 E2
Waterglades The
HP9 175 C6
Water Hall Prim Sch
MK2 58 D4
Waterhouse Cl MK16 22 D4
Water La
Berkhamsted HP4 135 C4
Bovingdon HP3 146 B1
Ford HP17 128 B7
Leighton Buzzard LU7 80 F7
Sherington MK16 13 E1
Speen HP27 150 C4
Waterlily [5] HP19 101 E4
Waterloo Ct MK3 46 E2
Waterloo Rd
Leighton Buzzard LU7 80 E6
Uxbridge UB8 201 C4
Waterlow Cl MK16 22 C2
Waterman Ct SL1 204 E5
Water Mdw HP5 154 B7
WATERMEAD 101 F4
Watermead HP19 101 E4
Watermeadow
HP19 101 F3
Water Meadow Way
HP22 131 B6
Watermill La MK11 32 F6
Watermill Way
HP22 116 F2
WATERPERRY 123 B1
Waterperry OX33 123 B1
WATERPERRY
COMMON 122 F8
Waterperry Common
Ledall Cottage
OX33 122 F5
Waterperry OX33 123 A3
Waterperry Gdns*
OX33 123 B1
Waterperry Mews
HP19 114 F8
Waterperry Rd
Holton OX33 122 E1
Worminghall HP18 123 D5
WATERSIDE 154 D6
Waterside
[14] Berkhamsted
HP4 135 D4
Berkhamsted HP4 135 D4
Chesham HP5 154 D6
Edlesborough LU6 92 F4
Milton Keynes MK6 47 C8
Uxbridge UB8 208 C8
Wooburn Green
HP10 185 E7
Waterside Ct HP5 154 C7
Waterside Dr SL3 207 A4
Waterside Lodge
SL6 203 C8
Waterside Pk MK12 33 C7
Waterside Prim Acad
HP5 154 D6
Waterside View LU7 80 E6
Waterslade Pens
HP17 126 F6
Watersmeet Cl MK4 46 D4
Waters Reach SL6 196 A1
WATER STRATFORD 40 A1
Water Stratford Rd
Finmere MK18 39 E1
Finmere MK18 50 E8
Tingewick MK18 51 A7
Water Tower Cl
UB8 201 E7
Watery La
Astrope HP23 104 B2
Beachampton MK19 44 B6
Brackley NN13 38 A7
Marsworth HP23 104 F1
Turville RG9 170 A2
Wooburn Green
HP10 185 E8
Watling Acad MK19 45 B8
Watling St
Abbey Hill MK8 33 D1
Bletchley MK2 47 D1
Bow Brickhill MK17 58 F8
Fairfields MK11 33 B2
Granby MK6 47 A3
Little Brickhill MK17 59 D6
Milton Keynes, Kiln Farm
MK8, MK11 33 B2
Milton Keynes, Shenley
Lodge MK6 46 C6
Paulerspury NN12 17 E7
Potterspury NN12 18 C3
Watling Terr MK2 47 E1
Watlington Ct HP16 152 A8
Watlington Hill
OX49 168 A8
Watlington Pk
OX49 168 A5
Watlington Rd
OX49 157 A7
Watling Way Pool
MK11 32 F4
Watlow Gdns MK18 41 E2
Watson Cl MK8 45 D6
Watson Dr MK17 37 B1
Watten Ct MK2 58 E4
Wattleton Rd HP9 175 E1
Watts Cl MK19 11 A3
Wavell Ct MK15 35 B7
Wavell Gdns SL2 197 F2
Wavell Rd
Beaconsfield HP9 176 B1
Maidenhead SL6 202 B6
WAVENDON 48 E7
Wavendon Comb Sch
MK7 48 D6

Wavendon Fields
Wavendon MK17......48 F6
Wavendon MK17......48 F7
WAVENDON GATE... 48 D6
Wavendon House Dr
MK17...............49 B8
Wavendon Lodge Mws
MK17...............37 B1
Wavendon MK17. 37 C2
Waveney Cl MK16... 22 E3
Waverley Croft MK10 36 A1
Waverley Rd SL1... 205 C8
Waverley Wlk HP20 101 D2
Waxwing Cl HP19 . 101 E3
Wayfarers End
HP27..............138 D7
Wayfarers Pk HP4. 134 F4
Waylands HP21..... 211 E1
Wayne Gdns MK4... 45 E3
Wayside
High Wycombe
HP13..............173 D7
Speen HP27.......150 C4
Wayside Ct HP6... 154 C1
Wayside Gdns SL9 188 D4
Wayside Mews SL6. 202 F8
Wealdstone Pl MK6. 35 A2
Weasel La MK3 .... 57 C6
Weatherby LU6.... 93 E8
Weathercock Cl
MK17..............49 B5
Weathercock Gdns
HP15..............163 C7
Weathercock La
MK17..............49 C4
Weaver Cl HP23.... 125 D7
Weavers Branch
HP23..............125 D1
Weavers Cl MK18....52 F6
Weavers End MK19... 11 B2
Weavers Hill MK11... 33 A4
Weavers La MK4 ... 21 C1
Weavers Rd HP23 . 118 E4
Webb Cl
Chesham HP5.....144 B1
Slough SL3........206 D2
Webber Heath MK7. 48 D4
Webber Independent
Sch The MK14.... 34 D7
Webb La HP22.... 102 C2
Webbs Home Cl
MK10..............36 A2
Webbs Mdw HP19.. 115 A8
Webster Cl
Maidenhead SL6.. 202 A5
Thame OX9.......125 F1
Webster Rd HP21 .. 116 A6
Websters Mdw MK4. 46 E2
Wedgewood Cl MK17 48 F7
Wedgewood St
HP19..............115 A8
Wedgwood Ave
MK14.............. 22 A1
Wedgwood Dr
HP14..............162 A6
WEEDON..............87 D1
Weedon Cl SL9.... 177 B2
Weedon Hill HP6... 153 D4
Weedon La HP6.... 154 A3
Weedon Rd
Aston Abbotts HP22... 88 A2
Aylesbury HP19....101 C2
Weekes Dr SL1.... 205 B4
Weill Rd HP21 ..... 116 A4
Weir Farm Cl OX25.. 81 A5
Weir La
Blackthorn OX25.... 81 A4
East Claydon MK18... 74 F1
Whitchurch HP22.....86 F6
Weirside Gdns
UB7...............208 D5
Welbeck Ave HP21. 116 C6
Welbeck Cl MK10 ... 35 F1
Welbeck Rd SL6.... 202 D5
Welburn Gr MK4 ... 46 E2
Welby Cl SL9...... 202 A4
Welchman Ct MK3 . 58 B8
Welden SL2........ 206 C7
Welders La
Chalfont St Giles
SL9...............177 A3
Seer Green SL9.... 177 B3
Weldon Rise MK5... 46 B8
Welford Rd MK18... 63 E3
Welford Way HP18. 112 F3
Welland Cl SL3.... 212 B8
Welland Dr MK16... 22 E3
Welland Ho MK3.... 57 E8
Welland Rd
Aylesbury HP21....115 C5
Longford TW6.....213 B4
Wellbank SL2...... 196 E1
Wellbrook Mews
HP23..............119 B4
Wellcroft LU7..... 105 F5
Wellcroft Rd SL1... 205 B5
WELL END...........184 F5
Well End Cotts SL8. 184 F5
Weller Cl HP6..... 154 E2
Weller Ct LU6...... 93 C7
Weller Rd HP6.... 154 E2
Wellesbourne Cres
HP13..............162 C3
Wellesbourne Gdns
HP13..............162 D2

Wellesbourne Rd
HP13..............162 D2
Welles La MK4 .... 45 D3
Wellesley Ave SL0.. 207 F4
Wellesley Ct SL0 ... 207 F4
Wellesley Ho SL4 . 210 B6
Wellesley Path SL1. 206 A4
Wellesley Rd SL1.. 206 A4
Welley Ave TW19... 211 E3
Welley Rd SL3,
TW19.............211 E3
Wellfield HP15..... 163 B3
Wellfield Ct MK15...35 D8
Wellfield Rd HP14.. 171 B8
Wellground
Stokenchurch HP14.. 157 F1
Stokenchurch HP14.. 158 B3
Wellhayes MK14 ....34 F8
WELL HEAD............93 D5
Well Head Rd LU6... 93 C6
Wellhouse Rd SL6.. 195 C2
Wellhouse Way
HP14..............161 E6
Wellingborough Rd
MK46................6 F5
Wellington Ave
HP27..............139 B4
Wellington Cl 1
SL6...............202 B8
Wellington Dr HP18. 98 A7
Wellington Gdns
SL2...............198 C6
Wellington Pl
Aylesbury HP21....115 E4
Milton Keynes MK3... 58 B7
Wellington Rd
Aylesbury HP21....115 E4
High Wycombe HP12. 172 E4
Maidenhead SL6...202 D7
Uxbridge UB8.....201 C4
Wellington St SL1.. 206 A4
Well La
Leighton Buzzard
LU7...............80 A1
Princes Risborough
HP27..............139 C6
Well Mdw HP19.... 101 D4
Wells Cl SL4...... 210 A7
Wells Gr MK17 .... 37 B1
Well St MK18...... 52 D8
Well Water Cl HP22 130 A8
Welsh La
Chackmore MK18 .... 40 C5
Chackmore MK18 ... 40 D3
Stowe MK18....... 40 C5
Syresham NN13 ....26 E8
Syresham NN13 .... 27 A7
Welsummer Gr MK5. 46 A3
Welton Rd HP21.... 116 B7
Wemyss Cl 1 MK3 ...46 F2
WENDOVER...........131 C4
Wendover Bypass
Wendover HP22...130 E7
Wendover HP22...130 F5
Wendover HP22...130 F8
Wendover CE Jun Sch
HP22..............131 B6
WENDOVER DEAN... 141 C5
Wendover Hts HP22 131 C6
Wendover Rd
Bourne End SL8...185 A5
Burnham SL1......204 B8
Ellesborough HP17.. 130 D3
Wendover St HP11.. 172 F7
Wendover Sta HP22 131 B4
Wendover Way
Aylesbury HP21....115 F6
High Wycombe HP11. 173 B6
Wendover Woods
(Forest Wlks)*
HP23..............131 F6
Wenford MK10..... 36 C3
Wenlack Cl UB9.... 190 A1
Wenlock Cl HP13... 174 A6
Wenning La MK4... 46 B2
Wensleydale Cres
MK14.............. 21 C1
Wentworth Ave SL2 198 A2
Wentworth Cl HP13 173 C8
Wentworth Cres
SL6...............202 C6
Wentworth Dr TW6. 213 B4
Wentworth Ind Ctr
SL2...............198 A1
Wentworth Way MK3 57 D4
Wenwell Cl HP22... 118 A3
Werner Ct HP21.... 115 E4
Werner Terr MK18.. 73 B6
Wernette Way
HP11..............173 C4
Werth Dr MK17.... 49 B2
Wescott Way UB8.. 201 C3
Wesley Cl HP20.... 102 A2
Wesley Dene 4
HP13..............173 B7
Wesley Hill 1 HP5. 144 B1
Wessex Ct
4 Stanwell TW19... 213 E1
11 Windsor SL4.... 210 C6
Wessex Prim Sch
SL6...............202 B3
Wessex Rd SL8..... 185 B2
Wessex Road Ind Est
Wessex Way SL6... 202 B4
Wessons Hill SL6... 195 C7
West Acres HP7.... 165 D7

Westanley Ave HP7 165 D8
West Ave HP10..... 163 C1
Westborne Ct MK13. 34 A6
Westborough Ct
SL6...............202 C6
Westborough Rd
SL6...............202 C6
Westbourne St 6
HP11..............172 F7
Westbrook End
MK17..............57 C3
Westbrook Hay Prep Sch
HP1...............146 D2
WESTBURY............39 B4
Westbury Cl
Bicester OX27.......71 E2
Newport Pagnell MK16 22 B4
Westbury Court Bsns Ctr
OX27................71 C4
Westbury Farm Studios
MK5................45 F4
Westbury Ho 3
HP20..............101 D1
Westbury La MK16.. 22 A5
Westbury Mill NN13 .38 F4
Westbury Rd
Biddlesden MK18....27 C1
Shalstone NN13 ....39 B8
Westbury Terr OX27.71 F7
West Cl SL7........193 D7
Westcliffe MK8 .... 33 C2
Westcoign Ho SL6.. 203 B8
West Comm SL9 ... 188 D6
West Common Cl
SL9...............188 E6
West Common Rd
UB8...............201 D6
WESTCOTT...........98 C7
Westcott CE Sch
HP18..............98 A7
Westcott Rd
Ashendon HP18......97 F2
Ashendon HP18.....98 A2
Westcott Venture Pk
Westcott HP18.....97 E7
Westcott HP18.....97 F6
Westcott Venture Pk
HP18..............98 A6
Westcott Venture Pk
Westcott HP18.....98 A8
Wotton Underwood
HP18..............97 E4
West Cres SL4..... 209 F6
WESTCROFT..........45 E2
Westcroft
Slough SL2.........198 B1
Tring HP23........119 A3
Westcroft Rbdt MK4. 46 A2
Westcroft Stables*
HP27..............150 B3
West Ct
Bray SL6..........203 C4
High Wycombe HP13 161 D3
West Dales MK13... 34 C5
West Dean SL6.... 202 F8
Westdean La HP17.. 130 C3
Westdown Gdns LU6 .93 F7
West Dr HP13...... 173 D8
WEST DRAYTON..... 208 D3
West Drayton Park Ave
UB7...............208 E3
West Drayton Prim Sch
UB7...............208 E4
West Drayton Sta
UB7...............208 E5
West Edge OX27... 71 C2
WEST END............63 C2
West End
Hoggeston MK18 ... 77 B7
Stagsden MK43.... 16 E3
Weston Turville
HP22..............116 B6
West End Cl MK18... 63 C2
West End Ct SL2... 198 F4
West End La SL2... 198 E4
West End Pl HP22.. 116 E2
West End Rd
Cheddington LU7...104 F7
High Wycombe HP11. 172 F7
13 High Wycombe
HP11..............172 A7
West End St HP11.. 172 F7
Westergate Ave
MK17..............36 E3
Western Ave
Buckingham MK18... 41 C1
Denham UB9.......190 C1
New Denham UB9... 201 D8
Western Dene
HP15..............163 A5
Western Dr
Hanslope MK19..... 11 A3
Wooburn Green
HP10..............185 E5
Western House Prim
Sch SL1...........204 F5
Western La MK18....65 F3
Western Link Rd
HP18..............100 E4
Western Perimeter Rd
Harmondsworth
TW6..............213 C6
Longford TW6.....213 B4
Western Perimeter Road
Rdbt TW19........213 C2
Western Rd
Great Horwood
MK17..............55 A3

Western Rd continued
Milton Keynes, Fenny
Stratford MK2.....47 D1
Milton Keynes, Wolverton
MK12.............. 33 C6
Tring HP23........118 F3
West Farm Way
MK4................13 E8
Westfield
Aylesbury HP21....115 E3
Hyde Heath HP6...153 C4
Westfield Ave MK19. 31 D5
Westfield Bglws
SL7...............192 F6
Westfield Cotts SL7 192 F5
Westfield Prim Sch
HP4...............134 F5
Westfield Rd
Beaconsfield HP9...175 C1
Berkhamsted HP4...134 E6
Dunstable LU6......93 F8
Henley-on-Thames
RG9...............191 D2
Long Crendon HP18. 124 E7
Long Crendon HP23. 125 A7
Maidenhead SL6...202 D7
Milton Keynes MK2. 58 C7
Slough SL1........198 B1
Wheatley OX33....122 A1
Westfields
Buckingham MK18... 52 C8
Princes Risborough
HP27..............139 D4
Westfield Sch SL8.. 185 A3
Westfield Wlk HP27 172 D6
West Furlong MK18. 53 A1
Westgate Cres SL1. 204 F6
Westgate Ct SL1... 174 A4
Westgate Ret Pk
SL1...............205 A6
Westgate Sch The
SL1...............205 A5
Westhill MK14..... 34 D8
West Hill MK17..... 49 D4
Westhorpe Farm La
SL7...............184 B4
Westhorpe Pk SL7.. 184 A4
Westhorpe Rd SL7.. 183 F3
WEST HYDE..........178 F5
West Hyde La SL9.. 178 A4
West La
Bledlow HP27......138 B1
Bledlow HP27......148 B8
Emberton MK46....13 E8
Henley-on-Thames
RG9...............191 D2
Westland Cl
Haddenham HP17... 126 E6
Stanwell TW19.....213 E1
Westlands Ave SL1. 204 C7
Westlands Cl SL1... 204 C7
Westlands Rd HP27 149 E5
WEST LEITH........118 F2
West Leith HP23... 118 F1
WESTLINGTON.......113 E1
Westlington La
HP17..............113 E1
Westlington Lea
HP17..............113 E2
Westmead
Monks Risborough
HP27..............139 B5
Windsor SL4......210 B4
West Mead SL6.... 195 F2
Westminster Cl
Brackley NN13......38 A7
High Wycombe HP11. 173 B4
Westminster Crcs
NN13.............. 38 A7
Westminster Dr
Aylesbury HP21....115 F6
Milton Keynes MK3... 47 A2
Westmorland Ave
HP21..............116 B6
Westmorland Ho
MK3................46 F2
Westmorland Rd
SL6...............202 D6
Westmount Ave
HP7...............165 C8
Weston Ct HP22.... 117 C5
Weston La OX9 .... 136 F5
Weston Rd
Aston Clinton HP22. 117 C5
Lewknor OX49.....157 A8
Olney MK46.........6 D3
Olney MK46.........6 E3
Ravenstone MK46.... 5 E2
Slough SL1........204 F8
WESTON
TURVILLE.........116 E3
Weston Turville CE Sch
HP22..............116 E3
Weston Turville Resr
Wildlife Reserve
HP22..............130 F8
WESTON
UNDERWOOD........6 B1
Weston Way HP22.. 116 A2
Weston Way Ind Est
HP22..............116 A2
Westover Ct HP13.. 161 D1
Westover Rd HP13 . 161 D2
West Pas 11 HP23.. 119 A3
Westpits MK46......13 E8
West Point SL1.... 204 D5
West Puxley Cl MK13 31 D5
West Rd
Berkhamsted HP4... 135 A5
Cranfield MK43.....24 D2

West Rd continued
Maidenhead SL6... 202 E7
West Drayton UB7.. 208 F3
Woburn Sands MK17. 49 B5
West Richardson St 2
HP11..............172 F7
Westrick Walk
HP16..............151 C5
West Ridge SL8.... 185 B4
Westridge Cl HP5 . 144 A1
Westron Gdns HP23 119 B4
Westside La MK16... 12 B6
West Side Rise MK46..6 F1
West Spur Rd UB8.. 201 D2
West Sq SL0...... 207 F7
West St
Adstock MK18.......53 F1
Aylesbury HP19....101 C1
Buckingham MK18... 41 C1
Dunstable LU6......93 F7
Henley-on-Thames
RG9...............191 D2
Leighton Buzzard LU7 .80 F7
Maidenhead SL6...202 F7
Marlow SL7........183 D1
Olney MK46.........6 D7
Steeple Claydon MK18 .62 F2
Steeple Claydon MK18 63 D2
West View
Chesham HP5......144 D2
Hardwick HP22......87 B3
High Wycombe HP13. 173 B8
Westward Dr HP23. 104 F8
West Way HP9..... 174 F1
West Waye HP13... 162 C2
West Well Cl MK18... 51 A6
West Well La MK18.. 51 A6
West Wlk MK9 .... 34 E2
Westwood HP12... 172 B3
Westwood Cl
Little Chalfont HP6. 166 D8
Milton Keynes MK8. 45 F8
Westwood Dr HP6.. 166 D8
Westwood Gn SL6.. 195 F6
Westwood Rd SL7.. 183 C1
Westwood Wlk 6
HP20..............101 F2
WEST WYCOMBE... 160 F2
West Wycombe Comb
Sch HP14.........160 F2
West Wycombe Park*
HP14..............161 A1
West Wycombe Pk
HP14..............160 F2
West Wycombe Rd
High Wycombe
HP12..............161 C1
High Wycombe HP13. 161 A2
West Yard Ind Est
HP14..............160 C8
Wetherby Gdns MK3. 57 D6
Wethered Pk SL7.. 183 C1
Wethered Rd
Burnham SL1......204 B8
Marlow SL7........183 D2
Wetheringsett 3
MK6................47 C4
Wexford Ct 2 SL6.. 203 B7
Wexham Court Prim Sch
SL3...............206 C8
Wexham Park SL2.. 199 B5
Wexham Park Hospl
SL3...............199 C1
Wexham Park La
SL3...............199 C1
Wexham Pl SL2.... 199 D6
Wexham Rd SL1,
SL2...............206 B6
Wexham Sch SL2.. 206 C8
Wexham St SL3... 199 B3
WEXHAM STREET.. 199 C4
Wexham Woods
SL3...............206 C8
Weybourne Rd 1
MK10..............36 A4
Wey La HP5....... 154 B7
WHADDON...........45 A1
Whaddon CE First Sch
MK17..............56 B8
Whaddon Chase
HP19..............101 D2
Whaddon Hall MK17. 45 B2
Whaddon Rd
Calverton MK19.....45 A6
Little Horwood MK17. 56 B4
Milton Keynes, Shenley
Brook End MK5....46 A3
Mursley MK17......56 C3
Nash MK17........44 D2
Newport Pagnell MK16 22 B3
Newton Longville
MK17..............57 D3
Newton Longville MK4. 56 F5
9 Shenley Brook End
MK4................56 E8
Whaddon Way MK3. 46 E2
Whales La OX27.... 71 E2
Whalley Dr
Bletchley MK3......47 A1
Milton Keynes MK3. 47 A2
Wharf Cl
Old Stratford MK19... 32 B7
Wendover HP22...131 B5
Wharf Ct UB8..... 201 C1
Wharfe La RG9.... 191 E2
Wharf La
Berkhamsted HP4... 134 C8
Bourne End SL8... 184 F3

Wharf La continued
Bourne End SL8.... 185 A3
Old Stratford MK19... 32 C7
Wharf Rd HP22.... 131 B5
Wharf Row HP22... 118 B4
Wharfside MK2..... 47 E1
Wharfside Pl MK18. 41 E1
Wharf The
Leighton Buzzard LU7. 80 E6
Milton Keynes MK2... 58 B8
Milton Keynes, Giffard Park
MK14..............21 E2
Wharf View MK18... 41 E1
WHARLEY END...... 24 D1
Wharton Ho 2
HP20..............101 D1
Whatmore Cl TW19. 213 A1
Wheatbutts The
SL4...............204 F2
Wheat Cl HP21.... 115 E3
Wheatcroft Cl MK6. 47 A5
Wheatfield OX39... 147 E8
Wheatfield Cl SL6. 202 A4
Wheathouse Copse
MK17..............55 A3
Wheatlands HP4 ... 92 D7
Wheatlands Rd
SL3...............206 C3
WHEATLEY...........122 A1
Wheatley Cl MK4... 46 C2
Wheatley Park Sch
OX33.............. 122 B2
Wheatley Rd
Aston Clinton HP22. 117 C6
Oxford OX33......122 A3
Wheatley Way SL9. 177 E4
Wheatsheaf Ho
HP10..............185 E7
Wheatsheaf Par
SL4...............211 A2
Wheatstone Cl SL3. 206 A3
Wheeler Ave HP10. 174 C8
Wheeler Cl HP20... 116 B8
WHEELER END...... 171 B6
Wheeler End Comm
HP14..............171 A4
Wheeler Pl
Beaconsfield HP9... 175 C1
5 Buckingham MK18. 41 E3
Wheelers Cl HP10... 174 C8
Wheelers End OX39 147 C5
Wheelers Flats
HP10..............174 D8
Wheelers La MK13 . 34 A6
Wheelers Pk HP13. 173 D7
Wheelers Orch SL9. 177 E4
Wheelers Yd MK16. 152 A7
Wheelwright Mews
MK14..............34 F4
Wheelwright Rd
HP27..............138 D7
Wheelwrights HP22 116 F2
Wheelwrights Pl
SL3...............212 C7
Wheelwrights Way
MK19..............32 C7
Wheelwrights Yd
HP22..............85 A5
WHELPLEY HILL.... 145 D5
Whelpley Hill Pk
HP5...............145 D5
Whet Stone Cl MK13. 34 B4
Whichcote Gdns
HP5...............154 D6
Whichert Cl HP9 ... 175 C6
Whichford MK14.... 22 A1
Whielden Cl HP7... 165 B7
Whielden Gate HP7 164 E4
Whielden Gn HP7... 165 B3
Whielden Hts HP7.. 165 A7
Whielden La
Coleshill HP7......164 E5
Winchmore Hill HP7. 164 D3
Whielden St HP7... 165 B7
Whinchat HP19.... 101 E3
Whincup Cl HP11.. 172 F5
Whinham Gn 1
HP18..............100 C5
Whinneys Rd HP10. 174 C3
Whipass Hill HP9... 176 A5
WHIPSNADE.........107 F2
Whipsnade Park
Homes LU6........93 F1
Whipsnade Rd LU6. 93 F5
Whipsnade Tree
Cathedral* LU6 ...93 F1
Whiskin Cl 1 HP21. 115 E4
Whistler Mws SL4.. 210 B5
Whitby Cl MK3..... 47 A2
Whitby Rd SL1..... 205 C6
WHITCHURCH........87 B6
Whitchurch Cl
Maidenhead SL6.. 195 E3
Westcott HP18.....98 C7
Whitchurch Comb Sch
HP22..............86 E7
Whitchurch Ho 5
SL6...............202 F7
Whitchurch La HP22. 86 D8
Whitchurch Rd
Cublington LU7.....78 E3
Cublington LU7.....88 A8
Oving HP22........86 D7
Whiteacres Dr SL6. 203 B1
White Alder MK12... 33 E5
Whitebaker Ct MK14 .34 F4
Whitebeam Chase
SL6...............202 E3

Whitebeam Cl
Aylesbury HP22. . . . . 116 C3
Uxbridge UB8. . . . . . 201 C5
Whitebred Chase
MK8. . . . . 45 C7
Whitebrook Pk SL6. 196 C4
White Canons Dr
MK46. . . . . 7 F7
Whitecastle Way 15
MK4. . . . . 56 E8
Whitechurch Cl
HP17. . . . . 114 C5
White Cl
High Wycombe
HP13. . . . . 161 D1
Slough SL1 . . . . 205 D5
White Cotts MK18. . 29 D4
White Cres HP22. . . 131 C5
Whitecross Green Wood
Whitecross Green Wood
Wildlife Reserve
OX5. . . . . 94 C2
Whitecross Rd
HP17. . . . . 126 F5
White End HP5. . . . 155 B6
Whitefield La HP16. 152 A6
Whiteford Rd SL2. . 206 B3
Whitegate Ct MK6. . 47 B6
Whitehall SL6. . . . . 196 B1
Whitehall Ave MK10. 36 D1
Whitehall Cl UB8. . . 201 D4
Whitehall Inf Sch
UB8. . . . . 201 C4
Whitehall Jun Sch
UB8. . . . . 201 C4
Whitehall La TW19. 212 A1
Whitehall Rd UB8. . 201 D3
Whitehall St 6
HP20. . . . . 101 D1
White Hart Cl
Chalfont St Giles
HP8. . . . . 177 A7
Ludgershall HP18 . . . 96 B8
White Hart Field
HP22. . . . . 85 B4
White Hart La HP17. 127 A5
White Hart Mdw
HP9. . . . . 175 E1
White Hart Rd
1 Maidenhead SL6. . 202 F7
Slough SL1 . . . . 205 D5
White Hart St 9
HP11. . . . . 173 A7
Whitehaven SL1. . . 205 F6
Whitehaven Cl 3
MK10. . . . . 36 B4
Whitehead Way
HP21. . . . . 115 E6
Whitehead Wy MK18. 41 D3
White Hermitage
SL4. . . . . 211 C2
Whitehill
Berkhamsted HP4. . . 135 C5
Berkhamsted HP4. . . 135 D5
Olney MK46. . . . . 6 E5
White Hill
Ashley Green HP4,
HP5. . . . . 145 C4
Beaconsfield HP9,
HP10. . . . . 185 F8
Chesham HP5. . . . . . 144 D1
High Wycombe HP13. 162 B2
Remenham Hill RG9 . 192 A2
White Hill Cl
Chesham HP5. . . . . . 144 D1
Marlow Bottom SL7. . 183 C6
Whitehill Ct HP4 . . 135 D5
Whitehill La LU7. . . 105 D3
White Hill La LU7. . 105 D3
White Horse Ct
HP6. . . . . 154 C2
White Horse Dr MK4. 46 C2
White Horse La HP22 87 A6
White Horse Rd
SL4. . . . . 209 D5
Whitehorse Yd MK11. 32 D5
White Hos MK18. . . . 50 D6
Whitehouse MK8. . . 45 D7
Whitehouse Cl
HP10. . . . . 174 E1
White House Cl SL9. 177 E3
White House Gdns
LU7. . . . . 118 F3
Whitehouse La
HP10. . . . . 174 E2
White House La
MK18. . . . . 29 D4
Whitehouse Prim Sch
NK19. . . . . 45 C8
Whitehouse Way
Iver Heath SL0 . . . . . 200 D2
Slough SL3 . . . . 206 D3
Whitelands Ave
WD3 . . . . 167 C5
Whitelands Rd
HP12. . . . . 172 D7
Whitelands Way
HP12. . . . . 172 D7
WHITELEAF. 139 D5
Whiteleaf Ctr The
HP20. . . . . 101 F1
Whiteleaf Hill Nature
Reserve HP27. . . . . 139 E4
Whiteleaf Way
HP27. . . . . 139 D5
Whiteley Cres MK3. . 57 F6
White Lilies Island
SL4. . . . . 210 B7

White Lion Cl HP7. . 166 A8
White Lion Rd HP7. . 166 B8
Whitelock Rd RG9. . 196 B1
White Lodge Cl SL7. 183 C6
White Paddock SL6. 202 A2
Whitepit La HP10. . . 185 D7
White Rock SL6. . . . 196 B1
Whites Cl MK18. . . . . 63 D3
Whites Croft MK6. . . 46 F6
Whites La SL3. . . . . 211 B8
White Spire Sch MK3. 46 F1
White Star Ct 14
MK10. . . . . 36 C4
Whiteswan La HP18 113 A3
Whitethorn Ave
UB7. . . . . 208 F6
Whitethorn Cl HP22 130 A8
Whitethorn Pl UB7. 208 F5
Whitethorns MK46 . . 6 E6
White View 14 HP20 101 F3
Whitewood Rd HP4 135 A4
WHITFIELD. 26 D3
Whitfield Rd
Biddlesden MK18 . . . . 27 B2
Biddlesden NN13. . . . 26 B2
Hughenden Valley
HP14. . . . . 162 A6
Radstone NN13. . . . . . 26 A4
Whitfield Way WD3 167 F1
Whitley Cl TW19 . . . 213 E1
Whitley Ct 1 HP21. 115 E4
Whitmees MK46 . . . . . 6 E4
Whitney Rdbt MK4 . . 45 E2
Whitsun Pasture
MK15 . . . . 35 B7
Whittaker Rd SL2. . 197 E1
Whittenham Cl SL2. 206 A5
Whittingham Ave
HP22. . . . . 131 D6
Whittington Chase
4 Church Hill MK4. . 56 E8
Milton Keynes MK4. . 45 E1
Whittlebury Cl
Deanshanger NN12. . 31 A6
Wicken MN12 . . . . . . 30 E7
Whittle Ct MK5. . . . . 46 C7
Whittle Parkway
SL1. . . . . 204 D7
Whitton Way MK16. . 22 C3
Whittlebury Rd
MK18. . . . . 17 C1
Whitworth La MK5. . 46 B7
Whurley Way SL6. . 195 E2
Whybrow Gdns HP4 135 E6
Whyteladyes La SL6 195 E6
Whytingham Rd
HP23. . . . . 119 C4
WICKEN. 31 B3
Wicken Park Rd
MK19 . . . . 31 B2
Wicken Rd
Deanshanger MK19 . . 31 E4
Leckhampstead MK18. 30 E1
Wickets The SL6. . . 202 C7
Wicket The SL1. . . . 205 E3
Wickfields HP27 . . . 138 D6
Wickham Cl HP19. . 101 E2
Wickham Field HP22 89 C3
Wick Rd HP23. . . . . 133 D8
Wickstead La MK4. . 45 D6
Widbrook Rd SL6 . . 196 B3
Widdenton View
HP14. . . . . 171 C5
Widdowson Pl 1
HP21. . . . . 115 E5
Widecroft Rd SL0. . 207 E7
Widewater Rd SL9. 190 C6
Widgeon Ho HP11. . 173 C6
Widgeon Rd TW6 . . 213 B4
Widmere Field
HP16. . . . . 151 C5
Widmere La SL7 . . . 183 A6
WIDMER END. 162 E6
Widmer End Com Comb
Sch HP15. . . . . 162 F6
WIDMOOR. 185 E3
Widmore Cl HP15. . 143 E5
Widnell La OX25 . . . . 95 C7
Wigans La HP14 . . . 148 C6
Wiggington Ho SL4 210 D7
Wiggington Rd
Cholesbury HP5 . . . . 134 B1
Cholesbury HP5 . . . . 144 B8
WIGGINTON. 119 D1
WIGGINTON
BOTTOM. 133 D8
Wigginton Bottom
HP23. . . . . 133 C8
Wiggles La HP23 . . . 118 F7
Wigmore Ct HP19 . . 101 A2
Wigmore Rd HP19 . . 101 A2
Wigwell Gdns MK17. 55 A2
Wilberforce Mews 7
SL6. . . . . 202 F7
Wildacre Rd MK5. . . 46 A6
Wilden Mws HP14. . 161 C8
Wilderness The
HP4. . . . . 135 C4
Wildgreen N SL3. . . 207 A2
Wildgreen S SL3. . . 207 A2
Wilds Cross MK14. . . 21 F3
Wildwood Ct WD3. . 167 F5
Wilford Cl MK15. . . . 35 C2
Wilford Rd SL3. . . . 206 F4
Wilfrids Wood Cl
HP10. . . . . 185 B6
Wilkie Ct 8 MK17 . . . 49 A5
Wilkinson Cl MK3. . . 58 A8

Wilkinson Cres MK12 33 B6
Wilks Croft MK5. . . . . 45 F7
WILLEN. 35 D7
Willen La MK14. . . . . 34 F8
WILLEN PARK. 35 C6
Willen Park Ave
MK15 . . . . 35 B6
Willen Prim Sch
MK15 . . . . 35 C7
Willen Rd
Milton Keynes MK10 . . 35 F3
Newport Pagnell
MK16 . . . . 22 D2
Newport Pagnell
MK16 . . . . 22 D3
Willets Rise MK5. . . . 46 A5
Willetts La HP7. . . . 200 F7
Willey Ct MK11. . . . . 32 F4
William Bandy Cl
LU7. . . . . 79 F3
William Burt Cl
HP22. . . . . 116 F1
William Ellis Cl SL4. 211 A1
William Fiske Ho 4
HP4. . . . . 135 C4
William Harding Cl
HP21. . . . . 115 E7
William Harding Comb
Sch HP21. . . . . 116 A5
William Hartley Yd
SL3. . . . . 199 B1
William Hill Dr
HP22. . . . . 102 C4
William Ho 4 HP13 173 F5
William Moulder Ct
HP5. . . . . 144 B3
Williams Circ MK7 . . 48 A4
Williams Cl
Aylesbury HP19. . . . 101 D1
Hanslope MK19. . . . . . 10 F3
Princes Risborough
HP27. . . . . 139 D3
Williams Ct LU7. . . . 105 C2
William Shakman Ho
HP8. . . . . 177 B8
William Smith Cl
MK15 . . . . 35 C3
Williamson Way
LU7. . . . . 105 E5
William St
Berkhamsted HP4. . . 135 D4
Slough SL1 . . . . 205 F5
Windsor SL4 . . . . . . 210 D6
William Sutton Ho
MK5. . . . . 46 A6
Williams Way HP27 138 D6
Willis Pl SL1. . . . . . 206 C1
Willis Rd HP17 . . . . 127 A6
Willis St MK17. . . . . . 58 C3
Willmott Cl HP19. . . 101 D4
Willoners
Slough SL2 . . . . 198 A1
Slough SL2 . . . . 205 A8
Willoughby Ave
UB10. . . . . 201 E3
Willoughby La HP17 127 B5
Willoughby Rd SL3. 207 B3
Willoughbys Wlk
HP13. . . . . 161 D2
Willow Ave
High Wycombe
HP12. . . . . 172 B4
New Denham UB9. . . 201 C4
West Drayton UB7. . . 208 F6
Willow Bank
Marlow Bottom SL7. . 183 D5
Wolverton MK12. . . . . 33 E7
Willowbank Terr 6
HP21. . . . . 115 E8
Willowbrook
Slough SL4 . . . . 205 D2
Wendover HP22 . . . . 131 B7
Willow Chase
Chesham HP5 . . . . . 144 B1
Hazlemere HP15. . . . 162 E3
Willow Cl
Chalfont St Peter
SL9. . . . . 177 E1
Colnbrook SL3. . . . . 212 C7
Flackwell Heath
HP10. . . . . 185 C6
Maidenhead SL6 . . . 195 D1
Moulsoe MK16 . . . . . . 36 E8
Willow Crescent E
UB9. . . . . 201 C7
Willow Crescent W
UB9. . . . . 201 C7
Willow Ct
2 Aylesbury, Quarrendon
HP19. . . . . 101 A2
Aylesbury, Walton Court
HP21. . . . . 115 C6
High Wycombe HP11. 173 E4
Walter's Ash HP14 . . 161 C8
Willow Dr
Buckingham MK18 . . . 52 F7
Maidenhead SL6 . . . 203 B2
Willow End HP22. . . 116 F2
Willowford MK13 . . . . 33 E5
Willow Gr MK19. . . . . 32 B6
Willow Herb HP19. . 101 E4
Willow Ho LU7. . . . . . 80 E7
Willow La
Amersham HP7 . . . . 165 E6
Ickford HP18. . . . . . 124 A4
Milton Keynes MK11. . 32 C5
Willowmead HP17 . . 114 F5
Willowmead Cl 10
SL7. . . . . 183 F3

Willowmead Gdns
SL7. . . . . 183 F3
Willowmead Rd 8
SL7. . . . . 183 F3
Willowmead Sq 9
SL7. . . . . 183 F3
Willow Parade SL3. 207 A3
Willow Pk SL2 . . . . . 199 A5
Willow Pl SL4 . . . . . 210 C8
Willow Prim Sch
SL2. . . . . 206 B6
Willow Rd
Aylesbury HP19. . . . 101 C1
Brackley NN13 . . . . . 38 A6
Chinnor OX39 . . . . . 147 C6
Great Horwood MK17. 55 A3
Poyle SL3 . . . . 212 E5
Thame OX9 . . . . 125 F1
Willow Rise HP17 . . 127 A7
Willows Rd SL8. . . . 185 B4
Willows Riverside Pk
SL4. . . . . 209 C7
Willows Riverside Pk
The SL4. . . . . 209 C7
Willows Sch The
MK6. . . . . 35 A2
Willows The
Amersham HP6 . . . . 154 B4
4 Bourne End SL8 . . 185 B3
Edlesborough LU6. . . 92 F3
High Wycombe HP12. 172 E8
Longwick HP27 . . . . 138 E6
Windsor SL4 . . . . . . 209 D7
Willow Tree Pl SL9. 177 B1
Willowvale Way
MK18 . . . . 63 C2
Willow Way
Loudwater HP11 . . . 174 B2
Milton Keynes MK2 . . 58 C7
Princes Risborough
HP27. . . . . 139 D3
Wing LU7 . . . . 79 E3
Willow Wlk HP15. . . 163 A3
Willow Wood Cl
SL1. . . . . 197 B3
Willow Wren MK14. . 21 F2
Wilmar Cl UB8. . . . . 201 D5
Wilmin Gr MK5. . . . . . 46 B7
Wilmot Rd SL1. . . . . 197 B2
Wilsley Pound MK7. . 48 B8
Wilson Ct MK8. . . . . . 45 E7
WILSTONE. 104 D1
WILSTONE GREEN. 118 D8
Wilstone Resr 水 HP22,
HP23. . . . . 118 C7
Wilstone St HP22. . . 102 C2
Wilstone Wharf
HP23. . . . . 104 C1
Wilton Ave MK3. . . . . 58 A8
Wilton Cl UB7. . . . . 213 D8
Wilton Cres
Beaconsfield HP9 . . . 175 D4
Windsor SL4 . . . . . . 209 D4
Wilton Hollow HP9. 175 D3
Wilton La HP9. . . . . 176 E4
WILTON PARK. 176 B1
Wilton Rd HP9 . . . . 175 E3
Wiltshire Ave SL2 . . 198 C1
Wiltshire Lodge 2
SL6. . . . . 202 F6
Wiltshire Rd 2 SL7 183 F3
Wiltshire Way MK3. . 46 E1
Wimbledon Pl MK13. 34 D1
Wimbledon Dr MK6 47 A4
Wimborne Cres MK4 45 F2
Wimpole Rd UB7. . . 208 D5
Winbury Ct SL6. . . . 202 E7
Winbury Pl SL6 . . . . 203 B3
Wincanton Hill MK3. 57 C6
Winchbottom La
High Wycombe
HP10. . . . . 173 B1
Little Marlow SL7,
HP10. . . . . 184 B7
Winchcombe Mdws
Stantonbury MK14 . . 21 C1
Stantonbury MK14 . . 34 C8
Winchendon Rd
Ashendon HP18 . . . . 111 F7
Nether Winchendon
HP18. . . . . 112 B6
Winchendon Ridge Rd
Nether Winchendon
HP18. . . . . 112 E6
Upper Winchendon
HP18. . . . . 99 A1
Upper Winchendon
HP18. . . . . 113 A8
Winchester Circ
MK10 . . . . 36 B1
Winchester Cl
Amersham HP7. . . . . 165 E8
Poyle SL3 . . . . 212 E6
Winchester Ct HP11 174 B3
Winchester Dr SL6. 202 B3
Winchester Ho
HP21. . . . . 115 F6
WINCHMORE HILL. 164 D2
Winch's Mdw SL1. . 197 B2
Winch Terr SL4. . . . 209 D5
Windermere Cl
Aylesbury HP21. . . . 116 B6
Chorleywood WD3. . 167 A4
Windermere Dr MK2 58 D5
Windermere Gdns
LU7. . . . . 80 C2
Windermere Way
Slough SL1 . . . . 204 C7

Windermere Way
continued
West Drayton UB7. . . 208 E5
Windmill Cl
Aylesbury HP19. . . . 115 B8
Buckingham MK18 . . . 41 F1
Chinnor OX39 . . . . . 147 B7
Ivinghoe LU7. . . . . . 105 F5
Windsor SL4 . . . . . . 210 B5
Windmill Hill
Chipperfield WD4 . . 156 F7
Coleshill HP7. . . . . . 164 F2
Princes Risborough
HP27. . . . . 139 B2
Windmill Hill Dr
MK3. . . . . 57 D7
Windmill Hill Rdbt
MK4. . . . . 46 C1
Windmill La
Bledlow Ridge
HP16. . . . . 159 F8
Hazlemere HP15. . . . 162 A2
Windmill Par HP15. 162 F6
Windmill Rd
Chalfont St Peter
SL9. . . . . 177 D3
Cookham Rise SL6. . 195 E6
Fulmer SL3 . . . . 199 D7
Haddenham HP17. . . 126 F6
Slough SL1 . . . . 205 D5
Thame OX9 . . . . 126 E1
Windmill St HP18 . . . 96 A1
Windmill Way
Cranfield MK43. . . . . . 25 C3
Tring HP23 . . . . 118 F4
Windmill Wood
MK6. . . . . 154 A2
Windrush Ave SL3. 207 B3
Windrush Cl
Ickenham UB10. . . . 201 F8
Milton Keynes MK15 . . 35 A6
Windrush Ct
Aylesbury HP21. . . . 115 D4
High Wycombe HP13. 173 E6
Windrush Dr HP13 . 173 F6
Windrush Ho SL8 . . 185 B4
Windrush Way SL6. 203 A8
WINDSOR. 210 E6
Windsor And Eton Relief
Rd Spur SL4. . . . . . 205 C2
Windsor Ave
Leighton Buzzard LU7. 80 F7
Newport Pagnell MK16 22 D2
Windsor Boys' Sch The
SL4. . . . . 210 B6
Windsor Bsns Ctr
SL4. . . . . 210 C6
Windsor Castle 水
SL4. . . . . 210 E7
Windsor Castle St 2
MK10 . . . . 36 D4
Windsor Cl
Bovingdon HP3 . . . . 146 A3
Burnham SL1. . . . . . 197 C1
Stanwell TW19 . . . . 213 A4
Windsor Cres HP10. 174 C2
Windsor Ct 5 HP6 . 154 D1
Windsor Dr SL3. . . . 162 D1
Windsor Rd HP9 . . . 186 F8
Windsor & Eton Central
Sta SL4. . . . . 210 D6
Windsor & Eton
Riverside Sta SL4. 210 D7
Windsor Girls' Sch
SL4. . . . . 210 A4
Windsor Great Pk
SL4. . . . . 210 D2
Windsor Great Pk
SL4. . . . . 210 D2
Windsor Hall SL4. . 210 F4
Windsor Hill
Monks Risborough
HP27. . . . . 139 C5
Wooburn Green
HP10. . . . . 185 F5
Windsor Ho 4 SL1. 205 F3
Windsor La
Burnham SL1. . . . . . 197 C1
Little Kingshill HP16 . 152 C3
Wooburn Green
HP10. . . . . 185 E5
Windsor Rd
Aylesbury HP21. . . . 116 A7
Beaconsfield HP9 . . . 186 F6
Chesham HP5 . . . . . 144 B3
Datchet SL3. . . . . . . 211 A7
Gerrards Cross SL9. . 188 C3
Hedgerley SL9. . . . . 188 A6
Maidenhead SL6. . . 203 C2
Oakley Green SL4 . . 209 A7
Pitstone LU7. . . . . . 105 C3
Slough SL1 . . . . 205 E4
Wraysbury TW19 . . . 211 E1
Windsor Royal Sta 1
SL4. . . . . 210 D6
Windsor St
Milton Keynes MK2 . . 58 C7
Milton Keynes, Wolverton
MK12 . . . . 33 C6
Uxbridge UB8. . . . . 201 C1
Winehouse Gr
Wavendon MK16 . . . . 36 E1
4 Wavendon MK17 . . 48 E8
Winemar Cl MK19 . . . 11 A3
Winfold La MK4. . . . . 46 B1
WING. 79 F2
Wingate Ave HP13 . 173 E7

Wingate Circ MK7. . . 48 A4
Wingate Cl
Hanslope MK19. . . . . 10 F2
High Wycombe HP13. 173 E7
Wingate Wlk HP20 . 116 A7
Wingbury Ctyd Bsns
Village HP22. . . . . . 89 D5
Wing Cl SL7. . . . . . . 183 C1
Wingfield Gr MK10 . . 36 A2
WINGRAVE. 89 C3
Wingrave CE Comb Sch
HP22. . . . . 89 A3
Wingrave Cross Rds
HP22. . . . . 88 F4
Wingrave Rd
Aston Abbotts HP22 . . 88 E4
Long Marston HP23. . 104 D1
Wing HP23 . . . . 119 B5
Wing Rd
Cublington LU7 . . . . . 78 C1
Leighton Buzzard LU7. 80 D5
Stewkley LU7. . . . . . . 78 F6
Winkers Cl SL9. . . . . 177 F2
Winkers La SL9 . . . . 177 F3
Winkfield La SL4. . . 209 A1
Winkfield Rd SL4. . . 209 A2
Winnock Rd UB7. . . 208 D5
Winsby Way MK17. . . 36 E3
Winsford Hill MK4. . . 46 E3
WINSLOW. 66 B4
Winslow CE Comb Sch
MK18 . . . . 66 B4
Winslow Field HP16 151 F8
Winslow Gdns
MK13 . . . . 174 A7
Winslow Rd
Adstock MK18. . . . . . 64 E8
East Claydon MK18. . 74 F8
East Claydon MK18. . 65 E1
Granborough MK18. . 65 E1
Granborough MK18. . 75 F7
Great Horwood MK17 . 54 F1
Hoggeston MK18 . . . . 76 F6
Little Horwood MK17 . 55 C1
Little Horwood MK17 . 66 C4
Middle Claydon MK18. 64 E1
Nash MK17. . . . . 55 C8
Padbury MK18. . . . . . 53 D1
Swanbourne MK17 . . 66 F3
Swanbourne MK17 . . 67 A3
Wingrave HP22 . . . . . 89 D2
Winstanley La MK5. . 46 C4
Winston Ct SL6. . . . 202 A8
Winstone Cl HP6. . . 154 B5
Winston Gdns HP4 . 134 F4
Winston Ho HP11 . . 174 A4
Winston Mews
HP18. . . . . 100 E5
Winterbottom Way
MK46. . . . . 7 F3
Winterburn MK13. . . . 34 B5
Winter Ct 6 SL7. . . . 183 E2
Wintergreen Bvd 1
UB7. . . . . 208 F4
WINTERHILL. 46 D8
Winter Hill SL6. . . . . 184 C1
Winter Hill Rd SL6. . 195 A4
Winters Acre SL1 . . 204 B8
Winters Way
Holmer Green
HP15. . . . . 163 D7
Steeple Claydon MK18 63 C2
Winterton Dr HP21. 115 E4
Wintoun Path SL2. . 197 E1
Winvale SL1. . . . . . . 205 E3
Winwood
Slough SL2 . . . . 206 C7
Windsor SL4 . . . . . . 209 F6
Winwood Cl MK19. . . 31 E1
Winwood Dr HP22. . . 85 A5
Wirecut Rise 3
MK17. . . . . 49 A5
Wirethorn Furlong 2
HP17. . . . . 126 F6
Wise La UB7. . . . . . 208 D2
Wiseman Cl HP21. . . 115 D3
Wisewood Rd MK4,
MK5. . . . . 45 E4
Wishart Gn MK7. . . . . 48 E5
Wisley Ave MK13. . . . 34 D3
Wistmans MK4. . . . . . 46 D4
Witan Ct MK9 . . . . . . 34 D2
Witan Gate East MK9 34 D2
Witan Gate West
MK9. . . . . 34 D1
Witchell HP22. . . . . 131 A6
Witham Ct MK3. . . . . 46 E1
Witham Way HP21. . 115 C4
Witheridge La HP9,
HP10. . . . . 175 B7
Withers Cl HP21. . . . 115 D5
Withey Cl SL4. . . . . 209 E6
Withington MK13. . . . 34 A5
Withycombe MK4. . . . 46 E3
Withycroft SL3. . . . . 206 F2
Witney Cl UB10 . . . . 201 F8
Wittington Cotts
SL7. . . . . 193 D6
Wittmills Oak MK18. . 41 E1
Witton Ho WD3 . . . . 167 D4
Wivelsfield LU6. . . . . 92 E6
Wixon Path HP19. . . 115 A8
Wizard Wy MK10. . . . 35 E2
Walker Pl HP21. . . . 115 E5

Woad La MK14 . . . . . . 34 E8
WOBURN 60 F7
Woburn Ave MK12 . . . 33 C6
Woburn Ct LU7 . . . . . 80 E6
Woburn La MK17 . . . . 49 E4
Woburn Lower Sch
MK17 . . . . .60 F7
Woburn Pk MK17 . . . . .60 F8
Woburn Rd
Aspley Heath MK17 . . . 49 C2
Little Brickhill MK17 . . 59 E6
Sheeplane MK17, LU7 . 60 C1
WOBURN SANDS 49 A5
Woburn Sands Rd
MK17 . . . . 48 D3
Woburn Sands Sta
MK17 . . . . 49 A5
Wodehouse Wlk
MK16 . . . . 22 A5
Wodell Dr 5 MK12 . . 33 A6
Wolf La SL4 . . . . 209 E4
Wolfscote La MK4 . . 46 B3
Wolseley Cl
Brackley NN13 . . . . . . 26 A1
Brackley NN13 . . . . . . 26 A1
Wolsey Gdns MK13 . . 34 A4
Wolstan Cl UB9 . . . . . 190 A1
Wolston Mdw MK10 . . 35 F3
WOLVERTON 33 C5
WOLVERTON MILL . . . 33 A6
Wolverton Park Rd
MK12 . . . . 33 D8
Wolverton Rd
Castlethorpe MK19 . . . 20 B5
Milton Keynes, Gifford Park
MK16 . . . . 21 E2
Milton Keynes, Stony
Stratford MK11 . . . . . . 32 E6
Milton Keynes, Wolverton
MK12, MK19 . . . . 33 E8
Wolverton Sta MK12 . 33 E7
WOOBURN 185 D4
Wooburn Common Rd
HP10, SL1 . . . . 186 A2
Wooburn Grange
HP10 . . . . 185 D3
WOOBURN GREEN . . 185 F7
Wooburn Green La
HP9 . . . . 186 A8
Wooburn Manor Pk
HP10 . . . . 185 E5
Wooburn Mead
HP10 . . . . 185 E6
Wooburn Mews
HP10 . . . . 185 E5
WOOBURN MOOR . . 174 E1
Wooburn Town
HP10 . . . . 185 E5
Woodall Cl MK10 . . . . 35 E3
Woodbank HP27 . . . . 149 C5
Woodbank Ave SL9 . . 188 D5
Woodbank Dr HP8 . . 177 D7
Woodbine Cl HP27 . . 138 E5
Woodbine Cotts
SL9 . . . . 188 D8
Woodbridge Ho
UB8 . . . . 201 C5
**WOODBURN
COMMON** 186 B3
Woodbury Cl
Bourne End SL8 . . . . . 185 C3
4 Maidenhead SL6 . . 202 B8
Woodchester Pk
HP9 . . . . 175 C6
Wood Cl SL4 . . . . 210 C3
Woodcock Ave
HP14 . . . . 161 B8
Woodcock Rd TW19 . 213 B3
Woodcock Way SL0 207 F7
Woodcote SL6 . . . . . 202 D6
Woodcote Gn HP13 161 D2
Woodcote Lawns
HP5 . . . . 144 A4
Woodcroft Rd HP5 . 144 D3
WOOD END
Little Horwood 55 E2
Nash 55 C8
Wood End
Little Horwood MK17 . 55 E2
Nash MK17 . . . . 55 C8
Wood End Cl SL2 . . 187 D1
Wood End Fst Sch
MK14 . . . . 34 D8
Woodend House Rd
SL7 . . . . 182 D4
Woodend La MK16 . . 36 E8
Wood End La MK16 . . 23 E1
Woodfield Dr SL6 . . 202 A6
Woodfield Pk HP6 . . 154 B3

Woodfield Rd HP27 139 C4
Woodford Cl HP19 . 115 B7
Woodford Way SL2 . 198 A2
Wood Gn MK10 . . . . .47 F8
WOOD GREEN
27 F2
Biddlesden MK18 . . . . .27 F1
Wood Green MK18 . . 39 E8
Woodgreens Sq
OX39 . . . . 147 C5
Woodhall Cl UB8 . . . 201 D7
WOODHAM 83 E1
Woodhill Ave SL9 . . 189 A5
Woodhill Ct
Amersham HP6 . . . . . 154 D2
Gerrards Cross SL9 . . 188 E4
Woodhouse Ct
MK14 . . . . 34 D6
Woodhurst Dr UB9 . 189 F6
Woodhurst Rd SL6 . 196 B1
Woodhurst South
SL6 . . . . 196 C1
Wood La
Aspley Guise MK17 . . 49 D4
Iver SL0 . . . . 207 C8
Milton Keynes MK14 . . 34 E8
Slough SL1 . . . . 205 A4
South Heath HP16 . . . 152 E8
Tingewick MK18 . . . . . 51 B6
Wendover HP22 . . . . 131 D6
Weston Underwood
MK46 . . . . .5 F4
Weston Underwood
MK46 . . . . .6 A2
Woodland Ave
Leighton Buzzard LU7 .70 F2
Slough SL1 . . . . 205 D6
Windsor SL4 . . . . 209 F3
Woodland Cl
High Wycombe
HP12 . . . . 172 C6
Marlow SL7 . . . . 183 E4
Tring HP23 . . . . 118 F2
Woodland Glade
SL2 . . . . 187 D1
Woodland Grange
SL0 . . . . 207 E3
Woodland La WD3 . 167 D6
Woodland Pl WD3 . 167 F5
Woodland Rd WD3 . 178 D5
Woodlands
Gerrards Cross SL9 . . 188 F5
Princes Risborough
HP27 . . . . 139 B3
Woodlands Ave
HP4 . . . . 135 C3
Woodlands Bsns Pk
Maidenhead SL6 . . . . 202 A2
Milton Keynes MK14 . . 34 C6
Woodlands Cl
Buckingham MK18 . . . 41 E2
Gerrards Cross SL9 . . 189 A5
Holmer Green HP15 . 163 C6
Woodlands Cotts 1
SL2 . . . . 198 C7
Woodlands Cres
MK18 . . . . 41 D2
Woodlands Dr
Beaconsfield HP9 . . . 175 C4
Walter's Ash HP14 . . 161 C8
Woodlands Farm
SL6 . . . . 195 C6
Woodlands Glade
HP9 . . . . 175 C4
Woodlands Hill HP9 186 E5
Woodlands Park Ave
SL6 . . . . 202 A2
**Woodlands Park Prim
Sch** SL6 . . . . 202 A1
Woodlands Park Rd
SL6 . . . . 202 A3
Woodlands The
Amersham HP6 . . . . . 154 C4
Tylers Green HP10 . . 162 F3
Woodlands View
HP13 . . . . 174 A7
Woodland View
Chesham HP5 . . . . . . 154 D6
Milton Keynes MK12 . . 33 D5
Saunderton HP14 . . . 160 C8
Woodland Way
Marlow SL7 . . . . 183 E4
Woburn Sands MK17 . . 49 B4
Woodlane Cl
Flackwell Heath
HP10 . . . . 173 F1
Flackwell Heath
HP10 . . . . 174 A1
Wood Lane Cl
Flackwell Heath
HP10 . . . . 173 F1
Iver Heath SL0 . . . . . 200 B2
Woodlane Gdns

Flackwell Heath
HP10 . . . . 173 F1
Flackwell Heath
HP10 . . . . 174 A1
Woodley Ct HP7 . . . 165 D8
Woodley Headland
MK6 . . . . 47 C7
Woodley Hill HP5 . . 154 D5
Woodman Cl LU7 . . . .79 F3
Woodmans Cl MK19 . 31 E4
Woodmans Croft
HP19 . . . . 115 A8
Woodmoor End SL6 196 B3
Woodpiece Rd OX25. 94 E7
Woodpits La MK46 . . . .6 E5
Wood Pond Cl HP9 . 176 C4
Wood Rd MK43. . . . . . .3 F7
WOODROW 164 D5
Wood Row HP23 . . . 133 E7
Woodruff Ave MK14 . 34 E4
Woodrush Cl MK6 . . .47 B4
Woodside
Aspley Guise MK17 . . 49 D3
Eaton Bray LU6 . . . . . 92 E6
Flackwell Heath
HP10 . . . . 185 C6
Milton Keynes MK11 . . 32 E6
Woodside Ave
Amersham HP6 . . . . . 154 D3
Beaconsfield HP9 . . . 175 C4
Flackwell Heath
HP10 . . . . 185 C7
Woodside Cl
Amersham HP6 . . . . . 154 D1
Beaconsfield HP9 . . . 175 C3
Chalfont St Peter SL9 177 E1
Loudwater HP11 . . . . 174 B2
Woodside Hill
Chalfont St Peter
SL9 . . . . 177 E1
Chalfont St Peter SL9 188 F8
Woodside Jun Sch
HP6 . . . . 154 E1
Woodside Rd
Amersham HP6 . . . . . 154 D1
Beaconsfield HP9 . . . 175 C3
High Wycombe HP13. 174 A8
Woodside Way
Leighton Buzzard
LU7 . . . . 80 D6
Tylers Green HP10 . . 174 C8
Woods La NN12 . . . . 18 E3
Woods Pl
13 Wendover HP22 . 119 A3
Wendover HP22 . . . . 131 B4
Woodspring Ct 2
MK10 . . . . .35 F1
Wood St
Milton Keynes MK13 . .33 F7
Waddesdon HP18 . . . 99 A4
Woburn Sands MK17. . 49 B4
Woodstock Ave SL3 206 D2
Woodstock Cl
Aylesbury HP21 . . . . 116 B6
Maidenhead SL6 . . . . 195 F1
Woodstock Ct SL4 . . 34 B7
Woodstock Dr UB10 201 F8
Woodview Cl HP12 . 161 B2
Wood View Cotts
HP5 . . . . 144 B7
Woodview Dr HP16 . 150 C5
Woodville OX39 . . . . 147 C5
Woodville Cres NN12 18 E6
Woodward Ho 4
MK2 . . . . 58 C8
Woodward Pl MK8 . . 34 A1
Woodwards Pcn
HP17 . . . . 127 B6
Woodway HP27 . . . . 149 D6
Wood Way HP27 . . . 174 F1
Woodway Farm Ind Est
HP18 . . . . 124 F8
Woodways HP17 . . . 127 A6
Wood White Dr
HP19 . . . . 101 B4
Woodwicks WD3 . . 178 D5
Woolbrock Cl 14
HP18 . . . . 100 D5
Woollerton Cres
HP22 . . . . 131 D5
Woollerton Ct HP27 139 B4
Woolmans MK11 . . . 33 A4
Woolpack Grange
Stantonbury MK14 . . . 21 C1
2 Stantonbury MK14 . 34 C8
Woolrich Gdns MK11 32 E5
WOOLSTONE 35 D3
Wooster Rd HP9 . . . 175 D4
Wooton Ct MK13 . . . .33 F8
**WOOTTON BOURNE
END** 25 E8
Wootton Dr HP10 . . 185 E8
Wootton Gn OX27 . . 72 E6

Wootton La HP17 . . . 113 E1
Wootton Way SL6 . . 202 C6
Worcester Cl
Maidenhead SL6 . . . . 202 D3
Newport Pagnell MK16 22 A3
Worcester Gdns
SL1 . . . . 205 D4
Worcester Ho MK3 . .46 F7
Worcester Rd UB8 . . 208 D8
Worcester Way
Olney MK46 . . . . .6 F6
Olney MK46 . . . . .7 A6
Wordsworth Ave
MK16 . . . . 22 A4
Wordsworth Dr MK3. 58 A7
Wordsworth Rd
High Wycombe
HP11 . . . . 173 A5
Slough SL2 . . . . 197 D1
Wordsworth Way
UB7 . . . . 208 E2
WORLD'S END 130 F7
World's End La
HP22 . . . . 130 F8
Worley Pl HP9 . . . . 176 D5
WORMINGHALL 123 E6
Worminghall Rd
Ickford HP18 . . . . . . 123 F4
Oakley HP18 . . . . 109 D4
Shabbington OX9 . . . 124 A4
Wormsley Cres
HP14 . . . . 158 C4
Wormsley Est HP14. 157 E2
WORMSTONE 99 C5
Wornal Pk HP18 . . . 123 C7
Wornal Pk HP18 . . . 123 C8
Worple The TW19 . . 211 F1
Worrall La UB8 . . . . 201 F6
Worrelle Ave
Milton Keynes MK10 . .35 F3
Milton Keynes MK10 . 36 A3
Worster Rd SL6 . . . 195 E6
Worth Ct MK10 . . . . . 36 B1
Worthies The HP7 . . 165 B7
Worthington Rd
LU6 . . . . 93 F8
Wotton End HP18 . . . 96 C7
Wotton Path 2
HP21 . . . . 115 E3
Wotton Rd
Ashendon HP18 . . . . . 97 E1
Brill HP18 . . . . 96 D3
Wotton Underwood
HP18 . . . . 97 D2
**WOTTON
UNDERWOOD** 97 C4
Wotton Underwood
Dorton HP18 . . . . .96 F3
Dorton HP18 . . . . 97 A3
**Wotton Underwood
Village** HP18 . . . . . . 97 A4
Woughton L Ctr MK6 .46 F7
**WOUGHTON ON THE
GREEN** 47 D8
WOUGHTON PARK . . 47 E6
Wraxall Way MK6 . . .47 D5
Wray Ct MK4 . . . . . . 46 A2
WRAYSBURY 211 E1
Wraysbury Dr UB7 . 208 D6
Wraysbury Prim Sch
TW19 . . . . 211 A3
Wraysbury Sta
TW19 . . . . 212 A1
Wren Ave UB10 . . . . 201 F4
Wren Cl MK18. . . . . . .52 F7
Wren Ct SL3 . . . . . . 207 A3
Wren Dr UB7 . . . . . . 208 D3
Wren Path HP19 . . . 114 F8
Wren Rd HP16 . . . . . 151 C5
Wrensfield SL7 . . . . 183 C2
Wrens Pk MK10 . . . . 36 B2
Wren Vale HP11 . . . 173 A8
Wren Wlk LU6 . . . . . 92 E4
Wreschner Cl MK19 . .31 F4
Wright SL4 . . . . 209 C4
Wrights Cl HP14 . . . 171 B5
Wright's La HP11 . . 151 C5
Wrights Mdw Rd
HP11 . . . . 173 F4
Wright Sq SL4 . . . . . 209 C4
Wrights Yd HP16 . . . 152 A7
Wright Way
Harmondsworth
SL3 . . . . 213 A7
Oakley Green SL4 . . . 209 C4
Wroughton Rd 4
HP22 . . . . 131 E6
Wulfstan Cl MK18 . . 52 B8
Wyatt Cl HP13 . . . . . 172 F8
Wyatt Rd SL4 . . . . . 209 D4
Wyatts Rd WD3 . . . 167 F5
Wyatt Wy HP11 . . . . 100 D4
Wychwood HP16 . . . 152 B4

Wychwood Gdns
HP12 . . . . 172 C6
Wychwood Rise
HP16 . . . . 152 B4
Wyclands Ho HP12 . 161 B2
Wycliffe End HP19 . 115 C8
Wycombe Abbey Sch
HP11 . . . . 173 A6
Wycombe Air Pk
SL7 . . . . 171 F2
Wycombe Cl HP21. . 116 B4
Wycombe End
Beaconsfield HP9 . . . 175 E1
Beaconsfield HP9 . . . 186 C8
**Wycombe Grange Pupil
Referral Unit The**
HP11 . . . . 173 C7
Wycombe High Sch
HP11 . . . . 172 F4
Wycombe Hospl
HP11 . . . . 173 A6
Wycombe Ind Mall
HP11 . . . . 172 F7
Wycombe La HP10 . 185 E7
WYCOMBE MARSH . 173 F4
Wycombe Mus *
HP13 . . . . 173 B7
Wycombe Mus & Gdn 18
HP13 . . . . 173 B7
Wycombe Rd
Beacon's Bottom
HP14 . . . . 159 D3
Burroughs Grove
HP10 . . . . 172 E1
Holmer Green HP15 . 163 B6
Lacey Green HP14 . . 149 B4
Marlow SL7 . . . . 183 C4
Marlow Bottom SL7 . . 183 E6
Prestwood HP15 . . . . 151 C5
Princes Risborough
HP27 . . . . 139 D3
Stokenchurch HP14 . 158 F5
Wycombe Ret Pk
HP11 . . . . 173 F4
Wycombe Sp Ctr
HP11 . . . . 172 F5
Wycombe Swan Theatre
HP11 . . . . 173 B6
Wycombe View
HP10 . . . . 174 A2
Wye Cl
Aylesbury HP21 . . . . 115 C5
Milton Keynes MK3 . . 46 E1
Wye Ct 3 SL8 . . . . . 185 A3
Wye Est HP11 . . . . . 173 E5
Wye Gdns HP12 . . . 172 D8
Wye Rd HP10 . . . . . 185 D8
Wye River Bsns Ctr 8
HP11 . . . . 172 F7
Wyeth Cl SL6 . . . . . 204 C6
Wye Valley Sch The
SL8 . . . . 185 B4
Wykeham Cl MK18 . . 51 B6
Wykeham Gate
HP17 . . . . 126 F5
Wykeham Rise
OX39 . . . . 147 C5
Wykeham Way
HP17 . . . . 126 F6
Wykeridge Cl HP5. . 144 B4
Wylands Rd SL3 . . . 207 A2
Wylie End MK13 . . . 34 A7
Wyman Chase MK4. . 45 D2
WYMBUSH 33 F2
Wymbush Ind Est
MK8 . . . . 33 E3
Wymering Rd HP21 163 B6
Wymers Cl SL1. . . . . 197 B3
Wymers Wood Rd
SL1 . . . . 197 A3
Wymondham MK10. . 36 B1
Wynbury Dr HP13 . . 162 E1
Wyndale Cl RG9 . . . 191 E1
Wyndham Ave
High Wycombe
HP13 . . . . 161 F2
High Wycombe HP13. 162 A1
Wyndham Cres
SL1 . . . . 197 B3
Wyness Ave MK17 . . 59 C5
Wynford Gn HP21 . . 115 F6
Wyngates LU7 . . . . . 80 E5
Wyngrave Pl HP9 . . 175 C5
Wynne-Jones Ctr
HP21 . . . . 115 F8
Wynn Gr HP15 . . . . 163 B3
Wynnstay Gdns
SL7 . . . . 183 C2
Wynnswick Rd HP9. 176 C5
Wynyard Ct MK6 . . . 46 E7

X

Xscape MK6 . . . . .34 F2

Y

Yalts Brow MK4 . . . . . 46 B2
Yardley Ave LU7 . . . 105 D4
Yardley Gn HP20 . . . 101 C5
YARDLEY GOBION 1 B6
**Yardley Gobion CE Prim
Sch** NN12 . . . . 18 E6
YARDLEY HASTINGS . . .1 B6
**Yardley Hastings Prim
Sch** NN7 . . . . .1 A7
Yardley Rd
Cosgrove MK19 . . . . . 19 D2
Olney MK46 . . . . .6 E6
Olney NN7 . . . . 1 D1
Potterspury NN12 . . . 18 E3
Potterspury NN12 . . . 18 F4
Yarmouth Rd SL1 . . 205 C6
Yarrow Pl MK14 . . . . 34 E4
Yarrowside HP7 . . . 166 B7
Yearl Stone Sq 7
MK6 . . . . 47 C4
Yeates Cl
Thame OX9 . . . . 125 F1
Winslow MK18 . . . . . .65 F4
Yeats Cl MK16 . . . . . 21 F5
Ye Meads SL6. . . . . . 203 E5
Ye Meads Cotts
SL6 . . . . 203 E5
Ye Meads Ho SL6 . . 203 E5
Yeomans Cl NN13 . . 38 A8
Yeomans Dr MK14. . 22 B1
Yeomans Keep
WD3 . . . . 167 F6
Yeovil Ent Ctr SL1 . 204 E8
Yeovil Rd SL1 . . . . . 204 E8
Yew Ave UB7 . . . . . . 208 E6
Yewtree Cl LU7 . . . . 105 E5
Yew Tree Cl
Beaconsfield HP9 . . . 175 F1
Botley HP5 . . . . 145 A1
Eaton Bray LU6 . . . . . .92 F5
Maidenhead SL6 . . . . 202 E8
Newton Longville
MK17 . . . . 57 C3
Stoke Mandeville
HP22 . . . . 116 A1
Yew Tree Dr
Bovingdon HP3 . . . . . 146 B3
Hazlemere HP15 . . . . 162 F6
Yew Tree Rd
Slough SL1 . . . . 206 A3
Uxbridge UB10 . . . . . 201 F4
Yew Wlk HP15 . . . . . 163 A3
Yiewsley Ct UB7 . . . 208 E5
Yolsum Cl HP17 . . . . 126 E6
Yonder Slade MK18 . 52 D6
York Ave
Slough SL1 . . . . 205 C7
Windsor SL4 . . . . 210 B5
York Cl HP7 . . . . 165 F8
York Cl 3 LU7 . . . . . .80 F7
Yorke HP22 . . . . 117 C5
York Ho
High Wycombe
HP13 . . . . 173 F8
Milton Keynes MK3 . . 57 E7
York Pl HP21 . . . . . . 115 D7
York Rd
Henley-on-Thames
RG9 . . . . 191 D2
Maidenhead SL6 . . . . 203 A7
Marlow SL7 . . . . 183 D2
Milton Keynes MK11 . . 32 D5
Uxbridge UB8 . . . . . . 201 D5
Windsor SL4 . . . . 210 B5
Yorkshire Cl MK3 . . .46 F1
York Way HP12 . . . . 172 E4
Youens Rd HP12 . . . 172 C5
Young Cl HP21 . . . . . 116 A6
Young People's Acad
UB7 . . . . 208 E6

Z

Zante Gr MK3 . . . . . . 58 A4
Zealand Ave UB7 . . 213 C7
Zebu Cres MK8. . . . . 45 C7
Zetland Ct SL6 . . . . 203 B8
Zodiac Bsns Pk
UB8 . . . . 208 D7
Zoe St HP18 . . . . . . 100 E4
ZSL Whipsnade Zoo *
HP4 . . . . 107 E8
Zubron Gr 7 MK8 . . 45 D8